GIPS® Standards Handbook for Firms

Explanation of the Provisions in Sections 1–8

November 2020

CFA Institute®
Global Investment
Performance Standards

ISBN 978-1-956563-06-1

CONTENTS

INTRODUCTION

The Global Investment Performance Standards (GIPS®) for Firms are divided into eight sections, which are as follows:

1. Fundamentals of Compliance
2. Input Data and Calculation Methodology
3. Composite and Pooled Fund Maintenance
4. Composite Time-Weighted Return Report
5. Composite Money-Weighted Return Report
6. Pooled Fund Time-Weighted Return Report
7. Pooled Fund Money-Weighted Return Report
8. GIPS Advertising Guidelines.

The Explanation of the Provisions in Sections 1–8 provides interpretation of each provision contained in Sections 1–8. Firms that choose to comply with the GIPS standards must comply with all applicable requirements of the GIPS standards, including any Guidance Statements, interpretations, and Questions and Answers (Q&As) published by CFA Institute and the GIPS standards governing bodies.

Section 1: Fundamentals of Compliance. The Fundamentals of Compliance section includes several core principles that create the foundation for the GIPS standards, including properly defining the firm, providing GIPS Reports to all prospective clients and pooled fund prospective investors, adhering to applicable laws and regulations, and ensuring that information presented is not false or misleading.

Section 2: Input Data and Calculation Methodology. Consistency of input data used to calculate performance is critical to effective compliance with the GIPS standards and establishes the foundation for full, fair, and comparable investment performance presentations. Achieving comparability among investment management firms' performance presentations requires uniformity in methods used to calculate returns. The GIPS standards mandate the use of certain calculation methodologies to facilitate comparability. The Input Data and Calculation Methodology section addresses these topics.

Section 3: Composite and Pooled Fund Maintenance. A composite is an aggregation of one or more portfolios managed according to a similar investment mandate, objective, or strategy. The composite return is the asset-weighted average of the performance of all portfolios in the composite. Creating meaningful composites is essential to the fair presentation, consistency, and comparability of performance over time and among firms. Pooled funds must be included in composites if they meet a composite definition.

Section 4: Composite Time-Weighted Return Report. Section 4 includes the requirements and recommendations for preparing a GIPS Composite Report that includes time-weighted returns. Firms that prepare a GIPS Composite Report that includes time-weighted returns must include the required numerical information and disclosures specified in Section 4, if applicable to the specific composite.

Section 5: Composite Money-Weighted Return Report. Section 5 includes the requirements and recommendations that apply to composites that include money-weighted returns in a GIPS Composite Report, when the firm meets the requirements specified in Provision 1.A.35 and chooses to present money-weighted returns.

Section 6: Pooled Fund Time-Weighted Return Report. Section 6 includes the requirements and recommendations for preparing a GIPS Pooled Fund Report that includes time-weighted returns. Firms that prepare a GIPS Pooled Fund Report that includes time-weighted returns must include the required numerical information and disclosures specified in Section 6, if applicable to the specific pooled fund.

Section 7: Pooled Fund Money-Weighted Return Report. Section 7 includes the requirements and recommendations that apply to pooled funds that include money-weighted returns in a GIPS Pooled Fund Report, when the firm meets the requirements specified in Provision 1.A.35 and chooses to present money-weighted returns.

Section 8: GIPS Advertising Guidelines. Section 8 includes the requirements and recommendations for preparing a GIPS Advertisement. Firms that prepare a GIPS Advertisement must include the required numerical information and disclosures specified in Section 8, if applicable to the specific composite or pooled fund.

Each provision in each section is included in a grey text box. Within the provisions are words appearing in small capital letters. This indicates defined terms that can be found in the GIPS Standards Glossary. Following each provision is a discussion that provides interpretive guidance to help readers understand the provision.

1. FUNDAMENTALS OF COMPLIANCE

1.A. Fundamentals of Compliance—Requirements

Provision 1.A.1

The GIPS standards MUST be applied on a FIRM-wide basis. Compliance MUST be met on a FIRM-wide basis and cannot be met on a COMPOSITE, POOLED FUND, or PORTFOLIO basis.

Discussion

The GIPS standards provide an ethical framework for calculating and presenting a firm's investment performance history. The definition of the firm is the foundation for firm-wide compliance and creates defined boundaries for determining total firm assets. Only firms that manage actual assets may claim compliance with the GIPS standards.

To claim compliance, a firm must comply with all the applicable requirements of the GIPS standards. Compliance cannot be met on a composite, pooled fund, or portfolio basis and can be met only on a firm-wide basis. For example, if a firm definition includes both equity and fixed income products, the firm cannot present only its equity products (strategies) as being in compliance with the GIPS standards. If a firm definition includes both segregated accounts and pooled funds, the firm must meet the GIPS standards requirements for both segregated accounts and pooled funds in order to claim compliance with the GIPS standards.

Provision 1.A.2

The FIRM MUST be defined as an investment firm, subsidiary, or division held out to the public as a DISTINCT BUSINESS ENTITY.

Discussion

It is the firm's responsibility to ensure that the definition of the firm is appropriate, rational, and fair, reflecting the way the firm is held out to the public. A firm's definition will take into account the specific circumstances of the firm and must reflect how it is held out to current and prospective clients or current and prospective pooled fund investors as a distinct business entity. A distinct business entity is a unit, division, department, or office that is organizationally and functionally segregated from other units, divisions, departments, or offices and that retains discretion over the assets it manages. The business entity should have autonomy over the investment decision-making process.

Possible criteria that can be used to determine what constitutes a distinct business entity include, but are not limited to, the following:

- being a legal entity,
- having a distinct market or client type (e.g., institutional, retail, or private client), and
- using a separate and distinct investment process.

It would be inappropriate for an organization to establish a business entity solely for GIPS compliance purposes unless the entity will be consistently held out to the investing public as an autonomous business unit through the firm's marketing efforts and other communications with the investing public. The separate business entity should be identified on the organization's website and in other forms of marketing communications, not solely in GIPS Reports.

The GIPS standards recommend that the firm adopt the broadest, most meaningful definition of the firm. The scope of this definition should include all geographic (country, regional, etc.) offices operating under the same brand name, if all of these offices together are held out to the public as a distinct business entity, regardless of the actual name of the individual investment management company. In some cases, however, it may be appropriate to define the firm based on geographic location if each location is held out to the public as a distinct business entity (e.g., the London office of ABC Firm). It may also be appropriate to have multiple defined firms that use the same brand name if each defined firm is managed separately and operates independently or if each firm serves distinctly different client types. A firm must not use a narrow definition of the firm simply to reduce the scope of work required to achieve and maintain compliance with the GIPS standards.

There may be changes within a defined firm, such as those resulting from a corporate restructuring or merger and acquisition activities, that cause a firm to reconsider the definition of the firm. When such a change occurs, the firm must determine which scenario applies:

- The change is so substantial that it is essentially a new firm, and there is no continuation of the track record;
- The change is material enough to warrant a disclosure of the change, but there is a continuation of the track record; or
- No change in the firm definition is necessary.

The following are examples of how a firm may be defined.

Example 1:

A firm consists of two legal entities. The two legal entities are held out to prospective clients and prospective investors as one business entity, and the firm definition states the following:

"For the purpose of complying with the GIPS® standards, the firm is defined as all assets managed by Treetown Investment Management, LLC and Treetown Investment Management, Inc., together Treetown Investment Management."

If Treetown Investment Management, LLC, and Treetown Investment Management, Inc. were each held out to prospective clients and prospective investors as a distinct business entity, each legal entity could be defined as a separate firm for the purpose of complying with the GIPS standards.

Example 2:

A legal entity has a division serving institutional clients and a division serving wrap fee clients. Each division is managed autonomously, and each has a distinct client type. The legal entity's marketing department decides that these two divisions of the firm will begin to use the same brand, regardless of client type, because of the significant cost savings in promoting a single brand.

Each division of the entity serves a distinctly different client type. The firm may define the institutional division and the wrap fee division as separate firms for the purposes of GIPS compliance if it wishes to do so, even if both divisions are operating under the same brand. However, the two firms must be consistently held out to that public as distinct business entities and be clearly defined to avoid potential confusion, particularly if one of the firms claims compliance with the GIPS standards but the other does not. A non-compliant firm must not receive any inappropriate benefit from a related firm's claim of compliance.

Example 3:

A parent corporation has three divisions: one serving Asia, one serving the United States, and one serving Europe. Each division uses a similar investment process.

The decision regarding how to define the firm must consider each division's characteristics. If each division is held out to the public as a distinct business entity, is organizationally and functionally segregated from the other divisions, and retains discretion over the assets it manages, the parent corporation may define each division as a separate firm for the purposes of GIPS compliance. Alternatively, if all of these divisions are held out to the public as a single business entity, the firm should be defined as a single firm that includes all three divisions.

Provision 1.A.3

To initially claim compliance with the GIPS standards, the FIRM MUST attain compliance for a minimum of five years or for the period since the FIRM inception if the FIRM has been in existence for less than five years.

Discussion

A firm cannot initially claim compliance with the GIPS standards until it meets the applicable requirements of the GIPS standards for at least a five-year period, or since inception of the firm if the firm has been in existence for less than five years. Being in compliance for a minimum five-year period, or since inception if less than five years, means that for this period, the firm has complied with all applicable requirements of the GIPS standards, including any Guidance Statements, interpretations, and Questions & Answers (Q&As) published by CFA Institute and the GIPS standards governing bodies.

Assuming a firm initially attains compliance for the minimum five-year period, and the firm is presenting time-weighted returns (TWRs) in a GIPS Report, it is required to present five years of GIPS-compliant performance, or performance since inception of the composite or pooled fund if it has been in existence less than five years. The ability to present five years of GIPS-compliant performance does not mean, however, that the firm is able to claim compliance with the GIPS standards. The firm must fulfill all of the requirements of the GIPS standards for at least the initial five-year period or since inception if the firm has been in existence for less than five years, not simply the requirements relating to the presentation of performance in a GIPS Report. If a firm initially claims compliance for a longer period than five years, the firm must present a track record for the entire period of time for which it claims compliance, or for at least 10 years if the firm claims compliance for a period longer than 10 years.

If a firm is presenting money-weighted returns (MWRs) in a GIPS Report, it is required to present only one return: the annualized since-inception MWR of the composite or pooled fund through the most recent annual period end. The number of years included in this since-inception MWR will depend on the length of time for which the composite or pooled fund has been in existence as of the most recent annual period end. Regardless of the period encompassed in this since-inception money-weighted return, the firm cannot claim compliance with the GIPS standards until it has fulfilled all of the requirements of the GIPS standards, including but not limited to all of the input data and calculation requirements, for a full five-year period or since inception of the composite or pooled fund if the composite or pooled fund has been in existence for less than five years. If the composite or pooled fund has been in existence for longer than five years but the firm is initially claiming compliance with the GIPS standards for the minimum five-year period, the firm is still required to present the since-inception MWR since the composite or pooled fund inception date—not only for the period for which the firm claims compliance with the GIPS standards.

Once a firm has claimed compliance for a five-year period, or since inception of the firm if the firm has existed for less than 5 years, the firm must include in GIPS Reports an additional year of performance each year, building up to a minimum of 10 years of GIPS-compliant performance. Although a firm is required to present only 10 years of performance in a GIPS Report when it is presenting TWRs, it is recommended that firms present more than 10 years of performance in a GIPS Report.

Consider the following examples of time periods required to be presented when first claiming compliance with the GIPS standards and TWRs are presented.

Example 1:

A firm has been in existence since 1 January 2011 and wishes to claim compliance starting with GIPS Reports for periods ending 31 December 2020. The firm decides to attain compliance for the minimum five-year period and chooses to present performance on a calendar-year basis.

The firm must comply with all applicable requirements of the GIPS standards on a firm-wide basis for an initial five-year period, in this case from 1 January 2016 through 31 December 2020. The firm must prepare GIPS Reports that include five years of GIPS-compliant performance in its first GIPS Reports for all composites or limited distribution pooled funds (LDPFs) that have a track record of at least five years. For all composites or LDPFs that have a track record of less than five years, the firm must present a since-inception track record. The firm must then continue to add one year of additional performance to its GIPS Reports each year, building to a minimum of 10 years of GIPS-compliant performance for each of its GIPS Reports.

Example 2:

A firm has been in existence since 2013 and wishes to claim compliance starting in 2020. For various reasons, the firm can create a GIPS-compliant track record only beginning 1 January 2017.

The firm may not claim compliance with the GIPS standards until it can present five years of GIPS-compliant performance. In this case, the firm must wait one more year until it has GIPS-compliant returns from 2017 through 2021. Only then can the firm claim compliance with the GIPS standards.

Example 3:

A firm has been in existence for two years and has two years of performance through 31 December 2019.

If a firm has been in existence for less than five years, the firm may initially claim compliance for the period since the firm's inception. The firm must present performance since the composite or pooled fund inception date and then build to a minimum of 10 years of GIPS-compliant performance. In this case, the firm may claim compliance with the GIPS standards with two years of GIPS-compliant performance (2018 and 2019) and add an additional year each year until it reaches a minimum of 10 years of compliant performance. A firm is not required to present a track record longer than 10 years but is recommended to do so.

Example 4:

A firm has been in existence for less than one year and has no annual composite or pooled fund returns to report.

The firm may claim compliance with the GIPS standards as soon as it meets all of the applicable requirements of the GIPS standards and has performance to report. If the firm is less than 12 months old, it is permitted to present since-inception performance in GIPS Reports for its composites and/or pooled funds and claim compliance with the GIPS standards.

Returns for periods of less than one year must not be annualized.

Provision 1.A.4

The FIRM MUST comply with all applicable REQUIREMENTS of the GIPS standards, including any Guidance Statements, interpretations, and Questions & Answers (Q&As) published by CFA Institute and the GIPS standards governing bodies.

Discussion

The GIPS standards are ethical standards for investment performance presentation to ensure fair representation and full disclosure of a firm's performance. Firms must comply with all requirements of the GIPS standards that apply to the firm, including requirements found within the provisions of the GIPS standards as well as within any Guidance Statements, interpretations, and Questions & Answers (Q&As) published by CFA Institute and the GIPS standards governing bodies. Firms must also comply with all updates and clarifications published by these entities. Firms must review all of the provisions and other requirements of the GIPS standards to determine each requirement's applicability.

The GIPS standards must be applied with the objectives of fair representation and full disclosure of investment performance. Meeting the objectives of fair representation and full disclosure will likely require compliance with more than the minimum requirements of the GIPS standards. If a firm applies the GIPS standards in a performance situation that is not addressed specifically by the GIPS standards or is open to interpretation, disclosures other than those required by the GIPS standards may be necessary. To fully explain the performance included in a GIPS Report, firms are encouraged to present all relevant information, beyond required and recommended information, that will help a prospective client or prospective investor understand the information presented. Firms are also encouraged to adopt the recommendations included in the GIPS standards.

Provision 1.A.5

The FIRM MUST:

a. Document its policies and procedures used in establishing and maintaining compliance with the REQUIREMENTS of the GIPS standards, as well as any RECOMMENDATIONS it has chosen to adopt, and apply them consistently.
b. Create policies and procedures to monitor and identify changes and additions to all of the Guidance Statements, interpretations, and Q&As published by CFA Institute and the GIPS standards governing bodies.

Discussion

Policies and procedures are essential to implementing adequate business controls at all stages of the investment performance process—from data input to preparing marketing materials—to ensure the validity of the claim of compliance. A firm must document all of the policies and procedures it follows for meeting the requirements of the GIPS standards, as well as any recommendations the firm has chosen to adopt. There is no requirement to create and document policies and procedures to comply with requirements that do not apply to the firm. However, firms must actively make a determination about the applicability of all the requirements of the GIPS standards and document their policies and procedures accordingly.

Once a firm establishes its policies and procedures, it must apply them consistently. Policies and procedures should be reviewed regularly to determine if they should be changed or improved, but it is not expected that they will change frequently. A firm must not change a policy retroactively solely to enhance performance or to present the firm in a better light. Retroactive changes to policies and procedures should be avoided.

Firms must also create policies and procedures to monitor and identify changes and additions to all of the Guidance Statements, interpretations, Q&As, and any other guidance published by CFA Institute and the GIPS standards governing bodies. A firm should assign at least one person internally who is responsible for monitoring its compliance with the GIPS standards. Depending on the firm's size and complexity, it might have a team of people responsible for GIPS compliance, and maintaining compliance may require coordination across multiple departments, including but not limited to operations, performance, compliance, and marketing.

Provision 1.A.6

The FIRM MUST:

a. Comply with all applicable laws and regulations regarding the calculation and presentation of performance.

b. Create policies and procedures to monitor and identify changes and additions to laws and regulations regarding the calculation and presentation of performance.

Discussion

The GIPS standards provide an ethical framework for calculating and presenting a firm's investment performance history. Firms must also comply with all applicable laws and regulations regarding the calculation and presentation of performance in the country or countries in which they are domiciled as well as those countries in which they do business. Firms must create policies and procedures to ensure that they adhere to all applicable laws and regulations regarding the calculation and presentation of performance. Firms must also have policies and procedures to identify and monitor changes and additions to laws and regulations regarding the calculation and presentation of performance.

Compliance with applicable laws and regulations does not necessarily result in compliance with the GIPS standards. Firms claiming compliance must comply with the GIPS standards in addition to all applicable laws and regulations. In the rare cases when laws and regulations conflict with the GIPS standards, firms are required to comply with the laws and regulations and disclose the manner in which the laws or regulations conflict with the GIPS standards.

Provision 1.A.7

The FIRM MUST NOT present performance or PERFORMANCE-RELATED INFORMATION that is false or misleading. This REQUIREMENT applies to all performance or PERFORMANCE-RELATED INFORMATION on a FIRM-wide basis and is not limited to those materials that reference the GIPS standards. The FIRM may provide any performance or PERFORMANCE-RELATED INFORMATION that is specifically requested by a PROSPECTIVE CLIENT or PROSPECTIVE INVESTOR for use in a one-on-one presentation.

Discussion

The underlying principles of the GIPS standards, fair representation and full disclosure, help to ensure that current and prospective clients and investors are not given performance or performance-related information that is incomplete, inaccurate, biased, or fraudulent. Firms must not present any performance or performance-related information that is known to be inaccurate or that may mislead either current or prospective clients or current or prospective investors. This concept applies to all performance and performance-related materials on a firm-wide basis and is not limited to those materials that reference the GIPS standards. Examples of information that is misleading and unrepresentative include the presentation of custom benchmark returns that have been reduced by model investment management fees (i.e., net-of-fees benchmark returns) when only gross-of-fees composite returns are presented, or model performance that is presented as actual performance.

Firms are not limited to providing only GIPS-compliant information to prospective clients, prospective investors, or other interested parties. Firms may present other performance or performance-related information as long as it is not false or misleading.

The following information has an especially high risk of being interpreted by prospective clients and prospective investors in a way that is likely to be false or misleading:

- Actual performance linked to model, hypothetical, backtested, or simulated historical results;
- Non-portable performance from a past firm linked to current ongoing results;
- Portable performance from a past firm linked to ongoing results, when there was a break in performance between the prior firm and the current firm; and
- Non-compliant data after the minimum effective compliance date linked to compliant data.

This linked information must not be presented in a GIPS Report.

Outside of a GIPS Report, firms may present this linked information if asked to do so by a prospective client or prospective investor. The linked information may be presented in a one-on-one presentation that is created for and will be used only by the prospective client or prospective investor.

The linked information may also be presented outside of a GIPS Report in marketing materials provided to other prospective clients or prospective investors if the following conditions are met:

- The linked information is presented in a one-on-one presentation that includes the delivery of a GIPS Report, if the corresponding GIPS Report has not been previously delivered to the prospective client or prospective investor;
- The linked information is presented only to prospective clients or prospective investors who the firm believes are sufficiently knowledgeable about investments and can understand the relevance and limitations of the track record being presented;
- There are sufficient disclosures regarding the linked information so that prospective clients and prospective investors understand that this is not a GIPS-compliant track record. Disclosure, however, does not necessarily prevent information from being false or misleading;
- The linked information is not presented if a GIPS-compliant track record is requested; and
- The linked information is not included in a consultant database.

A firm may wish to present performance for select time periods, other than the time period(s) required and recommended by the GIPS standards. For example, if the market experienced a sharp decline during the first two months of the calendar year and became more stable in March, the firm may want to show performance of its strategy from 1 January through 28 February and from 1 March through 31 December. If the performance for these select time periods is presented in addition to the performance for the required time periods, it may be presented in a GIPS Report. This is permitted because the select time periods are being presented in addition to the required time periods. To present only performance for the select time periods without performance for the required time periods, especially if the select time periods were chosen because the periods had the highest performance, would be misleading and is not permitted for firms that claim compliance with the GIPS standards. Firms may present performance for select time periods outside of GIPS Reports with the appropriate disclosure and labeling.

The firm may provide to a prospective client or prospective investor any information requested by that prospective client or prospective investor. Such information must be restricted to a one-on-one presentation for use with that specific prospective client or prospective investor and must be accompanied by comprehensive disclosures that explain the information being presented. A one-on-one presentation is not limited to a formal presentation or to information presented in a face-to-face meeting. A one-on-one presentation refers to a presentation that is created for and will be used only by the prospective client or prospective investor who made the request.

Provision 1.A.8

If the FIRM does not meet all the applicable REQUIREMENTS of the GIPS standards, the FIRM MUST NOT represent or state that it is "in compliance with the Global Investment Performance Standards except for..." or make any other statements that may indicate compliance or partial compliance with the GIPS standards.

Discussion

When a firm makes the claim of compliance with the GIPS standards, it is representing that all of the applicable requirements of the GIPS standards have been met on a firm-wide basis. Either a firm meets all of the applicable requirements of the GIPS standards and may claim compliance, or a firm does not meet all of the applicable requirements of the GIPS standards and must not claim compliance or partial compliance with the GIPS standards. If the firm does not meet all of the applicable requirements of the GIPS standards, the firm must not represent or state that it is "in compliance with the Global Investment Performance Standards except for..." or make any other statements that may indicate compliance or partial compliance with the GIPS standards.

Provision 1.A.9

Statements referring to the calculation methodology as being "in accordance," "in compliance," or "consistent" with the Global Investment Performance Standards, or similar statements, are prohibited.

Discussion

Only firms that manage actual assets may claim compliance with the GIPS standards. For firms that do manage actual assets, either directly or through the use of sub-advisors, compliance can be achieved only when the firm has met all of the applicable requirements of the GIPS standards on a firm-wide basis. Compliance with the GIPS standards involves more than just the use of a particular calculation methodology. To avoid any confusion, references to the GIPS standards must not be used in the context of reporting performance or performance presentations when the firm is not in compliance with the GIPS standards.

Software vendors, custodians, and other service providers do not manage actual assets and cannot claim compliance with the GIPS standards. They may make reference to the fact that their software or services may help an asset manager achieve or maintain compliance with the GIPS standards, if that is the case. For example, a software vendor may state that its software system calculates performance that satisfies the calculation requirements of the GIPS standards, but the vendor must not state or imply that using its system automatically makes a firm compliant with the GIPS standards or that its system complies with the GIPS standards.

Consultant databases or questionnaires often require investment management firms to fill in monthly or quarterly performance data. The databases or questionnaires then ask the manager to indicate whether or not the data presented has been prepared in accordance with the GIPS standards. When responding to such a database or questionnaire, a firm that claims compliance with the GIPS standards may state that the returns "are prepared in compliance with the GIPS standards" if the following conditions are met:

- The performance information used to complete the questionnaire is consistent with the information used to prepare the corresponding GIPS Report;
- If applicable, the performance information used to complete the questionnaire is more current than the information currently included in the corresponding GIPS Report but will be used in the future to update the corresponding GIPS Report; and
- If applicable, the performance information used to complete the questionnaire is older than the information currently included in the corresponding GIPS Report but could have been used to report the composite's or pooled fund's performance for periods prior to those currently included in the GIPS Report.

Provision 1.A.10

The FIRM MUST NOT make statements referring to the performance of a current client or POOLED FUND investor as being "calculated in accordance with the Global Investment Performance Standards," except for when a GIPS-compliant FIRM reports the performance of a SEGREGATED ACCOUNT to current clients or a POOLED FUND to current investors.

Discussion

The GIPS standards do not specifically address how a firm must report performance of an individual client's portfolio to current clients or how the performance of an investor's investment in a pooled fund must be reported to current pooled fund investors. The GIPS standards do provide an ethical framework for calculating and presenting a firm's investment performance history, allowing both prospective and current clients and pooled fund investors the best opportunity to fairly evaluate the firm's past performance.

The firm must not make statements referring to the performance of a current client or pooled fund investor as being "calculated in accordance with the Global Investment Performance Standards," except for when a GIPS-compliant firm reports the performance of a segregated account to current clients or a pooled fund to current investors. When a firm that claims compliance with the GIPS standards reports the performance of a current client's portfolio to that client or reports the performance of an investor's investment in a pooled fund to a current pooled fund investor, the firm may note on the current client's or investor's performance report that the return was calculated in accordance with the requirements of the GIPS standards if the statement is true.

Provision 1.A.11

The FIRM MUST make every reasonable effort to provide a GIPS COMPOSITE REPORT to all PROSPECTIVE CLIENTS when they initially become PROSPECTIVE CLIENTS. The FIRM MUST NOT choose to which PROSPECTIVE CLIENTS it presents a GIPS COMPOSITE REPORT.

Discussion

Firms claiming compliance with the GIPS standards must make every reasonable effort to provide all prospective clients with a GIPS Composite Report when they initially become prospective clients. The GIPS Composite Report must be one that represents the strategy being marketed to the prospective client. The firm must not choose to which prospective clients it presents a GIPS Composite Report.

A GIPS Composite Report is defined as a presentation for a composite that contains all the information required by the GIPS standards and may also include recommended information and supplemental information. It may also include other information that the firm believes would be helpful to interpreting the GIPS Report. A prospective client is defined as any person or entity that has expressed interest in one of the firm's composite strategies and qualifies to invest in the composite. Current clients may also qualify as prospective clients for any strategy that differs from their current investment strategy. Providing a GIPS Composite Report to current clients interested in a strategy different from their current strategy will help ensure that they have the information necessary to evaluate the new investment strategy and make an informed decision. Investment consultants, consultant databases, and other third parties are considered prospective clients if they represent individuals or entities that qualify as prospective clients.

It is up to the firm to establish policies and procedures for determining who is considered to be a prospective client. These include policies and procedures for determining when an interested party becomes a prospective client. An interested party becomes a prospective client when two tests are met. First, the interested party must have expressed interest in a specific composite strategy or strategies. Second, the firm must have determined that the interested party qualifies to invest in the respective composite strategy. For example, assume a firm is meeting with an interested party to introduce the firm to the interested party. At this initial meeting, the firm provides information about itself in an attempt to interest the interested party in investing with the firm. At this point, the two tests to qualify as a prospective client have not been met; therefore, the interested party is not yet a prospective client, and the firm is not obligated to provide a GIPS Composite Report. The firm should, however, communicate that it claims compliance with the GIPS standards and offer to provide a list of all composite and limited distribution pooled fund descriptions.

Once the interested party expresses interest in a specific composite strategy and the firm determines that the interested party qualifies to invest in the composite strategy, the interested party then becomes a prospective client. This is the point at which the firm must make every reasonable effort to provide the prospective client with the appropriate GIPS Composite Report, if the firm has not already provided it to the prospective client.

At times, a prospective client may ask the firm about a composite strategy that the firm does not yet manage. For example, assume a firm manages one equity and one fixed-income composite and has been meeting with a prospective client who originally was interested in (and qualified to invest in) the equity composite. The prospective client learns that the firm also manages fixed-income portfolios and inquires about a balanced strategy that blends the equity and fixed-income strategies. If the firm does not have an appropriate composite to present to the prospective client, the firm must inform the prospective client that it does not currently manage the specific style or strategy. The firm may present information regarding the hypothetical blended balanced strategy, but this must not be presented as a GIPS-compliant track record. The hypothetical blend may be included in a GIPS Report as supplemental information only if all the component composites on which the hypothetical blend is based are included in the respective GIPS Report. If a hypothetical blend based on the performance of actual component composites is presented outside of a GIPS Report, it is recommended but not required that the presentation include all the component composites on which the hypothetical blend is based.

A prospective client may request a GIPS Composite Report for a new composite for which the firm is not yet required to prepare a GIPS Composite Report. The firm may also wish to market a new composite for which a GIPS Composite Report has not yet been created. For example, a firm launches a strategy 1 June and is marketing the strategy in October. In such cases, the performance for the composite must be made available, but it is not required to be within a GIPS Composite Report. The firm must create a GIPS Composite Report for the new composite that includes performance from inception through the initial annual period end. If the prospective client for this new strategy is still a prospective client after the GIPS Composite Report is prepared with performance from composite inception through the initial annual period end, the firm must provide this GIPS Composite Report to the prospective client.

Because a firm is required to demonstrate that it made every reasonable effort to provide prospective clients with a GIPS Composite Report (see Provision 1.A.17), a firm should establish policies and procedures for tracking which GIPS Composite Reports or initial partial-period performance outside of a GIPS Composite Report were provided to which prospective clients, and when. Doing so will allow a firm to determine when ongoing prospective clients must receive an updated GIPS Composite Report. (See Provision 1.A.12 regarding the requirement to provide an updated GIPS Composite Report to ongoing prospective clients.) It will also allow a firm to know who must receive a corrected GIPS Composite Report in cases for which the firm determines that a previously distributed GIPS Composite Report contained a material error. (See Provision 1.A.20.)

It is the firm's obligation to make every reasonable effort to provide a GIPS Composite Report to prospective clients. The firm may do so by providing the GIPS Report directly to the prospective client or by providing the prospective client with an electronic link to the GIPS Report. The link provided must be a direct link to the GIPS Composite Report, however, and not simply a general link to firm information, such as a link to the firm's website.

Firms are not limited to providing only GIPS Composite Reports to prospective clients or interested parties. Firms may present other performance or performance-related information, in addition to the GIPS Composite Report, as long as it is not false or misleading. Firms may also provide any performance or performance-related information a prospective client requests for use in a one-on-one presentation. Such information must be restricted to a one-on-one presentation for use with that specific prospective client and must be accompanied by comprehensive disclosures that explain the information being presented. A one-on-one presentation is not limited to a formal presentation or to information presented in a face-to-face meeting. In this case, the one-on-one presentation refers to the presentation that is created for and will be used only by the prospective client who made the request.

Provision 1.A.12

Once the FIRM has provided a GIPS COMPOSITE REPORT to a PROSPECTIVE CLIENT, the FIRM MUST provide an updated GIPS COMPOSITE REPORT at least once every 12 months if the PROSPECTIVE CLIENT is still a PROSPECTIVE CLIENT.

Discussion

Some prospective clients remain prospective clients for extended periods. Once a firm has provided a GIPS Composite Report to a prospective client, the firm must provide an updated GIPS Composite Report at least once every 12 months if the prospective client is still a prospective client. If a firm provides performance information to an investment consultant or a database, these entities qualify as prospective clients and must receive the appropriate GIPS Composite Report(s). They must also receive an updated GIPS Composite Report at least once every 12 months.

Provision 1.A.13

The FIRM MUST make every reasonable effort to provide a GIPS REPORT to all LIMITED DISTRIBUTION POOLED FUND PROSPECTIVE INVESTORS when they initially become PROSPECTIVE INVESTORS. The GIPS REPORT may be either:

a. A GIPS POOLED FUND REPORT, or
b. A GIPS COMPOSITE REPORT. A GIPS COMPOSITE REPORT may be provided only if the LIMITED DISTRIBUTION POOLED FUND is included in the respective COMPOSITE.

The FIRM MUST NOT choose to which LIMITED DISTRIBUTION POOLED FUND PROSPECTIVE INVESTORS it presents a GIPS REPORT.

Discussion

The firm must make every reasonable effort to provide a GIPS Report to all limited distribution pooled fund (LDPF) prospective investors when they initially become prospective investors. The GIPS Report may be either a GIPS Pooled Fund Report or a GIPS Composite Report. A GIPS Composite Report may be provided only if the LDPF is included in the respective composite. The firm must not choose to which LDPF prospective investors it presents a GIPS Report. For purposes of complying with the GIPS standards, the firm must classify pooled funds as either broad distribution pooled funds (BDPFs) or LDPFs. Because the reporting requirements in Provision 1.A.13 apply only to LDPFs, firms that offer pooled funds must be able to correctly classify their pooled funds in order to determine whether this provision applies. The classification of pooled funds is made at the fund level, not the share class level.

A *broad distribution pooled fund* (BDPF) is a pooled fund that is:

- regulated under a framework that would permit the general public to purchase or hold the pooled fund's shares, and
- is not exclusively offered in one-on-one presentations.

A *limited distribution pooled fund* (LDPF) is any pooled fund that is not a broad distribution pooled fund.

Although the classification of pooled funds is often straightforward (e.g., a fund that may be purchased by the general public online is typically a BDPF), there are situations in which the appropriate classification of a pooled fund is less clear.

In some cases, a firm elects to offer or sell the pooled fund to only a subset of the general public, such as retirement accounts for individuals. For purposes of classifying funds as limited or broad, these funds are considered to be available to the general public because anyone within the limited group of investors may purchase or hold the pooled fund's shares.

Because the classification of a fund is made at the pooled fund level, no pooled fund will have some of its classes of shares classified as a BDPF and some as an LDPF. If the firm offers, or is permitted to offer, any of the pooled fund's share classes to the general public, and the shares are not sold exclusively in one-on-one presentations, the pooled fund may be classified as a BDPF. This would be the case even if some shares classes of the fund are not available to the general public or are offered only in a one-one-one presentation.

If a firm is the sub-advisor for a pooled fund that is marketed or distributed by another firm as either an LDPF or a BDPF, the firm acting as sub-advisor must treat the sub-advised pooled fund as a segregated account. It must be included in a composite if it is fee-paying and discretionary. Only if the firm offers participation in the pooled fund, either directly or through an agent, would the pooled fund be considered either a BDPF or LDPF.

The following table provides information about how to classify pooled funds as BDPF or LDPF.

Example	Description	BDPF/ LDPF	Not Offered Exclusively in One-on-One Presentations	Regulations Permit General Public to Purchase Shares	Explanation
1.	Pooled fund with one or more share classes that are offered to the general public (retail share classes). The share classes are not sold exclusively in one-on-one presentations.	BDPF	Yes	Yes	The fund is classified as a BDPF because it is regulated under a framework that would permit the general public to purchase or hold shares and is offered to the general public in a manner that does not exclusively involve one-on-one presentations.
2.	Pooled fund that is regulated under a framework that would permit the general public to purchase or hold shares, but the firm has chosen to offer institutional share classes only. All share classes are sold exclusively in one-on-one presentations.	LDPF	No	Yes	The fund is classified as an LDPF because it is offered exclusively in one-on-one presentations.
3.	Pooled fund that is regulated under a framework that would permit the general public to purchase or hold shares, but the firm has chosen to offer institutional share classes only. The fund is marketed in a variety of ways that do not always involve a one-on-one presentation with prospective institutional investors.	BDPF	Yes	Yes	The fund is classified as a BDPF because it is regulated under a framework that would permit the general public to purchase or hold share although the firm has chosen not to do so, and it is not offered exclusively in one-on-one presentations.
4.	Pooled fund regulated under a framework that would permit the general public to purchase or hold the pooled fund's shares. The firm offers shares of the fund exclusively in one-on-one presentations.	LDPF	No	Yes	The fund is classified as an LDPF because all share classes are offered exclusively in one-on-one presentations.

(continued)

Example	Description	BDPF/ LDPF	Not Offered Exclusively in One-on-One Presentations	Regulations Permit General Public to Purchase Shares	Explanation
5.	Pooled fund with one or more retail share classes and one or more institutional share classes.	BDPF	Yes	Yes	The fund is classified as a BDPF because it has retail share classes, whether or not its institutional classes are offered exclusively in one-on-one presentations.
6.	Pooled fund with one or more retail share classes that is classified as a BDPF in its home country, but it may be offered only as a private placement in other countries for regulatory reasons.	BDPF	Yes	Yes	The fund is classified as a BDPF because it has retail share classes, even though in other jurisdictions it may not be held by the general public and is offered in one-on-one presentations.
7.	Pooled fund with shares traded on an exchange.	BDPF	Yes	Yes	The fund is classified as a BDPF because it is regulated under a framework that would permit the general public to purchase or hold shares and is not offered exclusively in one-on-one presentations.
8.	Pooled fund that is regulated under a framework that would permit the general public to purchase or hold shares, but that for regulatory or business reasons is offered exclusively through intermediaries and/or via platforms that are accessible to investors that meet certain qualifications. The fund is not offered exclusively in one-on-one presentations.	BDPF	Yes	Yes	The fund is classified as a BDPF because it is regulated under a framework that would permit the general public to purchase or hold its shares and it is not offered exclusively in one-on-one presentations.

(continued)

Example	Description	BDPF/ LDPF	Not Offered Exclusively in One-on-One Presentations	Regulations Permit General Public to Purchase Shares	Explanation
9.	Pooled fund that is regulated under a framework that would permit certain members of the general public to purchase or hold shares, and is sold exclusively to investors with certain tax or affinity characteristics (e.g., retirement accounts). The fund is not offered exclusively in one-on-one presentations.	BDPF	Yes	Yes	Funds that are available only to a subset of investors with certain tax or affinity characteristics that are shared by a large portion of the public are considered to be available to the general public.
10.	Pooled fund that has a partnership structure and is exclusively offered in one-on-one presentations.	LDPF	No	No	The fund is classified as an LDPF because it is offered exclusively in one-on-one presentations and is not available to the general public.
11.	Pooled fund that is exclusively offered in one-on-one presentations to sponsors or agents that make investment decisions on behalf of beneficial owners (e.g., plan participants).	LDPF	No	No	The fund is classified as an LDPF because it is offered exclusively in one-on-one presentations to the sponsor or agent that makes investment decisions (determines which pooled funds will be offered to beneficial owners) on behalf of beneficial owners. In this scenario, the firm has no obligation to provide GIPS Reports to individual beneficial owners.

This table categorizes several common pooled fund structures as LDPFs or BDPFs. Because of the diversity of fund structures in various jurisdictions, these examples cannot address every possible structure, and many firms will need to make good faith determinations regarding the treatment of specific pooled funds.

Providing GIPS Reports to LDPF Prospective Investors

If a firm offers LDPFs, it is required to provide an LDPF prospective investor with a GIPS Report. The GIPS Report can be either a GIPS Pooled Fund Report or a GIPS Composite Report.

- A GIPS Pooled Fund Report is a presentation for a pooled fund that contains all the information required by the GIPS standards and may also include recommended information, supplemental information, and other information. Other information may be included as long as it is not false or misleading.

- A GIPS Composite Report is a presentation for a composite that contains all the information required by the GIPS standards and may also include recommended information, supplemental information, and other information. Other information may be included as long as it is not false or misleading.

A GIPS Composite Report may be provided to an LDPF prospective investor in lieu of a GIPS Pooled Fund Report but only if the LDPF is included in the respective composite.

An LDPF prospective investor is any person or entity that has expressed interest in one of the firm's LDPFs and is qualified to invest in the fund. Current pooled fund investors may also qualify as prospective investors for any pooled fund that is different from their current pooled fund. Providing a GIPS Report to current pooled fund investors interested in a pooled fund different from their current pooled fund will help ensure that they have information to better evaluate the new pooled fund and make an informed decision. Investment consultants, consultant databases, and other third parties are included as prospective investors if they represent individuals or entities that qualify as prospective investors.

It is up to the firm to establish policies and procedures for determining who is considered to be a pooled fund prospective investor, including policies and procedures for determining when an interested party becomes an LDPF prospective investor. An interested party becomes a pooled fund prospective investor when two tests are met. First, the interested party must have expressed interest in a specific LDPF. Second, the firm must have determined that the interested party qualifies to invest in the respective pooled fund. For example, assume a firm is meeting with an interested party to introduce the firm to the interested party. At this initial meeting, the firm provides information about itself in an attempt to attract the interested party to invest with the firm. At this point, the two tests to qualify as a pooled fund prospective investor have not been met; therefore, the interested party is not yet a prospective investor, and the firm is not obligated to provide a GIPS Report. However, the firm should communicate that it claims compliance with the GIPS standards and offer to provide a list of all composite and LDPF descriptions.

Once the interested party expresses interest in a specific LDPF and the firm determines that the interested party qualifies to invest in the pooled fund, the interested party then becomes a pooled fund prospective investor. At this point, the firm must make every reasonable effort to provide the prospective investor with the appropriate GIPS Report.

LDPFs with No Performance History

Participation in a new LDPF is often marketed by a firm before the pooled fund has a track record. If an LDPF has no performance history, there is no requirement to provide a GIPS Report. It is recommended, however, that the firm provide the most appropriate track record for the new fund if an appropriate track record is available. (See Provision 1.B.7.) The most appropriate track record would be a GIPS Report for a composite or another pooled fund that the firm manages according to the same or similar strategy as the LDPF that has not yet started. If an appropriate track record is presented to prospective investors, sufficient information should be provided so that pooled fund prospective investors understand the source and nature of the track record presented. As is always the case, the information presented must adhere to the principles of fair representation and full disclosure.

A prospective investor may request a GIPS Report for a new LDPF for which the firm is not yet required to prepare a GIPS Report. The firm may also wish to market a new LDPF for which a GIPS Report has not yet been created because the LDPF has not reached the initial annual period end. In such cases, the performance for the LDPF must be made available, but it is not required to be within a GIPS Report. If the prospective investor for this new LDPF is still a prospective investor after a GIPS Report with performance through the initial annual period end is prepared, the firm must provide this GIPS Report to the prospective investor.

Tracking Which GIPS Report Has Been Provided

Because a firm is required to demonstrate that it made every reasonable effort to provide LDPF prospective investors with a GIPS Composite Report or GIPS Pooled Fund Report (see Provision 1.A.17), a firm should establish policies and procedures for tracking which GIPS Report(s) or initial partial-period performance outside of a GIPS Report were provided to which LDPF prospective investors and when. Doing so will allow a firm to determine when ongoing LDPF prospective investors must receive an updated GIPS Report. (See Provision 1.A.14 regarding the requirement to provide an updated GIPS Report to ongoing prospective investors.) It will also allow a firm to know who must receive a corrected GIPS Report in cases where the firm determines that a previously distributed GIPS Report contained a material error. (See Provisions 1.A.20 and 1.A.21.)

Electronic Delivery

It is the firm's obligation to make every reasonable effort to provide a GIPS Report to prospective investors. This obligation may be met by providing the GIPS Report directly to the prospective investor or by providing the prospective investor with an electronic link to the GIPS Report. However, the link provided must be a direct link to either the GIPS Pooled Fund Report for the LDPF in which the prospective investor is interested or the GIPS Composite Report for the composite in which the LDPF is included, and not simply a general link to firm information, such as a link to the firm's website.

Performance Information Outside of a GIPS Report

Firms are not limited to providing only GIPS Reports to LDPF prospective investors or interested parties. Firms may present other performance or performance-related information, in addition to the GIPS Report, as long as it is not false or misleading. The firm may also provide any performance or performance-related information a prospective investor requests for use in a one-on-one presentation. Such information must be restricted to a one-on-one presentation for use with that specific prospective investor and must be accompanied with comprehensive disclosures that explain the information being presented. A one-on-one presentation is not limited to a formal presentation or to information presented in a face-to-face meeting. In this case, the one-on-one presentation refers to the presentation that is created for and will be used only by the prospective investor who made the request.

Provision 1.A.14

Once the FIRM has provided a GIPS POOLED FUND REPORT or GIPS COMPOSITE REPORT to a LIMITED DISTRIBUTION POOLED FUND PROSPECTIVE INVESTOR, the FIRM MUST provide an updated GIPS POOLED FUND REPORT or GIPS COMPOSITE REPORT at least once every 12 months if the LIMITED DISTRIBUTION POOLED FUND PROSPECTIVE INVESTOR is still a LIMITED DISTRIBUTION POOLED FUND PROSPECTIVE INVESTOR.

Discussion

Some limited distribution pooled fund (LDPF) prospective investors remain pooled fund prospective investors for extended periods of time. Once a firm has provided a GIPS Report, either a GIPS Pooled Fund Report or a GIPS Composite Report, to an LDPF prospective investor, the firm must provide an updated GIPS Report at least once every 12 months if the pooled fund prospective investor is still a prospective investor. If a firm provides performance information to an investment consultant or a database, these entities qualify as prospective investors and must receive the appropriate GIPS Report. They must also receive an updated GIPS Report at least once every 12 months.

Provision 1.A.15

The FIRM may provide a GIPS POOLED FUND REPORT or a GIPS COMPOSITE REPORT that includes the BROAD DISTRIBUTION POOLED FUND to BROAD DISTRIBUTION POOLED FUND PROSPECTIVE INVESTORS but is not REQUIRED to do so.

Discussion

A broad distribution pooled fund (BDPF) is a pooled fund that is regulated under a framework that would permit the general public to purchase or hold the pooled fund's shares and is not exclusively offered in one-on-one presentations. (More extensive guidance on the classification of a pooled fund as a BDPF can be found in the discussion of Provision 1.A.13.) BDPFs are typically highly regulated. Because of both the complexity and diversity of local laws and regulations applying to BDPFs, which typically specify what must be included in the materials for these funds, as well as what must not be included, it is not required that a GIPS Report be provided to BDPF prospective investors. If a firm wishes to provide a GIPS Pooled Fund Report or GIPS Composite Report that includes the BDPF to a BDPF prospective investor, however, it may do so.

Because a firm that manages and markets only BDPFs is not required to provide a GIPS Report to pooled fund prospective investors, if such a firm complies with the GIPS standards, a claim of compliance with the GIPS standards might not appear in any of its materials. If the firm wishes to present a claim of compliance with the GIPS standards to prospective investors, the claim of compliance may appear in a:

- GIPS Advertisement,
- GIPS Pooled Fund Report, or
- GIPS Composite Report for a composite that includes the BDPF.

The claim of compliance may also appear on the firm's website by including a GIPS Advertisement, or the website itself can adhere to the GIPS Advertising Guidelines. A claim of compliance may also appear in a GIPS Report that is posted on the firm's website.

Because the 2010 edition of the GIPS standards required all portfolios, both segregated accounts and pooled funds, to be included in a composite, many firms had included BDPFs and LDPFs in composites that included only one or more pooled funds. The 2020 edition of the GIPS standards does not require a firm to include a pooled fund in a composite unless the pooled fund is managed in a strategy that is managed for or offered as a segregated account, or the pooled fund meets a composite definition. When a firm adopts the 2020 edition of the GIPS standards, the firm may terminate any composite that contains only pooled funds whose strategy is not offered as a segregated account. However, a firm that wishes to continue to include pooled funds in composites that include only one or more pooled funds, even though the strategy of the pooled funds is not offered as a segregated account, may continue to do so.

Provision 1.A.16

When providing GIPS REPORTS to PROSPECTIVE CLIENTS and PROSPECTIVE INVESTORS, the FIRM MUST update these reports to include information through the most recent annual period end within 12 months of that annual period end.

Discussion

GIPS Composite Reports and GIPS Pooled Fund Reports are designed to provide information to prospective clients or prospective investors that will help them understand the investment mandate, characteristics, and performance of a specific composite or pooled fund managed by the firm. Although a GIPS Report contains important information, the value and relevance of that information are affected by the timeliness with which the GIPS Report is updated. A GIPS Report that presents returns that are significantly out of date is not helpful to prospective clients or prospective investors. It is therefore required that any GIPS Report that is provided to a prospective client or prospective investor must be updated within 12 months of the end of the most recent annual period end. As an example, suppose that a firm presents calendar-year returns in GIPS Reports. GIPS Reports with information through 31 December 2020 must be available no later than 31 December 2021. The lack of the completion of an annual verification is not a valid reason for delaying the updating of a GIPS Report.

If a specific composite or pooled fund is not being marketed, and as a result there are no prospective clients or prospective investors for the composite or pooled fund, the firm is not required to update the respective GIPS Report. As stated in Provision 1.A.24, however, a firm must provide a GIPS Report for any composite that is on the firm's list of composite descriptions, and any pooled fund that is on the firm's list of limited distribution pooled fund (LDPF) descriptions, to a prospective client or prospective investor upon request. While a firm is not required to annually update a GIPS Report when there are no prospective clients or prospective investors, the firm must be able to provide an updated GIPS Report, within a reasonable period of time, to a prospective client or prospective investor for the respective composite or LDPF.

Provision 1.A.17

The FIRM MUST be able to demonstrate how it made every reasonable effort to provide:

a. A GIPS COMPOSITE REPORT to those PROSPECTIVE CLIENTS REQUIRED to receive a GIPS COMPOSITE REPORT.

b. A GIPS POOLED FUND REPORT or GIPS COMPOSITE REPORT to those LIMITED DISTRIBUTION POOLED FUND PROSPECTIVE INVESTORS REQUIRED to receive a GIPS POOLED FUND REPORT or GIPS COMPOSITE REPORT.

Discussion

Firms are required to make every reasonable effort to provide a GIPS Composite Report to all prospective clients and a GIPS Pooled Fund Report or GIPS Composite Report to all limited distribution pooled fund (LDPF) prospective investors. A firm may provide a GIPS Composite

Report to an LDPF prospective investor in lieu of a GIPS Pooled Fund Report only if the respective LDPF is included in the composite. Firms are also required to have policies and procedures in place that are used to establish and maintain compliance with the requirements of the GIPS standards. Therefore, any firm claiming compliance with the GIPS standards must have specific policies and procedures to ensure that every reasonable effort is made to provide the required GIPS Composite Report to prospective clients and the required GIPS Report to LDPF prospective investors. These should include policies and procedures for tracking which GIPS Reports were provided to which prospective clients or prospective investors, and when. For example, a firm's policies and procedures might specify that the required GIPS Report will be included as part of the standard package of marketing materials prepared for prospective clients or pooled fund prospective investors, and that a checklist will be used to indicate the dates on which the GIPS Report was provided to the prospective client or prospective investor and which version of the GIPS Report was provided. Documenting the date on which the GIPS Report was last provided to the prospective client or prospective investor as well as the version of the GIPS Report will help a firm fulfill the requirement that the appropriate GIPS Report be provided to a prospective client or prospective investor who remains a prospect at least once every 12 months. The most effective policies and procedures for a firm will depend on the circumstances surrounding the typical interactions between the firm and its prospective clients or prospective investors.

To demonstrate that the firm made a reasonable effort to provide the appropriate GIPS Report to prospective clients and prospective investors, it is necessary for the firm to document both the relevant policies and procedures for providing the required reports to prospective clients and pooled fund investors and the steps taken to implement the relevant policies and procedures.

Provision 1.A.18

A COMPOSITE BENCHMARK used in a GIPS COMPOSITE REPORT MUST reflect the investment mandate, objective, or strategy of the COMPOSITE. The FIRM MUST NOT use a price-only BENCHMARK in a GIPS COMPOSITE REPORT.

Discussion

Benchmarks are important tools that aid in the planning, implementation, and evaluation of a portfolio's investment policy. They also help facilitate discussions with prospective clients regarding the relationship between risk and return. As a result, firms are required to present the total return for a benchmark that reflects the composite's investment mandate, objective, or strategy in all GIPS Composite Reports.

GIPS Composite Reports that include time-weighted returns must include composite returns for each annual period. GIPS Composite Reports that include money-weighted returns must include the composite return for the period from inception through the most recent annual period end. Firms must present benchmark returns for these required periods and for any additional periods for which composite returns are presented. For example, if a GIPS Composite Report includes quarterly composite returns, quarterly benchmark returns must also be included.

The benchmark that appears in a GIPS Composite Report may be different from the benchmark(s) used for the portfolios that are included in the composite. For example, a firm may decide that it is appropriate to include portfolios with different benchmarks in the same composite. Additionally, a firm may present more than one benchmark in a GIPS Composite Report. The firm must determine the appropriate benchmark or benchmarks for each composite.

There may be situations in which there is no appropriate benchmark for a composite—that is, no benchmark exists that reflects the composite's investment mandate, objective, or strategy. In such cases, the firm must not present a benchmark in the GIPS Composite Report and must disclose why no benchmark is presented. Outside of a GIPS Composite Report, a firm may present a benchmark that is not reflective of the composite's strategy. There must, however, be a valid reason for doing so. For example, if a firm believes that no appropriate benchmark exists, it might want to present a market index to represent the opportunity cost of investing in the composite's investment strategy. If such a benchmark is used outside of a GIPS Composite Report, there must be sufficient disclosure so that a prospective client or prospective investor understands the nature of the benchmark and why it is being presented. Disclosure, however, does not necessarily prevent information from being false or misleading. A firm must not select a benchmark for the purpose of providing a favorable comparison to the performance of the composite. To do so would be misleading, regardless of the disclosures accompanying the benchmark.

Because the GIPS standards require that the total return for the benchmark be presented, a price-only index will not satisfy the requirements of the GIPS standards. This also applies to benchmarks that are components of a blended benchmark. A blended benchmark is the combination of two or more indexes, such as a benchmark that consists of 50% of the ABC Index and 50% of the DEF Index. In this example, both the ABC Index and the DEF Index must be total return benchmarks, not price-only benchmarks. However, when there is an appropriate total return benchmark, a price-only benchmark may be presented in a GIPS Composite Report as supplemental information, as well as outside of a GIPS Composite Report if the price-only benchmark is accompanied by a total return benchmark. If a price-only benchmark is included in a GIPS Composite Report as supplemental information, or is presented outside of a GIPS Composite Report, it must be identified as a price-only benchmark, and there must be sufficient disclosures so that a prospective client or prospective investor understands the difference between the return of a price-only benchmark and the return of a total return benchmark. If no appropriate total return benchmark for the composite's strategy exists, the firm may not present a price-only benchmark in a GIPS Composite Report but may present it outside of a GIPS Composite Report. In such cases, "price only" must be included in the label or the name of the benchmark. As in all cases where a price-only benchmark is presented, there must be sufficient disclosures so that a prospective client or prospective investor understands the difference between the return of a price-only benchmark and the return of a total return benchmark.

Some benchmarks may appear to be price-only benchmarks because they do not include income, but they should be considered total return benchmarks. These include the following:

- private market equivalent (PME) benchmarks,
- commodity benchmarks, and similar benchmarks, that do not have income because of the nature of the benchmark constituents, and
- target returns, such as an 8% hurdle rate.

Provision 1.A.19

A POOLED FUND BENCHMARK used in a GIPS POOLED FUND REPORT MUST reflect the investment mandate, objective, or strategy of the POOLED FUND. The FIRM MUST NOT use a price-only BENCHMARK in a GIPS POOLED FUND REPORT.

Discussion

Benchmarks are important tools that aid in the planning, implementation, and evaluation of a pooled fund's investment policy. They also help facilitate discussions with pooled fund prospective investors regarding the relationship between risk and return. As a result, firms are required to present the total return for a benchmark that reflects the pooled fund's investment mandate, objective, or strategy in all GIPS Pooled Fund Reports.

GIPS Pooled Fund Reports that include time-weighted returns must include pooled fund returns for each annual period. GIPS Pooled Fund Reports that include money-weighted returns must include the pooled fund return for the period from inception through the most recent annual period end. Firms must present benchmark returns for these required periods and for any additional periods for which pooled fund returns are presented. For example, if a GIPS Pooled Fund Report includes quarterly pooled fund returns, quarterly benchmark returns must also be included.

The benchmark that appears in a GIPS Pooled Fund Report may differ from the benchmark that is required to be presented in the pooled fund's regulatory materials or that is presented in other fund marketing materials. A firm may also present more than one benchmark in a GIPS Pooled Fund Report. The firm must determine the appropriate benchmark or benchmarks for each pooled fund.

There may be situations in which there is no appropriate benchmark for a pooled fund—that is, no benchmark exists that reflects the pooled fund's investment mandate, objective, or strategy.

In such cases, the firm must not present a benchmark in the GIPS Pooled Fund Report and must disclose why no benchmark is presented. Outside of a GIPS Pooled Fund Report, a firm may present a benchmark that is not reflective of the pooled fund's strategy. There must, however, be a valid reason for doing so. For example, laws or regulations sometimes require the use of what would be considered an inappropriate benchmark for a broad distribution pooled fund. As another example, if a firm believes that no appropriate benchmark exists, it might want to present a market index to represent the opportunity cost of investing in the pooled fund. If such a benchmark is used outside of a GIPS Pooled Fund Report, there must be sufficient disclosure so that a pooled fund prospective investor understands the nature of the benchmark and why it is being presented. Disclosure, however, does not necessarily prevent information from being false or misleading. A firm must not select a benchmark for the purpose of providing a favorable comparison to the performance of the pooled fund. To do so would be misleading, regardless of the disclosures accompanying the benchmark.

Because the GIPS standards require that the total return for the benchmark be presented, a price-only index will not satisfy the requirements of the GIPS standards. This also applies to benchmarks that are components of a blended benchmark. A blended benchmark is the combination of two or more indexes, such as a benchmark that consists of 50% of the ABC Index and 50% of the DEF Index. In this example, both the ABC Index and the DEF Index must be total return benchmarks, not price-only benchmarks. However, when there is an appropriate total return benchmark, a price-only benchmark may be presented in a GIPS Pooled Fund Report as supplemental information, as well as outside of a GIPS Pooled Fund Report, if the price-only benchmark is accompanied by a total return benchmark. If a price-only benchmark is included in a GIPS Pooled Fund Report as supplemental information, or is presented outside of a GIPS Pooled Fund Report, it must be identified as a price-only benchmark, and there must be sufficient disclosures so that a prospective investor understands the difference between the return of a price-only benchmark and the return of a total return benchmark. If no appropriate total return benchmark for the pooled fund's strategy exists, the firm may not present a price-only benchmark in a GIPS Pooled Fund Report but may present it outside of a GIPS Pooled Fund Report. In such cases, "price only" must be included in the label or the name of the benchmark. As in all cases where a price-only benchmark is presented, there must be sufficient disclosures so that a prospective investor understands the difference between the return of a price-only benchmark and the return of a total return benchmark.

Some benchmarks may appear to be price-only benchmarks because they do not include income, but they should be considered total return benchmarks. These include the following:

- private market equivalent (PME) benchmarks,
- commodity benchmarks, and similar benchmarks, that do not have income due to the nature of the benchmark constituents, and
- target returns, such as an 8% hurdle rate.

Provision 1.A.20

The FIRM MUST correct MATERIAL ERRORS in GIPS COMPOSITE REPORTS and MUST:

a. Provide the corrected GIPS COMPOSITE REPORT to the current verifier.
b. Provide the corrected GIPS COMPOSITE REPORT to current clients, current investors,[a] and any former verifiers that received the GIPS COMPOSITE REPORT that had the MATERIAL ERROR.
c. Make every reasonable effort to provide the corrected GIPS COMPOSITE REPORT to all current PROSPECTIVE CLIENTS and PROSPECTIVE INVESTORS that received the GIPS COMPOSITE REPORT that had the MATERIAL ERROR. The FIRM is not REQUIRED to provide a corrected GIPS COMPOSITE REPORT to former clients, former investors, former PROSPECTIVE CLIENTS, or former PROSPECTIVE INVESTORS.

Discussion

Firms claiming compliance with the GIPS standards are likely to face situations in which errors are discovered that must be specifically addressed. Even with the tightest of controls, errors will occur. An error, which can be qualitative or quantitative, is any component of a GIPS Composite Report that is missing or inaccurate. Errors in GIPS Composite Reports can result from, but are not limited to, incorrect, incomplete, or missing:

- composite returns or assets,
- total firm assets,
- benchmark returns,
- number of portfolios in a composite,
- three-year annualized ex post standard deviation, and
- disclosures.

Firms must establish error correction policies and procedures, and materiality must be defined in the error correction policies.

If a GIPS Composite Report contains a material error, the GIPS Composite Report must be corrected and the corrected GIPS Composite Report that includes a disclosure of the error must be provided to the current verifier and to all current clients, current investors, and any former verifiers that received the GIPS Composite Report with the material error. Former verifiers that received the GIPS Composite Report with the material error must receive the corrected GIPS Composite Report with a disclosure of the error in case the error affects a previously issued verification report or performance examination report. The firm must also make every reasonable effort to provide the

[a] The 2020 edition of the GIPS standards incorrectly omitted the words "current investors" from this provision.

corrected GIPS Composite Report to all current prospective clients and prospective investors that received the GIPS Composite Report with the material error. The firm is not required to provide the corrected GIPS Composite Report to former prospective clients or former prospective investors that received the GIPS Composite Report that contained the material error.

The firm generally has three options for dealing with non-material errors in GIPS Composite Reports:

1. *Take no action.*

   The error is deemed immaterial and does not require a change to any data or disclosures in the GIPS Composite Report.
2. *Correct the GIPS Composite Report with no disclosure of the change and no distribution of the corrected GIPS Composite Report.*

   The correction of the error results in a change to one or more items in the GIPS Composite Report, but these changes are deemed not material and therefore do not require disclosure of the change or distribution of the corrected GIPS Composite Report.
3. *Correct the GIPS Composite Report with disclosure of the change and no distribution of the corrected GIPS Composite Report.*

   The correction of the error results in a change to one or more items in the GIPS Composite Report, but these changes are deemed not material. The firm does not distribute the corrected GIPS Composite Report but, according to the firm's pre-established error correction policies and procedures, the error does require disclosure in the corrected GIPS Composite Report.

A firm must decide what criteria it will use to determine materiality. The following is a definition of materiality that firms might find useful as a starting point:

> An error (or item) is material if the magnitude of the omission or misstatement of performance information, in light of surrounding circumstances, makes it probable that the judgment of a reasonable person relying on the information would have been changed by the omission or misstatement.

When determining materiality, a firm may consider the following factors:

- magnitude of the error, in absolute and relative terms,
- whether the error is material relative to the benchmark,
- whether returns are overstated or understated,
- significance of the missing or incorrect disclosures,
- whether the error affects returns over time or is a timing issue,
- period(s) affected by the error,
- if these policies will be applied firm-wide or on a composite-specific or pooled fund–specific basis, and
- whether the firm has any legal or regulatory obligations related to error correction.

The size and effect of the error may vary for different asset types (e.g., equities, fixed income, emerging market equities), reporting periods (e.g., monthly, quarterly, or annual returns), and by time period (e.g., prior to a specific date, more than five years ago).

It is important to remember that the omission of required information is considered an error, as well as a misstatement in the information presented. The GIPS Composite Report must be corrected to include the required information, and the firm must apply its error correction policies to determine if the error is material.

Firms must establish and document error correction policies and procedures and must implement them consistently. A firm should strive to create an unambiguous process that includes specific steps to discover errors.

Provision 1.A.21

The FIRM MUST correct MATERIAL ERRORS in GIPS POOLED FUND REPORTS and MUST:

a. Provide the corrected GIPS POOLED FUND REPORT to the current verifier.

b. Provide the corrected GIPS POOLED FUND REPORT to current investors and any former verifiers that received the GIPS POOLED FUND REPORT that had the MATERIAL ERROR.

c. Make every reasonable effort to provide the corrected GIPS POOLED FUND REPORT to all current PROSPECTIVE INVESTORS that received the GIPS POOLED FUND REPORT that had the MATERIAL ERROR. The FIRM is not REQUIRED to provide a corrected GIPS POOLED FUND REPORT[b] to former investors or former PROSPECTIVE INVESTORS.

Discussion

Firms claiming compliance with the GIPS standards are likely to face situations in which errors are discovered that must be specifically addressed. Even with the tightest of controls, errors will occur. An error, which can be qualitative or quantitative, is any component of a GIPS Pooled Fund Report that is missing or inaccurate. Errors in GIPS Pooled Fund Reports can result from, but are not limited to, incorrect, incomplete, or missing:

- pooled fund returns or assets,
- firm assets,
- benchmark returns, and
- disclosures.

[b] The 2020 edition of the GIPS standards incorrectly state GIPS Composite Report versus GIPS Pooled Fund Report.

Firms must establish error correction policies, and materiality must be defined in the error correction policies.

If a GIPS Pooled Fund Report contains a material error, the GIPS Pooled Fund Report must be corrected and the corrected GIPS Pooled Fund Report that includes a disclosure of the error must be provided to the current verifier, as well as to all current investors and any former verifiers that received the GIPS Pooled Fund Report with the material error. Former verifiers that received the GIPS Pooled Fund Report with the material error must receive the corrected GIPS Pooled Fund Report with a disclosure of the error in case the error affects a previously issued verification report or performance examination report. The firm must also make every reasonable effort to provide the corrected GIPS Pooled Fund Report to all current prospective investors that received the GIPS Pooled Fund Report with the material error. The firm is not required to provide the corrected GIPS Pooled Fund Report to former prospective investors that received the GIPS Pooled Fund Report that contained the material error.

The firm generally has three options for dealing with non-material errors in GIPS Pooled Fund Reports:

1. *Take no action.*

   The error is deemed immaterial and does not require a change to any data or disclosures in the GIPS Pooled Fund Report.
2. *Correct the GIPS Pooled Fund Report with no disclosure of the change and no distribution of the corrected GIPS Pooled Fund Report.*

   The correction of the error results in a change to one or more items in the GIPS Pooled Fund Report, but these changes are deemed not material and therefore do not require disclosure of the change or distribution of the corrected GIPS Pooled Fund Report.
3. *Correct the GIPS Pooled Fund Report with disclosure of the change and no distribution of the corrected GIPS Pooled Fund Report.*

   The correction of the error results in a change to one or more items in the GIPS Pooled Fund Report, but these changes are deemed not material. The firm does not distribute the corrected GIPS Pooled Fund Report but, according to the firm's pre-established error correction policies and procedures, the error does require disclosure in the corrected GIPS Pooled Fund Report.

A firm must decide what criteria it will use to determine materiality. The following is a definition of materiality that firms might find useful as a starting point:

> An error (or item) is material if the magnitude of the omission or misstatement of performance presentation information, in light of surrounding circumstances, makes it probable that the judgment of a reasonable person relying on the information would have been changed by the omission or misstatement.

When determining materiality, a firm may consider the following factors:

- magnitude of the error, in absolute and relative terms,
- whether the error is material relative to the benchmark,
- whether returns are overstated or understated,
- significance of the missing or incorrect disclosures,
- whether the error affects returns over time or is a timing issue,
- period(s) affected by the error,
- if these policies will be applied firm-wide or on a composite-specific or pooled fund–specific basis, and
- whether the firm has any legal or regulatory obligations related to error correction.

The size and effect of the error may vary for different asset types (e.g., equities, fixed income, emerging market equities), reporting periods (e.g., monthly, quarterly, or annual returns), and by time period (e.g., prior to a specific date, more than five years ago).

It is important to remember that the omission of required information is considered an error, as well as a misstatement in the information presented. The GIPS Pooled Fund Report must be corrected to include the required information, and the firm must apply its error correction policies to determine if the error is material.

Firms must establish and document error correction policies and procedures and must implement them consistently. A firm should strive to create an unambiguous process that includes specific steps to discover errors.

Provision 1.A.22

The FIRM MUST maintain:

a. A complete list of COMPOSITE DESCRIPTIONS. The FIRM MUST include terminated COMPOSITES on this list for at least five years after the COMPOSITE TERMINATION DATE.

b. A complete list of POOLED FUND DESCRIPTIONS for LIMITED DISTRIBUTION POOLED FUNDS. The FIRM is not REQUIRED to include terminated LIMITED DISTRIBUTION POOLED FUNDS on this list.

c. A complete list of BROAD DISTRIBUTION POOLED FUNDS. The FIRM is not REQUIRED to include terminated BROAD DISTRIBUTION POOLED FUNDS on this list.

Discussion

Firms must maintain a complete list of composite descriptions and limited distribution pooled fund (LDPF) descriptions. It must also maintain a list, without descriptions, of broad distribution pooled funds (BDPFs). Firms must include terminated composites on the firm's list of composite descriptions for at least five years after the composite termination date. One reason for this requirement is that a terminated composite may be re-started so a list of current and terminated composites may provide a more complete picture of a firm's capabilities.

In contrast, it is not required that a firm's list of LDPF descriptions or its list of BDPFs include terminated pooled funds. Once a pooled fund is closed, it is no longer available for investment and typically would not be restarted.

A firm that manages BDPFs is required to maintain a complete list of BDPFs. The list can be at the fund level; it does not have to be at the share class level. Firms are not required to maintain a complete list of BDPF descriptions. Instead, a firm must provide a description of any BDPF to any BDPF prospective investor upon request.

If a firm is the sub-advisor for a pooled fund that is marketed or distributed by another firm as either an LDPF or a BDPF, the firm acting as sub-advisor must treat the sub-advised pooled fund as a segregated account. It will not appear on the firm's list of LDPFs or BDPFs. Only if the firm offers participation in the pooled fund, either directly or through an agent, will the pooled fund be considered either a BDPF or LDPF.

Prior to the 2020 edition of the GIPS standards, firms were required to include all portfolios, both segregated accounts and pooled funds, in a composite. When a firm adopts the 2020 edition of the GIPS standards, it will no longer be required to include pooled funds in a composite unless the pooled fund is managed in a strategy that is managed for or offered as a segregated account, or the pooled fund meets a composite definition. Once a firm adopts the 2020 GIPS standards, any composites containing only one or more pooled funds whose strategy is not offered as a segregated account may be terminated. These terminated composites are not required to be included on the firm's list of composite descriptions. This is a one-time exemption to the requirement that terminated composites must be included on a firm's list of composite descriptions for five years after the composite termination date. This exemption applies only to those composites that contain only one or more pooled funds and whose strategy is not managed for or not offered as a segregated account.

If an LDPF or BDPF is included in a composite, the LDPF or BDPF must still appear on the required list of LDPF descriptions or the list of BDPFs, if the firm offers participation in the pooled fund, either directly or through an agent. The firm may combine its complete list of composite descriptions, complete list of LDPF descriptions, and complete list of BDPFs into one document if it wishes to do so. The firm may also prepare a list of all the strategies that it offers and indicate, as part of the strategy description, the vehicles (segregated account, LDPF, or BDPF) in which the strategy is available.

Composite and LDPF Descriptions

A composite or LDPF description provides key information about the investment strategy. The description is not meant to replace more comprehensive descriptions of the investment strategy included in the composite or pooled fund definition, investment management agreement, and/or fund offering documents, but it should provide enough information about the strategy to be informative while remaining concise. It must provide enough information to prospective clients or prospective investors to make them aware of any significant features of a composite or pooled fund investment strategy that may distinguish the strategy from similar strategies within and between firms.

A composite description must include the material risks of the composite's strategy. All investment products or strategies have some degree of inherent common risk, such as, but not limited to, market, currency, investment-specific, inflation, or interest rate risk. Firms may include these generic, systemic risks in a composite or pooled fund description but are not required to do so. It is not expected that the composite description or pooled fund description will include reference to every one of these generic, systemic risks unless any is materially more significant to a composite or pooled fund strategy than typically expected. The following are some of the risks that should be discussed in a composite or pooled fund description if the risks could have had significant influence on the historical returns or are a key feature of the strategy and need to be considered alongside the future expected returns:

- liquidity risk,
- leverage and derivatives risk,
- credit/issuer risk,
- counterparty risk,
- interest rate risk, and
- currency risk.

It is recognized that some strategies can be highly volatile or may be profoundly affected by market-driven events. Firms are reminded that composite descriptions and pooled fund descriptions must reflect material changes in the risks of the strategies that would be caused by market events or changes imposed by the firm.

Example of a Composite Description for a Constant Proportion Portfolio Insurance Strategy

> The strategy of this composite is based on the Constant Proportion Portfolio Insurance (CPPI) approach and is composed of a mix of risky assets (global large-cap equities) and short-term high-quality treasury bills. The strategy includes a dynamic allocation between the risky assets and treasury bills, which is adjusted on a monthly basis. The allocation to risky assets may vary from 0% to 100% and depends on the performance of the risky assets and the current risk tolerance limit (floor) expressed by the portfolio's calculated

minimum target value. The allocation to risky assets increases with positive performance of the risky assets and is reduced if the performance of the risky assets trends downwards. The strategy does not allow any leverage. This composite's performance is compared with the Global Large-Cap Equities Index as the composite benchmark.

A sample list of composite descriptions and pooled fund descriptions is provided in Appendix D of the GIPS standards.

Provision 1.A.23

The FIRM MUST provide:

a. The complete list of COMPOSITE DESCRIPTIONS to any PROSPECTIVE CLIENT that makes such a request.

b. The complete list of POOLED FUND DESCRIPTIONS for LIMITED DISTRIBUTION POOLED FUNDS to any LIMITED DISTRIBUTION POOLED FUND PROSPECTIVE INVESTOR that makes such a request. This list may include only the LIMITED DISTRIBUTION POOLED FUNDS for which the PROSPECTIVE INVESTOR is eligible.

c. The complete list of BROAD DISTRIBUTION POOLED FUNDS to any BROAD DISTRIBUTION POOLED FUND PROSPECTIVE INVESTOR that makes such a request. This list may include only the BROAD DISTRIBUTION POOLED FUNDS for which the PROSPECTIVE INVESTOR is eligible. If the FIRM maintains a complete list of BROAD DISTRIBUTION POOLED FUNDS on its website, the FIRM may instead direct the PROSPECTIVE INVESTOR to the FIRM'S website.

d. The POOLED FUND DESCRIPTION for any BROAD DISTRIBUTION POOLED FUND to any BROAD DISTRIBUTION POOLED FUND PROSPECTIVE INVESTOR that makes such a request.

Discussion

In addition to maintaining a complete list of composite descriptions, a complete list of limited distribution pooled fund (LDPF) descriptions, and a complete list of broad distribution pooled funds (BDPFs), as applicable to the firm, firms must provide these lists to prospective clients or pooled fund prospective investors upon request. The discussion of Provision 1.A.22 addresses the creation of these lists.

Requests by a Prospective Client for a Firm's List of Composite Descriptions

The complete list of composite descriptions must be provided to any prospective client upon request. This list must include all of the firm's composites, including those that have terminated within the past five years. Although firms are required to provide a complete list of composite descriptions to any prospective client that makes such a request, they are encouraged to provide this information to anyone else who makes the request.

Requests by a Prospective Investor for a Firm's List of LDPF Descriptions

The complete list of LDPF descriptions must be provided to any prospective investor upon request. Note that this list may be tailored to include only those LDPFs for which the prospective investor is eligible, but the firm is not required to do so. Although firms are required to provide a complete list of LDPF descriptions to any prospective investor who makes such a request, they are encouraged to provide this information to anyone else who makes the request.

Requests by a Prospective Investor for a Complete List of BDPFs

The complete list of a firm's BDPFs must be provided to any prospective investor upon request. Note that this list may be tailored to include only those BDPFs for which the prospective investor is eligible, but the firm is not required to do so. If the firm includes information about all of its BDPFs on its website, the firm may direct a prospective investor to its website rather than provide the list directly.

For BDPFs, a firm is required to maintain and provide only a complete list of BDPF names. Firms are not required to provide a complete list of BDPF descriptions. However, a firm must provide a description of a specific BDPF to any BDPF prospective investor who makes such a request. Firms may provide a prospectus or offering document for the BDPF to fulfill this request.

Although firms are required to provide a list of BDPFs or a description of a specific BDPF to any prospective investor who makes such a request, they are encouraged to provide this information to anyone else who makes the request.

Provision 1.A.24

The FIRM MUST provide:

a. A GIPS COMPOSITE REPORT for any COMPOSITE listed on the FIRM'S list of COMPOSITE DESCRIPTIONS to any PROSPECTIVE CLIENT that makes such a request.

b. A GIPS POOLED FUND REPORT or GIPS COMPOSITE REPORT, provided the LIMITED DISTRIBUTION POOLED FUND is included in the respective COMPOSITE, for any LIMITED DISTRIBUTION POOLED FUND listed on the FIRM'S list of POOLED FUND DESCRIPTIONS for LIMITED DISTRIBUTION POOLED FUNDS to any LIMITED DISTRIBUTION POOLED FUND PROSPECTIVE INVESTOR that makes such a request.

Discussion

Provisions 1.A.11 and 1.A.13 require firms to make every reasonable effort to provide the appropriate GIPS Report to all prospective clients who are interested in a particular composite strategy and to all prospective investors who are interested in a limited distribution pooled fund (LDPF). This provision requires a firm to provide a GIPS Report to a prospective client or prospective investor upon request.

This requirement is an acknowledgement that, before investing with a firm, a prospective client or a prospective investor will often want to gain knowledge of the firm that goes beyond information about the particular composite or pooled fund strategy in which they may want to invest. Requesting a GIPS Report for other composites or pooled funds may help the prospective client or prospective investor gain a fuller picture of the firm's investment activities and a deeper understanding of the firm with which they are considering investing.

A firm must provide a GIPS Composite Report for any composite listed on the firm's list of composite descriptions to a prospective client upon request. The firm must therefore have the ability to prepare and provide a GIPS Composite Report for any composite on the firm's list of composite descriptions, including composites that are not typically marketed or that have been terminated within the past five years.

A firm must provide a GIPS Report for any LDPF listed on the firm's list of LDPF descriptions to an LDPF prospective investor upon request. The report provided may be a GIPS Pooled Fund Report or a GIPS Composite Report if the LDPF is included in the respective composite. The firm must therefore have the ability to prepare and provide a GIPS Report for any LDPF listed on the firm's list of LDPF descriptions, including LDPFs that are not marketed.

Firms that manage sub-advised pooled funds that are marketed or distributed by another firm as either an LDPF or a broad distribution pooled fund (BDPF) must treat these portfolios as segregated accounts and not pooled funds for the purpose of determining the composite assignment and on which list they must be maintained.

Provision 1.A.25

All data and information necessary to support all items included in GIPS COMPOSITE REPORTS, GIPS POOLED FUND REPORTS, and GIPS ADVERTISEMENTS MUST be captured, maintained, and available within a reasonable time frame, for all periods presented in these reports and advertisements.

Discussion

A fundamental principle of the GIPS standards is the need for firms to be able to ensure the validity of their claim of compliance. It is, therefore, important for current and prospective clients and investors, verifiers, and regulators to have confidence that all items included in a GIPS Report or GIPS Advertisement are supported by the appropriate records. This provision applies to GIPS Composite Reports for all composites and to GIPS Pooled Fund Reports for all pooled funds, whether the composite or pooled fund is marketed or not.

Firms must maintain records to be able to recalculate their performance history as well as substantiate all other information, including supplemental information, included in a GIPS Report or GIPS Advertisement, for all periods shown. This requirement applies to all time periods for which performance is presented in the GIPS Report or GIPS Advertisement. This requirement is consistent with the regulatory requirements of many countries. In some jurisdictions, however, regulators require records to be kept for longer periods than those required by the GIPS standards. Care should be taken to ensure that the firm follows the strictest of the recordkeeping requirements applicable to the firm.

It is understood that the required data may not be immediately available. For example, data may need to be retrieved from an offsite location or from a third-party service provider. However, the data and information required to be maintained by this provision must be available in a usable format within a reasonable time frame. In all instances, either paper (hard-copy) records or electronically stored records will suffice. If records are stored electronically, the records must be accessible and able to be printed or downloaded, if needed. Records stored in a system that is not operable and from which data cannot be retrieved will not satisfy the recordkeeping requirements.

Although most firms are looking for a very precise list of the minimum documents that must be maintained to support all parts of the GIPS Report or GIPS Advertisement, including the ability to recalculate the firm's performance history, there is no single list of records that will suffice in all situations. Each firm must determine for itself which records must be maintained. The following lists include records that firms should consider maintaining to meet the recordkeeping requirements of this provision. None of these lists should be considered exhaustive. The actual records required will depend on the firm's particular circumstances.

Records to Support Portfolio-Level (Segregated Account and Pooled Fund) Returns

1. portfolio statements, including positions and valuations, as well as information supporting the determination of fair value,
2. information to prove that performance is based on actual assets, including bank/custodial statements and reconciliations,
3. portfolio transactions reports,
4. outstanding trades reports,
5. corporate action reports,

6. income received/earned reports,
7. accrued income reports,
8. foreign or other withholding tax reclaim reports,
9. cash flow/weighted cash flow reports,
10. foreign exchange rates,
11. information on calculation methodology used,
12. information provided by a third party (e.g., a sub-advisor or custodian) for which a firm may need to take additional steps to ensure the information can be relied on to meet the requirements of the GIPS standards,
13. investment management fee information, and
14. information specific to pooled funds:
    a. pooled fund net asset value (NAV) reports,
    b. pooled fund dividend and gain distributions,
    c. supporting documentation for a pooled fund's NAV (e.g., trial balances),
    d. fee data, including custody and administrative fees,
    e. pooled fund expense ratio information,
    f. shareholder/owner information and cash flow activity, and
    g. profit and loss allocation reports for limited distribution pooled funds (LDPFs).

Records to Support Composite-Level Returns and Other Composite-Level Data

1. portfolios included in the composite,
    a. when each portfolio entered (and exited, if applicable) the composite,
    b. each portfolio's return for each period, and
    c. value used to weight each portfolio (beginning value or beginning value plus weighted external cash flows) for each period,
2. number of portfolios in the composite and the composite assets as of each annual period end and any other period for which this information is presented in GIPS Reports,
3. internal dispersion calculation data,
4. investment management fee information, if composite returns are calculated using model investment management fees,
5. support for the three-year annualized ex post standard deviation calculation and any additional risk measures, and
6. exchange rates used to convert composite returns into different currencies.

 |

Records to Support the Inclusion of a Portfolio in a Specific Composite or Its Exclusion from All Composites

1. composite definition, particularly related to the composite inclusion criteria, including the definition of discretion,
2. portfolios excluded from all composites and the reasons for exclusion,
3. investment management agreements and investment guidelines, as well as amendments thereto,
4. reports provided to clients and investors if used to help determine composite assignment,
5. analytics used to support composite assignment or composite exclusion, and
6. e-mail/other correspondence with clients regarding documented changes to a portfolio's investment mandate, objective, or strategy.

Records to Support Other Information Included in a GIPS Report

1. advisory-only assets,
2. uncalled committed capital,
3. firm and composite overlay exposure,
4. composite investment management fee schedules,
5. pooled fund expense ratio and investment management fee schedules,
6. performance-based fee calculations,
7. benchmark returns, including custom benchmark calculations,
8. estimated transaction costs, and
9. supplemental information.

Records to Support a Firm's Claim of Compliance

1. GIPS standards policies and procedures, covering all periods for which the firm claims compliance with the GIPS standards,
2. definition of the firm, historically and current,
3. supporting calculation for total firm assets as of each annual period end and any other period for which total firm assets are presented in GIPS Reports,
4. composite inception and creation dates,
5. determination of whether each pooled fund is a broad distribution pooled fund (BDPF) or LDPF,
6. list of composite descriptions,
7. list of LDPF descriptions, including inception date,
8. list of BDPFs, if not maintained on the firm's website,

9. GIPS Composite Reports for all composites, and
10. GIPS Pooled Fund Reports for all pooled funds for which a GIPS Pooled Fund Report was created.

Any Additional Records Necessary to Support a Claim of Compliance

1. marketing output/request for proposal (RFP) responses,
2. system and control reports from independent accountants or other third parties (e.g., accounting reports, other internal controls/compliance reports for the client and/or custodians),
3. third-party (e.g., sub-advisory, custodial, performance data provider) agreements,
4. minutes of relevant decision-making committees (e.g., a board, an investment committee, a GIPS compliance committee),
5. client and investor fee schedules/agreements,
6. systems manuals, especially for the systems that generate the portfolio, pooled fund, and composite returns, as well as GIPS Reports (including both numerical information and disclosures),
7. documentation of efforts made to provide all prospective clients and prospective investors with GIPS Reports,
8. documentation that the firm followed its error correction policy, including efforts made to provide, in the case of a material error, a corrected GIPS Report, including disclosure of the error, to all appropriate parties in accordance with the firm's error correction policy,
9. underlying benchmark data (if not publicly available), and
10. documentation of providing the following to any prospective client or prospective investor who requested:
    a. a list of composite descriptions or LDPF descriptions,
    b. a list of BDPFs, if this information is not maintained on the firm's website,
    c. a BDPF description, if this information is not maintained on the firm's website,
    d. a GIPS Report,
    e. policies for valuing portfolios (segregated accounts and pooled funds),
    f. policies for calculating performance,
    g. policies for preparing GIPS Reports,
    h. verification report(s), and
    i. performance examination report(s).

It is expected that all firms will have disaster recovery plans to mitigate the loss of records for any reason, whether it is a catastrophic event beyond the control of the firm or a situation within the control of the firm. If a firm that claims compliance with the GIPS standards experiences a catastrophic event that destroys all of its records and electronic or other backup systems, the firm should try to reconstruct the necessary information by obtaining the information from clients, custodians, consultants, verifiers, or any other party outside the firm that might have duplicate copies of those records. If the underlying data to support the GIPS Report was destroyed because of extreme circumstances beyond the firm's control and is unavailable from other sources, however, the firm may continue to claim compliance and show performance if the lack of records for the unavailable period(s) is disclosed.

For example, assume Firm A claims compliance with the GIPS standards, and the records for Firm A from its inception on 1 January 2017 through 31 December 2017 were destroyed under extreme circumstances beyond the firm's control. The firm can claim compliance with the GIPS standards but must disclose that the firm's records for the period from 1 January 2017 through 31 December 2017 were destroyed under extreme circumstances beyond the firm's control and the data are unavailable from other sources. The firm must also consider any applicable regulatory requirements and must remember that the GIPS standards are ethical standards based on the principles of fair representation and full disclosure. Any performance information that is presented must adhere to these principles.

Firms that have not yet claimed compliance with the GIPS standards and want to do so but do not have records to support the recordkeeping requirements because they experienced a catastrophic event in the past cannot take advantage of this exception from the recordkeeping requirement. They cannot claim compliance until they have complied with all the requirements of the GIPS standards, including the requirement to have the records to support at least a five-year performance track record.

All firms are reminded that, above all else, they must follow all applicable laws and regulations regarding the calculation and presentation of performance, including all recordkeeping requirements.

Provision 1.A.26

The FIRM is responsible for its claim of compliance with the GIPS standards and MUST ensure that the records and information provided by any third party on which the FIRM relies meet the REQUIREMENTS of the GIPS standards.

Discussion

A firm that claims compliance with the GIPS standards is responsible for its claim of compliance. Therefore, a firm that uses a third party to provide any service (e.g., custody or performance measurement), and relies on that service, must ensure that the records and information provided by the third-party service provider meet the requirements of the GIPS standards. The firm is responsible for ensuring that the data received from various external sources is accurate and must be able to aggregate any information supplied by external service providers as needed. A firm should carefully research any third-party service provider and should engage only reputable service providers.

It is acknowledged that, in some cases, it may be challenging to obtain information from a third party that meets the requirements of the GIPS standards. A firm has the option of bringing performance in house rather than relying on a third party. A firm can also make adjustments to the information provided by a third party so that it meets the requirements of the GIPS standards. For example, if a firm received composite data from a third party, and the third party weighted portfolio returns by ending value instead of beginning value, the firm could weight the returns itself using beginning-of-period values to calculate composite returns. As another example, suppose that a custodian reflects interest income on a cash basis. The firm may make adjustments to the income information from the custodian to properly reflect accrued income.

When using third-party service providers, firms are encouraged to ensure that adequate service-level agreements are in place to provide the historical records necessary, both currently and as needed in the future. It may be helpful to partner with custodians, administrators, prime brokers, and investment managers that understand what is needed to comply with the GIPS standards.

Firms must establish policies and procedures to ensure that third-party information, such as the information provided by a custodian or an underlying external manager, adheres to the requirements of the GIPS standards, if the firm relies on that information. A thorough examination of third-party service providers' policies and procedures should be conducted when they are hired. It is recommended that firms that claim compliance with the GIPS standards conduct periodic testing or other monitoring procedures that ensure that the policies and procedures of any third-party service provider on which the firm relies have not changed since the service provider was first hired and are being applied consistently and appropriately.

Finally, this provision does not require a firm to "look through" net asset value (NAV) valuations of pooled funds that are investments in a portfolio. Firms may rely on NAVs of pooled funds that reflect the fund's tradable value and use that as the pooled fund's fair value.

Provision 1.A.27

The FIRM MUST NOT LINK actual performance with historical THEORETICAL PERFORMANCE.

Discussion

Theoretical performance is a broad term encompassing different types of performance that is not derived from a composite, portfolio, or pooled fund with actual assets invested in the strategy or fund presented ("non-actual" performance). There are several names for this type of information: model, back-tested, hypothetical, simulated, indicative, and forward-looking, among others. Firms may present theoretical performance but, within a GIPS Report, historical theoretical performance must not be linked to the performance of a composite that includes actual portfolios or to the performance of an actual pooled fund. As an example, a firm that has a composite with a one-year track record must not extend the history to five years using back-tested performance for four years linked to the actual one-year performance. As a second example, a composite that lost all its constituent portfolios for two months cannot continue the track record without interruption by using the benchmark return for the missing months of performance to simulate performance. Historical composite or pooled fund returns must represent performance of only actual discretionary assets managed by the firm.

Theoretical performance, such as simulated or model performance, may be included in a GIPS Report. If historical theoretical performance is included in a GIPS Report, it must not be linked to actual performance and must be clearly labeled as supplemental information. Theoretical performance should be provided only to clients and investors or prospective clients and prospective investors who are sufficiently experienced and knowledgeable to assess the relevance and limitations of theoretical performance.

Theoretical performance that is not linked to actual performance may be presented when responding to a request for proposal (RFP) or when providing information in a database for a strategy a firm does not currently manage, but it must be clearly identified as model or hypothetical information.

Outside of a GIPS Report, firms may present actual performance linked to historical theoretical performance if asked to do so by a prospective client or prospective investor. The linked information may be presented in a one-on-one presentation that is created for and will be used only by the prospective client or prospective investor.

The linked information may also be presented outside of a GIPS Report in marketing materials provided to other prospective clients or prospective investors if the following conditions are met:

- The linked information is presented in a one-on-one presentation that includes the delivery of a GIPS Report, if the corresponding GIPS Report has not been previously delivered to the prospective client or prospective investor;
- The linked information is presented only to prospective clients or prospective investors who the firm believes are sufficiently knowledgeable about investments and can understand the relevance and limitations of the track record being presented;

- There are sufficient disclosures regarding the linked information so that prospective clients and prospective investors understand that this is not a GIPS-compliant track record. Disclosure, however, does not necessarily prevent information from being false or misleading;
- The linked information is not presented if a GIPS-compliant track record is requested; and
- The linked information is not included in a consultant database.

Provision 1.A.28

Changes in the FIRM'S organization MUST NOT lead to alteration of historical performance.

Discussion

Over time, the organization of a firm may change. For example, a firm may transition from a private to a public corporation or a management buyout may result in a publicly traded company becoming a private entity. Regardless of the reason for the change in a firm's organization, historical composite or pooled fund performance must remain part of the firm's history. In considering issues regarding the use of historical performance, it is important to remember that performance is the record of the firm, not of the individual. For example, suppose that a sole investment decision maker for a composite or pooled fund leaves a firm and the new portfolio manager continues to manage the composite or pooled fund according to the same investment mandate or strategy as the previous portfolio manager. The firm must link the historical performance of the composite or pooled fund to the ongoing performance achieved by the new portfolio manager.

Provision 1.A.29

For TIME-WEIGHTED RETURNS presented in GIPS REPORTS, the FIRM MUST NOT LINK non-GIPS-compliant performance for periods beginning on or after the MINIMUM EFFECTIVE COMPLIANCE DATE to GIPS-compliant performance. The FIRM may LINK non-GIPS-compliant performance to GIPS-compliant performance in GIPS REPORTS provided that only GIPS-compliant performance is presented for periods beginning on or after the MINIMUM EFFECTIVE COMPLIANCE DATE.

Discussion

The minimum effective compliance date is the date after which a firm may present only GIPS-compliant performance in GIPS Reports. When presenting time-weighted returns in a GIPS Report, the firm must not link non-GIPS-compliant performance for periods beginning on or after the minimum effective compliance date to GIPS-compliant performance. Most composites and pooled funds have a minimum effective compliance date of 1 January 2000. Therefore, for these composites and pooled funds, performance for periods after 1 January 2000 that does not comply with the GIPS standards must not be presented as part of a GIPS Report. Real estate and private equity composites and pooled funds and wrap fee composites have a different minimum effective compliance date of 1 January 2006. For these composites and pooled funds, performance for periods beginning on or after 1 January 2006 that does not comply with the GIPS standards must not be presented in a GIPS Report. For any performance presented for periods beginning prior to the minimum effective compliance date that does not comply with the GIPS standards in a GIPS Report, firms must disclose the periods of non-compliance.

Outside of a GIPS Report, non-compliant performance for periods beginning on or after the minimum effective compliance date may be linked to compliant performance if the linking is requested by a prospective client or prospective investor. The linked information may be presented in a one-on-one presentation that is created for and will be used only by the prospective client or prospective investor.

The linked information may also be presented outside of a GIPS Report in marketing materials provided to other prospective clients or prospective investors if the following conditions are met.

- The linked information is presented in a one-on-one presentation that includes the delivery of a GIPS Report, if the corresponding GIPS Report has not been previously delivered to the prospective client or prospective investor;
- The linked information is presented only to prospective clients or prospective investors who the firm believes are sufficiently knowledgeable about investments and can understand the relevance and limitations of the track record being presented;
- There are sufficient disclosures regarding the linked information so that prospective clients and prospective investors understand that this is not a GIPS-compliant track record. Disclosure, however, does not necessarily prevent information from being false or misleading;
- The linked information is not presented if a GIPS-compliant track record is requested; and
- The linked information is not included in a consultant database.

In a GIPS Report, the GIPS standards allow firms to link non-GIPS-compliant performance to the composite's GIPS-compliant history provided that only GIPS-compliant performance is shown for periods beginning on or after the minimum effective compliance date.

For example, suppose that a firm has been in existence since 1997 and would like to show its entire performance history. It wants to claim compliance beginning 1 January 2005. Given the type of assets the firm manages, its minimum effective compliance date is 1 January 2000. The firm must present returns that meet the requirements of the GIPS standards for periods beginning on or after 1 January 2000. The firm may link non-compliant performance history for periods ended prior to 1 January 2000 to its GIPS-compliant performance. It must not link non-GIPS-compliant performance for periods beginning on or after 1 January 2000 to its GIPS-compliant performance. If any non-compliant performance is presented for periods ended prior to 1 January 2000, the firm must disclose that the performance for periods prior to 1 January 2000 is not in compliance with the GIPS standards. The firm is encouraged to bring its entire performance history into compliance but is not required to do so.

The purpose of this requirement is to ensure that all performance presented after the minimum effective compliance date complies with the GIPS standards so that prospective clients and prospective investors can more easily compare performance results between firms. Firms are reminded that they must comply with all applicable laws and regulations regarding the calculation and presentation of performance and they must not present performance or performance-related information that is false or misleading.

Provision 1.A.30

For MONEY-WEIGHTED RETURNS presented in GIPS REPORTS, the FIRM MUST NOT present non-GIPS-compliant performance for periods ending on or after the MINIMUM EFFECTIVE COMPLIANCE DATE. The FIRM may present non-GIPS-compliant performance in GIPS REPORTS for periods ending prior to the MINIMUM EFFECTIVE COMPLIANCE DATE.

Discussion

The minimum effective compliance date is the date after which only GIPS-compliant performance may be presented by a firm in GIPS Reports. For money-weighted returns, the firm must not present non-GIPS-compliant performance for periods ending on or after the minimum effective compliance date. Most composites and pooled funds have a minimum effective compliance date of 1 January 2000. For these composites and pooled funds, performance for periods ending on or after 1 January 2000 that does not comply with the GIPS standards must not be presented as part of a GIPS Report. Real estate and private equity composites and pooled funds have a minimum effective compliance date of 1 January 2006. For these composites and pooled funds, performance for periods ending on or after 1 January 2006 that does not comply with the GIPS standards must not be presented in a GIPS Report. For any performance presented for periods ended prior to the minimum effective compliance date that does not comply with the GIPS standards in a GIPS Report, firms must disclose the periods of non-compliance.

The measurement period for a since-inception money-weighted return (MWR) is the period from the inception date of the composite or pooled fund through the end of the period that is being reported. The beginning date remains constant and the ending date is extended as the measurement period becomes longer. The period-end date will determine what is a compliant time period for GIPS Report purposes.

The inception date is always incorporated into a since-inception MWR in contrast to a time-weighted return (TWR), which does not necessarily incorporate since-inception results. It could be argued that the since-inception basis of MWR reporting would mean that any period of historical non-compliance could make the current period also non-compliant because the current calculation includes inputs from periods for which the firm did not claim compliance with the GIPS standards. This is not the case, however—a firm may present returns that use inputs (i.e., cash flows) from periods for which the firm did not claim compliance as long as the inputs meet any applicable requirements of the GIPS standards. Daily external cash flows must be used within any GIPS-compliant since-inception MWR calculation as of 1 January 2020. Prior to 1 January 2020, quarterly or more-frequent external cash flows must be used.

Outside of a GIPS Report, non-compliant performance for periods ending on or after the minimum effective compliance date may be presented if the non-compliant performance is requested by a prospective client or prospective investor. The non-compliant performance may be presented in a one-on-one presentation that is created for and will be used only by the prospective client or prospective investor.

The non-compliant performance may also be presented outside of a GIPS Report to other prospective clients or prospective investors if the following conditions are met:

- The non-compliant performance is presented in a one-on-one presentation that includes the delivery of a GIPS Report, if the corresponding GIPS Report has not been previously delivered to the prospective client or prospective investor;
- The non-compliant performance is presented only to prospective clients or prospective investors who the firm believes are sufficiently knowledgeable about investments and can understand the relevance and limitations of the track record being presented;
- There are sufficient disclosures regarding the non-compliant performance so that prospective clients and prospective investors understand that this is not a GIPS-compliant track record. Disclosure, however, does not necessarily prevent information from being false or misleading;
- The non-compliant performance is not presented if a GIPS-compliant track record is requested; and
- The non-compliant performance is not included in a consultant database.

The purpose of this requirement is to ensure that all performance presented for periods ending after the minimum effective compliance date complies with the GIPS standards so that prospective clients and prospective investors can more easily compare performance results between firms.

Firms are reminded that they must comply with all applicable laws and regulations regarding the calculation and presentation of performance and they must not present performance or performance-related information that is false or misleading.

Provision 1.A.31

When the FIRM jointly markets with other firms, the FIRM claiming compliance with the GIPS standards MUST ensure that the FIRM is clearly defined and separate relative to other firms being marketed and also that it is clear which FIRM is claiming compliance.

Discussion

A firm that claims compliance with the GIPS standards may jointly market with another firm that may or may not comply with the GIPS standards. To avoid confusion when jointly marketing with another firm, a GIPS-compliant firm must be sure that it is clearly defined relative to the other firm with which it is jointly marketing, and it must be clear as to which firm is, or which firms are, claiming compliance with the GIPS standards. The clarity regarding which firm is, or which firms are, claiming compliance with the GIPS standards is necessary for the firm's joint marketing activities to meet the criterion of fair representation, a fundamental principle of the GIPS standards.

Provision 1.A.32

Performance from a past firm or affiliation may be used to represent the historical performance of the new or acquiring FIRM and LINKED to the performance of the new or acquiring FIRM if the FIRM meets the following REQUIREMENTS on a COMPOSITE-specific or POOLED FUND–specific basis:

a. Substantially all of the investment decision makers MUST be employed by the new or acquiring FIRM (e.g., research department staff, portfolio managers, and other relevant staff);
b. The decision-making process MUST remain substantially intact and independent within the new or acquiring FIRM;
c. The new or acquiring FIRM MUST have records to support the performance; and
d. There MUST be no break in the track record between the past firm or affiliation and the new or acquiring FIRM.

If any of the above REQUIREMENTS are not met, the performance from a past firm or affiliation MUST NOT be linked to the ongoing performance record of the new or acquiring FIRM.

Discussion

When a manager, group of managers, or an entire firm joins a new firm, the performance of the past firm or affiliation may be linked to or used to represent the historical performance of a new or acquiring firm if all of the following requirements are met on a composite-specific or pooled fund-specific basis:

- Substantially all of the investment decision makers (e.g., research department staff, portfolio managers, and other relevant staff) are employed by the new or acquiring firm;
- The decision-making process remains substantially intact and independent within the new or acquiring firm;
- The new or acquiring firm has records that document and support the performance; and
- There is no break in the track record between the past firm or affiliation and the new or acquiring firm.

If all of these portability requirements are met, the historical track record for the composite or pooled fund from the past or acquired firm may be ported and linked to the continuing composite or pooled fund track record at the new or acquiring firm and presented as a continuous track record. Although the linking of the track record is not required, it is best practice to do so. A firm should not use theoretical performance instead of actual performance to market a strategy when an actual portable track record is available.

If the firm does not meet all of these portability requirements, it may not link to the track record from the past or acquired firm. The actions that a firm may take with respect to the use of the composite or pooled fund track record from the past firm will depend on which requirement(s) cannot be met. In all cases, performance from a past firm must never be presented when the new or acquiring firm does not have records to document and support the performance. Suppose that the new or acquiring firm has records that document and support the performance from a past firm or affiliation but one or more of the other portability requirements are not met. In such a case, performance from the past or acquired firm must not be linked to performance at the new firm. For guidance on situations where there is a break in the track record between the past firm and the new or acquiring firm but all other portability requirements are met, see Provision 1.A.33.

For a firm to be able to link the track record from the past firm to the ongoing composite performance at the new firm in a GIPS Report, the track record must include all portfolios that were managed in the strategy at the past firm—that is, it must be composite performance. Where the provision states "on a composite-specific basis," the word "composite" refers to the entire composite from the past firm, not a subset of portfolios. This is true even if the past firm did not claim compliance with the GIPS standards. Although the GIPS standards do not have a requirement that all portfolios must transfer from the past firm to the new firm, the firm must have all the records needed to document and support the entire composite performance history. If the new or acquiring firm cannot create a complete composite track record from the past firm or affiliation and can only create the track record using a subset of portfolios, that information cannot be linked to the track record of the composite at the new or acquiring firm in a GIPS Report. The track record based on a subset of the portfolios from the past firm can be presented only as supplemental information in a GIPS Report and must not be linked to the track record of the composite at the new or acquiring firm.

Outside of a GIPS Report, an acquiring firm that has records for only a subset of portfolios in a composite from a past firm or affiliation may link the performance of the subset of portfolios in the composite to the ongoing performance of the composite at the new firm if the linking is requested by a prospective client or prospective investor. The linked information may be presented in a one-on-one presentation that is created for and will be used only by the prospective client or prospective investor.

The linked information may also be presented outside of a GIPS Report if the following conditions are met:

- The linked information is presented in a one-on-one presentation that includes the delivery of a GIPS Report, if the corresponding GIPS Report has not been previously delivered to the prospective client or prospective investor;
- The linked information is presented only to prospective clients or prospective investors who the firm believes are sufficiently knowledgeable about investments and can understand the relevance and limitations of the track record being presented;
- There are sufficient disclosures regarding the linked information so that prospective clients and prospective investors understand that this is not a GIPS-compliant track record. Disclosure, however, does not necessarily prevent information from being false or misleading;
- The linked information is not presented if a GIPS-compliant track record is requested; and
- The linked information is not included in a consultant database.

If an acquired firm is compliant with the GIPS standards, the performance history meets the portability requirements, and the new or acquiring firm chooses to port the performance, then the firm must port the entire compliant track record that was presented by the acquired firm. If the ported track record is greater than 10 years, the acquiring firm may choose to present only a 10-year track record in GIPS Reports.

If a firm that is compliant with the GIPS standards acquires a non-compliant firm, the GIPS standards permit a one-year grace period to bring the acquired assets of the non-compliant firm into compliance with the GIPS standards. (See Provision 1.A.34 for additional guidance on the one-year grace period.)

If a firm wishes to port performance from an acquired non-compliant firm and link it to the firm's ongoing performance, if it is possible, it must build a composite or pooled fund track record from the prior firm of at least five years, or since inception if the composite or pooled fund has been in existence for less than five years. If it is not possible to build a composite or pooled fund track record from the prior firm of at least five years, or since inception if the composite or pooled fund has been in existence for less than five years, it must build the history for as long as the firm is able to do so.

There may be cases in which a similar strategy is managed by the past firm or affiliation and the new or acquiring firm. The new or acquiring firm cannot combine the pre-acquisition track records or assets of a composite from the acquired firm with a composite from the acquiring firm and then show the combined track record or assets as GIPS-compliant information. The firm must determine if it will use the track record from the past firm or affiliation or use its own track record. On a prospective basis, the ongoing composite may consist of portfolios from the past firm or affiliation that have transferred to the new or acquiring firm and continue the same investment mandate or strategy as well as portfolios from the new or acquiring firm that meet the definition of the composite.

If a firm that is not compliant with the GIPS standards acquires a firm that is compliant, the non-compliant acquiring firm cannot then claim compliance with the GIPS standards, even if all the portability tests are met. The non-compliant acquiring firm will have to attain compliance for its own assets for at least a five-year period (or since the firm's inception if it has been in existence for less than five years) before it can claim compliance for the newly combined entity.

Example 1:

Firm A is acquired by and merges with Firm B to create Firm AB. The effective merger date is 1 August 2019. Both Firm A and Firm B claim compliance with the GIPS standards, and all portability requirements are met. Firm A has a large-cap growth equity composite (Composite A), and Firm B has a large-cap core equity composite (Composite B). It is decided that, after the acquisition, all large-cap equity portfolios will be managed based on the strategy of Composite A, which will be the "surviving" composite. The portfolios in Composite B will be modified to conform to the strategy of Composite A and moved into Composite A. Composite B will cease to exist and will be included on the list of composite descriptions as a terminated composite. Firm AB wants to present a track record for its large-cap composite that includes performance from Firm A and will use Composite A's historical track record.

Starting 1 August 2019, the effective date of the merger, the historical track record of Composite A will be linked to the ongoing performance of Composite A. Starting no earlier than 1 August 2019, Composite A will also include the portfolios from Composite B that have been modified to conform to the strategy of Composite A.

Example 2:

Firm A is acquired by and merges with Firm B to create Firm AB. The effective merger date is 1 August 2019. Both Firm A and Firm B claim compliance with the GIPS standards, and all of the portability requirements are met. At the time of the merger, each firm has a large-cap composite. Firm A's large-cap composite (Composite A) and Firm B's large-cap composite (Composite B) have the same benchmark and strategies that are very similar. Firm AB plans to combine the two composites and create one large-cap composite, Composite AB. Firm AB wants to present a track record for Composite AB that includes the pre-merger track record.

When presenting large-cap composite history through 31 July 2019:

- The large-cap composite history through 31 July 2019 may be the track record of either Composite A or Composite B, whichever is selected as the "surviving" composite.
- The track record presented for the large-cap composite history through 31 July 2019 must not be a combination of the track records of Composite A and Composite B.

When presenting the large-cap composite performance from 1 August 2019 forward:

- Starting no earlier than 1 August 2019, Firm AB may combine the portfolios in the surviving composite with the portfolios in the non-surviving composite. For example, if Composite B is the surviving composite, the firm can include the portfolios from Composite A in the surviving Composite B on or after 1 August 2019.
- The performance of Composite AB, which includes portfolios from Composite A for periods from 1 August 2019 forward, is linked to the pre-merger track record of Composite B.

The non-surviving composite, Composite A, must be included on the list of composite descriptions as a terminated composite.

Example 3:

Firm A is acquired by and merges with Firm B to create Firm AB. The effective merger date is 1 August 2019. Both Firm A and Firm B claim compliance with the GIPS standards, and all portability requirements are met. Firm A has a large-cap growth equity composite (Composite A), and Firm B has a large-cap core equity composite (Composite B). It is decided that Firm AB will create a new large-cap equity strategy that will blend the strategies of Composite A and Composite B. Therefore, neither the strategy of Composite A nor Composite B will be carried forward into the new merged firm. In this case, there is no "surviving" strategy. Firm AB's new large-cap composite will have no performance history. Performance for the firm's new large-cap composite will begin on or after the effective merger date of 1 August 2019.

The track records of Composite A and Composite B, based on pre-merger investment strategies, must be included on the list of composite descriptions as terminated composites.

Provision 1.A.33

Performance from a past firm or affiliation may be used to represent the historical performance of the new or acquiring FIRM when there is a break in the track record between the past firm or affiliation and the new or acquiring FIRM if the new or acquiring FIRM meets the following REQUIREMENTS on a COMPOSITE-specific or POOLED FUND–specific basis:

a. Substantially all of the investment decision makers MUST be employed by the new or acquiring FIRM (e.g., research department staff, portfolio managers, and other relevant staff);
b. The decision-making process MUST remain substantially intact and independent within the new or acquiring FIRM;
c. The new or acquiring FIRM MUST have records to support the performance;
d. The new or acquiring FIRM MUST separately present the performance before the break and after the break; and
e. The new or acquiring FIRM MUST NOT LINK performance prior to the break in the track record to the performance after the break in the track record.

Discussion

A break in the performance track record between the past firm or affiliation and the new firm may occur for a number of reasons. For example, an acquired team may be required to take a garden leave prior to joining the new firm, and the portfolios previously managed by the acquired team would not be managed by them during the garden leave, resulting in a gap in performance until a track record is established at the new firm. If there is a break in the performance track record between the past firm or affiliation and the new or acquiring firm, it may be permissible for performance from the past firm or affiliation to be used to represent the historical performance of the new or acquiring firm if certain requirements are met.

First, the firm must meet all of the other requirements for portability (listed in items a through c in the provision):

- Substantially all of the investment decision makers are employed by the new or acquiring firm;
- The decision-making process remains substantially intact and independent within the new or acquiring firm; and
- The new or acquiring firm has the records to support the performance.

Second, the firm must meet the requirements for the presentation of the performance from the past firm or affiliation (listed in items d through e in the provision):

- Performance before and after the break in the track record must be presented separately; and
- Performance prior to the break in the track record must not be linked to the performance after the break in the track record.

If the firm does not meet all of the tests specified in items a through c, the performance from the past firm or affiliation must not be used to represent the historical performance of the new or acquiring firm.

If all of the tests specified in items a through c are met, and the firm chooses to present the performance from the past firm or affiliation, the track record must be shown in two segments: one segment representing performance before the break in the track record and one segment representing performance after the break in the track record.

As an example, suppose that Firm A acquires Firm B, which has a large-cap growth composite. All conditions for portability are met, except that there is a break in the performance track record of the large-cap growth composite during the acquisition process. The performance track record for the large-cap growth composite at Firm B begins on 1 August 2014 and ends on 18 June 2019, the date of the acquisition. The track record resumes at Firm A on 1 July 2019. The complete track record for the large-cap growth composite may be shown, but it must be shown in two segments. Assuming that Firm A calculates composite performance on a monthly basis, Firm A may show performance from 1 August 2014 through 31 May 2019. It may then show performance from 1 July 2019 forward. These two segments of the large-cap growth composite track record must be presented separately and must not be linked. The following example shows how the performance of the large-cap growth composite could be presented in a GIPS Composite Report, with the break in performance clearly indicated.

Year	Composite Gross Return (%)	Composite Net Return (%)	XYZ Index (%)	Composite 3-Yr-St Dev (%)	Benchmark 3-Yr St Dev (%)	Number of Portfolios	Internal Dispersion (%)	Composite Assets ($ M)	Firm Assets ($ M)
2020	-0.84	-1.83	-0.65			2	4.8	493	12,989
1 Jul–31 Dec 2019[1]	3.98	3.46	3.58			2		475	12,678
1 Jan–31 May 2019[1]	1.22	0.81	3.46						5,367
2018	8.22	7.15	7.09	12.95	11.15	3	3.8	594	5,249
2017	6.52	5.47	5.67	12.51	10.68	5	3.1	682	5,439
2016	14.50	13.37	13.03			12	3.6	1,094	5,986
2015	41.16	39.80	33.36			22	2.7	2,012	8,401
2014[2]	18.66	17.49	15.48			20		1,978	7,423

[1] There were no portfolios in the composite from 19 June 2019 through 30 June 2019.

[2] Returns are for the period from 1 August 2014 (inception date) through 31 December 2014.

If the firm is asked to provide cumulative performance for the large-cap growth composite as of 31 December 2020, including performance for one-year, three-year, and five-year periods, the firm would be able to provide cumulative performance for only a one-year period. Three-year and five-year cumulative performance does not exist because of the break in performance in 2019.

In keeping with the principles of fair representation and full disclosure, the GIPS standards require firms to handle all situations involving a break in performance with the greatest transparency.

In order for a firm to be able to use the track record from the past firm or affiliation in a GIPS Report, the track record must include all portfolios that were managed in the strategy at the past firm—that is, it must be composite performance. Where the provision states "on a composite-specific basis", the word "composite" refers to the entire composite from the past firm, not a subset of portfolios. This is true even if the past firm did not claim compliance with the GIPS standards. While the GIPS standards do not have a requirement that all portfolios must transfer from the past firm to the new firm, the firm must have all the records needed to document and support the entire composite performance history. If the new or acquiring firm cannot create a complete composite track record from the past firm or affiliation and can only create the track record using a subset of portfolios, that information cannot be used at the new or acquiring firm in a GIPS Report. The track record based on a subset of the portfolios from the past firm can be presented only as supplemental information in a GIPS Report.

Outside of a GIPS Report, an acquiring firm that has records for only a subset of portfolios in a composite from a past firm or affiliation may use the performance of the subset of portfolios from the past firm or affiliation at the new firm if the information is requested by a prospective client or prospective investor. The subset information may be presented in a one-on-one presentation that is created for and will be used only by the prospective client or prospective investor.

The subset information may also be presented outside of a GIPS Report if the following conditions are met:

- The subset information is presented in a one-on-one presentation that includes the delivery of a GIPS Report, if the corresponding GIPS Report has not been previously delivered to the prospective client or prospective investor;
- The subset information is presented only to prospective clients or prospective investors who the firm believes are sufficiently knowledgeable about investments and can understand the relevance and limitations of the track record being presented;
- There are sufficient disclosures regarding the subset information so that prospective clients and prospective investors understand that this is not a GIPS-compliant track record. Disclosure, however, does not necessarily prevent information from being false or misleading;
- The subset information is not presented if a GIPS-compliant track record is requested; and
- The subset information is not included in a consultant database.

Provision 1.A.34

If the FIRM acquires another firm or affiliation, the FIRM has one year to bring any non-compliant assets into compliance. Assets of the acquired non-compliant firm or affiliation MUST meet all the REQUIREMENTS of the GIPS standards within one year of the acquisition date, on a going forward basis.

Discussion

The GIPS standards recognize the difficulties that firms encounter when transferring assets from one firm to another or when merging two firms. Similar to the idea of allowing a firm time to invest new portfolios before adding them to composites, in the case of an acquisition or merger, the GIPS standards permit a one-year grace period to bring the assets of a newly acquired or merged non-compliant firm into compliance with the GIPS standards. Assets of the non-compliant firm must meet all the requirements of the GIPS standards, on a going forward basis, as of the first full reporting period one year after the acquisition date.

The one-year grace period begins on the effective acquisition date—the date on which the acquirer obtains control of the acquired firm. The effective date of a merger typically depends on the date on which certain legal documents are filed. During the one-year grace period, the acquired assets are included in total firm assets, although not all assets managed by the compliant firm are in compliance with the GIPS standards because of the acquisition or merger. The compliant firm may continue to claim compliance with the GIPS standards, however.

The compliant firm must disclose all significant events that would help prospective clients and investors interpret the GIPS Report. An acquisition of or merger with another firm would normally be considered a significant event.

Example Timeline for the Grace Period:

- Acquisition date: 15 July 2018
- End of grace period, one year after the acquisition date: 15 July 2019
- First full reporting period one year after the acquisition date: August 2019

In this example, assuming the firm calculates composites using monthly portfolio returns, the firm would need to include all acquired portfolios in composites no later 1 August 2019. Note, however, that if the firm does not construct the composite retroactive to the acquisition date, a break in the track record will occur and the firm will be unable to link to the prior firm track record.

A firm is not required to but may decide to port a track record from an acquired firm at any point in the future, as long as the portability requirements are met. (Please see Provisions 1.A.32 and 1.A.33 for portability requirements.) There is no specific end-date by which all track records from the non-compliant acquired firm must be ported. A firm may decide to port a track record from an acquired firm at any point in the future, as long as the portability requirements are met.

The following is an example of the one-year grace period for a firm that is compliant with the GIPS standards that acquires a firm that is not compliant with the GIPS standards.

Coastire Capital Management, a firm that complies with the GIPS standards, acquires Fanglobe Investment Advisors on 15 July 2018. Fanglobe does not comply with the GIPS standards. Coastire completes the task of having all of Fanglobe's assets in compliance with the GIPS standards by 15 July 2019, the end of the one-year grace period. When Coastire calculates monthly performance for August 2019, all performance is in compliance with the GIPS standards.

Although Coastire has satisfied the requirements of the one-year grace period by having all of the firm's assets in compliance with the GIPS standards for reporting periods beginning on and after 15 July 2019, Fanglobe's assets for periods prior to 15 July 2019 are not in compliance with the GIPS standards. After several months, Coastire determines that it would like to port two track records from the acquired firm—a track record for Fanglobe's mid-cap value strategy, which has 6 years of history, and a track record for Fanglobe's large-cap value strategy, which has 13 years of history. Both track records meet the portability requirements.

Coastire may bring the historical assets of Fanglobe into compliance with the GIPS standards at any time in the future and may then port the two track records. Both track records, however, must be based on all of Fanglobe's portfolios managed in the respective strategies and not on a subset of portfolios. If Coastire ports the track record for Fanglobe's mid-cap value strategy, it must create a mid-cap value composite and port at least 5 of the 6 years of history, if possible. If Coastire ports the track record for Fanglobe's large-cap value strategy, it must create a large-cap value composite and port at least 5 of the 13 years of history, if possible.

Note that to be able to port the two track records from Fanglobe, the composites on which the track records are based must meet all of the requirements for composite construction and input data. For example, Coastire must be able to prove that all fee-paying discretionary portfolios that meet the composite definition for the mid-cap value strategy and large-cap value strategy have been included in the respective composites. To create a continuous composite history, Coastire must also create a composite history for these strategies from the acquisition date of 15 July 2018 through 31 July 2019.

Provision 1.A.35

The FIRM MUST present TIME-WEIGHTED RETURNS unless certain criteria are met, in which case the FIRM may present MONEY-WEIGHTED RETURNS. The FIRM may present MONEY-WEIGHTED RETURNS only if the FIRM has control over the EXTERNAL CASH FLOWS into the PORTFOLIOS in the COMPOSITE or POOLED FUND, and the PORTFOLIOS in the COMPOSITE have or the POOLED FUND has at least one of the following characteristics:

a. CLOSED-END
b. FIXED LIFE
c. FIXED COMMITMENT
d. ILLIQUID INVESTMENTS as a significant part of the investment strategy.

Discussion

The GIPS standards require firms to present time-weighted returns (TWRs) unless very specific circumstances are met. This requirement is because external cash flows are generally client driven and investment managers should not be rewarded or penalized for investment decisions outside of their control. In addition, by removing the effects of external cash flows, a TWR best reflects the firm's ability to manage the portfolio according to a specified investment mandate, objective, or strategy. This allows prospective clients and prospective investors the best opportunity to fairly evaluate the firm's past performance and to facilitate comparison between investment management firms.

There are some investment strategies and products, however, including many private market investment strategies for which the timing and the size of cash flows are controlled by the investment manager and are part of the investment decision process. In such cases, it is appropriate that performance reflects the results of the investment manager's cash flow timing decisions. Therefore, a firm may present composite or pooled fund money-weighted returns (MWRs) instead of, or in addition to, TWRs if the firm has control over the external cash flows into and out of the portfolios in the composite or the pooled fund, and the portfolios in the composite have or the pooled fund has at least one of the following characteristics:

- closed-end
- fixed life
- fixed commitment
- illiquid investments as a significant part of the investment strategy.

Illiquid investments would be considered a significant part of the investment strategy if the illiquidity is a key feature of the investment strategy and is likely to have a material effect on returns.

If these conditions are met for a specific composite or pooled fund, the firm may choose to present only MWRs in the respective GIPS Report. If these conditions are not met for a composite or pooled fund, the firm must present TWRs in the respective GIPS Report. When a firm does not meet the tests to present only MWRs for a composite or pooled fund, it may present MWRs in addition to TWRs in the respective GIPS Report as supplemental information.

Provision 1.A.36

The FIRM MUST choose if it will present TIME-WEIGHTED RETURNS, MONEY-WEIGHTED RETURNS, or both for each COMPOSITE or POOLED FUND, and it MUST consistently present the selected returns for each COMPOSITE or POOLED FUND.

Discussion

The firm must choose whether to present time-weighted returns (TWRs) or money-weighted returns (MWRs) for a composite or pooled fund, keeping in mind that MWRs may only be presented in the circumstances specified in Provision 1.A.35. If either TWRs or MWRs are permitted under the GIPS standards, the firm may choose to present TWRs, MWRs, or both TWRs and MWRs. If the firm does not meet the criteria for presenting MWRs for a specific composite or pooled fund, the firm must present TWRs and may present MWRs but only as supplemental information. Once a firm has chosen which return(s) it will present, the firm must consistently present the return(s) selected for each composite or pooled fund.

To "consistently present" the selected returns means that, once a firm has chosen the type of permitted return to present (TWR, MWR, or both), it must continue to present the selected return(s) unless there is a compelling reason to change the type of return presented. Doing so is important for consistency in the presentation of a firm's track record and to prevent the changing of the type of return presented in order to present more-favorable returns.

The following are some of the appropriate reasons for a firm to change the type of return presented:

- There is a change in the GIPS standards with respect to the criteria for the use of a TWR or MWR.
- There are new legal or regulatory requirements that require a change in the type of return presented.
- The firm decides to present both TWRs and MWRs in GIPS Reports, rather than the one type of return that had been presented, in order to provide a more comprehensive view of performance.

- A review of the firm's strategy leads to a changed view regarding the type of return that most accurately reflects the strategy. (This should be a very infrequent occurrence).
- There is a change in the strategy's key features that would require or permit a change in the type of return that is presented. (For example, a firm may change the structure of a fund from a closed-end fund to an open-end fund, or there may be a change in the investments used for the strategy).

Once a change in the type of return(s) presented is made, however, the newly selected return(s) type must be presented unless there is a compelling reason to make another change.

Provision 1.A.37

If the FIRM chooses to include a GIPS COMPOSITE REPORT or GIPS POOLED FUND REPORT in marketing materials, the FIRM MUST indicate this fact in the marketing materials.

Discussion

Provisions 1.A.11 and 1.A.13 require firms to make every reasonable effort to provide a GIPS Report to prospective clients and pooled fund prospective investors. If a GIPS Report is included in marketing materials, there must be a disclosure that will inform prospective clients or prospective investors that a GIPS Report is included in the marketing materials. The disclosure should be prominent (e.g., included in the table of contents) and is intended to help prospective clients and prospective investors locate the GIPS Report within the marketing materials. Such a disclosure will help to highlight the importance of the GIPS Report.

Provision 1.A.38

The FIRM MUST notify CFA Institute of its claim of compliance by submitting the GIPS COMPLIANCE NOTIFICATION FORM. This form:

a. MUST be filed when the FIRM initially claims compliance with the GIPS standards.
b. MUST be updated annually with information as of the most recent 31 December, with the exception of FIRM contact information, which MUST be current as of the form submission date.
c. MUST be filed annually thereafter by 30 June.

Discussion

Firms must notify CFA Institute of their claim of compliance by submitting the GIPS Compliance Notification Form, which can be found on the CFA Institute website (cfainstitute.org).

When a firm is first coming into compliance, the firm must submit the GIPS Compliance Notification Form to CFA Institute once it has met all of the requirements of the GIPS standards and is at the point of initially claiming compliance with the GIPS standards. The firm must not claim compliance with the GIPS standards unless the GIPS Compliance Notification Form has been submitted to CFA Institute.

After the initial filing, the form must be filed annually by 30 June. Information provided in the GIPS Compliance Notification Form must be as of the most recent 31 December, with the exception of the firm's contact information. Contact information must be current as of the form's submission date. The period of any verification performed would not impact the notification submission date or the date as of which the information is provided. Firms must establish policies and procedures to ensure the form is submitted by the deadline.

The GIPS Compliance Notification Form must reflect the definition of the firm used to determine firm-wide compliance with the GIPS standards even when the definition of the firm is different from the legal entity of the firm. If the overall legal entity contains multiple GIPS firms for GIPS compliance purposes, a separate GIPS Compliance Form must be submitted for each defined firm.

Provision 1.A.39

If the FIRM chooses to be verified, it MUST gain an understanding of the verifier's policies for maintaining independence and MUST consider the verifier's assessment of independence.

Discussion

Verification is a process by which a verification firm (verifier) conducts testing of a firm on a firm-wide basis, in accordance with the required verification procedures of the GIPS Standards for Verifiers. Verification provides assurance on whether the firm's policies and procedures related to composite and pooled fund maintenance, as well as the calculation, presentation, and distribution of performance, have been designed in compliance with the GIPS standards and have been implemented on a firm-wide basis. Crucial to the verification process is the assumption by all interested parties that the verifier performs its service in an unbiased manner and is not testing its own work. Therefore, verification must be performed by an independent third party. If a firm chooses to be verified, the firm must understand the verifier's policies for ensuring that the verifier is independent from the firm. To do so, the firm should obtain a summary of the verifier's policies for ensuring independence and should have sufficient discussions with the verifier to understand the policies.

Although a firm is not responsible for a verifier's independence assessment, the firm must understand the issues encountered and the conclusions reached by the verifier regarding independence from the firm, particularly when the verifier provides other GIPS-compliance related services. This understanding is important because the firm may have knowledge that the verifier does not have. The firm is obligated to inform the verifier if the firm believes that the verifier missed some factor in its independence assessment or if the firm believes the assessment is incorrect.

When considering verifier independence, both the firm and the verifier must keep in mind the following question: If a prospective client or prospective investor of the firm relies on the fact that the firm has been verified, could the prospective client's or prospective investor's perception of the verification's value potentially change if the prospective client or prospective investor knew about other existing relationships between the firm and the verifier? A firm must gain enough of an understanding of the verifier's policies and procedures for maintaining independence to lead to a strong answer of "no" to this question.

The firm's understanding of the verifier's policies and procedures for maintaining independence is not a one-time event. It is an ongoing process and must be performed in connection with each verification engagement.

It may be helpful for both the verifier and the firm to consider independence as a continuum. At one extreme of the continuum is a verifier that has no other relationships with the firm. At the other extreme is a verifier with existing relationships and independence issues with the firm that cannot be resolved, such that the verifier cannot conduct the engagement because independence cannot be achieved. The firm and the verifier must determine where their relationship lies on this continuum and whether it is appropriate to proceed with the verification engagement.

1.B. Fundamentals of Compliance—Recommendations

Provision 1.B.1

The FIRM SHOULD comply with the RECOMMENDATIONS of the GIPS standards, including RECOMMENDATIONS in any Guidance Statements, interpretations, and Q&As published by CFA Institute and the GIPS standards governing bodies.

Discussion

The recommendations contained in the GIPS standards are suggested tasks or actions that are considered best practice and should be followed or performed, although they are not required. The GIPS standards must be applied with the objectives of fair representation and full disclosure of investment performance. However, meeting the objectives of fair representation and full disclosure, which are the fundamental principles of the GIPS standards, may mean that a firm must follow the recommendations in addition to the requirements of the GIPS standards. If a firm chooses to adopt any recommendations, its policies and procedures must reflect how that recommendation is applied.

Provision 1.B.2

The FIRM SHOULD update GIPS COMPOSITE REPORTS and GIPS POOLED FUND REPORTS quarterly.

Discussion

GIPS Composite Reports and GIPS Pooled Fund Reports contain important information, but the value and relevance of that information are affected by the timeliness with which the GIPS Report is updated. A GIPS Report that includes returns that are significantly out of date is not helpful to prospective clients or prospective investors. For this reason, it is required that firms update GIPS Composite Reports and GIPS Pooled Fund Reports within 12 months of the end of the most recent annual period, even if a verification for the firm, or a performance examination of a composite or pooled fund, is not yet completed. In the interest of fair representation and full disclosure, however, it is recommended that GIPS Composite Reports and GIPS Pooled Fund Reports be updated quarterly to provide more timely information to prospective clients and prospective investors.

When updating a GIPS Report that presents time-weighted returns to include monthly, quarterly, or year-to-date returns, firms are required to update only the following information:

- composite or pooled fund returns,
- benchmark returns, and
- significant events that would help a prospective client or prospective investor understand the GIPS Report.

When performance in a GIPS Report that presents money-weighted returns is updated more frequently than the required annual update, firms are required to update only the following information:

- the composite or pooled fund return,
- the benchmark return,
- the required multiples, such as the paid-in capital (PIC) multiple, the investment multiple (TVPI), and the unrealized multiple (RVPI), as of the most recent quarter end or month end, and
- significant events that would help a prospective client or prospective investor understand the GIPS Report.

Firms may also update other information in the GIPS Report, such as total firm assets and the number of portfolios in the composite, but are not required to do so.

Provision 1.B.3

The FIRM SHOULD be verified.

Discussion

Verification is intended to provide a firm and its current and prospective clients and pooled fund investors additional confidence in the firm's claim of compliance with the GIPS standards. It is recommended that firms be verified for all period(s) for which compliance with the GIPS standards is claimed. Verification may increase the knowledge of the firm's performance measurement team and improve the consistency and quality of the firm's GIPS standards-related performance information. Verification may also result in improved internal policies and procedures as well as marketing advantages to the firm. Verification does not provide assurance, however, about the performance of any specific composite or pooled fund or the accuracy of any specific GIPS Report. Although verification brings additional credibility to the claim of compliance, it does not provide assurance on the firm's claim of compliance with the GIPS standards in its entirety.

Provision 1.B.4

The FIRM SHOULD adopt the broadest, most meaningful definition of the FIRM. The scope of this definition SHOULD include all geographical (country, regional, etc.) offices operating under the same brand name, regardless of the actual name of the individual investment management company.

Discussion

It is important that firms remember the overarching principles of fair representation and full disclosure when defining the firm. Although there are specific requirements that must be met related to defining the firm (see Provision 1.A.2), firms are recommended to define the firm as broadly as possible, encompassing all of the relevant locations and departments, so that the prospective client or prospective investor is given enough information about the investment strategies being managed and the firm as a whole to make an informed decision about whether or not to invest with the firm. It is recommended that the definition of the firm include all geographical offices operating under the same brand name, regardless of the actual name of the individual investment management company.

Examples of how a firm could be defined as broadly as possible include:

- all offices operating under the same brand name (e.g., XYZ Asset Management),
- other names resulting from mergers, acquisitions, and/or trading under a different name for branding purposes,
- financial service holding companies defined as one global firm with multiple brands, several legal entities, multiple offices, investment teams, and investment strategies,
- an investment management firm with one brand but multiple strategies and investment teams, and
- all offices trading under a globally recognizable trading name with regional/country-specific additions (e.g., XYZ Asset Management Asia).

The appropriate definition of the firm will depend on the firm's actual circumstances. In some cases, it may be appropriate to define the firm based on geographic location or to have different firms that use the same brand name if that is how the firm is held out to prospective clients and prospective investors.

Investment management firms in most countries must register with one or more governmental agencies or regulators. The GIPS standards recognize a regulatory registration as a possible definition of a firm for purposes of compliance but also require firms to consider the manner in which they are holding themselves out to the public when determining the firm definition.

Provision 1.B.5

The FIRM SHOULD provide to each current client, on an annual basis, a GIPS COMPOSITE REPORT of the COMPOSITE in which the client's PORTFOLIO is included.

Discussion

It is recommended, but not required, that a firm provide a GIPS Composite Report to a current client on an annual basis. It is likely to be helpful for a client to know how the client's own portfolio performed relative to other portfolios that are managed according to the same investment objective, mandate, or strategy. In addition to composite performance, GIPS Composite Reports include important disclosures and presentation items that a firm may not provide to current clients as part of client reporting. These disclosures and presentation items will likely provide useful information to current clients in their periodic assessment of the firm.

Provision 1.B.6

The FIRM SHOULD provide to each LIMITED DISTRIBUTION POOLED FUND current investor, on an annual basis, a GIPS POOLED FUND REPORT of the LIMITED DISTRIBUTION POOLED FUND in which the investor is invested.

Discussion

It is recommended, but not required, that a firm provide a GIPS Pooled Fund Report to a current investor in a limited distribution pooled fund (LDPF) on an annual basis. In addition to fund performance, GIPS Pooled Fund Reports include important disclosures and presentation items that a firm might not provide to current investors as a part of investor reporting. These disclosures and presentation items will likely provide useful information to current investors in their periodic assessment of the pooled fund. If the firm includes the LDPF in a composite, the firm may instead provide the GIPS Composite Report for the composite in which the fund is included.

Provision 1.B.7

If the FIRM is selling participation in a new LIMITED DISTRIBUTION POOLED FUND that does not yet have a track record, the FIRM SHOULD present the most appropriate track record for the new LIMITED DISTRIBUTION POOLED FUND, if available. The most appropriate track record is a GIPS REPORT for a COMPOSITE or another POOLED FUND that is managed according to the same or similar strategy as the new LIMITED DISTRIBUTION POOLED FUND.

Discussion

Participation in a new limited distribution pooled fund (LDPF) is often being marketed by a firm before the pooled fund has a track record. If an LDPF has no performance history, there is no requirement to provide a GIPS Report. In such cases, however, the firm should present the most appropriate track record for the new fund if an appropriate track record is available. The most appropriate track record would be a GIPS Report for a composite or another pooled fund that the firm manages according to the same or similar strategy as the new LDPF that has not yet started. If an appropriate track record is presented to prospective investors, sufficient information should be provided so that pooled fund prospective investors understand the track record presented. The firm should consider whether any adjustments to net returns should be made to align fees used to calculate net returns with the fees that will be charged by the new LDPF. As is always the case, the information presented must adhere to the principles of fair representation and full disclosure.

2. INPUT DATA AND CALCULATION METHODOLOGY

2.A. Input Data and Calculation Methodology—Requirements

Firm Assets, Composite Assets, and Pooled Fund Assets

Provision 2.A.1

TOTAL FIRM ASSETS:

a. MUST be the aggregate FAIR VALUE of all discretionary and non-discretionary assets managed by the FIRM. This includes both fee-paying and non-fee-paying PORTFOLIOS.[1]

b. MUST include assets assigned to a SUB-ADVISOR provided the FIRM has discretion over the selection of the SUB-ADVISOR.

c. MUST NOT include ADVISORY-ONLY ASSETS.

d. MUST NOT include uncalled COMMITTED CAPITAL.[2]

Discussion

Total firm assets include all discretionary and non-discretionary assets for which a firm has investment management responsibility. Total firm assets include assets assigned to a sub-advisor provided the firm has discretion over the selection of the sub-advisor. All portfolios included in total firm assets must be considered for inclusion in composites.

For periods beginning on or after 1 January 2011, firms must value all discretionary and non-discretionary assets in accordance with the definition of fair value. Fair value is defined in the GIPS standards as the amount at which an investment could be sold in an arm's-length transaction between willing parties in an orderly transaction. The valuation must be determined using the objective, observable, unadjusted quoted market price for an identical investment in an active market on the measurement date, if available. In the absence of an objective, observable, unadjusted quoted market price for an identical investment in an active market on the measurement date, the valuation must represent the firm's best estimate of the fair value. Fair value must include any accrued income.

[1] REQUIRED for periods beginning on or after 1 January 2011. For periods prior to 1 January 2011, TOTAL FIRM ASSETS MUST be the aggregate of either the FAIR VALUE or the MARKET VALUE of all discretionary and non-discretionary assets under management within the defined FIRM.

[2] REQUIRED for periods beginning on or after 1 January 2020.

The requirement to value all assets at fair value applies to assets in both fee-paying and non-fee-paying portfolios. Total firm assets must reflect the fair value of all discretionary and non-discretionary assets within the firm definition. For periods prior to 1 January 2011, total firm assets must be the aggregate of the fair value or market value of all discretionary and non-discretionary assets under management within the defined firm.

Some firms use a sub-advisor to manage part or all of a particular strategy. For example, if a firm specializes in managing equities, it might hire a sub-advisor to manage its fixed-income assets. If a firm has discretion over selecting (i.e., can hire and/or fire) the sub-advisor, the firm must include the assets managed by the sub-advisor in total firm assets. If the firm does not have discretion over sub-advisor selection, it must not include the sub-advised assets in total firm assets, composite assets, or pooled fund assets.

A firm retains the responsibility for its claim of compliance for all its assets, including its discretionary sub-advised assets and their reported performance. Therefore, all discretionary sub-advised assets must be treated by the firm in the same manner as assets managed internally and must be subject to the same policies and procedures as internally managed assets. If the firm intends to place reliance on information from sub-advisors, it must ensure that the records and information provided by the sub-advisor meet the requirements of the GIPS standards. For reliance on third-party records and information, please refer to Provision 1.A.26.

Total firm assets must include:

- assets for which the firm has either conditional or unconditional authority to make investment decisions,
- fee-paying assets (wherein a fee is payable to the firm for the ongoing management of a portfolio's assets) and non-fee-paying assets (wherein no fee is payable to the firm for the ongoing management of a portfolio's assets),
- assets managed outside the firm (e.g., by sub-advisors) for which the firm has asset allocation (assignment) authority (i.e., the firm has discretion over the selection of the sub-advisor), and
- cash and cash equivalents (substitutes).

Note that although non-fee-paying assets may be excluded from composites, they must be included in total firm assets.

Total firm assets must exclude:

- advisory-only assets,
- uncalled committed capital, and
- overlay exposure.

Advisory-Only Assets

Advisory-only assets are assets for which the firm provides investment recommendations and for which two conditions are met. The firm:

- has no control over implementation of investment decisions, and
- does not have trading authority over the assets.

There is an important distinction between advisory-only assets, which are excluded from total firm assets, and non-discretionary portfolios that are included in total firm assets. In the case of a non-discretionary segregated account that is included in total firm assets, the account has documented client-imposed restrictions that significantly hinder a firm from fully implementing its intended strategy. Although the account is considered non-discretionary because the intended strategy cannot be fully implemented, the firm is responsible for managing the account, including the trading of its assets. In the case of an advisory-only account, the firm does not manage the account and has no trading authority for the account. The firm offers investment advice only. Unlike non-discretionary accounts, an advisory-only account does not simply have restrictions that might prevent an intended strategy from being implemented. The firm has no direct authority to manage or trade the account. For this reason, the account must not be included in any composite and must not be included in total firm assets.

Although advisory-only assets may not be included in total firm assets, a firm may wish to report firm-wide advisory-only assets. If a firm chooses to present information on its advisory-only assets, it may present advisory-only assets as either:

- a separate value, or
- the combination of total firm assets and firm-wide advisory-only assets.

If the firm wishes to present a combination of total firm assets and firm-wide advisory-only assets, it must also present firm-wide advisory-only assets for the same periods for which the combination of total firm assets and firm-wide advisory-only assets is presented.

Uncalled Committed Capital

Committed capital is defined as pledges of capital to an investment vehicle by investors (limited partners and the general partner) or the firm and is typically drawn down over a period of time. Uncalled committed capital is the amount of capital that has not yet been drawn. For periods beginning on or after 1 January 2020, uncalled committed capital must not be included in total firm assets. Uncalled committed capital is excluded from total firm assets because it is not actively under management by the firm and there may be cases in which the committed capital is never called and will never be actively managed.

Although uncalled committed capital may not be included in total firm assets, a firm may wish to report firm-wide uncalled committed capital. If a firm wishes to present information about its uncalled committed capital, it may present uncalled committed capital as:

- a separate value, or
- the combination of total firm assets and firm-wide uncalled committed capital.

If the firm presents a combination of total firm assets and firm-wide uncalled committed capital, it must also present firm-wide uncalled committed capital for the same periods for which the combination of total firm assets and firm-wide uncalled committed capital is presented.

In certain regulatory filings, uncalled capital must be included in assets under management. Therefore, assets reported for regulatory purposes may differ from total firm assets.

For periods ending prior to 1 January 2020, firms may have included uncalled committed capital in total firm assets. If this is the case, firms are not required to restate total firm assets for periods ended prior to 1 January 2020, to remove uncalled committed capital from total firm assets.

Overlay

An overlay strategy is defined as a strategy in which the management of a certain aspect of an investment strategy is carried out separately from the underlying portfolio. Overlay strategies are typically designed either to limit or maintain a specified risk exposure that is present in the underlying portfolio or to profit from a tactical view on the market by changing a portfolio's specified risk exposure. For overlay strategies, overlay exposure is defined as the economic value for which a firm has investment management responsibility. Overlay exposure is the notional value of the overlay strategy being managed, the value of the underlying portfolios being overlaid, or a specified target exposure.

Firms must not include overlay exposure in total firm assets. However, firms may wish to present information about firm-wide overlay exposure. For overlay strategy composites, the firm is not required to present total firm assets and may instead choose to present total firm overlay exposure as of each annual period end. See Provision 4.A.15.

The following table provides examples of the type of assets that must be included in or excluded from total firm assets.

Type of Asset	Included in Total Firm Assets?	Reason
Discretionary assets for which the firm has unconditional authority to implement its strategy	Yes	Firm controls investment decisions.
Non-discretionary assets for which the firm has conditional authority to implement the strategy	Yes	Firm has limited control of investment decisions.
Non-fee-paying assets for which the firm has conditional or unconditional authority to implement the strategy	Yes	Firm has all or limited control of investment decisions.
Assets directed to a sub-advisor by the firm	Yes	Firm retains discretion over sub-advisor selection and has investment management responsibility.
Assets directed to a sub-advisor by the client	No	Firm does not retain discretion over sub-advisor selection and does not have investment management responsibility.
Assets within advisory-only client relationships	No	Firm has no control over implementation of investment decisions and no trading authority for the assets.
Uncalled committed capital	No	Firm is not actively managing uncalled committed capital and may never call the capital.
Overlay exposure	No	Firm is not managing the underlying assets.

The next table provides guidance on how to distinguish among discretionary, non-discretionary, and advisory-only assets.

Scenarios Regarding Investment Management and Trading Authority

Firm's Investment Management and Trading Authority	Type of Portfolio	Assets Included in or Excluded from Total Firm Assets
• Has authority to manage the portfolio according to a specific investment mandate • Has full trading authority for the portfolio	Discretionary	Included
• Has authority to manage the portfolio • Follows client-imposed restrictions on the management of the portfolio that prevents the portfolio from being representative of a specific investment mandate • Has full trading authority for the portfolio	Non-discretionary	Included
• Provides investment recommendations that must be approved by the client; the client may or may not accept the recommendations • Has full authority to trade the portfolio if the client approves the recommendations	Non-discretionary	Included
• Provides investment recommendations that must be approved by the client • Has no authority to trade the portfolio	Advisory-only	Excluded
• Delivers a model portfolio • Has no authority to trade the portfolio	Advisory-only	Excluded

Hedge fund structure

It is common for hedge funds to use a master-feeder structure, in which offshore and on-shore feeder funds invest in a centralized master fund. All portfolio investment activity occurs at the master fund level. Feeder funds own shares of the master fund. In a master-feeder structure, a firm may include in total firm assets either the master fund assets or the sum of the feeder fund assets.

For hedge funds registered offshore, the investment management function may be formally assigned to a third-party entity that is not actually performing the portfolio management function, and the firm may be named as having an advisory-only role. If the firm is actually performing the investment management function, however, these assets must be included in total firm assets.

Determining Discretion for Wrap Fee Portfolios, including Unified Managed Accounts (UMAs)

Wrap fee programs are offered by brokerage firms (often referred to as wrap fee sponsors). These programs give investors access to numerous investment managers through one platform. Wrap fee sponsors charge a single "wrap" or "bundled" fee for several combined services (e.g., investment management, trading, custodial, and other administrative services). An investor selects the investment manager (i.e., the firm) whose strategy appears to best suit his or her needs, and the firm assumes responsibility for managing the investor's wrap fee portfolio. The firm typically has full discretion to manage the wrap fee portfolio, and the wrap fee sponsor handles trade execution, custodial, and administrative services. For this type of wrap fee portfolio, wrap fee assets are discretionary and would be included in the firm's total firm assets.

Model delivery programs are a type of wrap fee program in which the firm does not direct trades and provides only a model portfolio to the wrap fee sponsor. From the firm's perspective, the service provided is characterized as investment advice because the firm has no control over whether the trades are executed as intended. Wrap fee assets included in model delivery programs would be considered advisory-only assets, because the firm is offering advice only and is not managing the account or directing trades. These assets would, therefore, not be included in total firm assets.

There is a type of wrap fee account called a Unified Managed Account (UMA) for which the determination of discretion, and whether or not the wrap fee portfolio should be included in total firm assets, are particularly challenging. A UMA program is similar to standard wrap fee programs in many ways. Investors have access to multiple managers through a single platform, and a single bundled fee is charged for a combination of services. The distinguishing feature of a UMA portfolio is the ability to combine multiple investment strategies into a single portfolio. A UMA portfolio may hold securities associated with multiple investment strategies and firms in one custodial or brokerage account.

Although firms generally dictate the investment strategy to be used for their designated portion of the assets in a UMA portfolio, their trading responsibilities can range from those of a standard wrap fee relationship to those of a model delivery program and often lie somewhere in between.

In a typical UMA program, the firm provides a model portfolio to the UMA platform and leaves the responsibility for executing trades to the wrap fee sponsor. In some UMA programs, the firm has discretionary authority to enter trades directly on the wrap fee sponsor's platform, although such an arrangement is not typical. It should also be noted that most UMA programs include an overlay component, whereby another firm (often the wrap fee sponsor) oversees the overall composition of, and coordinates all activity in, the wrap fee portfolio. This arrangement includes cash management (how cash will be distributed among the various firms) and asset allocation decisions (rebalancing or changing the asset allocation to each firm).

The discretion that a firm has regarding a UMA portfolio depends on the characteristics of the particular UMA program. Some UMA programs may be fully discretionary, others may have shared discretion between the wrap fee sponsor and the firm, and some may be model delivery only. Discretion may also be influenced by the presence and responsibilities of an overlay manager who may have the authority to override the firm's trading directives. Determining the level of discretion is important because it dictates whether the firm must include the UMA program assets in total firm assets. Because of the varying characteristics of different UMA programs, firms must evaluate each UMA program individually to determine whether its assets must be included in total firm assets.

The following are some factors to consider when determining whether to include UMA portfolios in total firm assets:

- The contract between the sponsor and the firm:
  - A contract that indicates that the firm has discretionary authority may suggest that the portfolios governed by the contract should be included in total firm assets. If this is the case, the level of control the firm actually has should be assessed.
  - In the case of "dual contracts," in which the firm has contracts with both the sponsor and the client, a contract with the client that specifies that the firm has discretionary authority would support including the UMA portfolios in total firm assets.
- Trading authority:
  - The firm must have trading authority for the UMA portfolios to be included in total firm assets. Some possible scenarios include the following:
    - The firm submits trades to the wrap fee sponsor's platform, but the wrap fee sponsor has final approval before execution. The firm may determine that it retains sufficient trading discretion for the wrap fee portfolios to be included in total firm assets.
    - The firm does not execute trades but has contractual assurance that the trades submitted will be executed in a timely manner and receives confirmation of execution. A firm could determine that these UMA portfolios should be included in total firm assets.
    - The wrap fee sponsor is responsible for all trading and can freely decide to deviate from the firm's trading instructions. This is an advisory-only relationship, and the UMA assets must not be included in total firm assets.

- Authority at the portfolio level:
  - If the firm is making trading decisions on a portfolio-specific basis, this scenario indicates the firm has discretion. Inclusion of UMA assets in total firm assets is likely permitted.
  - If the firm does not have access to the data necessary to make decisions at the portfolio-specific level, the firm is likely to have limited authority over the portfolio and assets would not likely qualify for inclusion in total firm assets.

Because of the complexities that often exist in determining the level of discretion for a firm's UMA assets, it is common for firms to exclude UMA assets from total firm assets and treat these assets as advisory-only assets. Firms must review all UMA programs to determine if the assets should be included in total firm assets and, if included, whether the portfolios should be included in a composite.

As described, firms have many decisions to make when establishing procedures for calculating total firm assets. Total firm assets reported for any given time period must be the same in all of the firm's GIPS Reports.

Provision 2.A.2

TOTAL FIRM ASSETS, COMPOSITE assets, and POOLED FUND assets MUST:

a. Include only actual assets managed by the FIRM.
b. Be calculated net of discretionary leverage and not grossed up as if the leverage did not exist.

Discussion

Total firm assets, composite assets, and pooled fund assets must include only actual assets managed by the firm. Assets represented by simulated, backtested, or model performance must not be included in total firm assets, composite assets, or pooled fund assets because such assets do not represent actual assets managed by the firm. Because uncalled committed capital is not considered to be actual assets managed by the firm, composite assets or pooled fund assets must not include uncalled committed capital for periods beginning on or after 1 January 2020. This is consistent with the requirement to not include uncalled committed capital in total firm assets for periods beginning on or after 1 January 2020. (See Provision 2.A.1.)

When a composite or pooled fund strategy employs discretionary leverage, the composite or pooled fund assets and total firm assets must be presented net of the discretionary leverage and not grossed up as if the leverage did not exist. Discretionary leverage refers to loans taken at the investment manager's discretion. For example, if the firm is managing a fund that has $200 million in assets and the firm chooses to borrow $50 million, the fund's net assets are $200 million and its gross assets are $250 million. Because the firm chose to lever the fund, the firm must use net assets of $200 million when calculating total firm assets.

In contrast, non-discretionary leverage refers to borrowings that are mandated by or undertaken by the client. Non-discretionary leverage is not deducted when calculating total firm assets, composite assets, or pooled fund assets. For example, if the client gave the firm $250 million to manage, of which the client has borrowed $50 million, the amount of assets included in total firm assets is $250 million. The fact that the client borrowed $50 million of the assets given to the firm does not influence the calculation of the firm's total firm assets.

Provision 2.A.3

The FIRM MUST NOT double count assets when calculating TOTAL FIRM ASSETS, COMPOSITE assets, or POOLED FUND assets.

Firms are prohibited from double counting assets when calculating total firm assets, composite assets, or pooled fund assets. If double counting is not eliminated, assets reported will be inflated and result in a misleading GIPS Report. For firms that include portfolios in more than one composite, create carve-outs, or manage portfolios that invest in the firm's pooled funds (e.g., portfolios that invest in the firm's short-term money market fund), care must be taken to ensure assets are not counted more than once.

As an example, suppose that Firm XYZ has one Eurozone fixed-income composite that contains the following three portfolios:

Portfolio 1: a pooled fund invested in Eurozone bonds with net assets of €20 million,

Portfolio 2: a second pooled fund invested in Eurozone bonds of several Eurozone countries with net assets of €30 million, and

Portfolio 3: a segregated account invested entirely in the two pooled funds already mentioned. Net assets of this segregated account are €10 million.

These three portfolios are the only portfolios within Firm XYZ. The firm asks the following questions:

- What is the correct number of portfolios in the Eurozone fixed-income composite?

  The Eurozone fixed-income composite would have three portfolios in the composite.

- What is the correct amount of composite assets in the Eurozone fixed-income composite?

  The Eurozone fixed-income composite would have three portfolios in the composite, with composite assets of €50 million. Presenting composite assets of €60 million—thus including €10 million from Portfolio 3, which is invested entirely in Portfolio 1 and Portfolio 2—is misleading, and those assets would be double counted.

Portfolio	Invested In	Net Assets (€ millions)	Composite Assets/ Firm Assets (€ millions)
1	Eurozone bonds	20	20
2	Eurozone bonds	30	30
3	Portfolios 1 and 2	10	
Total		60	50

- What is the correct amount of composite assets that should be included in total firm assets? Composite assets of €50 million would also be included in total firm assets. Total firm assets would also be €50 million.

Provision 2.A.4

COMPOSITE and POOLED FUND performance MUST be calculated using only actual assets managed by the FIRM.

Discussion

Composite and pooled fund performance must be calculated using only actual assets managed by the firm. This performance must include any sub-advised assets for which the manager has discretion when selecting the sub-advisor.

Simulated, backtested, or model performance must not be included in any composites or pooled funds because such performance does not represent actual assets managed by the firm. Similarly, firms must not blend the history of two existing composites or pooled funds to create simulated performance for a "hybrid" or model composite or pooled fund and present it as a GIPS-compliant track record. For example, if the performance of actual portfolios in an equity composite is combined with the performance of actual portfolios in a fixed-income composite to show what the results might have been had the equity and fixed-income portfolios been combined, the results would be considered a simulated strategy. This "hybrid" or model composite may be presented as supplemental information only if all of the component parts are presented. Even though the returns for the equity and fixed-income composites are based on actual assets managed by the firm, the arbitrary method of combining them historically is subject to manipulation and does not represent real-time, actual asset allocation decisions. The performance results of this simulated strategy would, therefore, be considered hypothetical performance. This would also be true for combinations of different pooled funds or carve-outs used to create a simulated strategy.

Firms may present theoretical performance in GIPS Reports. Theoretical performance is not derived from actual assets invested in the strategy presented, and it includes model, backtested, hypothetical, simulated, indicative, ex ante, and forward-looking performance. Theoretical performance must be clearly labeled as supplemental information. Firms must not link historical theoretical performance with actual performance. For example, assume a firm manages equity portfolios and fixed-income portfolios. The firm wishes to create a track record for a balanced strategy invested 50% in equities and 50% in fixed income, rebalanced monthly, but it does not manage any portfolios in this balanced strategy. The firm uses the equity composite and the fixed-income composite as building blocks to create a 50/50 blended balanced strategy. The performance of the balanced strategy is theoretical and may be presented as supplemental information when all of the underlying building block composites are presented—in this case, the equity and fixed-income composites. It must be clear, however, that the performance for the balanced strategy is theoretical performance, and the appropriate disclosures about theoretical performance must be included.

A ported composite or pooled fund track record (a track record from a past or acquired firm that meets the portability requirements and can be used by the new or acquiring firm) is considered to be an extension of the new or acquiring firm. The assets of the ported track record must be included in composite assets or pooled fund assets. While a ported track record is not based on actual assets that had been managed at the new or acquiring firm, it must be based on actual assets at the past or acquired firm.

Overlay Exposure

Provision 2.A.5

Total FIRM OVERLAY EXPOSURE MUST include all discretionary and non-discretionary OVERLAY STRATEGY PORTFOLIOS for which the FIRM has investment management responsibility.[3]

Discussion

For periods beginning on or after 1 January 2020, total firm overlay exposure must include all discretionary and non-discretionary overlay strategy portfolios for which the firm has investment management responsibility. When calculating total firm overlay exposure, firms must sum the overlay exposures of all overlay portfolios managed even if different allowable methods are used to calculate the portfolios' overlay exposure. To calculate overlay exposure, a firm may use the notional value of the overlay strategy portfolios, the value of the underlying portfolios being overlaid, or a specified target exposure. If overlay exposure is maintained in different currencies, the firm must convert the overlay exposure to the currency used in the GIPS Report. For purposes of calculating total firm overlay exposure, firms must not recalculate overlay exposures to a single method.

For example, assume Firm A offers two types of overlay strategies. In one strategy, called "Global Equity Beta Overlay," the composite overlay exposure of €500 million is calculated using the

[3] REQUIRED for periods beginning on or after 1 January 2020.

notional exposure of all portfolios in the composite at period end. In the second strategy, "Active Currency Overlay," the composite overlay exposure of €750 million is calculated using the value of the underlying portfolios at period end. Firm A would calculate total firm overlay exposure of €1,250 million by summing €500 million and €750 million.

Provision 2.A.6

When calculating OVERLAY EXPOSURE, the FIRM MUST:[4]

a. Use the notional exposure of the OVERLAY STRATEGY PORTFOLIOS, the value of the underlying PORTFOLIOS being overlaid, or a specified target exposure.
b. Use the same method for all PORTFOLIOS within a COMPOSITE.

Discussion

For periods beginning on or after 1 January 2020, there are three allowable methods for calculating overlay exposure. Overlay exposure must be calculated by using:

- the notional exposure of the overlay strategy portfolios being managed,
- the value of the underlying portfolios being overlaid, or
- a specified target exposure.

The same method for calculating overlay exposure must be used for all portfolios within a composite.

For periods ending prior to 1 January 2020, these same methods may be used, but firms are not required to use these methods.

Provision 2.A.7

When calculating OVERLAY STRATEGY PORTFOLIO returns, the FIRM MUST:[5]

a. Use as the denominator the notional exposure of the OVERLAY STRATEGY PORTFOLIOS, the value of the underlying PORTFOLIO being overlaid, or a specified target exposure.
b. Use the same method for all PORTFOLIOS within a COMPOSITE.

[4] REQUIRED for periods beginning on or after 1 January 2020.
[5] REQUIRED for periods beginning on or after 1 January 2020.

Discussion

When calculating returns for an overlay strategy portfolio, the denominator must be one of the following:

- the notional exposure of the overlay strategy portfolios as of the beginning of the period,
- the value of the underlying portfolio being overlaid as of the beginning of the period, or
- the specified target exposure as of the beginning of the period, which can be defined as a target exposure or determined by a formula used to calculate the target exposure for each period.

Some overlay strategies require the use of a specific denominator. For example, when an interest rate overlay is benchmarked to a set of cash flows, the notional amount of derivatives required to hedge the interest rate exposure will not equal the present value of the cash flows being hedged because the notional amount will vary depending on the instruments chosen to implement the hedge. An interest rate overlay return calculated by dividing the profit/loss earned by the portfolio during the period by the notional exposure of the instruments used would not be comparable to the change in present value of the cash flows being hedged. Therefore, the denominator for an interest rate overlay benchmarked to a set of cash flows must be the sum of the present value of the cash flows being hedged as of the beginning of the period.

The same method for calculating the denominator must be used for all portfolios within a composite when calculating overlay strategy portfolio returns. In addition, this same method must be used to calculate a composite's total overlay exposure.

General/Accounting

Provision 2.A.8

TOTAL RETURNS MUST be used.

Discussion

Total return, which is measured over a specified period, has two components: (1) the appreciation or depreciation (capital change) of the assets in the portfolio over the specified period and (2) the income earned on the assets in the portfolio over the specified period. When calculating the performance of a portfolio, firms are required to use a total return.

Provision 2.A.9

TRADE DATE ACCOUNTING MUST be used.[6]

Discussion

For periods beginning on or after 1 January 2005, trade date accounting must be used. For the purpose of complying with the GIPS standards, trade date accounting is defined as recognizing the asset or liability on the date of purchase or sale and not on the settlement date. Recognizing the asset or liability within three business days of the date the transaction is entered into (the trade date [T], T + 1, T + 2, or T + 3) satisfies the trade date accounting requirement for purposes of the GIPS standards. Settlement date accounting recognizes the asset or liability on the date when the exchange of cash and investments is completed.

For purchases, when using settlement date accounting, any movement in value between the trade date or booking date and the settlement date will not affect performance until the settlement date. For purchases, when using trade date accounting, the change in value will be reflected for each valuation between trade date and settlement date. Performance comparisons between portfolios and/or composites that use settlement date accounting and those that use trade date accounting may not be valid. The same problem occurs when comparing settlement date portfolios and composites with their benchmarks.

The principle behind requiring trade date accounting is to ensure there is not a significant lag between trade execution and reflecting the trade in the performance of a portfolio. For the purpose of compliance with the GIPS standards, portfolios are considered to satisfy the trade date accounting requirement provided that transactions are recorded and recognized consistently and within normal market practice—typically, a period between trade date and up to three business days after trade date (T + 3).

For some pooled funds, firms may need to differentiate between the date of placing a subscription/redemption order and the date of the effective asset ownership transfer. The date of the execution or transfer of ownership (in this case, when the definitive quantity and settlement price of the asset being purchased/sold is determined and becomes known) should be considered the trade date.

External cash flows are typically booked on the date when they are actually received or distributed. If a firm receives notification of incoming funds and trades on a pre-announced external cash inflow before it is received into the portfolio, the portfolio will become leveraged during the period between the trade date and the date when the external cash inflow is physically received. To "cover" this additional exposure and eliminate the leverage effect, firms may choose to apply

[6] REQUIRED for periods beginning on or after 1 January 2005.

the trade date and settlement date principles to pre-arranged external cash flows by booking the external cash flow with a trade date that reflects the date the firm may trade in advance of the external cash inflow and a settlement date that reflects the date when the cash is received. If the firm chooses to match the trade date of pre-announced external cash flows to the trade date of trades related to those external cash flows, it should establish this as its policy and treat all pre-announced external cash flows consistently.

Provision 2.A.10

ACCRUAL ACCOUNTING MUST be used for fixed-income securities and all other investments that earn interest income, except that interest income on cash and cash equivalents may be recognized on a cash basis. Any accrued income MUST be included in the beginning and ending PORTFOLIO values when performance is calculated.

Discussion

Accrual accounting allows the recording of financial transactions as they come into existence rather than when they are paid or settled. When determining the valuation for a security that pays interest income, firms must include the income that would have been received at the end of the performance period had the security actually paid interest income earned during the performance period.

Accrued interest income must be included in both the beginning and ending portfolio values when performance is calculated. Interest should be accrued for a security in the portfolio using whatever method is customary and appropriate for that security.

Some instruments already include accrued income as part of the security's market price. If income for these instruments is being accrued as part of the income recognition process, steps should be taken to ensure that the income is not double counted.

Income on cash and cash equivalents may be recognized on either an accrual or cash basis. Accrued income for cash and cash equivalents can be difficult to calculate. Unlike bonds with a known coupon rate, some short-term securities (e.g., overnight deposits) may not have a published interest rate. Firms must develop a methodology for accounting for short-term interest earnings and consistently apply the method selected. Firms could consider using the last actual known interest rate to accrue income for the most recent period. When the actual rate becomes known, an adjustment can then be made to allocate the actual income earned to the proper period. In this way, there is no systematic underestimation or overestimation of income, and income is also properly assigned to the period when earned. Cash-basis accounting (recording the income for short-term cash and cash equivalents as it is actually received) will tend to lag the suggested accrual method by recognizing income a month after it was earned. Either method is acceptable, however, and the method chosen must be used consistently.

An issue that may arise is how to calculate the performance of a bond, including the accrual of interest, when a bond goes into default. In this situation, the firm must recognize the loss when it occurred and the historical performance must not be recalculated. The accrual of interest must be included in the calculation method up until the point of the bond's default. At that point, the calculation method would reflect the loss of accrued interest by adjusting the amount of accrued interest to zero. When and if the bond comes out of default and there is a reasonable expectation that the bond will commence paying interest, including back interest, the firm must begin accruing for such interest payments. The firm must not allocate such payments over periods when they were originally due but not paid.

Provision 2.A.11

Returns from cash and cash equivalents MUST be included in all return calculations, even if the FIRM does not control the specific cash investment(s).

Discussion

Returns earned on cash and cash equivalents held in portfolios must be combined with the returns of other assets in the portfolio to calculate the portfolio's return. The firm's asset allocation decisions, including allocation to cash, are a component of investment strategy implementation and thus part of the portfolio's return.

If the firm does not control the actual investment of cash (e.g., cash is always invested in a custodial money market fund or invested separately by the client) but does control the amount of the portfolio that is allocated to cash, then the cash assets must be included in the firm's total assets and the performance of cash must be included in the portfolio performance.

This is true even if a client-selected cash vehicle "breaks" the $1.00 net asset value (NAV). A break occurs when the NAV of a money market fund falls below the $1.00 NAV. This scenario may happen when the money market fund's investment income does not cover operating expenses or investment losses. Because the firm chose to have portfolio assets "invested" in cash and cash equivalents, it is responsible for the performance of this investment and the change in NAV must be included in the total return of the portfolio. Additionally, the firm must continue to include the portfolio in the respective composite. The fact that the investment of cash is technically not under the firm's control will not generally affect the portfolio's returns as much as the allocation of assets to cash, which is under the firm's control.

Provision 2.A.12

Returns for periods of less than one year MUST NOT be annualized.

Discussion

Composite or pooled fund performance reflects only the performance of actual assets managed by the firm. When returns for periods of less than one year are annualized, the partial-year return is "extended" in order to create an annual return. The extrapolation of the partial-year return produces a simulated return and does not reflect the performance of actual assets. Therefore, performance for periods of less than one year must not be annualized.

Care must be taken when money-weighted returns (MWRs) are calculated and the composite or pooled fund has less than a year of performance. Many firms use Excel to calculate MWRs using the XIRR function. The XIRR function calculates an annualized internal rate of return (IRR) (an IRR is a method that can be used to calculate an MWR). When calculating an XIRR for a period of less than one year, the annualized return generated must be "de-annualized."

The non-annualized since inception IRR (SI-IRR) can be calculated as follows:

$$R_{SI\text{-}IRR} = \left[(1 + r_{SI\text{-}IRR})^{\frac{TD}{365}} \right] - 1,$$

where

$R_{SI\text{-}IRR}$ = non-annualized since-inception internal rate of return

$r_{SI\text{-}IRR}$ = annualized since-inception internal rate of return

TD = total number of calendar days in the measurement period (less than one year)

For example, a portfolio is funded with $1,000,000 cash on 1 September 2020. Another $75,000 is contributed on 10 September 2020. At the end of the month, 30 September 2020, the portfolio is valued at $1,100,000. Also assume that end-of-day cash flows are used. Using Excel's XIRR formula the annualized SI-IRR is 34.41%.

Dates	External Cash Flows & Ending Valuation		Explanation
1-Sep-2020	$	(1,000,000)	Contribution
10-Sep-2020	$	(75,000)	Contribution
30-Sep-2020	$	1,100,000	Portfolio value as of 30 September 2020
		34.41%	Calculated annualized return using XIRR

To calculate the non-annualized return in Excel, using the non-annualized SI-IRR formula, the calculation is as follows:

= (1 + 0.3441)^(29/365) – 1

= 2.38%

Provision 2.A.13

All returns MUST be calculated after the deduction of TRANSACTION COSTS incurred during the period. The FIRM may use estimated TRANSACTION COSTS only for those PORTFOLIOS for which actual TRANSACTION COSTS are not known.

Discussion

Transaction costs are defined as the costs of buying or selling investments. These costs typically take the form of brokerage commissions, exchange fees and/or taxes, and/or bid–offer spreads from either internal or external brokers. Custodial fees charged per transaction should be considered custody fees and not transaction costs. For real estate, private equity, and other private market investments, transaction costs include all legal, financial, advisory, and investment banking fees related to buying, selling, restructuring, and/or recapitalizing investments but do not include dead deal costs.

Both gross-of-fees returns and net-of-fees returns must reflect the deduction of transaction costs incurred in the purchase or sale of investments. Transaction costs must be deducted when calculating performance because these are costs that must be paid in order to implement the investment strategy. A firm may use estimated transaction costs only for those portfolios whose actual transaction costs are not known. It is the firm's responsibility to determine if there are any regulatory requirements that would prohibit the use of estimated transactions costs. If such regulatory requirements exist, estimated transaction costs must not be used.

When a portfolio's transaction costs are not known, a reasonable estimate of transactions costs (i.e., an estimate that the firm judges to be a fair approximation of actual transaction costs) may be used. Some approaches for determining a reasonable estimate of transactions costs include basing estimated transactions costs on:

- actual transaction costs for portfolios that the firm manages in the same or similar strategy, or
- actual transaction costs for similar securities that trade in a similar market.

The estimate of transaction costs may take the form of a percentage cost that can be applied to the portfolio return to determine the portfolio return after the deduction of those costs, or as a monetary value. If a monetary value is used, for costs that are based on the size of the transaction, the firm should scale the monetary transaction cost estimate sourced from a similarly managed portfolio to the monetary value of the portfolio.

For wrap fee portfolios, if the firm is able to obtain estimated transaction costs from wrap fee sponsors, it should use the highest estimated transaction costs. For the treatment of estimated transaction costs in bundled fee portfolios, please refer to Provision 2.A.14.

Regardless of the approach used, the firm must have documentation supporting the transaction costs on which the estimate is based.

Firms that use estimated transaction costs must document their policies and procedures for estimating transaction costs, along with the rationale for their method of estimating transaction costs, and apply the policies consistently. The methodology and assumptions used to estimate transactions costs must be periodically reviewed to ensure that the policies are still judged to result in a reasonable estimate of transaction costs.

Finally, in some markets brokers offer zero commission trades. If a portfolio is paying zero commissions, then it is appropriate to calculate portfolio gross-of-fees and net-of-fees returns that reflect zero transaction costs. However, the zero-transaction cost must not be used as a model transaction cost for other portfolios. When a composite includes portfolios that pay zero commissions, firms should disclose this fact. Not disclosing this fact could be misleading.

Provision 2.A.14

For PORTFOLIOS with BUNDLED FEES, if the FIRM cannot estimate TRANSACTION COSTS or if actual TRANSACTION COSTS cannot be segregated from a BUNDLED FEE:

a. When calculating GROSS-OF-FEES returns, returns MUST be reduced by the entire BUNDLED FEE or the portion of the BUNDLED FEE that includes the TRANSACTION COSTS.

b. When calculating NET-OF-FEES returns, returns MUST be reduced by the entire BUNDLED FEE or the portion of the BUNDLED FEE that includes the TRANSACTION COSTS and the INVESTMENT MANAGEMENT FEE.

Discussion

A bundled fee portfolio has a fee structure that combines multiple fees into one total or “bundled” fee. Bundled fees can include any combination of investment management fees, trading costs, custody fees, and/or administrative fees. Two examples of bundled fees are wrap fees and all-in fees. Calculations of gross-of-fees and net-of-fees returns for all portfolios, including bundled fee portfolios, must reflect the deduction of transaction costs incurred by the portfolio during the measurement period.

A gross-of-fees return is the return on investments reduced by any transaction costs incurred during the period. When calculating a bundled fee portfolio's gross-of-fees return, if the firm can identify the portion of the bundled fee that includes the transaction costs, that is the only portion of the bundled fee that must be reflected in the performance calculation. If the firm is unable to determine the portion of the bundled fee that includes the transaction costs and is unable to determine an appropriate estimate of transaction costs, then the entire bundled fee must be deducted when calculating the bundled fee portfolio's gross-of-fees return.

A net-of-fees return is the gross-of-fees return reduced by investment management fees, which include both performance-based fees and carried interest. A net-of-fees return must, therefore, reflect the deduction of both transaction costs and investment management fees. To meet the requirements of the GIPS standards when calculating a bundled fee portfolio's net-of-fees return, if the firm can identify the portion of the bundled fee that includes transaction costs and investment management fees, that is the only portion of the bundled fee that must be reflected in the performance calculation. If the firm is unable to identify the portion of the bundled fee that includes transaction costs and investment management fees, and it is unable to determine an appropriate estimate of transaction costs and an appropriate model investment management fee, then the entire bundled fee must be reflected (i.e., reduce performance) when calculating the bundled fee portfolio's net-of-fees return.

A pure gross-of-fees return is the return on investments that is not reduced by any transaction costs incurred during the period. When presenting returns for a composite of portfolios with bundled fees, it is permitted to show a pure gross-of-fees return as supplemental information.

Provision 2.A.15

All REQUIRED returns MUST be calculated net of discretionary leverage, unless otherwise specified.

Discussion

All required returns must be calculated net of discretionary leverage, unless otherwise specified. Discretionary leverage refers to loans taken at the firm's discretion. For example, suppose that a client gives the firm $1 million to manage. The firm then borrows another $500,000. The net of discretionary leverage amount (i.e., the assets on which performance is calculated) is $1 million, not $1.5 million, which is the gross of discretionary leverage amount.

In contrast, non-discretionary leverage refers to borrowings that are mandated by or undertaken by the client. For example, suppose that a client gives the firm $1.5 million to manage, of which the client has borrowed $500,000. In this case, the amount of assets on which performance is calculated is $1.5 million. The fact that the client borrowed $500,000 of the assets given to the firm does not influence the calculation of the firm's performance.

Firms that use subscription lines of credit and calculate and present since-inception money-weighted returns (MWRs) are required to present MWRs both with and without the subscription line of credit. Considering only the subscription line of credit, and ignoring any other leverage that may exist, the return with the subscription line of credit is considered a levered return and the return without the subscription line of credit would be considered an unlevered return. The one exception to the requirement to present MWRs both with and without the subscription line of credit is included in Provision 7.A.2. A firm is required to only present returns with the subscription line of credit, and not returns without the subscription line of credit, when it is presenting an MWR and the subscription line of credit has both of the following characteristics:

- The principal was repaid within 120 days using committed capital drawn down through a capital call;
- No principal was used to fund distributions.

Other than the exception for subscription lines of credit in Provision 7.A.2, the rationale for requiring that all returns be calculated net of discretionary leverage is that an unlevered return is hypothetical, and it is not appropriate for a firm to include such a return when calculating the performance of a portfolio or a composite. Unlevered performance that does not reflect the deduction of discretionary leverage is permitted to be presented only as supplemental information.

Provision 2.A.16

The FIRM MUST calculate performance in accordance with its COMPOSITE-specific or POOLED FUND–specific calculation policies.

Discussion

A firm must create composite-specific and/or pooled fund–specific policies for calculating the performance of its portfolios and composites. It must apply these policies consistently when calculating performance. A firm must ensure that its policies for calculating performance address not only assets managed internally but also those managed externally, or for which performance is calculated externally. A firm claiming compliance with the GIPS standards that uses external managers and service providers is responsible for having policies and procedures in place to ensure that the relevant outsourced services produce information on which the firm relies that is consistent with the requirements of the GIPS standards and that all GIPS standards requirements have been met.

Although it is not possible to list all of the items that must be included in a firm's policies and procedures for calculating the performance of its portfolios and any composites, the following are examples of some of the items that a firm must address in its policies and procedures relating to performance calculation:

- How the firm ensures that the information from third-party service providers meets the requirements of the GIPS standards and can be used, as necessary, to produce returns that comply with the GIPS standards;
- The policies for estimating transaction costs, if estimated transaction costs are used;
- The fees and expenses deducted when calculating gross-of-fees returns and net-of-fees returns;
- The methodology for calculating a time-weighted return (TWR) for portfolios and composites for which the firm presents a TWR;
- The methodology for calculating a money-weighted return (MWR) for portfolios and composites for which the firm presents an MWR;
- The calculation methodology for portfolios with external cash flows;
- The treatment of reclaimable withholding taxes when recording interest income and dividends;
- How model investment management fees are calculated, if used in calculating net-of-fees returns;
- The treatment of performance-based fee clawbacks, if any; and
- The treatment of side pockets, if any.

Although a firm must establish a composite-specific or pooled fund–specific calculation policy, that policy may differentiate calculations used for different types of portfolios in the composite. For example, suppose that a firm has a composite that includes pooled funds, which use a daily TWR calculation methodology, and segregated accounts, which use a Modified Dietz return (with revaluations for large cash flows) calculation methodology. The firm may have a different policy for the return calculation methodologies used for pooled funds versus segregated accounts that are included in the same composite. The firm must apply the composite-specific calculation policy consistently, however, based on the return calculation methodology for each type of portfolio in the composite.

It is possible that all of a firm's composites and pooled funds use the same calculation policy; however, the appropriate policy must be determined for each composite and/or pooled fund. The firm must not simply establish this policy on a firm-wide basis without considering whether the policy is appropriate for each composite or pooled fund.

A firm's policies and procedures for calculating performance must be designed to ensure that the firm adheres to all applicable laws and regulations regarding the calculation and presentation of performance. Firms must establish policies and procedures to ensure that performance and performance-related information does not include false or misleading information.

Policies and procedures should be reviewed regularly to determine if they should be changed or improved, but it is not expected that they will change frequently. A firm must not change a policy retroactively solely to increase performance or to present the firm in a better light. Retroactive changes to policies and procedures should be avoided.

The firm should also conduct periodic testing or other monitoring procedures to ensure that all outsourced policies and procedures are being applied consistently and appropriately.

Provision 2.A.17

For PORTFOLIOS invested in underlying POOLED FUNDS, all returns MUST reflect the deduction of all fees and expenses charged at the underlying POOLED FUND level, unless the FIRM controls the INVESTMENT MANAGEMENT FEES of the underlying POOLED FUNDS. When the FIRM controls the INVESTMENT MANAGEMENT FEES of the underlying POOLED FUNDS, the FIRM may calculate GROSS-OF-FEES returns that do not reflect the deduction of the underlying POOLED FUND INVESTMENT MANAGEMENT FEES.

Discussion

If presenting returns for portfolios invested in underlying pooled funds, all returns must reflect the deduction of all fees and expenses charged at the underlying pooled fund level, because investors must pay these fees. When the firm controls the investment management fees of the underlying pooled funds, however, it may calculate gross-of-fees returns that do not reflect the deduction of the underlying pooled fund investment management fees. An investment management fee includes both asset-based and performance-based fees. In such situations, the firm can present the gross-of-fees returns gross of the underlying funds' investment management fees but net of the underlying funds' transaction costs and other expenses. The following represent some situations in which this criterion is met:

- Both underlying funds and the fund-of-funds are managed by the same firm, and there is effectively a fee rebate or waiver at the fund-of-funds level for those fees charged at the underlying fund level.
- A fund-of-funds that resembles a master-feeder structure or a segregated portfolio that invests in one or multiple underlying funds managed by the same firm. Its investment management fee model is structured so that the investment management fee is either partially or fully charged at the underlying fund level.

Provision 2.A.18

When calculating ADDITIONAL RISK MEASURES:

a. The PERIODICITY of the COMPOSITE or POOLED FUND returns and the BENCHMARK returns MUST be the same.
b. The risk measure calculation methodology of the COMPOSITE or POOLED FUND and the BENCHMARK MUST be the same.

Discussion

Evaluating past performance requires an understanding of the risks taken to achieve the results. The firm may choose to present additional risk measures for a composite or pooled fund and for the benchmark that it determines are appropriate for the composite's or pooled fund's investment mandate, objective, or strategy. An additional risk measure is a risk measure included in a GIPS Report beyond those required to be presented. A firm may choose to present a proprietary measure of risk as an additional risk measure, but it must describe the proprietary measure of risk that is presented and explain why it was selected.

The periodicity of the composite or pooled fund and the benchmark must be identical when calculating additional risk measures. Periodicity refers to the length of the period over which a variable is measured (e.g., composite performance calculated monthly has monthly periodicity). As an example, if a firm is calculating an additional risk measure for a composite or pooled fund that has monthly returns and a benchmark that has quarterly returns, the firm would be required to use quarterly composite or pooled fund returns, not monthly returns, when calculating an additional risk measure. The firm must also determine that there are enough data points for the selected measure to be statistically significant so as not to be misleading.

It is also required that the risk measure calculation methodology of the composite or pooled fund and the benchmark be the same. Firms are required to select a calculation methodology on a composite-specific or pooled fund–specific basis, document the methodology in their policies and procedures, and consistently apply that methodology. Firms are required to maintain records supporting all calculations presented in GIPS Reports.

Valuation

Provision 2.A.19

PORTFOLIOS MUST be valued in accordance with the definition of FAIR VALUE.[7]

Discussion

The quality of a return depends on the quality of the valuations included in the calculation of that return. Performance reporting is of little value unless the underlying valuations are

[7] REQUIRED for periods beginning on or after 1 January 2011. For periods prior to 1 January 2011, PORTFOLIO valuations (excluding REAL ESTATE and PRIVATE EQUITY) MUST be based on FAIR VALUES or MARKET VALUES. For periods prior to 1 January 2011, REAL ESTATE investments MUST be valued at FAIR VALUE or MARKET VALUE (as previously defined for REAL ESTATE in the 2005 edition of the GIPS standards). For periods ending prior to 1 January 2011, PRIVATE EQUITY investments MUST be valued at FAIR VALUE, according to the GIPS Private Equity Valuation Principles in Appendix D of the 2005 edition of the GIPS standards, or the GIPS Valuation Principles in Chapter II of the 2010 edition of the GIPS standards.

based on sound valuation principles. Beginning 1 January 2011, portfolio valuations must be based on fair value.

Fair value is defined as the amount at which an investment could be sold in an arm's length transaction between willing parties in an orderly transaction. The valuation must be determined using the objective, observable, unadjusted quoted market price for an identical investment in an active market on the measurement date, if available. In the absence of an objective, observable, unadjusted quoted market price for an identical investment in an active market on the measurement date, the valuation must represent the firm's best estimate of the fair value. Fair value must include any accrued income.

As noted in the definition of fair value, when determining fair value, firms must use the objective, observable, unadjusted quoted market prices for identical investments in active markets on the measurement date, if available. Markets are not always liquid, however, and investment prices are not always objective and/or observable. For illiquid or hard-to-value investments, or for investments for which no observable market value or market price is available, additional steps are necessary. A firm's valuation policies and procedures must address situations in which the market prices may be available for similar but not identical investments, inputs to valuations are subjective rather than objective, and/or markets are inactive instead of active.

A very small number of circumstances exist in which cost or book value may be deemed to be fair value. Examples include stable value assets, such as guaranteed investment contracts (GICs) or real estate in the first year of the purchase of the property. In such cases, if a firm can support a determination that cost or book value and fair value are the same, it is acceptable for book value to be used when calculating asset values and returns.

It is important that a firm establish fair valuation policies that take into account the specific characteristics of asset classes or investment products. For example, to fair value an international pooled fund might require a firm to roll forward the valuation of the fund to the local market, in order to strike a Net Asset Value (NAV) based on more current prices than the local market close prices.

There is a recommended valuation hierarchy in provision 2.B.6. Firms are not required to follow the valuation hierarchy, but it is recommended that they do so.

Although a firm may use external third parties to value investments, the firm still retains responsibility for compliance with the GIPS standards, which includes the requirement to fairly value investments.

Over time, the type of valuation required and the minimum valuation frequency have changed. Prior editions of the GIPS standards included valuation guidance specific to private equity. The 2020 edition of the GIPS standards has no private equity–specific requirements. Instead, private equity is included in the broader category of private market investments. Please see the historical valuation requirements for various asset classes in the following exhibit.

Time Frame	Valuation Method	Minimum Valuation Frequency
Portfolios Except Private Market Investments		
1 Jan 2011 to Current	Fair Value	Monthly and on the date of all large cash flows
1 Jan 2010 to 31 Dec 2010	Fair Value or Market Value	Monthly and on the date of all large cash flows
1 Jan 2001 to 31 Dec 2009	Fair Value or Market Value	Monthly
Prior to 1 Jan 2001	Fair Value or Market Value	Quarterly
Private Market Investments (except real estate and private equity)		
1 Jan 2011 to Current	Fair Value	Quarterly
Prior to 1 Jan 2011	Fair Value or Market Value	Quarterly
Private Equity		
1 Jan 2011 to Current	Fair Value	Quarterly
1 Jan 2008 to 31 Dec 2010	Fair Value (According to the GIPS Private Equity Valuation Principles in Appendix D of the 2005 edition of the GIPS standards, or the GIPS Valuation Principles in Chapter II of the 2010 edition of the GIPS standards)	Quarterly
Prior to 1 Jan 2008	Fair Value (According to the GIPS Private Equity Valuation Principles in Appendix D of the 2005 edition of the GIPS standards, or the GIPS Valuation Principles in Chapter II of the 2010 edition of the GIPS standards)	Annually
Real Estate—Open-End Fund		
1 Jan 2011 to Current	Fair Value	Quarterly
1 Jan 2008 to 31 Dec 2010	Fair Value or Market Value (as previously defined for Real Estate in the 2005 edition of the GIPS standards)	Quarterly
Prior to 1 Jan 2008	Fair Value or Market Value (as previously defined for Real Estate in the 2005 edition of the GIPS standards)	Annually
1 Jan 2020 to Current	External Valuation	Every 12 months
1 Jan 2012 to 31 Dec 2019	External Valuation	Every 12 months unless client agreements stipulate otherwise, in which case investments must be externally valued every 36 months
1 Jan 06 to 31 Dec 2011	External Valuation	Every 36 months

(continued)

 |

Time Frame	Valuation Method	Minimum Valuation Frequency
Real Estate—Not in an Open-End Fund		
1 Jan 2011 to Current	Fair Value	Quarterly
1 Jan 2008 to 31 Dec 2010	Fair Value or Market Value (as previously defined for Real Estate in the 2005 edition of the GIPS standards)	Quarterly
Prior to 1 Jan 2008	Fair Value or Market Value (as previously defined for Real Estate in the 2005 edition of the GIPS standards)	Annually
1 Jan 2012 to Current	External Valuation	1. External valuation every 12 months unless client agreements stipulate otherwise, in which case investments must be externally valued every 36 months; or 2. Annual financial statement audit
1 Jan 2006 to 31 Dec 2011	External Valuation	Every 36 months

Provision 2.A.20

The FIRM MUST value PORTFOLIOS in accordance with the COMPOSITE-specific or POOLED FUND–specific valuation policy.

Discussion

When daily calculations are not used, a firm must not value a portfolio "opportunistically" and must follow its composite-specific or pooled fund-specific valuation policies consistently. For example, assume that a firm's valuation policy is to value portfolios for large cash flows, defined in the composite-specific valuation policy as a single external cash flow equal to or greater than 5% of the portfolio's beginning-of-month value. For any single external cash flow that is less than 5% of the portfolio's beginning-of-month value, the firm must not value the portfolio. For any single external cash flow that is equal to or greater than 5% of the portfolio's beginning-of-month value, the firm must value the portfolio. The firm must apply the composite-specific or pooled fund–specific valuation policy consistently and not "cherry-pick" when to value portfolios.

Although a firm must establish a composite-specific valuation policy, that policy may differentiate valuation frequency for different types of portfolios in the composite. For example, suppose that a firm has a composite that includes pooled funds, which are valued daily, and segregated accounts, which are valued monthly and for external cash flows above 5%. The firm may have a different policy for the frequency of valuing pooled funds versus segregated accounts that are included in the same composite. The firm must apply the composite-specific valuation policy consistently, however, based on the valuation frequency for each type of portfolio in the composite.

It is possible that all of a firm's composites and pooled funds use the same valuation policy; however, the appropriate policy must be determined for each composite and/or pooled fund. The firm must not simply establish this policy on a firm-wide basis without considering whether the policy is appropriate for each composite or pooled fund.

A firm must ensure that its policies for calculating performance address not only assets managed internally but also those managed externally or for which performance is calculated externally. A firm claiming compliance with the GIPS standards that uses external managers and service providers is responsible for having policies and procedures in place to ensure that the relevant outsourced services produce information on which the firm relies that is consistent with the requirements of the GIPS standards and that all GIPS standards requirements have been met.

Policies and procedures should be reviewed regularly to determine if they should be changed or improved, but it is not expected that they will change frequently. A firm must not change a policy retroactively solely to increase performance or to present the firm in a better light. Retroactive changes to policies and procedures should be avoided.

The firm should also conduct periodic testing or other monitoring procedures to ensure that all outsourced policies and procedures are being applied consistently and appropriately.

Provision 2.A.21

If the FIRM uses the last available historical price or preliminary, estimated value as FAIR VALUE, the FIRM MUST:

a. Consider it to be the best approximation of the current FAIR VALUE.
b. Assess the difference between the approximation and final value and the effect on COMPOSITE OR POOLED FUND assets, TOTAL FIRM ASSETS, and performance, and also make any adjustments when the final value is received.

Discussion

It is not uncommon for private market investments to be valued using preliminary, estimated values. If a firm uses the last available historical price or preliminary, estimated values as fair value, perhaps in order to produce a GIPS Report on a timely basis, the firm must consider the estimate of value to be the best approximation of the current fair value, and this must be defined in the firm's fair valuation policy. When using preliminary, estimated values, the firm should obtain an understanding of the process used to establish estimated values in order to determine whether reliance can be placed on the process.

Firms must define the use of the last available historical price or preliminary, estimated values, and the treatment of subsequent final values, in their composite-specific and/or pooled fund–specific fair valuation policies. The valuation policies must be followed consistently and made available upon request. If the firm uses the last available historical price or preliminary, estimated values, when final values are received the firm must assess the difference between the estimate of value and the final value, as well as the effect on composite or pooled fund assets, total firm assets, and performance. If the final values and resulting performance differ materially, firms must determine whether any adjustments to the composite or pooled fund must be made on a prospective basis or retroactively. If composite or pooled fund valuations are revised retroactively, firms must consider the requirements related to error correction and the firm's error correction policies. Differences between final and estimated values are not considered to be errors but are treated similarly.

It is important to remember the underlying principles of the GIPS standards: fair representation and full disclosure. If differences between the estimated and final values are consistently material, the firm should reassess whether it is proper to continue to use the estimates of fair value.

Provision 2.A.22

COMPOSITES and POOLED FUNDS MUST have consistent beginning and ending annual valuation dates. Unless the COMPOSITE or POOLED FUND is reported on a non-calendar fiscal year, the beginning and ending valuation dates MUST be at calendar year end or on the last business day of the year.[8]

Discussion

It is required that composites and pooled funds have consistent beginning and ending annual valuation dates. Such consistency will result in improved comparability of data. Unless the composite or pooled fund is reported on a non-calendar fiscal year, the beginning and ending valuation dates of the composite or pooled fund must be at calendar year end or on the last business day of the year. Portfolios in a composite must also have consistent beginning and ending valuation dates corresponding to the reporting period. If the composite or pooled fund beginning or ending annual valuation dates fall on a weekend or a holiday, the firm should use the valuation on the last business day of the period. If there is an available benchmark value on the same day as the ending valuation day for the composite or pooled fund, the firm should use the benchmark value from the ending valuation day for the composite or pooled fund. If the composite or pooled fund ending annual valuation date differs from that of the benchmark, this difference should be disclosed. For example, if the annual period end and the last valuation falls on 30 December because of the New Year's Eve holiday but the end of the annual period for the benchmark falls on

[8] REQUIRED for periods beginning on or after 1 January 2006.

31 December, any material difference in performance should be disclosed. The firm should use the benchmark value from 30 December if it is available.

Note that a firm's composites and/or pooled funds may have different year-end valuation dates if one or more of the firm's composites or pooled funds is reported on a non-calendar fiscal year, whereas other composites and/or pooled funds are reported as of calendar year end or on the last business day of the year. The annual valuation dates must correspond to the reporting dates for the composite or pooled fund. It is important, however, that the annual periods within a GIPS Report are consistent. For example, a GIPS Pooled Fund Report that reports a pooled fund's performance annually as of 30 June, its fiscal year end, must consistently report data for years ending 30 June for the pooled fund. The firm may decide in the future to create a GIPS Pooled Fund Report for the pooled fund based on a 31 December valuation and reporting date; however, the firm may not mix 30 June and 31 December annual reporting periods in the same GIPS Pooled Fund Report and must report all annual returns as of the calendar year end.

Portfolios—Time-Weighted Returns

Provision 2.A.23

When calculating TIME-WEIGHTED RETURNS for PORTFOLIOS that are included in COMPOSITES, all PORTFOLIOS except PRIVATE MARKET INVESTMENT PORTFOLIOS (see 2.A.40) MUST be valued:

a. At least monthly.[9]
b. As of the calendar month end or the last business day of the month.[10]
c. On the date of all LARGE CASH FLOWS. The FIRM MUST define LARGE CASH FLOW for each COMPOSITE to determine when PORTFOLIOS in that COMPOSITE MUST be valued.[11]

Discussion

The requirements contained in Provision 2.A.23 apply to a firm's portfolios that are included in composites, with the exception of private market investment portfolios. For the valuation requirements for private market investment portfolios, firms should refer to Provision 2.A.40 and related guidance.

[9] REQUIRED for periods beginning on or after 1 January 2001. For periods prior to 1 January 2001, PORTFOLIOS MUST be valued at least quarterly.
[10] REQUIRED for periods beginning on or after 1 January 2010.
[11] REQUIRED for periods beginning on or after 1 January 2010.

To improve the accuracy of time-weighted performance calculations, the GIPS standards have gradually increased the minimum required frequency of portfolio valuation from quarterly, to monthly, to the date of all large cash flows.

When calculating time-weighted returns for portfolios included in composites, all portfolios (with the exception of private market investment portfolios) must be valued at least monthly. Valuing portfolios included in the composite at different end dates does not allow for comparability of information. Firms must be consistent in defining the monthly valuation period to allow for comparability of data for all GIPS Composite Reports. It is also required that the calculation period must end on the same day as the reporting period. In other words, firms must value the portfolios included in a composite on the last day of the reporting period or the nearest business day. For periods beginning on or after 1 January 2010, firms must value portfolios as of the calendar month end or the last business day of the month.

In addition to the requirement for firms to value portfolios included in a composite at least monthly, firms are required to value all portfolios included in a composite on the date of all large cash flows, if the portfolios are not valued daily. A large cash flow, defined by the firm for each composite, is the level at which the firm determines that an external cash flow may distort performance if the portfolio is not valued. The firm must determine in advance (i.e., on an ex ante basis) what is considered to be a large cash flow on a composite-specific basis. Firms must define the amount in terms of the value of cash/asset flow or in terms of a percentage of the portfolio assets or the composite assets. Firms must also determine if a large cash flow is a single external cash flow or an aggregate of a number of external cash flows within a stated period. The determination of the large cash flow level may be influenced by a variety of factors, such as the strategy's nature, its historical and expected volatility, and its targeted cash level.

A firm must not establish a high large cash flow level solely for the purpose of reducing the number of instances when portfolios must be valued because of large cash flows. The firm also must not base the policy on the degree to which the large cash flow affects the return. The large cash flow level chosen by the firm on a composite-specific basis must represent the firm's estimate of the level of external cash flow that would potentially distort the accuracy of a portfolio's performance calculation if the portfolio is not valued at the time of the external cash flow.

It is possible that all of a firm's composites have the same level of large cash flows; however, the appropriate level must be determined for each composite. The firm must not simply establish this level on a firm-wide basis without considering whether the level is appropriate for each portfolio or composite.

Revaluing portfolios as of the close of the business day prior to a large external cash flow is acceptable if external cash flows are assumed to take place at the beginning of the day.

When applying these provisions, it should be remembered that private market investment portfolios have separate valuation requirements. Firms should refer to the valuation table included in Provision 2.A.19 for additional guidance on valuation requirements, including the valuation requirements for private market investments.

Provision 2.A.24

When calculating TIME-WEIGHTED RETURNS for all PORTFOLIOS except PRIVATE MARKET INVESTMENT PORTFOLIOS (see 2.A.41) included in COMPOSITES, the FIRM MUST:

a. Calculate returns at least monthly.[12]
b. Calculate monthly returns through the calendar month end or the last business day of the month.[13]
c. Calculate sub-period returns at the time of all LARGE CASH FLOWS, if daily returns are not calculated.[14]
d. For EXTERNAL CASH FLOWS that are not LARGE CASH FLOWS, calculate PORTFOLIO returns that adjust for daily-weighted EXTERNAL CASH FLOWS, if daily returns are not calculated.[15]
e. Treat EXTERNAL CASH FLOWS according to the FIRM'S COMPOSITE-specific policy.
f. Geometrically LINK periodic and sub-period returns.
g. Consistently apply the calculation methodology used for an individual PORTFOLIO.

Discussion

Provision 2.A.24 applies to all portfolios included in composites except private market investment portfolios. Please refer to Provision 2.A.41 for the requirements regarding the calculation of a time-weighted return (TWR) for private market investment portfolios included in composites.

TWRs measure the firm's performance and attempt to negate or neutralize the effect of external cash flows to or from the client. The GIPS standards do not require a specific method to be used to calculate TWRs but do require the return methodology to meet certain criteria.

Although it is required that TWRs be calculated at least monthly, many firms calculate daily returns. If daily returns are not calculated, a firm must calculate sub-period returns for portfolios at the time of all large cash flows in order to calculate a more accurate TWR. A large cash flow is the level at which the firm determines that an external cash flow may distort performance if the portfolio is not valued at the time of the external cash flow. A large cash flow is defined by the firm

[12] REQUIRED for periods beginning on or after 1 January 2001.
[13] REQUIRED for periods beginning on or after 1 January 2010.
[14] REQUIRED for periods beginning on or after 1 January 2010.
[15] REQUIRED for periods beginning on or after 1 January 2005.

for each composite to determine when the portfolios in that composite are to be valued for performance calculations. Firms must define the amount, for each composite, in terms of the value of the cash/asset flow or in terms of a percentage of the portfolio assets or the composite assets. Firms must also determine if a large cash flow is a single external cash flow or an aggregate of a number of external cash flows within a stated period of time.

For periods beginning on or after 1 January 2001, firms must calculate portfolio TWRs at least monthly. When calculating and presenting performance in a GIPS Composite Report, calculating returns for portfolios at different end dates does not allow for the comparability of information. Therefore, to facilitate comparability, for periods beginning on or after 1 January 2010, firms must calculate monthly returns as of the calendar month end or the last business day of the month.

The actual valuation of the portfolio's investments and calculation of return each time a large cash flow occurs will result in a more accurate TWR calculation than using either the Original Dietz method or the Modified Dietz method, but it is less accurate than a "true" TWR calculation methodology, which requires valuation and return calculation with every external cash flow.

The returns calculated for each sub-period are geometrically linked according to the following formula:

$$r_t^{TWR} = \left[(1+r_1)\times(1+r_2)\times\ldots\times(1+r_I)\right]-1,$$

where r_t^{TWR} is the time-weighted return for period t and period t consists of I sub-periods.

The chief advantage of valuing a portfolio at the time of large cash flows and calculating sub-period returns is that it calculates a better estimate than the midpoint or day-weighting methods. The major disadvantage is that it requires precise valuation of the portfolio each time a large cash flow occurs. In practice, this means that firms must have the ability to value portfolios on a daily basis. If all investments are not accurately priced for each sub-period valuation, errors generated in the return calculation may be greater than the errors caused by using the midpoint or day-weighting approximation methods. In such cases, it is important to be able to correct for errors, such as missed security splits, mispricings, and improperly booked transactions, because day-to-day compounding will not correct for them automatically if external cash flows occur.

As of 1 January 2005, the calculation of portfolio returns that adjust for daily-weighted external cash flows is required, if daily returns are not calculated. The denominator in the calculation of a TWR that adjusts for daily-weighted external cash flows reflects the weighting of external cash flows for the days they have been in the portfolio and available for investment during the period. A firm must create a composite-specific policy for the treatment of external cash flows and apply the policy consistently. Examples of acceptable methods for calculating returns that adjust for daily-weighted external cash flows are the Modified Dietz method and internal rate of return (IRR). These methods are estimates of TWRs.

Modified Dietz Method

The Modified Dietz method improves upon the Original Dietz method, which assumes that all external cash flows occur during the midpoint of the period. In an attempt to determine a more accurate return, the Modified Dietz method weights each external cash flow in the denominator by the amount of time it is held in the portfolio. The formula for estimating the TWR using the Modified Dietz method is

$$r_t^{MD} = \frac{V_t^E - V_t^B - \sum_{i=1}^{I} CF_{i,t}}{V_t^B + \sum_{i=1}^{I} \left(CF_{i,t} \times w_{i,t}\right)},$$

where

r_t^{MD} = the Modified Dietz return for the portfolio for period t

V_t^E = the ending value of the portfolio for period t

V_t^B = the beginning value of the portfolio for period t

i = the number of external cash flows (1, 2, 3, . . . I) in period t

$CF_{i,t}$ = the value of external cash flow i in period t

$w_{i,t}$ = the weight of external cash flow i in period t (assuming the external cash flow occurred at the end of the day), as calculated according to the following formula:

$$w_{i,t} = \frac{D_t - D_{i,t}}{D_t},$$

where

$w_{i,t}$ = the weight of external cash flow i in period t, assuming the external cash flow occurred at the end of the day

D_t = the total number of calendar days in period t

$D_{i,t}$ = the number of calendar days from the beginning of period t to external cash flow i

The numerator of $w_{i,t}$ is based on the assumption that the external cash flows occur at the end of the day. If external cash flows were assumed to occur at the beginning of the day, the numerator would be $[(D_t - D_{i,t}) + 1]$. A firm may choose to use a beginning-of-day or end-of-day external cash flow assumption or some combination of the two. The key is to establish a policy and treat external cash flows consistently.

The chief advantage of the Modified Dietz method is that it does not require portfolio valuation on the date of each external cash flow. Its chief disadvantage is that it provides a less accurate return than when the portfolio is valued at the time of each external cash flow. The estimate suffers most when a combination of the following conditions exists: (1) One or more large external cash flows occur, and (2) external cash flows occur during periods of high market volatility—that is, the portfolio's returns are significantly non-linear.

The following is an example of a return calculation using the Modified Dietz method. The example is for a portfolio with a beginning value of \$100,000 on 31 May, an ending value of \$135,000 on 30 June, and external cash flows of –\$2,000 on 6 June and \$20,000 on 11 June. Assume the external cash flows were reflected at the end of the day.

31 May	Beginning Value (BV)	\$100,000
6 June	Cash Flow (CF)	-\$2,000
11 June	Cash Flow (CF)	\$20,000
30 June	Ending Value (EV)	\$135,000

$$R_{\text{Modified Dietz}} = \frac{EV - BV - CF}{BV + (W \times CF)}$$

W is the weight of the external cash flow for the month. Because June has 30 days and the external cash flows were assumed to occur at the end of the day, the weights of the external cash flows are calculated as (30 – 6)/30 = 0.80 and (30 – 11)/30 = 0.6333, respectively.

$$R_{\text{Modified Dietz}} = \frac{135{,}000 - 100{,}000 - (-2{,}000 + 20{,}000)}{100{,}000 + (0.80 \times -2{,}000) + (0.6333 \times 20{,}000)}$$

$$R_{\text{Modified Dietz}} = \frac{17{,}000}{111{,}067} = 15.31\%$$

If the firm's policy was to treat external cash flows as occurring at the beginning of the day, the firm would have added one to the numerator in the weight calculation, and the weights to be multiplied by the external cash flows would be calculated as (30 – 6 + 1)/30 = 0.8333 and (30 – 11 + 1)/30 = 0.6667, respectively.

The following is an example of a return calculation using the Modified Dietz method and revaluing during the month for a large cash flow (assumed to be 10% in this example). To calculate performance for the month, we must calculate performance for the sub-periods before and after the large external cash flow and then geometrically link the sub-period returns. In this example, we use the same data as in the prior example but instead value the portfolio at the time of the large cash flow on 11 June.

31 May	Beginning Value (BV)	\$100,000
6 June	Cash Flow (CF)	-\$2,000
11 June	Cash Flow (CF)	\$20,000
11 June	Ending Value (EV)	\$125,000
30 June	Ending Value (EV)	\$135,000

Sub-period 1 calculation, from 31 May through 11 June:

Because sub-period 1 has 11 days and the external cash flows are assumed to occur at the end of the day, the weight of the external cash flow on the sixth day is (11 – 6)/11 = 0.4545. The weight of the cash flow on the 11th would be zero because it is assumed to happen at the end of the day on 11 June, which is when the portfolio was revalued.

$$R_{\text{Modified Dietz (sub-period 1)}} = \frac{125{,}000 - 100{,}000 - (-2{,}000 + 20{,}000)}{100{,}000 + (0.4545 \times -2{,}000) + (0 \times 20{,}000)}$$

$$R_{\text{Modified Dietz (sub-period 1)}} = \frac{7{,}000}{99{,}091} = 7.06\%$$

Sub-period 2 calculation, from 11 June through 30 June:

$$R_{\text{Modified Dietz (sub-period 2)}} = \frac{135{,}000 - 125{,}000}{125{,}000}$$

$$R_{\text{Modified Dietz (sub-period 2)}} = \frac{10{,}000}{125{,}000} = 8.00\%$$

To calculate the monthly return, geometrically link sub-period returns 1 and 2: (1 + 0.0706) × (1 + 0.08) – 1 = 0.1563, or 15.63%.

Other formulas in addition to the Modified Dietz method for calculating approximate TWRs are also permitted.

Internal Rate of Return (IRR) Method

The IRR, which is a money-weighted return, is the implied discount rate or effective compounded rate of return that equates the present value of cash outflows with the present value of cash inflows. The IRR method is an acceptable method to use to calculate a TWR when no large cash flows occur during the sub-period. To create a TWR, the IRRs before and after the large cash flow are calculated and then linked together geometrically.

The IRR is the value of R that satisfies the following equation:

$$V_E = \sum_{i=0}^{n} CF_i (1 + R)^{W_i},$$

where V_E and W_i are the same as for the Modified Dietz method.

The external cash flows, CF_i, are also the same as with the Modified Dietz method with one important exception: The value at the beginning of the period is also treated as an external cash flow—that is, $V_B = CF_0$.

The IRR is obtained by selecting values for R and solving the equation until the result equals V_E. For example, if three external cash flows (including the value at the beginning of the period) have occurred, the formula will have three terms:

$$V_E = CF_0(1+R)^{W_0} + CF_1(1+R)^{W_1} + CF_2(1+R)^{W_2}.$$

The first term deals with the first external cash flow, CF_0, which is the value of the portfolio at the beginning of the period; W_i is the proportion of the period when the external cash flow CF_i was held in the portfolio. Because CF_0 is in for the whole period, $W_0 = 1$. The larger the value of CF_i in the term, the more it will contribute to the total, but the smaller the exponent (i.e., the value of W_i), the less the term will contribute to the sum. The usual effect is that the first term, with a large CF_0 and W_0 equal to 1, will contribute far more than the other terms.

The advantages and disadvantages of the IRR method are the same as those of the Modified Dietz method. The IRR method has the additional disadvantage of requiring an iterative process solution. It is also possible to have multiple answers if both positive and negative external cash flows occur.

When calculating the TWR for portfolios, periodic and sub-period returns must be linked geometrically.

A firm must create a composite-specific policy for the treatment of external cash flows for each of its composites and must apply that policy consistently. For example, the same definition of a large cash flow must be used when evaluating a cash flow for all portfolios within the composite. Policies and procedures for the calculation methodology used for an individual portfolio must also be created and applied consistently.

Pooled Funds

Provision 2.A.25

When calculating TIME-WEIGHTED RETURNS for POOLED FUNDS that are not included in a COMPOSITE, POOLED FUNDS MUST be valued:

a. At least annually.
b. As of the calendar or fiscal year end.
c. Whenever there are subscriptions to or redemptions from the POOLED FUND.
d. As of the period end for any period for which performance is calculated.

Discussion

For some pooled funds, it may not be possible to strike a net asset value (NAV) or obtain valuations as frequently as is required of other types of portfolios, because of their illiquidity or because the pricing source does not provide the valuations on a monthly or more frequent basis.

If the underlying investments of a pooled fund that is not included in a composite do not lend themselves to monthly valuations and the fund itself is open to client cash flows only on a less frequent (e.g., quarterly) basis, it may be appropriate that valuations are performed on a less frequent than monthly basis. In all cases, valuations must be conducted at least on an annual basis and must take place as of the calendar or fiscal year end.

Although a pooled fund must be valued at least annually, the subscription and redemption cycle for the pooled fund would drive the choice of the periodicity for investment valuation and performance measurement. Therefore, in addition to the requirement for at least a valuation annually, the pooled fund must be valued whenever there are subscriptions to or redemptions from the pooled fund.

The pooled fund must also be valued as of the period end for any period for which performance is calculated.

There may be instances in which some investments in a pooled fund may not be valued because of a holiday. The firm's policy may be to not strike an NAV or value the pooled fund for that particular day because of the lack of valuations for all securities. For example, assume 31 December is a holiday in some markets and, as a result, 30% of the investments in the XYZ Fund are not valued. Assume the firm's policy is to not strike an NAV unless at least 75% of the assets are valued, so the last NAV struck is on 30 December. If the difference in performance is material, this fact should be disclosed. The firm should use the benchmark value from 30 December if it is available.

GIPS Reports must include information for annual periods. Many firms present annual returns on a calendar year basis as of 31 December but are not required to do so. For example, a firm may decide to present all performance on a fiscal year basis as of 30 June or some other month end. Firms may change their annual reporting period. For example, a firm may decide to change from calendar-year reporting as of 31 December to fiscal-year reporting as of 30 June. If the firm changes the annual reporting period, it must do so for all annual periods presented in the GIPS Report. The requirement to present returns for annual periods does not prevent the firm from presenting year-to-date returns.

 |

Provision 2.A.26

When calculating TIME-WEIGHTED RETURNS for POOLED FUNDS that are not included in a COMPOSITE, the FIRM MUST:

a. Calculate returns at least annually.
b. Calculate annual returns through the calendar or fiscal year end or the last business day of the year.
c. Calculate sub-period returns at the time of all subscriptions and redemptions.
d. Geometrically LINK periodic and sub-period returns.
e. When calculating POOLED FUND NET RETURNS, calculate POOLED FUND NET RETURNS that are net of TOTAL POOLED FUND FEES.

Discussion

If the underlying investments of a pooled fund that is not included in a composite do not lend themselves to monthly valuations and the pooled fund itself is open to client cash flows only on a less frequent (e.g., quarterly) basis, it may be appropriate to calculate time-weighted returns (TWRs) on a less frequent than monthly basis. In all cases, returns must be calculated at least annually through the calendar or fiscal year end or through the last business day of the year.

In addition to the requirement that TWRs be calculated at least annually, sub-period returns must be calculated whenever there are subscriptions to or redemptions from the pooled fund. This means that pooled funds use a "true" TWR calculation methodology, which requires valuation and return calculation with every external cash flow. The periodic and sub-period returns must be geometrically linked according to the following formula:

$$r_t^{TWR} = \left[(1+r_1)\times(1+r_2)\times\ldots\times(1+r_I)\right]-1,$$

where r_t^{TWR} is the time-weighted return for period t and period t consists of I sub-periods.

It is also required that, when calculating pooled fund net returns, the pooled fund net returns are net of total pooled fund fees. Total pooled fund fees include all of the fees and expenses charged to the pooled fund, including investment management fees, administrative fees, and other expenses. Total pooled fund fees do not include sales charges and loads that are associated with buying or selling shares of a pooled fund.

Provision 2.A.27

The FIRM MUST establish a POOLED FUND INCEPTION DATE for each POOLED FUND to determine when the POOLED FUND'S track record begins.[16]

Discussion

For periods beginning on or after 1 January 2020, firms must establish a pooled fund inception date for each pooled fund to determine when the pooled fund's track record begins. The inception date for a broad distribution pooled fund is typically the date when the fund strikes the first net asset value (NAV). For a limited distribution pooled fund, the pooled fund inception date may be based on the following dates: (1) when investment management fees are first charged, (2) when the first investment-related cash flow takes place, (3) when the first capital call is made, or (4) when the first committed capital is closed and legally binding. When presenting money-weighted returns (MWRs) with and without a subscription line of credit, firms must clearly label or identify the period covered by each MWR that is presented.

For example, assume a pooled fund track record with the line of credit begins 1 July 2020 and represents the date of the first capital call. The pooled fund track record without the line of credit begins 16 May 2019 and represents the date of the first fund investment.

For a pooled fund, the performance start date of the track record could be different depending on whether the pooled fund is included in a composite. For example, assume a unitized pooled fund started on 19 July and strikes its first NAV on that day. If the firm includes the pooled fund in a composite, it will follow the composite's new portfolio inclusion criteria and the pooled fund will be included in the composite according to the firm's composite inclusion criteria (e.g., first full month under management). If the firm creates a GIPS Pooled Fund Report for the same fund, the inception date for calculating performance to include in the GIPS Pooled Fund Report will likely be the date the pooled fund strikes its first NAV (i.e., 19 July).

Money-Weighted Returns

Provision 2.A.28

When calculating MONEY-WEIGHTED RETURNS, the FIRM MUST value PORTFOLIOS at least annually and as of the period end for any period for which performance is calculated.

[16] REQUIRED for periods beginning on or after 1 January 2020. For periods prior to 1 January 2020, PRIVATE EQUITY PRIMARY FUNDS MUST be included in at least one COMPOSITE defined by VINTAGE YEAR and investment mandate, objective, or strategy. For periods prior to 1 January 2020, PRIVATE EQUITY POOLED FUNDS OF FUNDS MUST be included in at least one COMPOSITE defined by VINTAGE YEAR of the POOLED FUND OF FUNDS and/or investment mandate, objective, or strategy.

Discussion

When calculating a money-weighted return (MWR), a firm must value portfolios at least annually and as of the period end for any period for which performance is calculated. Valuations must be in accordance with the definition of fair value. A more frequent valuation is considered good business practice and is recommended.

When calculating time-weighted returns (TWRs), valuations at the time of large cash flows and at period end are needed because those valuations are inputs to the TWR calculation. In a true TWR calculation, sub-period returns are calculated either daily or at the time of each external cash flow and then geometrically linked together to derive a return for the period.

For MWRs, valuations are needed only at the end of the period being measured. In addition, many portfolios for which MWRs are calculated involve private market investments with valuations that are generally performed on a less frequent basis because they are illiquid securities. For these reasons, when calculating an MWR, firms must value portfolios at least annually and as of the period end for any period for which performance is calculated, rather than monthly and at the time of large cash flows.

More-frequent valuations are generally required for client reporting purposes and are considered good business practice.

Provision 2.A.29

When calculating MONEY-WEIGHTED RETURNS, the FIRM MUST:

a. Calculate annualized SINCE-INCEPTION MONEY-WEIGHTED RETURNS.

b. Calculate MONEY-WEIGHTED RETURNS using daily EXTERNAL CASH FLOWS.[17]

c. Include stock DISTRIBUTIONS as EXTERNAL CASH FLOWS and value stock DISTRIBUTIONS at the time of DISTRIBUTION.

d. When calculating POOLED FUND NET RETURNS, calculate POOLED FUND NET RETURNS that are net of TOTAL POOLED FUND FEES.

Discussion

A money-weighted return (MWR) is a return that reflects the change in value and the timing and size of external cash flows. One commonly used method for calculating an MWR is to calculate an internal rate of return (IRR). In general, the IRR is the implied discount rate or effective

[17] Daily EXTERNAL CASH FLOWS are REQUIRED beginning 1 January 2020. Prior to 1 January 2020, quarterly or more frequent EXTERNAL CASH FLOWS MUST be used.

compounded rate of return that equates the present value of cash outflows with the present value of cash inflows. The since-inception internal rate of return (SI-IRR) is a specific version of the IRR in which the measurement period of the MWR covers the entire investment period since inception.

Unlike when using IRR to calculate a time-weighted return (TWR), using IRR to calculate an MWR does not involve the calculation or linking of sub-period returns. A single IRR is calculated for the entire period.

The IRR is the return for which the net present value of a cash flow series is equated to zero and is calculated by solving for the return that satisfies the following equation:

$$0=\sum_{i=0}^{I} CF_i\left(1+r_{IRR}\right)^{-\left(\frac{t_i}{365}\right)},$$

where

CF_i = external cash flow i [negative values for inflows (paid-in capital) and positive values for outflows (distributions)]

i = number of external cash flows (1, 2, 3, …, I) during the measurement period

r_{IRR} = annualized internal rate of return

t_i = number of calendar days between the beginning of the measurement period and the date of external cash flow i

The SI-IRR is a special version of the IRR in which the period-end value of the investment is treated as a synthetic terminal cash outflow, calculated as follows:

$$0=\left[\sum_{i=0}^{I} CF_i\left(1+r_{SI\text{-}IRR}\right)^{-\left(\frac{t_i}{365}\right)}\right]+\left[V_E\left(1+r_{SI\text{-}IRR}\right)^{-\left(\frac{TD}{365}\right)}\right],$$

where

CF_i = external cash flow i [negative values for inflows (paid-in capital) and positive values for outflows (distributions)]

i = number of external cash flows (1, 2, 3, …, I) during the measurement period

$r_{SI\text{-}IRR}$ = annualized since-inception internal rate of return

t_i = number of calendar days between the beginning of the measurement period and the date of external cash flow i

TD = total number of calendar days in the measurement period

V_E = value of the investment at the end of the measurement period. In the case of closed-end funds, this is typically the net asset value at the end of the measurement period.

Note that the above annualized formula assumes a 365-day year convention and thus may have slight inaccuracies when the measurement period contains one or more leap years.

Firms must calculate and present the annualized SI-IRR. If the period is less than a full year, firms must present the non-annualized SI-IRR. The non-annualized SI-IRR is calculated as follows:

$$R_{SI\text{-}IRR} = \left[\left(1 + r_{SI\text{-}IRR}\right)^{\frac{TD}{365}} \right] - 1,$$

where

$R_{SI\text{-}IRR}$ = non-annualized since-inception internal rate of return

$r_{SI\text{-}IRR}$ = annualized since-inception internal rate of return

TD = total number of calendar days in the measurement period

As of 1 January 2020, external cash flows must be reflected on a daily basis when calculating an MWR, which results in a more accurate return. Using daily external cash flows means that the external cash flows are dated on the date the external cash flows occur—for example, the date of a capital call or the date of a distribution. For periods prior to 1 January 2020, firms must calculate an MWR by using quarterly or more frequent external cash flows. However, firms should use daily external cash flows in calculating an MWR prior to 1 January 2020 if daily external cash flows are available.

In dealing with legacy cash flow streams that might be dated monthly for periods prior to 1 January 2020, the firm should assume that all external cash flows occurred on a particular date in the month regardless of the actual date of the external cash flow. The same is true if external cash flows are reflected on a quarterly basis. The firm could assume that all external cash flows within the month happened on the last business day of the respective month.

For example, the following table shows the date the cash flow could be reflected for performance purposes if cash flows are not reflected daily.

		Quarterly Cash Flows		Monthly Cash Flows	
Date	**Cash Flow**	**Cash Flow**	**Date**	**Cash Flow**	**Date**
4 Jan 2017	100			100	31 Jan 2017
7 Feb 2017	100			100	28 Feb 2017
9 Mar 2017	100	300	31 Mar 2017	100	31 Mar 2017
18 Apr 2017	100			100	30 Apr 2017
1 May 2017	100			100	31 May 2017
2 Jun 2017	100	300	30 Jun 2017	100	30 Jun 2017
14 Jul 2017	100			100	31 Jul 2017
8 Aug 2017	100			100	31 Aug 2017
9 Sep 2017	100	300	30 Sep 2017	100	30 Sep 2017

(continued)

		Quarterly Cash Flows		Monthly Cash Flows	
Date	Cash Flow	Cash Flow	Date	Cash Flow	Date
4 Oct 2017	100			100	31 Oct 2017
8 Nov 2017	100			100	30 Nov 2017
1 Dec 2017	100	300	31 Dec 2017	100	31 Dec 2017

Stock distributions must be included as external cash flows and must be valued at the time of distribution. The cash flow is reflected on the date the fund distributes the money to the investor.

It is also required that, when calculating pooled fund net returns for inclusion in a GIPS Pooled Fund Report, the pooled fund net returns are net of total pooled fund fees. Total pooled fund fees include all fees and expenses charged to the pooled fund, including investment management fees, administrative fees, and other expenses. Total pooled fund fees do not include sales charges and loads that are associated with buying or selling shares of a pooled fund.

In addition to SI-IRR, firms may calculate an MWR using the Modified Dietz method over the entire period. Unlike when being used to calculate a TWR, using the Modified Dietz method to calculate an MWR does not involve the calculation or linking of sub-period returns. A single MWR is calculated for the entire time period presented.

An example follows.

Modified Dietz								
Dates (MM/DD/YYYY)	Terminal Value	Cash Flows (CF)	Day of CF/ Valuation	Weighted CF	Numerator	Denominator	Return	
31 Dec 2016		2,000,000	0	2,000,000				
8 Jan 2017		200,000	8	198,905				
24 Dec 2017		(50,000)	358	(37,748)				
20 Feb 2018		(200,000)	416	(143,053)				
6 Mar 2018		150,000	430	105,852				
11 Dec 2018		(20,000)	710	(10,281)				
25 Jun 2019		100,000	906	37,988				
3 Jul 2019		30,000	914	11,232				
14 Aug 2019		(50,000)	956	(17,283)				
21 Mar 2020		(200,000)	1,176	(39,014)				
4 Jun 2020		80,000	1,251	11,499				
22 Nov 2020		(50,000)	1,422	(1,335)				
3 Dec 2020		150,000	1,433	2,875				
31 Dec 2020	2,300,000		1,461		160,000	2,119,637	7.55%	Cumulative
Total		2,140,000		2,119,637			1.84%	Annualized

 |

The numerator is the terminal value less the sum of the cash flows (2,300,000–2,140,000), or 160,000.

The denominator is the sum of the weighted cash flows (2,119,637).

The cumulative return is calculated as 160,000/2,119,637, or 7.55%.

To calculate the annualized return, the formula is (1 + r)^(1/n) – 1, where r is the cumulative return and n is the number of years. In this example, it would be:

= (1 + 0.0755)^(1/4) – 1

= 1.84%.

Net Returns

Provision 2.A.30

When calculating COMPOSITE NET-OF-FEES returns, INVESTMENT MANAGEMENT FEES used in the calculation MUST be either:

a. Actual INVESTMENT MANAGEMENT FEES incurred by each PORTFOLIO in the COMPOSITE, or

b. A model INVESTMENT MANAGEMENT FEE appropriate to PROSPECTIVE CLIENTS.

Discussion

For composites, a net-of-fees return is defined as the gross-of-fees return reduced by investment management fees. Investment management fees are the fees payable to the investment management firm for the ongoing management of a portfolio, and these fees include performance-based fees and carried interest. They are typically asset based (based on a percentage of assets), performance based (based on the performance of the portfolio on an absolute basis or relative to a benchmark), or a combination of the two, but they may take other forms as well.

When calculating net-of-fees returns for a composite, the investment management fees used in the calculation must be either the actual investment management fees incurred by each portfolio in the composite or a model investment management fee appropriate to prospective clients. Using either of these approaches provides a realistic representation of the expected effect of fees on performance and satisfies the GIPS standards fundamental principles of fair representation and full disclosure.

When initially calculating net-of-fees returns for historical periods using model fees, the firm must determine whether it is appropriate to use a model based on current investment management fees or the investment management fees that were in effect for the respective historical period.

The GIPS standards do not require a specific calculation methodology for accounting for investment management fees when calculating net-of-fees returns for either portfolios or composites. The firm must develop a calculation methodology that generates performance that is not misleading, presents performance fairly, and is applied consistently. The firm's choice regarding whether actual investment management fees or model investment management fees are used in calculating net-of-fees returns must be documented in the firm's policies and procedures on a composite-specific basis. The firm must also document whether current or historical model fees are used for historical periods when initially calculating net-of-fees returns.

Provision 2.A.31

If the FIRM uses model INVESTMENT MANAGEMENT FEES to calculate COMPOSITE NET-OF-FEES returns, the returns calculated MUST be equal to or lower than those that would have been calculated using actual INVESTMENT MANAGEMENT FEES.

Discussion

A firm may use model investment management fees to calculate composite net-of-fees returns. When calculating net-of-fees returns using model investment management fees, the model fees should reflect current fees. When initially calculating net-of-fees returns for historical periods, the firm must determine whether it is appropriate to use current fees or the fees that were in effect for the respective historical period. In all cases, net-of-fees returns calculated using model fees must result in net-of-fees returns that are equal to or lower than those that would have been calculated if actual investment management fees had been used. In other words, firms cannot enhance their net returns by switching from actual to model fees.

The model investment management fee must be appropriate to prospective clients. There are times when using the investment management fee that is appropriate to prospective clients as a model fee results in net-of-fees returns that are not equal to or lower than those that would have been calculated using actual investment management fees. If this is the case, to ensure this provision is met, the firm will need to use a model investment management fee that is higher than the current fee that is appropriate to prospective clients. When there are multiple investment management fee schedules, the appropriate model fee used to calculate composite net-of-fee returns may be the highest investment management fee that any prospective client would pay.

A firm may wish to include a second net-of-fees return in a GIPS Report that is created using a model fee specific to a prospective client. If this second net-of-fees return does not meet the requirement of being either equal to or lower than the return that would have been calculated using actual investment management fees, this second net-of-fees return must be labeled as supplemental information. In addition, there must be a disclosure explaining how the firm arrived at the return.

Provision 2.A.32

When calculating POOLED FUND NET RETURNS, TOTAL POOLED FUND FEES used in the calculation MUST be either:

a. Actual TOTAL POOLED FUND FEES, or

b. A model TOTAL POOLED FUND FEE appropriate to PROSPECTIVE INVESTORS.

Discussion

A pooled fund net return is defined as the pooled fund gross return reduced by all fees and costs, including investment management fees, administrative fees, and other costs. Pooled fund net returns do not reflect the deduction of sales charges and loads that are associated with buying or selling shares of a pooled fund.

When calculating a pooled fund net return, a firm may use either actual total pooled fund fees or a model total pooled fund fee appropriate to prospective investors. The firm may use the total expense ratio as the model total pooled fund fee, if the total expense ratio includes all fees and costs. If the total expense ratio does not include all fees and costs, such as performance-based fees, the firm must also deduct the additional fees and costs when calculating pooled fund net returns. Using either actual total pooled fund fees or a model total pooled fund fee appropriate to pooled fund prospective investors provides a realistic representation of the expected effect of fees on the pooled fund's returns and satisfies the GIPS standards fundamental principles of fair representation and full disclosure.

When initially calculating pooled fund net returns for historical periods using model fees, the firm must determine whether it is appropriate to use current total pooled fund fees or the total pooled fund fees that were in effect for the respective historical period.

The GIPS standards do not require a specific calculation methodology for accounting for total pooled fund fees when calculating net-of-fees returns for pooled funds. The firm must develop a calculation methodology that generates performance that is not misleading, presents performance fairly, and is applied consistently. The firm's choice regarding whether the actual total pooled fund fees or a model total pooled fund fee are used in calculating pooled fund net returns must be documented in the firm's policies and procedures on a pooled fund–specific basis. When using model fees, the firm must also document whether current or historical fees are used for historical periods when initially calculating pooled fund net returns.

Firms have the following options when calculating pooled fund net returns using actual fees where the pooled fund has multiple share classes:

- Deduct from the pooled fund gross return the highest total pooled fund fee of any individual share class in the fund.
- Calculate pooled fund net returns using a weighted average of actual pooled fund net returns from all share classes.

Different pooled fund share classes may be issued to differentiate among certain investor groups for tax reasons and/or to allow for different fee structures. In some situations, it may be impossible to definitively determine which total pooled fund fee is the highest among the share classes within the pooled fund, such as when each share class has a mix of fixed and performance-based investment management fees. In this instance, it is acceptable to use the model total pooled fund fee that is applicable to the specific pooled fund prospective investor, as long as doing so results in pooled fund net returns that are equal to or lower than those that would have been calculated if using actual (effectively charged) total pooled fund fees. (See Provision 2.A.33.)

The same concept applies when there are multiple series within a share class. Assuming there are multiple series within Share Class A, and the firm is presenting pooled fund net returns based on Share Class A, the firm should either present a weighted net return of all series within Share Class A or reduce the gross return by the total pooled fund fees from the oldest or initial series to reflect the performance a prospective investor would have received had the investor been invested in the pooled fund since its inception. The firm may take either approach as long as doing so results in pooled fund net returns that are equal to or lower than those that would have been calculated if using actual (effectively charged) total pooled fund fees. (See Provision 2.A.33.)

Although a firm must disclose if model or actual fees are used to calculate pooled fund net returns, when net returns are not straightforward and/or have multiple assumptions, additional disclosure about pooled fund net return calculations may be needed to ensure that the principle of full disclosure is met.

Provision 2.A.33

If the FIRM uses model TOTAL POOLED FUND FEES to calculate POOLED FUND NET RETURNS, the returns calculated MUST be equal to or lower than those that would have been calculated using actual TOTAL POOLED FUND FEES.

 |

Discussion

A firm may use model total pooled fund fees to calculate pooled fund net returns. When calculating pooled fund net returns using model total pooled fund fees, the model fees should reflect current fees. When initially calculating pooled fund net returns for historical periods, the firm must determine whether it is appropriate to use current total pooled fund fees or the total pooled fund fees that were in effect for the respective historical period. In all cases, pooled fund net returns calculated using model total pooled fund fees must result in pooled fund net returns that are equal to or lower than those that would have been calculated if actual total pooled fund fees had been used. In other words, firms cannot enhance their net returns by switching from actual to model fees.

The model total pooled fund fee must be appropriate to prospective investors. There are times when using the total pooled fund fee that is appropriate to prospective investors as a model fee results in net returns that are not equal to or lower than those that would have been calculated using actual total pooled fund fees. If this is the case, to ensure this provision is met, the firm will need to use a model total pooled fund fee that is higher than the current fee that is appropriate to prospective investors. When there are multiple total pooled fund fee schedules, the appropriate model fee may be the highest total pooled fund fee that any prospective investor would pay.

A firm may wish to include a second net return in a GIPS Report that is created using a model fee specific to a prospective investor. If this second net return does not meet the requirement of being either equal to or lower than the return that would have been calculated using actual total pooled fund fees, the second net return must be labeled as supplemental information. In addition, there must be a disclosure explaining how the firm arrived at the return.

Provision 2.A.34

When calculating COMPOSITE NET-OF-FEES returns and POOLED FUND NET RETURNS, the FIRM MUST reflect any PERFORMANCE-BASED FEE CLAWBACK in the period in which it is repaid.[18]

Discussion

A clawback is the repayment of previously earned performance-based fees resulting from subsequent underperformance. Beginning 1 January 2020, when calculating composite net-of-fees returns or pooled fund net returns, any performance-based fee clawback must be reflected in the period in which the firm determines previously earned performance fees must be repaid. A firm

[18] REQUIRED for periods beginning on or after 1 January 2020.

must not restate returns to eliminate performance-based fees that were previously reflected in returns.

Typically, performance fees reward positive outperformance, whereas no fee is charged when negative excess returns occur. Some performance fee models specify a penalty (negative fee) that must be paid by the manager in the case of negative excess returns, or they may require claw-backs wherein the manager must pay back the performance fee received in the past in the case of underperformance.

The firm may not restate historical net-of-fees performance because of performance fee claw-backs. The clawback is not an error correction of the performance fees accrued and crystallized in the previous periods but represents an actual penalty for the investment manager for underper-forming in the current period. Restating historical performance would be misleading. In addition, in the case of pooled funds the performance fee accrued in the previous periods would already have affected the past tradable net asset value (NAV) at which investors subscribed/redeemed fund units. Restating the NAV and performance of prior periods may result in legal obligations toward investors who may need to be compensated for the NAV price differences. Such compen-sation would be appropriate only in the case of a retrospective error correction. In such a case, the firm must comply with its error correction policies.

Composite Returns

Provision 2.A.35

COMPOSITE TIME-WEIGHTED RETURNS except PRIVATE MARKET INVESTMENT COMPOSITES (see 2.A.42) MUST be calculated at least monthly.[19]

Discussion

The more frequently composite returns are calculated, the more accurate the results will be. Quarterly composite calculations are permitted for periods prior to 1 January 2010; subsequently, composite returns must be calculated at least monthly. The portfolios included in the composite must be consistent for the entire performance measurement period (e.g., for the entire month if the composite is calculated using monthly portfolio returns).

[19] REQUIRED for periods beginning on or after 1 January 2010. For periods beginning on or after 1 January 2006 and ending prior to 1 January 2010, COMPOSITE returns MUST be calculated at least quarterly.

Private market investment composites are excluded from this provision because they are not required to be valued monthly.

Provision 2.A.36

COMPOSITE TIME-WEIGHTED RETURNS MUST be calculated by using one of the following approaches:

a. Asset-weighting the individual PORTFOLIO returns using beginning-of-period values;
b. Asset-weighting the individual PORTFOLIO returns using a method that reflects both beginning-of-period values and EXTERNAL CASH FLOWS; or
c. Using the aggregate method.

Discussion

A composite is defined as an aggregation of one or more portfolios managed according to a similar investment mandate, objective, or strategy. The objective in calculating the composite's return is to use a method that will conceptually produce the same value as if the assets of all the individual portfolios in the composite were aggregated and a return is calculated as if the composite were one portfolio.

The GIPS standards are based on the principle of asset-weighted composite returns. For example, if a composite contains two portfolios, one of which is 10 times the size of the other, the rate of return for the larger portfolio should have more of an effect on the composite return than the rate of return for the smaller portfolio. The asset-weighted return methods satisfy this principle by weighting each portfolio's contribution to the composite rate of return by its beginning value (as a percentage of the composite's beginning value) or by its beginning value plus weighted external cash flows (as a percentage of the composite's beginning value plus weighted external cash flows). The GIPS standards require asset weighting of the portfolio returns within a composite by using beginning-of-period values, by using beginning-of-period values plus weighted external cash flows, or by aggregating portfolio assets and external cash flows to calculate performance as a single master portfolio.

When calculating composite returns for a specific period, only portfolios that are included in the composite for the entire performance period are included in the calculation. For example, when calculating monthly composite returns, only those portfolios that are managed on a discretionary basis for the full month are included in the composite return calculation. Portfolios that begin during the month, close during the month, or are otherwise determined to not qualify for inclusion in the composite for the full month must not be included in the composite return calculation. If a firm wishes to include in composite returns portfolios that do not have a full month of performance, the firm must calculate composite returns more frequently than monthly (e.g., daily). Assuming a firm calculates composite returns daily, the firm would include in the daily composite return calculation only those portfolios that were managed for the full day. Firms must create and document policies and procedures for calculating composite returns and follow those policies and procedures consistently.

The following are examples of methods that a firm may use when asset-weighting individual portfolio returns when calculating composite time-weighted returns.

The *Beginning Assets Weighting* method for calculating composite returns, R_t, uses the formula

$$R_t = \frac{\sum_{k=1}^{K}\left(V_{k,t}^{B} \times r_{k,t}\right)}{\sum_{k=1}^{K} V_{k,t}^{B}},$$

where

R_t = the beginning assets weighted return for the composite for period t

k = the number of portfolios (1, 2, 3, . . . , K) in the composite at the beginning of period t

$V_{k,t}^{B}$ = the beginning value of portfolio k for period t

$r_{k,t}$ = the return of portfolio k for period t

The Beginning Assets Weighting method can also be expressed as

$$R_t = \sum_{k=1}^{K}\left(\frac{V_{k,t}^{B}}{\sum_{k=1}^{K} V_{k,t}^{B}} \times r_{k,t}\right) = \sum_{k=1}^{K} w_{k,t}^{B} r_{k,t},$$

where $w_{k,t}^{B}$ is the weight of the value of portfolio k as a fraction of total composite asset value based on beginning asset values for period t and can be calculated according to the following formula:

$$w_{k,t}^{B} = \frac{V_{k,t}^{B}}{\sum_{k=1}^{K} V_{k,t}^{B}}.$$

The *Beginning Assets Plus Weighted External Cash Flow* method represents a refinement to the Beginning Assets Weighting method. Consider the case in which one of two portfolios in a composite doubles in value as the result of a contribution on the third day of a performance period. Under the Beginning Assets Weighting method, this portfolio would be weighted in the composite based solely on its beginning value (i.e., not including the contribution). The Beginning Assets Plus Weighted External Cash Flow method resolves this problem by including the effect of external cash flows in the calculation. Assuming that external cash flows occur at the end of the day, the weighting factor for each external cash flow is calculated using the same methodology as in the Modified Dietz method as follows:

$$w_{i,k,t} = \frac{D_t - D_{i,k,t}}{D_t},$$

where

$w_{i,k,t}$ = the weight of external cash flow i in portfolio k in period t, assuming the external cash flow occurred at the end of the day

D_t = the total number of calendar days in period t

$D_{i,k,t}$ = the number of calendar days from the beginning of period t to external cash flow i in portfolio k

The numerator of $w_{i,k,t}$ is based on the assumption that the external cash flows occur at the end of the day. If external cash flows were assumed to occur at the beginning of the day, the numerator would be $[(D_t - D_{i,k,t}) + 1]$. A firm may choose to use a beginning-of-day or end-of-day external cash flow assumption or some combination of the two. The key is to establish a policy and treat external cash flows consistently.

The Beginning Assets Plus Weighted External Cash Flow composite return can be calculated as follows:

$$R_t = \frac{\sum_{k=1}^{K}\left\{\left[V_{k,t}^{B} + \sum_{i=1}^{I_k}\left(CF_{i,k,t} \times w_{i,k,t}\right)\right] \times r_{k,t}\right\}}{\sum_{k=1}^{K}\left[V_{k,t}^{B} + \sum_{i=1}^{I_k}\left(CF_{i,k,t} \times w_{i,k,t}\right)\right]},$$

where

R_t = the beginning assets plus weighted external cash flow composite return for period t

$V_{k,t}^{B}$ = the beginning value of portfolio k for period t

i_k = the number of external cash flows $(1, 2, 3, \ldots, I_k)$ in portfolio k

$CF_{i,k,t}$ = the ith external cash flow in portfolio k for period t

$w_{i,k,t}$ = the weight of external cash flow i in portfolio k for period t

$r_{k,t}$ = the return for portfolio k for period t

The Beginning Assets Plus Weighted External Cash Flow composite return method can also be expressed by the following formula:

$$R_t = \sum_{k=1}^{K} \left(\frac{V_{k,t}}{\sum_{k=1}^{K} V_{k,t}} \times r_{k,t} \right),$$

where

R_t = the beginning assets plus weighted external cash flow composite return for period t

$r_{k,t}$ = the return for portfolio k for period t

$V_{k,t}$ = the beginning value plus weighted external cash flows of portfolio k for period t, as calculated by the following formula:

$$V_{k,t} = V_{k,t}^{B} + \sum_{i=1}^{I_k} \left(CF_{i,k,t} \times w_{i,k,t} \right),$$

where

$V_{k,t}$ = the value of portfolio k's beginning assets plus weighted external cash flows for period t

$V_{k,t}^{B}$ = the beginning value of portfolio k for period t

i_k = the number of external cash flows (1, 2, 3, . . . , I_k) in portfolio k

$CF_{i,k,t}$ = the ith external cash flow in portfolio k for period t

$w_{i,k,t}$ = the weight of external cash flow i in portfolio k for period t

The *Aggregate Return* method combines all the composite assets and external cash flows before any calculations occur to calculate returns as if the composite were one portfolio. Therefore, unlike the Beginning Assets Weighting method or the Beginning Assets Plus Weighted External Cash Flow method, the Aggregate Return method does not use portfolio returns.

The following examples show how to calculate a composite return using the Beginning Assets Weighting method, the Beginning Assets Plus Weighted External Cash Flow method, and the Aggregate Return method, assuming that external cash flows occur at the end of the day.

Composite Return

Beginning Assets Weighting method:

Portfolio	BMV	Portfolio Weight	Portfolio Return	Weighted Return
A	450,000	17.08%	12.00%	2.05%
B	785,000	29.79%	14.00%	4.17%
C	1,400,000	53.13%	11.00%	5.84%
Total	2,635,000	100.00%		12.06%

$$R_{BMV} = \frac{(450{,}000 \times 0.12) + (785{,}000 \times 0.14) + (1{,}400{,}000 \times 0.11)}{(450{,}000 + 785{,}000 + 1{,}400{,}000)} = 12.06\%$$

Beginning Assets Plus Weighted External Cash Flow method:

Portfolio	BMV	Weighted Cash Flows	BMV plus Wtd CFs	BMV plus Wtd CFs	Portfolio Return	Weighted Return
A	450,000	75,000	525,000	18.95%	12%	2.27%
B	785,000	120,000	905,000	32.67%	14%	4.57%
C	1,400,000	(60,000)	1,340,000	48.38%	11%	5.32%
Total	2,635,000	135,000	2,770,000	100.00%		12.17%

$$R_{BMV+CF} = \frac{[(450{,}000 + 75{,}000) \times 0.12] + [(785{,}000 + 120{,}000) \times 0.14] + [(1{,}400{,}000 - 60{,}000) \times 0.11]}{(450{,}000 + 75{,}000 + 785{,}000 + 120{,}000 + 1{,}400{,}000 - 60{,}000)} = 12.17\%$$

Aggregate Return method (using Modified Dietz method):

(Assuming the large cash flow level is established at the composite level, and none of the cash flows qualify as a large cash flow)

Portfolio	BMV	EMV	Cash Flows	Weighted CFs	Portfolio Return
A	450,000	665,000	150,000	75,000	12%
B	785,000	1,140,000	240,000	120,000	14%
C	1,400,000	1,440,000	(120,000)	(60,000)	11%
Total	2,635,000	3,245,000	270,000	135,000	

Composite Return ($R_{Aggregate}$) = (Total EMV – Total BMV – Total CF)/(Total BMV + Total Wtd CF)

$$R_{Aggregate} = \frac{(3{,}245{,}000 - 2{,}635{,}000 - 270{,}000)}{(2{,}635{,}000 + 135{,}000)} = 12.27\%.$$

When using the aggregate method, a manager may encounter a situation in which the composite return falls outside the range of portfolio-level returns for a given period. This scenario can occur if the policies used to calculate portfolio-level returns do not flow through to the aggregate composite-level return calculation policies. "Flowing through" to the composite means that if any portfolio is valued during the month because of a large cash flow, the entire composite would also be valued and the sub-period return calculated for both the portfolio and the composite. A firm may establish large cash flow policies, however, such that only those portfolios in the composite that experience a large cash flow during the month are valued at the time of the large cash flow and any portfolios that did not experience a large cash flow are not valued during the month. In such a situation, the composite return may be outside the range of portfolio-level returns for a given period. To prevent this situation from occurring, the firm should consider establishing a policy wherein all portfolios in the composite are valued if any portfolio in the composite is valued during the month because of large cash flows. Once a firm has established large cash flow policies for a composite, the firm must apply the large cash flow policies consistently.

Provision 2.A.37

COMPOSITE GROSS-OF-FEES returns MUST reflect the deduction of TRANSACTION COSTS.

Discussion

Transaction costs are the costs of buying or selling investments. These costs typically take the form of brokerage commissions, exchange fees and/or taxes, and/or bid–offer spreads from either internal or external brokers. Custodial fees charged per transaction should be considered custody fees, not transaction costs. For real estate, private equity, and other private market investments, transaction costs include all legal, financial, advisory, and investment banking fees related to buying, selling, restructuring, and/or recapitalizing investments but do not include dead deal costs. When calculating composite gross-of-fees returns, transaction costs must be deducted from the underlying portfolio returns.

Other fees or expenses, such as custody fees, may also be deducted. If this is the case, the firm must disclose which additional fees or costs have been deducted when calculating the gross-of-fees returns.

For additional information on deduction of transaction costs, please refer to Provision 2.A.13.

Provision 2.A.38

COMPOSITE NET-OF-FEES returns MUST reflect the deduction of TRANSACTION COSTS and INVESTMENT MANAGEMENT FEES.

Discussion

Transaction costs are the costs of buying or selling investments. These costs typically take the form of brokerage commissions, exchange fees and/or taxes, and/or bid–offer spreads from either internal or external brokers. Custodial fees charged per transaction should be considered custody fees and not transaction costs. For real estate, private equity, and other private market investments, transaction costs include all legal, financial, advisory, and investment banking fees related to buying, selling, restructuring, and/or recapitalizing investments but do not include dead deal costs.

For portfolios invested in underlying pooled funds, the firm must deduct all fees and expenses charged at the underlying pooled fund level, unless the firm controls the investment management fees of the underlying pooled funds. When the firm controls the investment management fees of the underlying pooled funds, the firm may calculate gross-of-fees returns that do not reflect the deduction of the underlying investment management fees.

Investment management fees are the fees payable to the investment management firm for the ongoing management of a portfolio. They are typically asset based (based on a percentage of assets), performance based (based on the performance of the portfolio on an absolute basis or relative to a benchmark), or a combination of the two, but they may take other forms as well. Investment management fees also include carried interest. A net-of-fees return is the gross-of-fees return from which investment management fees are deducted. Therefore, composite net-of-fees returns must reflect the deduction of both transaction costs and investment management fees.

The GIPS standards do not require a specific calculation methodology for accounting for investment management fees when calculating net-of-fees returns for either portfolios or composites. The firm must develop a calculation methodology that generates performance that is not misleading, presents performance fairly, and is applied consistently.

Provision 2.A.39

When calculating COMPOSITE MONEY-WEIGHTED RETURNS, the FIRM MUST calculate COMPOSITE returns by aggregating the PORTFOLIO-level information for those PORTFOLIOS included in the COMPOSITE.

Discussion

When calculating composite money-weighted returns, a firm is required to aggregate the portfolio-level information for all portfolios included in the composite. This method combines the assets and external cash flows from all portfolios in the composite, so the return is calculated as if the composite were one portfolio. The following example shows how since-inception internal rates of return (SI-IRRs) can be calculated for a composite that includes multiple portfolios.

In 2019, the composite includes only Fund 1. The composite SI-IRR will be based solely on the cash flows and terminal value of Fund 1. In 2020, Fund 2 joins the composite, and at the end of 2020, the two-year annualized SI-IRR will be based on the combined cash flows and terminal values of Funds 1 and 2. In 2021, Fund 3 joins the composite, and at the end of 2021, the three-year annualized SI-IRR will be based on the combined cash flows and terminal values of Funds 1, 2, and 3.

	A	B	C	D	E	F	G
1							
2							
3	Date	CF or TV	Fund 1	Fund 2	Combined Fund 1 & 2	Fund 3	Combined Fund 1, 2 & 3
4	31-Dec-2018	Cash Flow	(1,000,000)		(1,000,000)		(1,000,000)
5	15-Jan-2019	Cash Flow	(10,000)		(10,000)		(10,000)
6	31-Dec-2019	Terminal Value	1,090,000				
7	15-Feb-2020	Cash Flow		(5,000,000)	(5,000,000)		(5,000,000)
8	30-Jun-2020	Cash Flow		(1,000,000)	(1,000,000)		(1,000,000)
9	31-Dec-2020	Terminal Value	1,100,000	6,500,000	7,600,000		
10	12-Feb-2021	Cash Flow				(4,000,000)	(4,000,000)
11	15-Mar-2021	Cash Flow	500,000				500,000
12	31-Dec-2021	Terminal Value	900,000	6,700,000		4,200,000	11,800,000
13							
14							
15							
16	Year	IRR Calc	Formula				
17	2019	7.92%	=XIRR(C4:C6,A4:A6,0.1)				
18	2020	8.47%	=XIRR(E4:E9,A4:A9,0.1)				
19	2021	7.33%	=XIRR(G4:G12,A4:A12,0.1)				

Private Market Investments

Provision 2.A.40

When calculating TIME-WEIGHTED RETURNS for PRIVATE MARKET INVESTMENT PORTFOLIOS that are included in COMPOSITES, PRIVATE MARKET INVESTMENT PORTFOLIOS MUST be valued:

a. At least quarterly.[20]

b. As of each quarter end or the last business day of the quarter.[21]

[20] REQUIRED for periods beginning on or after 1 January 2008.

[21] REQUIRED for periods beginning on or after 1 January 2010.

Discussion

A portfolio is considered a private market investment portfolio when it has an investment objective to invest primarily in private market investments. Private market investments include real assets (e.g., real estate, insurance-linked securities, collectibles, and infrastructure), private equity, and similar investments that are illiquid, not publicly traded, and not traded on an exchange.

Investments that are not private market investments must be valued at least monthly and at the time of large cash flows. Because of the illiquidity of private market investments, private market investments that are included in composites must be valued at least quarterly if time-weighted returns are being calculated, and they are not required to be valued at the time of large cash flows. Firms may use the Modified Dietz method to calculate the quarterly return. Firms are not required to value private market investment portfolios at the time of large cash flows but may do so. The firm must establish a composite-specific valuation policy, but that policy may specify a different valuation frequency for different types of portfolios in the composite. There may also be cases in which a firm may establish different valuation frequency policies for the same types of portfolios within a composite. For example, the firm may have a private market investment portfolio in a composite that provides for monthly subscriptions and redemptions, and the firm's policy is to value this portfolio monthly. Another portfolio in this same composite may have the same structure but provides for quarterly subscriptions and redemptions, and so the firm values this portfolio quarterly. The firm must apply the composite-specific valuation policy consistently based on the specified valuation frequency for the portfolios in the composite, but that policy may differentiate valuation frequency for different types of portfolios in the composite. For example, segregated accounts may be valued quarterly, whereas pooled funds are valued monthly. The firm must apply the composite-specific valuation policy consistently based on the valuation frequency for the type of portfolio.

In all cases, however, each private market investment portfolio in the composite must be valued at quarter end or on the last business day of the quarter.

Quarterly valuations are important for investors to be able to compare performance with private market investment benchmarks, which are typically not updated monthly. Quarterly valuations are also needed for comparability with other asset classes and for comparability of data in GIPS Reports. This quarterly valuation requirement can be met by either internal or external valuations.

Private market investments include real estate. For periods prior to 1 January 2008, real estate investments must be valued at least once every 12 months. The annual valuation requirement for periods prior to 1 January 2008 can be met either by internal or external valuations. An internal valuation is a firm's best estimate of value based on the most current and accurate information available to the firm. Internal valuation methodologies can include applying a discounted cash flow model, using a sales comparison or replacement cost approach, or conducting a review of all significant events (both general market events and asset-specific events) that could have a material effect on the investment. External valuations for real estate are discussed in Provisions 2.A.43 and 2.A.44.

Provision 2.A.41

When calculating TIME-WEIGHTED RETURNS for PRIVATE MARKET INVESTMENT PORTFOLIOS that are included in COMPOSITES, the FIRM MUST:

a. Calculate returns at least quarterly.[22]

b. Calculate quarterly returns through the calendar quarter end or the last business day of the quarter.[23]

c. Calculate PORTFOLIO returns that adjust for daily-weighted EXTERNAL CASH FLOWS.[24]

d. Treat EXTERNAL CASH FLOWS according to the FIRM'S COMPOSITE-specific policy.

e. Geometrically LINK periodic and sub-period returns.

f. Consistently apply the calculation methodology used for an individual PORTFOLIO.

Discussion

A portfolio is considered a private market investment portfolio when it has an investment objective to invest primarily in private market investments.

Private market investments include real assets (e.g., real estate, insurance-linked securities, collectibles, and infrastructure), private equity, and similar investments that are illiquid, not publicly traded, and not traded on an exchange.

Because private market investments do not trade publicly like stocks and bonds do, the return calculation requirements differ for private market investments. The portfolio calculation frequency is aligned with the minimum valuation frequency, which is quarterly; therefore, firms must calculate portfolio returns at least quarterly.

As of 1 January 2010, firms must calculate quarterly returns through the calendar quarter end or the last business day of the quarter when calculating time-weighted returns (TWRs) for private market investment portfolios included in composites. Consistency in return calculation dates will result in improved comparability of data for all GIPS Reports.

Because most portfolios within a composite experience external cash flows, which can often be unpredictable and are usually client driven, it is important that the calculation of portfolio TWRs adjust for daily-weighted external cash flows that occur during the calculation period. This is required for periods beginning on or after 1 January 2010. When calculating TWRs that adjust for daily-weighted external cash flows, periodic and sub-period returns must be geometrically linked.

Private market investments do not trade publicly like marketable securities do, and thus they do not have valuations readily available on a monthly basis or at the time of external cash flows.

[22] REQUIRED for periods beginning on or after 1 January 2008.

[23] REQUIRED for periods beginning on or after 1 January 2010.

[24] REQUIRED for periods beginning on or after 1 January 2010.

Therefore, firms are not required to value private market investment portfolios and to calculate sub-period returns at the time of large cash flows and to geometrically link these sub-period returns to calculate monthly TWRs, as is required for portfolios that are not private market investment portfolios. Instead, firms must calculate returns for private market investment portfolios at least quarterly and may use methods that adjust for daily-weighted external cash flows, such as the Modified Dietz or the internal rate of return (IRR) methods.

As explained in the discussion for Provision 2.A.24, the Modified Dietz and IRR methods are money-weighted return methods. By means of geometric linking of the periodic Modified Dietz or IRR returns, TWRs can be approximated. Firms must create composite-specific policies with respect to the methodology used in calculating returns for private market investment portfolios and must apply these policies consistently to the individual portfolios included in the composite.

Provision 2.A.42

COMPOSITE TIME-WEIGHTED RETURNS for PRIVATE MARKET INVESTMENT COMPOSITES MUST be calculated at least quarterly.

Discussion

Composite time-weighted returns for private market investment composites must be calculated at least quarterly. Quarterly returns are important for investors to be able to compare performance with private market investment benchmarks, which are typically reported on a quarterly basis. Quarterly returns are also needed for comparability with other asset classes and for comparability of data in GIPS Reports.

Real Estate

Provision 2.A.43

REAL ESTATE investments in a REAL ESTATE OPEN-END FUND MUST have an EXTERNAL VALUATION at least once every 12 months.[25]

[25] REQUIRED for periods beginning on or after 1 January 2020. For periods beginning on or after 1 January 2012 and ending prior to 1 January 2020, REAL ESTATE investments MUST have an EXTERNAL VALUATION at least once every 12 months unless client agreements stipulate otherwise, in which case REAL ESTATE investments MUST have an EXTERNAL VALUATION at least once every 36 months or per the client agreement if the client agreement REQUIRES EXTERNAL VALUATIONS more frequently than every 36 months. For periods beginning on or after 1 January 2006 and ending prior to 1 January 2012, REAL ESTATE investments MUST have an EXTERNAL VALUATION at least once every 36 months.

Discussion

An open-end fund is a pooled fund in which the number of investors is not fixed and the fund is open for subscriptions and redemptions. An open-end fund is considered a real estate open-end fund when it has an investment objective to invest primarily in real estate. An open-end fund that invests in any real estate and uses a real estate benchmark is also considered a real estate open-end fund.

Real estate investments include wholly owned or partially owned:

- investments in land, including products grown from the land (e.g., timber, crops),
- buildings under development, completed buildings, and other structures or improvements,
- equity-oriented debt (e.g., participating mortgage loans), and
- private interest in a property for which some portion of the return to the investor at the time of investment is related to the performance of the underlying real estate.

The following investments are not considered real estate investments, and portfolios that have these investments must follow the provisions of the GIPS standards that are not related to real estate:

- publicly traded real estate securities,
- mortgage-backed securities (MBS) and commercial mortgage-backed securities (CMBS), and
- private debt investments, including commercial and residential loans for which the expected return is solely related to contractual interest rates without any participation in the economic performance of the underlying real estate.

In addition to the requirement to fair value quarterly, real estate investments in a real estate open-end fund are required to have an external valuation at least once every 12 months.

An external valuation is an assessment of value performed by an independent third party who is a professionally designated or certified commercial property valuer or appraiser. In markets where these professionals are not available, steps must be taken to ensure that only qualified independent property valuers or appraisers are used. For additional information regarding an external valuation, please refer to Provision 2.A.45.

An external valuation is not required for a property when the property is under a sales contract and the firm believes that the sale will be finalized.

Provision 2.A.44

REAL ESTATE investments that are not in a REAL ESTATE OPEN-END FUND MUST:[26]

a. Have an EXTERNAL VALUATION at least once every 12 months unless client agreements stipulate otherwise, in which case REAL ESTATE investments MUST have an EXTERNAL VALUATION at least once every 36 months or per the client agreement if the client agreement REQUIRES EXTERNAL VALUATIONS more frequently than every 36 months; or

b. Be subject to an annual financial statement audit performed by an independent public accounting firm. The REAL ESTATE investments MUST be accounted for at FAIR VALUE, and the most recent audited financial statements available MUST contain an unmodified opinion issued by an independent public accounting firm.

Discussion

This provision applies to all real estate investments that are not included in a real estate open-end fund, including real estate investments held in a multi-asset-class portfolio. This provision does not apply to real estate that may be held by pooled funds in which the firm invests.

Real estate investments include wholly owned or partially owned:

- investments in land, including products grown from the land (e.g., timber, crops),
- buildings under development, completed buildings, and other structures or improvements,
- equity-oriented debt (e.g., participating mortgage loans), and
- private interest in a property for which some portion of the return to the investor at the time of investment is related to the performance of the underlying real estate.

The following investments are not considered to be real estate investments and must follow the provisions of the GIPS standards that are not related to real estate:

- publicly traded real estate securities,
- mortgage-backed securities (MBS) and commercial mortgage-backed securities (CMBS), and
- private debt investments, including commercial and residential loans in which the expected return is solely related to contractual interest rates without any participation in the economic performance of the underlying real estate.

[26] REQUIRED for periods beginning on or after 1 January 2012. For periods beginning on or after 1 January 2006 and ending prior to 1 January 2012, REAL ESTATE investments MUST have an EXTERNAL VALUATION at least once every 36 months or be subject to annual financial statement audit performed by an independent public accounting firm.

In addition to the requirement to fair value quarterly, real estate investments that are not in a real estate open-end fund must have either:

- an external valuation: an assessment of value performed by an independent third party who is a professionally designated or certified commercial property valuer or appraiser. In markets where these professionals are not available, steps must be taken to ensure that only qualified independent property valuers or appraisers are used; or
- a financial statement audit: an audit of a segregated account's or pooled fund's financial statements that includes the real estate investments.

If a firm chooses an external valuation to satisfy this requirement, the real estate investments must have an external valuation at least every 12 months unless client agreements stipulate a different frequency for external valuations. For example, if a client agreement stipulates that external valuations will take place every 24 months, the real estate investments in the portfolio must have an external valuation completed at least once every 24 months. Regardless of the terms of the client agreement, each real estate investment must have an external valuation at least once every 36 months. Firms are encouraged to discuss the importance of external valuation with their clients, because valuation is the major element used in the return calculation and the external appraisal typically provides a point of reference for subsequent internal valuations performed by the firm. A firm may not always be successful in convincing its clients to move to more frequent external valuations because typically the client pays the cost of the appraisal. In many markets, however, the cost of obtaining external appraisals, including subsequent updates, are not significant because of technological advances as well as increased availability of market data. For additional information regarding an external valuation, please refer to Provision 2.A.45.

Firms that opt to have an external valuation are not required to obtain an external valuation for a property when the property is under a sales contract and the firm believes that the sale will be finalized.

Instead of an external valuation, a firm may choose to have a financial statement audit. The audit must be performed by an independent, qualified (i.e., professionally designated, certified, or licensed) accounting firm. The accounting firm chosen must be knowledgeable of the accounting rules and principles that apply to the firm's financial statements, including all relevant laws and regulatory requirements. The financial statement audit may be at either the property level or portfolio level.

Although the most recent financial statement audit does not need to be through the most recent period for which the firm is claiming compliance with the GIPS standards, a financial statement audit must be performed annually. The real estate investments must be accounted for at fair value, and the most recent audited financial statements available must contain an unmodified opinion issued by the independent public accounting firm.

Provision 2.A.45

EXTERNAL VALUATIONS for REAL ESTATE investments MUST be performed by an independent third party who is a professionally designated or certified commercial property valuer or appraiser. In markets where these professionals are not available, the FIRM MUST take necessary steps to ensure that only qualified independent property valuers or appraisers are used.

Discussion

An external valuation must be performed by an independent third party who is a professionally designated or certified commercial property valuer/appraiser. In Europe, Canada, and parts of Southeast Asia, the predominant professional designation is that of the Royal Institution of Chartered Surveyors (RICS). In the United States, the professional designation is Member of the Appraisal Institute (MAI). In Australia, the designation is Certified Practicising Valuer from the Australian Property Institute. In markets where these professionals are unavailable, steps must be taken to ensure that only qualified independent valuers or appraisers are used. Even if no credentialed professionals are available, it would be unusual to not find a well-qualified independent valuer or appraiser who can value a property in a particular market.

The external valuation process must adhere to practices of the relevant valuation governing and standard setting body. Although appraisal standards may allow for a range of estimated values, it is recommended that a single value (final value conclusion) be obtained from external valuers or appraisers because only one value can be used for performance reporting.

Provision 2.A.46

The FIRM MUST NOT use EXTERNAL VALUATIONS for REAL ESTATE investments when the valuer's or appraiser's fee is contingent upon the investment's appraised value.

Discussion

The firm must not use external valuations when the valuer's or appraiser's fee is contingent upon the investment's appraised value. To do so could damage the objectivity of the valuer or appraiser and lead to a higher valuation than would otherwise be the case. The linking of a valuer's or appraiser's fee to the investment's appraised value will also lead to the perception that the investment's appraised value may have an upward bias, reducing the confidence of those evaluating the investment and the resulting valuation.

Carve-Outs

Provision 2.A.47

When calculating NET-OF-FEES returns of COMPOSITES containing CARVE-OUTS, the INVESTMENT MANAGEMENT FEES for the CARVE-OUTS MUST be representative of the INVESTMENT MANAGEMENT FEES charged or that would be charged to the PROSPECTIVE CLIENT:

a. When presenting performance to a PROSPECTIVE CLIENT for a standalone PORTFOLIO, the INVESTMENT MANAGEMENT FEE MUST be representative of the INVESTMENT MANAGEMENT FEES for a standalone PORTFOLIO managed according to that strategy.

b. When presenting performance to a PROSPECTIVE CLIENT for a multi-asset strategy PORTFOLIO, the INVESTMENT MANAGEMENT FEE MUST be representative of the INVESTMENT MANAGEMENT FEES for a multi-asset strategy PORTFOLIO managed according to that strategy.

Discussion

A carve-out is a portion of a portfolio that is by itself representative of a distinct investment strategy. It is used to create a track record for a narrow mandate from a multi-strategy portfolio managed to a broader mandate. For example, an equity composite may include the equity portions of balanced accounts wherein these equity portions are managed according to the same investment strategy as standalone portfolios.

For a composite that includes carve-outs, the presentation of performance to a prospective client must adhere to the fundamental GIPS standards principle of fair representation. The net-of-fees performance for a composite that includes carve-outs that is presented to a prospective client for a standalone portfolio must be calculated using an investment management fee that is representative of the investment management fees for a standalone portfolio managed to that strategy. Similarly, the net-of-fees performance for a composite that includes carve-outs that is presented to a prospective client for a multi-asset strategy portfolio must be calculated using an investment management fee that is representative of the investment management fees that would be charged for a multi-asset strategy portfolio managed according to that multi-asset strategy.

For example, assume Firm B manages a balanced strategy that contains both an equity and a fixed-income component, and the firm wants to carve out the equity component to create an equity composite. Firm B charges a 0.50% investment management fee for its balanced strategy. The equity strategy will charge a 0.75% investment management fee. When calculating and presenting net-of-fees returns to prospective clients interested in the equity strategy, the firm must use 0.75% as the investment management fee when calculating net-of-fees returns.

Wrap Fee

Provision 2.A.48

When calculating returns to be presented to a WRAP FEE PROSPECTIVE CLIENT, returns MUST be calculated net of the entire WRAP FEE. This is applicable to all WRAP FEE PORTFOLIOS in the COMPOSITE as well as any non–WRAP FEE PORTFOLIOS in the COMPOSITE.

Discussion

A wrap fee is a type of bundled fee specific to a particular investment product. The wrap fee is charged by a wrap fee sponsor for investment management services and typically includes associated transaction costs that cannot be separately identified. Wrap fees can be all-inclusive, asset-based fees, and they may include a combination of investment management fees, transaction costs, custody fees, and/or administrative fees.

When presenting performance to a wrap fee prospective client, performance must be shown net of the entire wrap fee. This requirement applies to all wrap fee portfolios in the composite as well as any non–wrap fee portfolios that are included in the composite.

If a firm has not managed actual wrap fee portfolios in a specific strategy, the firm may create a history from that strategy's non–wrap fee composite. The wrap fee performance history for that specific strategy may be calculated by using that strategy's gross-of-fees non–wrap fee composite history reduced by the highest total wrap fee charged to the client (end user) by the wrap fee sponsor for the strategy (product), resulting in net-of-fees wrap fee performance.

It is up to the firm to determine the appropriate highest wrap fee to deduct. This highest wrap fee should be obtained from the prospective wrap fee sponsor and should be comparable to the investment mandate, objective, or strategy of the wrap fee composite.

It is recognized that, when starting with the gross-of-fees non–wrap fee composite history, the gross-of-fees performance already reflects the deduction of actual transaction costs incurred. By then reducing the composite performance by the highest total wrap fee, which includes a portion attributable to transaction costs, performance will reflect the deduction of transaction costs twice (actual transaction costs and a portion of the highest wrap fee). If the firm can identify the portion of the highest total wrap fee attributable to transaction costs, or if the firm can estimate appropriate transaction costs, the firm may first calculate performance reflecting the deduction of both transaction costs and the highest wrap fee. The firm may then increase this result by the identifiable portion of the wrap fee attributable to actual or estimated transaction costs in order to compute a net-of-fees return.

To assist prospective clients and their understanding of the fees charged in these situations, when presenting gross-of-fees returns, firms must disclose if other fees are deducted in addition to the transaction costs. When presenting net-of-fees returns, firms must disclose if any other fees are deducted in addition to the investment management fees and transaction costs.

"Pure" gross-of-fees returns, which represent the return on investments that is not reduced by any transaction costs incurred during the period, are permitted only as supplemental information in a GIPS Composite Report and must be clearly labelled as such.

The following table describes the various returns that can be calculated for wrap fee portfolios:

Examples of Gross-of-Fees and Net-of-Fees Calculations

Non-wrap Composite	**Presenting to Current Wrap Fee Sponsors and Clients When Unbundling Wrap Fee**	**Presenting to Prospective Wrap Fee Sponsors and Clients**
Return on investments ("pure gross")[(a)]	Return on investments ("pure gross")[(a)]	Return on investments ("pure gross")[(a)]
– Transaction Costs	– Portion of wrap fee that includes transaction costs that can be segregated *Or* – Estimated transaction costs	
Gross-of-fees return	**Gross-of-fees return**	
– Investment management fee	– Portion of wrap fee that includes an investment management fee that can be segregated *Or* – Model investment management fee	– Model Wrap Fee *Or* – Actual Wrap Fee
Net-of-fees return	**Net-of-fees return**	
– Administrative Fee	– Remaining portion of wrap fee (administrative fees, if any)	
Client return[(b)]	**Client return**[(b)]	**Gross-of-fees return** **Net-of-fees return** **Client return**[(c)]

[(a)] Although the "pure gross" return is not required or recommended by the GIPS standards, it may be presented as supplemental information.

[(b)] The client return is not required by the GIPS standards and is presented here as additional information that may be helpful for existing clients.

[(c)] For wrap fee portfolios, the net-of-fees return is equal to the client return. If the firm does not have the ability to unbundle the wrap fee or estimate transaction costs, the net-of-fees return will also equal the gross-of-fees return.

Side Pockets and Subscription Lines of Credit

Provision 2.A.49

All COMPOSITE and POOLED FUND returns MUST include the effect of any discretionary SIDE POCKETS held by PORTFOLIOS in the COMPOSITE or the POOLED FUND.[27]

Discussion

A side pocket is a segregated investment that is used mainly in alternative investment pooled funds, such as hedge funds, funds of funds, and other alternative investment funds, to separate illiquid or distressed assets from other, more liquid investments or to segregate investments held for a special purpose from other investments. Side pockets are typically not available for investing for new pooled fund investors that invest after the side pocket has been created. All composite and pooled fund returns must include the effect of any discretionary side pockets held by portfolios in the composite or the pooled fund. The fact that future investors will not be participating in the performance of the side pocket is not a valid argument to exclude the side pocket from composite or pooled fund performance.

Firms may choose to also present returns without side pockets. Prospective clients and investors may be interested in the performance history without the effect of the side pocket because they will not be participating in the performance of the side pocket going forward.

A firm may exclude the effect of a non-discretionary side pocket on composite or pooled fund returns, just as firms may exclude non-discretionary assets from a portfolio's performance. A side pocket can be classified as non-discretionary only when all of the following criteria are met:

- The side pocket is segregated in a separate sub-portfolio (e.g., at the custodian bank or in the portfolio management system of the firm).
- The side-pocketed assets are no longer considered in the asset allocation and portfolio investment process.
- There are no investment decisions for the side-pocketed assets, except for monitoring and liquidating.
- There are no or reduced investment management fees charged on the side-pocketed assets.

A side pocket created at the express direction of a client may be considered non-discretionary and excluded from the performance of the composite or pooled fund, as if it were an unmanaged asset.

[27] REQUIRED for periods beginning on or after 1 October 2012.

Provision 2.A.50

When calculating MONEY-WEIGHTED RETURNS for COMPOSITES and POOLED FUNDS without the SUBSCRIPTION LINES OF CREDIT, the FIRM MUST include the cash flows from the SUBSCRIPTION LINES OF CREDIT.[28]

Discussion

A subscription line of credit is a loan facility that is usually put in place to facilitate administration when firms are calling for funds from investors. It is secured by limited partner commitments.

Subscription lines of credit are being used by more firms and for longer periods. These lines of credit can have a significant effect on returns. As has been widely discussed in the industry, there has also been a lack of consistency in return calculations when lines of credit are used. The purpose of Provision 2.A.50 is to help standardize the calculation of returns for composites and pooled funds that include a subscription line of credit, thereby increasing the comparability of returns from one firm to another.

Firms that use subscription lines of credit must calculate and present the since-inception money-weighted return (MWR) that includes the subscription line of credit. Firms are required to also calculate a since-inception MWR that does not include the subscription line of credit unless the subscription line of credit has the following two characteristics:

- The principal was repaid within 120 days using committed capital drawn down through a capital call.
- No principal was used to fund distributions.

The following example illustrates the MWRs calculated with and without the subscription line of credit. Note that the return with the subscription line of credit, which some may think of as being a levered return, is the return for which the period for the performance calculation is shortened, resulting in a higher return in an up market and a lower return in a down market. We refer to this as the return "with" the subscription line of credit because the period could not be shortened unless the subscription line of credit was used. The return without the subscription line of credit assumes the line of credit was not used and capital was called to fund investments. In the following example, we can think of the return without the subscription line of credit as being the return on the investment, whereas the return with the subscription line of credit is the return the investor (limited partner) would earn if a subscription line of credit was used.

[28] REQUIRED for MONEY-WEIGHTED RETURNS for periods ending on or after 31 December 2020.

	A	B	C	D
1			Net MWR	Net MWR
2			With	Without
3			Subscription	Subscription
4			Line of Credit	Line of Credit
5				
6	**Date**	**Transaction Type**	**Cash Flow**	**Cash Flow**
7	6-Jan-2020	Subscription LOC Drawdown		(1,000,000)
8	1-Jul-2020	Subscription LOC Drawdown		(500,000)
9	1-Oct-2020	Subscription LOC Drawdown		(500,000)
10	15-Dec-2020	Capital Call	(2,000,000)	
11	1-Oct-2021	Capital Call	(1,000,000)	(1,000,000)
12	31-Dec-2021	Ending Fair Value	3,500,000	3,500,000
13		SI-MWR	21.47%	13.28%

When using the XIRR formula in Excel, firms must include the first cell that contains the first capital call or subscription line of credit drawdown. For example, the XIRR formula for the Net MWR with Subscription Line of Credit is =XIRR(C10:C12,A10:A12,0.1), where C10:C12 reflects the cash flows and ending value. A10:A12 reflects the dates of the cash flows and ending value, and the 0.1 is a guess of what the IRR will be. If firms omit the guess, Excel assumes it is 10% or 0.1. Generally, a guess is not required. Note that the XIRR annualizes the result. If calculating for a period that is less than a year, firms will need to calculate the non-annualized return. See Provision 2.A.12 for the formula to calculate the non-annualized return.

Firms that are required to present returns both with and without the subscription line of credit must present comparable returns in GIPS Reports. If presenting gross returns, the firm must present gross returns with the subscription line of credit and without the subscription line of credit. The same is true for net returns. If presenting net returns, the firm must present net returns with the subscription line of credit and without the subscription line of credit.

When calculating returns without the subscription line of credit, firms may also exclude interest expense associated with the subscription line of credit. Firms should consider disclosing whether interest expense and other subscription line of credit costs are or are not reflected in the return without the subscription line of credit.

2.B. Input Data and Calculation Methodology—Recommendations

Provision 2.B.1

The FIRM SHOULD value PORTFOLIOS on the date of all EXTERNAL CASH FLOWS.

Discussion

To improve the accuracy of time-weighted performance calculations, the GIPS standards have gradually increased the minimum required frequency of portfolio valuation for many portfolio types from quarterly, to monthly, to the date of all large cash flows for periods beginning on or after 1 January 2010. Best practice, however, is to value portfolios on the date of all external cash flows. Firms are encouraged to create a policy to value portfolios on the date of all external cash flows as part of the composite-specific valuation policy where possible.

Provision 2.B.2

Valuations SHOULD be obtained from a qualified independent third party.

Discussion

The quality of valuations used as inputs to calculate performance has a significant effect on the accuracy of portfolio and composite returns; therefore, it is important that the valuations used are accurate. It is recommended that firms obtain valuations from an independent source because a third party can provide the most objective investment valuations. In most instances, obtaining valuations from an independent third party is considered to be a best practice. A firm claiming compliance with the GIPS standards is responsible for its claim of compliance and must ensure that the valuations obtained from a third party can be used to satisfy the requirements of the GIPS standards.

Provision 2.B.3

ACCRUAL ACCOUNTING SHOULD be used for dividends (as of the ex-dividend date).

Discussion

Accrual accounting determines the correct economic value of the portfolio assets and allows the recording of financial transactions as they come into existence rather than when they are paid or settled. It is recommended that dividends be recognized when earned on ex-date (accrual basis) versus when paid (cash basis).

Provision 2.B.4

The FIRM SHOULD accrue INVESTMENT MANAGEMENT FEES.

Discussion

Investment management fees are the fees payable to the investment management firm for the ongoing management of a portfolio. They are typically asset based (based on a percentage of assets), performance based (based on the portfolio's performance either on an absolute basis or relative to a benchmark), or a combination of the two, but they may take other forms as well. Investment management fees also include carried interest.

To calculate a net-of-fees return for a portfolio or composite, the gross-of-fees return must be reduced by investment management fees. To calculate a pooled fund net return, the pooled fund gross return must be reduced by investment management fees as well as by administrative fees and other costs. To reflect the most accurate net-of-fees return, investment management fees should be accrued when possible. Accrual accounting allows the recording of financial transactions as they come into existence rather when they are paid or settled. Net-of-fees returns can be skewed if investment management fees are reflected in the calculation as they are paid, particularly when portfolio values change significantly.

Provision 2.B.5

Returns SHOULD be calculated net of non-reclaimable withholding taxes on dividends, interest, and capital gains. Reclaimable withholding taxes SHOULD be accrued.

Discussion

Global investing requires recognition of the tax consequences of investing in different countries. The GIPS standards recommend that performance be reported net of non-reclaimable withholding taxes on dividends, interest, and capital gains. Some countries allow certain types of foreign investors to reclaim a portion of the foreign withholding taxes that are paid. These reclaimable foreign withholding taxes may be credited back to the investor at a later date. It is recommended that reclaimable foreign withholding taxes be accrued, meaning that the refund for reclaimable withholding taxes should be recorded when the reclaimable withholding taxes become a receivable owed to the firm, rather than when the refund is actually received.

Provision 2.B.6

The FIRM SHOULD incorporate the following hierarchy into its policies and procedures for determining FAIR VALUE for PORTFOLIO investments on a COMPOSITE-specific or POOLED FUND–specific basis.

a. Investments MUST be valued using objective, observable, unadjusted quoted market prices for identical investments in active markets on the measurement date, if available. If such prices are not available, then investments SHOULD be valued using;
b. Objective, observable quoted market prices for similar investments in active markets. If such prices are not available or appropriate, then investments SHOULD be valued using;
c. Quoted prices for identical or similar investments in markets that are not active (markets in which there are few transactions for the investment, the prices are not current, or price quotations vary substantially over time and/or between market makers). If such prices are not available or appropriate, then investments SHOULD be valued based on;
d. Market-based inputs, other than quoted prices, that are observable for the investment. If such inputs are not available or appropriate, then investments SHOULD be valued based on;
e. Subjective, unobservable inputs for the investment where markets are not active at the measurement date. Unobservable inputs SHOULD be used to measure FAIR VALUE only when observable inputs and prices are not available or appropriate. Unobservable inputs reflect the FIRM'S own assumptions about the assumptions that market participants would use in pricing the investment and SHOULD be developed based on the best information available under the circumstances.

Discussion

The GIPS standards include a recommended valuation hierarchy as presented in Provision 2.B.6. It is recommended that firms incorporate this hierarchy into their policies for determining fair value for portfolio investments on a composite-specific or pooled fund–specific basis. For further information regarding fair valuation and the frequency of internal and external valuation requirements, please refer to Provision 2.A.19.

 |

Provision 2.B.7

The FIRM SHOULD use GROSS-OF-FEES returns when calculating risk measures.

Discussion

Acknowledging that there are many acceptable calculation variations for various risk measures, the GIPS standards do not prescribe a specific methodology for calculating risk measures. It is recommended, however, that gross-of-fees returns be used when calculating risk measures. It is recommended that firms use gross-of-fees returns because these are not affected by investment management fees, which may introduce additional variability of returns.

Firms are required to select a calculation methodology, on a composite-specific or pooled fund-specific basis, for each risk measure presented in a GIPS Report. They must document the chosen calculation methodology in their policies and procedures, and then consistently apply the methodology selected.

Provision 2.B.8

PRIVATE MARKET INVESTMENTS SHOULD have an EXTERNAL VALUATION at least once every 12 months.

Discussion

For periods beginning on or after 1 January 2020, it is recommended that private market investments have an external valuation at least once every 12 months. (This is a requirement for real estate investments in a real estate open-end fund. Real estate investments not in a real estate open-end fund must have an external valuation at least once every 12 months, unless client agreements stipulate a less frequent external valuation, or be subject to an annual financial statement audit. See Provisions 2.A.43 and 2.A.44.)

Those evaluating a firm's private market investments, including prospective clients or investors, typically prefer an external valuation because it is independent, unbiased, and an "expert" estimate of value that is perceived by the marketplace to be more reliable than an internal valuation.

An external valuation is an assessment of value performed by an independent third party who is a professionally designated or certified commercial property valuer or appraiser. In markets where these professionals are unavailable, steps must be taken to ensure that only qualified independent property valuers or appraisers are used. For additional information regarding an external valuation, please refer to Provision 2.A.45.

3. COMPOSITE AND POOLED FUND MAINTENANCE

3.A. Composite and Pooled Fund Maintenance—Requirements

Provision 3.A.1

The FIRM MUST create COMPOSITES for the FIRM'S strategies that are managed for or offered as a SEGREGATED ACCOUNT.

Discussion

A composite is an aggregation of one or more portfolios (segregated accounts and/or pooled funds) managed according to a similar investment mandate, strategy, or objective. A firm must create a composite for each of the firm's strategies that is managed for or offered as a segregated account. A segregated account is a portfolio owned by a single client. A portfolio with a pooled fund wrapper (i.e., a single-investor pooled fund), which is unitized but is not available to other investors, is considered a segregated account. If a firm is a sub-advisor for a pooled fund, the firm must treat the sub-advised pooled fund as a segregated account. A composite will contain only one portfolio if the firm has only one portfolio that is managed for or offered as a segregated account for a particular strategy.

For periods beginning on or after 1 January 2020, firms are not required to create or maintain composites that include only one or more pooled funds if the strategy of the pooled fund(s) is not offered as a segregated account.

It is important to remember that the GIPS standards do not differentiate between "marketed" and "non-marketed" composites. The requirement to create composites applies to all strategies that are offered as a segregated account, or managed for a segregated account, whether or not the strategy is marketed by the firm. All composites must be included on the list of composite descriptions (see Provision 1.A.22), and the firm must be able to provide a GIPS Composite Report for any composite that is included on this list (see Provision 1.A.24).

If a firm manages portfolios with overlay strategies, the firm is required to create an overlay composite for an overlay strategy when the overlay strategy is managed separately from the underlying portfolio and the firm offers the overlay strategy as a segregated account. Firms are not required to create an overlay strategy composite when the overlay strategy is implemented as part of a broader strategy but may do so.

Provision 3.A.2

All actual, fee-paying, discretionary SEGREGATED ACCOUNTS MUST be included in at least one COMPOSITE. Non-discretionary PORTFOLIOS MUST NOT be included in COMPOSITES.

Discussion

A segregated account is a portfolio owned by a single client. As noted in Provision 3.A.1, a segregated account with a pooled fund wrapper (i.e., a single-investor pooled fund), which is unitized but not available to other investors, is treated as a segregated account. In addition, a firm that is a sub-advisor for one or more pooled funds must treat the sub-advised pooled funds as segregated accounts.

An actual segregated account is a portfolio that is invested in real, tangible assets and is differentiated from a hypothetical, simulated, or backtested track record for a portfolio or an advisory-only (model) portfolio.

A fee-paying segregated account incurs investment management fees, which are fees paid to the firm, either directly or indirectly, for the management of the segregated account. If a segregated account pays no investment management fees, it is considered a non-fee-paying segregated account.

If a firm temporarily waives the investment management fee for a segregated account that is normally charged a fee, the segregated account is still considered a fee-paying segregated account (with a fee of zero for that period) and must be included in the appropriate composite. Some firms may manage segregated accounts that have a minimal investment management fee that is meant to cover operating or transaction costs. This arrangement is common for segregated accounts that are owned by friends and employees of the firm. If a segregated account has a very small investment management fee that is not representative of the investment management fee that a segregated account would typically pay, the firm must consider such a segregated account as a fee-paying account for purposes of composite inclusion. However, because the segregated account has only a minimal investment management fee that is not representative of the firm's investment management fee for that strategy, the segregated account should be included in the percentage of composite assets that is non–fee paying. The percentage of composite assets that is non–fee paying is a required disclosure in GIPS Composite Reports when net-of-fees composite returns are presented and are calculated using actual investment management fees.

A firm is not required to include non-fee-paying segregated accounts in a composite but may choose to do so. Examples of non-fee-paying segregated accounts are portfolios consisting of the firm's own pension plan assets or portfolios managed for friends or employees of the firm that are not charged investment management fees. If the firm chooses to include non-fee-paying discretionary segregated accounts in one or more of its composites, the firm is not required to include all non-fee-paying discretionary segregated accounts in composites. If a firm chooses to include non-fee-paying discretionary segregated accounts in a specific composite, however, all non-fee-paying segregated accounts meeting the definition of that composite must be included.

If the firm includes non-fee-paying discretionary segregated accounts in its composites, they are subject to the same rules as fee-paying segregated accounts (e.g., the firm must not move non-fee-paying segregated accounts into and out of a composite unless documented changes in client guidelines or the redefinition of the composite makes it appropriate).

A discretionary segregated account is one for which the firm has the ability to implement its intended strategy. If documented client-imposed restrictions significantly hinder the firm from fully implementing its intended strategy, the firm may determine that the segregated account is non-discretionary. There are degrees of discretion, and not all client-imposed restrictions will necessarily cause a segregated account to be non-discretionary. The firm must determine if the restrictions will, or could, interfere with implementing the intended strategy to the extent that the segregated account is no longer representative of the strategy. Firms are responsible for determining whether account restrictions render a segregated account non-discretionary. Discretion may be defined at the segregated account, pooled fund, composite, asset class, or firm level. Once the definition of discretion has been determined, it must be documented in the firm's policies and procedures and applied consistently. Firms must also document the reasons for classifying each non-discretionary segregated account as non-discretionary.

Firms should, where possible and appropriate, consider classifying segregated accounts with defined restrictions as discretionary and grouping them with any other portfolios that have similar restrictions and are managed in the same strategy in a composite.

Non-discretionary segregated accounts must not be included in a firm's composites. Some firms, however, may group together some or all of the firm's non-discretionary segregated accounts in order to simplify account administration. For purposes of complying with the GIPS standards, such a group is not a composite and must not be included on the firm's list of composite descriptions.

Because the intent of the GIPS standards is to accurately and fairly represent firm performance, all actual, fee-paying, discretionary segregated accounts must be included in at least one of the firm's composites. This requirement helps ensure that a firm presents a complete performance record. Without this requirement, firms could potentially exclude poorly performing segregated accounts from composites.

Each composite must contain all segregated accounts that meet the composite's definition. (See Provision 3.A.5 for guidance on the creation of composite definitions.) Therefore, firms must include a segregated account in more than one composite if it satisfies the definition of more than one composite. If the firm includes portfolios in more than one composite, care must be taken to ensure that assets are not double counted when calculating total firm assets. A segregated account must be counted only once, even if it is included in more than one composite. (See Provision 2.A.3.)

In addition to segregated accounts, firms may have created carve-outs managed with their own cash balance, or carve-outs with allocated cash. A carve-out is a portion of a portfolio that is by itself representative of a distinct investment strategy. It is used to create a track record for a narrower mandate from a multi-strategy or multi-asset-class portfolio managed to a broader mandate. If a firm has included carve-outs with their own cash balance in a composite, all carve-outs with their own cash balance that have been created and that meet the composite definition for that strategy must be included in that composite. If a firm has included carve-outs with allocated cash in a composite, it must create carve-outs from all similar portfolios within the firm, and all carve-outs with allocated cash that meet the composite definition must be included in that composite.

Multi-Strategy or Multi-Asset-Class Portfolios

Some firms offer a multi-strategy or multi-asset-class segregated account, with each of the underlying strategies or asset classes included in the segregated account represented by "building blocks" for the strategy, which may be portfolios or carve-outs. A carve-out is a portion of a portfolio that is by itself representative of a distinct investment strategy. It may be used to create a track record for a narrower mandate from a multi-strategy or multi-asset-class portfolio managed to a broader mandate. For example, a multi-strategy fixed-income segregated account might include portfolios or carve-outs that represent different fixed-income strategies, such as long- and short-duration strategies or high-yield and high-quality strategies. A multi-asset class portfolio might include portfolios or carve-outs that represent equity and fixed-income strategies.

All actual, fee-paying discretionary segregated accounts must be included in at least one composite. This can be accomplished either by including total multi-strategy and multi-asset-class segregated accounts in composites or by including each of the underlying portfolios or carve-outs of total segregated accounts in composites. With the issuance of the 2020 edition of the GIPS standards, a multi-strategy or multi-asset-class segregated account is no longer required to be included in a composite if each of the segregated account's underlying portfolios or carve-outs are included in appropriate composites. This guidance replaces guidance included in a Q&A issued in November 2012 stating that a discretionary multi-strategy portfolio was required to be included in a multi-strategy composite, even if all of the underlying portfolio segments were included in composites. This change applies to all periods for which the firm claims compliance.

A firm may also choose to include both multi-strategy or multi-asset-class segregated accounts and the underlying portfolio or carve-out segments in a composite. The firm may then present the multi-strategy or multi-asset-class composites or the segment composites to prospective clients, or it may choose to present both. If the firm chooses to present segment composites and not present multi-strategy or multi-asset-class composites to prospective clients of a multi-asset-class or multi-strategy composite, it must present all segment composites of the multi-strategy or multi-asset-class strategy.

When the firm chooses to maintain both multi-strategy or multi-asset-class composites and the segment composites, it must be careful not to double count when calculating total firm assets.

It is the firm's responsibility to ensure that all of its actual, fee-paying, discretionary segregated accounts are included in any composite for which they meet the composite definition. Accordingly, firms must have policies and procedures to identify changes to a segregated account (both discretionary and non-discretionary) that would require a segregated account to be reclassified for composite assignment purposes. If a segregated account changes from discretionary to non-discretionary status because of a new restriction and must be removed from a composite, the segregated account must be removed from the composite on a prospective basis only.

Provision 3.A.3

All actual, fee-paying, discretionary POOLED FUNDS MUST be included in at least one COMPOSITE if they meet a COMPOSITE DEFINITION. The FIRM is not REQUIRED to create a COMPOSITE that only includes one or more POOLED FUNDS unless the FIRM offers the strategy as a SEGREGATED ACCOUNT. The FIRM may terminate any COMPOSITE that was created solely to include one or more POOLED FUNDS if the COMPOSITE is not representative of the FIRM'S strategy offered as a SEGREGATED ACCOUNT.

Discussion

A pooled fund is a fund whose ownership interests may be held by more than one investor and is managed to a defined strategy on behalf of fund investors. A portfolio with a pooled fund wrapper (i.e., a single-investor pooled fund), which is unitized but not available to other investors, is treated as a segregated account and not a pooled fund. If a firm is the sub-advisor for a pooled fund, the firm must treat the pooled fund as a segregated account and not a pooled fund.

An actual pooled fund is a pooled fund invested in real, tangible assets and is differentiated from a hypothetical, simulated, or backtested track record for a pooled fund.

A fee-paying pooled fund incurs investment management fees, which are fees paid to the firm, either directly or indirectly, for the management of the pooled fund. If a pooled fund pays no investment management fees, it is considered a non-fee-paying pooled fund.

A firm is not required to include non-fee-paying pooled funds in a composite but may choose to do so. Examples of non-fee-paying pooled funds are pooled funds that include assets of only friends or employees of the firm that are not charged investment management fees, or a feeder fund in a master/feeder fund structure where all fees are charged at the master fund level. If the firm chooses to include non-fee-paying discretionary pooled funds in one or more of its composites, the firm is not required to include all non-fee-paying discretionary pooled funds in composites. If a firm chooses to include non-fee-paying discretionary portfolios in a specific composite, however, all non-fee-paying pooled funds meeting the definition of that composite must be included.

If the firm includes non-fee-paying discretionary pooled funds in its composites, they are subject to the same rules as fee-paying pooled funds (e.g., the firm must not move non-fee-paying pooled funds into and out of a composite unless documented changes in pooled fund guidelines or the redefinition of the composite makes it appropriate).

A discretionary pooled fund is one for which the firm has the ability to implement its intended strategy. Firms make the ultimate decision as to whether or not pooled fund restrictions render a pooled fund non-discretionary. Discretion may be defined at the segregated account, pooled fund, composite, asset class, or firm level. Once the definition of discretion has been determined, it must be documented in a firm's GIPS standards policies and procedures and applied consistently. Firms should, where possible and appropriate, consider classifying pooled funds with defined restrictions as discretionary and grouping them with any other portfolios that have similar restrictions and are managed in the same strategy in a composite.

Non-discretionary pooled funds must not be included in a firm's composites. Some firms, however, may group together some or all of the firm's non-discretionary pooled funds in order to simplify account administration. For purposes of complying with the GIPS standards, such a group is not a composite and must not be included on the firm's list of composite descriptions.

Because the intent of the GIPS standards is to accurately and fairly represent firm performance, all actual, fee-paying, discretionary pooled funds must be included in at least one composite if they meet a composite definition. A firm must include a pooled fund in more than one composite if it satisfies the definition of more than one composite. This requirement ensures that a firm presents a complete picture of its performance record. Without this requirement, there is a potential for firms to exclude poorly performing pooled funds from composites. If the firm includes portfolios in more than one composite, care must be taken to ensure that assets are not double counted when calculating total firm assets. A pooled fund must be counted only once, even if it is included in more than one composite. (See Provision 2.A.3.) Prior to 1 January 2020, firms were allowed to differentiate between segregated accounts and pooled funds when defining composites. For example, a firm could choose to create one composite for segregated accounts managed in the firm's large-cap equity strategy and another composite for pooled funds managed in the same strategy. As of 1 January 2020, firms may no longer take this approach. On a prospective basis, pooled funds that are managed in a strategy that is managed for or offered as a segregated account must be included in the same composite as any segregated accounts managed or offered in that strategy. Under prior editions of the GIPS standards, a firm was required to include all portfolios, including pooled funds, in at least one composite. Under the 2020 edition of the GIPS standards, a firm is not required to create or maintain a composite that includes only one or more pooled funds if the firm does not offer the pooled fund strategy as a segregated account strategy.

Firms that complied with prior editions of the GIPS standards may terminate any composite that includes only one or more pooled funds if that composite is not representative of a strategy offered as a segregated account. A firm may choose to create a composite that includes only one or more pooled funds, however, even if the pooled fund strategy is not offered as a segregated account strategy.

There may be situations in which a firm offers a certain strategy only as a pooled fund but at a later date decides to offer the strategy as a segregated account as well. Once the firm begins to offer the strategy as a segregated account, it must then create a composite that will include only the pooled fund until it begins to manage segregated accounts in the strategy. The initial track record for the composite will be based on the pooled fund's track record. It is also possible that the firm might begin to manage a segregated account in the strategy at the request of a client, even though the firm did not offer the strategy as a segregated account. Once the firm begins to manage a segregated account in the strategy, it must create a composite that includes both the pooled fund and the segregated account. The track record would be based on the track record of the pooled fund initially, because it is the first portfolio in the composite, and would subsequently include any segregated accounts managed in the strategy.

A pooled fund must be assigned to a composite if it meets a composite definition. A composite definition includes not only the composite strategy but also the criteria that determine whether and when a portfolio managed in the strategy represented by the composite is included in the composite. For a more complete explanation of a composite definition, please see Provision 3.A.5.

Pooled funds with different base currencies may be included in the same composite, but their assets and returns must be expressed in the same currency as that of the composite. If pooled funds managed in a specific strategy have different base currencies, firms should consider whether the effect of any hedging justifies creating multiple composites defined by both the mandate and hedging. If a pooled fund has multiple share classes, each of which is invested similarly but has a different base currency and there is no currency hedging, each share class may be included in the composite, but the firm must convert the returns and assets for all of the share classes to the same currency for inclusion in the composite. Alternatively, the firm may include in the composite one share class as a proxy for the total fund, if the converted returns for all share classes are the same or very similar. The firm would include the fair value of the assets of the total fund instead of the proxy share class.

It is the firm's responsibility to ensure that all of its actual, fee-paying, discretionary pooled funds are included in any composite for which they meet the composite definition. Accordingly, firms must have policies and procedures to identify changes to a pooled fund (both discretionary and non-discretionary) that would require a pooled fund to be reclassified for composite assignment purposes. If a pooled fund changes from discretionary to non-discretionary status because of a new restriction and must be removed from a composite, the pooled fund must be removed from the composite on a prospective basis only.

Provision 3.A.4

Non-fee-paying discretionary PORTFOLIOS may be included in a COMPOSITE. If the FIRM includes non-fee-paying discretionary PORTFOLIOS in a COMPOSITE, those PORTFOLIOS MUST be subject to the same policies and procedures as fee-paying PORTFOLIOS.

Discussion

If a portfolio (a segregated account or pooled fund) pays no investment management fee, it is considered a non-fee-paying portfolio. Examples of non-fee-paying portfolios are portfolios consisting of the firm's own pension plan assets, a portfolio for a new strategy that currently consists only of a firm's seed capital, or portfolios managed for friends or employees that are not charged investment management fees.

If a firm temporarily waives the investment management fee for a portfolio that is normally charged a fee, the portfolio is still considered a fee-paying portfolio (with a fee of zero for that period) and must be included in the appropriate composite. Some firms may manage portfolios that have a minimal investment management fee that is meant to cover operating or transaction costs. This arrangement is common for portfolios that are owned by friends and employees of the firm. If a portfolio has a very small investment management fee that is not representative of the investment management fee that a segregated account would typically pay, the firm must consider such a portfolio as fee-paying for purposes of composite inclusion. However, because the portfolio has only a minimal investment management fee that is not representative of the firm's investment management fee for that strategy, the segregated account should be included in the percentage of composite assets that is non–fee paying. The percentage of composite assets that is non–fee paying is a required disclosure in GIPS Composite Reports when net-of-fees composite returns are presented and are calculated using actual investment management fees.

A firm is not required to include non-fee-paying discretionary portfolios in a composite but may choose to do so. Examples of non-fee-paying portfolios are portfolios consisting of the firm's own pension plan assets or portfolios managed for friends or employees of the firm that are not charged investment management fees. If the firm chooses to include non-fee-paying discretionary portfolios in one or more of its composites, the firm is not required to include all non-fee-paying discretionary portfolios in composites. All non-fee-paying discretionary pooled funds meeting the definition of that composite must be included.

If the firm includes non-fee-paying discretionary portfolios in one or more of its composites, they are subject to the same policies and procedures as fee-paying portfolios (e.g., the firm must not move the non-fee-paying portfolio into and out of a composite without documented changes in client or pooled fund guidelines or unless the redefinition of the composite makes it appropriate).

Provision 3.A.5

COMPOSITES MUST be defined according to investment mandate, objective, or strategy. COMPOSITES MUST include all PORTFOLIOS, including SEGREGATED ACCOUNTS and POOLED FUNDS, that meet the COMPOSITE DEFINITION. The FIRM MUST NOT exclude PORTFOLIOS from COMPOSITES based solely on legal structure differences.

Discussion

A composite is an aggregation of one or more portfolios (segregated accounts or pooled funds) managed according to a similar investment mandate, objective, or strategy. Creating meaningful composites is critical to fair presentation, consistency, and comparability of results over time and among firms. Firms make the ultimate decision as to which portfolios belong in each composite. Pooled funds are required to be included in a composite only if they are managed according to a strategy that is managed for or offered as a segregated account and they meet the composite definition.

To create appropriate composites, it is important to understand what is meant by a composite description and a composite definition. For many of the provisions of the GIPS standards, it is important to understand the difference between a composite description and a composite definition.

A *composite description* is defined as general information regarding the investment mandate, objective, or strategy of the composite. The composite description may be more abbreviated than the composite definition but must include all key features of the composite and must include enough information to allow a prospective client to understand the key characteristics of the composite's investment mandate, objective, or strategy, including:

- the material risks of the composite's strategy.
- how leverage, derivatives, and short positions may be used, if they are a material part of the strategy.
- if illiquid investments are a material part of the strategy.

A *composite definition* is defined as detailed criteria that determine the assignment of portfolios to composites. Criteria may include, but are not limited to, investment mandate, style or strategy, asset class, the use of derivatives, leverage and/or hedging, targeted risk metrics, investment constraints or restrictions, and/or portfolio type (e.g., segregated account or pooled fund; taxable versus tax exempt).

To differentiate between a composite definition and a composite description, it might be helpful to think of a composite description as focused on a description of the strategy represented by the composite. In contrast, a composite definition includes not only the composite strategy, as represented by the composite description, but also the detailed criteria that determine whether and when a portfolio is included in a composite. These additional criteria include such factors as the new portfolio inclusion policy, as well as any policies regarding significant cash flows or minimum asset size that are applicable to the composite. Firms must use their judgment when determining what information is appropriate to include in a composite description and composite definition for a specific strategy. Firms are encouraged to include more than the required minimum information in a composite description or composite definition if doing so will help a prospective client or prospective investor understand both the nature of the portfolios included in the composite and the strategy used.

Composite descriptions are disclosed in GIPS Composite Reports and on the List of Composite Descriptions. Composite definitions must be documented in the firm's policies and procedures.

The following table shows some examples of the items typically included in a composite description and a composite definition. An actual composite description and composite definition will be specific to the composite and may include items not on this list and may not include some items on this list.

Item	Included in Composite Description	Included in Composite Definition
Description of Strategy		
Investment mandate, objective, or strategy	X	X
Portfolio type	X	X
Asset class	X	X
Investments used	X	X
Client type (institutional, retail)	X	X
Investment constraints/restrictions	X	X
Material risks of strategy	X	X
How leverage, derivatives, and short positions may be used, if a material part of strategy	X	X
If illiquid investments are a material part of strategy	X	X
Benchmark	*	X
Composite Inclusion/Exclusion Policies (if applicable)		
Timing of inclusion of new portfolios		X
Timing of exclusion of closed portfolios		X
Minimum size policy		X
Significant cash flow policy		X
Tax status	**	X
Targeted risk metrics		X

* Often included in composite descriptions but required in composite description if the benchmark is one of the criteria for assigning portfolios to a composite—that is, portfolios must be managed against a particular index to be included in the composite.

** If portfolios are assigned to the composite based on tax status, the composite description must include the tax status. If tax status is simply information about the type of portfolios included in the composite, it can be included in the composite definition only.

The following are examples of composite descriptions and composite definitions.

Intermediate-Maturity Fixed-Income Composite

Composite Description

The Intermediate-Maturity Fixed-Income Composite includes all institutional portfolios that invest in intermediate-maturity government and corporate bonds. All bonds have a credit rating of BBB or higher. Key risks include the risk of default of corporate bonds and the negative effect of rising interest rates on bond prices.

Composite Definition

The Intermediate-Maturity Fixed-Income Composite includes all institutional portfolios that invest in intermediate-maturity government and corporate bonds. All bonds have a credit rating of BBB or higher. Key risks include the risk of default of corporate bonds and the negative effect of rising interest rates on bond prices. New portfolios are added to the composite when they are fully invested, as indicated by a cash position of 5% or less. The minimum size for inclusion of new portfolios in the composite is $5 million. Before a new portfolio is added to a composite, it must be at or above the minimum size for the composite as of the prior month end. Tolerance for violation of the minimum size is established at 10%. If a portfolio falls below 10% of the minimum size at the end of one month, it is removed from the composite the following month. When the portfolio has returned to the minimum size by month end, it is returned to the composite in the following month. If a portfolio experiences a 15% cash inflow during a calendar month, it is automatically removed from the composite for that month. Following the policy for inclusion of new portfolios in the composite, if the cash level is 5% or less at month end, the portfolio will be returned to the composite in the following month. A cash outflow of 15% during a calendar month will trigger an automatic removal of a portfolio from the composite. The portfolio will be returned to the composite in the month following the outflow if it continues to meet other composite criteria, such as size. A portfolio may be removed from a composite prior to the month of the actual cash flow if there is a significant buildup of cash to prepare for the outflow.

US Large-Cap Growth Composite

Composite Description

The US Large-Cap Growth Composite includes all tax-exempt, institutional segregated accounts that invest in large-capitalization US stocks considered to have earnings growth prospects that are superior to that of the average company within the benchmark, the XYZ Large-Cap Growth Index. The targeted tracking error is less than 4% per annum.

Composite Definition

The US Large-Cap Growth Composite includes all tax exempt, institutional segregated accounts that invest in large-capitalization US stocks considered to have earnings growth prospects that are superior to that of the average company within the benchmark, the XYZ Large-Cap Growth Index. The targeted tracking error is less than 4% per annum.

The US Large-Cap Growth Composite includes only discretionary institutional tax-exempt portfolios. A portfolio is defined as discretionary if it is free of any unique client needs or restrictions that will materially affect performance. The minimum size for inclusion in the composite is $1 million. When a new large-cap growth portfolio is fully invested (a cash level of 10% or less) at month end, it will be added to the composite in the following month. Terminated portfolios are included in the composite through the last full month for which the firm has discretion. The termination date is based on the notification date of the loss of the portfolio (i.e., the date on which discretion was lost) rather than the date of the actual closing of the portfolio.

A Significant Cash Flow (SCF) policy was adopted for the Large-Cap Growth Composite starting 1 February 2015. The SCF policy is triggered by a net cash inflow or outflow of 15% or more of portfolio assets during a calendar month. If a portfolio in the composite experiences a 15% or greater cash inflow during a calendar month, it is automatically removed from the composite for that month. If the cash level is 10% or less at month end, the portfolio will be returned to the portfolio in the following month. A cash outflow of 15% or more will trigger an automatic removal of a portfolio from the composite. The portfolio will be returned to the composite in the month following the outflow if it continues to meet other composite criteria, such as size. A portfolio may be removed from the composite prior to the month of the actual cash flow if there is a significant buildup of cash to prepare for the outflow.

The Large-Cap Growth Composite has a composite inception date of 1 July 2012 and a composite creation date of 1 April 2014.

The firm must determine what definition of the composite is most appropriate: either a broad, "inclusive" definition, with a potential for a wide internal dispersion of portfolio returns, or a narrow, "exclusive" definition, with a potential for a smaller internal dispersion of portfolio returns.

The GIPS standards require firms to develop objective criteria for defining composites. The following are guiding principles that firms must consider when defining composites:

- Composites should enable current and prospective clients and investors to compare the performance of one firm with that of another.
- Firms must apply the criteria for defining composites consistently. For example, the firm may not select only certain, specific portfolios that meet the composite definition (i.e., "cherry-picking") but must include all portfolios that satisfy the criteria for inclusion.
- Firms are not permitted to include portfolios with materially dissimilar investment mandates, objectives, or strategies in the same composite. The performance of such a composite is meaningless. When there are many portfolios that have unique, defining investment characteristics and these portfolios have a strategy that is managed for or offered as a segregated account, it may be necessary for the firm to create numerous single-portfolio composites.

- Portfolios must not be moved from one composite to another unless documented changes to a portfolio's investment mandate, objective, or strategy or the redefinition of the composite makes such a move appropriate. The historical performance of the portfolio must remain with the original composite.

The firm may create broader composites, sometimes referred to as "umbrella" or "parent" composites, that include portfolios from more narrowly defined composites. For example, a firm may create a composite of all fixed-income portfolios with an intermediate-maturity mandate that includes portfolios from different intermediate-maturity-term composites that are based on specific benchmarks. Please see Provision 3.A.19 for additional guidance on this point.

Composite Definition Hierarchy

The following suggested hierarchy may be helpful as firms consider how to define composites. Firms are not required to define their composites according to each level of the hierarchy. When considering this suggested hierarchy for composite definition, it is important to keep in mind that pooled funds are required to be included in a composite if they meet a composite definition.

Investment Mandate, Objective, or Strategy

Composites may be based on the overall investment mandate, objective or strategy, or overall product description.

> Examples: Large-cap global equities, long-maturity international bonds, small-cap stocks, global long/short equity, or private equity

Asset Class

Composites based on a broad asset class are the most basic and should be representative of the firm's products. Firms may further define asset classes by country or region.

> Examples: Equity, fixed income, balanced, real estate, venture capital, US fixed income, European equities

Style or Sector

Firms may further define a composite based on the style or sector.

> Examples: Growth, value, active, indexed, asset class sector (e.g., telecommunications)

Benchmark

Firms may define composites based on the portfolios' benchmark, provided the benchmark reflects the investment mandate, objective, or strategy. This situation is often the case if the benchmark also defines the investment universe.

Examples: Swiss Performance Index, S&P 500 Index, FTSE 100 Index

Risk/Return Characteristics

Portfolios with different risk characteristics (e.g., targeted tracking error, beta, volatility, and information ratio) and return objectives may be grouped together into different composites.

Example: A Japanese equity portfolio with a targeted excess return of 1% and targeted tracking error of 2% would be in a separate composite from a Japanese equity portfolio with a targeted excess return of 3% and targeted tracking error of 6%.

Constraints/Guidelines

Firms may choose to further define their composites based on relevant client constraints or guidelines. The following are examples of constraints or guidelines that could result in materially different strategies and, therefore, justify separate composites.

Extent of the Use of Derivatives, Hedging, Short Positions, and/or Leverage

Portfolios that use derivatives, hedging, short positions, and/or leverage may have a different investment strategy from those portfolios that do not use these techniques or instruments. Accordingly, firms must consider whether portfolios that use derivatives, hedging, short positions, and/or leverage should be included in separate composites from portfolios that are restricted from using, or do not use, such instruments or strategies.

Tax Considerations

The firm should define separate composites for portfolios with specific tax considerations if such considerations hinder the firm's ability to implement a specific investment strategy as compared with similar portfolios without specific tax considerations. The different tax situations of institutional and private clients may require different investment strategies. For example, private clients may have restrictions against selling an investment at a loss and rebuying the same investment within a specific time period, but institutional portfolios typically do not have such restrictions. If tax considerations result in different strategies based on the portfolio's tax status, firms are required to define separate composites appropriate to the different strategies.

Type of Client (e.g., pension fund, private client, endowment)

Client type alone must not be used as the primary criterion for defining a composite. In some cases, however, the client type determines the investment strategy because of characteristics that are unique to the client type. If portfolios of different client types have materially different investment strategies and/or styles that are specific to the type of client, the firm must create separate composites representing each of the different strategies that is managed for or offered as a segregated account.

One example would be a wrap fee client. Wrap fee portfolios involve a bundled fee that is specific to the particular investment product. Although the firm can use the same investment strategy for both wrap fee and non–wrap fee portfolios, it may not always have a direct relationship with the end user of its investment management services, even though these portfolios are often considered discretionary assets of the firm. Instead, multiple parties are involved in this business model, with a wrap fee sponsor serving as the intermediary between the firm and the end user of investment services. These factors are what distinguishes wrap fee portfolios and necessitates additional guidance for creating composites. For information on creating appropriate composites to show to prospective wrap fee clients, both before and after a firm obtains wrap fee portfolios, please see Provision 3.A.14.

Instruments Used

The firm may define separate composites based on the specific instruments used for a strategy. An example would be portfolios managed in a commodity strategy, wherein some portfolios choose to invest in the commodity strategy using futures while other portfolios invest in the commodity strategy using physical commodities.

Portfolio Size

Differences in portfolio size may result in meaningful, material differences in investment strategy and justify the creation of separate composites. For example, smaller segregated accounts managed according to a mid-cap equity strategy may be invested in pooled funds while larger segregated accounts managed in the same strategy are invested in individual securities.

Client Characteristics (e.g., cash flow needs, risk tolerances)

Firms may create composites based on multiple client characteristics. For example, a firm may choose to create a growth equity composite for clients that require a 15% cash balance because they withdraw cash on a regular basis versus clients whose portfolios are fully invested. Cash flow considerations and how they affect the investment strategy are often key factors when firms consider whether to include pooled funds in composites.

Portfolio Types/Legal Structure

A composite must include all portfolios that are managed according to the same strategy. Differences in portfolio types or legal structure alone would not warrant a separate composite definition. If differences in portfolio types, such as limited partnerships and segregated accounts, lead to differences in how the strategy is implemented, then the firm would split limited partnerships and segregated accounts into separate composites. Differences driven by a portfolio's legal structure may also arise in implementing a strategy. For example, some portfolio types may be prohibited from investing in 144(a) securities or new-issue IPOs. If the portfolio type or legal structure does not affect the management of the portfolio, then portfolio type or legal structure must not be used as a criterion for composite definition. If the portfolio type or legal structure affects the management of the portfolio, then the firm must create separate composites based on portfolio type or legal structure.

Prior to 1 January 2020, firms were allowed to differentiate between segregated accounts and pooled funds when defining composites. For example, a firm could choose to create one composite for segregated accounts managed in the firm's large-cap equity strategy and another composite for pooled funds managed in the same strategy. As of 1 January 2020, firms may no longer take this approach. On a prospective basis, pooled funds managed in a strategy that is managed for or offered as a segregated account must be included in the same composite as any segregated accounts managed or offered in that strategy.

Currencies

Reporting currency must not be used as a criterion for composite definition unless it affects the investment strategy. For example, suppose that a firm manages portfolios invested in a S&P 500 Index strategy. Some investors in this strategy require reporting in Swiss francs (CHF), some require reporting in British pounds (GBP), and others require reporting in US dollars (USD). If the difference in reporting currencies does not create a difference in the underlying portfolios, the firm may not create different composites based on the client reporting currencies.

In contrast, differences in portfolio base currencies that have a material effect on strategy implementation must be considered when defining composites. For example, if a client instructs the firm to invest cash balances in a different currency, this cash restriction could be used as a criterion for composite definition. Additionally, if currency hedging is part of the investment strategy, different composites may be required. Although the hedged returns of portfolios denominated in different currencies are intended to be similar if they are managed to the same strategy, there will be a difference in returns (even with perfect hedging) equivalent to the cost (or benefit) of hedging. This cost (or benefit) of hedging caused by the interest rate differential between currencies can be significant over time.

 |

Additional Considerations

Multi-Strategy or Multi-Asset-Class Portfolios

Some firms offer a multi-strategy or multi-asset-class segregated account, with each of the underlying strategies or asset classes included in the segregated account represented by "building blocks" for the strategy, which may be portfolios or carve-outs. A carve-out is a portion of a portfolio that is by itself representative of a distinct investment strategy. It may be used to create a track record for a narrower mandate from a multi-strategy or multi-asset-class portfolio managed to a broader mandate. For example, a multi-strategy fixed-income segregated account might include portfolios or carve-outs that represent different fixed-income strategies, such as long- and short-duration strategies or high-yield and high-quality strategies. A multi-asset-class portfolio might include portfolios or carve-outs that represent equity and fixed-income strategies.

All actual, fee-paying discretionary segregated accounts must be included in at least one composite. This can be accomplished either by including total multi-strategy and multi-asset-class segregated accounts in composites or by including each of the underlying portfolios or carve-outs of total segregated accounts in composites. With the issuance of the 2020 edition of the GIPS standards, a multi-strategy or multi-asset-class segregated account is no longer required to be included in a composite if each of the segregated account's underlying portfolios or carve-outs are included in appropriate composites. This guidance replaces guidance included in a Q&A issued in November 2012 stating that a discretionary multi-strategy portfolio was required to be included in a multi-strategy composite, even if all of the underlying portfolio segments were included in composites. This change applies to all periods for which the firm claims compliance.

A firm may also choose to include both multi-strategy or multi-asset-class segregated accounts and the underlying portfolio or carve-out segments in a composite. The firm may then present the multi-strategy or multi-asset-class composites or the segment composites to prospective clients, or it may choose to present both. If the firm chooses to present segment composites and not present multi-strategy or multi-asset-class composites to prospective clients of a multi-asset-class or multi-strategy composite, it must present all segment composites of the multi-strategy or multi-asset-class strategy.

When the firm chooses to maintain both multi-strategy or multi-asset-class composites and segment composites, it must be careful not to double count when calculating total firm assets.

Example 1:

A firm creates balanced portfolios with different weights for equity and fixed income based on a client's investment needs. The firm may determine that each segregated account is so customized that the composites for total segregated accounts would not be meaningful. The firm decides to include the segments of each segregated account in asset class composites and does not create balanced composites.

Example 2:

A firm might decide to create composites based on ranges that represent various blends of a balanced strategy with an equity component and a fixed-income component. There might be an "aggressive" balanced composite for portfolios whose equity segment represents 70% to 100% of the balanced portfolio, a "moderate" balanced composite for portfolios whose equity portion represents 40% to 69%, and a "conservative" composite for portfolios whose equity segment represents 0% to 39%. The firm may also choose to create both balanced and asset class composites.

It is important to remember that if a firm chooses to include a total multi-strategy or multi-asset-class portfolio in a composite, the composite must be constructed according to strategic ranges of asset mixes provided in the client investment guidelines, not according to the tactical percentage of assets invested in the different asset classes. Firms often have discretion to tactically alter the asset allocation in an effort to add value. Portfolios must not be moved into or out of composites in response to changes in tactical asset allocation. Only in the case of client-documented strategic asset allocation changes can portfolios be moved into different composites. Client-documented strategic asset allocation changes include those situations in which the client has given contractual authority to the portfolio manager to make strategic changes in asset allocation. Please see Provision 3.A.10 for additional guidance on this point.

Inception Date

Because composites represent an investment strategy over time, a composite based solely on the composite's inception date would, generally, not show representative results of how the strategy performed over time in changing market conditions. Therefore, in general, firms are not permitted to create composites based solely on the composite inception date.

In very specific situations, however, such as for private equity or real estate closed-end fund composites, it may be appropriate to group portfolios into composites according to inception date (i.e., by vintage year) and strategy. Vintage year is typically based on either the year of the investment vehicle's first drawdown or capital call from its investors or the year when the first committed capital from outside investors is closed and legally binding. For certain investments, the vintage year will drive the investment opportunities in a certain strategy.

Firms with Multiple Offices, Branches, or Investment Divisions

Firms are permitted to define different composites for offices, branches, or investment divisions within the defined firm only if the portfolios are managed according to investment mandates, objectives, or strategies that are unique to each particular office, branch, or division. Thus, it is the investment mandate, objective, or strategy that determines the composite, not the location or group. Composites may, therefore, include portfolios from different offices within the firm that are managed according to the same investment mandate, objective, or strategy. However, composites must include only portfolios within the definition of the firm.

Internal Dispersion of Portfolio Returns within a Composite

Although internal dispersion is one measure to determine how consistently a firm has implemented its strategy across the portfolios in the composite, it can be measured only on an ex post basis and, therefore, must not be used as a criterion to define a composite. An internal dispersion figure may serve as a good indicator of whether the criteria for composite definition are suitable or whether the firm should consider redefining the composite. There is no general rule for a maximum amount of composite internal dispersion. The firm should contemplate the definition of a broad, "inclusive" composite with a wide internal dispersion of portfolio returns versus a narrow, "exclusive" composite with a narrower internal dispersion measure.

Treatment of Fees

Firms must not define a composite based on either the type of fees that are paid or the portfolios' fee schedule. For example, it would not be appropriate to create two versions of a composite that differ only because some portfolios in the composite have a performance-based investment management fee while others do not. A firm may not exclude a pooled fund from a composite for which the fund meets the composite definition solely because the fund pays higher fees than segregated accounts.

Firms should include non-fee-paying portfolios in composites. The GIPS standards do not, however, require that non-fee-paying portfolios be included in composites.

Portfolio Manager

Composites must not be defined solely based on portfolio manager. For example, if a firm uses five portfolio managers to manage portfolios invested in its Growth Equity strategy, and all portfolio managers follow the same investment strategy, the firm must not create composites based on individual portfolio managers. Composites must be defined by the strategy according to which portfolios are managed and not by the person who manages the portfolios.

Inclusion of Segregated Accounts and Pooled Funds in Composites

Once a firm has established composite definitions, all actual, fee-paying, discretionary segregated accounts must be assigned to at least one appropriate composite, as well as to all composites for which they meet the composite definition. All actual, fee-paying discretionary pooled funds must be assigned to any composite for which they meet a composite definition. If a segregated account or pooled fund meets more than one composite definition, the segregated account or pooled fund must be included in each of the relevant composites.

Provision 3.A.6

Any change to a COMPOSITE DEFINITION MUST NOT be applied retroactively.

Discussion

Although investment strategies can change over time, in most cases firms should not change the definition of a composite. Generally, changes in strategy result in the creation of a new composite. In some cases, however, it may be appropriate to redefine a composite. If a firm determines that it is appropriate to redefine a composite, it must disclose the date and description of the redefinition. Changes to composites must not be applied retroactively.

When there are changes related to strategy implementation, the firm must determine if the changes to the composite's investment process or personnel result in a change in the investment strategy of the portfolios in the composite. If the firm determines that the changes result in a new investment strategy offered by the firm, a new composite must be started with a current composite creation date and no composite history. The firm must clearly document its decision and rationale. If the changes in resources, process, and personnel do not result in a change in investment strategy, the firm must not create a new composite but must revise the composite description and composite definition where appropriate.

Note that if a firm chooses to create a new composite to reflect a new investment strategy, the firm may move portfolios that meet the new composite definition into the new composite. The history of existing portfolios must remain with the original composite.

The following are some examples of changes in investment strategy and resulting composite changes.

Example 1: Evolution of a Composite Strategy

A firm has a mid-cap equity composite. It is decided that the composite will begin using futures to fully invest any cash balances. Most client guidelines permit the use of futures, but some do not. The firm does not wish to continue to offer a mid-cap strategy that does not use futures.

The firm is permitted to view this change as an evolution of its existing mid-cap strategy rather than as the creation of a new strategy. It must change its composite description and composite definition to indicate the use of futures and the date on which the use of futures began. The portfolios that allow the use of futures remain in the composite.

Because the firm did not wish to continue to offer a mid-cap strategy that does not use futures, the firm would consider the mid-cap portfolios that do not allow the use of futures to be non-discretionary portfolios and exclude these portfolios from all composites on a prospective basis.

If instead the firm wished to continue to also offer a mid-cap strategy that does not use futures, as a variation of its mid-cap strategy, the firm would create a new composite for mid-cap portfolios that do not use futures. The mid-cap portfolios that do not use futures would be moved to the new composite with a new composite creation date.

Example 2: Combining Composite Strategies

A firm currently has two small-cap equity composites. The investment mandate is the same for both composites, but the permissible market-cap range differs. One composite invests in small-cap stocks with market caps ranging between $100 million and $1.0 billion. The second composite invests in stocks ranging from $500 million to $1.5 billion. The firm would like to expand, with client acceptance, the market-cap range for all portfolios in each composite so that all of the firm's small-cap portfolios could invest in stocks ranging from $100 million to $1.5 billion, eliminating the need for two composites.

If the firm decides to create a new strategy by expanding the permissible size range for all small-cap portfolios, the firm must create a new composite. The new composite will consist of all the small-cap portfolios in the two composites. The two existing small-cap composites will cease to exist. The new small-cap composite will not have historical performance results because the new composite's strategy (the expanded market-cap range) is newly implemented. The firm must include the two terminated small-cap composites on the list of composite descriptions for at least five years after the composites' termination date. The firm must obtain any needed client approval for the change in investment mandate and must appropriately document the creation of the new small-cap composite and the termination of the former small-cap composites.

Example 3: Redefinition of a Composite Based on Historical Tactical Decisions

For the past five years, a firm has offered a global equity composite. The firm defined the strategy to allow investments in equity securities from any geographic area, but the firm tactically did not hold any Japanese equities during that time. The firm has now decided that its global equity strategy will not allow investments in Japanese stocks. It therefore wants to redefine the composite as global equities ex-Japan.

Redefining the composite as a global equities ex-Japan composite is not permitted. Historically, the firm did not actually manage the assets in a global equities ex-Japan style. The original composite had a broad global investment mandate that could have included investments in Japan. The firm made a tactical decision not to own Japanese equity securities. Redefining the composite's strategy more narrowly would not accurately reflect the composite's historical investment strategy and would not provide an accurate history of the mandate. The firm is accountable for the tactical decision not to own any Japanese securities. If the firm wishes to offer a global equities ex-Japan composite, it must create a new composite with an investment mandate that reflects the lack of Japanese investments as a strategic decision and not a tactical one. With clients' permission, the firm may move clients into the new global equities ex-Japan composite. The new composite would have no historical track record. The firm may continue the existing global equity strategy or terminate the global equity composite and find other investment options for clients who do not wish to move into the global equities ex-Japan composite.

Example 4: Umbrella Composites

A firm manages two composites in a mid-cap equity strategy. One composite is based on fundamental research, and the other is a quantitative strategy. The firm would like to create an "umbrella" composite to illustrate the performance of its mid-cap strategies while continuing to market both of its mid-cap strategies.

An umbrella composite is a broadly defined composite that includes portfolios from more narrowly defined composites. In this case, the umbrella composite represents the firm's mid-cap equity strategies. The firm will include all of the portfolios from its two mid-cap equity composites in the umbrella composite. The umbrella composite's track record will therefore be a combination of the track records of both mid-cap equity composites. The two mid-cap equity composites will continue to exist.

Umbrella composites may be created retroactively and would include the track records of the underlying composites. For an additional discussion of umbrella composites, please refer to Provision 3.A.19.

Provision 3.A.7

COMPOSITES MUST include new PORTFOLIOS on a timely and consistent COMPOSITE-specific basis after each PORTFOLIO comes under management.

Discussion

The firm is responsible for setting reasonable guidelines for each composite regarding the inclusion of new portfolios. Firms are encouraged to establish a policy that includes new portfolios in composites as soon as possible, preferably at the start of the next full performance measurement period. The measurement period is the period for which the composite performance is calculated.

Firms may need time to invest the assets of a new portfolio to reflect the firm's investment strategy, and the GIPS standards allow firms flexibility in determining when to add the new portfolio to the composite. Different strategies may result in different time frames for inclusion based on the liquidity of the assets involved. Although in most situations it is fairly easy to purchase and sell securities, some securities may be more illiquid and, therefore, a longer period of time may initially be required to implement the firm's strategy. Firms must establish a policy on a composite-specific basis and apply it on a timely and consistent basis.

In the case of specific instructions from the client, firms may delay including a new portfolio in a composite. For example, a client may indicate to the firm that assets will be deposited over an extended period, which may delay the full implementation of the firm's strategy until all assets are received. This scenario can result in an exception to the composite's new portfolio inclusion policy. If a firm determines that the incremental investing does not affect the implementation of the style or strategy, however, the firm must follow its composite-specific policy for including new portfolios in the composite.

Provision 3.A.8

COMPOSITES MUST include only those PORTFOLIOS that are managed for the full performance measurement period for which the COMPOSITE return is calculated. PORTFOLIOS that are not managed for the full performance measurement period MUST NOT be included in the COMPOSITE.

Discussion

When calculating composite time-weighted returns, firms must include in the composite only those portfolios that are managed for the full performance measurement period. This requirement applies to all methodologies for calculating composite performance, including the aggregate method.

When considering a composite for which time-weighted returns are presented, if performance intervals are calculated on a monthly basis, only portfolios that are managed for the full month are included in the composite return calculation. Including portfolios that were not managed for the full month would result in returns that are not truly representative of the strategy for the performance period being calculated. For example, assume the firm calculates composite returns monthly. When calculating the composite return for the month of March, only portfolios that have a full month of performance are included. A portfolio with an inception date of 5 March would not be included, nor would a portfolio that terminated on 23 March. To illustrate why the returns are not truly representative, assume the composite contains three portfolios for the full month of March for which the monthly portfolio returns are 3.4%, 3.5%, and 3.6%. The firm gets a new portfolio that starts 5 March, and because the first few days of March had strong performance that the new portfolio did not experience, the return of that portfolio is 1%. Another portfolio that was originally in the composite terminated on 23 March, and there was negative performance at the end of the month that the portfolio did not experience, so that portfolio's return is 5%. To calculate a monthly composite return for March, it would not make sense to include the partial-period returns for the new and terminating portfolios, 1% and 5%, because those returns are missing part of the month. Additionally, there would be no beginning weight for the portfolio that opened on 5 March.

However, the first portfolio in a composite may be included in the composite when the portfolio is fully invested when it is the only portfolio in the composite for the full performance measurement period. Also, the last portfolio in a composite may be included in the composite until the day on which the firm loses discretion to manage the portfolio. A firm must create policies and procedures regarding the inclusion of new portfolios in a composite and the exclusion of terminated portfolios from a composite, and it must apply those policies and procedures consistently. The policies may be composite specific.

For a composite for which a money-weighted return (MWR) is presented, there is only a single since-inception MWR. If a composite for which a MWR is presented includes more than one portfolio, the MWR can be calculated by combining the cash flows and values of the individual portfolios using the aggregate method. Portfolios must be included in the composite calculation for the full period for which the portfolio is under management.

Provision 3.A.9

Terminated PORTFOLIOS MUST be included in the historical performance of the COMPOSITE up to the last full measurement period that each PORTFOLIO was under management and for which the FIRM has discretion.

Discussion

The requirement to include terminated portfolios in the composite's historical performance up to the last full measurement period during which each portfolio was under management and for which the firm has discretion prevents survivorship bias by retaining the performance history of the portfolio while it was managed to the composite's strategy. Once a client notifies the firm of the termination, the firm generally loses its discretion over the portfolio because the firm is restricted in its management of the portfolio. If this is the case, the firm must include the portfolio in the composite through the last full measurement period for which the firm has discretion and exclude it from the composite for subsequent periods. As an example, suppose that a firm was notified on 25 May of the termination of a portfolio and was instructed to immediately commence liquidating the portfolio. Assuming monthly performance measurement periods, because the firm lost discretion to manage the portfolio effective 25 May, the portfolio must be included in the composite return calculation for April and excluded from the composite return calculation for May. A firm must create policies and procedures regarding the handling of the termination of portfolios in a composite, and it must apply those policies and procedures consistently. The policies may be composite specific.

A change in the legal status of a portfolio alone would not be a valid reason to remove the portfolio from the composite. As an example, suppose that a firm managed a portfolio for an individual and, when the client passed away, the portfolio had to be closed and reopened as part of a trust rather than in the individual's name. From the firm's perspective, the portfolio was not terminated because the portfolio did not leave the firm and the firm never lost discretion over the portfolio. The change in the legal status of the portfolio alone is not a valid reason to remove the portfolio from the composite if the assets never left the portfolio, the firm was never restricted in its management of the portfolio, and the portfolio strategy remained unchanged. If the firm had to suspend trading for an extended period to allow for the change in legal status, however, it would be appropriate for the firm to temporarily remove the portfolio from the composite and re-include it when the transition to the trust was complete.

If all of the portfolios are removed from a composite, for any reason, the composite's performance record comes to an end. If, after some period of time, portfolios are again included in the composite, the prior performance history of the composite must be presented. If time-weighted returns are being presented and the break in performance occurred more than 10 years ago, or before the firm claimed compliance with the GIPS standards, the performance prior to the break is not required to be presented. The composite's prior performance history must not be linked to the ongoing composite performance results. If money-weighted returns (MWR) are being presented, MWRs may not be calculated across the break in performance. The firm must present a MWR for the period from inception to the break in performance. If portfolios in the composite have committed capital, the firm must present the information required by Provision 5.A.4 (e.g., committed capital and ratios) as of the end date of this return calculation. When portfolios are once again included in the composite, the firm must begin to calculate a MWR for the period after the break in performance through the most recent annual period end. If the break in performance occurred more than 10 years ago or before the firm claimed compliance with the GIPS standards, the MWR and the information required by Provision 5.A.4 (e.g., committed capital and ratios) prior to the break in performance are not required to be presented.

Provision 3.A.10

PORTFOLIOS MUST NOT be moved from one COMPOSITE to another unless documented client-directed changes to a PORTFOLIO'S investment mandate, objective, or strategy or the redefinition of the COMPOSITE make it appropriate. The historical performance of the PORTFOLIO MUST remain with the original COMPOSITE. PORTFOLIOS MUST NOT be moved into or out of COMPOSITES as a result of the FIRM'S tactical changes.

Discussion

Firms are permitted to move portfolios (segregated accounts and pooled funds) into and out of composites only because of documented changes to a portfolio's investment mandate, objective, or strategy or in the case where the redefinition of a composite makes it appropriate. Documentation of the client-directed change can include, but is not limited to, letters, e-mails, and internal memorandums documenting conversations with clients.

This requirement seeks to preclude or at least minimize the movement of portfolios into, out of, and between composites. Theoretically, once a firm creates composites based on its various investment strategies, portfolios will be managed to those strategies on a long-term basis. As a result, defining composites is a critical issue when complying with the GIPS standards.

Over time, however, a client's investment objective may change, a pooled fund's investment mandate may be modified, and firms may adopt new investment strategies. In those instances, moving a portfolio from one composite to another may be necessary. In the case of segregated accounts, wherein the client selects the strategy, the move must be based on a change in the segregated account's strategy that is directed by the client and is clearly identified and documented. In the case of a pooled fund, there must be a documented change in the pooled fund's investment strategy. Portfolios must not be moved from one composite to another because of changes in tactical asset allocation. Portfolios can be moved into different composites only in the case of client-documented strategic asset allocation changes for segregated accounts or changes in the investment mandate for pooled funds, or when the redefinition of a composite makes such a move appropriate.

If the firm suggests a change in strategy that would result in a client's portfolio moving to a new composite, the firm must make every reasonable effort to provide the client with a GIPS Composite Report for the new composite. If the client requests a change that would result in the firm moving the client's portfolio to a new composite, the firm should provide the client with a GIPS Composite Report for the new composite but is not required to do so.

There are situations in which a client has contractually given the firm authority over the allocation of a multi-strategy or multi-asset-class portfolio. In such cases, the documentation of an allocation change should be considered "client-directed" documentation for the change when combined with a client contract that assigns the firm authority over asset allocation within a portfolio. The documentation of the change must include the timing of and reason for the change and must be recorded. A memo to the client file or a record in the client management system would suffice.

The transfer of a portfolio from one composite to another is treated like a portfolio termination when it is removed from the former composite and treated like a new portfolio when moved to the new composite. The portfolio's prior history must remain in the former composite through the last full measurement period during which the portfolio was managed in the former style.

Provision 3.A.11

If the FIRM sets a minimum asset level for PORTFOLIOS to be included in a COMPOSITE, the FIRM:

a. MUST NOT include PORTFOLIOS below the COMPOSITE-specific minimum asset level in that COMPOSITE.

b. MUST NOT apply retroactively any changes to that COMPOSITE-specific minimum asset level.

Discussion

When a firm establishes a minimum asset level for including portfolios in a composite, the firm has determined that portfolios below that level are too small to be representative of the strategy. Once this level has been established, the firm must not include portfolios below the composite-specific minimum asset level in the composite.

Although firms may not retroactively change a composite-specific minimum asset level, firms attaining compliance may apply a composite minimum asset level retroactively. If a firm is initially coming into compliance with the GIPS standards and is building a compliant track record, it may establish a minimum asset level for a composite and apply that minimum asset level as it constructs the composite's history. Firms must document and disclose any subsequent changes to the composite's minimum asset level and must not retroactively apply the new limit.

Portfolios may fall below the minimum asset level as a result of client withdrawals or depreciation (decrease in asset value). A firm's policies regarding minimum asset levels must define, for each composite with a minimum asset level, whether the composite minimum asset level policy is applied only when a portfolio is first invested in the composite or if it is applied for all periods. There are different approaches to establishing policies and procedures for minimum asset levels.

- Some firms see the composite minimum asset level as a limitation only when initially investing the portfolio and believe that portfolios that subsequently fall below the minimum asset level continue to reflect the composite strategy. These firms establish a composite minimum asset level that applies only to the portfolio's initial size.
- Some firms have policies that apply to the portfolio's initial size and also to subsequent decreases in market value that result from external cash flows and not to market activity. Firms that leave portfolios in the composite when they fall below the minimum asset level as a result of market activity must have policies that address the appropriate action when a portfolio that is below the minimum asset level has a withdrawal and the portfolio cannot be rebalanced to the composite strategy.

- Some firms believe that assigning a composite minimum asset level means that the firm must have a certain amount of assets to manage the portfolio on an ongoing basis as well as to initially invest the portfolio. Such firms view a portfolio falling below the minimum asset level for any reason, including external cash flows or market activity, as non-discretionary.

If a firm's policies regarding minimum asset levels require that a portfolio be removed from a composite solely as a result of market activity, and the firm calculates composite returns monthly, the portfolio should remain in the composite during the first month it drops below the composite minimum because of market fluctuations. A decrease in value resulting from market fluctuations reflects the portfolio manager's performance and, therefore, should be captured in the composite return. When firms test the composite minimum using the end-of-month value, this has the unintended consequence of creating an upward bias for the composite return because the firm is removing portfolios with negative performance from the composite. The test for minimum assets should therefore be done using beginning-of-month values, not ending values.

Each of these approaches is consistent with the requirements regarding minimum asset levels. It is critical that if a firm establishes a minimum asset level for a composite, it must document its policies regarding how portfolios will be treated if they fall below the minimum and must apply these policies consistently.

When establishing policies and procedures regarding a minimum asset level, firms may consider establishing a threshold for applying both the minimum asset level and a minimum time period in order to minimize portfolio movement into or out of a composite. For example, a firm's policies might establish a threshold of 10% below the minimum asset level when determining if a portfolio should be removed from the composite. The firm's policies might also indicate that a portfolio must remain below/above the minimum for at least two periods prior to removal/addition.

If a portfolio is removed from a composite because it falls below the composite-specific minimum asset level, the portfolio's prior history must remain in the composite. Like all policies, once the firm establishes a policy regarding the minimum asset level, it must be applied consistently. Once a portfolio is removed, the firm must determine if the portfolio meets any other composite definition and, if so, must include it in the appropriate composite(s) in a timely and consistent manner. For example, a firm might determine it needs a minimum of $5 million to implement its Broad Large-Cap strategy. Portfolios below the $5 million minimum are invested in a concentrated variation of this strategy and are included in the Concentrated Broad Large-Cap Composite. In this case, although the investment mandate may be the same, the strategy is implemented differently based on the portfolio's size.

Firms should bear in mind that if all the portfolios in a composite fall below the minimum asset level and, according to the firm's policies, are removed from the composite, the composite's performance record would come to an end. If, after some period of time, portfolios move above the minimum asset level or new portfolios are added to the composite, the composite's prior performance history must be shown but not linked to the ongoing composite performance results.

Note that a composite's historical performance does not change if a firm establishes a new minimum asset level for the composite. If a firm chooses to implement a new minimum asset level or change the minimum asset level for an existing composite, the firm must document and disclose the new minimum or change to the minimum and apply the new minimum consistently going forward. The firm must not go back and restate historical performance to include or exclude portfolios using the new minimum asset level. Prospectively, the firm will include in the composite only those portfolios that meet the new minimum asset level for the composite. As pointed out earlier, however, if a firm is initially coming into compliance with the GIPS standards and is building a compliant track record, the firm may establish a minimum asset level for a composite and apply that minimum asset level as it constructs a composite's history.

It is important to be aware of the difference between a composite minimum and a product minimum. A composite minimum represents the size below which a portfolio is considered too small to be managed to a specific strategy because the strategy cannot be fully implemented. A composite minimum determines whether a portfolio is included in a composite. A product minimum is used for marketing purposes as a guideline for accepting new segregated accounts. A firm may accept new clients that have less than the stated product minimum. A firm may have a product minimum and no composite minimum, a composite minimum and no product minimum, or different amounts for a product minimum and a composite minimum. As Provision 3.B.1 points out, if a firm has one or more composite minimums, it should not present a GIPS Composite Report to a prospective client for any composite for which the prospective client is known not to meet the composite's minimum asset level.

Provision 3.A.12

A FIRM that removes PORTFOLIOS from COMPOSITES because of SIGNIFICANT CASH FLOWS MUST define "significant" on an EX ANTE, COMPOSITE-specific basis and MUST consistently follow the COMPOSITE-specific policy.

Discussion

For the purposes of the GIPS standards, an external cash flow is defined as capital (cash or investments) that enters or exits a portfolio. A significant cash flow is defined as the level at which the firm determines that a client-directed external cash flow may temporarily prevent the firm from implementing the composite strategy. The firm may define a significant cash flow as a single flow or an aggregate of a number of flows within a stated period of time. Transfers of assets between asset classes within a portfolio or firm-initiated cash flows must not be considered significant cash flows and must not be used to move portfolios out of composites on a temporary basis.

Firms that wish to remove portfolios from composites in cases of significant cash flows must define "significant" on an ex ante, composite-specific basis and must consistently follow the composite-specific policy. Note that a significant cash flow policy is not appropriate for a composite that presents money-weighted returns (MWRs) and is intended only for composites that present time-weighted returns. This is because, in the case of MWRs, the timing of cash flows is under the firm's control. The concept of a significant cash flow also does not apply to a pooled fund presented in a GIPS Pooled Fund Report.

Once a significant cash flow policy is established for a composite, the firm must remove from the composite all portfolios that experience a significant cash flow. Firms must establish policies for the timing of excluding portfolios that experience significant cash flows from composites, as well as policies for the timing of re-including those portfolios in composites. These policies must be established on a composite-specific basis. A significant cash flow definition or policy may be changed, as long as it is done prospectively and the change is documented in the firm's policies and procedures. Changes to a significant cash flow definition or policy must not be applied retroactively. If a firm is initially coming into compliance with the GIPS standards and is building a compliant track record, however, the firm may establish a significant cash flow policy for a composite and apply that significant cash flow policy as it constructs a composite's history. If a significant cash flow policy is being constructed historically for a newly created composite, a significant cash flow level must not be established with the intent of increasing composite performance.

The significant cash flow definition for a composite may be influenced by the characteristics of the asset class(es) within the strategy, such as market liquidity, and/or by the firm's trading capabilities. For instance, a significant cash flow may be considered 10% of a portfolio's value for an emerging market fixed-income composite but may be in excess of 50% of a portfolio's value for a more liquid composite, such as European equities. In theory, the determination of significance should be based primarily on the liquidity of the asset class and the investment strategy employed. Because of the dynamic nature of global markets and the inherent subjectivity involved, it is impractical to establish absolute levels of significance for each asset class.

The measure of significance must be determined as either a specific monetary amount (e.g., €50,000,000) or a percentage of portfolio assets (based on the most recent valuation). No other criteria, such as the impact or lack of impact of the significant cash flow on the respective portfolio's performance, may be considered.

If a firm has a single portfolio in a composite and that portfolio is temporarily removed from the composite because of the firm's significant cash flow policy, the composite's track record is broken and its continuous performance history ends. Once the portfolio is added back to the composite and the composite performance is restarted, the performance history must be presented for periods both before and after the break and cannot be linked across the break. If the break in performance occurred more than 10 years ago or before the firm claimed compliance with the GIPS standards, the performance prior to the break does not need to be presented. In all other cases, the firm must present the performance both prior to and after the performance break.

It is important to be aware of the difference between a large cash flow and a significant cash flow. Large cash flows apply only when daily returns are not calculated. A large cash flow is the level at which the firm determines that an external cash flow may distort the return if the portfolio is not valued and a sub-period return is not calculated. Portfolios that experience a large cash flow remain in the composite. A significant cash flow is the level at which the firm determines that one or more client-directed external cash flows may temporarily prevent the firm from implementing the composite strategy. Portfolios that experience a significant cash flow are temporarily removed from the composite.

As an example, suppose that a firm is establishing policies and procedures for a newly established long-maturity bond strategy. The firm currently values portfolios monthly. As part of determining the valuation policies for this strategy, the performance team asks the following question: Is there a level at which an external cash flow could distort a portfolio's monthly return if the portfolio is not valued and a sub-period return is not calculated? When discussing this issue with the fixed-income team, the performance team determines that an external cash flow of 5% or more could distort a portfolio's return. The firm, therefore, establishes a large cash flow policy for the composite that states that any portfolio managed in the strategy would be revalued in the event of an external cash flow of 5% or greater. The next question is whether there is a level at which an external cash flow would be so significant that it would actually prevent the firm from implementing the composite strategy for the portfolio. A cash flow of 5% would require valuation at the time of the cash flow, but the portfolio would still be considered to be representative of the strategy. It would therefore have to be a bigger external cash flow to cause the portfolio to be no longer representative of the composite strategy. Discussion with the fixed-income team determines that total external cash flows of 15% or more during a calendar month would be significant enough to prevent a portfolio from being representative of the style. The firm therefore establishes a large cash flow policy of 5% and a significant cash flow policy of 15% for its long-maturity bond strategy.

As the example illustrates, the levels used to define large cash flows and significant cash flows will not be the same. The significant cash flow level for a composite must be higher than the large cash flow level. This is because a large cash flow is the level that would require a portfolio to be valued (where daily returns are not calculated) but the portfolio is still considered to be discretionary and remains in the composite. In contrast, a significant cash flow is the level at which the portfolio is no longer representative of the composite strategy and is removed from the composite because the external cash flow disrupts implementation of the investment strategy.

A firm must not adopt a significant cash flow policy solely for the purpose of reducing or eliminating the number of instances when portfolios must be valued because of large cash flows. The significant cash flow level chosen by the firm for a specific composite must represent the firm's estimate of the level of cash flows that would potentially disrupt the investment strategy's implementation. Significant cash flow levels and large cash flow levels must be established independently.

As an alternative to a significant cash flow policy, when a portfolio is removed from the composite, it is recommended that a firm use a temporary new account. (See Provision 3.B.2.) This approach allows a firm to create a new portfolio into which a client's contributions and withdrawals are directed. Provision 3.A.13 provides a further discussion of the use of temporary new accounts to remove the effects of significant cash flows.

Firms may establish a significant cash flow policy that exempts certain types of external cash flows. For example, a client may use a transition manager to move a cash inflow to the firm in the form of assets that the firm has directed to be purchased. The inflow does not prevent the firm from implementing the composite's strategy, so the significant cash flow policy for this composite would not apply in this instance.

Provision 3.A.13

A FIRM that uses TEMPORARY NEW ACCOUNTS to remove the effect of a SIGNIFICANT CASH FLOW MUST establish policies on an EX ANTE, COMPOSITE-specific basis. TEMPORARY NEW ACCOUNTS MUST NOT be included in COMPOSITE performance.

Discussion

As discussed in Provision 3.A.12, a firm may establish a significant cash flow policy that allows the firm to remove a portfolio from a composite if it experiences a client-directed external cash flow that may temporarily prevent the firm from implementing the composite strategy. An alternative method for removing the effect of a significant cash flow is to use temporary new accounts.

If a portfolio experiences a significant cash inflow, the firm would create a temporary new account for the inflow of assets. The funds would remain in the temporary new account until they are invested and reflect the portfolio's investment mandate. The performance of the assets in the temporary new account would not be reflected in the main portfolio's performance until these assets are transferred into the main portfolio. The temporary new account must not be included in composite performance. The assets of the temporary new account would be reflected in total firm assets if the temporary new account is in existence at the end of a reporting period, but they would not be included in composite assets.

If the portfolio experiences a cash outflow that qualifies as a significant cash flow, the firm may create a temporary new account for the outflow of assets. The temporary new account would be funded with the assets the firm will distribute to the client or will liquidate to meet the cash flow needs of the client. The portfolio with the remaining assets would continue in the composite and would reflect the outflow in the performance calculation at the date of transfer to the temporary new account. The temporary new account must not be included in composite performance.

The assets of the temporary new account would be reflected in total firm assets if it is in existence at the end of a reporting period but would not be included in composite assets.

A firm that uses temporary new accounts to remove the effect of a significant cash flow must establish policies on an ex ante composite-specific basis. A temporary new account may also be used for pooled funds to deal with cash flows from subscriptions and redemptions. For example, assume a pooled fund has quarterly openings. Fund investors contribute cash prior to the quarterly subscription date, and the firm puts the cash into a temporary new account. On the first day of the quarter, the firm transfers the cash to the fund. The temporary new account used to hold the contributions is not included in any composite or reflected in the pooled fund's performance.

Wrap Fee

Provision 3.A.14

The FIRM MUST include the performance record of actual WRAP FEE PORTFOLIOS in appropriate COMPOSITES in accordance with the FIRM's established PORTFOLIO inclusion policies. Once established, these COMPOSITES (containing actual WRAP FEE PORTFOLIOS) MUST be used when presenting GIPS COMPOSITE REPORTS to WRAP FEE PROSPECTIVE CLIENTS.

Discussion

A wrap fee is a type of bundled fee specific to a particular investment product. The wrap fee is charged by a wrap fee sponsor for investment management services and typically includes associated transaction costs that cannot be separately identified. Wrap fees can be all-inclusive, asset-based fees and may include a combination of investment management fees, transaction costs, custody fees, and/or administrative fees. A wrap fee portfolio is sometimes referred to as a "separately managed account" or "managed account."

Although the firm can use the same investment strategy for both wrap fee and non–wrap fee portfolios, it may not always have a direct relationship with the end user of its investment management services, even though these portfolios are often considered discretionary assets of the firm. Instead, multiple parties are involved in this business model, with a wrap fee sponsor serving as the intermediary between the firm and the end user of investment services. These factors are what distinguishes wrap fee portfolios and necessitates additional guidance for creating and maintaining composites that include wrap fee portfolios.

Prior to Managing Wrap Fee Portfolios

A firm may wish to present performance to wrap fee prospective clients for a specific strategy for which the firm does not yet manage wrap fee portfolios. In such a case, the firm must not present the GIPS Composite Report created for non-wrap fee clients. Instead, the firm must calculate a wrap fee performance history for that specific strategy by using that strategy's gross-of-fees non–wrap fee composite history reduced by the highest total wrap fee charged to the client (end user) by the wrap fee sponsor for the strategy (product). The result is net-of-fees wrap fee performance. Note that this approach is permissible only if the firm has no wrap fee portfolios under management for the strategy during the time periods for which the firm compiles the wrap fee performance using only non–wrap fee portfolios. As stated in Provision 4.A.16, when presenting performance to a wrap fee prospective client, the firm must present the percentage of composite assets represented by wrap fee portfolios as of each annual period end. If there are no wrap fee portfolios in the composite as of the annual period end, then the percentage of composite assets represented by wrap fee portfolios for that year end would be 0%. For an example of a GIPS Composite Report prepared for a wrap fee prospective client prior to the firm's managing actual wrap fee portfolios, please refer to Appendix A.

Once a Firm Acquires One or More Wrap Fee Portfolios

Once a firm acquires one or more wrap fee portfolios for management, the firm must include the performance of the actual wrap fee portfolio(s) in a composite that reflects the specific strategy of the wrap fee portfolios in accordance with the firm's established portfolio inclusion policies. The firm must determine if it will combine wrap fee portfolios in a composite with non–wrap fee portfolios with the same strategy or if it will have a separate composite for non–wrap fee portfolios.

The firm has three options to consider:

1. Retain the calculated history that had been shown to clients prior to the acquisition of a wrap fee portfolio (i.e., the strategy's gross-of-fees non–wrap fee composite history reduced by the total model wrap fee), redefine the composite to include only actual wrap fee portfolios going forward, and include relevant disclosures related to the redefinition;
2. Continue to include the ongoing performance of the non–wrap fee portfolios and combine it with performance of actual wrap fee portfolios; or
3. Create a new composite that includes only wrap fee portfolios. The new composite will have no history prior to the date that wrap fee portfolios are first managed.

When presenting wrap fee performance to wrap fee prospective clients, the firm must choose one of these three options.

Firms must not redefine a composite on a retroactive basis. If a firm has chosen Option 2 and combines the ongoing performance of non–wrap fee portfolios with the performance of wrap fee portfolios, it may not retroactively strip those portfolios out of the composite at a later date in order to create a "wrap fee" composite history. At any point in time, however, the firm may choose to create a new composite that includes only wrap fee portfolios on a prospective basis. This composite would have no history prior to the composite creation date. The firm could then terminate the composite that includes both non-wrap fee portfolios and wrap fee portfolios if it wishes to do so.

The 2010 edition of the GIPS standards included the concept of a sponsor-specific wrap fee composite for the internal use of a wrap fee sponsor only. A sponsor-specific wrap fee composite included only the wrap fee portfolios that were managed for the particular wrap fee sponsor. The concept of sponsor-specific wrap fee composites is considered to be client reporting to a specific wrap fee sponsor and has been eliminated in the 2020 edition of the GIPS standards. A wrap fee composite must include all wrap fee portfolios managed in a specific investment strategy and must not be limited solely to the wrap fee portfolios managed for a specific wrap fee sponsor. Prospective clients for a specific wrap fee strategy must receive information about all portfolios managed in that strategy. Firms that previously maintained sponsor-specific composites would terminate any sponsor-specific wrap fee composites. Firms may remove these composites from the list of composite descriptions and are not required to include them on this list as terminated composites.

Carve-Outs

Provision 3.A.15

Any CARVE-OUT included in a COMPOSITE MUST include cash and any related income. Cash may be:

a. Accounted for separately, or
b. Allocated synthetically to the CARVE-OUT on a timely and consistent basis.

Discussion

A carve-out is a portion of a portfolio that is by itself representative of a distinct investment strategy. It is used to create a track record for a narrower mandate from a multi-strategy or multi-asset-class portfolio managed to a broader mandate. A carve-out is sometimes managed with its own cash. In other cases, cash is synthetically allocated to a carve-out. For periods beginning on or after 1 January 2010, firms were prohibited from including carve-outs with allocated cash in composites. To be included in a composite, a carve-out had to be managed with its own cash. When complying with the 2020 edition of the GIPS standards, firms are once again allowed to include carve-outs with allocated cash in composites and may do so for all periods, both retrospectively and prospectively. A carve-out included in a composite must include cash and any related income, with the cash either accounted for separately or allocated synthetically. If firms choose to synthetically allocate cash to a carve-out, they must do so on a timely and consistent basis and must create carve-outs with allocated cash from all portfolios and portfolio segments within the firm managed to that strategy.

Note that carve-outs managed with their own cash balance are not subject to the requirements that apply to carve-outs with allocated cash. However, if a firm includes a carve-out that is managed with its own cash balance in a composite, all similar carve-outs that have been created and have their own cash balance must also be included in that composite.

The following are some acceptable methods that may be used to allocate cash synthetically to a carve-out:

- *Beginning-of-Period Cash Allocation.* Cash is allocated based on the beginning value of the carve-out as a percentage of the beginning value of the total portfolio excluding cash.
- *Beginning-of-Period Plus Weighted Cash Flow Allocation.* Cash is allocated based on the beginning value plus weighted cash flows of the carve-out as a percentage of the beginning value plus weighted cash flows of the total portfolio, excluding cash.
- *Strategic Asset Cash Allocation (true up actual).* The cash allocation is based directly on the target strategic asset allocation. For example, if the portfolio is targeted to have 40% in equities and 60% in bonds, then the allocation of cash will be the difference between the targeted allocation and the actual allocation. If the portfolio had a target allocation of 40% but at the beginning of the period held only 35% in equities, then the cash allocation would constitute the difference (5%).
- *Strategic Asset Cash Allocation (target weights).* An alternative method for strategic asset cash allocation is to allocate cash solely on the basis of target strategic asset allocation and not on the actual beginning-of-period allocation. In this case, 40% of the cash would be allocated to equities and 60% of the cash to bonds, regardless of the actual beginning-of-period allocation to equities and bonds.

Firms must determine which method to use for each composite, document it in their policies and procedures, and apply the method consistently. In all cases, the cash return must be the portfolio's actual cash return. A cash return proxy must not be used.

It is important for firms to be aware that when calculating returns for carve-outs, cash flows that are considered to be internal cash flows for the total portfolio may need to be treated as external cash flows at the carve-out level. For example, the sale of an equity position would be considered an internal cash flow at the total portfolio level, but it must be treated like an external cash flow when calculating performance at the equity carve-out level (the sold assets transfer out of the equity segment and the cash proceeds are an inflow to the cash segment). Firms must establish policies for carve-outs that address valuation frequency, calculation methods, large cash flows, and significant cash flows.

Provision 3.A.16

Any CARVE-OUT included in a COMPOSITE MUST be representative of a standalone PORTFOLIO managed or intended to be managed according to that strategy.

Discussion

A carve-out is a portion of a portfolio that is by itself representative of a distinct investment strategy. It may be used to create a track record for a narrower mandate from a multi-strategy or multi-asset-class portfolio managed to a broader mandate. A composite is an aggregation of one or more portfolios that are managed according to a similar investment mandate, objective, or strategy. If a firm includes a carve-out in a composite, the firm must believe that the carve-out is representative of a standalone portfolio that is managed or is intended to be managed according to that composite's strategy. (A standalone portfolio is a portfolio that is not a portion of a larger portfolio.) If the carve-out is not representative of the composite's investment strategy, it would be misleading to include the carve-out in the composite.

For example, suppose that a firm manages a global equity strategy. A typical portfolio managed in that strategy holds 100 stocks. The firm decides that it would like to offer a strategy that includes only Japanese equities. Portfolios managed in the global equity strategy currently include holdings of only four Japanese stocks. The firm may not create a carve-out of these four Japanese stocks to represent a Japanese equity strategy. A carve-out representing only four positions in a portfolio of 100 stocks is not representative of a standalone portfolio managed according to a Japanese equity strategy.

In contrast, suppose that the firm manages an Asian equity strategy. A typical portfolio managed in the Asian equity strategy includes 50 stocks, with 30 holdings representing Japanese companies. In this case, a carve-out of the 30 positions representing Japanese companies would likely be representative of a Japanese equity strategy the firm might offer. The number of positions, however, is only one indicator of whether the carve-out would be a representative carve-out. The firm would have to determine that the carve-out is truly representative of the Japanese equity strategy it is planning to offer.

Provision 3.A.17

When the FIRM creates a CARVE-OUT of a particular strategy, allocates cash to the CARVE-OUT, and includes the CARVE-OUT in a COMPOSITE, the FIRM MUST create CARVE-OUTS with allocated cash from all PORTFOLIOS and PORTFOLIO segments within the FIRM managed to that strategy and MUST include those CARVE-OUTS with allocated cash in the COMPOSITE.

Discussion

A carve-out is a portion of a portfolio that is by itself representative of a distinct investment strategy. It may be used to create a track record for a narrower mandate from a multi-strategy or multi-asset-class portfolio managed to a broader mandate. The GIPS standards are based on the principles of fair representation and full disclosure. It would not be in keeping with these principles to "cherry pick" which carve-outs managed to a particular strategy are included in a composite. When a firm creates a carve-out of a particular strategy, allocates cash to the carve-out, and includes the carve-out in a composite, the firm must create carve-outs with allocated cash from all portfolios and portfolio segments within the firm that are managed to that strategy and include all such carve-outs in the relevant composite. This must be done for all periods for which the carve-out is included in the composite.

When creating a composite that includes carve-outs with allocated cash, firms are encouraged to go as far back into the history of the carve-out strategy as possible. The longer the performance history provided for a composite that includes carve-outs with allocated cash, the more representative of the strategy the composite will be. A firm must not select the periods to include in GIPS Reports by cherry-picking periods that present the firm in a better light.

Provision 3.A.18

When the FIRM has or obtains standalone PORTFOLIOS managed in the same strategy as the CARVE-OUTS with allocated cash, the FIRM MUST create a separate COMPOSITE for the standalone PORTFOLIOS.

Discussion

A carve-out is a portion of a portfolio that is by itself representative of a distinct investment strategy. It may be used to create a track record for a narrower mandate from a multi-strategy or multi-asset-class portfolio managed to a broader mandate. At some point, a firm may obtain standalone portfolios managed in the same strategy as the carve-outs with allocated cash. (A standalone portfolio is a portfolio that is not a portion of a larger portfolio.) The firm must then create a separate composite that contains only the standalone portfolios. The returns and composite assets of the composite that includes only standalone portfolios must be presented in the GIPS Composite Report for the composite that includes carve-outs with allocated cash. This presentation will allow a prospective client to compare the returns of the composite that includes carve-outs with allocated cash to the returns of the composite that contains only standalone portfolios. If the two composites have a significant performance difference, the prospective client has a chance to ask questions about the difference in returns. This provision applies only to situations in which the firm has created a composite that includes carve-outs with synthetically allocated cash.

It does not apply to composites in which the carve-outs included are carve-outs with their own cash balance.

Once a firm has obtained one or more standalone portfolios managed in the same style as the carve-outs with allocated cash, the firm has the following options for the maintenance of the composite that includes carve-outs with allocated cash. It can:

- continue to include only carve-outs with allocated cash in the composite;
- include both carve-outs with allocated cash and standalone portfolios in the composite;
- terminate the composite that includes carve-outs with allocated cash and maintain the composite that includes only standalone portfolios managed in the strategy; or
- redefine the composite to exclude carve-outs with allocated cash going forward.

Firms that wish to continue including carve-outs with allocated cash in the composite should also include standalone portfolios in the composite once standalone portfolios are obtained. Although firms are permitted to continue to include only carve-outs with allocated cash in the composite after they have obtained one or more standalone portfolios managed in the same strategy as the carve-outs with allocated cash, it is not encouraged or expected that many firms will do so.

Firms are reminded that, for all cases in which the firm has a composite that includes carve-outs with allocated cash, as well as standalone portfolios managed in the same strategy, the returns and composite assets of the composite that includes only standalone portfolios must be presented in the GIPS Composite Report for the composite that includes carve-outs with allocated cash.

If a carve-out with allocated cash is included in a composite for any period, the words "carve-out" must be indicated in the name of the composite. (See Provisions 4.C.28.a and 5.C.27.a.)

Carve-outs with allocated cash were permitted in composites prior to 1 January 2010 and prohibited from 1 January 2010 through 31 December 2019. Carve-outs with allocated cash are permitted for all periods, both prospectively and retrospectively, for firms that comply with the 2020 edition of the GIPS standards. The following examples provide guidance on what is required regarding the use of carve-outs with allocated cash that were created and used for periods prior to 1 January 2010.

Example 1

A firm used carve-outs with allocated cash for one of its composites from 1 January 2007 through 31 December 2009. Starting 1 January 2010, when carve-outs with allocated cash were no longer permitted in composites, the firm created and used carve-outs with their own cash balance for that strategy. Even though the firm is permitted to use carve-outs with allocated cash once it complies with the 2020 edition of the GIPS standards, the firm will continue to use carve-outs with their own cash balance. The firm will continue to use the track record from carve-outs with allocated cash it had created and used for the periods prior to 1 January 2010. The firm asks whether it has to create a composite of standalone portfolios, as required by Provision 3.A.18, for the period prior to 1 January 2010 when carve-outs with allocated cash are included in the composite.

The firm may use the carve-outs it had created and used for the strategy prior to 1 January 2010 without adhering to Provision 3.A.18 regarding the creation of a separate composite for the strategy containing only standalone portfolios. In addition, the firm is not required to apply Provision 4.C.28.a and 4.C.28.d for GIPS Composite Reports that present time-weighted returns or 5.C.27.a and 5.C.28.d for GIPS Composite Reports that present money-weighted returns. These provisions require the indication of "carve-out" in the name of the composite and a disclosure that a GIPS Composite Report for a composite of standalone portfolios is available upon request. It is important to note that this exception applies only to carve-outs with allocated cash that were previously created and used prior to 1 January 2010. If the firm decides to create and use carve-outs with allocated cash for any periods after 1 January 2010, the requirements regarding the creation and presentation of a composite with standalone portfolios would apply, as would the disclosure requirements.

Example 2

A firm notes that, in the 2020 edition of the GIPS standards, the use of carve-outs with allocated cash is permitted for all time periods. The firm had been using carve-outs with their own cash balances for one of their strategies from 1 January 2010 forward but now decides that it would like to extend its track record for that strategy by creating carve-outs with allocated cash for periods prior to 1 January 2010. It is unable to create carve-outs with their own cash balances for periods prior to that date.

If the firm retroactively creates carve-outs with allocated cash for any period, it must adhere to Provision 3.A.18. If the firm manages standalone portfolios in this strategy, it must create a composite for the standalone portfolios managed in the same strategy as the carve-outs with allocated cash and present the returns and composite assets of the composite that includes only standalone portfolios in the GIPS Composite Report for the carve-outs with allocated cash. The firm must also adhere to the disclosure requirements contained in 4.C.28.a and 4.C.28.d for GIPS Composite Reports that present time-weighted returns, as well as to the disclosure requirements in 5.C.27.a and 5.C.27.d for GIPS Composite Reports that present money-weighted returns.

Provision 3.A.19

The FIRM MUST NOT combine different COMPOSITES, POOLED FUNDS, or CARVE-OUTS to create a simulated strategy and present it as a COMPOSITE.

Discussion

All composite assets must include only actual assets managed by the firm in the respective strategy. (See Provision 2.A.2.) Therefore, a firm must not combine different composites, pooled funds, or carve-outs to create a simulated strategy and present it as a composite. For example, if the performance of actual portfolios in an equity composite is combined with the performance of actual portfolios in a fixed-income composite to show what the results might have been had the equity strategy and fixed-income strategy been combined, the results would be considered a simulated strategy. Even though the returns for the equity and fixed-income composites are based on actual assets managed by the firm, the arbitrary method of combining them historically is subject to manipulation and does not represent real-time, actual asset allocation decisions. The performance results of this simulated strategy would, therefore, be considered hypothetical performance. This would also be true for combinations of different composites, pooled funds, or carve-outs to create a simulated strategy.

A hypothetical blend based on the performance of actual component composites may be included in a GIPS Report as supplemental information only if all the component composites, and the associated GIPS Reports on which the hypothetical blend is based, are included in the GIPS Report. In addition, the hypothetical blend must relate to all composites represented in the GIPS Report. For example, when combining a fixed-income composite and an equity composite to create a balanced portfolio, the blend may be shown as supplemental information in a GIPS Report if it includes the GIPS Report for both the fixed-income composite and the equity composite.

The prohibition against combining different composites, pooled funds, or carve-outs to create a simulated strategy does not prohibit the creation and presentation of composites that are often referred to as "umbrella" or "parent" composites. An umbrella composite is a broadly defined composite that includes portfolios from more narrowly defined composites. Umbrella composites are commonly used for fixed-income composites, in which the umbrella composite is based on the investment mandate and the more narrowly defined subset or "child" composites are based on specific benchmarks. As an example, a firm might have an Intermediate-Maturity Fixed-Income Composite as an umbrella composite that includes all fixed-income portfolios with an intermediate-maturity mandate. A subset composite might include the Intermediate-Maturity ABC Index Composite (all intermediate-maturity fixed-income portfolios with the ABC US Intermediate Aggregate Index as the benchmark) and the Intermediate-Maturity XYZ Index Composite (all intermediate-maturity fixed-income portfolios with the XYZ Intermediate Aggregate Index as the benchmark).

Another example of an umbrella or parent composite would be a Large-Cap Composite that includes all of the firm's large-cap portfolios. Subsets of this composite might include a Large-Cap Growth Composite (all of the firm's large-cap growth portfolios) and a Large-Cap Value Composite (all of the firm's large-cap value portfolios).

3.B. Composite and Pooled Fund Maintenance—Recommendations

Provision 3.B.1

If the FIRM sets a minimum asset level for PORTFOLIOS to be included in a COMPOSITE, the FIRM SHOULD NOT present a GIPS COMPOSITE REPORT to a PROSPECTIVE CLIENT known not to meet the COMPOSITE's minimum asset level.

Discussion

When a firm establishes a minimum asset level for including portfolios in a composite, the firm is indicating that portfolios below that level are too small to be representative of that strategy. In the spirit of fair representation, it would not be in the prospective client's best interest to be shown a GIPS Composite Report for a composite with a strategy that is not available to the prospective client. (See Provision 3.A.11 for a discussion of a composite minimum asset level.)

Provision 3.B.2

To remove the effect of a SIGNIFICANT CASH FLOW, the FIRM SHOULD use a TEMPORARY NEW ACCOUNT.

Discussion

In some situations, a client-directed external cash flow may temporarily prevent a firm from implementing the composite strategy. Firms may choose to keep portfolios that experience such cash flows in the composite. Instead, as discussed in Provision 3.A.12, a firm may establish a significant cash flow policy that allows the firm to remove a portfolio from a composite if it experiences a client-directed external cash flow that may temporarily prevent the firm from implementing the composite strategy. Another method for removing the effect of a significant cash flow, as discussed in Provision 3.A.13, is to use temporary new accounts. If a portfolio experiences a cash inflow that qualifies as a significant cash flow, the firm can create a temporary new account for the inflow of assets. The funds remain in the temporary new account until they are invested and reflect the portfolio's investment mandate. If the portfolio experiences a cash outflow that qualifies as a significant cash flow, the firm can create a temporary new account funded with the assets that the firm will distribute to the client or will liquidate to meet the client's cash flow needs. Significant cash flows are not applicable to composites that present performance using money-weighted returns.

It is recommended that a firm use a temporary new account to remove the effect of a significant cash flow rather than removing the portfolio from the composite. The use of temporary new accounts is the most direct method of dealing with significant cash flows and reduces the movement of portfolios into and out of a composite. Please refer to Provisions 3.A.12 and 3.A.13 for a more detailed discussion of a significant cash flow policy and the creation of temporary new accounts.

4. COMPOSITE TIME-WEIGHTED RETURN REPORT

Firms that prepare a GIPS Composite Report that includes time-weighted returns must include the following required numerical information and disclosures, if applicable to the specific composite.

4.A. Presentation and Reporting—Requirements

Provision 4.A.1

The FIRM MUST present in each GIPS COMPOSITE REPORT:

a. At least five years of performance (or for the period since the COMPOSITE INCEPTION DATE if the COMPOSITE has been in existence less than five years) that meets the REQUIREMENTS of the GIPS standards. After the FIRM presents a minimum of five years of GIPS-compliant performance (or for the period since the COMPOSITE INCEPTION DATE if the COMPOSITE has been in existence less than five years), the FIRM MUST present an additional year of performance each year, building up to a minimum of 10 years of GIPS-compliant performance.

Discussion

To claim compliance, a firm is required to meet all applicable requirements of the GIPS standards on a firm-wide basis for at least a five-year period, or since inception of the firm if the firm has been in existence for less than five years. When initially claiming compliance with the GIPS standards, a firm must present a minimum of five years of composite performance or performance since the inception of the composite if the composite has been in existence for less than five years.

Once the firm has its initial minimum five years of GIPS-compliant history, the firm must continue to add annual returns to each GIPS Composite Report, so that five years after initially claiming compliance with the GIPS standards, the firm will have a 10-year performance record for its composites. It is recommended that firms present a composite's history for more than the minimum required periods. (See Provision 4.B.6.)

Provision 4.A.1

The FIRM MUST present in each GIPS COMPOSITE REPORT:

b. COMPOSITE returns for each annual period.

Discussion

The GIPS standards require the presentation of annual composite returns. Firms must clearly label the annual presentation periods. Firms must define the annual reporting period on a composite-by-composite basis and apply it consistently. For purposes of comparability, best practice would be for a firm to report composite performance on a calendar year-end basis.

Within each GIPS Composite Report, the annual periods must be consistent. For example, a firm that reports a composite's performance annually as of 30 June must consistently report data for years ending 30 June for that composite. The firm may decide in the future to change to a 31 December valuation and reporting date; however, the firm may not mix 30 June and 31 December valuation and reporting dates in the same GIPS Composite Report.

Although the GIPS standards require the presentation of annual returns, it is recommended that firms present more frequent returns, such as quarterly or monthly returns. (See Provision 4.B.2.c.) More frequent returns help prospective clients evaluate a composite's track record.

Composite returns may be presented either gross-of-fees or net-of-fees, with one exception. Wrap fee composite returns must be presented net of the entire wrap fee. Firms may also choose to present both gross-of-fees and net-of fees composite returns in a GIPS Composite Report.

Provision 4.A.1

The FIRM MUST present in each GIPS COMPOSITE REPORT:

c. When the initial period is less than a full year, the return from the COMPOSITE INCEPTION DATE through the initial annual period end.[29]

Discussion

When a composite has an initial period that is less than a full year, the GIPS standards require that the return be presented for the partial year from the composite inception date through the initial

[29] REQUIRED for COMPOSITES with a COMPOSITE INCEPTION DATE of 1 January 2011 or later.

 |

annual period end. This is required for composites that begin on or after 1 January 2011. Although not required to do so for composites that begin prior to this date, firms should consider presenting the initial partial year of performance for all composites.

For example, assume that a firm presents composite returns for annual periods ended 31 December, and a new composite is created with a track record beginning 1 April 2018. The initial GIPS Composite Report for this composite must include the composite return for the period from 1 April 2018 through 31 December 2018. Subsequently, the firm must add annual returns, building up to a minimum 10-year track record.

Partial-year returns must not be annualized. As an example, a composite that began on 1 December 2020 and has a one-month initial return through 31 December 2020 of 3% (which equates to an annualized return of 42.6%) would be required to present that 3% as the partial year's performance. The annualized return of 42.6% must not be presented. Some spreadsheet and software applications automatically annualize all returns, and firms are reminded that for periods of less than a year, the firm must "de-annualize" any annualized returns that are calculated.

The method chosen to de-annualize a return is at the discretion of the firm, but it must be a geometric calculation. In the situation just presented, the 42.6% annualized return could be de-annualized by one of the following formulas:

$$\left\{\left[(1+0.426)^{\left(\frac{1}{12}\right)}\right]-1\right\}\times 100 = 3\% \quad \textit{or} \quad \left\{\left[(1+0.426)^{\left(\frac{31}{365}\right)}\right]-1\right\}\times 100 = 3\%,$$

both resulting in a non-annualized one-month return of 3%.

Provision 4.A.1

The FIRM MUST present in each GIPS COMPOSITE REPORT:

d. When the COMPOSITE terminates, the return from the last annual period end through the COMPOSITE TERMINATION DATE.[30]

Discussion

The GIPS standards require that returns from the last annual period end through the composite termination date be presented for composites with a termination date of 1 January 2011 or later. Assume that a firm presents composite returns for annual periods ended 31 December and a composite terminates so that the track record ends 31 August 2017. The GIPS Composite Report

[30] REQUIRED for COMPOSITES with a COMPOSITE TERMINATION DATE of 1 January 2011 or later.

for this composite must include the composite return for the period from 1 January 2017 through 31 August 2017. Partial-year returns must not be annualized. As an example, a composite that terminates on 31 January 2020 and has a one-month return for January 2020 of 3% (which equates to an annualized return of 42.6%) would be required to present that 3% as the partial year's performance. The annualized return of 42.6% must not be presented. Some spreadsheet and software applications automatically annualize all returns, and firms are reminded that for periods of less than a year, the firm must "de-annualize" any annualized returns that are calculated.

The method chosen to de-annualize a return is at the discretion of the firm, but it must be a geometric calculation. In the situation just presented, the 42.6% annualized return could be de-annualized by one of the following formulas:

$$\left\{\left[(1+0.426)^{\left(\frac{1}{12}\right)}\right]-1\right\}\times 100=3\% \quad or \quad \left\{\left[(1+0.426)^{\left(\frac{31}{365}\right)}\right]-1\right\}\times 100=3\%,$$

both resulting in a non-annualized one-month return of 3%.

Provision 4.A.1

The FIRM MUST present in each GIPS COMPOSITE REPORT:

e. The TOTAL RETURN for the BENCHMARK for each annual period and for all other periods for which COMPOSITE returns are presented, unless the FIRM determines there is no appropriate BENCHMARK.

Discussion

Benchmarks are important tools that aid in the planning, implementation, and evaluation of a portfolio's investment policy. They also help facilitate discussions with prospective clients regarding the relationship between risk and return. As a result, firms are required to present a total return for the benchmark that reflects the composite's investment mandate, objective, or strategy for each annual period. A firm may choose to present more than one benchmark in a GIPS Composite Report and, if it does so, it must include all required information for all benchmarks included in a GIPS Composite Report.

In addition to the required annual benchmark returns, firms must also present benchmark returns for the same periods for which composite returns are presented. For example, if the GIPS Composite Report includes quarterly composite returns, quarterly benchmark returns must also be included.

Because the GIPS standards require that the total return for the benchmark be presented, a price-only index would not satisfy the requirements of the GIPS standards. This scenario also applies to benchmarks that are components of a blended benchmark. A price-only benchmark may be presented in a GIPS Composite Report as supplemental information only if it is presented in addition to a total return benchmark. It must be labeled as a price-only benchmark, and there must be sufficient disclosures so that a prospective client understands the difference between the return of a price-only benchmark and the return of a total return benchmark. Firms must not present only a price-only benchmark even if no appropriate total return benchmark is available for a specific strategy. If a firm determines that no appropriate benchmark for the composite exists, it must not present a benchmark and must disclose why no benchmark is presented. (See Provision 4.C.31.)

Some benchmarks, such as commodity benchmarks, may not have income because the asset class does not create income, but they are still considered to be total return benchmarks. Target returns, such as an 8% hurdle rate, may also not have income, but this is not considered a price-only return.

Provision 4.A.1

The FIRM MUST present in each GIPS COMPOSITE REPORT:

f. The number of PORTFOLIOS in the COMPOSITE as of each annual period end. If the COMPOSITE contains five or fewer PORTFOLIOS at period end, the number of PORTFOLIOS is not REQUIRED.

Discussion

Each GIPS Composite Report must include information about the number of portfolios included in the composite. These figures must be presented as of the end of each annual period that is included in the GIPS Composite Report. This requirement provides information to prospective clients on whether the composite is composed of a small number of portfolios or many. In cases where there are five portfolios or fewer in a composite at period end, the firm may choose to not present the number of portfolios in the composite. The firm might choose to do this to protect the identity and confidentiality of its clients. Because firms must present information about the number of portfolios in the composite, however, firms must either (1) state that the composite contains "five or fewer portfolios," "less than six portfolios," or use similar language, or (2) present the actual number of portfolios in the composite. (See Provision 4.C.39.)

Note that "five or fewer portfolios in the composite" refers to the number of portfolios in the composite at the annual period end and not the number of portfolios in the composite for the full year. For example, if there were four portfolios in the composite for the full year but eight portfolios in the composite at year end, the firm would present eight, the actual number of portfolios in the composite at year end. The number of portfolios in the composite also must not include those portfolios that are joining the composite as of the next period. For example, assume a firm reports performance on a calendar year basis. A new portfolio that is funded during December and will be included in the composite beginning 1 January must not be included in the number of portfolios in the composite as of 31 December.

Provision 4.A.1

The FIRM MUST present in each GIPS COMPOSITE REPORT:

g. COMPOSITE assets as of each annual period end.

Discussion

Each GIPS Composite Report must include the amount of composite assets as of the end of each annual period that is included in the GIPS Composite Report. This requirement provides information to prospective clients on the size of the composite, measured by the amount of assets it contains. When the composite strategy uses discretionary leverage, composite assets must be presented net of the discretionary leverage and not grossed up as if the discretionary leverage did not exist. Discretionary leverage refers to loans taken at the discretion of the firm. In contrast, non-discretionary leverage refers to borrowings that are mandated by the client. For example, if a composite has $200 million in assets, including $50 million of assets borrowed by the firm, the composite's net assets are $200 million and its gross assets are $250 million. When calculating composite assets, the firm must use $200 million.

If a portfolio is temporarily excluded from a composite because of the composite's minimum asset size policy or significant cash flow policy, or is excluded for any other reason, the portfolio's assets would not be included in composite assets for the period(s) for which the portfolio was excluded. However, the portfolio's assets would be included in total firm assets for all periods for which the portfolio is under management, whether or not it is excluded from the composite. Composite assets do not include assets of those portfolios that are joining the composite as of the next period. For example, assume a firm reports performance on a calendar year basis. A new portfolio that is funded during December and will be included in the composite beginning 1 January must not be included in composite assets as of 31 December.

Provision 4.A.1

The FIRM MUST present in each GIPS COMPOSITE REPORT:

h. TOTAL FIRM ASSETS as of each annual period end.[31]

[31] REQUIRED for periods ending on or after 31 December 2020. For periods ending prior to 31 December 2020, the FIRM may present either TOTAL FIRM ASSETS or COMPOSITE assets as a percentage of TOTAL FIRM ASSETS.

 |

Discussion

For annual periods ending on or after 31 December 2020, the firm must present total firm assets as of each annual period end. For annual periods ending prior to this date, the firm must present either total firm assets or composite assets as a percentage of total firm assets. Discretionary leverage must be deducted when calculating total firm assets. Discretionary leverage refers to loans taken at the discretion of the firm. In contrast, non-discretionary leverage refers to borrowings that are mandated by the client. For example, if a composite has $200 million in assets, including $50 million borrowed by the firm, the firm must use $200 million when calculating total firm assets, not $250 million. The inclusion of both composite assets and total firm assets in a GIPS Composite Report will help a prospective client understand the composite size in relation to total firm assets.

Non-discretionary portfolios that are excluded from composites are included in total firm assets. Portfolios that are temporarily excluded from a composite because of the composite's minimum asset size policy or significant cash flow policy, or are excluded for any other reason, are also included in total firm assets.

Firms must be sure that assets are not double-counted because counting assets more than once would not fairly represent total firm assets.

See the discussion of Provision 2.A.1 for additional guidance on the calculation of total firm assets.

Provision 4.A.1

The FIRM MUST present in each GIPS COMPOSITE REPORT:

i. A measure of INTERNAL DISPERSION of individual PORTFOLIO annual returns for each annual period. If the COMPOSITE contains five or fewer PORTFOLIOS for the full year, a measure of INTERNAL DISPERSION is not REQUIRED.

Discussion

Internal dispersion is a measure of the spread of the annual returns of individual portfolios within a composite. It allows prospective clients to determine how consistently the firm implemented its strategy across the portfolios in the composite for the full annual period. Internal dispersion measures include high–low, range, quartiles, interquartile range, or standard deviation (asset weighted or equal weighted) of portfolio returns as well as other statistical measures.

The GIPS standards do not require or recommend a specific measure to calculate internal dispersion. Instead, the firm is permitted to choose a measure for each composite and apply it consistently. The firm may change which internal dispersion measure is presented for a specific composite but should apply a measure consistently once it is adopted. A widely used internal dispersion measure is standard deviation. Firms are required to disclose which internal dispersion measure is presented.

Because the internal dispersion measure represents the spread of annual returns of individual portfolios within the composite for the full year, only the portfolios that have been managed for the full annual period are included in the internal dispersion calculation. Firms must identify the portfolios in the composite that have been included for the full annual period and calculate the annual return for each of those portfolios. Firms must use those annual returns to calculate the composite's internal dispersion. The GIPS standards acknowledge that, by using only portfolios that have been included in the composite for the full year in the annual internal dispersion calculation, the internal dispersion number will not precisely correlate with the actual composite performance but will inform a prospective client of the dispersion of annual returns of those portfolios included in the composite for the year.

If the firm presents only gross-of-fees returns in the GIPS Composite Report, the firm should use gross-of-fees returns to calculate the internal dispersion measure. If the firm presents only net-of-fees returns in the GIPS Composite Report, the firm should use net-of-fees returns to calculate the internal dispersion measure. If the firm presents both gross-of-fees and net-of-fees returns, it is recommended that the firm use gross-of-fees returns to calculate the internal dispersion measure. (See Provision 2.B.7.) The firm must disclose which returns (gross-of-fees or net-of-fees) are used to calculate the internal dispersion measure. (See Provision 4.C.44.)

The internal dispersion of the individual portfolio returns must be presented for each annual period that is included in the GIPS Composite Report. In cases where there are five or fewer portfolios in a composite for the full annual period, the measure of internal dispersion is not required to be presented. Because firms must include information about the internal dispersion of individual portfolio returns, however, firms must indicate that the internal dispersion measure is not applicable or include other similar language. (See Provision 4.C.40.)

The following are explanations of commonly used measures of internal dispersion.

Equal-Weighted Standard Deviation

A widely used measure of internal dispersion is the standard deviation across equal-weighted annual portfolio returns. The formula is as follows:

$$\text{Equal-weighted standard deviation} = \sqrt{\frac{\Sigma\left[R_{PORTi} - MEAN(R)\right]^2}{n}},$$

where R_{PORTi} is the annual return on the ith portfolio that has been in the composite for the full annual period, n is the number of portfolios in the composite for the full annual period (the use of n is best practice and preferable, but either n or $n - 1$ in the denominator of the standard deviation calculation is acceptable), and $MEAN(R)$ is the equal-weighted mean return of the portfolios in the composite for the full annual period, where

$$MEAN\ (R) = \frac{R_{PORT1} + R_{PORT2} + \ldots + R_{PORTi}}{n},$$

where R_{PORT1} is the time-weighted return for the first portfolio in the composite for the full annual period, R_{PORTi} is the time-weighted return for the ith portfolio in the composite for the full annual period, and n is the number of portfolios in the composite for the full annual period. Because only portfolios that are included in the composite for the full annual period are included in the internal dispersion calculation, n may be different from the number of portfolios at period end shown in the GIPS Composite Report.

Asset-Weighted Standard Deviation

Another widely used measure of internal dispersion is the asset-weighted standard deviation of annual portfolio returns. The formula is as follows:

$$\text{Asset-weighted standard deviation} = \sqrt{\Sigma W_i \left[R_{PORTi} - \left(\Sigma W_i R_{PORTi} \right) \right]^2},$$

where W_i is the individual portfolio weight and R_{PORTi} is the individual portfolio annual return.

High–Low and Range

The high–low and the range are the simplest and most easily understood measures of internal dispersion. Their key advantages are simplicity, ease of calculation, and ease of interpretation. One disadvantage of these measures is that one extreme value or outlier can skew the internal dispersion measure.

Interquartile Range

Another measure of internal dispersion is the interquartile range, which measures the difference between the median value of ranked data sets Q_1 and Q_3.

$$\text{Interquartile range: } Q_R = Q_1 - Q_3$$

where

Q_1 = first or upper quartile return

Q_3 = third or lower quartile return

The following is an example of the calculation of the various internal dispersion measures.

Firm A has a composite that consists of 15 portfolios. Ten of the portfolios have been in the composite for the entire year.

	A	B	C	D	E	F	G	H	I	J
1	Portfolio	BMV	Annual Return	Weight (BMV)	Contribution (BMV)	Difference to Equal Weighted Mean	Squared Difference (equal weighted mean)	Difference to Asset Weighted Mean	Squared Difference (asset weighted mean)	Weighted Squared Difference
2	1	100,000	5.2%	3.85%	0.20%	0.07%	0.0000%	0.02%	0.0000%	0.0000%
3	2	300,000	4.9%	11.54%	0.57%	-0.23%	0.0005%	-0.28%	0.0008%	0.0001%
4	3	200,000	5.5%	7.69%	0.42%	0.37%	0.0014%	0.32%	0.0010%	0.0001%
5	4	500,000	5.6%	19.23%	1.08%	0.47%	0.0022%	0.42%	0.0018%	0.0003%
6	5	100,000	5.1%	3.85%	0.20%	-0.03%	0.0000%	-0.08%	0.0001%	0.0000%
7	6	250,000	4.7%	9.62%	0.45%	-0.43%	0.0018%	-0.48%	0.0023%	0.0002%
8	7	450,000	5.2%	17.31%	0.90%	0.07%	0.0000%	0.02%	0.0000%	0.0000%
9	8	200,000	4.8%	7.69%	0.37%	-0.33%	0.0011%	-0.38%	0.0014%	0.0001%
10	9	300,000	5.3%	11.54%	0.61%	0.17%	0.0003%	0.12%	0.0001%	0.0000%
11	10	200,000	5.0%	7.69%	0.38%	-0.13%	0.0002%	-0.18%	0.0003%	0.0000%
12	Sample formulas for portfolio 10			=B11/B13	=C11*D11	=(C11-D16)	=F11^2	=(C11-E13)	=H11^2	=D11*I11
13	Sum (Portfolios 1–10)	2,600,000		100.00%	5.18%					0.0009%
14										
15	Asset Weighted Mean			5.18%	=E13					
16	Equal Weighted Mean			5.13%	=AVERAGE(C2:C11)					
17	Count of Portfolios			10	=COUNT(C2:C11)					
18	Sum of Squared Differences (to equal weighted mean)			0.0076%	=SUM(G2:G11)					
19	Sum of Squared Differences (to asset weighted mean)			0.0078%	=SUM(I2:I11)					
20	Equal Weighted Standard Deviation			0.2759%	=SQRT(D18/D17)					
21	Asset Weighted Standard Deviation			0.2976%	=SQRT(J13)					
22	High			5.6%	=MAX(C2:C11)					
23	Low			4.7%	=MIN(C2:C11)					
24	Range			0.9%	=D22-D23					
25	First Quartile Return			5.3%	=QUARTILE(C2:C11,3)					
26	Third Quartile Return			4.9%	=QUARTILE(C2:C11,1)					
27	Interquartile Range			0.4%	=D25-D26					

 |

Provision 4.A.1

The FIRM MUST present in each GIPS COMPOSITE REPORT:

j. For COMPOSITES for which monthly COMPOSITE returns are available, the three-year annualized EX POST STANDARD DEVIATION (using monthly returns) of the COMPOSITE and the BENCHMARK as of each annual period end.[32]

Discussion

Evaluating past performance requires an understanding of the risks taken to achieve the results. Standard deviation is universally defined as a measure of the variability of returns. For composites for which monthly returns are available, the GIPS standards require the presentation of ex post standard deviation, often referred to as external standard deviation. Ex post standard deviation is a measure of the volatility of a strategy and benchmark over time, and it is intended to measure the risk of investing in the strategy. In contrast, internal standard deviation, discussed in Provision 4.A.1.i, is used to measure the dispersion of portfolio returns within a composite. For periods ending on or after 1 January 2011, firms must present, as of each annual period end, the three-year annualized ex post standard deviation using monthly returns for both the composite and the benchmark.

Standard deviation for both the composite and the benchmark must be calculated using 36 monthly returns. The same formula must be used to calculate standard deviation for the composite and the benchmark.

Some composites, such as those for private market investments, may not have monthly returns. For these composites, if the composite has at least three annual periods of performance, firms must disclose if the three-year annualized ex post standard deviation of the composite and/or benchmark is not presented because 36 monthly returns are not available. (See Provision 4.C.36.)

Ex Post Standard Deviation (External)

Ex post standard deviation is calculated as follows:

$$\text{Composite or benchmark ex post standard deviation} = \sqrt{\frac{\Sigma\left[R_i - MEAN(R)\right]^2}{n}},$$

where R_i is the return on the *i*th monthly composite or benchmark return, n is the number of monthly returns used for the external standard deviation calculation (the use of n is best practice and preferable, but either n or $n - 1$ in the denominator of the standard deviation calculation is

[32] REQUIRED for periods ending on or after 1 January 2011.

acceptable), and *MEAN*(*R*) is the mean monthly return of the composite or the benchmark over the period for which the external standard deviation is being calculated, where

$$MEAN(R) = \frac{R_1 + R_2 + \ldots + R_i}{n},$$

where R_1 is the time-weighted return for the first monthly composite or benchmark return, R_i is the *i*th monthly composite or benchmark return, and n is the number of returns used in the calculation (required to be 36 monthly returns to satisfy this requirement).

Firms are required to select a methodology (i.e., the use of n or $n - 1$) on a composite-specific basis, document it in their policies and procedures, and consistently apply that methodology.

To annualize the three-year ex post standard deviation calculated using monthly returns, the result of the foregoing standard deviation formula must be multiplied by the square root of 12.

If the firm presents only gross-of-fees returns in the GIPS Composite Report, the firm should use gross-of-fees returns to calculate the external standard deviation. If a firm presents only net-of-fees returns in the GIPS Composite Report, the firm should use net-of-fees returns to calculate the external standard deviation. If the firm presents both gross-of-fees and net-of-fees returns, it is recommended that the firm use gross-of-fees returns to calculate the external standard deviation. (See Provision 2.B.7.) The firm must disclose which returns (gross-of-fees or net-of-fees) were used to calculate the external standard deviation. (See Provision 4.C.44.)

Provision 4.A.2

The FIRM MUST present the percentage of the total FAIR VALUE of COMPOSITE assets that were valued using subjective unobservable inputs (as described in Provision 2.B.6.e) as of the most recent annual period end, if such investments represent a material amount of COMPOSITE assets.

Discussion

Markets are not always liquid, and investment prices are not always objective and/or observable. As the last level of the recommended valuation hierarchy indicates (see Provision 2.B.6), it may be necessary for a firm to use subjective unobservable inputs to value an investment for which markets are not active at the measurement date. Examples of subjective unobservable inputs include an assumed discount rate, an assumed occupancy rate for a commercial building, and the default rate used for the valuation of a security in default. Examples related to insurance-linked securities include assumptions regarding hurricane damage and mortality rates. Unobservable inputs should be used to measure fair value only when observable inputs and prices are not available or appropriate. Unobservable inputs reflect the firm's own assumptions about the assumptions that market participants would use in pricing the investment and should be developed based on the best information available under the circumstances.

Firms must present the percentage of the total fair value of composite assets that were valued using subjective unobservable inputs as of the most recent annual period end, if such investments represent a material amount of composite assets. The amount of composite assets valued using subjective unobservable inputs would be considered material if it would likely influence a reader's judgment regarding the reliability of the valuation. The firm must decide on the criteria it will use to determine when subjective unobservable inputs represent a material amount of composite assets, include these criteria in its policy and procedures, and apply these criteria consistently.

Sample Disclosure:

"As of 31 December 2020, 29% of composite assets were valued using subjective, unobservable inputs. These inputs are not supported by market activity and instead are based on internal proprietary pricing models."

Provision 4.A.3

The FIRM MUST clearly label or identify:

a. The periods that are presented.
b. If COMPOSITE returns are GROSS-OF-FEES or NET-OF-FEES.

Discussion

All periods presented in a GIPS Composite Report must be clearly labeled or identified. This includes annual periods, partial-year periods, and any additional periods presented.

Firms may present either gross-of-fees composite returns or net-of-fees composite returns in a GIPS Composite Report and may also choose to present both gross-of-fees and net-of-fees returns. For prospective clients to understand the nature of the returns being presented, all returns presented must be clearly labeled or identified as gross-of-fees or net-of-fees.

Provision 4.A.4

If the FIRM includes more than one BENCHMARK in the GIPS COMPOSITE REPORT, the FIRM MUST present and disclose all REQUIRED information for all BENCHMARKS presented.

Discussion

It is permissible to include more than one benchmark in a GIPS Composite Report. All benchmarks included in a GIPS Composite Report must adhere to the requirements of the GIPS standards that are applicable to benchmarks. Firms may label benchmarks as primary and secondary benchmarks, but the same requirements and recommendations apply to all benchmarks included in a GIPS Composite Report. For example, a GIPS Composite Report must include:

- a description for all benchmarks
- a disclosure of changes to (or deletion of) any benchmark
- the three-year annualized ex post standard deviation of all benchmarks

If the firm designates benchmarks as primary and secondary benchmarks, it must disclose when these designations change (e.g., if a primary benchmark becomes a secondary benchmark), because such a change in designation is considered a benchmark change. In all instances, if multiple benchmarks are presented in a GIPS Composite Report and one or more of the benchmarks is removed from the GIPS Composite Report, the firm must disclose this fact.

An appropriate benchmark for a composite reflects the investment mandate, strategy, or objective of the composite. Additional benchmarks beyond appropriate benchmarks may be presented in a GIPS Composite Report as supplemental information. There must be sufficient disclosure so that a prospective client or prospective investor understands the nature of the benchmark and why it is being presented. Disclosure, however, does not necessarily prevent information from being false or misleading. An additional benchmark must never be presented for the sole purpose of providing a favorable comparison to the performance of the composite. To do so would be misleading, regardless of the disclosures accompanying the benchmark.

Provision 4.A.5

If the COMPOSITE loses all of its member PORTFOLIOS, the COMPOSITE track record MUST end. If PORTFOLIOS are later added to the COMPOSITE, the COMPOSITE track record MUST restart. The periods both before and after the break in track record MUST be presented, with the break in performance clearly shown. The FIRM MUST NOT LINK performance prior to the break in track record to the performance after the break in track record.

Discussion

If all of the portfolios in a composite are either terminated or removed from the composite for some other reason, such as the application of a minimum account size or significant cash flow policy, the composite's performance record would come to an end. After a period of time, portfolios may move above the minimum or new portfolios may be added to the composite, and the composite's performance record would begin again. In such a case, there will be a break in the composite's performance record. The composite's prior performance history must not be linked to the ongoing composite performance results. A firm must not use the performance of a benchmark to link the performance track record from before and after the break in the composite's track record. Any performance table in a GIPS Report must clearly indicate the break.

For firms that claim compliance for a period longer than 10 years, if the break in performance occurred more than 10 years ago, the performance prior to the break does not need to be presented. In all other cases, the firm must present the performance both prior to and after the performance break.

If a firm is also presenting a since-inception money-weighted return (SI-MWR) and there is a break in performance, the SI-MWR must not be calculated across the break. A current SI-MWR must be calculated using only the performance after the break. If the break in performance occurred less than 10 years ago, and it occurred during the period for which the firm claims compliance, an SI-MWR from the beginning of the track record up until the break must also be presented. The current SI-MWR and the SI-MWR representing performance prior to the break must not be linked and must be presented separately. The SI-MWRs before and after the break in performance must be clearly labeled so a prospective client or prospective investor can understand the periods reflected in the two returns.

Consider the following example for a firm that calculates performance on a monthly basis:

The firm has a composite that temporarily lost all of its portfolio members, resulting in a break in performance. The inception date for the composite is 1 January 2014, and there were four portfolios in the composite on 31 July 2015. During August 2015, two portfolios were liquidated and two fell below the minimum account size, leaving the composite with no portfolios. During April 2016, the two portfolios that had previously fallen below the composite minimum finally exceeded the minimum account size and were added back to the composite as of 1 May 2016, effectively reinstating the composite's performance. During 2017, three new portfolios were added to the composite.

Because all of the portfolios in the composite were either terminated or fell below the minimum level and, according to the firm's policies, were removed from the composite, the performance record of the composite comes to an end as of 31 July 2015. The performance record begins again on 1 May 2016 when two portfolios again met the minimum size criterion and were added back to the composite. When presenting the performance of this composite, the prior performance history of the composite through 31 July 2015 must be shown but must not be linked to the ongoing composite performance results beginning 1 May 2016.

For the purpose of performance presentation, as of 31 December 2017, the composite had an uninterrupted performance track record from 1 January 2014 to 31 July 2015, a performance break from 1 August 2015 to 30 April 2016, and an uninterrupted performance track record from 1 May 2016 to 31 December 2017.

Under the principles of fair representation and full disclosure, the GIPS standards require firms to handle such cases with the highest transparency. In this instance, the firm must present both periods of performance. The periods before and after the break must be presented separately. The GIPS Composite Report could present the information in this scenario as follows:

Period	Period Returns (%)		Internal Dispersion (%)	Number of Portfolios as of Period End	Assets as of Period End (USD millions)	
	Composite (gross of fees)	Benchmark			Composite	Total Firm
1 Jan–31 Dec 2017	X%	X%	X%	5	X	X
1 May–31 Dec 2016*	X%	X%	–	2	X	X
1 Jan–31 Jul 2015*	X%	X%	–	–	–	–
1 Jan–31 Dec 2014	X%	X%	X%	4	X	X

* There were no portfolios in the composite from 1 August 2015 through 30 April 2016.

It is important that the composite data is presented in a way that makes it clear that there were no portfolios in the composite from 1 August 2015 through 30 April 2016 and that the performance presented in the GIPS Composite Report is not linked across the break. The periods presented must be clearly labeled.

Although the firm may present a cumulative return for the period from 1 January 2014 through 31 July 2015, it must not link periods across performance breaks and present a cumulative and/or annualized return over such periods (e.g., from 1 January 2014 to 31 December 2017). The same would apply to the presentation of any required or recommended risk measures based on cumulative periods (e.g., three-year annualized ex post standard deviation).

The firm may not choose to omit performance for the incomplete years (e.g., for 2015 and 2016 in the previous example) because they are not annual returns. Such an interpretation would not meet the goals of fair representation and full disclosure.

Provision 4.A.6

If the COMPOSITE includes CARVE-OUTS with allocated cash, the FIRM MUST present the percentage of COMPOSITE assets represented by CARVE-OUTS with allocated cash as of each annual period end.

Discussion

A carve-out is a portion of a portfolio that is, by itself, representative of a distinct investment strategy, such as the domestic equity portion of a balanced portfolio. A carve-out may have its own dedicated cash balance, or cash may be allocated to the carve-out synthetically. With the issuance of the 2020 edition of the GIPS standards, firms are once again allowed to include carve-outs that include cash that has been allocated synthetically in composites. (Doing so was prohibited from 1 January 2010 through 31 December 2019.)

A composite that includes carve-outs with allocated cash may also include carve-outs with their own cash balance and standalone portfolios. (A standalone portfolio is a portfolio that is not a portion of a larger portfolio.) Because prospective clients should have sufficient information to understand the nature of the portfolios included in a composite, a firm must, therefore, present the percentage of composite assets represented by carve-outs with allocated cash as of each annual period end. Carve-outs with their own dedicated cash are not included in this percentage. This approach allows prospective clients to understand how much of the composite's assets are represented by standalone portfolios and/or by carve-outs with their own cash and how much of the composite's assets are represented by carve-outs with allocated cash. Provision 4.A.6 applies only to carve-outs with allocated cash. It does not apply to carve-outs with their own dedicated cash.

Provision 4.A.7

If the COMPOSITE includes non-fee-paying PORTFOLIOS, the FIRM MUST present the percentage of COMPOSITE assets represented by non-fee-paying PORTFOLIOS as of each annual period end when NET-OF-FEES returns are presented and are calculated using actual INVESTMENT MANAGEMENT FEES.

Discussion

A firm may choose whether or not to include non-fee-paying portfolios in composites. This decision may be made on a composite-by-composite basis. If the firm has chosen to include a non-fee-paying portfolio in a composite, it must also include all other non-fee-paying discretionary portfolios meeting the definition of the composite. (See Provision 3.A.4 for further guidance on non-fee-paying portfolios.)

If a firm has included non-fee-paying portfolios in a composite and is presenting net-of-fees returns that are calculated using actual investment management fees, the firm is required to present the percentage of composite assets represented by non-fee-paying portfolios as of each annual period end. This may be done as a written disclosure, such as "This composite contained 15% non-fee-paying portfolios as of 31 December 2015, 17% as of 31 December 2016, 5% as of 31 December 2017, and 2% as of 31 December 2018." Alternatively, the firm could add a column to its performance table titled "% composite assets composed of non-fee-paying portfolios" and list the percentage at the end of each annual period.

If the composite contains non-fee-paying portfolios but only gross-of-fees returns are presented, or if model fees are used to calculate composite net-of-fees returns, this information is not required to be presented. This guidance differs from the requirement in the 2010 edition of the GIPS standards, which required this information to be presented whenever a composite included non-fee-paying portfolios. Firms may apply this current guidance to all periods presented in GIPS Composite Reports.

Provision 4.A.8

If the FIRM chooses to present COMPOSITE uncalled COMMITTED CAPITAL or a combination of COMPOSITE assets and COMPOSITE uncalled COMMITTED CAPITAL, the FIRM MUST:

a. Present COMPOSITE uncalled COMMITTED CAPITAL for the same periods for which the combination of COMPOSITE assets and COMPOSITE uncalled COMMITTED CAPITAL is presented.
b. Clearly label COMPOSITE uncalled COMMITTED CAPITAL as such.
c. Clearly label the combination of COMPOSITE assets and COMPOSITE uncalled COMMITTED CAPITAL as such.

Discussion

Committed capital is defined as pledges of capital to an investment vehicle by investors (limited partners and the general partner) or the firm and is typically drawn down over a period of time. Uncalled committed capital is the amount of capital that has not yet been drawn. Because uncalled committed capital is not considered actual composite assets, composite uncalled committed capital must not be included in the calculation of composite assets as of 1 January 2020. This is consistent with the requirement to not include uncalled committed capital in total firm assets for periods beginning on or after 1 January 2020. (See Provision 2.A.1.) A firm may report composite uncalled committed capital in addition to the required presentation of composite assets, if it wishes to do so. The inclusion of information on composite uncalled committed capital provides prospective clients with a more complete picture of the firm's investments and the amount of capital that is currently committed to a future investment. If a firm chooses to present information on composite uncalled committed capital, it may present composite uncalled committed capital as either:

- a separate value, or
- the combination of composite assets and composite uncalled committed capital.

If a firm chooses to present composite uncalled committed capital as a separate value, the information must be clearly labeled.

If a firm chooses to present the combination of composite assets and composite uncalled committed capital, the firm must present composite uncalled committed capital for the same periods for which the combination of composite assets and composite uncalled committed capital is presented. Both composite uncalled committed capital and the combination of composite assets and composite uncalled committed capital must be clearly labeled as such.

Provision 4.A.9

If the FIRM chooses to present FIRM-wide uncalled COMMITTED CAPITAL or a combination of TOTAL FIRM ASSETS and FIRM-wide uncalled COMMITTED CAPITAL, the FIRM MUST:

a. Present FIRM-wide uncalled COMMITTED CAPITAL for the same periods for which the combination of TOTAL FIRM ASSETS and FIRM-wide uncalled COMMITTED CAPITAL is presented.

b. Clearly label FIRM-wide uncalled COMMITTED CAPITAL as such.

c. Clearly label the combination of TOTAL FIRM ASSETS and FIRM-wide uncalled COMMITTED CAPITAL as such.

Discussion

Committed capital is defined as pledges of capital to an investment vehicle by investors (limited partners and the general partner) or the firm and is typically drawn down over a period of time. Uncalled committed capital is the amount of capital that has not yet been drawn. For periods beginning on or after 1 January 2020, uncalled committed capital must not be included in total firm assets. (See Provision 2.A.1.) Although firm-wide uncalled committed capital must not be included in the calculation of total firm assets as of 1 January 2020, a firm may report firm-wide uncalled committed capital in addition to the required presentation of total firm assets, if it wishes to do so. The inclusion of information on firm-wide uncalled committed capital provides prospective clients with a more complete picture of the firm's investments and the amount of capital that is currently committed to a future investment. If a firm chooses to present information on firm-wide uncalled committed capital, it may present firm-wide uncalled committed capital as either:

- a separate value, or
- the combination of total firm assets and firm-wide uncalled committed capital.

If a firm chooses to present firm-wide uncalled committed capital as a separate value, the information must be clearly labeled.

If a firm chooses to present the combination of total firm assets and firm-wide uncalled committed capital, the firm must present firm-wide uncalled committed capital for the same periods for which the combination of total firm assets and firm-wide uncalled committed capital is presented. Both firm-wide uncalled committed capital and the combination of total firm assets and firm-wide uncalled committed capital must be clearly labeled as such.

Provision 4.A.10

If the FIRM chooses to present ADVISORY-ONLY ASSETS that reflect the COMPOSITE's investment mandate, objective, or strategy, or a combination of COMPOSITE assets and ADVISORY-ONLY ASSETS that reflect the COMPOSITE's investment mandate, objective, or strategy, the FIRM MUST:

a. Present ADVISORY-ONLY ASSETS that reflect the COMPOSITE's investment mandate, objective, or strategy for the same periods for which the combination of COMPOSITE assets and ADVISORY-ONLY ASSETS that reflect the COMPOSITE's investment mandate, objective, or strategy is presented.
b. Clearly label ADVISORY-ONLY ASSETS that reflect the COMPOSITE's investment mandate, objective, or strategy as such.
c. Clearly label the combination of COMPOSITE assets and ADVISORY-ONLY ASSETS that reflect the COMPOSITE's investment mandate, objective, or strategy as such.

Discussion

Advisory-only assets are assets for which the firm provides investment recommendations in line with the composite strategy but for which the firm has no control over implementation of investment decisions and no trading authority for the assets. Although composite advisory-only assets must not be included in the calculation of composite assets because the firm does not manage these assets, a firm may wish to provide information on composite advisory-only assets in addition to the required presentation of composite assets. The inclusion of information on composite advisory-only assets provides prospective clients additional information about a firm's business model and the types of investment-related services that it provides. If a firm chooses to present information on composite advisory-only assets, it may present composite advisory-only assets as either:

- a separate value, or
- the combination of composite assets and composite advisory-only assets.

If a firm chooses to present composite advisory-only assets as a separate value, the information must be clearly labeled.

If a firm chooses to present the combination of composite assets and composite advisory-only assets, the firm must present composite advisory-only assets for the same periods for which the combination of composite assets and composite advisory-only assets is presented. Both composite advisory-only assets and the combination of composite assets and composite advisory-only assets must be clearly labeled as such.

Provision 4.A.11

If the FIRM chooses to present FIRM-wide ADVISORY-ONLY ASSETS or a combination of TOTAL FIRM ASSETS and FIRM-wide ADVISORY-ONLY ASSETS, the FIRM MUST:

a. Present FIRM-wide ADVISORY-ONLY ASSETS for the same periods for which the combination of TOTAL FIRM ASSETS and FIRM-wide ADVISORY-ONLY ASSETS is presented.
b. Clearly label FIRM-wide ADVISORY-ONLY ASSETS as such.
c. Clearly label the combination of TOTAL FIRM ASSETS and FIRM-wide ADVISORY-ONLY ASSETS as such.

Discussion

Advisory-only assets are assets for which the firm provides investment recommendations but for which the firm has no control over implementation of investment decisions and no trading authority for the assets. Although firm-wide advisory-only assets must not be included in the calculation of total firm assets because the firm does not manage these assets, a firm may wish to provide information on firm-wide advisory-only assets in addition to the required presentation of total firm assets. The inclusion of information on firm-wide advisory-only assets provides prospective clients additional information about a firm's business model and the types of investment-related services that it provides. If a firm chooses to present information on firm-wide advisory-only assets, it may present firm-wide advisory-only assets as either:

- a separate value, or
- the combination of total firm assets and firm-wide advisory-only assets.

If a firm chooses to present firm-wide advisory-only assets as a separate value, the information must be clearly labeled.

If a firm chooses to present the combination of total firm assets and firm-wide advisory-only assets, the firm must present firm-wide advisory-only assets for the same periods for which the combination of total firm assets and firm-wide advisory-only assets is presented. Both the firm-wide advisory-only assets and the combination of total firm assets and firm-wide advisory-only assets must be clearly labeled as such.

Provision 4.A.12

All REQUIRED and RECOMMENDED information in the GIPS COMPOSITE REPORT MUST be presented in the same currency.

Discussion

Firms must present all required and recommended information in a GIPS Composite Report in the same currency (e.g., composite and benchmark returns, composite assets, and risk and internal dispersion measures). This requirement is not applicable to the fee schedule. Supplemental information should also be presented in the same currency. If it is not, that fact must be disclosed. Not disclosing this fact could be misleading.

If a firm chooses to present a composite in a different currency, the firm must convert all of the required information into the new currency. If the firm chooses to present performance in multiple currencies in the same GIPS Composite Report, the firm must convert all of the required information into each of the currencies and ensure it is clear in which currencies performance is reported. The firm must also convert any recommended information it chooses to present in the GIPS Composite Report containing the converted information.

In cases where a composite contains portfolios with different currencies, the firm must convert the individual portfolio returns to a single currency in order to calculate a composite return. It is not permissible to do so by applying the exchange rate as of the current period end to historical data.

The GIPS standards do not require or recommend a particular method for converting portfolio performance from one currency to another. Two possible options for converting returns into a different currency are as follows:

- When using the aggregate method of composite calculation, convert the underlying data (values and external cash flows) into the selected currency using the exchange rate on the date of each cash flow and valuation, and then calculate the composite returns based on the converted data; or
- When using the weighted average method of composite calculation, first calculate the individual portfolio returns, then convert the portfolio returns into the selected currency, and calculate the weighted average composite return using the converted returns.

A firm may instead convert composite returns. Starting with composite returns calculated in its base currency, a composite return can be converted using the movement in the exchange rate between the base currency and the reporting currency over the period of the return. The following example illustrates this method:

Suppose that the return of a composite in euros for the year 2018 is +5.00%. The exchange rate for 1 euro to the US dollar at the start of the year was 1.2008, and at the end of the year it is 1.14315. First calculate the movement in the exchange rate over the year:

$$FX\ return = \frac{FX_{end}}{FX_{start}} - 1$$

$$FX\ return = \frac{1.14315}{1.2008} - 1 = -0.0480 \quad or \quad -4.80\%$$

The exchange rate movement and the euro composite return are then multiplied to determine the USD composite return:

$$USD\ Composite\ Return = (1+0.05) \times (1-0.0480) - 1 = (1.05 \times 0.952) - 1 = -0.00041 \quad or \quad -0.041\%$$

It is not acceptable to convert returns by applying the exchange rate as of the current period end to the historical data, including cash flows and valuations, used to calculate returns.

It is up to the firm to determine the composite-specific conversion method. Policies and procedures for converting returns must be established, documented, and applied consistently.

Provision 4.A.13

When the FIRM presents the performance of a COMPOSITE that includes CARVE-OUTS with allocated cash and also has a COMPOSITE of standalone PORTFOLIOS managed according to the same strategy, the FIRM MUST present for the COMPOSITE of standalone PORTFOLIOS:

a. The COMPOSITE returns for each annual period for which the COMPOSITE of standalone PORTFOLIOS exists, and

b. The COMPOSITE assets as of each annual period end for which the COMPOSITE of standalone PORTFOLIOS exists.

This information MUST be included in the GIPS COMPOSITE REPORT of the COMPOSITE that includes CARVE-OUTS with allocated cash.

Discussion

A carve-out is a portion of a portfolio that is by itself representative of a distinct investment strategy, such as the domestic equity portion of a balanced portfolio. A carve-out may have its own dedicated cash balance, or cash may be allocated to the carve-out synthetically. If a firm has created carve-outs with allocated cash, the firm is likely, at some point, to obtain standalone portfolios managed in the same strategy as the carve-outs with allocated cash. (A standalone portfolio is a portfolio that is not a portion of a larger portfolio.) The firm must then create a separate composite that contains only the standalone portfolios. (See Provision 3.A.18.) If such a composite of standalone portfolios exists, the returns and assets of the composite that includes only standalone portfolios must be presented in the GIPS Composite Report for the composite that includes carve-outs with allocated cash. This will allow a prospective client to compare the returns and assets of the composite that includes carve-outs with allocated cash to the returns and assets of the composite that contains only standalone portfolios managed in the same strategy. If there are significant performance differences between the two composites, the prospective client has a chance to ask questions about the difference in returns between the two composites.

This provision applies only to carve-outs with allocated cash. It does not apply to carve-outs with their own cash.

Provision 4.A.14

For OVERLAY STRATEGY COMPOSITES, the FIRM MUST present COMPOSITE OVERLAY EXPOSURE as of each annual period end. For those periods for which the FIRM presents COMPOSITE OVERLAY EXPOSURE, the FIRM may choose not to present COMPOSITE assets.[33]

Discussion

An overlay strategy is one in which the management of a certain aspect of an investment strategy is carried out separately from the underlying portfolio and it is offered as a separate strategy. If the overlay element is part of the overall portfolio, it may be carved out to represent the overlay strategy, but this is not required. Overlay strategies are typically designed to either limit or maintain a specified risk exposure that is present in the underlying portfolio or to profit from a tactical view on the market by changing a portfolio's specified risk exposure. There are also overlay strategies that seek to add value against a specified target allocation or allocated capital at risk. Common types of overlay strategies include, but are not limited to, currency overlay, asset allocation overlay, interest rate overlay, and option overwrite overlay.

Overlay exposure is the economic value of the assets underlying the overlay portfolios for which a firm has investment management responsibility. For periods beginning on or after 1 January 2020, overlay exposure must be calculated using one of the following approaches: (1) the notional value of the overlay strategy being managed, (2) the value of the underlying portfolios being overlaid, or (3) a specified target exposure as of the beginning of the period, which can either be defined as a target exposure or determined by a formula used to calculate the target exposure for each period. The same method for calculating overlay exposure must be used for all portfolios within a composite. (See Provision 2.A.6.) For periods ending on or after 31 December 2020, it is required that firms present composite overlay exposure as of each annual period end in a GIPS Composite Report for overlay strategy composites.

Overlay strategies are often unfunded and are implemented by using derivatives, which can lead to the fair value of overlay portfolios being very small, negative, or even zero. For those periods

[33] REQUIRED for periods ending on or after 31 December 2020.

for which the firm presents composite overlay exposure, the firm may choose not to present composite assets because the amount of composite assets may be immaterial or may not be a good indication of the volume of overlay assets being managed.

Provision 4.A.15

For OVERLAY STRATEGY COMPOSITES, the FIRM is not REQUIRED to present TOTAL FIRM ASSETS and may instead choose to present total FIRM OVERLAY EXPOSURE as of each annual period end.

Discussion

Overlay exposure is the economic value of the assets underlying the overlay portfolios for which a firm has investment management responsibility. For periods beginning on or after 1 January 2020, overlay exposure must be calculated using one of the following approaches: (1) the notional value of the overlay strategy being managed, (2) the value of the underlying portfolios being overlaid, or (3) a specified target exposure as of the beginning of the period, which can either be defined as a target exposure or determined by a formula used to calculate the target exposure for each period.

Overlay strategies are often unfunded and are implemented by using derivatives, which can lead to the fair value of overlay portfolios being very small, negative, or even zero. Total firm assets for an overlay manager may therefore be quite small. The more meaningful information for an overlay manager would be total firm overlay exposure. Therefore, firms may choose not to present total firm assets because the amount may not be material or may not be a good indication of the volume of assets being managed by the firm. The firm may instead present total firm overlay exposure. However, total firm assets or total firm overlay exposure must be presented as of each annual period end. Firms may also choose to present both total firm assets and total firm overlay exposure.

Provision 4.A.16

For WRAP FEE COMPOSITES, when the FIRM presents performance to a WRAP FEE PROSPECTIVE CLIENT, the FIRM MUST present:

a. The COMPOSITE that includes the performance of all actual WRAP FEE PORTFOLIOS, if any, managed according to the COMPOSITE investment mandate, objective, or strategy, regardless of the WRAP FEE sponsor.

b. COMPOSITE performance that is net of the entire WRAP FEE.

c. The percentage of COMPOSITE assets represented by WRAP FEE PORTFOLIOS as of each annual period end.

Discussion

A wrap fee is a type of bundled fee specific to a particular investment product. The wrap fee is charged by a wrap fee sponsor for investment management services and typically includes associated transaction costs that cannot be separately identified. Wrap fees can be all-inclusive, asset-based fees and may include a combination of investment management fees, transaction costs, custody fees, and/or administrative fees.

The GIPS standards require firms to define composites according to investment mandates, objectives, and/or strategies. To facilitate the comparability of performance results and prevent firms from cherry-picking their best-performing portfolios for presentation, firms must group all appropriate wrap fee portfolios in a composite managed according to a specific investment objective, mandate, or strategy (creating a style-defined composite) regardless of the wrap fee sponsor. If the firm has no actual wrap fee portfolios under management for the specified strategy, this style-defined composite will include only non–wrap fee portfolios managed to the specified strategy. (See Provision 3.A.14 for a more detailed discussion of the creation of wrap fee composites.)

The 2010 edition of the GIPS standards included the concept of a sponsor-specific composite that included only the wrap fee portfolios managed for a specific wrap fee sponsor in the composite strategy. The concept of a sponsor-specific wrap fee composite was removed in the 2020 edition of the GIPS standards. Sponsor-specific performance may still be used when creating materials for the use of a specific wrap fee sponsor, but such materials are considered to be client reporting and not a GIPS-compliant composite.

When presenting performance to a wrap fee prospective client, performance must be shown net of the entire wrap fee. This is required whether the composite includes wrap fee portfolios or non-wrap fee portfolios. This is because a wrap fee is a bundled fee that includes transaction costs that cannot be separately identified, and the prospective client must pay the total wrap fee. Firms may present gross-of-fees returns in addition to returns that are net of the entire wrap fee. A gross-of-fees return must reflect the deduction of transaction costs. To calculate a gross-of-fees return, firms may deduct the portion of the wrap fee that includes transaction costs, if this is known. Firms may also deduct estimated transaction costs, if actual transaction costs are not known and they have the ability to determine a reasonable estimate of transaction costs. (For the treatment of estimated transaction costs in bundled fee portfolios, please see Provision 2.A.14.) Pure gross-of-fees returns may be presented as supplemental information. A pure gross-of-fees return is one that is not reduced by any transaction costs incurred during the period. It is common, however, for wrap fee managers to present returns that are net of the entire wrap fee and pure gross-of-fees returns—and to not present a gross-of-fees return. See Provision 2.A.48 for information about calculating wrap fee portfolio returns.

It is also required that when a firm presents performance to a wrap fee prospective client, the GIPS Composite Report for the wrap fee composite must include the percentage of composite assets represented by wrap fee portfolios as of each annual period end. This allows prospective clients to understand how much of the composite's assets is represented by actual wrap fee portfolios.

Provision 4.A.17

For WRAP FEE COMPOSITES, when the FIRM presents PURE GROSS-OF-FEES returns, the FIRM MUST:

a. Clearly label returns as PURE GROSS-OF-FEES.
b. Identify PURE GROSS-OF-FEES returns as SUPPLEMENTAL INFORMATION.

Discussion

The GIPS standards require that transaction costs be deducted when calculating both gross-of-fees and net-of-fees returns. A pure gross-of-fees return is the return on investments that is not reduced by any transaction costs incurred during the period. If a firm presents pure gross-of-fees returns for a wrap fee composite, the returns must be clearly labeled as pure gross-of-fees returns and must also be identified as supplemental information. Supplemental information is any performance-related information included as part of a GIPS Composite Report that supplements or enhances the requirements and/or recommendations of the GIPS standards. The required labeling of a pure gross-of-fees return and its designation as supplemental information helps prospective clients distinguish pure gross-of-fees returns, which do not reflect the deduction of transaction costs, and gross-of-fees returns, which do reflect the deduction of transaction costs. (See Provision 4.A.18 for a discussion of supplemental information.)

Provision 4.A.18

Any SUPPLEMENTAL INFORMATION included in the GIPS COMPOSITE REPORT:

a. MUST relate directly to the COMPOSITE.
b. MUST NOT contradict or conflict with the REQUIRED OR RECOMMENDED information in the GIPS COMPOSITE REPORT.
c. MUST be clearly labeled as SUPPLEMENTAL INFORMATION.

Discussion

Supplemental information is any performance-related information included as part of a GIPS Composite Report that supplements or enhances the requirements and/or recommendations of the GIPS standards. Performance-related information includes:

- information expressed in terms of investment return and risk, and
- other information and input data that directly relate to the calculation of investment return and risk (e.g., portfolio holdings), as well as information derived from investment return and risk input data (e.g., performance contribution or attribution).

Supplemental information should provide users of the GIPS Composite Report with the proper context in which to understand the performance results. Common examples of supplemental information include the following:

- segment returns that do not include cash,
- after-tax returns,
- money-weighted returns (MWRs) when the firm does not meet the tests for presenting only MWRs, and
- pure gross-of-fees returns for wrap fee composites.

Supplemental information must relate directly to the composite and must not contradict or conflict with the required or recommended information in the GIPS Composite Report. Examples of information that relates directly to the composite and would be considered supplemental information include segment returns (e.g., country or sector), performance attribution, and composite or portfolio-level holdings. An example of information that would conflict with the GIPS standards is a non-portable track record from a past firm that is linked to composite performance of the new firm.

The following is a more complete list of the principles that apply when supplemental information is presented. Supplemental information must:

- satisfy the spirit and principles of the GIPS standards—fair representation and full disclosure,
- comply with all applicable laws and regulations regarding the calculation and presentation of performance,
- not include performance or performance-related information that is false or misleading,
- relate directly to the composite and supplement or enhance the required or recommended information included in the composite's GIPS Composite Report,
- not contradict or conflict with the required or recommended information in the GIPS Composite Report,
- be clearly labeled as supplemental information, and
- not be shown with greater prominence than the required composite information.

4.B. Presentation and Reporting—Recommendations

Provision 4.B.1

The FIRM SHOULD present both GROSS-OF-FEES and NET-OF-FEES COMPOSITE returns.

Discussion

For all composites except wrap fee composites, a firm may choose to present either gross-of-fees or net-of-fees composite returns in a GIPS Composite Report. For wrap fee composites, firms are required to present composite returns that are net of the entire wrap fee. Each type of return provides important information to prospective clients.

Because a gross-of-fees return is the return on investments reduced by any transaction costs, it is the best measure of the firm's investment management ability and can be thought of as the "investment return." In addition, because fees are sometimes negotiable, presenting gross-of-fees returns shows the firm's expertise in managing assets without the effect of the firm's or client's negotiating skills. Gross-of-fees returns also allow prospective clients to better compare performance between firms.

Net-of-fees composite returns reflect the deduction of transaction costs and investment management fees. Net-of-fees returns therefore provide the best indication to prospective clients of the returns that the firm's clients received or would have received over time, after taking into account the effect of investment management costs.

Because both gross-of-fees and net-of-fees returns provide important information to prospective clients, it is recommended that firms present both gross-of-fees and net-of-fees composite returns in a GIPS Composite Report.

Provision 4.B.2

The FIRM SHOULD present the following items:

a. Cumulative returns of the COMPOSITE and the BENCHMARK for all periods.

Discussion

Cumulative returns of the composite and benchmark provide additional useful information to prospective clients by indicating the total rate of return for a defined period of performance. It is therefore recommended that cumulative returns for all periods be provided in addition to the required annual returns.

To calculate cumulative returns of a composite for any period, the historical daily, monthly, quarterly, or annual sub-period returns are geometrically linked according to the following formula:

$$R_{CUM} = \left[(1+R_1)\times(1+R_2)\times\ldots\times(1+R_n)\right]-1,$$

where R_1 is the composite return for Period 1 and R_n is the composite return for the most recent period.

Example:

Firm ABC has the following annual returns that were calculated from monthly composite returns:

	Composite	$1 + R_n$
2015	2.3%	1.023
2016	−4.7%	0.953
2017	6.9%	1.069
2018	3.2%	1.032
2019	0.9%	1.009
Jan 2020–Jun 2020	−3.1%	0.969

To calculate the composite cumulative return for the period from January 2015 through June 2020, the returns are linked:

$$\begin{aligned}\text{Composite cumulative return} &= \left[(1.023)\times(0.953)\times(1.069)\times(1.032)\times(1.009)\times(0.969)\right]-1\\ &= 0.052, \quad \text{or} \quad 5.2\%.\end{aligned}$$

If the composite experiences a break in the track record, the periods before and after the break must not be linked. Therefore, in such a case, a cumulative return may be calculated up to the break and a separate cumulative return may be calculated for the performance period that begins after the break. However, the firm must not calculate a cumulative return across the periods that include the break. Additional guidance on how to calculate performance if there is a break in the track record is included in the discussion of Provision 4.A.5.

Provision 4.B.2

The FIRM SHOULD present the following items:

b. Equal-weighted COMPOSITE returns.

 |

Discussion

The GIPS standards require that composite time-weighted returns be calculated by asset-weighting the individual portfolio returns or by using the aggregate method. (See Provision 2.A.36.) This allows for a larger portfolio to have more weight on a composite's return than a smaller portfolio. Equal-weighted composite returns, however, provide another useful perspective on composite performance. The simple average, together with a measure of internal dispersion, provides a measure of the manager's ability to obtain consistent returns for all portfolios regardless of size. It is therefore recommended that firms also include equal-weighted composite returns in a GIPS Composite Report.

The formula for the equal-weighted composite return, R_{EQUAL}, is

$$R_{EQUAL} = \frac{R_{PORT1} + R_{PORT2} + \ldots + R_{PORTi}}{n},$$

where R_{PORT1} is the time-weighted return for the first portfolio in the composite, R_{PORTi} is the time-weighted return for the ith portfolio in the composite, and n is the number of portfolios in the composite.

Provision 4.B.2

The FIRM SHOULD present the following items:

c. Quarterly and/or monthly returns.

Discussion

Although the GIPS standards require the presentation of annual returns for the composite and benchmark (Provisions 4.A.1.b and 4.A.1.e), it is recommended that firms present more-frequent returns, such as quarterly or monthly returns. More-frequent returns help prospective clients evaluate a composite's track record. Firms must present benchmark returns for the same periods for which composite returns are presented. If the GIPS Composite Report includes annual and quarterly composite returns, annual and quarterly benchmark returns must also be presented.

Provision 4.B.2

The FIRM SHOULD present the following items:

d. Annualized COMPOSITE and BENCHMARK returns for periods longer than 12 months.

Discussion

It is recommended that firms show the results of both the composite and the benchmark for periods longer than 12 months in annualized terms to help prospective clients in the evaluation of the composite's track record. Annualized returns are created by calculating the geometric mean, not the arithmetic mean, and represent the geometric average annual compound return achieved over the defined period of more than one year. Sub-period returns during the investment period are geometrically linked to calculate the cumulative return. Then the *n*th root of the cumulative return is calculated, where *n* is the number of years in the period. Annualized performance is permitted only for periods of one year or more.

The formula for calculating annualized performance is as follows:

$$\text{Annualized return (\%)} = [(1 + R)^{1/n}] - 1,$$

where R is the cumulative return for the period and n is the number of years in the period.

For example, assume a composite's cumulative return for a five-year period is 150.0%. It has a five-year average annual compound return, or annualized return, of 20.11%, which is calculated as:

$$\left[(1+1.5)^{\frac{1}{5}}\right]-1=0.2011=20.11\%.$$

If instead the 150% is achieved over 12.5 years, the 12.5-year average annual compound return, or annualized return, is 7.61%, which is calculated as:

$$\left[(1+1.5)^{\frac{1}{12.5}}\right]-1=0.0761=7.61\%.$$

If the composite experiences a break in the track record, the periods before and after the break must not be linked, and annualized returns must not be calculated across the break in performance.

Provision 4.B.3

For all periods for which an annualized EX POST STANDARD DEVIATION of the COMPOSITE and the BENCHMARK are presented, the FIRM SHOULD present the corresponding annualized return of the COMPOSITE and the BENCHMARK.

Discussion

To provide context so that the prospective client can better understand the ex post standard deviation, it is recommended that firms present annualized returns for the composite and benchmark for the same periods for which annualized standard deviation is presented. For example, if a firm chooses to present the 5-year, 7-year, and 10-year annualized standard deviations in addition to the required 3-year annualized standard deviation, firms are encouraged to also present the corresponding 3-year, 5-year, 7-year, and 10-year annualized returns for the composite and the benchmark. This will help prospective clients to better interpret risk and return in the context of the return distribution for all periods for which an annualized standard deviation is presented.

Provision 4.B.4

For all periods greater than three years for which an annualized return of the COMPOSITE and the BENCHMARK are presented, the FIRM SHOULD present the corresponding annualized EX POST STANDARD DEVIATION (using monthly returns) of the COMPOSITE and the BENCHMARK.

Discussion

To provide context so that the prospective client can interpret the annualized composite and benchmark returns, it is recommended that firms present the annualized ex post standard deviation (using monthly returns) for both the composite and benchmark for the same periods that annualized composite and benchmark returns are presented. For example, if a firm chooses to present the 5-year, 7-year, and 10-year annualized composite and benchmark returns, firms are encouraged to also present the corresponding 5-year, 7-year, and 10-year annualized ex post standard deviation of the composite and benchmark. This will help prospective clients to assess and compare risk and return for all periods for which annualized returns are presented.

Provision 4.B.5

The FIRM SHOULD present relevant EX POST ADDITIONAL RISK MEASURES for the COMPOSITE and the BENCHMARK.

Discussion

For composites for which monthly composite returns are available, firms must present the three-year annualized ex post standard deviation (using monthly returns) of the composite and the benchmark as of each annual period end. This is required for periods ending on or after 1 January 2011. (See Provision 4.A.1.j.) Additional risk measures are risk measures included in a GIPS Composite Report beyond those required to be presented. It is recommended that firms present relevant ex post additional risk measures for the composite and benchmark in a GIPS Composite Report. Currently, there is no single risk measure that comprehensively and consistently captures every risk to which an asset class, product, or strategy is exposed or sensitive. Also, there may be additional risk measures that would be especially helpful to prospective clients when interpreting a composite's return. There are many risk and quantitative measures that are routinely calculated to help a reader evaluate and understand the return and risk characteristics of a particular investment strategy. Determining which risk measures are relevant to a strategy requires an understanding of the characteristics and limitations of each measure and insight into the portfolio construction process and investment strategy. Several risk measures are commonly used within the industry, but there is less of a consensus over what constitutes relevant risk measures when evaluating portfolios containing derivatives, alternatives, and/or illiquid assets. Some firms have developed proprietary measures, which, despite providing insight into the strategy, make comparisons across managers problematic.

A number of factors should be considered when selecting relevant risk measures, including the following:

- Comparability: The risk measure selected should allow objective comparisons across firms to be made.
- Computational transparency: All inputs to the calculation should be readily available and understood.
- Interpretational transparency: In isolation as a single figure or presented as a time series, the risk measure should aid interpretation and provide context to the performance figures presented.
- Investment process or strategy consistency: The risk measure should provide insight into the underlying investment process.
- Risk measure stability: The selected risk measure should be sensitive to market and portfolio movements but should not exhibit excessive range swings such that interpretation of the absolute and relative values is compromised.

Provision 4.B.6

The FIRM SHOULD present more than 10 years of annual performance in the GIPS COMPOSITE REPORT.

Discussion

Once the composite has its initial minimum 5-year (or since-inception) compliant history, the firm must continue to add annual returns to each GIPS Composite Report for the next 5 years, at a minimum, so that the firm will build up to a 10-year compliant performance record for its composites.

At some point, a firm will have a minimum 10-year compliant track record for a specific composite. When the firm eventually adds an additional annual return to a 10-year track record in a GIPS Composite Report, the firm may delete the information for the oldest year included or may instead present a longer track record. It is recommended that firms include more than the minimum 10 years of annual performance in a GIPS Composite Report to provide more information to prospective clients. If any performance is presented that does not comply with the GIPS standards (only allowed for periods prior to 1 January 2006 for wrap fee, real estate, and private equity composites and prior to 1 January 2000 for all other composites), firms must disclose the period(s) of non-compliance.

Provision 4.B.7

The FIRM SHOULD present PROPRIETARY ASSETS as a percentage of COMPOSITE assets as of each annual period end.

Discussion

Proprietary assets are assets owned by the firm, the firm's management, and/or the firm's parent company that are managed by the firm. Knowing how much of a composite's assets are proprietary and how much are managed for external clients provides prospective clients with additional insight regarding the composite, especially when a significant percentage of the composite's assets are proprietary assets. If a composite includes proprietary assets, it is recommended that firms present proprietary assets as a percentage of composite assets as of each annual period end.

Provision 4.B.8

If the FIRM uses preliminary, estimated values as FAIR VALUE, the FIRM SHOULD present the percentage of assets in the COMPOSITE that were valued using preliminary, estimated values as of each annual period end.

Discussion

The use of preliminary, estimated values as fair value is common for some alternative strategies, including those that invest in underlying funds for which the firm relies on valuations provided by the underlying fund managers. When using preliminary, estimated values as fair value, it is important to remember the underlying principles of the GIPS standards: fair representation and full disclosure. If using preliminary, estimated values, firms must disclose this fact in the relevant

GIPS Composite Report (Provision 4.C.41). It is recommended that the firm also present the percentage of assets in the composite that were valued using preliminary, estimated values as of each annual period end. This provides important information that allows prospective clients to better assess the valuations and performance record presented.

Provision 4.B.9

For REAL ESTATE COMPOSITES, the FIRM SHOULD present COMPOSITE and BENCHMARK COMPONENT RETURNS for all periods presented.

Discussion

For real estate composites, it is recommended that firms also present composite and benchmark component returns in addition to total returns. Component returns separate the total return into a capital return and an income return. Component returns provide additional information to prospective clients regarding the sources of the total return and the nature of the investment strategy. The income return is generally viewed as more stable than the capital return. Real estate investors typically want to know the contribution from the income and capital returns.

The following are examples of formulas that may be used to calculate the income return and capital return for a real estate investment. The formulas presented use the following terms:

r_t^{GFI} = gross-of-fees income return for period t

r_t^{NFI} = net-of-fees income return for period t

r_t^{GFC} = gross-of-fees capital return for period t

r_t^{NFC} = net-of-fees capital return for period t

r_t^{GFT} = gross-of-fees total return for period t

r_t^{NFT} = net-of-fees total return for period t

NII_t = net investment income (after interest expense, advisory fees, and any performance-based fees allocated to the income component for performance calculation purposes) for period t

AF_t = advisory fee (asset-based portion of investment management fee expensed, including any acquisition and disposition fees that are included as an advisory fee and excluding any performance-based fees) for period t

PF_t^C = performance-based fees allocated to the capital component (for performance calculation purposes) for period t

PF_t^I = performance-based fees allocated to the income component (for performance calculation purposes) for period t

V_t^B = the beginning value of the portfolio for period t

V_t^E = the ending value of the portfolio for period t

FC_t = fees charged by the firm and capitalized for accounting purposes but treated as an investment management fee for performance purposes for period t (including acquisition and disposition fees)

j = the number of external cash flows (1, 2, 3, . . . , J) in period t

$CF_{j,t}$ = the value of cash flow j in period t

$W_{j,t}$ = the weight of cash flow j in period t (assuming the cash flow occurred at the end of the day) as calculated according to the following formula:

$$w_{j,t} = \frac{D_t - D_{j,t}}{D_t},$$

where

$w_{j,t}$ = the weight of cash flow j in period t, assuming the cash flow occurred at the end of the day

D_t = the total number of calendar days in period t

$D_{j,t}$ = the number of calendar days from the beginning of period t to cash flow j

Acquisition, disposition, and financing services performed by the firm, an affiliate of the firm, or a third party on a particular transaction are considered transaction costs and must be deducted from both gross-of-fees and net-of-fees returns. These items (also referred to as "brokerage expenses") are direct costs incurred upon implementation of a particular investment transaction and are considered transaction costs. It is recommended that these transaction costs be accounted for through the capital returns. Please note that the acquisition and disposition transaction costs described earlier are different from investment management fees specifically associated with acquisition and disposition services performed by the firm. It is common practice in the real estate industry to have investment management agreements separate the investment management fee into one or more of the following components: base investment management, acquisition, disposition, and financing. In this scenario, the fees specifically relating to acquisition and disposition are typically considered to be part of the investment management fee because these relate to the investment management responsibilities performed by the firm in formulating its investment decisions as part of the normal investment decision-making process. Financing fees, if applicable, are typically identified separately in the investment management agreement and are classified as transaction costs because they are usually related to post-acquisition refinancing.

The term "net investment income" is intended to reflect the effect of ownership and financing structures and includes all underlying property-level activity. Investment-level returns are distinct from property-level returns. Investment-level returns reflect the effect of ownership and financing structures and include all underlying property-level activity. Property-level returns exclude all of the non-property (investment-level) balance sheet items, as well as income and expenses, and include only those income and expenses that directly relate to the operation of the property. Property-level returns are not used for reporting performance in compliance with the GIPS standards, although they may be shown as supplemental information.

Income Return

The income return measures the investment income earned on all investments (including cash and cash equivalents) during the measurement period, net of all non-recoverable expenditures, interest expense on debt, and property taxes. The income return is computed as a percentage of the capital employed. Capital employed is defined as the "weighted average equity" (weighted average capital) during the measurement period. Capital employed does not include any income return or capital return earned during the measurement period. Beginning capital is adjusted by weighting the external cash flows that occurred during the period.

The numerator in the gross-of-fees income return represents the investment income for the portfolio during the period, including any income earned during the period at the investment level, and also reflects all income, fees, and expenses at the property level.

The formula for gross-of-fees income return is as follows:

$$r_t^{GFI} = \frac{NII_t + AF_t + PF_t^I}{V_t^B + \sum_{j=1}^{J}(CF_{j,t} \times W_{j,t})}.$$

The numerator in the net-of-fees income return represents the net investment income for the portfolio during the period. This figure would include any income earned and expenses and fees deducted at the investment level and all income, fees, and expenses at the property level.

The formula for net-of-fees income return is as follows:

$$r_t^{NFI} = \frac{NII_t}{V_t^B + \sum_{j=1}^{J}(CF_{j,t} \times W_{j,t})}.$$

Capital Return

The capital return is the change in value of the real estate investments and cash and/or cash equivalent assets held throughout the measurement period, adjusted for all capital expenditures (subtracted) and net proceeds from sales (added). The capital return is computed as a percentage of the capital employed. Capital return is also known as "capital appreciation return" or "appreciation return."

The capital return numerator reflects the change (increase or decrease) in investment value adjusted for capital improvements, sales, refinancing, and net investment income activity.

The numerator includes both realized gains/losses and the change in unrealized gains/losses from the prior period.

The net-of-fees capital return reflects the deduction of any performance-based (incentive) fees attributable to the capital component for performance calculation purposes. This figure would exclude any performance-based fees attributable to the income component for performance calculation purposes.

The formula for gross-of-fees capital return is as follows:

$$r_t^{GFC} = \frac{V_t^E - V_t^B - \sum_{j=1}^{J} CF_{j,t} - NII_t + PF_t^C + FC_t}{V_t^B + \sum_{j=1}^{J} (CF_{j,t} \times W_{j,t})}.$$

The formula for net-of-fees capital return is as follows:

$$r_t^{NFC} = \frac{V_t^E - V_t^B - \sum_{j=1}^{J} CF_{j,t} - NII_t}{V_t^B + \sum_{j=1}^{J} (CF_{j,t} \times W_{j,t})}.$$

Total Return

The total return is the percentage change in value of real estate investments, including all capital return and income return components, expressed as a percentage of the capital employed over the measurement period. The total return numerator measures the change (increase or decrease) in investment value from both income (loss) and realized and unrealized gains and losses.

The formula for total return gross-of-fees is as follows:

$$r_t^{GFT} = \frac{V_t^E - V_t^B - \sum_{j=1}^{J} CF_{j,t} + AF_t + PF_t^I + PF_t^C + FC_t}{V_t^B + \sum_{j=1}^{J} (CF_{j,t} \times W_{j,t})}.$$

The formula for total return net-of-fees is as follows:

$$r_t^{NFT} = \frac{V_t^E - V_t^B - \sum_{j=1}^{J} CF_{j,t}}{V_t^B + \sum_{j=1}^{J} (CF_{j,t} \times W_{j,t})}.$$

All performance results, both total returns and component returns, must be clearly identified so that prospective clients can properly interpret and compare performance. To interpret performance data, prospective clients need to know what the performance results represent.

Provision 4.B.10

If the FIRM has COMMITTED CAPITAL, the FIRM SHOULD present FIRM-wide uncalled COMMITTED CAPITAL as of each annual period end.

Discussion

Committed capital is defined as pledges of capital to an investment vehicle by investors (limited partners and the general partner) or the firm and is typically drawn down over a period of time. Uncalled committed capital is the amount of capital that has not yet been drawn. If a firm has committed capital, it is recommended that the firm present total firm-wide uncalled committed capital as of each annual period end. This information provides prospective clients a more complete picture of the capital that is currently committed to a future investment. If the firm chooses to present firm-wide uncalled committed capital, it may present this amount separately from total firm assets. The firm may also choose to present the combination of total firm assets and firm-wide uncalled committed capital. Provision 4.A.9 discusses the requirements relating to the presentation of firm-wide uncalled committed capital in a GIPS Composite Report.

4.C. Disclosure—Requirements

Provision 4.C.1

Once the FIRM has met all the applicable REQUIREMENTS of the GIPS standards, the FIRM MUST disclose its compliance with the GIPS standards using one of the following compliance statements. The compliance statement for a COMPOSITE MUST only be used in a GIPS COMPOSITE REPORT.

a. For a FIRM that is verified:

"[Insert name of FIRM] claims compliance with the Global Investment Performance Standards (GIPS®) and has prepared and presented this report in compliance with the GIPS standards. [Insert name of FIRM] has been independently verified for the periods [insert dates]. The verification report(s) is/are available upon request."

"A firm that claims compliance with the GIPS standards must establish policies and procedures for complying with all the applicable requirements of the GIPS standards. Verification provides assurance on whether the firm's policies and procedures related to composite and pooled fund maintenance, as well as the calculation, presentation, and distribution of performance, have been designed in compliance with the GIPS standards and have been implemented on a firm-wide basis. Verification does not provide assurance on the accuracy of any specific performance report."

b. For COMPOSITES of a verified FIRM that have also had a PERFORMANCE EXAMINATION:

"[Insert name of FIRM] claims compliance with the Global Investment Performance Standards (GIPS®) and has prepared and presented this report in compliance with the GIPS standards. [Insert name of FIRM] has been independently verified for the periods [insert dates]."

"A firm that claims compliance with the GIPS standards must establish policies and procedures for complying with all the applicable requirements of the GIPS standards. Verification provides assurance on whether the firm's policies and procedures related to composite and pooled fund maintenance, as well as the calculation, presentation, and distribution of performance, have been designed in compliance with the GIPS standards and have been implemented on a firm-wide basis. The [insert name of COMPOSITE] has had a performance examination for the periods [insert dates]. The verification and performance examination reports are available upon request."

The compliance statement for a FIRM that is verified or for COMPOSITES of a verified FIRM that have also had a PERFORMANCE EXAMINATION is complete only when both paragraphs are shown together, one after the other.

c. For a FIRM that has not been verified:

"[Insert name of FIRM] claims compliance with the Global Investment Performance Standards (GIPS®) and has prepared and presented this report in compliance with the GIPS standards. [Insert name of FIRM] has not been independently verified."

The FIRM MUST NOT exclude any portion of the respective compliance statement. Any modifications to the compliance statement MUST be additive.

Discussion

A firm meeting all the requirements of the GIPS standards must use one of the three compliance statements in each of its GIPS Composite Reports. The English version of the compliance statements is the controlling version. If a firm chooses to translate the claim of compliance into a language for which there is no official translation of the GIPS standards, the firm must take care to ensure that the translation used reflects the required wording of the claim of compliance used in Provisions 4.C.1.a, 4.C.1.b, or 4.C.1.c.

It is acceptable to combine both paragraphs of the claim of compliance for a verified firm (Provision 4.C.1.a) into a single paragraph. If the paragraphs are not combined, the claim of compliance for a verified firm is complete only when both paragraphs are shown together, one after the other. A firm may not separate the two required paragraphs from each other.

The same is true for the claim of compliance for a composite that has also had a performance examination (Provision 4.C.1.b). Both paragraphs of the claim of compliance may be combined into a single paragraph. If the paragraphs are not combined, the claim of compliance is complete only when both paragraphs are shown together, one after the other. A firm may not separate the two required paragraphs from each other.

When preparing the GIPS Composite Report for a composite that has had a performance examination, the firm may choose to use either the verification or performance examination claim of compliance. For example, a firm might choose to use the verification claim of compliance for all GIPS Reports, including GIPS Reports for composites and pooled funds that have had a performance examination, if it wishes to standardize the claim of compliance for all GIPS Reports throughout the firm. In this situation, the firm may also disclose that a specific composite or pooled fund has had a performance examination.

The language in each compliance statement must not exclude any portion of the respective compliance statement, with one exception. In the second paragraph of both 4.C.1.a and 4.C.1.b, there is a reference to "composite and pooled fund maintenance." The firm may delete the words "and pooled fund" if no broad distribution pooled funds or limited distribution pooled funds are included within the definition of the firm.

There may also be instances where it may be appropriate for a firm to modify the language slightly. For example, a firm may modify the language to include the name of the firm's verifier, if the firm wishes to disclose this information. A firm may also need to modify the language to add more details about the name of the firm that has been verified or the dates of the verification if the verification period was not continuous. Any modifications must be additive and must not result in a claim of compliance that is false or misleading.

Provision 4.C.2

The FIRM MUST disclose the following: "GIPS® is a registered trademark of CFA Institute. CFA Institute does not endorse or promote this organization, nor does it warrant the accuracy or quality of the content contained herein."

Discussion

"GIPS®" is a registered trademark of CFA Institute, and firms are required to acknowledge this in all GIPS Composite Reports. The required disclosure may appear in the body of the GIPS

Composite Report or in a footnote to the report. The term "this organization", which is included in the required disclosure, refers to any entity associated with the GIPS Composite Report, either the firm or the verifier.

CFA Institute (owner of the GIPS® trademark) may take appropriate action against any firm that misuses the mark "GIPS®" or any compliance statement, including false claims of compliance with the GIPS standards. CFA Institute members, CFA Program charterholders, CFA candidates, CIPM Program certificants, and CIPM candidates who misuse the term "GIPS" or any compliance statement, misrepresent their performance history or the performance history of their firm, or falsely claim compliance with the GIPS standards are also subject to disciplinary sanctions under the CFA Institute Code of Ethics and Standards of Professional Conduct. Possible disciplinary sanctions include public censure, suspension of membership, and revocation of the CFA charter or CIPM certificate.

Regulators with jurisdiction over firms claiming compliance with the GIPS standards may also take enforcement actions against firms that falsely claim compliance with the GIPS standards.

Firms may also use the following language to replace the first sentence in this required disclosure: "GIPS® is a registered trademark owned by CFA Institute." See the GIPS Standards Trademark Usage Guidelines on the CFA Institute website (www.cfainstitute.org) for additional guidance on the proper use of "GIPS".

Provision 4.C.3

The FIRM MUST disclose the definition of the FIRM used to determine TOTAL FIRM ASSETS and FIRM-wide compliance.

Discussion

To claim compliance with the GIPS standards, a firm must comply with all applicable requirements of the GIPS standards on a firm-wide basis. Accordingly, the firm must determine exactly how it will be defined for the purpose of compliance. The GIPS standards require that a firm must be defined as an investment firm, subsidiary, or division held out to the public as a distinct business entity.

A distinct business entity is a unit, division, department, or office that is organizationally and functionally segregated from other units, divisions, departments, or offices, that retains discretion over the assets it manages, and that should have autonomy over the investment decision-making process.

Possible criteria that can be used to determine this status include:

- being a legal entity,
- having a distinct market or client type (e.g., institutional, retail, private client), and
- using a separate and distinct investment process.

See Provision 1.A.2 for a more detailed discussion of defining the firm.

Because there are often a number of closely related units or divisions within larger investment management entities, it is critical to disclose the precise definition of the firm that is presenting the performance results and would be responsible for the management of the prospective client's assets. This provision requires the firm to disclose sufficient details of the entity that is presenting investment performance such that the firm is clearly identified.

Sample Disclosures:

Example 1:

Firm A is a multinational investment firm with offices around the world, including in Japan, Australia, the United Kingdom, and the United States. Although all of its offices are part of the global parent company, each office is registered with the appropriate national regulatory authority, and each is held out to clients and prospective clients as a distinct business entity. The firm has defined its offices in Japan, Australia, the United Kingdom, and the United States as separate firms for the purpose of complying with the GIPS standards. The offices in Japan, the United Kingdom, and the United States claim compliance with the GIPS standards. Firm A's Australia office, however, does not claim compliance with the GIPS standards.

Sample Disclosure for Firm A—US:

"For the purpose of complying with the GIPS standards, the firm is defined as Firm A—US, which serves US clients and investors and is a subsidiary of Firm A, a multinational investment firm with offices globally. Firm A also has subsidiaries in the United Kingdom, Australia, and Japan, which are not included in the definition of the firm for purposes of compliance with the GIPS standards."

Example 2:

Firm B has two divisions, each of which serves a distinct client type. Firm B Institutional Investment Management manages institutional assets. Firm B Retail Investors manages retail assets. The firm has determined that it will create two separate firms for the purpose of complying with the GIPS standards.

Sample Disclosure for Firm B Institutional Investment Management:

"For the purpose of complying with the GIPS standards, the firm is defined as Firm B Institutional Investment Management, the institutional asset management division of Firm B."

Example 3:

Firm C is an investment management firm that offers both active and passive (indexed) investment strategies. For the purpose of complying with the GIPS standards, the firm has decided to create two separate firms: one that offers active investment strategies and one that offers indexed investment strategies.

Sample Disclosure for Firm C—Indexed Investing:

"For the purpose of complying with the GIPS standards, the firm is defined as Firm C—Indexed Investing. Firm C—Indexed Investing is the division of Firm C that offers indexed investment strategies to clients."

Provision 4.C.4

The FIRM MUST disclose the COMPOSITE DESCRIPTION.

Discussion

The composite description is defined as general information regarding the investment mandate, objective, or strategy of the composite. The composite description may be more abbreviated than the composite definition but must include all key features of the composite and must include enough information to allow a prospective client to understand the key characteristics of the composite's investment mandate, objective, or strategy, including:

- the material risks of the composite's strategy,
- how leverage, derivatives, and short positions may be used, if they are a material part of the strategy, and
- if illiquid investments are a material part of the strategy.

The composite definition goes a step further than the composite description and includes the detailed criteria that determine the assignment of portfolios to composites, such as investment constraints or restrictions. Although the composite description is a required disclosure, the composite definition is not a required disclosure. (See the discussion of Provision 3.A.5 for additional information regarding composite definitions and composite descriptions.)

The required disclosure of the composite description provides information about the composite's investment strategy that is intended to help a prospective client who is considering an investment product or strategy and is reviewing a GIPS Composite Report for that product or strategy. The composite description should provide sufficient information to prospective clients to allow them to differentiate the significant features of the strategy from other strategies within the firm and to compare products across firms. The disclosed strategy features will likely affect both the historical and expected risk and returns. Along with the required benchmark description (see Provision 4.C.5), the GIPS Composite Report will allow prospective clients to understand both the investment strategy employed and the benchmark against which the composite's performance is evaluated. This will help prospective clients to compare investments across firms.

If leverage, derivatives, and short positions may be used, and they are a material part of the strategy, this must be disclosed in the composite description. Provision 4.C.17 requires that the firm disclose how leverage, derivatives, and short positions have been used historically, if material. Taken together, these two required disclosures provide a more complete picture about the presence, use, and extent of leverage, derivatives, and short positions. When determining what would be material, the firm must consider whether the disclosure of how leverage, derivatives, and/or short positions may be used and/or have been used historically is likely to affect a prospective client's or prospective investor's view of the risk involved in the strategy. If so, it would be misleading for the firm to fail to disclose their use to these prospective clients or prospective investors when describing the strategy.

Generally, all investment products or strategies have some degree of inherent risk (e.g., market risk), but it is not intended that the composite description identifies every risk of the strategy. Instead, firms must identify those material risks of the strategy, if any, and must disclose those risks. For example, investment concentration, correlation (or lack thereof), liquidity, and exposure to counterparties are features that may need to be included in the composite description.

The key characteristics of some strategies may change given market events. Firms should periodically review composite descriptions to ensure they are current.

Sample Disclosures:

"The Large Cap Equity Growth Composite includes all institutional portfolios that invest in large-capitalization US stocks that are considered to have growth in earnings prospects that is superior to that of the average company within the benchmark, the XYZ Large Cap Growth Index. The targeted tracking error between the composite and the benchmark is less than 3%."

"The Leveraged Bond Composite includes all segregated accounts invested in a diversified range of high-yield corporate and government bonds with the aim of providing investors with a high level of income while seeking to maximize the total return. The portfolios are invested in domestic and international fixed income securities of varying maturities. The strategy allows investment in exchange-traded and OTC derivative contracts (including, but not limited to, options, futures, swaps, and forward currency contracts) for the purposes of risk, volatility, and currency exposure management. The strategy allows leverage up to but not exceeding twice the value of a portfolio's investments through the use of repurchase financing arrangements with counterparties. Inherent in derivative instrument investments is the risk of counterparty default. Leverage may also magnify losses as well as gains to the extent that leverage is employed. The benchmark is the XYZ Capital Global Aggregate Bond Index."

A Sample List of Composite Descriptions can be found in Appendix D of the GIPS standards.

Provision 4.C.5

The FIRM MUST disclose:

a. The BENCHMARK DESCRIPTION, which MUST include the key features of the BENCHMARK or the name of the BENCHMARK for a readily recognized index or other point of reference.
b. The PERIODICITY of the BENCHMARK if BENCHMARK returns are calculated less frequently than monthly.

Discussion

Firms are required to disclose a description of each benchmark included in a GIPS Composite Report. The benchmark description is defined as general information regarding the investments, structure, and/or characteristics of the benchmark, and it must include the key features of the benchmark. In the case of a widely recognized benchmark, such as the S&P 500® Index, the name of the benchmark will satisfy this requirement. (S&P 500® is a registered trademark of Standard & Poor's Financial Services LLC.) Each firm must decide for itself whether a benchmark is widely recognized. If the firm is not certain as to whether the benchmark is widely known, the firm must include the benchmark description.

If the benchmark returns are calculated less frequently than monthly, the periodicity of the benchmark must be disclosed.

Sample Disclosure for a Widely Recognized Benchmark:

"The benchmark is the S&P 500® Index."

Sample Disclosure for a Benchmark That Is Not Widely Recognized:

"The benchmark is the XYZ World Index, which is designed to measure the equity market performance of developed market countries. The benchmark is market-cap weighted and is composed of all XYZ country-specific developed market indices."

Sample Disclosure for an Index with Returns Calculated Less Frequently than Monthly:

"The ABC Property Index (API) is a quarterly, unleveraged composite total return for private commercial real estate properties held for investment purposes only. All properties in the API have been acquired, at least in part, on behalf of tax-exempt institutional investors."

Provision 4.C.6

When presenting GROSS-OF-FEES returns, the FIRM MUST disclose if any other fees are deducted in addition to TRANSACTION COSTS.

Discussion

A gross-of-fees return is the return on investments reduced by any transaction costs. If a firm presents a gross-of-fees return in a GIPS Composite Report, the firm must disclose if any other fees are deducted in addition to transaction costs (e.g., custody fees). In cases where fees other than transactions costs have been deducted from the gross-of-fees returns, this disclosure helps prospective clients understand the gross-of-fees returns being presented and therefore compare performance across firms.

In some markets, brokers offer zero-commission trades. If a portfolio is paying zero commissions, then it is appropriate to calculate portfolio gross-of-fees returns that reflect zero transaction costs. When a composite includes portfolios that pay zero commissions, firms should disclose this fact. Not disclosing this fact could be misleading.

Sample Disclosure:

"Gross-of-fees returns reflect the deduction of transaction costs and custodian fees but do not reflect the deduction of investment management fees."

Provision 4.C.7

When presenting NET-OF-FEES returns, the FIRM MUST disclose:

a. If any other fees are deducted in addition to INVESTMENT MANAGEMENT FEES and TRANSACTION COSTS.
b. If NET-OF-FEES returns are net of any PERFORMANCE-BASED FEES or CARRIED INTEREST.
c. If model or actual INVESTMENT MANAGEMENT FEES are used.
d. If model INVESTMENT MANAGEMENT FEES are used, and COMPOSITE GROSS-OF-FEES returns are not presented, the model INVESTMENT MANAGEMENT FEE used to calculate NET-OF-FEES returns.[34]
e. If model INVESTMENT MANAGEMENT FEES are used, the methodology used to calculate NET-OF-FEES returns.

[34] REQUIRED for periods ending on or after 31 December 2020.

Discussion

When presenting returns, it is important that there are sufficient disclosures so that prospective clients can understand what the returns actually represent.

Net-of-fees returns for composites are required to reflect only the deduction of transaction costs and investment management fees. Investment management fees include both asset-based fees and performance-based fees or carried interest. Other expenses may also be deducted (e.g., custody fees). If other fees are deducted from the net-of-fees returns, this must be disclosed to help prospective clients understand the net-of-fees returns presented and to compare performance across firms. If the net-of-fees returns are net of any performance-based fees or carried interest, that must be disclosed as well.

In some markets, brokers offer zero-commission trades. If a portfolio is paying zero commissions, then it is appropriate to calculate portfolio net-of-fees returns that reflect zero transaction costs. When a composite includes portfolios that pay zero commissions, firms should disclose this fact. Not disclosing this fact could be misleading.

A firm must also disclose whether model or actual investment management fees are used to calculate net-of-fees returns. (See Provision 2.A.31 for an explanation of when model investment management fees may be used.) If gross-of-fees returns are presented along with the net-of-fees returns, prospective clients can easily determine the model fee used by deducting the net-of-fee returns from the gross-of-fee returns. For periods ending on or after 31 December 2020, however, if model investment management fees have been used and composite gross-of-fees returns are not presented, the firm must disclose the model fee used to calculate net-of-fees returns. The methodology used in the calculation of net-of-fees returns must be disclosed if model investment management fees are used.

Sample Disclosure for Actual Fees:

"Net-of-fees returns are calculated using actual management fees, which include performance fees. These fees are accounted for on an accrual basis."

Sample Disclosure for Model Fees:

"Net-of-fees returns are calculated by reducing monthly composite returns by a model fee of 0.0830%. This equates to a model annual fee of 1.0%, which is the highest tier of the standard fee schedule."

Provision 4.C.8

The FIRM MUST disclose which fees and expenses other than INVESTMENT MANAGEMENT FEES (e.g., research costs) are separately charged by the FIRM to clients, if material.

Discussion

Clients typically bear investment management fees and transaction costs. In some cases, however, firms may charge fees or expenses, such as investment research costs, directly to clients. When any fees or expenses other than investment management fees are separately charged by the firm to clients, and these fees or expenses are material, the firm must disclose which fees and expenses are separately charged. When determining if additional fees or expenses would be considered material, a firm must consider whether the additional fees or expenses are significant enough to reduce a prospective client's assessment of the attractiveness of the expected returns of the strategy relative to total fees charged. If so, the firm's failure to disclose these additional fees or expenses would violate the principle of full disclosure.

Sample Disclosure:

"In addition to investment management fees and transaction costs, certain investment research costs are charged directly to clients, as stipulated in client agreements."

Provision 4.C.9

The FIRM MUST disclose or otherwise indicate the reporting currency.

Discussion

The GIPS standards require that firms disclose the currency used to report the numerical information presented in a GIPS Composite Report. If the firm presents performance in multiple currencies in the same GIPS Composite Report, the firm must ensure it is clear which currencies are used to calculate and report performance and assets.

Labeling the columns within a GIPS Composite Report with the appropriate currency symbol would satisfy this requirement, as would a written disclosure. If firms market the strategy outside their home market, they should consider whether the currency symbol alone is sufficient. For example, a Canadian firm marketing only in Canada may decide to present only the $ symbol. If the firm markets the strategy in both the United States and Canada, the firm must disclose whether the currency is USD or CAD, because both currencies use the same currency symbol.

All required and recommended information presented in a GIPS Composite Report must be presented in the same currency. (See Provision 4.A.12.)

Sample Disclosures:

"Valuations are computed and all information is reported in Canadian dollars."

"All numerical information is reported in Japanese yen."

Provision 4.C.10

The FIRM MUST disclose which measure of INTERNAL DISPERSION is presented.

Discussion

The GIPS standards do not mandate that a specific measure of a composite's internal dispersion must be included in a GIPS Composite Report. Instead, firms are permitted to choose a measure for each composite and apply it consistently. (See Provision 4.A.1.i.) Because firms may choose which measure of internal dispersion to present, disclosure of the chosen measure is required in the GIPS Composite Report to help prospective clients understand which measure of internal dispersion is being presented.

Sample Disclosure:

"Internal dispersion is calculated using the equal-weighted standard deviation of the annual gross returns of those portfolios that were included in the composite for the entire year."

Provision 4.C.11

The FIRM MUST disclose the current FEE SCHEDULE appropriate to PROSPECTIVE CLIENTS or PROSPECTIVE INVESTORS.

a. When presenting performance to a PROSPECTIVE CLIENT for a standalone PORTFOLIO, the FEE SCHEDULE MUST reflect the FEE SCHEDULE for a standalone PORTFOLIO managed according to that strategy.
b. When presenting performance of a COMPOSITE that includes CARVE-OUTS to a PROSPECTIVE CLIENT for a multi-asset strategy PORTFOLIO, the FEE SCHEDULE MUST reflect the FEE SCHEDULE for a multi-asset strategy PORTFOLIO managed according to that strategy.
c. When presenting a WRAP FEE COMPOSITE to a WRAP FEE PROSPECTIVE CLIENT, the FEE SCHEDULE MUST reflect the total WRAP FEE.
d. When presenting a GIPS COMPOSITE REPORT to a PROSPECTIVE INVESTOR for a POOLED FUND included in the COMPOSITE, the FIRM MUST disclose the POOLED FUND's current FEE SCHEDULE and EXPENSE RATIO.

Discussion

Firms must disclose the current fee schedule that is applicable to prospective clients or prospective investors for the specific composite. The fee schedule can be asset based, performance based, or a combination of both. Determining which fee schedule is appropriate depends on the recipient of the information.

Prospective Client for a Standalone Portfolio

A standalone portfolio is a portfolio that is not a portion of a larger portfolio. If the performance of a composite is being presented to a prospective client for a standalone portfolio, the fee schedule must reflect the fee schedule for a standalone portfolio managed according to that strategy.

Prospective Client for a Multi-Asset-Class Strategy Portfolio When the Composite Includes Carve-Outs

If the performance of a multi-asset-class strategy model composite that includes carve-outs is being presented to a prospective client as supplemental information to the single-asset-class composites that represent the "building blocks" for the strategy, the fee schedule must reflect the fee schedule for a multi-asset-class portfolio managed according to the strategy, not the fees associated with the individual building blocks. The same is true if the building blocks do not include carve-outs. The firm may provide the fee schedules for the individual building blocks for the strategy, in addition to the fee schedule for the multi-asset-class strategy, if it wishes to do so. Note that the firm must also present the GIPS Composite Reports for the underlying, building block composites to the prospective client. (See Provision 3.A.2.)

Wrap Fee Prospective Client

If a wrap fee composite is being presented to a wrap fee prospective client, the fee schedule must reflect the total wrap fee that will be charged to the wrap fee prospective client. The firm may also present the fee schedule that it charges for managing the wrap fee portfolios, which is a component of the total wrap fee, but this disclosure must be in addition to the total wrap fee schedule. Firms should also consider disclosing when clients are expected to incur significant trade away fees. Trade away fees, also known as step-out fees, are fees charged on trade orders that a portfolio manager for a wrap fee portfolio places with a broker/dealer other than the broker/dealer designated by the wrap fee sponsor.

Prospective Investor for a Pooled Fund Included in the Composite

When presenting performance to a prospective investor for a pooled fund, a firm may provide a GIPS Pooled Fund Report that includes performance of that pooled fund. If the pooled fund is included in a composite, the firm may instead provide a GIPS Composite Report to the prospective investor. If the firm provides a GIPS Composite Report to the prospective investor, the firm must include the fee schedule that is appropriate to the pooled fund, rather than (or in addition to) the fee schedule for the composite. If the pooled fund has multiple fee schedules, the firm may use the highest fee schedule as the appropriate fee that can be used for all prospective investors. The firm may also include multiple fee schedules in the GIPS Composite Report.

Firms must present the total expense ratio that is applicable to prospective investors for the specific pooled fund. The pooled fund expense ratio is the ratio of total pooled fund expenses to average net assets. The expense ratio should not reflect transaction costs. The expense ratio gives prospective investors important insight into the total fees and expenses involved in an investment in the fund. For example, a pooled fund expense ratio of 2% indicates that an investor will pay $20 in expenses each year for every $1,000 invested, in addition to transaction costs. An expense ratio also helps investors compare expenses across funds, because even a small difference in fees can have a significant effect over time.

If the pooled fund has multiple share classes, the firm may present multiple expense ratios or may present only the expense ratio appropriate to the prospective investor. The firm may also use the highest expense ratio as the expense ratio that can be used for all prospective investors of the fund. Expense ratios must reflect any performance-based fees or carried interest, if accrued or charged to the pooled fund.

Because expense ratios can change over time, firms must determine which expense ratio to present. A firm might choose to present the expense ratio as of the most recent annual period end, or the last known expense ratio. When the expense ratio has had a material change resulting from a change in assets or costs, the firm should present a more current expense ratio that reflects what a prospective investor is likely to pay at the current time.

Pooled fund expense ratios that are calculated for periods of less than one year must be annualized. For example, assume that a pooled fund starts on 1 April, and the firm calculates an expense ratio of 0.75% for the period from 1 April 2019 through 31 December 2019. The firm must present an annualized rate of 1.00%, representing a pooled fund expense ratio for the entire year, rather than the 0.75% that represents an expense ratio for only nine months. Presenting an annualized expense ratio facilitates the comparison of expense ratios across funds and firms. Firms may also present the non-annualized expense ratio but must clearly disclose or indicate that the expense ratio is not annualized.

When a firm uses a single GIPS Composite Report for prospective investors for multiple pooled funds that are included in the composite, it must disclose fee schedules and expense ratios for each pooled fund. The firm may instead choose to tailor the GIPS Composite Report to include the fee schedule and expense ratio that are appropriate for the prospective investor.

The fee schedule presented to a prospective client or prospective investor is typically listed by asset level ranges and should be appropriate to the particular prospective client or prospective investor. The fee schedule must be current. Although a current fee schedule may not assist a prospective client or prospective investor when interpreting historical performance because the actual fees paid may differ from the fee schedule disclosed, it is the most relevant to the prospective client or prospective investor. The actual fee that the prospective client or prospective investor may pay (if it hires the firm) could also differ from the fee schedule disclosed in the GIPS Composite Report. For example, a prospective client or prospective investor may be able to negotiate a lower fee.

This disclosure requirement is not satisfied if the firm does not include the fee schedule and expense ratio, if applicable, in the GIPS Composite Report and instead makes reference to another document that includes the fee schedule or expense ratio, such as Form ADV, which is a US regulatory document, or a fund prospectus. The fee schedule and expense ratios may be an exhibit attached to the GIPS Composite Report.

Sample Disclosure for a Composite to a Prospective Client for a Segregated Account:

"The annual fee schedule is as follows:

First €10 million	0.80%
Next €40 million	0.60%
Above €50 million	0.30%"

Sample Disclosure for a Model Composite That Includes Carve-Outs or Other "Building Blocks" to a Prospective Client for a Multi-Asset-Class Strategy Portfolio:

"The current standard management fee schedule for a segregated account managed to the Balanced strategy, which is a blend of the Large-Cap Equity Composite and the Intermediate-Term Fixed Income Composite, is as follows:

- 0.70% on the first $25 million
- 0.55% on the next $75 million
- 0.45% on all assets above $100 million.

The fee schedules for the Large-Cap Equity Composite and the Intermediate-Term Fixed Income Composite are as follows:

Large-Cap Equity Composite	*Intermediate-Term Fixed Income Composite*
0.90% on the first $25 million	0.50% on the first $25 million
0.70% on the next $75 million	0.40% on the next $75 million
0.60% on all assets above $100 million	0.30% on all assets about $100 million"

Sample Disclosure for a Wrap Fee Composite:

"The standard wrap fee schedule in effect is 3.00% of total assets. The wrap fee includes transaction costs, investment management fees, custody fees, and other administrative fees."

Sample Disclosure for a Composite That Includes a Pooled Fund:

"The investment management fee schedule for Global Equity segregated accounts is as follows: 1.00% on the first $25 million; 0.75% thereafter. The investment management fee schedule for the Global Equity Pooled Fund, which is included in the Global Equity Composite, is 0.80% on all assets. The total expense ratio as of 31 December 2019 for the Global Equity Pooled Fund was 0.95%."

Sample Disclosure for a Composite That Includes Two Pooled Funds:

Vehicle	Fee Schedule	Expense Ratio
Segregated account	0.50% on all assets	n/a
Limited partnership	0.45% on all assets	0.75%
Collective fund	0.40% on all assets	0.68%

Provision 4.C.12

If the FEE SCHEDULE includes PERFORMANCE-BASED FEES or CARRIED INTEREST, the FIRM MUST disclose the PERFORMANCE-BASED FEE DESCRIPTION or CARRIED INTEREST DESCRIPTION.

Discussion

Sufficient information must be included with any fee schedule included in a GIPS Composite Report to allow prospective clients to understand the nature of the firm's compensation.
If performance-based fees or carried interest are included in the fee schedule, the firm must disclose a description of the performance-based fees and/or carried interest. Relevant information for a performance-based fee includes the performance-based fee rate, hurdle rate, clawback, high watermark, reset frequency, accrual frequency, crystallization schedule, and on what basis fees are charged. Relevant information for carried interest includes the hurdle rate, crystallization schedule, and high watermark.

Sample Disclosures:

"The standard fee schedule is as follows:

Management fee is 0.75% per annum, charged on a quarterly basis on the period-end value of the portfolio assets.

Performance fee:

The performance fee is earned when the portfolio's total return, reduced by the pro rata accrued fixed management fee, exceeds the benchmark return (the excess return) and the portfolio's net asset value is above the high watermark, which is the portfolio's net asset value as of the last year end when the performance fee crystallized. The performance fee is 10% of the excess return, which is calculated arithmetically, accrued daily, and crystallizes annually. Further details of the performance fee calculation are available upon request."

Provision 4.C.13

The FIRM MUST disclose the COMPOSITE INCEPTION DATE.

Discussion

When reviewing the performance data in a GIPS Composite Report, it is important that prospective clients have sufficient information regarding the length of the composite track record to put the performance presented in the GIPS Composite Report in perspective. Therefore, the inception date of the composite being presented in the GIPS Composite Report must be disclosed. Prospective clients can then compare the periods of performance presented in the GIPS Composite Report with the length of the composite's track record, and they can request additional information for historical periods not included in the GIPS Composite Report. If there has been a break in the performance record of a composite, the initial inception date before the break is the date that would be disclosed.

Sample Disclosures:

"The Small Cap Value Composite has an inception date of 1 May 2010, the date on which the first portfolio in the composite was fully invested."

"The Global Fixed Income Composite has an inception date of 1 November 2015. There was a break in performance from 1 March 2019 through 30 November 2019. During that period, there were no portfolios in the composite. Composite performance began again on 1 December 2019."

"The Asia Pacific Equities Composite has an inception date of 1 March 1998. Returns for periods prior to the 10-year track record presented in this report are available upon request."

 |

Provision 4.C.14

The FIRM MUST disclose the COMPOSITE CREATION DATE.

Discussion

Firms must disclose the composite creation date, which is the date on which the firm first grouped one or more portfolios together to create the composite. The composite creation date is not necessarily the same as the composite inception date. The composite inception date is the initial date of the composite's performance record and is a required disclosure. (See Provision 4.C.13.) The composite creation date can be significantly after the composite inception date, depending on when the firm first grouped the individual portfolios together to create the composite. This information allows prospective clients to compare the composite creation date with the composite inception date to determine whether the firm grouped portfolios together into a composite retroactively or created the composite at the beginning of the composite's performance track record. The intent of this disclosure is to enable prospective clients to determine if the composite was created with the benefit of hindsight.

For those firms that created composites many years ago, it may be impossible to know the specific day a composite was created. Some firms disclose a composite creation date as a month, or even a year, when the composite was created in the very distant past. Newly created composites should have more-precise composite creation dates.

Sample Disclosures:

"The Growth Opportunities Composite was created on 17 July 2019. This is the date on which portfolios were first grouped together to create the composite."

"The Core Fixed Income Composite was created in November 2009."

Provision 4.C.15

The FIRM MUST disclose that the following lists are available upon request, if applicable:

a. List of COMPOSITE DESCRIPTIONS.
b. List of POOLED FUND DESCRIPTIONS for LIMITED DISTRIBUTION POOLED FUNDS.
c. List of BROAD DISTRIBUTION POOLED FUNDS.

Discussion

In each GIPS Composite Report, firms must disclose that a list of composite descriptions and a list of pooled fund descriptions for limited distribution pooled funds (LDPFs) are available upon request, if applicable to the firm. The firm must also disclose that a list of broad distribution pooled funds (BDPFs) is available upon request, if BDPFs are included within the definition of the firm. The required list of LDPF descriptions and of BDPFs is at the fund level and not the share class level.

If the firm does not sell participation in a fund (e.g., the firm manages the assets but another legal entity distributes the fund and the firm does not sell shares in the fund), the firm must consider the portfolio a segregated account and would include the portfolio in a composite. This would include sub-advised pooled funds. The segregated account would not be included on the list of LDPF descriptions or the list of BDPFs. In addition, a portfolio with a pooled fund wrapper, (i.e., a single-investor pooled fund), which is unitized but is not available to other investors, is also considered a segregated account, would be included in a composite, and would not appear on a list of LDPF descriptions or a list of BDPFs.

As noted in Provision 1.A.22, if a pooled fund is included in a composite but the firm offers participation in the fund, either directly or through an agent, the pooled fund must still appear on the required list of LDPF descriptions or the list of BDPFs, as appropriate.

The firm may combine its list of composite descriptions, its list of LDPF descriptions, and its list of BDPFs into one document if it wishes to do so. The firm may also prepare a list of all the strategies that it offers and may indicate, as part of the strategy description, the types of portfolios (segregated account, LDPF, or BDPF) in which the strategy is available. This list of strategies can be in narrative or table format.

This requirement exists to provide prospective clients with a complete picture of the firm's composites and pooled funds. Prospective clients may then request information that will allow them to evaluate whether the GIPS Composite Report they have received is the most appropriate and to determine if there are any other GIPS Composite Reports or GIPS Pooled Fund Reports that they should also request to see.

a. List of COMPOSITE DESCRIPTIONS.

The firm must disclose, in each GIPS Composite Report, that the firm's list of composite descriptions is available upon request. The list of composite descriptions itself does not need to be included in each GIPS Composite Report but must be available upon request. The list of composite descriptions must include the composite description for each current composite, as well as a description for all composites that have terminated in the past five years. The composite descriptions disclosed in GIPS Composite Reports must be consistent with the descriptions included in the list of composite descriptions.

An explanation of composite descriptions can be found in the discussion of Provision 1.A.22. A Sample List of Composite Descriptions can be found in Appendix D of the GIPS standards.

b. List of POOLED FUND DESCRIPTIONS for LIMITED DISTRIBUTION POOLED FUNDS.

If LDPFs are included within the definition of a firm, the firm must disclose, in each GIPS Composite Report, that the firm's list of descriptions of LDPFs is available upon request. An LDPF is any pooled fund that is not a BDPF. A BDPF is any pooled fund that is regulated under a framework that would permit the general public to purchase or hold the pooled fund's shares and is not exclusively offered in one-on-one presentations. LDPFs are often referred to as "private funds." These funds are typically sold in one-on-one presentations and may not be highly regulated. The list of LDPF descriptions does not need to be included in each GIPS Composite Report but must be available upon request. The list of LDPF descriptions must include the pooled fund description for each current pooled fund but does not have to include terminated funds. Terminated LDPFs are treated differently from terminated composites because, although a firm can restart a composite strategy when a prospective client hires the firm for a strategy that was previously closed, the firm does not have the same ability to restart a pooled fund. The pooled fund descriptions disclosed in GIPS Pooled Fund Reports must be consistent with the descriptions included in the list of pooled fund descriptions.

The list of LDPF descriptions may be tailored to include only those LDPFs for which a prospective investor is eligible, but the firm is not required to do this.

An explanation of LDPF descriptions can be found in the discussion of Provision 1.A.22. A Sample List of Pooled Fund Descriptions can be found in Appendix D of the GIPS standards.

c. List of BROAD DISTRIBUTION POOLED FUNDS.

In addition to the lists of composite descriptions and LDPF descriptions, firms must also disclose, in each GIPS Composite Report, that a list of BDPFs is available upon request, if applicable to the firm. A BDPF is any pooled fund that is regulated under a framework that would permit the general public to purchase or hold the pooled fund's shares and is not exclusively offered in one-on-one presentations. These funds are typically sold to the general public and are highly regulated.

Note that the required list of BDPFs is a list of the names of the firm's BDPFs only. No descriptions of the BDPFs are required. The list of BDPF names does not need to be included in each GIPS Composite Report but must be available upon request. The list of BDPFs must include the names of all current BDPFs but does not need to include terminated BDPFs. Terminated BDPFs are treated differently from terminated composites because, although a firm can restart a composite strategy when a prospective client hires the firm for a strategy that was previously closed, the firm does not have the same ability to restart a pooled fund. If a firm includes information about all of its BDPFs on its website, the firm may provide a link to the website to fulfill the requirement to provide the list of BDPFs upon request.

This list may be tailored to include only those BDPFs for which a prospective investor is eligible, but the firm is not required to do this.

Sample Disclosures:

For Firms with Composites Only

"A list of composite descriptions is available upon request."

For Firms with Composites and Limited Distribution Pooled Funds

"A list of composite descriptions and a list of limited distribution pooled fund descriptions are available upon request."

For Firms with Composites, Limited Distribution Pooled Funds, and Broad Distribution Pooled Funds

"A list of composite descriptions, a list of limited distribution pooled fund descriptions, and a list of broad distribution pooled funds are available upon request."

For Firms That Offer Strategies in Multiple Vehicles

"A list of all composite and pooled fund investment strategies offered by the firm, with a description of each strategy, is available upon request. The type of portfolios in which each strategy is available (segregated account, limited distribution pooled fund, or broad distribution pooled fund) is indicated in the description of each strategy."

Provision 4.C.16

The FIRM MUST disclose that policies for valuing investments, calculating performance, and preparing GIPS REPORTS are available upon request.

Discussion

In each GIPS Composite Report, firms must disclose the availability of policies for valuing investments, calculating performance, and preparing GIPS Reports. The policies are not required to be included in each GIPS Composite Report but must be available upon request. Firms are not required to provide the related procedures, in addition to the policies, but may do so.

Sample Disclosure:

"Firm XYZ's policies for valuing investments, calculating performance, and preparing GIPS Reports are available upon request."

Provision 4.C.17

The FIRM MUST disclose how leverage, derivatives, and short positions have been used historically, if material.

Discussion

Firms must provide enough information in a GIPS Composite Report to allow a prospective client to understand how leverage, derivatives, and short positions have been employed historically and may be used going forward. Although the composite description includes disclosure of the firm's ability to use leverage, derivatives, and short positions (See Provision 4.C.4), Provision 4.C.17 requires that the firm disclose the leverage, derivatives, and short positions that have been used historically, if material. Taken together, these two required disclosures provide a more complete picture of the presence, use, and extent of leverage, derivatives, and short positions.

For example, assume a firm discloses in the composite description that the strategy may employ up to 200% leverage. To satisfy the disclosure requirement in Provision 4.C.17, the firm might state, "Since the inception of the strategy, the leverage has averaged 110% of the composite's value; however, during 2019 the leverage averaged 160%, which greatly increased the sensitivity to market volatility and the potential for realized gains and/or losses."

No disclosure is required if leverage, derivatives, and short positions have not been used or if their use has not been material. When determining what would be material, the firm must consider whether the disclosure of how leverage, derivatives, and/or short positions have been used historically is likely to affect a prospective client's view of the risk involved in the strategy. If so, it would be misleading for the firm to fail to disclose their use to these prospective clients when describing the strategy.

Provision 4.C.18

If estimated TRANSACTION COSTS are used, the FIRM MUST disclose:

a. That estimated TRANSACTION COSTS were used.
b. The estimated TRANSACTION COSTS used and how they were determined.

Discussion

Gross-of-fees and net-of-fees composite returns must reflect the deduction of transaction costs, which are the costs of buying or selling investments. Firms may use either actual or estimated transaction costs when calculating returns. Estimated transaction costs may be used only for portfolios for which the actual transaction costs are not known. Provision 2.A.13 provides guidance on the use of estimated transaction costs.

If estimated transaction costs are used in calculating returns, there must be a disclosure that estimated transaction costs were used. A firm must also disclose the estimated transaction costs used and how they were determined. A firm might, for example, determine estimated transaction costs based on other portfolios whose transaction costs are known.

In some markets, brokers offer zero-commission trades. If a portfolio is paying zero commissions, then it is appropriate to calculate portfolio gross-of-fees returns and net-of-fees returns that reflect zero transaction costs. When a composite includes portfolios that pay zero commissions, firms should disclose this fact. Not disclosing this fact could be misleading.

Sample Disclosures:

"Some portfolios in the composite do not pay explicit transaction costs for security purchases and sales. Estimated transaction costs for these portfolios are used, and these are determined based on the average transaction cost per share incurred by portfolios in the composite that pay explicit transaction costs. The average transaction cost was determined to be $0.031 per share. We apply a model transaction cost per share of $0.04 to each investment transaction."

"The transaction costs for some portfolios in the composite are not known and must be estimated. The estimated transaction costs for these portfolios is 12 Swiss francs per trade."

"Effective 1 January 2020, a majority of portfolio trades are made through brokers that no longer charge commissions on standard equity trades. Portfolios that trade options and futures continue to pay transaction costs for options/futures contract trades."

Provision 4.C.19

The FIRM MUST disclose all significant events that would help a PROSPECTIVE CLIENT interpret the GIPS COMPOSITE REPORT. This disclosure MUST be included for a minimum of one year and for as long as it is relevant to interpreting the track record.

Discussion

The GIPS standards are based on the principles of fair representation and full disclosure. Meeting these objectives requires a good faith commitment on the part of the firm to adhere to the spirit of the GIPS standards. The GIPS standards cannot foresee and cover every situation that might occur. Therefore, this provision requires that firms disclose all significant events that would help explain the firm's GIPS Composite Report to a prospective client. The primary goal of this requirement is to provide relevant information to prospective clients so that they can understand the potential effect of the significant event on the composite's investment strategy and the firm.

Significant events are determined by the firm and would include, as examples, a material change in personnel responsible for investment management, significant changes to the investment management process, the loss of historical records resulting from a catastrophic event, or a change in firm ownership. The acquisition of a new entity or selling off part of a firm would also qualify as a significant event, as would the departure of someone who was the single investment decision maker for a strategy.

Depending on the situation, a general statement describing the significant event that has occurred may be sufficient. Other situations may require firms to disclose specific information pertaining to the significant event. The disclosure regarding the significant event must be included in the GIPS Composite Report for a minimum of one year and for as long as it is relevant to interpreting the performance track record. As an example, a firm that acquires another firm, resulting in a large increase in total firm assets, may disclose this significant event for as long as the large change in total firm assets is included in the GIPS Composite Report. In contrast, a change in a firm's chief investment officer (CIO) is a change that a firm may believe should be disclosed for one year only.

The firm must consider the underlying principles of the GIPS standards, which are fair representation and full disclosure, when determining how long the disclosure will be included in the GIPS Composite Report.

Sample Disclosures:

"In June 2017, Firm G determined that the custodian bank used by all of the firm's proprietary mutual funds had failed to file reclaimable withholding tax refund requests with the appropriate authorities. At that time, all accrued reclaimable withholding taxes were written off, decreasing the composite's monthly return by 1.06%."

"On 15 April 2018, the quantitative asset management division of Firm Z was sold, resulting in the 2018 decrease in Firm Z's assets."

"In February 2020, the parent company of Firm M announced plans to exit the investment management business and sell Firm M. As of April 2020, a tentative sale of Firm M has been agreed upon but not yet finalized."

Provision 4.C.20

For any performance presented for periods prior to the MINIMUM EFFECTIVE COMPLIANCE DATE that does not comply with the GIPS standards, the FIRM MUST disclose the periods of non-compliance.

Discussion

Firms may link non-GIPS compliant performance to their GIPS-compliant performance provided that only GIPS-compliant performance is presented for periods beginning on or after the minimum effective compliance date, which is 1 January 2006 for private equity and real estate composites and pooled funds and wrap fee composites, and 1 January 2000 for all other composites and pooled funds. If the firm chooses to present non-compliant performance for periods prior to the minimum effective compliance date, the firm must disclose which periods are not in compliance. Prospective clients and existing clients can then inquire about the reasons why the periods prior to the minimum effective compliance date are not compliant and consider the effects of non-compliance on the historical performance.

If non-compliant performance is included in a GIPS Composite Report after the minimum effective date, it must be labeled as supplemental information and must not be linked to the GIPS-compliant performance.

Sample Disclosure:

"The performance record for 1995 through 1999 is not in compliance with the GIPS standards."

Provision 4.C.21

If the FIRM is redefined, the FIRM MUST disclose the date and description of the redefinition.

Discussion

A firm redefinition occurs when something changes with how the firm is held out to the public or when any of its distinct business entity criteria significantly change. Changes in investment style or personnel are not events that typically cause a firm redefinition. A simple firm name change is also not a sufficient reason to redefine the firm. Corporate restructuring may cause a change with how the firm is held out to the public. As an example, a firm that was defined to include only the institutional division would be redefined when it consolidated the institutional division with the mutual fund/retail division. A merger or acquisition may cause a change in the definition of the firm, but that is not always the case.

Suppose that a firm defines itself as an investment management firm offering active equity strategies to clients. An acquisition that expanded the firm's offerings to include fixed-income strategies would result in a redefinition of the firm, because there would be a change in how the firm holds itself out to the public. An acquisition that simply added additional equity strategies to the firm's offerings would not result in a redefinition of the firm. However, the acquisition is likely to be a significant event that must be disclosed in a GIPS Composite Report. (See Provision 4.C.19.)

In some cases, as a result of a significant alteration in a firm's structure or organization, a change can be so great that it creates a new firm. See Provision 1.A.2 for guidance on firm definitions.

The GIPS standards require that changes in a firm's organization must not lead to alteration of historical performance (see Provision 1.A.28).

Sample Disclosures:

"As of 1 August 2019, XYZ Firm was redefined to include both the London and Tokyo office of XYZ Company. Previously, the firm was defined to include only the London office."

"As of 1 January 2020, XYZ Investment Management was redefined to include the wrap division."

"Effective 1 January 2019, ABC Capital Management was redefined as an investment management firm offering both equity and fixed-income strategies. Prior to the 31 December 2018 acquisition of Curtone Capital Management, an investment firm offering fixed-income strategies, ABC Capital Management offered only equity strategies."

Provision 4.C.22

If the COMPOSITE is redefined, the FIRM MUST disclose the date and description of the redefinition.

Discussion

Investment strategies can change over time. In some cases, such a change results in the termination of one composite and the creation of a new composite. In other cases, it may be appropriate to redefine the composite. If a composite is redefined, the firm must disclose the date and description of the redefinition. See Provision 3.A.5 for guidance on composite definitions.

Sample Disclosures:

"Effective 1 January 2018, the Small Cap Composite was redefined to exclude mutual funds from the composite because of liquidity constraints; subsequently, only institutional portfolios are included."

"As of 1 July 2019, the fixed-income strategy includes the use of interest rate futures to modify duration and manage interest rate risk. Prior to this date, the Composite's strategy did not involve the active management of interest rate risk."

Provision 4.C.23

The FIRM MUST disclose changes to the name of the COMPOSITE. This disclosure MUST be included for a minimum of one year and for as long as it is relevant to interpreting the track record.

Discussion

When prospective clients are evaluating composites over time and across firms, it is important that they understand exactly which composites they are assessing. If a firm changes the name of a composite, the change must be disclosed in the GIPS Composite Report. The name change must be disclosed for a minimum of one year and potentially for more than one year if the firm determines the disclosure is still relevant and meaningful. The firm must consider the underlying principles of the GIPS standards, which are fair representation and full disclosure, when determining how long the disclosure will be included in the GIPS Composite Report.

Sample Disclosure:

"As of 1 January 2016, the XYZ Index Composite was renamed the US Equity Large Cap Composite."

Provision 4.C.24

The FIRM MUST disclose:

a. The minimum asset level, if any, below which PORTFOLIOS are not included in the COMPOSITE.

b. Any changes to the minimum asset level.

Discussion

The firm may establish a minimum asset level for a composite to exclude portfolios that are too small to be representative of the intended strategy. Firms must disclose the minimum asset level of the composite, if one exists, in each respective GIPS Composite Report. If any changes have been made to the minimum asset level of a composite, the firm must document and disclose changes to the minimum asset level and must not retroactively apply the new limit. See the discussion of Provision 3.A.11 for additional guidance on composite minimums.

Sample Disclosure:

"The minimum portfolio size for inclusion in the LMN Composite is €500,000. Prior to 2018, portfolios with assets below €400,000 were not included in the LMN Composite."

Provision 4.C.25

The FIRM MUST disclose if COMPOSITE returns are gross or net of withholding taxes, if material.

Discussion

Global investing requires recognition of the tax consequences of investing in different countries. The GIPS standards do not require firms to reflect withholding taxes, either reclaimable or non-reclaimable taxes, in a certain manner. Firms may choose whether or not to reflect the effect of withholding taxes when calculating performance. The GIPS standards do recommend that performance be reported net of non-reclaimable withholding taxes on dividends, interest, and capital gains and also recommend that reclaimable foreign withholding taxes be accrued (see Provision 2.B.5). If withholding taxes are material, firms must disclose how withholding taxes are treated when calculating performance. A firm must determine the level at which withholding taxes become material, document this level in its policies and procedures, and apply it consistently.

Sample Disclosure:

"Portfolio returns are net of all foreign non-reclaimable withholding taxes. Reclaimable withholding taxes are reflected as income if and when received."

Provision 4.C.26

The FIRM MUST disclose if BENCHMARK returns are net of withholding taxes if this information is available.

Discussion

Global investing requires recognition of the tax consequences of investing in different countries. The GIPS standards do not require firms to reflect withholding taxes, either reclaimable or non-reclaimable taxes, in a certain manner. Firms may choose whether or not to reflect the effect of withholding taxes when calculating composite performance and, similarly, whether or not to use a benchmark that reflects the effect of withholding taxes.

As Provision 4.C.25 indicates, if withholding taxes are material, firms must disclose how withholding taxes are treated when calculating performance. To facilitate the comparison of composite returns and benchmark returns, firms must also disclose if the benchmark returns are net of withholding taxes if this information is available. If the benchmark name indicates that the benchmark is net of withholding taxes, no additional disclosure is necessary.

Sample Disclosure:

"Benchmark returns are net of withholding taxes."

Provision 4.C.27

If the GIPS COMPOSITE REPORT conforms with laws and/or regulations that conflict with the REQUIREMENTS of the GIPS standards, the FIRM MUST disclose this fact and disclose the manner in which the laws and/or regulations conflict with the GIPS standards.

Discussion

Firms must comply with all applicable laws and regulations regarding the calculation and presentation of performance. Compliance with applicable laws and regulations, however, does not necessarily result in compliance with the GIPS standards. Firms must also comply with all of the applicable requirements of the GIPS standards. In the rare cases where laws and regulations conflict with the GIPS standards, firms are required to comply with the laws and regulations and disclose the manner in which the laws and/or regulations conflict with the GIPS standards.

This disclosure will assist prospective clients in comparing GIPS Composite Reports among firms where reporting requirements may differ because of local laws or regulations.

Sample Disclosure:

"Local laws do not allow the presentation of returns of less than one year to prospective clients, which is in conflict with the GIPS standards. Therefore, no performance is presented for this composite for the period from 1 July 2018 (the inception date of the composite) through 31 December 2018."

Provision 4.C.28

If CARVE-OUTS with allocated cash are included in the COMPOSITE, the FIRM MUST:

a. Indicate CARVE-OUT in the COMPOSITE name.
b. Disclose that the COMPOSITE includes CARVE-OUTS with allocated cash.
c. Disclose the policy used to allocate cash to CARVE-OUTS.
d. Disclose that the GIPS COMPOSITE REPORT for the COMPOSITE of standalone PORTFOLIOS is available upon request, if the COMPOSITE of standalone PORTFOLIOS exists.

Discussion

With the issuance of the 2020 edition of the GIPS standards, firms are once again allowed to include carve-outs with cash that has been allocated synthetically in composites. (This was prohibited from 1 January 2010 through 31 December 2019.) In the spirit of fair representation and full disclosure, it is important that prospective clients have sufficient information to understand the nature of the portfolios included in a composite. If carve-outs with allocated cash are included in a composite, the name of the composite must include "carve-out" or otherwise indicate this. In addition to "carve-out" being indicated in the name of the composite, there must be a disclosure that the composite includes carve-outs with allocated cash. These two requirements signal to prospective clients that there are assets in the composite that do not represent standalone portfolios and for which they might want to request additional information. (A standalone portfolio is a portfolio that is not a portion of a larger portfolio.) Firms are not required to indicate "carve-out" in the composite name if the composite includes carve-outs with allocated cash that were created in compliance with prior editions of the GIPS standards.

Because the methodology for allocating cash to carve-outs can have a significant effect on a composite's return, it is required that the firm disclose the policy used to allocate cash to the carve-outs in the composite. See the discussion of Provision 3.A.15 for methods that may be used to allocate cash.

Once a firm obtains one or more standalone portfolios managed in the same strategy as the carve-outs with allocated cash, the firm must create a separate composite that includes only the standalone portfolios. (See Provision 3.A.18.) The returns and composite assets of the composite that includes only standalone portfolios must be presented in the GIPS Composite Report for the composite that includes carve-outs with allocated cash. In addition, in the GIPS Composite Report for the composite that includes carve-outs with allocated cash, the firm must disclose that the GIPS

Composite Report for the composite of standalone portfolios managed in the same strategy as the composite with carve-outs with allocated cash is available upon request. This disclosure will inform prospective clients that they can compare the GIPS Composite Reports for the composite with carve-outs with allocated cash and the composite with only standalone portfolios if they wish to do so. This disclosure is required only when the firm has standalone portfolios managed in the same strategy as the composite with carve-outs with allocated cash and has therefore created the required composite of standalone portfolios.

Once a firm has obtained standalone portfolios managed in the same strategy as the carve-outs with allocated cash, the firm may present prospective clients with the GIPS Composite Report that includes only the standalone portfolios, rather than the GIPS Composite Report that includes carve-outs with allocated cash.

Sample Disclosure:

"The Large-Cap Carve-Out Equity Composite includes carve-outs with allocated cash. Cash and cash returns are allocated to carve-outs based on each carve-out's size relative to its total portfolio, using beginning-of-month values. A GIPS Composite Report for the Large-Cap Equity Composite that includes only standalone portfolios is available upon request."

Provision 4.C.29

The FIRM MUST disclose the use of a SUB-ADVISOR and the periods a SUB-ADVISOR was used.[35]

Discussion

Some firms use a sub-advisor to manage part or all of a particular strategy. For example, if a firm specializes in managing equities, it might hire a sub-advisor (a third-party investment manager) to manage the fixed income portion of its balanced portfolios. The GIPS standards require that firms include the performance of assets assigned to a sub-advisor in a composite provided the firm has the authority to allocate the assets to a sub-advisor. In the spirit of full disclosure, a firm must disclose the fact that a sub-advisor was used in the management of the composite strategy and the periods for which a sub-advisor was used. It is not necessary to disclose the name of the sub-advisor. This is required for periods beginning on or after 1 January 2006.

[35] REQUIRED for periods beginning on or after 1 January 2006.

Sample Disclosures:

"A sub-advisor is used to manage the international equity allocation of the Asia Growth Balanced Composite."

"A sub-advisor was used for the management of the Targeted Duration Fixed Income Composite from its inception in 2001 through 31 December 2018."

Provision 4.C.30

The FIRM MUST disclose if the COMPOSITE'S valuation hierarchy materially differs from the RECOMMENDED valuation hierarchy. (See Provision 2.B.6 for the RECOMMENDED valuation hierarchy.)[36]

Discussion

Firms must establish policies and procedures for determining portfolio valuations. For periods beginning on or after 1 January 2011, those valuations must be determined in accordance with the definition of fair value. Provision 2.B.6 includes a recommended valuation hierarchy that firms should incorporate into their policies and procedures for determining fair value for portfolio investments. Firms must establish a valuation hierarchy on a composite-specific basis. It is acceptable for firms to apply a different valuation hierarchy to specific composites provided the valuation methodology conforms to the definition of fair value. If the valuation hierarchy materially differs from the recommended valuation hierarchy, the firm must disclose this fact. Prospective clients will be informed and then may request additional information about the firm's valuation policies.

Sample Disclosure:

"All portfolio investments are valued using the firm's proprietary valuation models to determine fair value. Our valuation procedures materially differ from the recommended valuation hierarchy in the GIPS standards."

Provision 4.C.31

If the FIRM determines no appropriate BENCHMARK for the COMPOSITE exists, the FIRM MUST disclose why no BENCHMARK is presented.

[36] REQUIRED for periods beginning on or after 1 January 2011.

Discussion

Benchmarks are important tools that aid in the planning, implementation, and evaluation of an investment strategy. They also help facilitate discussions with prospective clients regarding the relationship between composite risk and return. As a result, the GIPS standards require firms to provide benchmark total returns in all GIPS Composite Reports. The benchmark must reflect the investment mandate, objective, or strategy of the composite. Although there is typically an appropriate benchmark for traditional strategies, it is more common for managers of alternative strategies to determine that no appropriate benchmark for the composite exists. If this is the case, the firm must disclose why no benchmark is presented.

Sample Disclosure:

"Because the composite's strategy is absolute return where investments are permitted in all asset classes, no benchmark is presented because we believe that no benchmark that reflects this strategy exists."

Provision 4.C.32

If the FIRM changes the BENCHMARK, the FIRM MUST disclose:

a. For a prospective BENCHMARK change, the date and description of the change. Changes MUST be disclosed for as long as returns for the prior BENCHMARK are included in the GIPS COMPOSITE REPORT.

b. For a retroactive BENCHMARK change, the date and description of the change. Changes MUST be disclosed for a minimum of one year and for as long as they are relevant to interpreting the track record.

Discussion

Firms must disclose the date and description of any changes to the benchmark over time. A benchmark change can take two forms:

- The benchmark is changed from one benchmark to another on a prospective basis only.
- The benchmark is changed for all periods (i.e., retroactively).

In most cases, the firm should only change the benchmark going forward and not change the benchmark retroactively.

If the firm changes the benchmark prospectively and presents benchmark returns that combine two different benchmarks, the date and description of the change must be disclosed for as long as returns for the prior benchmark are included in the GIPS Composite Report. For example, assume a firm changes the benchmark for a composite in June 2015, and the change is made prospectively. As long as benchmark returns from 2015 or prior periods are included in the GIPS Composite Report, the firm must include this disclosure. Firms must also carefully identify the benchmark as a custom benchmark in the GIPS Composite Report and must make clear that the benchmark returns are not those of the current benchmark for all periods. It would not be appropriate to label the benchmark returns with the name of the current benchmark. The firm must provide information, including labeling of the benchmark, that is sufficient to allow a prospective client to distinguish the prior benchmark returns from the current benchmark returns.

There may be times when a firm determines that it is appropriate to change the benchmark for a given composite retroactively. For example, because benchmarks are continually evolving, if the firm finds that a new benchmark is a better comparison for an investment strategy, the firm may consider changing the benchmark retroactively. In the case of a retroactive benchmark change, there must be a disclosure of the date and description of the benchmark change, including the fact that the benchmark was changed retroactively. Disclosures related to a retroactive change in a benchmark must be included in the respective GIPS Composite Report for a minimum of one year and for as long as the disclosures are relevant to interpreting the performance track record. The firm must consider the underlying principles of the GIPS standards, which are fair representation and full disclosure, when determining how long this disclosure will be included in the GIPS Composite Report.

When a firm changes a benchmark retroactively, the firm is encouraged to continue to also present the old benchmark.

This provision applies to a fundamental change in the benchmark—for example, a change in an index used in calculating the benchmark—rather than to periodic minor changes in benchmark weights and components. If a firm uses a custom benchmark that is a blend of one or more benchmarks, a change in the weights of the constituent benchmarks is not considered a benchmark change within the scope of this provision. For example, the benchmark may change every quarter as part of the normal procedure. In this instance, it is appropriate to disclose that the benchmark is rebalanced quarterly using the weights of the asset classes in the composite's model portfolio. A firm is not required to disclose how the asset class weights have changed each quarter but may do so.

Changes to the benchmark primarily intended to make performance look better by lowering the benchmark return violate the spirit of the GIPS standards.

Sample Disclosure for a Prospective Change:

"Benchmark results presented are a combination of two indices. ABC Index was used prior to 30 September 2015; ABC Value Index is used subsequently."

Sample Disclosure for a Retroactive Change:

"In January 2017, the benchmark was changed from ABC Index to XYZ Index for all periods."

Provision 4.C.33

If a custom BENCHMARK or combination of multiple BENCHMARKS is used, the FIRM MUST:

a. Disclose the BENCHMARK components, weights, and rebalancing process, if applicable.

b. Disclose the calculation methodology.

c. Clearly label the BENCHMARK to indicate that it is a custom BENCHMARK.

Discussion

When custom benchmarks are used, the firm must disclose the benchmark components, weights, and rebalancing process, if applicable, as well as the calculation methodology. For example, if the firm combines two indices, WW Index and XX Index, to create the WWXX benchmark for the composite, the following would be an appropriate disclosure:

"The WWXX benchmark is a combination of 50% WW Index and 50% XX Index, calculated by weighting the respective index returns on a monthly basis."

It is also required that the benchmark be clearly labeled to indicate that it is a custom benchmark. For example, the label for the benchmark returns in a GIPS Report would read "Custom Benchmark." The benchmark description and required disclosures might read as follows:

"*Custom Benchmark*: The benchmark is 100% hedged. The benchmark is based on a zero-cost one-month rolling hedge, whereby mid spot rates and one-month bid–offer forward points are applied."

In some markets, it has become more common to use benchmarks that reflect the deduction of model fees or other expenses. These net benchmarks are considered custom benchmarks. A firm must not present net benchmark returns compared with only gross-of-fees composite returns. For example, assume the firm wishes to include a custom benchmark that reflects the deduction of model or actual investment management fees, but the firm presents only gross-of-fees composite returns in the GIPS Composite Report. The firm must not present net benchmark returns when only gross-of-fees composite returns are presented. The firm may use net benchmark returns only when composite net-of-fees returns are presented. The use of net benchmark returns when only gross-of-fees composite returns are presented is one instance where disclosure is not sufficient to prevent the information presented from being false and misleading. When a firm includes net benchmark returns in a GIPS Composite Report, the firm must clearly label the benchmark as a custom net benchmark and disclose the calculation methodology.

It is becoming more common for exchange-traded funds (ETFs) to be used as benchmarks. An ETF is a pooled fund that tracks a specific investment universe that is expressed by an index or a basket and that is listed on an exchange. Unlike a market index, an ETF incurs trading costs and other charges, including taxes. Because of the incurred costs, an ETF may underperform the market index that it tracks. If an ETF is chosen as the benchmark for a strategy, the firm should present net-of-fees composite returns. As part of the benchmark description for an ETF, the firm must disclose the following items:

- if ETF returns are gross or net of fees and other costs, including transaction costs;
- the ETF expense ratio, if ETF net returns are presented;
- if ETF returns are based on market prices or net asset values (NAVs);
- the timing of the market close used to determine the ETF's valuations; and
- if ETF returns are gross or net of withholding taxes, if this information is available.

If the firm also presents composite gross-of-fees returns, it should present ETF returns that are grossed up, but it is not required to do so.

Sample Disclosures:

"Benchmark returns are a customized version of the XYZ Index, which is calculated monthly by XYZ Company. The benchmark reflects the deduction of a model fee of 1.00% per annum, which is calculated monthly by deducting 1/12 of 1% from the benchmark return."

"The benchmark is the Special ETF, which tracks the securities included in the Special Index. The ETF returns reflect the deduction of all expenses and transaction costs incurred by the Special ETF and are net of withholding taxes. As of 31 December 2019 the expense ratio was 0.14%. The Special ETF returns reflect market prices, which are determined by the midpoint between the bid and ask prices as of the closing time of the New York Stock Exchange."

Provision 4.C.34

If a PORTFOLIO-WEIGHTED CUSTOM BENCHMARK is used, the FIRM MUST disclose:

a. That the BENCHMARK is rebalanced using the weighted average returns of the BENCHMARKS of all of the PORTFOLIOS included in the COMPOSITE.
b. The frequency of the rebalancing.

c. The components that constitute the PORTFOLIO-WEIGHTED CUSTOM BENCHMARK, including the weights that each component represents, as of the most recent annual period end.
d. That the components that constitute the PORTFOLIO-WEIGHTED CUSTOM BENCHMARK, including the weights that each component represents, are available for prior periods upon request.

Discussion

Firms may use a portfolio-weighted custom benchmark, which is created using the benchmarks of the individual portfolios in the composite. If such a benchmark is used, firms must disclose that the benchmark is calculated using the weighted average returns of the benchmarks of all of the portfolios included in the composite, along with the frequency of the rebalancing. Firms are not required to disclose how the underlying portfolio benchmarks and weights have changed each period.

Additionally, in the spirit of full disclosure and fair representation, firms must disclose the components that constitute the portfolio-weighted custom benchmark, including the weight that each component represents, as of the most recent annual period end. It is also required that firms disclose that the information regarding the components of the portfolio-weighted custom benchmark, as well as the component weights, is available for prior periods upon request.

Sample Disclosure:

"The Long US Government/Credit Custom Benchmark is calculated using the benchmarks of the portfolios in the composite. The benchmark is rebalanced monthly based on the beginning values of portfolios included in the composite. As of 31 December 2018, the breakdown of the benchmark is 88.2% XYZ US Long Government/Credit Index and 11.8% XYZ US Long Government/Credit A+ Index. The breakdown of the custom benchmark for different time periods is available upon request."

Provision 4.C.35

If the FIRM has adopted a SIGNIFICANT CASH FLOW policy for the COMPOSITE, the FIRM MUST disclose how the FIRM defines a SIGNIFICANT CASH FLOW for the COMPOSITE and for which periods.

Discussion

A significant cash flow is defined as the level at which the firm determines that one or more client-directed external cash flows may temporarily prevent the firm from implementing the composite strategy. The cash flow may be defined by the firm as a single flow or an aggregate of a number of flows within a stated period. The measure of significance must be determined as either a specific monetary amount (e.g., €50,000,000) or a percentage of portfolio assets (based on the most recent valuation). If a firm has adopted a significant cash flow policy for a specific composite, the firm must disclose how the firm defines a significant cash flow for that composite and for which periods.

Sample Disclosures:

"Firm ABC defines a significant cash flow for the European Developed Markets Equity Composite as an external cash flow within a portfolio equal to or greater than €50,000,000. If a portfolio experiences a cash inflow of €50,000,000 or more during a calendar month, it is removed from the composite for that month. Following the policy for inclusion of new portfolios in the composite, if the cash level is 5% or less of the portfolio's assets at month end, the portfolio will be returned to the composite in the following month. A cash outflow of €50,000,000 or more during a calendar month will trigger removal of a portfolio from the composite for that month. The portfolio will be returned to the composite in the month following the outflow if it continues to meet other composite criteria, such as size. A portfolio may be removed from a composite prior to the month of the actual cash outflow if there is a significant buildup of cash to prepare for the outflow. The significant cash flow policy for the European Developed Markets Equity Composite was adopted in May 2017."

"A Significant Cash Flow (SCF) policy was adopted for the Large-Cap Growth composite starting 1 February 2015. The SCF policy is triggered by a net cash inflow or outflow of 15% or more during a calendar month. If a portfolio in the composite experiences a 15% or greater cash inflow during a calendar month, it is removed from the composite for that month. If the cash level is 10% or less of portfolio assets at month-end, the portfolio will be returned to the composite in the following month. A cash outflow of 15% or more will trigger removal of a portfolio from the composite. The portfolio will be returned to the composite in the month following the outflow if it continues to meet other composite criteria, such as size."

Provision 4.C.36

For COMPOSITES with at least three annual periods of performance, the FIRM MUST disclose if the three-year annualized EX POST STANDARD DEVIATION of the COMPOSITE and/or BENCHMARK is not presented because 36 monthly returns are not available.

Discussion

For periods ending on or after 1 January 2011, firms must present the three-year annualized ex post standard deviation of the composite and benchmark, which must be calculated using 36 monthly returns, as of each annual period end.

The 2010 edition of the GIPS standards required that a firm disclose, in all cases, if the three-year annualized ex post standard deviation of the composite and/or benchmark is not presented because 36 monthly returns are not available. The 2020 edition of the GIPS standards modifies this requirement. This disclosure is required only if the three-year annualized ex post standard deviation is not presented for composites that have at least three annual periods of performance. This change applies to all periods presented in a GIPS Composite Report.

If a composite has at least three annual periods of performance but 36 monthly returns are not available for the composite, firms are not required to present the three-year annualized ex post standard deviation for either the benchmark or the composite. This scenario often applies to private market investment composites because they are not required to have monthly returns. Firms must disclose that 36 monthly returns are not available for the composite. (If private market investment composites do have monthly valuations and 36 monthly returns are available, the three-year annualized ex post standard deviation must be presented.) If 36 monthly returns are not available for the composite but are available for the benchmark, a firm is not required to present the three-year annualized ex post standard deviation for the benchmark but may do so.

If 36 monthly returns are not available for the benchmark but are available for the composite, firms are required to present only the three-year annualized ex post standard deviation for the composite. In this instance, because 36 monthly returns are not available for the benchmark, firms must not present a three-year annualized ex post standard deviation for the benchmark using data points other than monthly. Firms must disclose that 36 monthly returns are not available for the benchmark.

Sample Disclosure If 36 Monthly Returns Are Available for the Composite but Not for the Benchmark:

"The three-year annualized ex post standard deviation of the benchmark is not presented because the benchmark returns are calculated quarterly."

Sample Disclosure If 36 Monthly Returns Are Not Available for the Composite:

"The three-year annualized ex post standard deviation of the composite and benchmark are not presented because the composite returns are calculated quarterly."

Provision 4.C.37

The FIRM MUST disclose if performance from a past firm or affiliation is presented, and for which periods.

Discussion

Provision 1.A.32 includes the portability tests that must be met to determine if performance from a past firm or affiliation may be used to represent the historical performance of a new or acquiring firm and if that performance can be linked to the ongoing performance of the new or acquiring firm. Provision 1.A.33 includes the portability tests that must be met for the new or acquiring firm to use performance from a past firm or affiliation to represent its historical performance when there is a break in the track record between the past firm or affiliation and the new or acquiring firm. In this instance, the track record from the past firm or affiliation may be used if the tests are met, but it must not be linked to the performance of the new or acquiring firm.

If the firm meets the required portability tests and presents performance from a past firm or affiliation in the GIPS Composite Report, the firm must disclose this fact, as well as the periods for which performance from the past firm or affiliation is presented.

Sample Disclosure:

"Performance shown prior to 2017 represents results achieved by the Small-Cap Team while it was a part of ABC Investments. The Small-Cap Team joined the firm on 2 January 2017."

Provision 4.C.38

The FIRM MUST disclose any change to the GIPS COMPOSITE REPORT resulting from the correction of a MATERIAL ERROR. Following the correction of the GIPS COMPOSITE REPORT, this disclosure MUST be included for a minimum of one year and for as long as it is relevant to interpreting the track record. The disclosure is not REQUIRED to be included in a GIPS COMPOSITE REPORT that is provided to a PROSPECTIVE CLIENT or PROSPECTIVE INVESTOR that did not receive the GIPS COMPOSITE REPORT containing the MATERIAL ERROR.

Discussion

Firms claiming compliance with the GIPS standards are likely to be faced with situations in which errors are discovered that must be specifically addressed. An error, which can be qualitative or quantitative, can be related to any component of a GIPS Composite Report that is missing or inaccurate. Errors in GIPS Composite Reports can result from, but are not limited to, incorrect, incomplete, or missing:

- composite returns or assets,
- firm assets,
- benchmark returns,
- number of portfolios in a composite,
- three-year annualized ex post standard deviation, or
- disclosures.

Any material error in a GIPS Composite Report must be corrected and disclosed in a revised GIPS Composite Report. A firm must define materiality within its error correction policies and procedures.

To adhere to this requirement, a firm must determine the criteria it will use to determine materiality. The following is a definition of materiality that firms might find useful as a starting point for their determination of materiality. "An error is material if the magnitude of the omission or misstatement of performance information, in light of surrounding circumstances, makes it probable that the judgment of a reasonable person relying on the information would have been changed by the omission or misstatement." Firms should have a defined process for determining the objective criteria it will use in determining materiality.

Disclosure of the change in the corrected GIPS Composite Report resulting from a material error must be included in the GIPS Composite Report for a minimum of 12 months following the correction of the report and for as long as it is relevant to interpreting the track record. The firm must consider the underlying principles of the GIPS standards, which are fair representation and full disclosure, when determining how long the disclosure will be included in the GIPS Composite Report that contained the material error.

Disclosure of the change resulting from a material error is not required to be included in a GIPS Composite Report that is provided to new prospective clients or prospective investors.

The discussion for Provision 1.A.20 provides additional information on error correction, including the determination of materiality, the actions that must be taken when an error in a GIPS Composite Report is discovered, and an explanation of who must receive the revised GIPS Composite Report.

Sample Disclosure:

"This GIPS Composite Report includes a correction of the information provided for the XYZ Index. The annual return for the XYZ Index for 2017 was originally presented as 3.4%. The correct return is 4.3%, as shown in this revised GIPS Composite Report."

 |

Provision 4.C.39

If the FIRM chooses to not present the number of PORTFOLIOS in the COMPOSITE because there are five or fewer PORTFOLIOS in the COMPOSITE, the FIRM MUST disclose that the COMPOSITE contains five or fewer PORTFOLIOS or use similar language.

Discussion

Each GIPS Composite Report must include information about the number of portfolios included in the composite. These figures must be presented as of the end of each annual period that is included in the GIPS Composite Report. (See Provision 4.A.1.f.) This requirement provides information to prospective clients on whether the composite is composed of a small number of portfolios or many.

In cases where there are five portfolios or fewer in a composite at period end, the firm may choose to not present the actual number of portfolios in the composite. The firm might choose to do this to protect the identity and confidentiality of its clients. Because firms must include information about the number of portfolios in the composite, however, firms must either state or indicate that the composite contains "five or fewer portfolios", "fewer than six portfolios", (or use similar language) or present the actual number of portfolios in the composite.

Note that "five or fewer portfolios in the composite" refers to the number of portfolios in the composite at the annual period end, not the number of portfolios in the composite for the full year. If there were four portfolios in the composite for the full year but seven portfolios in the composite at the annual period end, the firm would be required to present the actual number of portfolios (in this example, seven) in the composite at the annual period end.

Sample Disclosure:

"ABC's policy is to not present the number of portfolios in the composite when there are fewer than six portfolios included in the composite as of year end."

Sample Disclosure as Part of a Table:

The column where the number of portfolios in the composite at the annual period end is presented would simply note "<6" or "≤5" for any annual period end for which there were five or fewer portfolios in the composite at the annual period end.

Provision 4.C.40

If the FIRM chooses to not present the INTERNAL DISPERSION of individual PORTFOLIO returns because there are five or fewer PORTFOLIOS in the COMPOSITE for the full year, the FIRM MUST disclose that the INTERNAL DISPERSION measure is not applicable or use similar language.

Discussion

The internal dispersion of the individual portfolio annual returns must be presented for each annual period that is included in a GIPS Composite Report. In cases where there are five or fewer portfolios in a composite for the full year, the measure of internal dispersion is not required to be presented. Because firms must include some information about the internal dispersion of individual portfolio returns, however, firms must indicate that the internal dispersion measure is not applicable or include similar language. The firm may instead choose to present an internal dispersion measure.

Note that "five or fewer portfolios in the composite" refers to the number of portfolios in the composite for the full year, not the number of portfolios in the composite at the annual period end. For example, if there were four portfolios in the composite for the full year but seven portfolios in the composite at year-end, the firm would not be required to present the measure of internal dispersion for the composite.

Sample Disclosure:

"ABC's policy is to not present the internal dispersion when there are five or fewer portfolios included in the composite for the full year."

Sample Disclosure as Part of a Table:

The column where the measure of internal dispersion is presented for each annual period would simply note N.A. for any annual period for which there were five or fewer portfolios included in the composite for the full year.

Provision 4.C.41

The FIRM MUST disclose if preliminary, estimated values are used to determine FAIR VALUE.

 |

Discussion

The use of preliminary, estimated values as fair value is common for some alternative strategies, including those that invest in underlying funds for which the firm relies on valuations provided by the underlying fund managers. When using preliminary, estimated values as fair value, it is important to remember the underlying principles of the GIPS standards: fair representation and full disclosure. If using preliminary, estimated values, firms must disclose this fact in the relevant GIPS Composite Report.

Firms that use preliminary, estimated values to determine fair value and subsequently change valuations when final values are received must determine how the firm's error correction policies will be applied. (Please see Provision 1.A.20 for guidance on error correction policies.) Differences between the final and estimated values are not necessarily errors but are treated in a similar manner because the correction of previously presented information may be involved.

In addition to this required disclosure, it is recommended (see Provision 4.B.8) that firms present the percentage of assets in the composite that were valued using preliminary, estimated values as of each annual period end. This information will help prospective clients to interpret the performance record.

Sample Disclosure:

"Preliminary, estimated values were used in the determination of the fair value of the composite's assets."

Provision 4.C.42

If the FIRM changes the type of return(s) presented for the COMPOSITE (e.g., changes from MONEY-WEIGHTED RETURNS to TIME-WEIGHTED RETURNS), the FIRM MUST disclose the change and the date of the change. This disclosure MUST be included for a minimum of one year and for as long as it is relevant to interpreting the track record.

Discussion

A firm must present time-weighted returns (TWRs) in a GIPS Composite Report unless certain criteria are met that allow money-weighted returns (MWRs) to be presented instead of TWRs. Firms may choose to present MWRs instead of TWRs for a specific composite only if the firm controls the external cash flows into the portfolios in the composite and the portfolios in the composite have at least one of the following characteristics: They are closed-end, fixed life, fixed commitment, or illiquid investments are a significant part of the strategy. (See Provision 1.A.35.)

If the firm changes the type of return presented for a composite, the firm must disclose, in the respective GIPS Composite Report, the change in the type of return (from MWR to TWR or from TWR to MWR) and the date of the change. This disclosure must be included in the GIPS Composite Report for a minimum of one year and for as long as it is relevant and helpful to the firm's prospective clients in interpreting the composite's track record. The firm must consider the underlying principles of the GIPS standards, which are fair representation and full disclosure, when determining how long the disclosure will be included in the GIPS Composite Report.

When a firm changes the type of return presented for a composite, for example from MWRs to TWRs, the firm must change the returns for all periods. As an example, suppose that a firm is presenting performance for the period from the inception of a composite on 1 January 2013 through 31 December 2020. It decides that it will switch to present TWRs as of 1 January 2020. The firm cannot present MWRs through 31 December 2019 and TWRs from 1 January 2020 through 31 December 2020. The firm must present TWRs from 1 January 2013 (the inception date of the composite) through 31 December 2020 in the GIPS Composite Report for the period ended 31 December 2020.

Sample Disclosure:

"Beginning with the GIPS Composite Report for the period ended 31 December 2020, the returns presented for the XYZ Composite were changed from money-weighted returns to time-weighted returns."

Provision 4.C.43

If the FIRM presents ADDITIONAL RISK MEASURES, the FIRM MUST:

a. Describe any ADDITIONAL RISK MEASURE.
b. Disclose the name of the risk-free rate if a risk-free rate is used in the calculation of the ADDITIONAL RISK MEASURE.

Discussion

Understanding and interpreting investment performance requires the consideration of both risk and return. It is therefore recommended that firms present additional risk measures (i.e., beyond those required to be presented) for the composite and the benchmark. (See Provision 4.B.5.) It is important to keep in mind that additional risk measures should be consistent with the composite's strategy. For example, if the strategy is to track the benchmark, then tracking error would be consistent with that objective.

The GIPS Composite Report must include a description of any additional risk measure presented. If a risk-free rate is used in the calculation of an additional risk measure, the name of the risk-free rate must be disclosed. The disclosure of the name of the risk-free rate used in the calculation of an additional risk measure is required because of the importance of the selection of an appropriate risk-free rate. With a disclosure regarding the risk-free rate, the firm's prospective clients can better understand and interpret the additional risk measure(s) presented.

Provision 4.C.44

The FIRM MUST disclose if GROSS-OF-FEES or NET-OF-FEES returns are used to calculate presented risk measures.

Discussion

To help prospective clients interpret the risk measures presented in a GIPS Composite Report, the firm must disclose which returns are used in the calculation of the presented risk measures. This applies to both required risk measures (e.g., the three-year annualized ex post standard deviation and internal dispersion) and any additional risk measures. As discussed in Provision 2.B.7, it is recommended that firms use gross-of-fees returns when calculating risk measures.

For wrap fee composites, it is sometimes not possible for a firm to calculate gross-of-fees returns. Because of the bundled fee for wrap fee composites, the firm may be unable to identify the transactions costs that must be deducted from the return on investments to arrive at gross-of-fees returns. Firms may therefore use pure gross-of-fees returns (the return on investments that is not reduced by any transaction costs incurred during the period) or returns that are net of the entire wrap fee when calculating risk measures presented in a GIPS Composite Report for a wrap fee composite.

Sample Disclosures:

"Gross-of-fees returns were used to calculate the three-year annualized ex post standard deviation of the composite."

"Gross returns were used to calculate all risk measures presented in this GIPS Composite Report."

"Net-of-fees returns were used to calculate the three-year annualized ex post standard deviation and the internal dispersion of the composite."

Sample Disclosure for a Wrap Fee Composite:

"Pure gross returns were used to calculate the three-year annualized ex post standard deviation and the internal dispersion of the composite. A pure gross return is the return on investments that is not reduced by any transactions costs incurred during the period."

Provision 4.C.45

For OVERLAY STRATEGY COMPOSITES, the FIRM MUST disclose:

a. The methodology used to calculate COMPOSITE OVERLAY EXPOSURE.
b. If collateral and collateral income are reflected in the COMPOSITE returns.

Discussion

According to Provision 2.A.6, for periods beginning on or after 1 January 2020, overlay exposure must be calculated by using one of the following options: (1) the notional exposure of the overlay strategies being managed; (2) the value of the underlying portfolios being overlaid; or (3) a specified target exposure as of the beginning of the period, which can either be defined as a target exposure or determined by a formula used to calculate the target exposure for each period. Because there are different allowable calculation methods, firms must disclose the methodology used in calculating composite overlay exposure. This disclosure will help prospective clients interpret the information presented.

Overlay strategies typically require collateral (sometimes referred to as margin or a margin account). The collateral provided may be for the required minimum or for a larger amount. The required minimum amount may be determined by law or regulation. There are different ways the collateral can be managed, which can affect the overlay portfolio return calculation. Firms must establish a policy for the treatment of collateral in the portfolio return calculation on a composite-specific basis. To help prospective clients interpret the composite returns presented, the firm must disclose whether collateral and collateral income are included in composite returns.

Sample Disclosure:

"Composite overlay exposure represents the total value of all underlying portfolios being overlaid in this composite. Returns include collateral and the associated income."

Provision 4.C.46

For REAL ESTATE investments that are not in a REAL ESTATE OPEN-END FUND, the FIRM MUST disclose that:[37]

a. EXTERNAL VALUATIONS are obtained, and the frequency with which they are obtained, or

b. The FIRM relies on valuations from financial statement audits.

Discussion

According to Provision 2.A.44, for periods beginning on or after 1 January 2012, real estate investments included in any portfolio except a real estate open-end fund must either:

- have an external valuation at least once every 12 months unless client agreements stipulate otherwise, in which case real estate investments must have an external valuation at least once every 36 months or per the client agreement if the client agreement requires external valuations more frequently than every 36 months; or
- be subject to an annual financial statement audit performed by an independent public accounting firm. The real estate investments must be accounted for at fair value, and the most recent audited financial statements available must contain an unmodified opinion issued by an independent public accounting firm.

Because valuation is such an important issue for real estate investments, firms must inform prospective clients whether they externally value real estate investments and, if so, how frequently, or instead place reliance on valuations from audited financial statements. This disclosure is required for periods ending on or after 31 December 2020.

Sample Disclosures:

"ABC Company obtains external valuations for all real estate investments annually."

"XYZ Company relies on valuations from audited financial statements. The audits are performed by an independent public accounting firm."

[37] REQUIRED for periods ending on or after 31 December 2020.

Provision 4.C.47

For WRAP FEE COMPOSITES, when the FIRM presents PURE GROSS-OF-FEES returns, the FIRM MUST disclose that PURE GROSS-OF-FEES returns do not reflect the deduction of TRANSACTION COSTS.

Discussion

When presenting information for a wrap fee composite to a wrap fee prospective client, firms may present pure gross-of-fees returns as supplemental information. Unlike a gross-of-fees or net-of-fees return, a pure gross-of-fees return is one that does not reflect the deduction of any transaction costs incurred during the period. Some prospective clients may not be aware of what a pure gross-of-fees return represents. Therefore, in addition to requiring that a pure gross-of-fees return be clearly labeled and identified as supplemental information (Provision 4.A.17), it is required that the firm disclose that pure gross-of-fees returns do not reflect the deduction of transaction costs.

Sample Disclosure:

"The pure gross-of-fees returns do not reflect the deduction of transaction costs."

Provision 4.C.48

When the GIPS COMPOSITE REPORT includes THEORETICAL PERFORMANCE as SUPPLEMENTAL INFORMATION, the FIRM MUST:

a. Disclose that the results are theoretical, are not based on the performance of actual assets, and if the THEORETICAL PERFORMANCE was derived from the retroactive or prospective application of a model.
b. Disclose a basic description of the methodology and assumptions used to calculate the THEORETICAL PERFORMANCE sufficient for the PROSPECTIVE CLIENT or PROSPECTIVE INVESTOR to interpret the THEORETICAL PERFORMANCE, including if it is based on model performance, backtested performance, or hypothetical performance.
c. Disclose whether the THEORETICAL PERFORMANCE reflects the deduction of actual or estimated INVESTMENT MANAGEMENT FEES, TRANSACTION COSTS, or other fees and charges that an actual client PORTFOLIO would have paid or will pay.
d. Clearly label the THEORETICAL PERFORMANCE as SUPPLEMENTAL INFORMATION.

 |

Discussion

To be presented as supplemental information in a GIPS Composite Report, theoretical performance must relate to the respective composite. The following are examples of theoretical performance that may be included in a GIPS Composite Report as supplemental information:

- Results created by applying a composite investment strategy or methodology to historical data to indicate how a strategy constructed with the benefit of hindsight would have performed during a certain period in the past had the strategy been in existence during that period.
- Ex ante performance that is linked to actual composite performance, or that is calculated using actual composite performance.
- Results that include the effect of currency hedging that has been applied after-the-fact to the composite when the composite was not originally managed including the currency hedging strategy, and the hedging is not part of the actual composite returns.

When theoretical performance is included as supplemental information in a GIPS Composite Report, a firm is required to include a number of disclosures to ensure that the recipients of the report, including prospective clients, understand the nature of the information being presented. Among the required disclosures are the source of the theoretical performance, the methodology and assumptions used to calculate the theoretical performance, and the treatment of fees and costs.

Firms must also clearly label the theoretical performance as supplemental information.

Sample Disclosure:

"A return history has been constructed for the period from 1 January 2015 through 31 December 2018 that reflects the application of an investment model used by XYZ Investment Management. The results are theoretical and are not based on the performance of actual portfolios. The return history is derived from the retroactive application of a model. Taking the constituents of the large-cap index at each month end, those securities that have an above-average dividend yield and an above-average dividend payout ratio were identified and reweighted by market capitalization. The next-month's performance was then applied to those stock weights to derive a model return for the month. These monthly model returns are then linked to provide annual returns. The theoretical performance presented does not reflect the deduction of investment management fees, transaction costs, or other fees and charges."

4.D. Disclosure—Recommendations

Provision 4.D.1

The FIRM SHOULD disclose material changes to valuation policies and/or methodologies.

Discussion

Valuation is a critical component of the performance calculation. Therefore, if a change to a firm's valuation policies and/or methodologies is material, firms should disclose the change in order to enable prospective clients to understand the potential effect of such a change.

Some examples of a material change include, but are not limited to, the following:

- new valuation principles adopted by a local accounting standards board,
- adoption of new international standards in lieu of local standards,
- change of economic criteria used to value investments, and
- change from a discounted cash flow basis to a comparables basis.

Sample Disclosure for a Policy Change:

"Prior to 1 March 2016, illiquid securities were valued internally. Subsequently, illiquid securities are valued using a third-party pricing service."

Sample Disclosure for a Methodology Change:

"For periods prior to 1 August 2019, real estate investments were valued on a discounted cash flow basis. As of 1 August 2019, real estate investments are valued on a comparables basis."

Provision 4.D.2

The FIRM SHOULD disclose material changes to calculation policies and/or methodologies.

Discussion

Firms have discretion to determine which policies and methodologies are used for calculating performance. Although these policies and methodologies must adhere to all applicable calculation requirements, firms may choose from a wide variety of policies and methodologies. Firms may change calculation policies and/or methodologies; however, firms must not change a calculation policy or methodology for the sole purpose of increasing performance. If a change to the calculation policies and/or methodologies is material, firms should disclose the change in order to enable prospective clients to understand the potential effect of such a change.

Sample Disclosure:

"Effective 1 January 2010, portfolio returns are calculated daily, using a true time-weighted return methodology. Previously, portfolio returns were calculated monthly using the Modified Dietz method."

Provision 4.D.3

The FIRM SHOULD disclose material differences between the BENCHMARK and the COMPOSITE'S investment mandate, objective, or strategy.

Discussion

Firms are required to disclose the composite description (see Provision 4.C.4) and the benchmark description (see Provision 4.C.5) in a GIPS Composite Report. It is recommended that firms also disclose any material differences between the benchmark and the composite's investment mandate, objective, or strategy. Prospective clients will be better able to evaluate the performance of the strategy relative to the benchmark presented if they understand any material differences between the composite and the benchmark.

Sample Disclosure:

"The Concentrated Equity Composite invests in only the top 20 stocks (as determined by the firm's Investment Committee) of the stocks that are included in its benchmark, the XYZ Index."

Provision 4.D.4

The FIRM SHOULD disclose the key assumptions used to value investments.

Discussion

Firms are required to disclose that valuation policies are available upon request. (See Provision 4.C.16.) Because valuation is a critical component of the performance calculation, it is recommended that firms also disclose the key assumptions used when valuing portfolio investments. This will help prospective clients better understand how the firm values investments and compare valuation assumptions for similar strategies used by different firms.

Sample Disclosure:

"Investments are valued using recent market quotations. If there is no publicly traded reference, equity investments are valued using a market multiples approach for similar investments in active markets, and fixed-income investments are valued using inputs such as interest rates, yield curve shape, volatility, prepayments, and credit risk."

Provision 4.D.5

If a parent company contains multiple firms, each FIRM within the parent company SHOULD disclose a list of the other firms contained within the parent company.

Discussion

The term "firm" is used in two different ways in Provision 4.D.5. "FIRM" is used to indicate an entity that claims compliance with the GIPS standards, whereas "firm" is used to indicate an entity that may or may not claim compliance with the GIPS standards. The definition of a firm will be based on the specific circumstances of the firm but must reflect how the firm is held out to the public as a distinct business entity. In some cases, a parent company may have two or more units, divisions, departments, or offices that are defined as separate firms within the context of the GIPS standards. To avoid confusion, a firm claiming compliance with the GIPS standards must be sure that it is clearly defined relative to the other firms within the parent company and that it is apparent which firm is claiming compliance. In the interest of fair representation and full disclosure, firms should disclose a list of the other organizations within the parent company. Firms should also consider indicating which organizations within the parent company claim compliance with the GIPS standards.

Sample Disclosure:

"ABC Institutional Investment Management is the institutional division of ABC parent company. The private banking division of ABC parent company also claims compliance with the GIPS standards, whereas the retail division of ABC parent company does not claim compliance with the GIPS standards."

Provision 4.D.6

If the COMPOSITE contains PORTFOLIOS with BUNDLED FEES, the FIRM SHOULD disclose the types of fees included in the BUNDLED FEE.

Discussion

A bundled fee is a fee that combines multiple fees into one total or "bundled" fee. Bundled fees can include any combination of investment management fees, transaction costs, custody fees, and/or administrative fees. Two examples of bundled fees are all-in fees and wrap fees.

All-In Fee: An all-in fee is a type of bundled fee that can include any combination of investment management fees, transaction costs, custody fees, and administrative fees. All-in fees are typically offered in certain jurisdictions where asset management, brokerage, and custody services are offered by the same company.

Wrap Fee: A wrap fee is a type of bundled fee that is specific to a particular investment product. The wrap fee is charged by a wrap fee sponsor for investment management services and typically includes associated transaction costs that cannot be separately identified. Wrap fees can be all-inclusive, asset-based fees and may include a combination of investment management fees, transaction costs, custody fees, and/or administrative fees.

To help prospective clients better understand the nature of the fees charged for a particular investment product, and to facilitate comparison of bundled fee products offered by different firms, it is recommended that firms disclose the types of fees included in the bundled fee.

Sample Disclosure:

"Portfolios within the composite pay a bundled fee, which includes all charges for transaction costs, portfolio management fees, and custody fees."

Provision 4.D.7

If the FIRM adheres to any industry valuation guidelines in addition to the GIPS valuation REQUIREMENTS, the FIRM SHOULD disclose which guidelines have been applied.

Discussion

Some market segments, such as private equity, have developed their own valuation guidelines. For these markets, it is not uncommon for the GIPS standards valuation requirements to be supplemented by other local or international standards because other standards may be more stringent in their requirements.

The disclosure of which industry's valuation guidelines have been used in addition to the GIPS standards valuation requirements will help prospective clients to determine the comparability of GIPS Composite Reports from different firms and/or jurisdictions.

Sample Disclosure:

"The Global Diversified Distressed Composite adheres to the XYZ Venture Capital Association's valuation guidelines as well as the GIPS standards valuation requirements. The XYZ valuation standards are based on fair value but provide more prescriptive advice in terms of how to value specific investments, such as secondary investments and distressed debt investments."

Provision 4.D.8

When using BENCHMARKS that have limitations, such as peer group BENCHMARKS, the FIRM SHOULD disclose these limitations.

Discussion

Firms must determine which benchmark(s) are most appropriate for composite(s). When determining which benchmarks to present in a GIPS Composite Report, firms should be guided by the ethical spirit of the GIPS standards.

Some benchmarks with known limitations are often used for certain types of investments. For example, peer group benchmarks, such as hedge fund peer group universe indices, are often used for hedge funds and other alternative investment strategies. Although peer group benchmarks are frequently used to evaluate hedge funds, there are some common problems with hedge fund peer group benchmarks, including the following:

- self-reporting bias (only some hedge funds choose to report performance data),
- survivorship bias (historical returns of closed hedge funds are removed from the peer group benchmark),
- inability to obtain returns for the same periods as the composite, and
- lack of investability (some hedge funds within a peer group benchmark are closed to new investors).

When using benchmarks that exhibit limitations, firms should describe these limitations in the relevant GIPS Composite Report. This helps prospective clients understand the nature of the benchmark and be aware of any known drawbacks in comparing the risk and return of the benchmark and composite.

Sample Disclosure:

"The benchmark is the Hedge Fund Aggregate Multi-Style Index, which includes more than 100 hedge funds of various styles and strategies. Because this index is based on the data self-reported by the constituent funds, it may have a self-reporting bias. In addition, some funds are closed to new investors and are no longer investable. We believe that no better index exists as a comparison for this composite."

Provision 4.D.9

The FIRM SHOULD disclose how research costs are reflected in returns.

Discussion

The focus on research costs has grown in certain markets. Although research costs are often absorbed by the firm, some firms instead charge research costs directly to clients. To allow prospective clients to understand the firm's policy for the treatment of research costs, firms should disclose if returns do or do not reflect the deduction of research costs.

Sample Disclosures:

"ABC Company bears the costs of investment research. Research costs are not separately charged to clients."

"Certain investment research costs are charged directly to clients outside the managed portfolio. Therefore, composite returns do not reflect the research costs that are charged directly to clients."

5. COMPOSITE MONEY-WEIGHTED RETURN REPORT

The following provisions apply to COMPOSITES that include MONEY-WEIGHTED RETURNS in a GIPS COMPOSITE REPORT when the FIRM meets the REQUIREMENTS specified in Provision 1.A.35 and chooses to present MONEY-WEIGHTED RETURNS.

5.A. Presentation and Reporting—Requirements

Provision 5.A.1

The FIRM MUST present in each GIPS COMPOSITE REPORT:

a. The annualized COMPOSITE SINCE-INCEPTION MONEY-WEIGHTED RETURN through the most recent annual period end.

Discussion

To claim compliance, a firm is required to meet all applicable requirements of the GIPS standards on a firm-wide basis for at least a five-year period, or since inception of the firm if the firm has been in existence for less than five years. See Provision 1.A.3 for a discussion of the required periods for initially claiming compliance.

If a firm meets the requirements for presenting money-weighted returns in a GIPS Composite Report (see Provision 1.A.35) and chooses to do so, the firm must present the annualized composite since-inception money-weighted return (SI-MWR) through the most recent annual period end.

For example, assume a firm presents returns on a calendar year-end basis. If a composite has an inception date of 1 March 2015 and the most recent annual period end is 31 December 2019, the firm must present an annualized composite SI-MWR from 1 March 2015 through 31 December 2019. Although only the annualized composite SI-MWR through the most recent annual period end is required, it is recommended that firms present annualized composite SI-MWRs through each annual period end. (See Provision 5.B.1.) In this example, doing so would mean presenting SI-MWRs from 1 March 2015 through 31 December 2015, 1 March 2015 through 31 December 2016, 1 March 2015 through 31 December 2017, and 1 March 2015 through 31 December 2018. The SI-MWR from 1 March 2015 through 31 December 2015 must not be annualized because the return is for a period of less than one year.

Firms must clearly label the periods for which SI-MWRs are presented. Firms must select the annual period end for which SI-MWRs will be presented on a composite-specific basis and apply it consistently. For purposes of comparability, best practice would be for a firm to report composite SI-MWRs for periods ending on 31 December.

Firms may present either gross-of-fees or net-of-fees composite returns. Firms may also choose to present both gross-of-fees and net-of-fees composite returns in a GIPS Composite Report.

Provision 5.A.1

The FIRM MUST present in each GIPS COMPOSITE REPORT:

b. When the COMPOSITE has a track record that is less than a full year, the non-annualized COMPOSITE SINCE-INCEPTION MONEY-WEIGHTED RETURN through the initial annual period end.

Discussion

When a composite has a track record of less than a full year, the firm must present the non-annualized since-inception money-weighted return (SI-MWR) through the initial annual period end. Subsequently, the firm must extend the measurement period for the SI-MWR to include the next annual period and calculate an annualized SI-MWR through the most recent annual period end.

SI-MWRs for periods of less than a full year must not be annualized. As an example, a composite that began on 1 December 2020 and has a one-month initial return through 31 December 2020 of 3% (which equates to an annualized return of 42.6%) would be required to present that 3% as the partial year's performance. The annualized return of 42.6% must not be presented. Some spreadsheet and software applications automatically annualize all returns, and firms are reminded that for periods of less than a year, the firm must "de-annualize" any annualized returns that are calculated.

The method chosen to de-annualize a return is at the discretion of the firm, but it must be a geometric calculation. In the situation just presented, the 42.6% annualized return could be de-annualized by one of the following formulas:

$$\left\{\left[(1+0.426)^{\left(\frac{1}{12}\right)}\right]-1\right\}\times 100=3\% \quad \text{or} \quad \left\{\left[(1+0.426)^{\left(\frac{31}{365}\right)}\right]-1\right\}\times 100=3\%,$$

both resulting in a non-annualized one-month return of 3%.

Provision 5.A.1

The FIRM MUST present in each GIPS COMPOSITE REPORT:

c. When the COMPOSITE terminates, the annualized COMPOSITE SINCE-INCEPTION MONEY-WEIGHTED RETURN through the COMPOSITE TERMINATION DATE.

Discussion

When a composite terminates, the firm must present the annualized composite since-inception money-weighted return (SI-MWR) through the composite termination date. For example, if a composite has an inception date of 1 July 2012 and terminates on 31 August 2019, the GIPS Composite Report for this composite must include a composite SI-MWR for the period from 1 July 2012 through 31 August 2019.

Provision 5.A.1

The FIRM MUST present in each GIPS COMPOSITE REPORT:

d. The SINCE-INCEPTION MONEY-WEIGHTED RETURN for the BENCHMARK for the same periods as presented for the COMPOSITE, unless the FIRM determines there is no appropriate BENCHMARK.

Discussion

Benchmarks are important tools that aid in the planning, implementation, and evaluation of a composite's investment policy. They also help facilitate discussions with prospective clients regarding the relationship between risk and return. As a result, firms are required to present the since-inception money-weighted return (SI-MWR) for the benchmark for the same periods as presented for the composite, unless the firm determines there is no appropriate benchmark.

The benchmark presented must be one that reflects the composite's investment mandate, objective, or strategy. A firm may choose to present more than one benchmark in a GIPS Composite Report but must include all required information for all benchmarks presented in the GIPS Composite Report.

Because the benchmark selected for a composite must be appropriate for comparison with the composite's performance, a firm must not compare a time-weighted return (TWR) benchmark with a composite's SI-MWR. Public market indexes by themselves are not directly comparable to an MWR because the market indexes typically use TWRs. The public market equivalent (PME) is a method in which a public market index is used to create a comparable MWR from a series of cash flows that replicate those of the composite and that can be compared with the composite's MWR. When the firm uses a PME, the market index used must be a total return benchmark.

For composites that have a subscription line of credit (LOC), and the firm is required to present composite returns both with and without the subscription line of credit (see Provision 5.A.2), the firm must present benchmark returns for the same periods as both composite returns. If the benchmark is a PME, the firm must calculate a PME using the composite cash flows with the subscription LOC as well as using composite cash flows without the subscription LOC.

See Provision 1.A.19 for a discussion of total return benchmarks. See the discussion of Provision 5.C.33 for additional information regarding a PME.

Provision 5.A.1

The FIRM MUST present in each GIPS COMPOSITE REPORT:

e. The number of PORTFOLIOS in the COMPOSITE as of the most recent annual period end. If the COMPOSITE contains five or fewer PORTFOLIOS at period end, the number of PORTFOLIOS is not REQUIRED.

Discussion

Each GIPS Composite Report must include information about the number of portfolios included in the composite. This figure must be presented as of the most recent annual period end that is included in the GIPS Composite Report. This requirement provides information to prospective clients on whether the composite is composed of a small number of portfolios or many. In cases where there are five portfolios or fewer in a composite at the most recent annual period end, the firm may choose to not present the number of portfolios in the composite. The firm might choose to do this to protect the identity and confidentiality of its clients. Because firms must present information about the number of portfolios in the composite, however, firms must either (1) state that the composite contains "five or fewer portfolios," "less than six portfolios," or use similar language, or (2) present the actual number of portfolios in the composite. (See Provision 5.C.38.)

Note that "five or fewer portfolios in the composite" refers to the number of portfolios in the composite at the most recent annual period end and not the number of portfolios in the composite for the full period for which the SI-MWR is presented. For example, if there were four portfolios in the composite for the full period but eight portfolios in the composite at year end, the firm would present eight, the actual number of portfolios in the composite at year end. The number of portfolios in the composite also must not include those portfolios that are joining the composite as of the next period. For example, assume a firm reports performance for periods ending on 31 December. A new portfolio that is funded during December and will be included in the composite beginning 1 January in accordance with the composite-specific policy must not be included in the number of portfolios in the composite as of 31 December.

Provision 5.A.1

The FIRM MUST present in each GIPS COMPOSITE REPORT:

f. COMPOSITE assets as of the most recent annual period end.

Discussion

Each GIPS Composite Report must include the amount of composite assets as of the most recent annual period end. This requirement provides information to prospective clients on the size of the composite, measured by the amount of assets it contains. When the composite strategy uses discretionary leverage, composite assets must be presented net of the discretionary leverage and not grossed up as if the discretionary leverage did not exist. Discretionary leverage refers to loans taken at the discretion of the firm. In contrast, non-discretionary leverage refers to borrowings undertaken by the client. For example, if the firm is managing a composite that has $200 million in assets, including $50 million of assets borrowed by the firm, the composite's net assets are $200 million and its gross assets are $250 million. When calculating composite assets, the firm must use $200 million.

If a portfolio is temporarily excluded from a composite because of the composite's minimum asset size policy, or is excluded for any other reason, the portfolio's assets would not be included in composite assets for the period(s) for which the portfolio was excluded. However, the portfolio's assets would be included in total firm assets for all periods for which the portfolio is under management, whether or not it is excluded from the composite. Composite assets do not include assets of those portfolios that are joining the composite as of the next period. For example, assume a firm reports performance for periods ending on 31 December. A new portfolio that is funded during December and will be included in the composite beginning 1 January in accordance with the composite-specific policy must not be included in composite assets as of 31 December.

Provision 5.A.1

The FIRM MUST present in each GIPS COMPOSITE REPORT:

g. TOTAL FIRM ASSETS as of the most recent annual period end.[38]

Discussion

For periods ending on or after 31 December 2020, the firm must present total firm assets as of the most recent annual period end. For periods ending prior to this date, the firm must present either total firm assets or composite assets as a percentage of total firm assets. Discretionary leverage must be deducted when calculating total firm assets. Discretionary leverage refers to loans taken at the discretion of the firm. In contrast, non-discretionary leverage refers to borrowings undertaken by the client. For example, if the firm is managing a composite that has $200 million in assets, including $50 million of assets borrowed by the firm, the firm must use $200 million when calculating total firm assets, not $250 million. The inclusion of both composite assets and total firm assets in a GIPS Composite Report will help a prospective client understand the composite size in relation to total firm assets.

Non-discretionary portfolios that are excluded from composites are included in total firm assets. Portfolios that are temporarily excluded from a composite because of the composite's minimum asset size policy, or are excluded for any other reason, are also included in total firm assets.

Firms must be sure that assets are not double-counted because counting assets more than once would not fairly represent total firm assets.

See the discussion of Provision 2.A.1 for additional guidance on the calculation of total firm assets.

Provision 5.A.2

If a SUBSCRIPTION LINE OF CREDIT is used, the FIRM MUST present the COMPOSITE SINCE-INCEPTION MONEY-WEIGHTED RETURN both with and without the SUBSCRIPTION LINE OF CREDIT through the most recent annual period end. The FIRM is not REQUIRED to present returns without the SUBSCRIPTION LINE OF CREDIT when the SUBSCRIPTION LINE OF CREDIT has all of the following characteristics:[39]

[38] REQUIRED for periods ending on or after 31 December 2020. For periods ending prior to 31 December 2020, FIRMS may present either TOTAL FIRM ASSETS or COMPOSITE assets as a percentage of TOTAL FIRM ASSETS.

[39] REQUIRED for periods ending on or after 31 December 2020.

a. The principal was repaid within 120 days using COMMITTED CAPITAL drawn down through a capital call.
b. No principal was used to fund DISTRIBUTIONS.

Discussion

A subscription line of credit (LOC) is a loan facility that is usually put in place to facilitate administration when firms are calling for funds from investors. A subscription LOC can have a significant effect on returns. However, there has been a lack of consistency in return calculations when a subscription LOC is used. For comparability and transparency, firms that use a subscription LOC must calculate and present the since-inception money-weighted return (SI-MWR) that includes the subscription LOC. For periods ending on or after 31 December 2020, firms are required to also calculate and present an SI-MWR that does not include the subscription LOC, unless the subscription LOC has the following two characteristics:

- The principal was repaid within 120 days using committed capital drawn down through a capital call; and
- No principal was used to fund distributions.

If the subscription LOC has both of these characteristics, the firm is not required to calculate and present an SI-MWR that does not include the subscription LOC.

Presenting composite returns with and without the subscription LOC provides prospective clients with a more complete understanding of the composite's performance and the effect of the subscription LOC on the composite's returns.

If returns both with and without the subscription LOC are required to be presented in a GIPS Composite Report, these returns must be comparable. If the firm presents gross-of-fees returns only, gross-of-fees returns with and without the subscription LOC must be presented. If the firm presents net-of-fees returns only, net-of-fees returns with and without the subscription LOC must be presented. If the firm presents both gross-of-fees and net-of-fees returns, the firm must present gross-of-fees returns with and without the subscription LOC and net-of-fees returns with and without the subscription LOC.

The SI-MWRs with and without the subscription LOC are required for the SI-MWR that is presented through the most recent annual period end. If a firm chooses to also include SI-MWRs through each annual period end, the SI-MWRs with and without the subscription LOC must be presented in the GIPS Composite Report.

See Provision 2.A.50 for guidance for calculating returns with and without the subscription LOC.

Provision 5.A.3

The FIRM MUST present the percentage of the total FAIR VALUE of COMPOSITE assets that were valued using subjective, unobservable inputs (as described in provision 2.B.6.e) as of the most recent annual period end, if such investments represent a material amount of COMPOSITE assets.

Discussion

Markets are not always liquid, and investment prices are not always objective and/or observable. As the last level of the recommended valuation hierarchy indicates (see Provision 2.B.6), it may be necessary for a firm to use subjective unobservable inputs to value an investment for which markets are not active on the measurement date. Examples of subjective unobservable inputs include an assumed discount rate, an assumed occupancy rate for a commercial building, and the default rate used for the valuation of a security in default. Examples related to insurance-linked securities include assumptions regarding hurricane damage and mortality rates. Unobservable inputs should be used to measure fair value only when observable inputs and prices are not available or appropriate. Unobservable inputs reflect the firm's own assumptions about the assumptions that market participants would use in pricing the investment and should be developed based on the best information available under the circumstances.

Firms must present the percentage of the total fair value of composite assets that were valued using subjective unobservable inputs as of the most recent annual period end, if such investments represent a material amount of composite assets. The amount of composite assets valued using subjective unobservable inputs would be considered material if it would likely influence a reader's judgment regarding the reliability of the valuation. The firm must decide on the criteria it will use to determine when subjective unobservable inputs represent a material amount of composite assets, include these criteria in its policy and procedures, and apply these criteria consistently.

Sample Disclosure:

"As of 31 December 2020, 29% of composite assets were valued using subjective, unobservable inputs. These inputs are not supported by market activity and instead are based on internal proprietary pricing models."

Provision 5.A.4

If PORTFOLIOS in the COMPOSITE have COMMITTED CAPITAL, the FIRM MUST present the following items as of the most recent annual period end:

a. COMPOSITE SINCE-INCEPTION PAID-IN CAPITAL.

b. COMPOSITE SINCE-INCEPTION DISTRIBUTIONS.

c. COMPOSITE cumulative COMMITTED CAPITAL.

d. TOTAL VALUE to SINCE-INCEPTION PAID-IN CAPITAL (INVESTMENT MULTIPLE or TVPI).

e. SINCE-INCEPTION DISTRIBUTIONS to SINCE-INCEPTION PAID-IN CAPITAL (REALIZATION MULTIPLE or DPI).

f. SINCE-INCEPTION PAID-IN CAPITAL to cumulative COMMITTED CAPITAL (PIC MULTIPLE).

g. RESIDUAL VALUE to SINCE-INCEPTION PAID-IN CAPITAL (UNREALIZED MULTIPLE or RVPI).

Discussion

Although the money-weighted return (MWR) is the basic metric used to report performance for composites in which the firm has control over the cash flows, has met the other requirements for presenting an MWR, and has chosen to present MWRs, it is not the only useful metric used to gauge performance. Other measures are also useful to provide additional insight. The MWR by its nature is sensitive to early cash flow events, and the MWR calculation assumes that the residual value, or fair value, of a composite is totally liquid—whereas, in reality, the residual value may be illiquid. Other metrics have been developed that allow a prospective client to examine aspects of performance other than simply a rate of return.

a. COMPOSITE SINCE-INCEPTION PAID-IN CAPITAL.

The composite since-inception paid-in capital consists of all capital inflows to portfolios within a composite by clients or investors (e.g., limited partners). These inflows are also referred to as contributions to a composite by clients or investors. Paid-in capital also includes distributions that are subsequently recalled and reinvested into the composite.

b. COMPOSITE SINCE-INCEPTION DISTRIBUTIONS.

The composite since-inception distributions includes all cash and stock distributed to composite clients or investors (e.g., limited partners).

c. COMPOSITE cumulative COMMITTED CAPITAL.

The composite cumulative committed capital represents the total pledges of capital to a composite by clients or investors (e.g., limited partners). Committed capital can be either drawn (paid-in) or undrawn (dry powder).

d. TOTAL VALUE to SINCE-INCEPTION PAID-IN CAPITAL (INVESTMENT MULTIPLE or TVPI).

The investment multiple, or TVPI, provides prospective clients or investors with a multiple that indicates how many times more the investment is worth compared with the original investment without taking into account the time value of money. Also known as the Multiple of Investment Capital (MOIC), it is equal to the sum of the composite since-inception distributions and its residual value (i.e., fair value) divided by the composite since-inception paid-in capital. The investment multiple is calculated as follows:

$$\text{TVPI} = \frac{\text{Since} - \text{Inception Distributions} + \text{Residual Value}}{\text{Since} - \text{Inception Paid} - \text{In Capital}}$$

TVPI can also be calculated as DPI + RVPI, where

DPI = realization multiple (see Provision 5.A.4.e)

RVPI = unrealized multiple (see Provision 5.A.4.g)

e. SINCE-INCEPTION DISTRIBUTIONS to SINCE-INCEPTION PAID-IN CAPITAL (REALIZATION MULTIPLE or DPI).

The DPI, or realization multiple, measures how much invested capital has actually been returned to clients or investors. It is the amount of invested capital that has been "realized" by clients or investors and is often viewed as the amount of the TVPI that is "realized." TVPI, also known as the investment multiple, is calculated as total value divided by since-inception paid-in capital. (See Provision 5.A.4.d.) DPI is calculated as follows:

$$\text{DPI} = \frac{\text{Since} - \text{Inception Distributions}}{\text{Since} - \text{Inception Paid} - \text{In Capital}}$$

f. SINCE-INCEPTION PAID-IN CAPITAL to cumulative COMMITTED CAPITAL (PIC MULTIPLE).

The paid-in capital multiple, also known as the PIC multiple or PIC ratio, gives prospective clients or investors information regarding how much committed capital has actually been drawn down or called. It is also known as the "dry-powder ratio" because it measures how much capital has already been invested and therefore indicates how much capital is left to invest. The PIC multiple is calculated as follows:

$$PIC = \frac{\text{Since} - \text{Inception Paid} - \text{In Capital}}{\text{Cumulative Committed Capital}}$$

Distributions can be either recallable or non-recallable. If a distribution is recallable, after the firm distributes proceeds to its clients or investors, it can draw down the same capital again, which makes it possible for the composite to have since-inception paid-in capital in excess of its total committed capital. A recallable distribution must be treated as an actual distribution and, if and when that distribution is recalled (drawn again), it must be treated as additional paid-in capital.

Recallable distributions affect the performance metric calculations. Firms may wish to consider additional disclosure when there is a material effect on the PIC or realization multiples. If a recallable distribution is re-contributed and reflected as paid-in capital a second time, the result will be that cumulative paid-in capital since inception is higher than total committed capital. It also means that the realization multiple (DPI), unrealized multiple (RVPI), and investment multiple (TVPI) will be lower. (For more information on DPI, RVPI, and TVPI, please see Provisions 5.A.4.e, 5.A.4.g, and 5.A.4.d, respectively.) All else being equal, for composites that have had recallable distributions, the denominator will be increased and the PIC multiple will be higher.

g. RESIDUAL VALUE to SINCE-INCEPTION PAID-IN-CAPITAL (UNREALIZED MULTIPLE or RVPI).

The unrealized multiple, or RVPI, is the converse of the realization multiple. It is equal to the composite's residual value (or fair value) at the end of the period divided by since-inception paid-in capital. It is calculated as follows:

$$RVPI = \frac{\text{Residual Value}}{\text{Since} - \text{Inception Paid} - \text{In Capital}}$$

Provision 5.A.5

The FIRM MUST clearly label or identify:

a. The periods that are presented.

b. If COMPOSITE returns are GROSS-OF-FEES or NET-OF-FEES.

c. If COMPOSITE returns do or do not reflect the SUBSCRIPTION LINE OF CREDIT. This information is REQUIRED only if the FIRM presents returns both with and without the SUBSCRIPTION LINE OF CREDIT.

Discussion

All periods presented in a GIPS Composite Report must be clearly labeled or identified.

Firms may present either gross-of-fees composite returns or net-of-fees composite returns in a GIPS Composite Report and may also choose to present both gross-of-fees and net-of-fees returns. For prospective clients to understand the nature of the returns being presented, the returns included in a GIPS Composite Report must be clearly labeled or identified as either gross-of-fees or net-of-fees.

If a firm uses a subscription line of credit (LOC), and it is required to present returns both with and without the subscription LOC, the firm must clearly indicate whether the composite returns do or do not reflect the subscription LOC. If no subscription LOC is used, or the firm is not required to present returns both with and without the subscription LOC, this disclosure is not required.

Provision 5.A.6

If the FIRM includes more than one BENCHMARK in the GIPS COMPOSITE REPORT, the FIRM MUST present and disclose all REQUIRED information for all BENCHMARKS presented.

Discussion

It is permissible to include more than one benchmark in a GIPS Composite Report. All benchmarks included in a GIPS Composite Report must adhere to the requirements of the GIPS standards that are applicable to benchmarks. Firms may label benchmarks as primary and secondary benchmarks, but the same requirements and recommendations apply to all benchmarks included in a GIPS Composite Report. For example, a GIPS Composite Report must include the following:

- a description for all benchmarks, and
- a disclosure of changes to (or deletion of) any benchmark.

If the firm designates benchmarks as primary and secondary benchmarks, it must disclose when these designations change (e.g., if a primary benchmark becomes a secondary benchmark), because such a change in designation is considered a benchmark change. In all instances, if multiple benchmarks are presented in a GIPS Composite Report and one or more of the benchmarks is removed from the GIPS Composite Report, the firm must disclose this fact. (See Provision 5.C.31.)

An appropriate benchmark for a composite reflects the investment mandate, objective, or strategy of the composite. Additional benchmarks beyond appropriate benchmarks may be presented in a GIPS Composite Report as supplemental information. There must be sufficient disclosure so that a prospective client understands the nature of the benchmark and why it is being presented.

Disclosure, however, does not necessarily prevent information from being false or misleading. An additional benchmark must never be presented for the sole purpose of providing a favorable comparison to the performance of the composite. To do so would be misleading, regardless of the disclosures accompanying the benchmark.

Provision 5.A.7

If the COMPOSITE includes CARVE-OUTS with allocated cash, the FIRM MUST present the percentage of COMPOSITE assets represented by CARVE-OUTS with allocated cash as of the most recent annual period end.

Discussion

A carve-out is a portion of a portfolio that is, by itself, representative of a distinct investment strategy, such as the domestic equity portion of a balanced portfolio. A carve-out may have its own dedicated cash balance, or cash may be allocated to the carve-out synthetically. With the issuance of the 2020 edition of the GIPS standards, firms are once again allowed to include carve-outs that include cash that has been allocated synthetically in composites. (Doing so was prohibited from 1 January 2010 through 31 December 2019.)

A composite that includes carve-outs with allocated cash may also include carve-outs with their own cash balance and standalone portfolios. (A standalone portfolio is a portfolio that is not a portion of a larger portfolio.) Because prospective clients should have sufficient information to understand the nature of the portfolios included in a composite, a firm must, therefore, present the percentage of composite assets represented by carve-outs with allocated cash as of the most recent annual period end. Carve-outs with their own dedicated cash are not included in this percentage. This approach allows prospective clients to understand how much of the composite's assets are represented by standalone portfolios and/or by carve-outs with their own cash and how much of the composite's assets are represented by carve-outs with allocated cash. Provision 5.A.7 applies only to carve-outs with allocated cash. It does not apply to carve-outs with their own dedicated cash.

Provision 5.A.8

If the COMPOSITE includes non-fee-paying PORTFOLIOS, the FIRM MUST present the percentage of COMPOSITE assets represented by non-fee-paying PORTFOLIOS as of the most recent annual period end when NET-OF-FEES returns are presented and are calculated using actual INVESTMENT MANAGEMENT FEES.

Discussion

A firm may choose whether or not to include non-fee-paying portfolios in composites. This decision may be made on a composite-by-composite basis. If the firm has chosen to include a non-fee-paying portfolio in a composite, it must also include all other non-fee-paying discretionary portfolios meeting the definition of the composite. (See Provision 3.A.4 for further guidance on non-fee-paying portfolios.)

If a firm has included non-fee-paying portfolios in a composite and is presenting net-of-fees returns that are calculated using actual investment management fees, the firm is required to present the percentage of composite assets represented by non-fee-paying portfolios as of the most recent annual period end. This may be done as a written disclosure, such as "This composite contained 15% non-fee-paying portfolios as of 31 December 2020." Alternatively, the firm could add a column to its performance table titled "% composite assets composed of non-fee-paying portfolios" and list the percentage as of the most recent annual period end.

If the composite contains non-fee-paying portfolios but only gross-of-fees returns are presented, or if model fees are used to calculate composite net-of-fees returns, this information is not required to be presented. This guidance differs from the requirement in the 2010 edition of the GIPS standards, which required this information to be presented whenever a composite included non-fee-paying portfolios. Firms may apply this current guidance to all periods presented in GIPS Composite Reports.

Provision 5.A.9

If the FIRM chooses to present COMPOSITE uncalled COMMITTED CAPITAL or a combination of COMPOSITE assets and COMPOSITE uncalled COMMITTED CAPITAL, the FIRM MUST:

a. Present COMPOSITE uncalled COMMITTED CAPITAL for the same periods for which the combination of COMPOSITE assets and COMPOSITE uncalled COMMITTED CAPITAL is presented.
b. Clearly label COMPOSITE uncalled COMMITTED CAPITAL as such.
c. Clearly label the combination of COMPOSITE assets and COMPOSITE uncalled COMMITTED CAPITAL as such.

Discussion

Committed capital is defined as pledges of capital to an investment vehicle by investors (limited partners and the general partner) or the firm and is typically drawn down over a period of time. Uncalled committed capital, also known as dry powder, is the amount of capital that has not yet

 |

been drawn. Because uncalled committed capital is not considered actual composite assets, composite uncalled committed capital must not be included in the calculation of composite assets as of 1 January 2020. This is consistent with the requirement to not include uncalled committed capital in total firm assets for periods beginning on or after 1 January 2020. (See Provision 2.A.1.) A firm may report composite uncalled committed capital in addition to the required presentation of composite assets, if it wishes to do so. The inclusion of information on composite uncalled committed capital provides prospective clients with a more complete picture of the firm's investments and the amount of capital that is currently committed to a future investment. If a firm chooses to present information on composite uncalled committed capital, it may present composite uncalled committed capital as either:

- a separate value, or
- the combination of composite assets and composite uncalled committed capital.

If a firm chooses to present composite uncalled committed capital as a separate value, the information must be clearly labeled.

If a firm chooses to present the combination of composite assets and composite uncalled committed capital, the firm must present composite uncalled committed capital for the same periods for which the combination of composite assets and composite uncalled committed capital is presented. Both composite uncalled committed capital and the combination of composite assets and composite uncalled committed capital must be clearly labeled as such.

Provision 5.A.10

If the FIRM chooses to present FIRM-wide uncalled COMMITTED CAPITAL or a combination of TOTAL FIRM ASSETS and FIRM-wide uncalled COMMITTED CAPITAL, the FIRM MUST:

a. Present FIRM-wide uncalled COMMITTED CAPITAL for the same periods for which the combination of TOTAL FIRM ASSETS and FIRM-wide uncalled COMMITTED CAPITAL is presented.
b. Clearly label FIRM-wide uncalled COMMITTED CAPITAL as such.
c. Clearly label the combination of TOTAL FIRM ASSETS and FIRM-wide uncalled COMMITTED CAPITAL as such.

Discussion

Committed capital is defined as pledges of capital to an investment vehicle by investors (limited partners and the general partner) or the firm and is typically drawn down over a period of time. Uncalled committed capital, also known as dry powder, is the amount of capital that has not yet been drawn. For periods beginning on or after 1 January 2020, uncalled committed capital must not be included in total firm assets. (See Provision 2.A.1.) Although firm-wide uncalled committed capital must not be included in the calculation of total firm assets as of 1 January 2020, a firm may report firm-wide uncalled committed capital in addition to the required presentation of total firm assets, if it wishes to do so. The inclusion of information on firm-wide uncalled committed capital provides prospective clients with a more complete picture of the firm's investments and the amount of capital that is currently committed to a future investment. If a firm chooses to present information on firmwide uncalled committed capital, it may present firm-wide uncalled committed capital as either:

- a separate value, or
- the combination of total firm assets and firm-wide uncalled committed capital.

If a firm chooses to present firm-wide uncalled committed capital as a separate value, the information must be clearly labeled.

If a firm chooses to present the combination of total firm assets and firm-wide uncalled committed capital, the firm must present firm-wide uncalled committed capital for the same periods for which the combination of total firm assets and firm-wide uncalled committed capital is presented. Both firm-wide uncalled committed capital and the combination of total firm assets and firm-wide uncalled committed capital must be clearly labeled as such.

Provision 5.A.11

If the FIRM chooses to present ADVISORY-ONLY ASSETS that reflect the COMPOSITE'S investment mandate, objective, or strategy or a combination of COMPOSITE assets and ADVISORY-ONLY ASSETS that reflect the COMPOSITE'S investment mandate, objective, or strategy, the FIRM MUST:

a. Present ADVISORY-ONLY ASSETS that reflect the COMPOSITE'S investment mandate, objective, or strategy for the same periods for which the combination of COMPOSITE assets and ADVISORY-ONLY ASSETS that reflect the COMPOSITE'S investment mandate, objective, or strategy is presented.
b. Clearly label ADVISORY-ONLY ASSETS that reflect the COMPOSITE'S investment mandate, objective, or strategy as such.
c. Clearly label the combination of COMPOSITE assets and ADVISORY-ONLY ASSETS that reflect the COMPOSITE'S investment mandate, objective, or strategy as such.

Discussion

Composite advisory-only assets are assets for which the firm provides investment recommendations in line with the composite's strategy but for which the firm has no control over implementation of investment decisions and no trading authority for the assets. Although composite advisory-only assets must not be included in the calculation of composite assets because the firm does not manage these assets, a firm may wish to provide information on composite advisory-only assets in addition to the required presentation of composite assets. The inclusion of information on composite advisory-only assets provides prospective clients additional information about a firm's business model and the types of investment-related services that it provides. If a firm chooses to present information on composite advisory-only assets, it may present composite advisory-only assets as either:

- a separate value, or
- the combination of composite assets and composite advisory-only assets.

If a firm chooses to present composite advisory-only assets as a separate value, the information must be clearly labeled.

If a firm chooses to present the combination of composite assets and composite advisory-only assets, the firm must present composite advisory-only assets for the same periods for which the combination of composite assets and composite advisory-only assets is presented. Both composite advisory-only assets and the combination of composite assets and composite advisory-only assets must be clearly labeled as such.

Provision 5.A.12

If the FIRM chooses to present FIRM-wide ADVISORY-ONLY ASSETS or a combination of TOTAL FIRM ASSETS and FIRM-wide ADVISORY-ONLY ASSETS, the FIRM MUST:

a. Present FIRM-wide ADVISORY-ONLY ASSETS for the same periods for which the combination of TOTAL FIRM ASSETS and FIRM-wide ADVISORY-ONLY ASSETS is presented.
b. Clearly label FIRM-wide ADVISORY-ONLY ASSETS as such.
c. Clearly label the combination of TOTAL FIRM ASSETS and FIRM-wide ADVISORY-ONLY ASSETS as such.

Discussion

Advisory-only assets are assets for which the firm provides investment recommendations but for which the firm has no control over implementation of investment decisions and no trading authority for the assets. Although firm-wide advisory-only assets must not be included in the calculation of total firm assets because the firm does not manage these assets, a firm may wish to provide information on firm-wide advisory-only assets in addition to the required presentation of total firm assets. The inclusion of information on firm-wide advisory-only assets provides prospective clients additional information about a firm's business model and the types of investment-related services that it provides. If a firm chooses to present information on firm-wide advisory-only assets, it may present firm-wide advisory-only assets as either:

- a separate value, or
- the combination of total firm assets and firm-wide advisory-only assets.

If a firm chooses to present firm-wide advisory-only assets as a separate value, the information must be clearly labeled.

If a firm chooses to present the combination of total firm assets and firm-wide advisory-only assets, the firm must present firm-wide advisory-only assets for the same periods for which the combination of total firm assets and firm-wide advisory-only assets is presented. Both the firm-wide advisory-only assets and the combination of total firm assets and firm-wide advisory-only assets must be clearly labeled as such.

Provision 5.A.13

All REQUIRED and RECOMMENDED information in the GIPS COMPOSITE REPORT MUST be presented in the same currency.

Discussion

Firms must present all required and recommended information in a GIPS Composite Report in the same currency (e.g., composite and benchmark returns, composite assets, and total firm assets). This requirement is not applicable to the fee schedule. Supplemental information should also be presented in the same currency. If it is not, that fact must be disclosed. Not disclosing this fact could be misleading.

If a firm chooses to present a composite in a different currency, the firm must convert all of the required information into the new currency. If the firm chooses to present performance in multiple currencies in the same GIPS Composite Report, the firm must convert all of the required information into each of the currencies and ensure it is clear in which currencies performance is reported. The firm must also convert any recommended information it chooses to present in the GIPS Composite Report containing the converted information.

In cases where a composite contains portfolios with different currencies, the firm must convert the individual portfolio cash flows and valuations to a single currency in order to calculate a composite return. It is not permissible to do so by applying the exchange rate as of the current period end to historical data.

It is up to the firm to determine the composite-specific conversion method. Policies and procedures for converting returns must be established, documented, and applied consistently.

Provision 5.A.14

When the FIRM presents the performance of a COMPOSITE that includes CARVE-OUTS with allocated cash and also has a COMPOSITE of standalone PORTFOLIOS managed according to the same strategy, the FIRM MUST present the COMPOSITE SINCE-INCEPTION MONEY WEIGHTED RETURN through the most recent annual period end and the COMPOSITE assets of the COMPOSITE of standalone PORTFOLIOS as of the most recent annual period end in the GIPS COMPOSITE REPORT of the COMPOSITE that includes CARVE-OUTS with allocated cash.

Discussion

A carve-out is a portion of a portfolio that is by itself representative of a distinct investment strategy, such as the domestic equity portion of a balanced portfolio. A carve-out may have its own dedicated cash balance, or cash may be allocated to the carve-out synthetically. If a firm has created carve-outs with allocated cash, the firm is likely, at some point, to obtain standalone portfolios managed in the same strategy as the carve-outs with allocated cash. (A standalone portfolio is a portfolio that is not a portion of a larger portfolio.) The firm must then create a separate composite that contains only the standalone portfolios. (See Provision 3.A.18.) If such a composite of standalone portfolios exists, the firm must present information about this composite in the GIPS Composite Report for the composite that includes carve-outs with allocated cash. The firm must present the since-inception-money weighted return (SI-MWR) through the most recent annual period end and the composite assets as of the most recent annual period end. Even though the time periods for the two SI-MWRs will be different, this will allow a prospective client to compare the return and assets of the composite that includes carve-outs with allocated cash to the return and assets of the composite that contains only standalone portfolios managed in the same strategy. If there are significant performance differences between the two composites, the prospective client has a chance to ask questions about the difference in returns between the two composites.

This provision applies only to carve-outs with allocated cash. It does not apply to carve-outs with their own cash.

Provision 5.A.15

Any SUPPLEMENTAL INFORMATION included in the GIPS COMPOSITE REPORT:

a. MUST relate directly to the COMPOSITE.
b. MUST NOT contradict or conflict with the REQUIRED OR RECOMMENDED information in the GIPS COMPOSITE REPORT.
c. MUST be clearly labeled as SUPPLEMENTAL INFORMATION.

Discussion

Supplemental information is any performance-related information included as part of a GIPS Composite Report that supplements or enhances the requirements and/or recommendations of the GIPS standards. Performance-related information includes:

- information expressed in terms of investment return and risk, and
- other information and input data that directly relate to the calculation of investment return and risk (e.g., composite holdings), as well as information derived from investment return and risk input data (e.g., performance contribution or attribution).

Supplemental information should provide users of the GIPS Composite Report with the proper context in which to understand the performance results. Common examples of supplemental information for a GIPS Composite Report that presents money-weighted returns (MWRs) include the following:

- segment MWRs that do not include cash,
- projected investment-level MWRs,
- projected multiples, and
- benchmark time-weighted returns.

Supplemental information must relate directly to the composite and must not contradict or conflict with the required or recommended information in the GIPS Composite Report. Examples of information that relates directly to the composite and would be considered supplemental information include segment returns (e.g., country or sector), performance attribution, and composite or portfolio-level holdings. An example of information that would conflict with the GIPS standards is an MWR that includes data from a past firm when the data does not meet the portability tests specified in Provision 1.A.32.

 |

The following is a more complete list of the principles that apply when supplemental information is presented. Supplemental information must:

- satisfy the spirit and principles of the GIPS standards—fair representation and full disclosure,
- comply with all applicable laws and regulations regarding the calculation and presentation of performance,
- not include performance or performance-related information that is false or misleading,
- relate directly to the composite and supplement or enhance the required or recommended information included in the GIPS Composite Report,
- not contradict or conflict with the required or recommended information in the GIPS Composite Report,
- be clearly labeled as supplemental information, and
- not be shown with greater prominence than the required composite information.

5.B. Presentation and Reporting—Recommendations

Provision 5.B.1

The FIRM SHOULD present annualized SINCE-INCEPTION MONEY-WEIGHTED RETURNS as of each annual period end.

Discussion

Although a firm is required to present only the annualized composite since-inception money-weighed return (SI-MWR) through the most recent annual period end, it is recommended that the firm also present SI-MWRs as of each annual period end. Doing so will provide prospective clients with a more complete picture of the performance of the composite over time.

Provision 5.B.2

If PORTFOLIOS in the COMPOSITE have COMMITTED CAPITAL, the FIRM SHOULD present the following items as of each annual period end:

a. COMPOSITE SINCE-INCEPTION PAID-IN CAPITAL.

b. COMPOSITE SINCE-INCEPTION DISTRIBUTIONS.

c. COMPOSITE cumulative COMMITTED CAPITAL.
d. TOTAL VALUE to SINCE-INCEPTION PAID-IN CAPITAL (INVESTMENT MULTIPLE or TVPI).
e. SINCE-INCEPTION DISTRIBUTIONS to SINCE-INCEPTION PAID-IN CAPITAL (REALIZATION MULTIPLE or DPI).
f. SINCE-INCEPTION PAID-IN CAPITAL to cumulative COMMITTED CAPITAL (PIC MULTIPLE).
g. RESIDUAL VALUE to SINCE-INCEPTION PAID-IN CAPITAL (UNREALIZED MULTIPLE or RVPI).

Discussion

Firms are required to present the composite since-inception money-weighted return (SI-MWR) through the most recent annual period end, as well as the since-inception paid-in capital, since-inception distributions, cumulative committed capital, investment multiple (TVPI), realization multiple (DPI), PIC multiple, and unrealized multiple (RVPI), as of the most recent annual period end. If firms choose to present additional SI-MWRs through prior annual period ends, firms are recommended to also present the same metrics as of each additional period end for which returns are presented. See Provision 5.A.4 for further discussion of these metrics.

Provision 5.B.3

The FIRM SHOULD present both annualized GROSS-OF-FEES and NET-OF-FEES COMPOSITE SINCE-INCEPTION MONEY-WEIGHTED RETURNS.

Discussion

A firm is required to present either an annualized gross-of-fees or net-of-fees composite since-inception money-weighted return (SI-MWR) in a GIPS Composite Report that presents money-weighed returns. Each type of return provides important information to prospective clients.

Because a gross-of-fees composite SI-MWR is the return on investments reduced by any transaction costs, it is the best measure of the firm's investment management ability and can be thought of as the "investment return." In addition, because fees are sometimes negotiable, presenting gross-of-fees SI-MWRs shows the firm's expertise in managing assets without the effect of the firm's or client's negotiating skills. Gross-of-fees returns also allow prospective clients to better compare performance between firms.

Net-of-fees composite SI-MWRs reflect the deduction of transaction costs and investment management fees. Net-of-fees composite returns therefore provide the best indication to prospective clients of the returns that the firm's clients received or would have received over time, after taking into account the effect of investment management costs.

Because both gross-of-fees and net-of-fees composite SI-MWRs provide important information to prospective clients, it is recommended that firms present both gross-of-fees and net-of-fees composite SI-MWRs in a GIPS Composite Report.

Provision 5.B.4

The FIRM SHOULD present PROPRIETARY ASSETS as a percentage of COMPOSITE assets as of the most recent annual period end.

Discussion

Proprietary assets are assets owned by the firm, the firm's management, and/or the firm's parent company that are managed by the firm. Knowing how much of a composite's assets are proprietary and how much are managed for external clients provides prospective clients with additional insight regarding the composite, especially when a significant percentage of the composite's assets are proprietary assets. If a composite includes proprietary assets, it is recommended that firms present proprietary assets as a percentage of composite assets as of the most recent annual period end.

Provision 5.B.5

The FIRM SHOULD present an appropriate EX POST risk measure for the COMPOSITE and the BENCHMARK. The same EX POST risk measure SHOULD be presented for the COMPOSITE and the BENCHMARK.

Discussion

Evaluating past performance requires an understanding of the risks taken to achieve the results. Although firms are required to include a qualitative narrative of material risks as part of the composite description, firms should also include an ex post risk measure for the composite and benchmark. Any risk measure presented must be calculated on an ex post basis and be based on actual historical data. Some examples of ex post risk measures that may be presented include drawdown measures, interest rate risk measures (e.g., duration), credit risk measures (e.g., credit spread), and liquidity risk measures. Because no quantitative risk measure is required for composites that present money-weighted returns, all risk measures presented are considered additional risk measures.

If the firm chooses to present an ex post risk measure for the composite and benchmark, the same ex post risk measure should be presented for the composite and benchmark. The risk measure must be one that the firm determines is appropriate for the composite. When choosing an appropriate ex post risk measure to present, the firm should satisfy itself that there are sufficient data points for the selected risk measure to be statistically significant so as not to be misleading. Firms are required to describe any additional risk measure that is included in the GIPS Composite Report (see Provision 5.C.41).

Provision 5.B.6

If the FIRM uses preliminary, estimated values as FAIR VALUE, the FIRM SHOULD present the percentage of assets in the COMPOSITE that were valued using preliminary, estimated values as of the most recent annual period end.

Discussion

The use of preliminary, estimated values as fair value is common for some alternative strategies, including those that invest in underlying funds for which the firm relies on valuations provided by the underlying fund managers. When using preliminary, estimated values as fair value, it is important to remember the underlying principles of the GIPS standards: fair representation and full disclosure. If using preliminary, estimated values, firms must disclose this fact in the relevant GIPS Composite Report (see Provision 5.C.39). It is recommended that the firm also present the percentage of assets in the composite that were valued using preliminary, estimated values as of the most recent annual period end. This provides important information that allows prospective clients to better assess the valuations and performance record presented.

Provision 5.B.7

If the FIRM has COMMITTED CAPITAL, the FIRM SHOULD present FIRM-wide uncalled COMMITTED CAPITAL as of the most recent annual period end.

Discussion

Committed capital is defined as pledges of capital to an investment vehicle by investors (limited partners and the general partner) or the firm and is typically drawn down over a period of time.

Uncalled committed capital, also known as dry powder, is the amount of capital that has not yet been drawn. If a firm has committed capital, it is recommended that the firm present total firm-wide uncalled committed capital as of the most recent annual period end. This information provides prospective clients a more complete picture of the capital that is currently committed to a future investment. If the firm chooses to present firm-wide uncalled committed capital, it may present this amount separately from total firm assets. The firm may also choose to present the combination of total firm assets and firmwide uncalled committed capital. Provision 5.A.10 discusses the requirements relating to the presentation of firm-wide uncalled committed capital in a GIPS Composite Report.

5.C. Disclosure—Requirements

Provision 5.C.1

Once the FIRM has met all the applicable REQUIREMENTS of the GIPS standards, the FIRM MUST disclose its compliance with the GIPS standards using one of the following compliance statements. The compliance statement for a COMPOSITE MUST only be used in a GIPS COMPOSITE REPORT.

a. For a FIRM that is verified:

"[Insert name of FIRM] claims compliance with the Global Investment Performance Standards (GIPS®) and has prepared and presented this report in compliance with the GIPS standards. [Insert name of FIRM] has been independently verified for the periods [insert dates]. The verification report(s) is/are available upon request.

"A firm that claims compliance with the GIPS standards must establish policies and procedures for complying with all the applicable requirements of the GIPS standards. Verification provides assurance on whether the firm's policies and procedures related to composite and pooled fund maintenance, as well as the calculation, presentation, and distribution of performance, have been designed in compliance with the GIPS standards and have been implemented on a firm-wide basis. Verification does not provide assurance on the accuracy of any specific performance report."

b. For COMPOSITES of a verified FIRM that have also had a PERFORMANCE EXAMINATION:

"[Insert name of FIRM] claims compliance with the Global Investment Performance Standards (GIPS®) and has prepared and presented this report in compliance with the GIPS standards. [Insert name of FIRM] has been independently verified for the periods [insert dates].

> "A firm that claims compliance with the GIPS standards must establish policies and procedures for complying with all the applicable requirements of the GIPS standards. Verification provides assurance on whether the firm's policies and procedures related to composite and pooled fund maintenance, as well as the calculation, presentation, and distribution of performance, have been designed in compliance with the GIPS standards and have been implemented on a firm-wide basis. The [insert name of COMPOSITE] has had a performance examination for the periods [insert dates]. The verification and performance examination reports are available upon request."
>
> The compliance statement for a FIRM that is verified or for COMPOSITES of a verified FIRM that have also had a PERFORMANCE EXAMINATION is complete only when both paragraphs are shown together, one after the other.
>
> c. For a FIRM that has not been verified:
>
> "[Insert name of FIRM] claims compliance with the Global Investment Performance Standards (GIPS®) and has prepared and presented this report in compliance with the GIPS standards. [Insert name of FIRM] has not been independently verified."
>
> The FIRM MUST NOT exclude any portion of the respective compliance statement. Any modifications to the compliance statement MUST be additive.

Discussion

A firm meeting all the requirements of the GIPS standards must use one of the three compliance statements in each of its GIPS Composite Reports. The English version of the compliance statements is the controlling version. If a firm chooses to translate the claim of compliance into a language for which there is no official translation of the GIPS standards, the firm must take care to ensure that the translation used reflects the required wording of the claim of compliance used in Provisions 5.C.1.a, 5.C.1.b, or 5.C.1.c.

It is acceptable to combine both paragraphs of the claim of compliance for a verified firm (Provision 5.C.1.a) into a single paragraph. If the paragraphs are not combined, the claim of compliance for a verified firm is complete only when both paragraphs are shown together, one after the other. A firm may not separate the two required paragraphs from each other.

The same is true for the claim of compliance for a composite that has also had a performance examination (Provision 5.C.1.b). Both paragraphs of the claim of compliance may be combined into a single paragraph. If the paragraphs are not combined, the claim of compliance is complete only when both paragraphs are shown together, one after the other. A firm may not separate the two required paragraphs from each other.

When preparing the GIPS Composite Report for a composite that has had a performance examination, the firm may choose to use either the verification or performance examination compliance statement. For example, a firm might choose to use the verification compliance statement for all GIPS Reports, including GIPS Reports for composites and pooled funds that have had a performance examination, if it wishes to standardize the compliance statement for all GIPS Reports throughout the firm. In this situation, the firm may also disclose that a specific composite or pooled fund has had a performance examination.

The language in each compliance statement must not exclude any portion of the respective compliance statement, with one exception. In the second paragraph of both 5.C.1.a and 5.C.1.b, there is a reference to "composite and pooled fund maintenance." The firm may delete the words "and pooled fund" if no broad distribution pooled funds or limited distribution pooled funds are included within the definition of the firm.

There may also be instances where it may be appropriate for a firm to modify the language slightly. For example, a firm may modify the language to include the name of the firm's verifier, if the firm wishes to disclose this information. A firm may also need to modify the language to add more details about the name of the firm that has been verified or the dates of the verification if the verification period was not continuous. Any modifications must be additive and must not result in a compliance statement that is false or misleading.

Provision 5.C.2

The FIRM MUST disclose the following: "GIPS® is a registered trademark of CFA Institute. CFA Institute does not endorse or promote this organization, nor does it warrant the accuracy or quality of the content contained herein."

Discussion

"GIPS®" is a registered trademark of CFA Institute, and firms are required to acknowledge this in all GIPS Composite Reports. The required disclosure may appear in the body of the GIPS Composite Report or in a footnote to the report. The term "this organization", which is included in the required disclosure, refers to any entity associated with the GIPS Composite Report, either the firm or the verifier.

CFA Institute (owner of the GIPS® trademark) may take appropriate action against any firm that misuses the mark "GIPS®" or any compliance statement, including false claims of compliance with the GIPS standards. CFA Institute members, CFA Program charterholders, CFA candidates, CIPM Program certificants, and CIPM candidates who misuse the term "GIPS" or any compliance statement, misrepresent their performance history or the performance history of their firm, or falsely claim compliance with the GIPS standards are also subject to disciplinary sanctions under the CFA Institute Code of Ethics and Standards of Professional Conduct. Possible disciplinary sanctions include public censure, suspension of membership, and revocation of the CFA charter or CIPM certificate.

Regulators with jurisdiction over firms claiming compliance with the GIPS standards may also take enforcement actions against firms that falsely claim compliance with the GIPS standards.

Firms may also use the following language to replace the first sentence in this required disclosure: "GIPS® is a registered trademark owned by CFA Institute." See the GIPS Standards Trademark Usage Guidelines on the CFA Institute website (www.cfainstitute.org) for additional guidance on the proper use of "GIPS".

Provision 5.C.3

The FIRM MUST disclose the definition of the FIRM used to determine TOTAL FIRM ASSETS and FIRM-wide compliance.

Discussion

To claim compliance with the GIPS standards, a firm must comply with all applicable requirements of the GIPS standards on a firm-wide basis. Accordingly, the firm must determine exactly how it will be defined for the purpose of compliance. The GIPS standards require that a firm must be defined as an investment firm, subsidiary, or division held out to the public as a distinct business entity.

A distinct business entity is a unit, division, department, or office that is organizationally and functionally segregated from other units, divisions, departments, or offices, that retains discretion over the assets it manages, and that should have autonomy over the investment decision-making process.

Possible criteria that can be used to determine this status include:

- being a legal entity,
- having a distinct market or client type (e.g., institutional, retail, private client), and
- using a separate and distinct investment process.

See Provision 1.A.2 for a more detailed discussion of defining the firm.

Because there are often a number of closely related units or divisions within larger investment management entities, it is critical to disclose the precise definition of the firm that is presenting the performance results and would be responsible for the management of the prospective client's assets. This provision requires the firm to disclose sufficient details of the entity that is presenting investment performance such that the firm is clearly identified.

Sample Disclosures:

Example 1:

Firm A is a multinational investment firm with offices around the world, including in Japan, Australia, the United Kingdom, and the United States. Although all of its offices are part of the global parent company, each office is registered with the appropriate national regulatory authority, and each is held out to the public as a distinct business entity. The firm has defined its offices in Japan, Australia, the United Kingdom, and the United States as separate firms for the purpose of complying with the GIPS standards. The offices in Japan, the United Kingdom, and the United States claim compliance with the GIPS standards. Firm A's Australia office, however, does not claim compliance with the GIPS standards.

Sample Disclosure for Firm A—US:

"For the purpose of complying with the GIPS standards, the firm is defined as Firm A—US, which serves US clients and investors and is a subsidiary of Firm A, a multinational investment firm with offices globally. Firm A also has subsidiaries in the United Kingdom, Australia, and Japan, which are not included in the definition of the firm for purposes of compliance with the GIPS standards."

Example 2:

Firm B has two divisions, each of which serves a distinct client type. Firm B Institutional Investment Management manages institutional assets. Firm B Retail Investors manages retail assets. The firm has determined that it will create two separate firms for the purpose of complying with the GIPS standards.

Sample Disclosure for Firm B Institutional Investment Management:

"For the purpose of complying with the GIPS standards, the firm is defined as Firm B Institutional Investment Management, the institutional asset management division of Firm B."

Example 3:

Firm C is an investment management firm that offers both active and passive (indexed) investment strategies. For the purpose of complying with the GIPS standards, the firm has decided to create two separate firms: one that offers active investment strategies and one that offers indexed investment strategies.

Sample Disclosure for Firm C—Indexed Investing:

"For the purpose of complying with the GIPS standards, the firm is defined as Firm C—Indexed Investing. Firm C—Indexed Investing is the division of Firm C that offers indexed investment strategies to clients."

Provision 5.C.4

The FIRM MUST disclose the COMPOSITE DESCRIPTION.

Discussion

The composite description is defined as general information regarding the investment mandate, objective, or strategy of the composite. The composite description may be more abbreviated than the composite definition but must include all key features of the composite and must include enough information to allow a prospective client to understand the key characteristics of the composite's investment mandate, objective, or strategy, including:

- the material risks of the composite's strategy,
- how leverage, derivatives, and short positions may be used, if they are a material part of the strategy, and
- if illiquid investments are a material part of the strategy.

The composite definition goes a step further than the composite description and includes the detailed criteria that determine the assignment of portfolios to composites, such as investment constraints or restrictions. Although the composite description is a required disclosure, the composite definition is not a required disclosure. (See the discussion of Provision 3.A.5 for additional information regarding composite definitions and composite descriptions.)

The required disclosure of the composite description provides information about the composite's investment strategy that is intended to help a prospective client who is considering an investment product or strategy and is reviewing a GIPS Composite Report for that product or strategy. The composite description should provide sufficient information to prospective clients to allow them to differentiate the significant features of the strategy from other strategies within the firm and to compare products across firms. The disclosed strategy features will likely affect both the historical and expected risk and returns. Along with the required benchmark description (see Provision 5.C.5), the GIPS Composite Report will allow prospective clients to understand both the investment strategy employed and the benchmark against which the composite's performance is evaluated. This will help prospective clients to compare investments across firms.

If leverage, derivatives, and short positions may be used, and they are a material part of the strategy, this must be disclosed in the composite description. Provision 5.C.16 requires that the firm disclose how leverage, derivatives, and short positions have been used historically, if material. Taken together, these two required disclosures provide a more complete picture about the presence, use, and extent of leverage, derivatives, and short positions. When determining what would be material, the firm must consider whether the disclosure of how leverage, derivatives, and/or short positions may be used and/or have been used historically is likely to affect a prospective

 |

client's or prospective investor's view of the risk involved in the strategy. If so, it would be misleading for the firm to fail to disclose their use to these prospective clients or prospective investors when describing the strategy.

Generally, all investment products or strategies have some degree of inherent risk (e.g., market risk), but it is not intended that the composite description identifies every risk of the strategy. Instead, firms must identify those material risks of the strategy, if any, and must disclose those risks. For example, investment concentration, correlation (or lack thereof), liquidity, and exposure to counterparties are features that may need to be included in the composite description.

The key characteristics of some strategies may change given market events. Firms should periodically review composite descriptions to ensure they are current.

Sample Disclosure:

"The Armor Distressed Debt Composite invests at least 85% of its assets in distressed euro-denominated bonds that have credit ratings of CCC or lower by at least one major credit rating agency. Key risks include widening corporate spreads and defaults, high levels of government debt, and elevated political tensions, which could lead to abrupt changes in monetary policy by the European Central Bank (ECB). A material amount of the composite's investments may be illiquid."

A Sample List of Composite Descriptions can be found in Appendix D of the GIPS standards.

Provision 5.C.5

The FIRM MUST disclose the BENCHMARK DESCRIPTION, which MUST include the key features of the BENCHMARK or the name of the BENCHMARK for a readily recognized index or other point of reference.

Discussion

Firms are required to disclose a description of each benchmark included in a GIPS Composite Report. The benchmark description is defined as general information regarding the investments, structure, and/or characteristics of the benchmark, and it must include the key features of the benchmark. In the case of a widely recognized benchmark, the name of the benchmark will satisfy this requirement. There are few money-weighted return benchmarks that would be considered widely recognized. If the firm presents a public market equivalent (PME) as a benchmark, the benchmark description must include the name of the market index that is used to calculate the PME. Given the unique nature of a PME, if the market index used to calculate the PME is not readily recognized, the firm must also disclose the description of this benchmark. See the discussion of Provision 5.C.33 for an explanation of a PME. Each firm must decide for itself whether a benchmark is widely recognized. If the firm is not certain as to whether the benchmark is widely known, the firm must include the benchmark description.

Sample Disclosure:

"The custom benchmark return is calculated by applying the investment cash flows of the Armor Distressed Debt Composite to the XYZ Eurozone Distressed Debt Bond Index. The index reflects a portfolio of euro-denominated distressed debt bonds issued in Eurozone countries that generally have credit ratings of CCC or lower from the main rating agencies and are listed on the XYZ platforms."

Provision 5.C.6

When presenting GROSS-OF-FEES returns, the FIRM MUST disclose if any other fees are deducted in addition to TRANSACTION COSTS.

Discussion

A gross-of-fees return is the return on investments reduced by any transaction costs. If a firm presents a gross-of-fees return in a GIPS Composite Report, the firm must disclose if any other fees are deducted in addition to transaction costs (e.g., custody fees).

In cases where fees other than transactions costs have been deducted from the gross-of-fees returns, this disclosure helps prospective clients understand the gross-of-fees returns being presented and therefore compare performance across firms.

In some markets, brokers offer zero-commission trades. If a portfolio is paying zero commissions, then it is appropriate to calculate portfolio gross-of-fees returns that reflect zero transaction costs. When a composite includes portfolios that pay zero commissions, firms should disclose this fact. Not disclosing this fact could be misleading.

Sample Disclosure:

"Gross-of-fees returns reflect the deduction of transaction costs and custodian fees but do not reflect the deduction of investment management fees."

Provision 5.C.7

When presenting NET-OF-FEES returns, the FIRM MUST disclose:

a. If any other fees are deducted in addition to INVESTMENT MANAGEMENT FEES and TRANSACTION COSTS.
b. If NET-OF-FEES returns are net of any PERFORMANCE-BASED FEES or CARRIED INTEREST.
c. If model or actual INVESTMENT MANAGEMENT FEES are used.
d. If model INVESTMENT MANAGEMENT FEES are used, and COMPOSITE GROSS-OF-FEES returns are not presented, the model INVESTMENT MANAGEMENT FEE used to calculate NET-OF-FEES returns.[40]
e. If model INVESTMENT MANAGEMENT FEES are used, the methodology used to calculate NET-OF-FEES returns.

Discussion

When presenting returns, it is important that there are sufficient disclosures so that prospective clients can understand what the returns actually represent.

Net-of-fees returns for composites are required to reflect only the deduction of transaction costs and investment management fees. Investment management fees include both asset-based fees and performance-based fees or carried interest. Other expenses may also be deducted (e.g., custody fees). If other fees are deducted from the net-of-fees returns, this must be disclosed to help prospective clients understand the net-of-fees returns presented and to compare performance across firms. If the net-of-fees returns are net of any performance-based fees or carried interest, that must be disclosed as well.

In some markets, brokers offer zero-commission trades. If a portfolio is paying zero commissions, then it is appropriate to calculate portfolio net-of-fees returns that reflect zero transaction costs. When a composite includes portfolios that pay zero commissions, firms should disclose this fact. Not disclosing this fact could be misleading.

A firm must also disclose whether model or actual investment management fees are used to calculate net-of-fees returns. (See Provision 2.A.31 for an explanation of when model investment management fees may be used.) Given the nature of a money-weighted return calculation, in most instances firms will use actual investment management fees. In some cases, however, it may be appropriate to use model fees, such as when a composite is seeded with firm capital and no investment management fees are charged. If model fees are used, and gross-of-fees returns are presented along with the net-of-fees returns, prospective clients can easily determine the model

[40] REQUIRED for periods ending on or after 31 December 2020.

fee used by deducting the net-of-fee returns from the gross-of-fee returns. For periods ending on or after 31 December 2020, however, if model investment management fees have been used and composite gross-of-fees returns are not presented, the firm must disclose the model fee used to calculate net-of-fees returns. The methodology used in the calculation of net-of-fees returns must also be disclosed if model investment management fees are used.

Sample Disclosure for Actual Fees:

"Net-of-fees returns are net of actual investment management fees, including incentive fees, which are recorded on an accrual basis."

Sample Disclosure for Model Fees:

"Net-of-fees returns are calculated by applying a model fee of 0.4125% on a quarterly basis. This equates to a model annual fee of 1.65%, which is the highest tier of the standard fee schedule."

Provision 5.C.8

The FIRM MUST disclose which fees and expenses other than INVESTMENT MANAGEMENT FEES (e.g., research costs) are separately charged by the FIRM to clients, if material.

Discussion

Clients typically bear investment management fees and transaction costs. In some cases, however, firms may charge fees or expenses, such as investment research costs, directly to clients. When any fees or expenses other than investment management fees are separately charged by the firm to clients, and these fees or expenses are material, the firm must disclose which fees and expenses are separately charged. When determining if additional fees or expenses would be considered material, a firm must consider whether the additional fees or expenses are significant enough to reduce a prospective client's assessment of the attractiveness of the expected returns of the strategy relative to total fees charged. If so, the firm's failure to disclose these additional fees or expenses would violate the principle of full disclosure.

Sample Disclosure:

"In addition to investment management fees and transaction costs, certain investment research costs are charged directly to clients, as stipulated in client agreements."

Provision 5.C.9

The FIRM MUST disclose or otherwise indicate the reporting currency.

Discussion

The GIPS standards require that firms disclose the currency used to report the numerical information presented in a GIPS Composite Report. If the firm presents performance in multiple currencies in the same GIPS Composite Report, the firm must ensure it is clear which currencies are used to calculate and report performance and assets.

Labeling the columns within a GIPS Composite Report with the appropriate currency symbol would satisfy this requirement, as would a written disclosure. If firms market the strategy outside their home market, they should consider whether the currency symbol alone is sufficient. For example, a Canadian firm marketing only in Canada may decide to present only the $ symbol. If the firm markets the strategy in both the United States and Canada, the firm must disclose whether the currency is USD or CAD, because both currencies use the same currency symbol.

All required and recommended information presented in a GIPS Composite Report must be presented in the same currency. (See Provision 5.A.13.)

Sample Disclosures:

"Valuations are computed and all information is reported in Canadian dollars."

"All numerical information is reported in Japanese yen."

Provision 5.C.10

The FIRM MUST disclose the current FEE SCHEDULE appropriate to PROSPECTIVE CLIENTS or PROSPECTIVE INVESTORS.

a. When presenting performance to a PROSPECTIVE CLIENT for a standalone PORTFOLIO, the FEE SCHEDULE MUST reflect the FEE SCHEDULE for a standalone PORTFOLIO managed according to that strategy.
b. When presenting performance of a COMPOSITE that includes CARVE-OUTS to a PROSPECTIVE CLIENT for a multi-asset strategy PORTFOLIO, the FEE SCHEDULE MUST reflect the FEE SCHEDULE for a multi-asset strategy PORTFOLIO managed according to that strategy.

c. When presenting a GIPS COMPOSITE REPORT to a PROSPECTIVE INVESTOR for a POOLED FUND included in the COMPOSITE, the FIRM MUST disclose the POOLED FUND'S current FEE SCHEDULE and EXPENSE RATIO.

Discussion

Firms must disclose the current fee schedule that is applicable to prospective clients or prospective investors for the specific composite. The fee schedule can be asset based, performance based, or a combination of both. Determining which fee schedule is appropriate depends on the recipient of the information.

Prospective Client for a Standalone Portfolio

A standalone portfolio is a portfolio that is not a portion of a larger portfolio. If the performance of a composite is being presented to a prospective client for a standalone portfolio, the fee schedule must reflect the fee schedule for a standalone portfolio managed according to that strategy.

Prospective Client for a Multi-Asset-Class Strategy Portfolio When the Composite Includes Carve-Outs

If the performance of a multi-asset-class strategy model composite that includes carve-outs is being presented to a prospective client as supplemental information to the single-asset-class composites that represent the "building blocks" for the strategy, the fee schedule must reflect the fee schedule for a multi-asset-class portfolio managed according to the strategy, not the fees associated with the individual building blocks. The same is true if the building blocks do not include carve-outs. The firm may provide the fee schedules for the individual building blocks for the strategy, in addition to the fee schedule for the multi-asset-class strategy, if it wishes to do so. Note that the firm must also present the GIPS Composite Reports for the underlying, building block composites to the prospective client. (See Provision 3.A.2.)

Prospective Investor for a Pooled Fund Included in the Composite

When presenting performance to a prospective investor for a pooled fund, a firm may provide a GIPS Pooled Fund Report that includes performance of that pooled fund. If the pooled fund is included in a composite, the firm may instead provide a GIPS Composite Report to the prospective investor. If the firm provides a GIPS Composite Report to the prospective investor, the firm must include the fee schedule that is appropriate to the pooled fund, rather than (or in addition to) the fee schedule for the composite.

If the pooled fund has multiple fee schedules, the firm may use the highest fee schedule as the appropriate fee that can be used for all prospective investors. The firm may also include multiple fee schedules in the GIPS Composite Report. Including a range of fee schedules (e.g., management fees range from 0.50% to 0.95%) would not satisfy this requirement.

Firms must present the total expense ratio that is applicable to prospective investors for the specific pooled fund. The pooled fund expense ratio is the ratio of total pooled fund expenses to average net assets. The expense ratio should not reflect transaction costs. The expense ratio gives prospective investors important insight into the total fees and expenses involved in an investment in the fund. For example, a pooled fund expense ratio of 2% indicates that an investor will pay $20 in expenses each year for every $1,000 invested, in addition to transaction costs. An expense ratio also helps investors compare expenses across funds, because even a small difference in fees can have a significant effect over time.

If the pooled fund has multiple share classes, the firm may present multiple expense ratios or may present only the expense ratio appropriate to the prospective investor. The firm may also use the highest expense ratio as the expense ratio that can be used for all prospective investors of the fund. Expense ratios must reflect any performance-based fees or carried interest, if accrued or charged to the pooled fund. Presenting a range of expense ratios (e.g., the expense ratio for all share classes ranges between 1.40% and 1.85%) would not satisfy this requirement.

Because expense ratios can change over time, firms must determine which expense ratio to present. A firm might choose to present the expense ratio as of the most recent annual period end, or the last known expense ratio. When the expense ratio has had a material change resulting from a change in assets or costs, the firm should present a more current expense ratio that reflects what a prospective investor is likely to pay at the current time.

Pooled fund expense ratios that are calculated for periods of less than one year must be annualized. For example, assume that a pooled fund starts on 1 April, and the firm calculates an expense ratio of 0.75% for the period from 1 April 2019 through 31 December 2019. The firm must present an annualized rate of 1.00%, representing a pooled fund expense ratio for the entire year, rather than the 0.75% that represents an expense ratio for only nine months. Presenting an annualized expense ratio facilitates the comparison of expense ratios across funds and firms. Firms may also present the non-annualized expense ratio but must clearly disclose or indicate that the expense ratio is not annualized.

When a firm uses a single GIPS Composite Report for prospective investors for multiple pooled funds that are included in the composite, it must disclose fee schedules and expense ratios for each pooled fund. The firm may instead choose to tailor the GIPS Composite Report to include the fee schedule and expense ratio that are appropriate for the prospective investor.

The fee schedule presented to a prospective client or prospective investor is typically listed by asset level ranges and should be appropriate to the particular prospective client or prospective investor. The fee schedule must be current. Although a current fee schedule may not assist a prospective client or prospective investor when interpreting historical performance because the actual fees paid may differ from the fee schedule disclosed, it is the most relevant to the prospective client or prospective investor. The actual fee that the prospective client or prospective investor may pay (if it hires the firm) could also differ from the fee schedule disclosed in the GIPS Composite Report. For example, a prospective client or prospective investor may be able to negotiate a lower fee.

This disclosure requirement is not satisfied if the firm does not include the fee schedule and expense ratio, if applicable, in the GIPS Composite Report and instead makes reference to another document that includes the fee schedule or expense ratio, such as Form ADV, which is a US regulatory document, or a fund prospectus. The fee schedule and expense ratios may be an exhibit attached to the GIPS Composite Report. The exhibit may be the pooled fund's offering documents, if the offering documents include the appropriate fee schedule and expense ratio.

Sample Disclosure for a Composite to a Prospective Client for a Segregated Account:

"The annual fee schedule is as follows:

First €10 million	0.80%
Next €40 million	0.60%
Above €50 million	0.30%"

Sample Disclosure for a Model Composite That Includes Carve-Outs or Other "Building Blocks" to a Prospective Client for a Multi-Asset-Class Strategy Portfolio:

"The current standard management fee schedule for a segregated account managed to the Balanced strategy, which is a blend of the Private Equity Composite and the Distressed Debt Fixed Income Composite, is as follows:

- 0.70% on the first $25 million
- 0.55% on the next $75 million
- 0.45% on all assets above $100 million

The fee schedules for the Private Equity Composite and the Distressed Debt Fixed Income Composite are as follows:

Private Equity Composite	Distressed Debt Fixed Income Composite
0.90% on the first $25 million	0.50% on the first $25 million
0.70% on the next $75 million	0.40% on the next $75 million
0.60% on all assets above $100 million	0.30% on all assets above $100 million"

Sample Disclosure for a Composite That Includes a Pooled Fund:

"The investment management fee schedule for Global Equity segregated accounts is as follows: 1.00% on the first $25 million; 0.75% thereafter. The investment management fee schedule for the Global Equity Pooled Fund, which is included in the Global Equity Composite, is 0.80% on all assets. The total expense ratio as of 31 December 2019 for the Global Equity Pooled Fund was 0.95%."

Sample Disclosure for a Composite That Includes Two Pooled Funds:

Vehicle	Fee Schedule	Expense Ratio
Segregated account	0.50% on all assets	n/a
Limited partnership	0.45% on all assets	0.75%
Collective fund	0.40% on all assets	0.68%

Provision 5.C.11

If the FEE SCHEDULE includes PERFORMANCE-BASED FEES or CARRIED INTEREST, the FIRM MUST disclose the PERFORMANCE-BASED FEE DESCRIPTION or CARRIED INTEREST DESCRIPTION.

Discussion

Sufficient information must be included with any fee schedule included in a GIPS Composite Report to allow prospective clients to understand the nature of the firm's compensation. If performance-based fees or carried interest are included in the fee schedule, the firm must disclose a description of the performance-based fees and/or carried interest. Relevant information for a performance-based fee includes the performance-based fee rate, hurdle rate, clawback, high watermark, reset frequency, accrual frequency, crystallization schedule, and on what basis fees are charged. Relevant information for carried interest includes the hurdle rate, crystallization schedule, and high watermark.

Sample Disclosure:

"The standard fee schedule is as follows:

Management fee is 0.75% per annum, charged on a quarterly basis on the period-end value of the portfolio assets.

Performance fee:

The performance fee is earned when the portfolio's total return, reduced by the pro rata accrued fixed management fee, exceeds the benchmark return (the excess return) and the portfolio's net asset value is above the high watermark, which is the portfolio's net asset value as of the last year end when the performance fee crystallized. The performance fee is 10% of the excess return, which is calculated arithmetically, accrued quarterly, and crystallizes annually. Further details of the performance fee calculation are available upon request."

Provision 5.C.12

The FIRM MUST disclose the COMPOSITE INCEPTION DATE.

Discussion

When reviewing the performance data in a GIPS Composite Report, it is important that prospective clients have sufficient information regarding the length of the composite track record to put the performance presented in the GIPS Composite Report in perspective. Therefore, the inception date of the composite being presented in the GIPS Composite Report must be disclosed. If there has been a break in the performance record of a composite, the initial inception date before the break is the date that would be disclosed.

Sample Disclosures:

"The Global Growth Composite has an inception date of 15 September 2019, the date on which the first portfolio in the composite experienced its first capital call from the limited partners."

"The Global Fixed Income Composite has an inception date of 1 November 2015. There was a break in performance from 1 March 2019 through 30 November 2019. During that period, there were no portfolios in the composite. Composite performance began again on 1 December 2019."

Provision 5.C.13

The FIRM MUST disclose the COMPOSITE CREATION DATE.

Discussion

Firms must disclose the composite creation date, which is the date on which the firm first grouped one or more portfolios together to create the composite. The composite creation date is not necessarily the same as the composite inception date. The composite inception date is the initial date of the composite's performance record and is a required disclosure. (See Provision 5.C.12.) The composite creation date can be significantly after the composite inception date, depending on when the firm first grouped the individual portfolios together to create the composite. This information allows prospective clients to compare the composite creation date with the composite inception date to determine whether the firm grouped portfolios together into a composite retroactively or created the composite at the beginning of the composite's performance track record. The intent of this disclosure is to enable prospective clients to determine if the composite was created with the benefit of hindsight.

For those firms that created composites many years ago, it may be impossible to know the specific day a composite was created. Some firms disclose a composite creation date as a month, or even a year, when the composite was created in the very distant past. Newly created composites should have more-precise composite creation dates.

Sample Disclosure:

"The Growth Opportunities Composite was created on 17 July 2019. This is the date on which portfolios were first grouped together to create the composite."

Provision 5.C.14

The FIRM MUST disclose that the following lists are available upon request, if applicable:

a. List of COMPOSITE DESCRIPTIONS.

b. List of POOLED FUND DESCRIPTIONS for LIMITED DISTRIBUTION POOLED FUNDS.

c. List of BROAD DISTRIBUTION POOLED FUNDS.

Discussion

In each GIPS Composite Report, firms must disclose that a list of composite descriptions and a list of pooled fund descriptions for limited distribution pooled funds (LDPFs) are available upon request, if applicable to the firm. The firm must also disclose that a list of broad distribution pooled funds (BDPFs) is available upon request, if BDPFs are included within the definition of the firm. The required list of LDPF descriptions and of BDPFs is at the fund level and not the share class level.

If the firm does not sell participation in a fund (e.g., the firm manages the assets but another legal entity distributes the fund and the firm does not sell shares in the fund), the firm must consider the portfolio a segregated account and would include the portfolio in a composite. This would include sub-advised pooled funds. The segregated account would not be included on the list of LDPF descriptions or the list of BDPFs. In addition, a portfolio with a pooled fund wrapper (i.e., a single-investor pooled fund), which is unitized but is not available to other investors, is also considered a segregated account, would be included in a composite, and would not appear on a list of LDPF descriptions or a list of BDPFs.

As noted in Provision 1.A.22, if a pooled fund is included in a composite but the firm offers participation in the fund, either directly or through an agent, the pooled fund must still appear on the required list of LDPF descriptions or the list of BDPFs, as appropriate.

The firm may combine its list of composite descriptions, its list of LDPF descriptions, and its list of BDPFs into one document if it wishes to do so. The firm may also prepare a list of all the strategies that it offers and may indicate, as part of the strategy description, the types of portfolios (segregated account, LDPF, or BDPF) in which the strategy is available. This list of strategies can be in narrative or table format.

This requirement exists to provide prospective clients with a complete picture of the firm's composites and pooled funds. Prospective clients may then request information that will allow them to evaluate whether the GIPS Composite Report they have received is the most appropriate and to determine if there are any other GIPS Composite Reports or GIPS Pooled Fund Reports that they should also request to see.

a. List of COMPOSITE DESCRIPTIONS.

The firm must disclose, in each GIPS Composite Report, that the firm's list of composite descriptions is available upon request. The list of composite descriptions itself does not need to be included in each GIPS Composite Report but must be available upon request. The list of composite descriptions must include the composite description for each current composite, as well as a description for all composites that have terminated in the past five years. The composite descriptions disclosed in GIPS Composite Reports must be consistent with the descriptions included in the list of composite descriptions.

An explanation of composite descriptions can be found in the discussion of Provision 1.A.22. A Sample List of Composite Descriptions can be found in Appendix D of the GIPS standards.

 |

b. List of POOLED FUND DESCRIPTIONS for LIMITED DISTRIBUTION POOLED FUNDS.

If LDPFs are included within the definition of a firm, the firm must disclose, in each GIPS Composite Report, that the firm's list of descriptions of LDPFs is available upon request. An LDPF is any pooled fund that is not a BDPF. A BDPF is any pooled fund that is regulated under a framework that would permit the general public to purchase or hold the pooled fund's shares and is not exclusively offered in one-on-one presentations. LDPFs are often referred to as "private funds." These funds are typically sold in one-on-one presentations and may not be highly regulated. The list of LDPF descriptions does not need to be included in each GIPS Composite Report but must be available upon request. The list of LDPF descriptions must include the pooled fund description for each current pooled fund but does not have to include terminated funds. Terminated LDPFs are treated differently from terminated composites because, although a firm can restart a composite strategy when a prospective client hires the firm for a strategy that was previously closed, the firm does not have the same ability to restart a pooled fund. The pooled fund descriptions disclosed in GIPS Pooled Fund Reports must be consistent with the descriptions included in the list of pooled fund descriptions.

The list of LDPF descriptions may be tailored to include only those LDPFs for which a prospective investor is eligible, but the firm is not required to do this.

An explanation of LDPF descriptions can be found in the discussion of Provision 1.A.22. A Sample List of Pooled Fund Descriptions can be found in Appendix D of the GIPS standards.

c. List of BROAD DISTRIBUTION POOLED FUNDS.

In addition to the lists of composite descriptions and LDPF descriptions, firms must also disclose, in each GIPS Composite Report, that a list of BDPFs is available upon request, if applicable to the firm. A BDPF is any pooled fund that is regulated under a framework that would permit the general public to purchase or hold the pooled fund's shares and is not exclusively offered in one-on-one presentations. These funds are typically sold to the general public and are highly regulated.

Note that the required list of BDPFs is a list of the names of the firm's BDPFs only. No descriptions of the BDPFs are required. The list of BDPF names does not need to be included in each GIPS Composite Report but must be available upon request. The list of BDPFs must include the names of all current BDPFs but does not need to include terminated BDPFs. Terminated BDPFs are treated differently from terminated composites because, although a firm can restart a composite strategy when a prospective client hires the firm for a strategy that was previously closed, the firm does not have the same ability to restart a pooled fund. If a firm includes information about all of its BDPFs on its website, the firm may provide a link to the website to fulfill the requirement to provide the list of BDPFs upon request.

This list may be tailored to include only those BDPFs for which a prospective investor is eligible, but the firm is not required to do this.

Sample Disclosures:

For Firms with Composites Only

"A list of composite descriptions is available upon request."

For Firms with Composites and Limited Distribution Pooled Funds

"A list of composite descriptions and a list of limited distribution pooled fund descriptions are available upon request."

For Firms with Composites, Limited Distribution Pooled Funds, and Broad Distribution Pooled Funds

"A list of composite descriptions, a list of limited distribution pooled fund descriptions, and a list of broad distribution pooled funds are available upon request."

For Firms That Offer Strategies in Multiple Vehicles

"A list of all composite and pooled fund investment strategies offered by the firm, with a description of each strategy, is available upon request. The type of portfolios in which each strategy is available (segregated account, limited distribution pooled fund, or broad distribution pooled fund) is indicated in the description of each strategy."

Provision 5.C.15

The FIRM MUST disclose that policies for valuing investments, calculating performance, and preparing GIPS REPORTS are available upon request.

Discussion

In each GIPS Composite Report, firms must disclose the availability of policies for valuing investments, calculating performance, and preparing GIPS Reports. The policies are not required to be included in each GIPS Composite Report but must be readily available upon request. Firms are not required to provide the related procedures, in addition to the policies, but may do so.

Sample Disclosure:

"Firm XYZ's policies for valuing investments, calculating performance, and preparing GIPS Reports are available upon request."

Provision 5.C.16

The FIRM MUST disclose how leverage, derivatives, and short positions have been used historically, if material.

Discussion

Firms must provide enough information in a GIPS Composite Report to allow a prospective client to understand how leverage, derivatives, and short positions have been employed historically and may be used going forward. Although the composite description includes disclosure of the firm's ability to use leverage, derivatives, and short positions (see Provision 5.C.4), Provision 5.C.16 requires that the firm disclose the leverage, derivatives, and short positions that have been used historically, if material. Taken together, these two required disclosures provide a more complete picture of the presence, use, and extent of leverage, derivatives, and short positions.

For example, assume a firm discloses in the composite description that the strategy may employ up to 200% leverage. To satisfy the disclosure requirement in Provision 5.C.16, the firm might state, "Since the inception of the strategy, the leverage has averaged 110% of the composite's value; however, during 2019 the leverage averaged 160%, which greatly increased the sensitivity to market volatility and the potential for realized gains and/or losses."

No disclosure is required if leverage, derivatives, and short positions have not been used or if their use has not been material. When determining what would be material, the firm must consider whether the disclosure of how leverage, derivatives, and/or short positions have been used historically is likely to affect a prospective client's view of the risk involved in the strategy. If so, it would be misleading for the firm to fail to disclose their use to these prospective clients when describing the strategy.

Provision 5.C.17

If estimated TRANSACTION COSTS are used, the FIRM MUST disclose:

a. That estimated TRANSACTION COSTS were used.

b. The estimated TRANSACTION COSTS used and how they were determined.

Discussion

Gross-of-fees and net-of-fees composite returns must reflect the deduction of transaction costs, which are the costs of buying or selling investments. Firms may use either actual or estimated transaction costs when calculating returns. Estimated transaction costs may be used only for portfolios for which the actual transaction costs are not known. Provision 2.A.13 provides guidance on the use of estimated transaction costs.

If estimated transaction costs are used in calculating returns, there must be a disclosure that estimated transaction costs were used. A firm must also disclose the estimated transaction costs used and how they were determined. A firm might, for example, determine estimated transaction costs based on other portfolios whose transaction costs are known.

In some markets, brokers offer zero-commission trades. If a portfolio is paying zero commissions, then it is appropriate to calculate portfolio gross-of-fees returns and net-of-fees returns that reflect zero transaction costs. When a composite includes portfolios that pay zero commissions, firms should disclose this fact. Not disclosing this fact could be misleading.

Sample Disclosures:

"Some portfolios in the composite do not pay explicit transaction costs for security purchases and sales. Estimated transaction costs for these portfolios are used, and these are determined based on the average transaction cost per share incurred by portfolios in the composite that pay explicit transaction costs. The average transaction cost was determined to be $0.031 per share. We apply a model transaction cost per share of $0.04 to each investment transaction."

"The transaction costs for some portfolios in the composite are not known and must be estimated. The estimated transaction costs for these portfolios is 12 Swiss francs per trade."

"Effective 1 January 2020, a majority of portfolio trades are made through brokers that no longer charge commissions on standard equity trades. Portfolios that trade options and futures continue to pay transaction costs for options/futures contract trades."

Provision 5.C.18

The FIRM MUST disclose all significant events that would help a PROSPECTIVE CLIENT interpret the GIPS COMPOSITE REPORT. This disclosure MUST be included for a minimum of one year and for as long as it is relevant to interpreting the track record.

Discussion

The GIPS standards are based on the principles of fair representation and full disclosure. Meeting these objectives requires a good faith commitment on the part of the firm to adhere to the spirit of the GIPS standards. The GIPS standards cannot foresee and cover every situation that might occur. Therefore, this provision requires that firms disclose all significant events that would help explain the firm's GIPS Composite Report to a prospective client. The primary goal of this requirement is to provide relevant information to prospective clients so that they can understand the potential effect of the significant event on the composite's investment strategy and the firm.

Significant events are determined by the firm and would include, as examples, a material change in personnel responsible for investment management, significant changes to the investment management process, the loss of historical records resulting from a catastrophic event, or a change in firm ownership. The acquisition of a new entity or selling off part of a firm would also qualify as a significant event, as would the departure of someone who was the single investment decision maker for a strategy.

Depending on the situation, a general statement describing the significant event that has occurred may be sufficient. Other situations may require firms to disclose specific information pertaining to the significant event. The disclosure regarding the significant event must be included in the GIPS Composite Report for a minimum of one year and for as long as it is relevant to interpreting the performance track record. As an example, a firm that acquires another firm, resulting in a large increase in total firm assets, may disclose this significant event for as long as the large change in total firm assets is included in the GIPS Composite Report. In contrast, a change in a firm's chief investment officer (CIO) is a change that a firm may believe should be disclosed for one year only.

The firm must consider the underlying principles of the GIPS standards, which are fair representation and full disclosure, when determining how long the disclosure will be included in the GIPS Composite Report.

Sample Disclosures:

"In February 2020, the portfolio manager responsible for managing the composite left the firm. The composite is now managed by a team of three of the firm's portfolio managers who are experienced in managing portfolios with similar strategies."

"On 15 April 2018, the quantitative asset management division of Firm Z was sold, resulting in the 2018 decrease in Firm Z's assets."

"In February 2020, the parent company of Firm M announced plans to exit the investment management business and sell Firm M. As of April 2020, a tentative sale of Firm M has been agreed upon but not yet finalized."

Provision 5.C.19

For any performance presented for periods prior to the MINIMUM EFFECTIVE COMPLIANCE DATE that does not comply with the GIPS standards, the FIRM MUST disclose the periods of non-compliance.

Discussion

In a GIPS Composite Report that includes money-weighted returns (MWRs), firms may present non-GIPS-compliant performance only for periods ending before the minimum effective compliance date, which is 1 January 2006 for private equity and real estate composites and 1 January 2000 for all other composites. (See Provision 1.A.30.) If the firm chooses to present non-compliant performance for periods prior to the minimum effective compliance date, the firm must disclose which periods are not in compliance. Prospective clients and existing clients can then inquire about the reasons why the performance prior to the minimum effective compliance date is not compliant and consider the effects of non-compliance on the historical performance.

The measurement period for a composite's since-inception money-weighted return (SI-MWR) is the period from the inception date of the composite through the end of the period being reported. The beginning date remains constant and the ending date is extended as the measurement period becomes longer. It is necessary to use the period-end date of an SI-MWR to determine the non-compliant period.

Determining the period of compliance for an MWR calculation requires consideration of cash flows and valuations. When calculating MWRs, quarterly or more frequent cash flows must be used prior to 1 January 2020, and daily cash flows must be used as of 1 January 2020. For periods ending on or after 1 January 2011, portfolios in the composite must be valued in accordance with the definition of fair value. See the discussion of Provision 2.A.19 for information on valuation requirements for periods ending prior to that date.

Given that the minimum effective compliance dates are so distant, and that firms are required to present only one SI-MWR (the SI-MWR through the most recent annual period end), it is not expected that the minimum effective compliance date will have an effect on many firms that present composite MWRs.

If non-compliant performance for periods ending on or after the minimum effective compliance date is included in a GIPS Composite Report, it must be labeled as supplemental information.

Sample Disclosure:

"The returns for the XYZ Private Equity Composite for periods ending prior to 31 December 2005 are not in compliance with the GIPS standards."

Provision 5.C.20

If the FIRM is redefined, the FIRM MUST disclose the date and description of the redefinition.

 |

Discussion

A firm redefinition occurs when something changes with how the firm is held out to the public or when any of its distinct business entity criteria significantly change. Changes in investment style or personnel are not events that typically cause a firm redefinition. A simple firm name change is also not a sufficient reason to redefine the firm. Corporate restructuring may cause a change with how the firm is held out to the public. As an example, a firm that was defined to include only the institutional division would be redefined when it consolidated the institutional division with the mutual fund/retail division. A merger or acquisition may cause a change in the definition of the firm, but that is not always the case.

Suppose that a firm defines itself as an investment management firm offering active equity strategies to clients. An acquisition that expanded the firm's offerings to include fixed-income strategies would result in a redefinition of the firm, because there would be a change in how the firm holds itself out to the public. An acquisition that simply added additional equity strategies to the firm's offerings would not result in a redefinition of the firm. However, the acquisition is likely to be a significant event that must be disclosed in a GIPS Composite Report. (See Provision 5.C.18.)

In some cases, as a result of a significant alteration in a firm's structure or organization, a change can be so great that it creates a new firm. See Provision 1.A.2 for guidance on firm definitions.

The GIPS standards require that changes in a firm's organization must not lead to alteration of historical performance (see Provision 1.A.28).

Sample Disclosures:

"As of 1 August 2019, XYZ Firm was redefined to include both the London and Tokyo office of XYZ Company. Previously, the firm was defined to include only the London office."

"As of 1 January 2020, XYZ Investment Management was redefined to include the wrap division."

"Effective 1 January 2019, ABC Capital Management was redefined as an investment management firm offering both equity and fixed-income strategies. Prior to the 31 December 2018 acquisition of Curtone Capital Management, an investment firm offering fixed-income strategies, ABC Capital Management offered only equity strategies."

Provision 5.C.21

If the COMPOSITE is redefined, the FIRM MUST disclose the date and description of the redefinition.

Discussion

Investment strategies can change over time. In some cases, such a change results in the termination of one composite and the creation of a new composite. In other cases, it may be appropriate to redefine the composite. If a composite is redefined, the firm must disclose the date and description of the redefinition. See Provision 3.A.5 for guidance on composite definitions.

Sample Disclosure:

"As of 1 July 2017, the fixed-income strategy includes the use of interest rate futures to modify duration and manage interest rate risk. Prior to this date, the Composite's strategy did not involve the active management of interest rate risk."

Provision 5.C.22

The FIRM MUST disclose changes to the name of the COMPOSITE. This disclosure MUST be included for a minimum of one year and for as long as it is relevant to interpreting the performance track record.

Discussion

When prospective clients are evaluating composites over time and across firms, it is important that they understand exactly which composites they are assessing. If a firm changes the name of a composite, the change must be disclosed in the GIPS Composite Report. The name change must be disclosed for a minimum of one year and potentially for more than one year if the firm determines the disclosure is still relevant and meaningful. The firm must consider the underlying principles of the GIPS standards, which are fair representation and full disclosure, when determining how long the disclosure will be included in the GIPS Composite Report.

Sample Disclosure:

"As of 1 January 2016, the Small-Cap Composite was renamed the US Equity Opportunity Composite."

 |

Provision 5.C.23

The FIRM MUST disclose:

a. The minimum asset level, if any, below which PORTFOLIOS are not included in the COMPOSITE.

b. Any changes to the minimum asset level.

Discussion

The firm may establish a minimum asset level for a composite to exclude portfolios that are too small to be representative of the intended strategy. Firms must disclose the minimum asset level of the composite, if one exists, in each respective GIPS Composite Report. If any changes have been made to the minimum asset level of a composite, the firm must document and disclose changes to the minimum asset level and must not retroactively apply the new limit. See the discussion of Provision 3.A.11 for additional guidance on composite minimums.

Sample Disclosure:

"The minimum portfolio size for inclusion in the LMN Composite is €500,000. Prior to 2018, there was no minimum."

Provision 5.C.24

The FIRM MUST disclose if COMPOSITE returns are gross or net of withholding taxes, if material.

Discussion

Global investing requires recognition of the tax consequences of investing in different countries. The GIPS standards do not require firms to reflect withholding taxes, either reclaimable or non-reclaimable taxes, in a certain manner. Firms may choose whether or not to reflect the effect of withholding taxes when calculating performance. The GIPS standards do recommend that performance be reported net of non-reclaimable withholding taxes on dividends, interest, and capital gains and also recommend that reclaimable foreign withholding taxes be accrued (see Provision 2.B.5). If withholding taxes are material, firms must disclose how withholding taxes are treated when calculating performance. A firm must determine the level at which withholding taxes become material, document this level in its policies and procedures, and apply it consistently.

Sample Disclosure:

"Portfolio returns are net of all foreign non-reclaimable withholding taxes. Reclaimable withholding taxes are reflected as income if and when received."

Provision 5.C.25

The FIRM MUST disclose if BENCHMARK returns are net of withholding taxes if this information is available.

Discussion

Global investing requires recognition of the tax consequences of investing in different countries. The GIPS standards do not require firms to reflect withholding taxes, either reclaimable or non-reclaimable taxes, in a certain manner. Firms may choose whether or not to reflect the effect of withholding taxes when calculating composite performance and, similarly, whether or not to use a benchmark that reflects the effect of withholding taxes.

As Provision 5.C.24 indicates, if withholding taxes are material, firms must disclose how withholding taxes are treated when calculating performance. To facilitate the comparison of composite returns and benchmark returns, firms must also disclose if the benchmark returns are net of withholding taxes if this information is available. If the benchmark name indicates that the benchmark is net of withholding taxes, no additional disclosure is necessary.

Sample Disclosure:

"Benchmark returns are net of withholding taxes."

Provision 5.C.26

If the GIPS COMPOSITE REPORT conforms with laws and/or regulations that conflict with the REQUIREMENTS of the GIPS standards, the FIRM MUST disclose this fact and disclose the manner in which the laws and/or regulations conflict with the GIPS standards.

Discussion

Firms must comply with all applicable laws and regulations regarding the calculation and presentation of performance. Compliance with applicable laws and regulations, however, does not necessarily result in compliance with the GIPS standards. Firms must also comply with all of the applicable requirements of the GIPS standards. In the rare cases where laws and regulations conflict with the GIPS standards, firms are required to comply with the laws and regulations and disclose the manner in which the laws and/or regulations conflict with the GIPS standards.

This disclosure will assist prospective clients in comparing GIPS Composite Reports among firms where reporting requirements may differ because of local laws or regulations.

Sample Disclosure:

"We present since-inception money-weighted returns through each annual period end. Local laws do not allow the presentation of returns of less than one year to prospective clients, which is in conflict with the GIPS standards. Therefore, no performance is presented for this composite for the period from 1 July 2018 (the inception date of the composite) through 31 December 2018."

Provision 5.C.27

If CARVE-OUTS with allocated cash are included in the COMPOSITE, the FIRM MUST:

a. Indicate CARVE-OUT in the COMPOSITE name.
b. Disclose that the COMPOSITE includes CARVE-OUTS with allocated cash.
c. Disclose the policy used to allocate cash to CARVE-OUTS.
d. Disclose that the GIPS COMPOSITE REPORT for the COMPOSITE of standalone PORTFOLIOS is available upon request, if the COMPOSITE of standalone PORTFOLIOS exists.

Discussion

With the issuance of the 2020 edition of the GIPS standards, firms are once again allowed to include carve-outs with cash that has been allocated synthetically in composites. (This was prohibited from 1 January 2010 through 31 December 2019.) In the spirit of fair representation and full disclosure, it is important that prospective clients have sufficient information to understand the nature of the portfolios included in a composite. If carve-outs with allocated cash are included in a composite, the name of the composite must include "carve-out" or otherwise indicate this. In addition to "carve-out" being indicated in the name of the composite, there must be a disclosure that the composite includes carve-outs with allocated cash. These two requirements signal to prospective clients that there are assets in the composite that do not represent standalone portfolios and for which they might want to request additional information. (A standalone portfolio is a portfolio that is not a portion of a larger portfolio.) Firms are not required to indicate "carve-out" in the composite name if the composite includes carve-outs with allocated cash that were created in compliance with prior editions of the GIPS standards.

Because the methodology for allocating cash to carve-outs can have a significant effect on a composite's return, it is required that the firm disclose the policy used to allocate cash to the carve-outs in the composite. See the discussion of Provision 3.A.15 for methods that may be used to allocate cash.

Once a firm obtains one or more standalone portfolios managed in the same strategy as the carve-outs with allocated cash, the firm must create a separate composite that includes only the standalone portfolios. (See Provision 3.A.18.) The returns and composite assets of the composite that includes only standalone portfolios must be presented in the GIPS Composite Report for the composite that includes carve-outs with allocated cash. In addition, in the GIPS Composite Report for the composite that includes carve-outs with allocated cash, the firm must disclose that the GIPS Composite Report for the composite of standalone portfolios managed in the same strategy as the composite with carve-outs with allocated cash is available upon request. This disclosure will inform prospective clients that they can compare the GIPS Composite Reports for the composite with carve-outs with allocated cash and the composite with only standalone portfolios if they wish to do so. This disclosure is required only when the firm has standalone portfolios managed in the same strategy as the composite with carve-outs with allocated cash and has therefore created the required composite of standalone portfolios.

Once a firm has obtained standalone portfolios managed in the same strategy as the carve-outs with allocated cash, the firm may present prospective clients with the GIPS Composite Report that includes only the standalone portfolios, rather than the GIPS Composite Report that includes carve-outs with allocated cash.

Sample Disclosure:

"The Private Equity Carve-Out Composite includes carve-outs with allocated cash. Cash and cash returns are allocated to carve-outs based on each carve-out's size relative to its total portfolio at the time of the last valuation. A GIPS Composite Report for the Private Equity Composite that includes only standalone portfolios is available upon request."

Provision 5.C.28

The FIRM MUST disclose the use of a SUB-ADVISOR and the periods a SUB-ADVISOR was used.[41]

[41] REQUIRED for periods beginning on or after 1 January 2006.

 |

Discussion

Some firms use a sub-advisor to manage part or all of a particular strategy. For example, if a firm specializes in managing equities, it might hire a sub-advisor (a third-party investment manager) to manage the fixed-income portion of its balanced portfolios. The GIPS standards require that firms include the performance of assets assigned to a sub-advisor in a composite, provided the firm has the authority to allocate the assets to a sub-advisor. In the spirit of full disclosure, a firm must disclose the fact that a sub-advisor was used in the management of the composite strategy and the periods for which a sub-advisor was used. It is not necessary to disclose the name of the sub-advisor. This is required for periods beginning on or after 1 January 2006.

Sample Disclosures:

"A sub-advisor is used to manage the international equity allocation of the Asia Growth Balanced Composite."

"A sub-advisor was used for the management of the Global Private Equity Composite from its inception in 2001 through 31 December 2018."

Provision 5.C.29

The FIRM MUST disclose if the COMPOSITE'S valuation hierarchy materially differs from the RECOMMENDED valuation hierarchy. (See provision 2.B.6 for the RECOMMENDED valuation hierarchy.)[42]

Discussion

Firms must establish policies and procedures for determining portfolio valuations. For periods beginning on or after 1 January 2011, those valuations must be determined in accordance with the definition of fair value. Provision 2.B.6 includes a recommended valuation hierarchy that firms should incorporate into their policies and procedures for determining fair value for portfolio investments. Firms must establish a valuation hierarchy on a composite-specific basis. It is acceptable for firms to apply a different valuation hierarchy to specific composites provided the valuation methodology conforms to the definition of fair value. If the valuation hierarchy materially differs from the recommended valuation hierarchy, the firm must disclose this fact. Prospective clients will be informed and then may request additional information about the firm's valuation policies.

[42] REQUIRED for periods beginning on or after 1 January 2011.

Sample Disclosure:

"All portfolio investments are valued using the firm's proprietary valuation models to determine fair value. Our valuation procedures materially differ from the recommended valuation hierarchy in the GIPS standards."

Provision 5.C.30

If the FIRM determines no appropriate BENCHMARK for the COMPOSITE exists, the FIRM MUST disclose why no BENCHMARK is presented.

Discussion

Benchmarks are important tools that aid in the planning, implementation, and evaluation of an investment strategy. They also help facilitate discussions with prospective clients regarding the relationship between composite risk and return. As a result, the GIPS standards require firms to provide benchmark total returns in all GIPS Composite Reports. The benchmark must reflect the investment mandate, objective, or strategy of the composite. Although there is typically an appropriate benchmark for traditional strategies, it is more common for managers of alternative strategies to determine that no appropriate benchmark for the composite exists. If this is the case, the firm must disclose why no benchmark is presented.

Sample Disclosure:

"Because the composite's strategy is absolute return where investments are permitted in all asset classes, no benchmark is presented because we believe that no benchmark that reflects this strategy exists."

Provision 5.C.31

If the FIRM changes the BENCHMARK, the FIRM MUST disclose:

a. For a prospective BENCHMARK change, the date and description of the change. Changes MUST be disclosed for as long as returns for the prior BENCHMARK are included in the GIPS COMPOSITE REPORT.

b. For a retroactive BENCHMARK change, the date and description of the change. Changes MUST be disclosed for a minimum of one year and for as long as they are relevant to interpreting the track record.

Discussion

Firms must disclose the date and description of any changes to the benchmark over time. A benchmark change can take two forms:

- The benchmark is changed from one benchmark to another on a prospective basis only.
- The benchmark is changed for all periods (i.e., retroactively).

In most cases, the firm should only change the benchmark going forward and not change the benchmark retroactively.

If the firm changes the benchmark prospectively and presents benchmark returns that combine two different benchmarks, the date and description of the change must be disclosed for as long as returns for the prior benchmark are included in the GIPS Composite Report. Given the nature of a money-weighted return (MWR), however, it is not expected that this situation would apply to a GIPS Composite Report that includes MWRs.

There may be times when a firm determines that it is appropriate to change the benchmark for a given composite retroactively. For example, because benchmarks are continually evolving, if the firm finds that a new benchmark is a better comparison for an investment strategy, the firm may consider changing the benchmark retroactively. In the case of a retroactive benchmark change, there must be a disclosure of the date and description of the benchmark change, including the fact that the benchmark was changed retroactively. Disclosures related to a retroactive change in a benchmark must be included in the respective GIPS Composite Report for a minimum of one year and for as long as the disclosures are relevant to interpreting the performance track record. The firm must consider the underlying principles of the GIPS standards, which are fair representation and full disclosure, when determining how long this disclosure will be included in the GIPS Composite Report.

When a firm changes a benchmark retroactively, the firm is encouraged to continue to also present the old benchmark.

Changes to the benchmark primarily intended to make performance look better by lowering the benchmark return violate the spirit of the GIPS standards.

Sample Disclosure:

"In January 2017, the benchmark was changed from ABC Index to XYZ Index for all periods."

Provision 5.C.32

If a custom BENCHMARK or combination of multiple BENCHMARKS is used, the FIRM MUST:

a. Disclose the BENCHMARK components, weights, and rebalancing process, if applicable.
b. Disclose the calculation methodology.
c. Clearly label the BENCHMARK to indicate that it is a custom BENCHMARK.

Discussion

When custom benchmarks are used, the firm must disclose the benchmark components, weights, and rebalancing process, if applicable. Given the nature of money-weighted return (MWR) calculations, this disclosure will rarely apply to a GIPS Composite Report that presents MWRs.

Instead, it is expected that a firm would use a public market equivalent (PME) as a custom benchmark. See the discussion of Provision 5.C.33 for an explanation of a PME. A PME must be clearly labeled as such, and the methodology used to calculate the PME must be disclosed.

A firm may calculate a PME that is a gross-of-fees or net-of-fees return. A PME that is a net-of-fees return is calculated using the same cash flows that are used to calculate the composite's net-of-fees return. A firm may use a net-of-fees PME benchmark only when composite net-of-fees returns are presented. The use of a net benchmark when only composite gross-of-fees returns are presented is one instance where disclosure is not sufficient to prevent the information presented from being false and misleading. When a firm includes a net-of-fees benchmark in a GIPS Composite Report, the firm must clearly label the benchmark as a custom benchmark and disclose the calculation methodology.

Sample Disclosure for a PME Benchmark:

"The benchmark is the public market equivalent (PME) of the ABC Mid-Cap Equity Index, which tracks the performance of US mid-cap companies. The PME is a method by which a public market index is used to create a since-inception money-weighted return that is comparable to a composite's since-inception money-weighted return from a series of cash flows that are the same as those of the composite and uses a theoretical investment value. The theoretical investment value is derived by buying and selling the public market index using the dates and amounts of actual composite cash flows."

Provision 5.C.33

The FIRM MUST disclose the calculation methodology used for the BENCHMARK. If the FIRM presents the PUBLIC MARKET EQUIVALENT of the COMPOSITE as a BENCHMARK, the FIRM MUST also disclose the index used to calculate the PUBLIC MARKET EQUIVALENT.

Discussion

The benchmark selected for a composite must be appropriate for comparison with the performance of the composite. Unlike benchmarks for publicly traded securities, however, industry benchmarks for private market investments are not as widely available or are available only through certain commercial vendors. Firms may use public market indices as a benchmark for private market investments, but the public market indices by themselves are not directly comparable to a money-weighted return (MWR) because the market indices typically use a time-weighted return. The public market equivalent (PME) is a method where a public market index is used to create a comparable MWR from a series of cash flows that replicate those of the composite and that can be compared with the MWR of the composite.

The GIPS standards require that the calculation methodology for the benchmark be disclosed. This information provides transparency as to the comparability of the performance of the composite and the benchmark. If a PME is used as a benchmark, the firm must disclose which public market index is used to create the PME.

Sample Disclosure for a Non-PME Benchmark:

"The benchmark is the since-inception money-weighted return for the ACME Advisory US Venture Capital Funds Universe—2018 Vintage Year. The vintage year is determined by the date of the first capital call for each fund in the universe."

Sample Disclosure for a PME Benchmark:

"The benchmark is the public market equivalent (PME) of the ABC Mid-Cap Equity Index, which tracks the performance of US mid-cap companies. The PME is a method by which a public market index is used to create a since-inception money-weighted return that is comparable to a composite's since-inception money-weighted return from a series of cash flows that are the same as those of the composite and uses a theoretical investment value. The theoretical investment value is derived by buying and selling the public market index using the dates and amounts of actual composite cash flows."

Provision 5.C.34

The FIRM MUST disclose if performance from a past firm or affiliation is presented, and for which periods.

Discussion

Although firms often think about time-weighted returns when considering portability issues, it is also possible for a money-weighted return to span two firms. Provision 1.A.32 includes the tests that must be met to determine if performance from a past firm or affiliation may be used to represent the historical performance of a new or acquiring firm and if that performance can be linked to the ongoing performance of the new or acquiring firm. Provision 1.A.33 includes the portability tests that must be met for the new or acquiring firm to use performance from a past firm or affiliation to represent its historical performance when there is a break in the track record between the past firm or affiliation and the new or acquiring firm. In this instance, the track record from the past firm or affiliation may be used if the tests are met, but the track record must not be linked to performance of the new or acquiring firm. A current since-inception money-weighted return (SI-MWR) must be calculated using only the performance after the break. A SI-MWR from the beginning of the track record up until the break may also be presented if the tests in Provision 1.A.33 are met. However, the current SI-MWR for the period after the break in performance and the SI-MWR representing performance prior to the break must not be linked and must be clearly labeled.

If the firm meets the required portability tests and presents performance from a past firm or affiliation in the GIPS Composite Report, the firm must disclose this fact, as well as the periods for which performance from the past firm or affiliation is presented.

Sample Disclosure:

"The Opportunity Composite has an inception date of March 2016 and was managed by the Distressed Debt Team at a prior firm. On 15 December 2017, the prior firm sold the line of business that included the Distressed Debt Team to ABC Investments. Composite activity prior to 15 December 2017 is from the prior firm."

Provision 5.C.35

The FIRM MUST disclose the frequency of EXTERNAL CASH FLOWS used in the MONEY-WEIGHTED RETURN calculation if daily frequency was not used.

Discussion

When calculating money-weighted returns (MWRs), quarterly or more frequent cash flows must be used prior to 1 January 2020, and daily cash flows must be used as of 1 January 2020. A historical cash flow stream may therefore include daily, monthly and/or quarterly cash flows. When constructing such a cash flow stream historically, and daily cash flows are not used, the firm must assume that all quarterly and monthly cash flows occurred on a particular date in the month or quarter regardless of the actual date of the cash flow. For example, all monthly or quarterly cash flows might be dated as if they occurred on the last day of the month, regardless of the actual date of the cash flow. See Provision 2.A.29 for an example of how quarterly and monthly cash flows can be reflected in an MWR calculation.

The MWR calculation is sensitive to the relative timing of cash flows and, especially early in the life of a composite, returns calculated using a quarterly cash flow dating convention can differ from returns calculated using a monthly or daily convention. Accordingly, firms are required to disclose the frequency of cash flows used in the MWR calculation if daily cash flows are not used for periods prior to 1 January 2020. It is recommended that firms use daily cash flows for all periods.

Sample Disclosure:

"The money-weighted return calculation incorporates monthly cash flows for periods prior to 1 January 2020 and daily cash flows thereafter."

Provision 5.C.36

If a SUBSCRIPTION LINE OF CREDIT is used, and the FIRM is REQUIRED to present returns both with and without the SUBSCRIPTION LINE OF CREDIT, the FIRM MUST disclose:

a. The purpose for using the SUBSCRIPTION LINE OF CREDIT.
b. The size of the SUBSCRIPTION LINE OF CREDIT as of the most recent annual period end.
c. The SUBSCRIPTION LINE OF CREDIT amount outstanding as of the most recent annual period end.

Discussion

Subscription lines of credit are being used by more firms and for longer periods, and they may have a significant effect on returns. It is therefore important that prospective clients have sufficient information about any subscription line of credit (LOC) that could influence composite performance.

In those situations in which a subscription LOC is used and the firm is required to present returns both with and without the subscription LOC (see Provision 5.A.2), the firm must disclose the purpose of the subscription LOC so that prospective clients can better understand why the subscription LOC exists. In some cases, the subscription LOC is short term in nature and is put in place simply to facilitate administration when capital is being called from investors. In other cases, the subscription LOC is longer term and is used to delay the capital calls from investors. To help prospective clients put the subscription LOC in perspective, the firm must also disclose both the size of the subscription LOC and the subscription LOC amount outstanding as of the most recent annual period end.

Sample Disclosures:

"A $100M subscription line of credit is in place as bridge financing to reduce the number of capital calls made to investors. As of 31 December 2020, $40M is outstanding."

"A $250M subscription line of credit is in place and is used to finance investments. During the past two years, the subscription LOC was fully drawn but was repaid as of 31 December 2019."

Provision 5.C.37

The FIRM MUST disclose any change to the GIPS COMPOSITE REPORT resulting from the correction of a MATERIAL ERROR. Following the correction of the GIPS COMPOSITE REPORT, this disclosure MUST be included for a minimum of one year and for as long as it is relevant to interpreting the track record. The disclosure is not REQUIRED to be included in a GIPS COMPOSITE REPORT that is provided to a PROSPECTIVE CLIENT or PROSPECTIVE INVESTOR that did not receive the GIPS COMPOSITE REPORT containing the MATERIAL ERROR.

Discussion

Firms claiming compliance with the GIPS standards are likely to be faced with situations in which errors are discovered that must be specifically addressed. An error, which can be qualitative or quantitative, can be related to any component of a GIPS Composite Report that is missing or inaccurate. Errors in GIPS Composite Reports can result from, but are not limited to, incorrect, incomplete, or missing:

- composite returns or assets,
- firm assets,
- benchmark returns,
- number of portfolios in a composite, or
- disclosures.

Any material error in a GIPS Composite Report must be corrected and disclosed in a revised GIPS Composite Report. A firm must define materiality within its error correction policies and procedures.

To adhere to this requirement, a firm must determine the criteria it will use to determine materiality. The following is a definition of materiality that firms might find useful as a starting point for their determination of materiality. "An error is material if the magnitude of the omission or misstatement of performance information, in light of surrounding circumstances, makes it probable that the judgment of a reasonable person relying on the information would have been changed by the omission or misstatement." Firms should have a defined process for determining the objective criteria it will use in determining materiality.

Disclosure of the change in the corrected GIPS Composite Report resulting from a material error must be included in the GIPS Composite Report for a minimum of 12 months following the correction of the report and for as long as it is relevant to interpreting the track record. The firm must consider the underlying principles of the GIPS standards, which are fair representation and full disclosure, when determining how long the disclosure will be included in the GIPS Composite Report that contained the material error.

Disclosure of the change resulting from a material error is not required to be included in a GIPS Composite Report that is provided to new prospective clients or prospective investors.

The discussion for Provision 1.A.20 provides additional information on error correction, including the determination of materiality, the actions that must be taken when an error in a GIPS Composite Report is discovered, and an explanation of who must receive the revised GIPS Composite Report.

Sample Disclosure:

"This GIPS Composite Report includes a correction of the information provided for the XYZ Peer Universe. The since-inception internal rate of return for the XYZ Peer Universe through 31 December 2020 was originally incorrectly presented as 3.4%. The correct return is 4.3%, as shown in this revised GIPS Composite Report."

Provision 5.C.38

If the FIRM chooses to not present the number of PORTFOLIOS in the COMPOSITE because there are five or fewer PORTFOLIOS in the COMPOSITE, the FIRM MUST disclose that the COMPOSITE contains five or fewer PORTFOLIOS or use similar language.

Discussion

Each GIPS Composite Report must include information about the number of portfolios included in the composite as of the most recent annual period end. (See Provision 5.A.1.e.) This requirement provides information to prospective clients on whether the composite is composed of a small number of portfolios or many.

In cases where there are five portfolios or fewer in a composite at period end, the firm may choose to not present the actual number of portfolios in the composite. The firm might choose to do this to protect the identity and confidentiality of its clients. Because firms must include information about the number of portfolios in the composite, however, firms must either state or indicate that the composite contains "five or fewer portfolios", "fewer than six portfolios", (or use similar language) or present the actual number of portfolios in the composite.

Note that "five or fewer portfolios in the composite" refers to the number of portfolios in the composite at the annual period end, not the number of portfolios in the composite for the full period for which the since-inception money-weighted return is presented. If there were four portfolios in the composite for the full period but eight portfolios in the composite at the annual period end, the firm would be required to present the actual number of portfolios (in this example, eight) in the composite at the annual period end.

Sample Disclosure:

"ABC's policy is to not present the number of portfolios in the composite when there are fewer than six portfolios included in the composite as of year end."

Sample Disclosure as Part of a Table:

The column where the number of portfolios in the composite at the most recent annual period end is presented would simply note "<6" or "≤5" if there were five or fewer portfolios in the composite at the most recent annual period end.

Provision 5.C.39

The FIRM MUST disclose if preliminary, estimated values are used to determine FAIR VALUE.

Discussion

The use of preliminary, estimated values as fair value is common for some alternative strategies, including those that invest in underlying funds for which the firm relies on valuations provided by the underlying fund managers. When using preliminary, estimated values as fair value, it is important to remember the underlying principles of the GIPS standards: fair representation and full disclosure. If using preliminary, estimated values, firms must disclose this fact in the relevant GIPS Composite Report.

Firms that use preliminary, estimated values to determine fair value and subsequently change valuations when final values are received must determine how the firm's error correction policies will be applied. (Please see Provision 1.A.20 for guidance on error correction policies.) Differences between the final and estimated values are not necessarily errors but are treated in a similar manner because the correction of previously presented information may be involved.

In addition to this required disclosure, it is recommended (see Provision 5.B.6) that firms present the percentage of assets in the composite that were valued using preliminary, estimated values as of the most recent annual period end. This information will help prospective clients to interpret the performance record.

Sample Disclosure:

"Preliminary, estimated values were used in the determination of the fair value of the composite's assets."

Provision 5.C.40

If the FIRM changes the type of return(s) presented for the COMPOSITE (e.g., changes from TIME-WEIGHTED RETURNS to MONEY-WEIGHTED RETURNS), the FIRM MUST disclose the change and the date of the change. This disclosure MUST be included for a minimum of one year and for as long as it is relevant to interpreting the track record.

Discussion

A firm must present time-weighted returns (TWRs) in a GIPS Composite Report unless certain criteria are met that allow money-weighted returns (MWRs) to be presented instead of TWRs. Firms may choose to present MWRs instead of TWRs for a specific composite only if the firm controls the external cash flows into the portfolios in the composite and the portfolios in the composite have at least one of the following characteristics: They are closed-end; fixed life; fixed commitment; or illiquid investments are a significant part of the strategy. (See Provision 1.A.35.)

When a firm changes the type of return presented for a composite, the firm must disclose, in the respective GIPS Composite Report, the change in the type of return (e.g., from TWR to MWR) and the date of the change. This disclosure must be included in the GIPS Composite Report for a minimum of one year and for as long as it is relevant and helpful to the firm's prospective clients in interpreting the composite's track record. The firm must consider the underlying principles of the GIPS standards, which are fair representation and full disclosure, when determining how long the disclosure will be included in the GIPS Composite Report.

When a firm changes the type of return presented for a composite, for example from TWRs to MWRs, the firm must change the returns for all periods. As an example, suppose that a firm is presenting TWRs for a composite from the inception of the composite on 1 January 2013 through 31 December 2019. It decides that it will switch to present MWRs as of 1 January 2020. The firm cannot present TWRs through 31 December 2019 and an MWR from 1 January 2020 through 31 December 2020. The firm must present the since-inception MWR for the period from 1 January 2013 (the inception date of the composite) through 31 December 2020 in the GIPS Composite Report for the period ended 31 December 2020.

Sample Disclosure:

"Beginning with the GIPS Composite Report for the period ended 31 December 2020, the returns presented for the XYZ Composite were changed from time-weighted returns to money-weighted returns.

Provision 5.C.41

If the FIRM presents ADDITIONAL RISK MEASURES, the FIRM MUST:

a. Describe any ADDITIONAL RISK MEASURE.
b. Disclose the name of the risk-free rate if a risk-free rate is used in the calculation of the ADDITIONAL RISK MEASURE.

Discussion

There is no required risk measure for a GIPS Composite Report that presents money-weighted returns. However, understanding and interpreting investment performance requires the consideration of both risk and return. It is therefore recommended that firms present additional risk measures for the composite and the benchmark. (Because no quantitative risk measure is required for composites that present money-weighted returns, all risk measures presented are considered additional risk measures. See Provision 5.B.5.) It is important to keep in mind that additional risk measures should be consistent with the composite's strategy. For example, if the strategy includes managing foreign currency risk, the presentation of a hedge ratio would be consistent with that objective.

The GIPS Composite Report must include a description of any additional risk measure presented. If a risk-free rate is used in the calculation of an additional risk measure, the name of the risk-free rate must be disclosed. The disclosure of the name of the risk-free rate used in the calculation of an additional risk measure is required because of the importance of the selection of an appropriate risk-free rate. With a disclosure regarding the risk-free rate, the firm's prospective clients can better understand and interpret the additional risk measure(s) presented.

Provision 5.C.42

The FIRM MUST disclose if GROSS-OF-FEES or NET-OF-FEES returns are used to calculate presented risk measures.

Discussion

To help prospective clients interpret the risk measures presented in a GIPS Composite Report, the firm must disclose which returns—gross-of-fees or net-of-fees returns—are used in the calculation of the presented risk measures.

Sample Disclosure:

"Net-of-fees returns were used to calculate drawdown."

Provision 5.C.43

For REAL ESTATE investments that are not in a REAL ESTATE OPEN-END FUND, the FIRM MUST disclose that:[43]

a. EXTERNAL VALUATIONS are obtained, and the frequency they are obtained, or
b. The FIRM relies on valuations from financial statement audits.

Discussion

According to Provision 2.A.44, for periods beginning on or after 1 January 2012, real estate investments included in any portfolio except a real estate open-end fund must either:

- have an external valuation at least once every 12 months unless client agreements stipulate otherwise, in which case real estate investments must have an external valuation at least

[43] REQUIRED for periods ending on or after 31 December 2020.

once every 36 months or per the client agreement if the client agreement requires external valuations more frequently than every 36 months; or

- be subject to an annual financial statement audit performed by an independent public accounting firm. The real estate investments must be accounted for at fair value, and the most recent audited financial statements available must contain an unmodified opinion issued by an independent public accounting firm.

Because valuation is such an important issue for real estate investments, firms must inform prospective clients whether they externally value real estate investments and, if so, how frequently, or instead place reliance on valuations from audited financial statements. This disclosure is required for real estate investments that are not in a real estate open-end fund, for periods ending on or after 31 December 2020.

Sample Disclosures:

"ABC Company obtains external valuations for all real estate investments annually."

"XYZ Company relies on valuations from audited financial statements. The audits are performed by an independent public accounting firm."

Provision 5.C.44

When the GIPS COMPOSITE REPORT includes THEORETICAL PERFORMANCE as SUPPLEMENTAL INFORMATION, the FIRM MUST:

a. Disclose that the results are theoretical, are not based on the performance of actual assets, and if the THEORETICAL PERFORMANCE was derived from the retroactive or prospective application of a model.
b. Disclose a basic description of the methodology and assumptions used to calculate the THEORETICAL PERFORMANCE sufficient for the PROSPECTIVE CLIENT or PROSPECTIVE INVESTOR to interpret the THEORETICAL PERFORMANCE, including if it is based on model performance, backtested performance, or hypothetical performance.
c. Disclose whether the THEORETICAL PERFORMANCE reflects the deduction of actual or estimated INVESTMENT MANAGEMENT FEES, TRANSACTION COSTS, or other fees and charges that an actual client PORTFOLIO would have paid or will pay.
d. Clearly label the THEORETICAL PERFORMANCE as SUPPLEMENTAL INFORMATION.

Discussion

To be presented as supplemental information in a GIPS Composite Report, theoretical performance must relate to the respective composite. The following are examples of theoretical performance that may be included in a GIPS Composite Report as supplemental information:

- Results created by applying a composite investment strategy or methodology to historical data to indicate how a strategy constructed with the benefit of hindsight would have performed during a certain period in the past had the strategy been in existence during that period.
- Ex ante performance that is calculated by combining actual composite cash flows with projected future cash flows.
- Results that include the effect of currency hedging that has been applied after the fact to the composite when the composite was not originally managed including the currency hedging strategy, and the hedging is not part of the actual composite returns.

When theoretical performance is included as supplemental information in a GIPS Composite Report, a firm is required to include a number of disclosures to ensure that the recipients of the report, including prospective clients, understand the nature of the information being presented. Among the required disclosures are the source of the theoretical performance, the methodology and assumptions used to calculate the theoretical performance, and the treatment of fees and costs.

Firms must also clearly label the theoretical performance as supplemental information.

Sample Disclosure:

"A return history has been constructed for the period from 1 January 2015 through 31 December 2018 that reflects the application of an investment model used by XYZ Investment Management. The results are theoretical and are not based on the performance of actual portfolios. The return history is derived from the retroactive application of a model. The model assumes that an investment was made in the top 20 individual funds that have been identified as funds that meet the model's ESG screening criteria currently, and it assumes an equal amount was invested in each fund on an assumed quarterly capital call. The first capital call was assumed to occur on 31 December 2014. The since-inception internal rate of return for the model does not reflect the deduction of investment management fees, transaction costs, or other fees and charges."

5.D. Disclosure—Recommendations

Provision 5.D.1

The FIRM SHOULD disclose material changes to valuation policies and/or methodologies.

Discussion

Valuation is a critical component of the performance calculation. Therefore, if a change to a firm's valuation policies and/or methodologies is material, firms should disclose the change in order to enable prospective clients to understand the potential effect of such a change.

Some examples of a material change include, but are not limited to, the following:

- new valuation principles adopted by a local accounting standards board,
- adoption of new international standards in lieu of local standards,
- change of economic criteria used to value investments, and
- change from a discounted cash flow basis to a comparables basis.

Sample Disclosure for a Policy Change:

"Prior to 1 March 2016, illiquid securities were valued internally. Subsequently, illiquid securities are valued using a third-party pricing service."

Sample Disclosure for a Methodology Change:

"For periods prior to 1 August 2019, real estate investments were valued on a discounted cash flow basis. As of 1 August 2019, real estate investments are valued on a comparables basis."

Provision 5.D.2

The FIRM SHOULD disclose material changes to calculation policies and/or methodologies.

Discussion

Firms have discretion to determine which policies and methodologies are used for calculating performance. Although these policies and methodologies must adhere to all applicable calculation requirements, firms may choose from a wide variety of policies and methodologies. Firms may change calculation policies and/or methodologies; however, firms must not change a calculation policy or methodology for the sole purpose of increasing performance. If a change to the calculation policies and/or methodologies is material, firms should disclose the change in order to enable prospective clients to understand the potential effect of such a change.

Sample Disclosure:

"Prior to 2019, the internal rate of return method was used to calculate since-inception money-weighted returns. Subsequently, the Modified Dietz method is used for all periods."

Provision 5.D.3

The FIRM SHOULD disclose material differences between the BENCHMARK and the COMPOSITE'S investment mandate, objective, or strategy.

Discussion

Firms are required to disclose the composite description (see Provision 5.C.4) and the benchmark description (see Provision 5.C.5) in a GIPS Composite Report. It is recommended that firms also disclose any material differences between the benchmark and the composite's investment mandate, objective, or strategy. Prospective clients will be better able to evaluate the performance of the strategy relative to the benchmark presented if they understand any material differences between the composite and the benchmark.

Sample Disclosure:

"The Small-Cap Opportunities Composite is a venture capital composite that invests in small-cap startups in all sectors, with a focus on the health care and financial services sectors. The benchmark for the composite is the public market equivalent (PME) of the ABC Small-Cap Index, which tracks the performance of US small-cap companies. The investment strategy of the composite differs from the small-cap investment strategies represented by the PME because the composite concentrates its investments. As of 31 December 2019, 62% of the composite was invested in the health care and financial services sectors, and 18% of the index was invested in these two sectors."

Provision 5.D.4

The FIRM SHOULD disclose the key assumptions used to value investments.

Discussion

Firms are required to disclose that valuation policies are available upon request. (See Provision 5.C.15.) Because valuation is a critical component of the performance calculation, it is recommended that firms also disclose the key assumptions used when valuing portfolio investments. This will help prospective clients better understand how the firm values investments and compare valuation assumptions for similar strategies used by different firms.

Sample Disclosures:

"Investments are valued using recent market quotations. If there is no publicly traded reference, equity investments are valued using a market multiples approach for similar investments in active markets, and fixed-income investments are valued using inputs such as interest rates, yield curve shape, volatility, prepayments, and credit risk."

"The firm uses valuations reported by the general partners of the underlying pooled funds."

Provision 5.D.5

If a parent company contains multiple firms, each FIRM within the parent company SHOULD disclose a list of the other firms contained within the parent company.

Discussion

The term "firm" is used in two different ways in Provision 5.D.5. "FIRM" is used to indicate an entity that claims compliance with the GIPS standards, whereas "firm" is used to indicate an entity that may or may not claim compliance with the GIPS standards. The definition of a firm will be based on the specific circumstances of the firm but must reflect how the firm is held out to the public as a distinct business entity. In some cases, a parent company may have two or more units, divisions, departments, or offices that are defined as separate firms within the context of the GIPS standards. To avoid confusion, a firm claiming compliance with the GIPS standards must be sure that it is clearly defined relative to the other firms within the parent company and that it is apparent which firm is claiming compliance. In the interest of fair representation and full disclosure, firms should disclose a list of the other organizations within the parent company. Firms should also consider indicating which organizations within the parent company claim compliance with the GIPS standards.

 |

Sample Disclosure:

"ABC Institutional Investment Management is the institutional division of ABC parent company. The private banking division of ABC parent company also claims compliance with the GIPS standards, whereas the retail division of ABC parent company does not claim compliance with the GIPS standards."

Provision 5.D.6

If the COMPOSITE contains PORTFOLIOS with BUNDLED FEES, the FIRM SHOULD disclose the types of fees included in the BUNDLED FEE.

Discussion

A bundled fee is a fee that combines multiple fees into one total or "bundled" fee. Bundled fees can include any combination of investment management fees, transaction costs, custody fees, and/or administrative fees. An example of a bundled fee is an all-in fee, which is a type of bundled fee that can include any combination of investment management fees, transaction costs, custody fees, and administrative fees. All-in fees are typically offered in certain jurisdictions where asset management, brokerage, and custody services are offered by the same company.

To help prospective clients better understand the nature of the fees charged for a particular investment product, and to facilitate comparison of bundled fee products offered by different firms, it is recommended that firms disclose the types of fees included in the bundled fee.

Sample Disclosure:

"Portfolios within the composite pay a bundled fee, which includes all charges for transaction costs, portfolio management fees, and custody fees."

Provision 5.D.7

If the FIRM adheres to any industry valuation guidelines in addition to the GIPS valuation REQUIREMENTS, the FIRM SHOULD disclose which guidelines have been applied.

Discussion

Some market segments, such as private equity, have developed their own valuation guidelines. For these markets, it is not uncommon for the GIPS standards valuation requirements to be supplemented by other local or international standards because other standards may be more stringent in their requirements.

The disclosure of which industry's valuation guidelines have been used in addition to the GIPS standards valuation requirements will help prospective clients to determine the comparability of GIPS Composite Reports from different firms and/or jurisdictions.

Sample Disclosure:

"The Global Diversified Distressed Composite adheres to the XYZ Venture Capital Association's valuation guidelines as well as the GIPS standards valuation requirements. The XYZ valuation standards are based on fair value but provide more prescriptive advice in terms of how to value specific investments, such as secondary investments and distressed debt investments."

Provision 5.D.8

When using BENCHMARKS that have limitations, such as peer group BENCHMARKS, the FIRM SHOULD disclose these limitations.

Discussion

Firms must determine which benchmark(s) are most appropriate for composite(s). When determining which benchmarks to present in a GIPS Composite Report, firms should be guided by the ethical spirit of the GIPS standards.

Some benchmarks with known limitations are often used for certain types of investments. For example, peer group benchmarks, such as hedge fund peer group universe indices, are often used for hedge funds and other alternative investment strategies. Although peer group benchmarks are frequently used to evaluate hedge funds, there are some common problems with hedge fund peer group benchmarks, including the following:

- self-reporting bias (only some hedge funds choose to report performance data),
- survivorship bias (historical returns of closed hedge funds are removed from the peer group benchmark),
- inability to obtain returns for the same periods as the composite, and
- lack of investability (some hedge funds within a peer group benchmark are closed to new investors).

When using benchmarks that exhibit limitations, firms should describe these limitations in the relevant GIPS Composite Report. This helps prospective clients understand the nature of the benchmark and be aware of any known drawbacks in comparing the risk and return of the benchmark and composite.

Sample Disclosure:

"The benchmark is the Hedge Fund Aggregate Multi-Style Index, which includes more than 100 hedge funds of various styles and strategies. Because this index is based on the data self-reported by the constituent funds, it may have a self-reporting bias. In addition, some funds are closed to new investors and are no longer investable. We believe that no better index exists as a comparison for this composite."

Provision 5.D.9

The FIRM SHOULD disclose how research costs are reflected in returns.

Discussion

The focus on research costs has grown in certain markets. Although research costs are often absorbed by the firm, some firms instead charge research costs directly to clients. To allow prospective clients to understand the firm's policy for the treatment of research costs, firms should disclose if returns do or do not reflect the deduction of research costs.

Sample Disclosures:

"ABC Company bears the costs of investment research. Research costs are not separately charged to clients."

"Certain investment research costs are charged directly to clients outside the managed portfolio. Therefore, composite returns do not reflect the research costs that are charged directly to clients."

6. POOLED FUND TIME-WEIGHTED RETURN REPORT

The following provisions apply to POOLED FUNDS that include TIME-WEIGHTED RETURNS in a GIPS POOLED FUND REPORT.

6.A. Presentation and Reporting—Requirements

Provision 6.A.1

The FIRM MUST present in each GIPS POOLED FUND REPORT:

a. At least five years of performance (or for the period since the POOLED FUND INCEPTION DATE if the POOLED FUND has been in existence less than five years) that meets the REQUIREMENTS of the GIPS standards. After the FIRM presents a minimum of five years of GIPS-compliant performance (or for the period since the POOLED FUND INCEPTION DATE if the POOLED FUND has been in existence less than five years), the FIRM MUST present an additional year of performance each year, building up to a minimum of 10 years of GIPS-compliant performance.

Discussion

To claim compliance, a firm is required to meet all applicable requirements of the GIPS standards on a firm-wide basis for at least a five-year period, or since inception of the firm if the firm has been in existence for less than five years. When initially claiming compliance with the GIPS standards, a firm must present a minimum of five years of pooled fund performance or performance since the inception of the pooled fund if the pooled fund has been in existence for less than five years.

Once the firm has its initial minimum five years of GIPS-compliant history, the firm must continue to add annual returns to each GIPS Pooled Fund Report, so that five years after initially claiming compliance with the GIPS standards, the firm will have a 10-year performance record for its pooled funds. It is recommended that firms present a pooled fund's history for more than the minimum required periods. (See Provision 6.B.6.)

Provision 6.A.1

The FIRM MUST present in each GIPS POOLED FUND REPORT:

b. POOLED FUND returns for each annual period.

Discussion

The GIPS standards require the presentation of annual pooled fund returns. Firms must clearly label the annual presentation periods. Firms must define the annual reporting period on a pooled fund-by-pooled fund basis and apply it consistently. For purposes of comparability, best practice would be for a firm to report pooled fund performance on a calendar year-end basis.

Within each GIPS Pooled Fund Report, the annual periods must be consistent. For example, a firm that reports a pooled fund's performance annually as of 30 June must consistently report data for years ending 30 June for that pooled fund. The firm may decide in the future to change to a 31 December valuation and reporting date; however, the firm may not mix 30 June and 31 December valuation and reporting dates in the same GIPS Pooled Fund Report.

Although the GIPS standards require the presentation of annual returns, it is recommended that firms present more frequent returns, such as quarterly or monthly returns. (See Provision 6.B.2.b.) More frequent returns help prospective investors evaluate a pooled fund's track record.

Firms may present either pooled fund gross returns or pooled fund net returns. Firms may also choose to present both pooled fund gross returns and pooled fund net returns in a GIPS Pooled Fund Report.

Provision 6.A.1

The FIRM MUST present in each GIPS POOLED FUND REPORT:

c. When the initial period is less than a full year, the return from the POOLED FUND INCEPTION DATE through the initial annual period end.[44]

Discussion

When a pooled fund has an initial period that is less than a full year, the GIPS standards require that the return be presented for the partial year from the pooled fund inception date through the

[44] REQUIRED for POOLED FUNDS with a POOLED FUND INCEPTION DATE of 1 January 2011 or later.

 |

initial annual period end. This is required for pooled funds that begin on or after 1 January 2011. Although not required to do so for pooled funds that begin prior to this date, firms should consider presenting the initial partial year of performance for all pooled funds.

For example, assume that a firm presents pooled fund returns for annual periods ended 31 December, and a new pooled fund is created with a track record beginning 1 April 2018. The initial GIPS Pooled Fund Report for this pooled fund must include the pooled fund return for the period from 1 April 2018 through 31 December 2018. Subsequently, the firm must add annual returns, building up to a minimum 10-year track record.

Partial-year returns must not be annualized. As an example, a pooled fund that began on 1 December 2020 and has a one-month initial return through 31 December 2020 of 3% (which equates to an annualized return of 42.6%) would be required to present that 3% as the partial year's performance. The annualized return of 42.6% must not be presented. Some spreadsheet and software applications automatically annualize all returns, and firms are reminded that for periods of less than a year, the firm must "de-annualize" any annualized returns that are calculated.

The method chosen to de-annualize a return is at the discretion of the firm, but it must be a geometric calculation. In the situation just presented, the 42.6% annualized return could be de-annualized by one of the following formulas:

$$\left\{\left[(1+0.426)^{\left(\frac{1}{12}\right)}\right]-1\right\}\times 100=3\% \quad \text{or} \quad \left\{\left[(1+0.426)^{\left(\frac{31}{365}\right)}\right]-1\right\}\times 100=3\%,$$

both resulting in a non-annualized one-month return of 3%.

Provision 6.A.1

The FIRM MUST present in each GIPS POOLED FUND REPORT:

d. When the POOLED FUND terminates, the return from the last annual period end through the POOLED FUND TERMINATION DATE.[45]

Discussion

The GIPS standards require that returns from the last annual period end through the pooled fund termination date be presented for pooled funds with a termination date of 1 January 2011 or later. Assume that a firm presents pooled fund returns for annual periods ended 31 December and a pooled fund terminates so that the track record ends 31 August 2017. The GIPS Pooled Fund

[45] REQUIRED for POOLED FUNDS with a POOLED FUND TERMINATION DATE of 1 January 2011 or later.

Report for this pooled fund must include the pooled fund return for the period from 1 January 2017 through 31 August 2017. Partial-year returns must not be annualized. As an example, a pooled fund that terminates on 31 January 2020 and has a one-month return for January 2020 of 3% (which equates to an annualized return of 42.6%) would be required to present that 3% as the partial year's performance.

The annualized return of 42.6% must not be presented. Some spreadsheet and software applications automatically annualize all returns, and firms are reminded that for periods of less than a year, the firm must "de-annualize" any annualized returns that are calculated.

The method chosen to de-annualize a return is at the discretion of the firm, but it must be a geometric calculation. In the situation just presented, the 42.6% annualized return could be de-annualized by one of the following formulas:

$$\left\{\left[(1+0.426)^{\left(\frac{1}{12}\right)}\right]-1\right\}\times 100 = 3\% \quad \text{or} \quad \left\{\left[(1+0.426)^{\left(\frac{31}{365}\right)}\right]-1\right\}\times 100 = 3\%,$$

both resulting in a non-annualized one-month return of 3%.

Provision 6.A.1

The FIRM MUST present in each GIPS POOLED FUND REPORT:

e. The TOTAL RETURN for the BENCHMARK for each annual period and for all other periods for which POOLED FUND returns are presented, unless the FIRM determines there is no appropriate BENCHMARK.

Discussion

Benchmarks are important tools that aid in the planning, implementation, and evaluation of a pooled fund's investment policy. They also help facilitate discussions with prospective investors regarding the relationship between risk and return. As a result, firms are required to present a total return for the benchmark that reflects the pooled fund's investment mandate, objective, or strategy for each annual period. A firm may choose to present more than one benchmark in a GIPS Pooled Fund Report and, if it does so, it must include all required information for all benchmarks included in a GIPS Pooled Fund Report.

In addition to the required annual benchmark returns, firms must also present benchmark returns for the same periods for which pooled fund returns are presented. For example, if the GIPS Pooled Fund Report includes quarterly pooled fund returns, quarterly benchmark returns must also be included.

Because the GIPS standards require that the total return for the benchmark be presented, a price-only index would not satisfy the requirements of the GIPS standards. This scenario also applies to benchmarks that are components of a blended benchmark. A price-only benchmark may be presented in a GIPS Pooled Fund Report as supplemental information only if it is presented in addition to a total return benchmark. It must be labeled as a price-only benchmark, and there must be sufficient disclosures so that a prospective investor understands the difference between the return of a price-only benchmark and the return of a total return benchmark. Firms must not present only a price-only benchmark even if no appropriate total return benchmark is available for a specific pooled fund. If a firm determines that no appropriate benchmark for the pooled fund exists, it must not present a benchmark and must disclose why no benchmark is presented. (See Provision 6.C.26.)

Some benchmarks, such as commodity benchmarks, may not have income because the asset class does not create income, but they are still considered to be total return benchmarks. Target returns, such as an 8% hurdle rate, may also not have income, but this is not considered a price-only return.

Provision 6.A.1

The FIRM MUST present in each GIPS POOLED FUND REPORT:

f. POOLED FUND assets as of each annual period end.

Discussion

Each GIPS Pooled Fund Report must include the amount of pooled fund assets as of the end of each annual period that is included in the GIPS Pooled Fund Report. This requirement provides information to prospective investors on the size of the pooled fund, measured by the amount of assets it contains. When the pooled fund strategy uses discretionary leverage, pooled fund assets must be presented net of the discretionary leverage and not grossed up as if the discretionary leverage did not exist. Discretionary leverage refers to loans taken at the discretion of the firm. In contrast, non-discretionary leverage refers to borrowings undertaken by the investor. For example, if the firm is managing a fund that has $200 million in assets, and the firm chooses to borrow $50 million, the fund's net assets are $200 million and its gross assets are $250 million. When calculating pooled fund assets, the firm must use $200 million.

Provision 6.A.1

The FIRM MUST present in each GIPS POOLED FUND REPORT:

g. TOTAL FIRM ASSETS as of each annual period end.[46]

Discussion

For annual periods ending on or after 31 December 2020, the firm must present total firm assets as of each annual period end. For annual periods ending prior to this date, the firm must present either total firm assets or pooled fund assets as a percentage of total firm assets. Discretionary leverage must be deducted when calculating total firm assets. Discretionary leverage refers to loans taken at the discretion of the firm. In contrast, non-discretionary leverage refers to borrowings that are undertaken by the investor. For example, if the firm is managing a pooled fund that has $200 million in assets, and the firm chooses to borrow $50 million, the firm must use $200 million when calculating total firm assets, not $250 million. The inclusion of both pooled fund assets and total firm assets in a GIPS Pooled Fund Report will help a prospective investor understand the pooled fund size in relation to total firm assets.

Firms must be sure that assets are not double-counted because counting assets more than once would not fairly represent total firm assets.

See the discussion of Provision 2.A.1 for additional guidance on the calculation of total firm assets.

Provision 6.A.1

The FIRM MUST present in each GIPS POOLED FUND REPORT:

h. For POOLED FUNDS for which monthly POOLED FUND returns are available, the three-year annualized EX POST STANDARD DEVIATION (using monthly returns) of the POOLED FUND and the BENCHMARK as of each annual period end.[47]

Discussion

Evaluating past performance requires an understanding of the risks taken to achieve the results. Standard deviation is universally defined as a measure of the variability of returns. For pooled

[46] REQUIRED for periods ending on or after 31 December 2020. For periods ending prior to 31 December 2020, FIRMS may present either TOTAL FIRM ASSETS or POOLED FUND assets as a percentage of TOTAL FIRM ASSETS.

[47] REQUIRED for periods ending on or after 1 January 2011.

funds for which monthly returns are available, the GIPS standards require the presentation of ex post standard deviation, often referred to as external standard deviation. Ex post standard deviation is a measure of the volatility of pooled fund and benchmark returns over time, and it is intended to measure the risk of investing in the pooled fund. For periods ending on or after 1 January 2011, firms must present, as of each annual period end, the three-year annualized ex post standard deviation using monthly returns for both the pooled fund and the benchmark.

Standard deviation for both the pooled fund and the benchmark must be calculated using 36 monthly returns. The same formula must be used to calculate standard deviations for the pooled fund and the benchmark.

Some pooled funds, such as those for private market investments, may not have monthly returns. For these pooled funds, if the pooled fund has at least three annual periods of performance, firms must disclose if the three-year annualized ex post standard deviation of the pooled fund and/or benchmark is not presented because 36 monthly returns are not available. (See Provision 6.C.29.)

Ex Post Standard Deviation (External)

Ex post standard deviation is calculated as follows:

$$\text{Pooled fund or benchmark ex post standard deviation} = \sqrt{\frac{\Sigma\left[R_i - MEAN(R)\right]^2}{n}},$$

where R_i is the ith monthly pooled fund or benchmark return, n is the number of monthly returns used for the external standard deviation calculation (the use of n is best practice and preferable, but either n or $n - 1$ in the denominator of the standard deviation calculation is acceptable), and $MEAN(R)$ is the mean monthly return of the pooled fund or the benchmark over the period for which the external standard deviation is being calculated, where:

$$MEAN(R) = \frac{R_1 + R_2 + \ldots + R_i}{n},$$

where R_1 is the time-weighted return for the first monthly pooled fund or benchmark return, R_i is the ith monthly pooled fund or benchmark return, and n is the number of returns used in the calculation (required to be 36 monthly returns to satisfy this requirement).

Firms are required to select a methodology (i.e., the use of n or $n - 1$) on a pooled fund–specific basis, document it in their policies and procedures, and consistently apply that methodology.

To annualize the three-year ex post standard deviation calculated using monthly returns, the result of the foregoing standard deviation formula must be multiplied by the square root of 12.

If the firm presents only pooled fund gross returns in the GIPS Pooled Fund Report, the firm should use gross returns to calculate the external standard deviation. If a firm presents only pooled fund net returns in the GIPS Pooled Fund Report, the firm should use net returns to calculate the external standard deviation. If the firm presents both pooled fund gross returns and net returns, it is recommended that the firm use pooled fund gross returns to calculate the external standard deviation. (See Provision 2.B.7.) The firm must disclose which returns (pooled fund gross returns or pooled fund net returns) were used to calculate the external standard deviation. (See Provision 6.C.35.)

Provision 6.A.2

The FIRM MUST present the percentage of the total FAIR VALUE of POOLED FUND assets that were valued using subjective unobservable inputs (as described in provision 2.B.6.e) as of the most recent annual period end, if such investments represent a material amount of POOLED FUND assets.

Discussion

Markets are not always liquid, and investment prices are not always objective and/or observable. As the last level of the recommended valuation hierarchy indicates (see Provision 2.B.6), it may be necessary for a firm to use subjective unobservable inputs to value an investment for which markets are not active on the measurement date. Examples of subjective unobservable inputs include an assumed discount rate, an assumed occupancy rate for a commercial building, and the default rate used for the valuation of a security in default. Examples related to insurance-linked securities include assumptions regarding hurricane damage and mortality rates. Unobservable inputs should be used to measure fair value only when observable inputs and prices are not available or appropriate. Unobservable inputs reflect the firm's own assumptions about the assumptions that market participants would use in pricing the investment and should be developed based on the best information available under the circumstances.

Firms must present the percentage of the total fair value of pooled fund assets that were valued using subjective unobservable inputs as of the most recent annual period end, if such investments represent a material amount of pooled fund assets. The amount of pooled fund assets valued using subjective unobservable inputs would be considered material if it would likely influence a reader's judgment regarding the reliability of the valuation. The firm must decide on the criteria it will use to determine when subjective unobservable inputs represent a material amount of pooled fund assets, include these criteria in its policy and procedures, and apply these criteria consistently.

Sample Disclosure:

"As of 31 December 2020, 29% of pooled fund assets were valued using subjective unobservable inputs. These inputs are not supported by market activity and instead are based on internal proprietary pricing models."

Provision 6.A.3

The FIRM MUST clearly label or identify:

a. The periods that are presented.

b. If POOLED FUND returns are POOLED FUND GROSS RETURNS or POOLED FUND NET RETURNS.

Discussion

All periods presented in a GIPS Pooled Fund Report must be clearly labeled or identified. This includes annual periods, partial-year periods, and any additional periods presented.

Firms may present either pooled fund gross returns or pooled fund net returns in a GIPS Pooled Fund Report and may also choose to present both pooled fund gross returns and pooled fund net returns. For prospective investors to understand the nature of the returns being presented, all returns presented must be clearly labeled or identified as gross returns or net returns.

Provision 6.A.4

If the FIRM includes more than one BENCHMARK in the GIPS POOLED FUND REPORT, the FIRM MUST present and disclose all REQUIRED information for all BENCHMARKS presented.

Discussion

It is permissible to include more than one benchmark in a GIPS Pooled Fund Report. All benchmarks included in a GIPS Pooled Fund Report must adhere to the requirements of the GIPS standards that are applicable to benchmarks. Firms may label benchmarks as primary and secondary benchmarks, but the same requirements and recommendations apply to all benchmarks included in a GIPS Pooled Fund Report. For example, a GIPS Pooled Fund Report must include:

- a description for all benchmarks,
- a disclosure of changes to (or deletion of) any benchmark, and
- the three-year annualized ex post standard deviation of all benchmarks.

If the firm designates benchmarks as primary and secondary benchmarks, it must disclose when these designations change (e.g., if a primary benchmark becomes a secondary benchmark), because such a change in designation is considered a benchmark change. In all instances, if multiple benchmarks are presented in a GIPS Pooled Fund Report and one or more of the benchmarks is removed from the GIPS Pooled Fund Report, the firm must disclose this fact. (See Provision 6.C.27.)

An appropriate benchmark for a pooled fund reflects the investment mandate, objective, or strategy of the pooled fund. Additional benchmarks beyond appropriate benchmarks may be presented in a GIPS Pooled Fund Report as supplemental information. There must be sufficient disclosure so that a prospective investor understands the nature of the benchmark and why it is being presented. Disclosure, however, does not necessarily prevent information from being false or misleading. An additional benchmark must never be presented for the sole purpose of providing a favorable comparison to the performance of the pooled fund. To do so would be misleading, regardless of the disclosures accompanying the benchmark.

Provision 6.A.5

The FIRM MUST present the POOLED FUND EXPENSE RATIO appropriate to PROSPECTIVE INVESTORS.

Discussion

Firms must present the pooled fund expense ratio that is applicable to prospective investors for the specific pooled fund. The pooled fund expense ratio is the ratio of total pooled fund expenses to average net assets. The expense ratio should not reflect transaction costs.

The pooled fund expense ratio gives prospective investors important insight into the total fees and expenses paid by investors in the fund. For example, a pooled fund expense ratio of 2% indicates that an investor will pay $20 in expenses each year for every $1,000 invested, in addition to transaction costs. An expense ratio also helps investors compare expenses across funds, because even a small difference in fees can have a significant effect over time.

If the pooled fund has multiple share classes, the firm may present multiple expense ratios or may present only the expense ratio appropriate to the prospective investor. The firm may also use the highest expense ratio as the expense ratio that can be used for all prospective investors of the fund. Expense ratios must reflect any performance-based fees or carried interest, if accrued or charged to the pooled fund. Presenting a range of expense ratios (e.g., the expense ratio for all share classes ranges between 0.40% and 0.85%) would not satisfy this requirement.

Because expense ratios can change over time, firms must determine which expense ratio to present. A firm might choose to present the expense ratio as of the most recent annual period end, or the last known expense ratio. When the expense ratio has had a material change resulting from a change in assets or costs, the firm should present a more current expense ratio that reflects what a prospective investor is likely to pay at the current time.

Pooled fund expense ratios that are calculated for periods of less than one year must be annualized. Assume that a pooled fund starts on 1 April, and the firm calculates an expense ratio of

0.75% for the period from 1 April 2019 through 31 December 2019. The firm must present an annualized rate of 1.00%, representing a pooled fund expense ratio for the entire year, rather than the 0.75% that represents an expense ratio for only nine months. Presenting an annualized expense ratio facilitates the comparison of expense ratios across funds and firms. Firms may also present the non-annualized expense ratio but must clearly disclose or indicate that the expense ratio is not annualized.

This presentation requirement is not satisfied if the firm does not include the expense ratio in the GIPS Pooled Fund Report and instead makes reference to another document that includes the expense ratio, such as a fund prospectus. The expense ratio may be an exhibit attached to the GIPS Pooled Fund Report. The exhibit may be the pooled fund's offering documents, if the offering documents include the appropriate expense ratio.

Provision 6.A.6

If the FIRM chooses to present POOLED FUND uncalled COMMITTED CAPITAL or a combination of POOLED FUND assets and POOLED FUND uncalled COMMITTED CAPITAL, the FIRM MUST:

a. Present POOLED FUND uncalled COMMITTED CAPITAL for the same periods for which the combination of POOLED FUND assets and POOLED FUND uncalled COMMITTED CAPITAL is presented.

b. Clearly label POOLED FUND uncalled COMMITTED CAPITAL as such.

c. Clearly label the combination of POOLED FUND assets and POOLED FUND uncalled COMMITTED CAPITAL as such.

Discussion

Committed capital is defined as pledges of capital to an investment vehicle by investors (limited partners and the general partner) or the firm and is typically drawn down over a period of time. Uncalled committed capital, also known as dry powder, is the amount of capital that has not yet been drawn. Because uncalled committed capital is not considered actual pooled fund assets, pooled fund uncalled committed capital must not be included in the calculation of pooled fund assets as of 1 January 2020. This is consistent with the requirement to not include uncalled committed capital in total firm assets for periods beginning on or after 1 January 2020. (See Provision 2.A.1.)

A firm may report pooled fund uncalled committed capital in addition to the required presentation of pooled fund assets, if it wishes to do so. The inclusion of information on pooled fund uncalled committed capital provides prospective investors with a more complete picture of the firm's investments and the amount of capital that is currently committed to a future investment.

If a firm chooses to present information on pooled fund uncalled committed capital, it may present pooled fund uncalled committed capital as either:

- a separate value, or
- the combination of pooled fund assets and pooled fund uncalled committed capital.

If a firm chooses to present pooled fund uncalled committed capital as a separate value, the information must be clearly labeled.

If a firm chooses to present the combination of pooled fund assets and pooled fund uncalled committed capital, it must present pooled fund uncalled committed capital for the same periods for which the combination of pooled fund assets and pooled fund uncalled committed capital is presented. Both pooled fund uncalled committed capital and the combination of pooled fund assets and pooled fund uncalled committed capital must be clearly labeled as such.

Provision 6.A.7

If the FIRM chooses to present FIRM-wide uncalled COMMITTED CAPITAL or a combination of TOTAL FIRM ASSETS and FIRM-wide uncalled COMMITTED CAPITAL, the FIRM MUST:

a. Present FIRM-wide uncalled COMMITTED CAPITAL for the same periods for which the combination of TOTAL FIRM ASSETS and FIRM-wide uncalled COMMITTED CAPITAL is presented.
b. Clearly label FIRM-wide uncalled COMMITTED CAPITAL as such.
c. Clearly label the combination of TOTAL FIRM ASSETS and FIRM-wide uncalled COMMITTED CAPITAL as such.

Discussion

Committed capital is defined as pledges of capital to an investment vehicle by investors (limited partners and the general partner) or the firm and is typically drawn down over a period of time. Uncalled committed capital, also known as dry powder, is the amount of capital that has not yet been drawn. For periods beginning on or after 1 January 2020, uncalled committed capital must not be included in total firm assets. (See Provision 2.A.1.) Although firm-wide uncalled committed capital must not be included in the calculation of total firm assets as of 1 January 2020, a firm may report firm-wide uncalled committed capital in addition to the required presentation of total firm assets, if it wishes to do so. The inclusion of information on firm-wide uncalled committed capital provides prospective investors with a more complete picture of the firm's investments and the amount of capital that is currently committed to a future investment. If a firm chooses to present information on firm-wide uncalled committed capital, it may present firm-wide uncalled committed capital as either:

- a separate value, or
- the combination of total firm assets and firm-wide uncalled committed capital.

If a firm chooses to present firm-wide uncalled committed capital as a separate value, the information must be clearly labeled.

If a firm chooses to present the combination of total firm assets and firm-wide uncalled committed capital, the firm must present firm-wide uncalled committed capital for the same periods for which the combination of total firm assets and firm-wide uncalled committed capital is presented. Both firm-wide uncalled committed capital and the combination of total firm assets and firm-wide uncalled committed capital must be clearly labeled as such.

Provision 6.A.8

If the FIRM chooses to present ADVISORY-ONLY ASSETS that reflect the POOLED FUND'S investment mandate, objective, or strategy or a combination of POOLED FUND assets and ADVISORY-ONLY ASSETS that reflect the POOLED FUND'S investment mandate, objective, or strategy, the FIRM MUST:

a. Present ADVISORY-ONLY ASSETS that reflect the POOLED FUND'S investment mandate, objective, or strategy for the same periods for which the combination of POOLED FUND assets and ADVISORY-ONLY ASSETS that reflect the POOLED FUND'S investment mandate, objective, or strategy is presented.

b. Clearly label ADVISORY-ONLY ASSETS that reflect the POOLED FUND'S investment mandate, objective, or strategy as such.

c. Clearly label the combination of POOLED FUND assets and ADVISORY-ONLY ASSETS that reflect the POOLED FUND'S investment mandate, objective, or strategy as such.

Discussion

Pooled fund advisory-only assets are assets for which the firm provides investment recommendations in line with the pooled fund's strategy but for which the firm has no control over implementation of investment decisions and no trading authority for the assets. Although pooled fund advisory-only assets must not be included in the calculation of pooled fund assets because the firm does not manage these assets, a firm may wish to provide information on pooled fund advisory-only assets in addition to the required presentation of pooled fund assets. The inclusion of information on pooled fund advisory-only assets provides prospective investors additional information about a firm's business model and the types of investment-related services that it provides. If a firm chooses to present information on pooled fund advisory-only assets, it may present pooled fund advisory-only assets as either:

- a separate value, or
- the combination of pooled fund assets and pooled fund advisory-only assets.

If a firm chooses to present pooled fund advisory-only assets as a separate value, the information must be clearly labeled.

If a firm chooses to present the combination of pooled fund assets and pooled fund advisory-only assets, the firm must present pooled fund advisory-only assets for the same periods for which the combination of pooled fund assets and pooled fund advisory-only assets is presented. Both pooled fund advisory-only assets and the combination of pooled fund assets and pooled fund advisory-only assets must be clearly labeled as such.

Provision 6.A.9

If the FIRM chooses to present FIRM-wide ADVISORY-ONLY ASSETS or a combination of TOTAL FIRM ASSETS and FIRM-wide ADVISORY-ONLY ASSETS, the FIRM MUST:

a. Present FIRM-wide ADVISORY-ONLY ASSETS for the same periods for which the combination of TOTAL FIRM ASSETS and FIRM-wide ADVISORY-ONLY ASSETS is presented.
b. Clearly label FIRM-wide ADVISORY-ONLY ASSETS as such.
c. Clearly label the combination of TOTAL FIRM ASSETS and FIRM-wide ADVISORY-ONLY ASSETS as such.

Discussion

Advisory-only assets are assets for which the firm provides investment recommendations but for which the firm has no control over implementation of investment decisions and no trading authority for the assets. Although firm-wide advisory-only assets must not be included in the calculation of total firm assets because the firm does not manage these assets, a firm may wish to provide information on firm-wide advisory-only assets in addition to the required presentation of total firm assets. The inclusion of information on firm-wide advisory-only assets provides prospective investors additional information about a firm's business model and the types of investment-related services that it provides. If a firm chooses to present information on firm-wide advisory-only assets, it may present firm-wide advisory-only assets as either:

- a separate value, or
- the combination of total firm assets and firm-wide advisory-only assets.

If a firm chooses to present firm-wide advisory-only assets as a separate value, the information must be clearly labeled.

If a firm chooses to present the combination of total firm assets and firm-wide advisory-only assets, the firm must present firm-wide advisory-only assets for the same periods for which the combination of total firm assets and firm-wide advisory-only assets is presented. Both the firm-wide advisory-only assets and the combination of total firm assets and firm-wide advisory-only assets must be clearly labeled as such.

Provision 6.A.10

All REQUIRED and RECOMMENDED information in the GIPS POOLED FUND REPORT MUST be presented in the same currency.

Discussion

Firms must present all required and recommended information in a GIPS Pooled Fund Report in the same currency (e.g., pooled fund and benchmark returns, pooled fund assets, and total firm assets). This requirement is not applicable to the fee schedule. Supplemental information should also be presented in the same currency. If it is not, that fact must be disclosed. Not disclosing this fact could be misleading.

If a firm chooses to present a pooled fund in a different currency, the firm must convert all of the required information into the new currency. If the firm chooses to present performance in multiple currencies in the same GIPS Pooled Fund Report, the firm must convert all of the required information into each of the currencies and ensure it is clear in which currencies performance is reported. The firm must also convert any recommended information it chooses to present in the GIPS Pooled Fund Report containing the converted information.

The GIPS standards do not require or recommend a particular method for converting pooled fund performance from one currency to another. One option for converting returns into a different currency is to convert the underlying data (values and external cash flows) into the selected currency using the exchange rate on the date of each cash flow and valuation, and then calculate the pooled fund returns based on the converted data.

A firm may instead convert pooled fund returns. Starting with pooled fund returns calculated in its base currency, a pooled fund return can be converted using the movement in the exchange rate between the base currency and the reporting currency over the period of the return. The following example illustrates this method:

Suppose that the return of a pooled fund in euros for the year 2018 is +5.00%. The exchange rate for 1 euro to the US dollar at the start of the year was 1.2008, and at the end of the year it is 1.14315. First calculate the movement in the exchange rate over the year:

$$FX\ return = \frac{FX_{end}}{FX_{start}} - 1$$

$$FX\ return = \frac{1.14315}{1.2008} - 1 = -0.0480, \text{or} - 4.80\%$$

The exchange rate movement and the euro pooled fund return are then multiplied to determine the USD pooled fund return:

$$\text{USD Pooled Fund Return} = (1 + 0.05) \times (1 - 0.0480) - 1 = (1.05 \times 0.952) - 1$$
$$= -0.00041, \text{ or } -0.041\%$$

It is not acceptable to convert returns by applying the exchange rate as of the current period end to the historical data, including cash flows and valuations, used to calculate returns.

It is up to the firm to determine the pooled fund–specific conversion method. Policies and procedures for converting returns must be established, documented, and applied consistently.

Provision 6.A.11

Any SUPPLEMENTAL INFORMATION included in the GIPS POOLED FUND REPORT:

a. MUST relate directly to the POOLED FUND.

b. MUST NOT contradict or conflict with the REQUIRED or RECOMMENDED information in the GIPS POOLED FUND REPORT.

c. MUST be clearly labeled as SUPPLEMENTAL INFORMATION.

Discussion

Supplemental information is any performance-related information included as part of a GIPS Pooled Fund Report that supplements or enhances the requirements and/or recommendations of the GIPS standards. Performance-related information includes:

- information expressed in terms of investment return and risk, and
- other information and input data that directly relate to the calculation of investment return and risk (e.g., pooled fund holdings), as well as information derived from investment return and risk input data (e.g., performance contribution or attribution).

Supplemental information should provide users of the GIPS Pooled Fund Report with the proper context in which to understand the performance results. Common examples of supplemental information include the following:

- segment returns that do not include cash,
- money-weighted returns (MWRs) when the firm does not meet the tests for presenting only MWRs, and
- a price-only benchmark presented in addition to a total return benchmark.

Supplemental information must relate directly to the pooled fund and must not contradict or conflict with the required or recommended information in the GIPS Pooled Fund Report. Examples of information that relates directly to the pooled fund and would be considered supplemental information include segment returns (e.g., country or sector), performance attribution, and pooled fund holdings. An example of information that would conflict with the GIPS standards is the presentation of a price-only benchmark when no total return benchmark is presented.

The following is a more complete list of the principles that apply when supplemental information is presented. Supplemental information must:

- satisfy the spirit and principles of the GIPS standards—fair representation and full disclosure,
- comply with all applicable laws and regulations regarding the calculation and presentation of performance,
- not include performance or performance-related information that is false or misleading,
- relate directly to the pooled fund and supplement or enhance the required or recommended information included in the pooled fund's GIPS Pooled Fund Report,
- not contradict or conflict with the required or recommended information in the GIPS Pooled Fund Report,
- be clearly labeled as supplemental information, and
- not be shown with greater prominence than the required pooled fund information.

6.B. Presentation and Reporting—Recommendations

Provision 6.B.1

The FIRM SHOULD present both POOLED FUND GROSS RETURNS and POOLED FUND NET RETURNS.

Discussion

A firm may choose to present either pooled fund gross returns or pooled fund net returns in a GIPS Pooled Fund Report. A firm may also choose to present both pooled fund gross returns and pooled fund net returns in a GIPS Pooled Fund Report. Each type of return provides important information to prospective investors.

Because a pooled fund gross return is the return on investments reduced by any transaction costs, it is the best measure of the firm's investment management ability and can be thought of as the "investment return." In addition, because fees are sometimes negotiable, presenting pooled fund gross returns shows the firm's expertise in managing assets without the effect of the firm's or investor's negotiating skills. Pooled fund gross returns also allow prospective investors to better compare performance between firms.

A pooled fund net return reflects the deduction of all pooled fund fees and costs, including investment management fees, administrative fees, and other costs. Pooled fund net returns therefore provide the best indication to prospective investors of the returns that the firm's investors in a particular fund received or would have received over time, after taking into account the effect of all fees and costs associated with the pooled fund.

Because both pooled fund gross returns and pooled fund net returns provide important information to prospective investors, it is recommended that firms present both pooled fund gross returns and pooled fund net returns in a GIPS Pooled Fund Report.

Provision 6.B.2

The FIRM SHOULD present the following items:

a. Cumulative returns of the POOLED FUND and the BENCHMARK for all periods.

Discussion

Cumulative returns of the pooled fund and benchmark provide additional useful information to prospective investors by indicating the total rate of return for a defined period of performance. It is therefore recommended that cumulative returns for all periods be provided in addition to the required annual returns.

To calculate cumulative returns of a pooled fund for any period, the historical daily, monthly, quarterly, or annual sub-period returns are geometrically linked according to the following formula:

$$R_{CUM} = \left[(1+R_1)\times(1+R_2)\times\ldots\times(1+R_n)\right]-1,$$

where R_1 is the pooled fund return for Period 1 and R_n is the pooled fund return for the most recent period.

Example:

Firm ABC has the following annual returns that were calculated from monthly pooled fund returns:

	Pooled Fund	$1 + R_n$
2015	2.3%	1.023
2016	-4.7%	0.953
2017	6.9%	1.069
2018	3.2%	1.032
2019	0.9%	1.009
Jan 2020–Jun 2020	-3.1%	0.969

To calculate the pooled fund cumulative return for the period from January 2015 through June 2020, the returns are linked:

$$\text{Pooled fund cumulative return} = \left[(1.023)\times(0.953)\times(1.069)\times(1.032)\times(1.009)\times(0.969)\right]-1=0.052, \text{or } 5.2\%.$$

Provision 6.B.2

The FIRM SHOULD present the following items:

b. Quarterly and/or monthly returns.

Discussion

Although the GIPS standards require the presentation of annual returns for the pooled fund and benchmark (Provisions 6.A.1.b and 6.A.1.e), it is recommended that firms present more-frequent returns, such as quarterly or monthly returns. More-frequent returns help prospective investors evaluate a pooled fund's track record. Firms must present benchmark returns for the same periods for which pooled fund returns are presented. If the GIPS Pooled Fund Report includes annual and quarterly pooled fund returns, annual and quarterly benchmark returns must also be presented.

Provision 6.B.2

The FIRM SHOULD present the following items:

c. Annualized POOLED FUND and BENCHMARK returns for periods longer than 12 months.

Discussion

It is recommended that firms show the results of both the pooled fund and the benchmark for periods longer than 12 months in annualized terms to help prospective investors evaluate the pooled fund's track record. Annualized returns are created by calculating the geometric mean, not the arithmetic mean, and represent the geometric average annual compound return achieved over the defined period of more than one year. Sub-period returns during the investment period are geometrically linked to calculate the cumulative return. Then the nth root of the cumulative return is calculated, where n is the number of years in the period. Annualized performance is permitted only for periods of one year or more.

The formula for calculating annualized performance is as follows:

$$\text{Annualized return (\%)} = [(1 + R)^{1/n}] - 1,$$

where R is the cumulative return for the period and n is the number of years in the period.

For example, assume a pooled fund's cumulative return for a five-year period is 150.0%. It has a five-year average annual compound return, or annualized return, of 20.11%, calculated as:

$$\left[(1+1.5)^{\frac{1}{5}}\right]-1=0.2011=20.11\%.$$

If instead the 150% is achieved over 12.5 years, the 12.5-year average annual compound return, or annualized return, is 7.61%, calculated as:

$$\left[(1+1.5)^{\frac{1}{12.5}}\right]-1=0.0761=7.61\%.$$

Provision 6.B.3

For all periods for which an annualized EX POST STANDARD DEVIATION of the POOLED FUND and the BENCHMARK are presented, the FIRM SHOULD present the corresponding annualized return of the POOLED FUND and the BENCHMARK.

Discussion

To provide context so that the prospective investor can better understand the ex post standard deviation, it is recommended that firms present annualized returns for the pooled fund and benchmark for the same periods for which annualized standard deviation is presented. For example, if a firm chooses to present the 5-year, 7-year, and 10-year annualized standard deviations in addition to the required 3-year annualized standard deviation, firms are encouraged to also present the corresponding 3-year, 5-year, 7-year, and 10-year annualized returns for the pooled fund and the benchmark. Doing so will help prospective investors to better interpret risk and return in the context of the return distribution for all periods for which an annualized standard deviation is presented.

Provision 6.B.4

For all periods greater than three years for which an annualized return of the POOLED FUND and the BENCHMARK are presented, the FIRM SHOULD present the corresponding annualized EX POST STANDARD DEVIATION (using monthly returns) of the POOLED FUND and the BENCHMARK.

Discussion

To provide context so that the prospective investor can interpret the annualized pooled fund and benchmark returns, it is recommended that firms present the annualized ex post standard deviation (using monthly returns) for both the pooled fund and benchmark for the same periods that annualized pooled fund and benchmark returns are presented. For example, if a firm chooses to present the 5-year, 7-year, and 10-year annualized pooled fund and benchmark returns, firms are encouraged to also present the corresponding 5-year, 7-year, and 10-year annualized ex post standard deviations of the pooled fund and benchmark. Doing so will help prospective investors to assess and compare risk and return for all periods for which annualized returns are presented.

Provision 6.B.5

The FIRM SHOULD present relevant EX POST ADDITIONAL RISK MEASURES for the POOLED FUND and the BENCHMARK.

Discussion

For pooled funds for which monthly pooled fund returns are available, firms must present the three-year annualized ex post standard deviation (using monthly returns) of the pooled fund and the benchmark as of each annual period end. This is required for periods ending on or after 1 January 2011. (See Provision 6.A.1.h.) Additional risk measures are risk measures included in a GIPS Pooled Fund Report beyond those required to be presented. It is recommended that firms present relevant ex post additional risk measures for the pooled fund and benchmark in a GIPS Pooled Fund Report. Currently, there is no single risk measure that comprehensively and consistently captures every risk to which an asset class, product, or strategy is exposed or sensitive. Also, there may be additional risk measures that would be especially helpful to prospective investors when interpreting a pooled fund's return. There are many risk and quantitative measures that are routinely calculated to help a reader evaluate and understand the return and risk characteristics of a particular investment strategy. Determining which risk measures are relevant to a pooled fund requires an understanding of the characteristics and limitations of each measure and insight into the portfolio construction process and investment strategy. Several risk measures are commonly used within the industry, but there is less of a consensus over what constitutes relevant risk measures when evaluating pooled funds containing derivatives, alternatives, and/or illiquid assets. Some firms have developed proprietary measures, which, despite providing insight into the strategy, make comparisons across managers problematic.

A number of factors should be considered when selecting relevant risk measures, including the following:

- Comparability: The risk measure selected should allow objective comparisons across firms to be made.
- Computational transparency: All inputs to the calculation should be readily available and understood.
- Interpretational transparency: In isolation as a single figure or presented as a time series, the risk measure should aid interpretation and provide context to the performance figures presented.
- Investment process or strategy consistency: The risk measure should provide insight into the underlying investment process.
- Risk measure stability: The selected risk measure should be sensitive to market and portfolio movements but should not exhibit excessive range swings such that interpretation of the absolute and relative values is compromised.

Provision 6.B.6

The FIRM SHOULD present more than 10 years of annual performance in the GIPS POOLED FUND REPORT.

 |

Discussion

Once the pooled fund has its initial minimum 5-year (or since-inception) compliant history, the firm must continue to add annual returns to each GIPS Pooled Fund Report for the next 5 years, at a minimum, so that the firm will build up to a 10-year compliant performance record for its pooled funds.

At some point, a firm will have a minimum 10-year compliant track record for a specific pooled fund. When the firm eventually adds an additional annual return to a 10-year track record in a GIPS Pooled Fund Report, the firm may delete the information for the oldest year included or may instead present a longer track record. It is recommended that firms include more than the minimum 10 years of annual performance in a GIPS Pooled Fund Report to provide more information to prospective investors. If any performance is presented that does not comply with the GIPS standards (only allowed for periods prior to 1 January 2006 for real estate and private equity pooled funds and prior to 1 January 2000 for all other pooled funds), firms must disclose the period(s) of non-compliance.

Provision 6.B.7

The FIRM SHOULD present PROPRIETARY ASSETS as a percentage of POOLED FUND assets as of each annual period end.

Discussion

Proprietary assets are assets owned by the firm, the firm's management, and/or the firm's parent company that are managed by the firm. Knowing how much of a pooled fund's assets are proprietary and how much are managed for external investors provides prospective investors with additional insight regarding the pooled fund, especially when a significant percentage of the pooled fund's assets are proprietary assets. If a pooled fund includes proprietary assets, it is recommended that firms present proprietary assets as a percentage of pooled fund assets as of each annual period end.

Provision 6.B.8

If the FIRM uses preliminary, estimated values as FAIR VALUE, the FIRM SHOULD present the percentage of assets in the POOLED FUND that were valued using preliminary, estimated values as of each annual period end.

Discussion

The use of preliminary, estimated values as fair value is common for some alternative strategies, including those that invest in underlying funds for which the firm relies on valuations provided by the underlying fund managers. When using preliminary, estimated values as fair value, it is important to remember the underlying principles of the GIPS standards: fair representation and full disclosure. If using preliminary, estimated values, firms must disclose this fact in the relevant GIPS Pooled Fund Report (Provision 6.C.32). It is recommended that the firm also present the percentage of assets in the pooled fund that were valued using preliminary, estimated values as of each annual period end. This provides important information that allows prospective investors to better assess the valuations and performance record presented.

Provision 6.B.9

For REAL ESTATE POOLED FUNDS, the FIRM SHOULD present POOLED FUND and BENCHMARK COMPONENT RETURNS for all periods presented.

Discussion

For real estate pooled funds, it is recommended that firms also present pooled fund and benchmark component returns in addition to total returns. Component returns separate the total return into a capital return and an income return. Component returns provide additional information to prospective investors regarding the sources of the total return and the nature of the investment strategy. The income return is generally viewed as more stable than the capital return. Real estate investors typically want to know the contribution from the income and capital returns.

The following are examples of formulas that may be used to calculate the income return and capital return for a real estate pooled fund. The formulas presented use the following terms:

r_t^{GI} = gross income return for period t

r_t^{NI} = net income return for period t

r_t^{GC} = gross capital return for period t

r_t^{NC} = net capital return for period t

r_t^{GT} = gross total return for period t

r_t^{NT} = net total return for period t

NII_t = net investment income (after interest expense, advisory fees, and any performance-based fees allocated to the income component for performance calculation purposes) for period t

 |

AF_t = advisory fee (asset-based portion of investment management fee expensed, including any acquisition and disposition fees that are included as an advisory fee and excluding any performance-based fees) for period t

PF_t^C = performance-based fees allocated to the capital component (for performance calculation purposes) for period t

PF_t^I = performance-based fees allocated to the income component (for performance calculation purposes) for period t

V_t^B = the beginning value of the pooled fund for period t

V_t^E = the ending value of the pooled fund for period t

FC_t = fees charged by the firm and capitalized for accounting purposes but treated as an investment management fee for performance purposes for the period t (including acquisition and disposition fees)

j = the number of external cash flows (1, 2, 3, . . . , J) in period t

$CF_{j,t}$ = the value of cash flow j in period t

$W_{j,t}$ = the weight of cash flow j in period t (assuming the cash flow occurred at the end of the day) as calculated according to the following formula:

$$w_{j,t} = \frac{D_t - D_{j,t}}{D_t},$$

where

$w_{j,t}$ = the weight of cash flow j in period t, assuming the cash flow occurred at the end of the day

D_t = the total number of calendar days in period t

$D_{j,t}$ = the number of calendar days from the beginning of period t to cash flow j

Acquisition, disposition, and financing services performed by the firm, an affiliate of the firm, or a third party on a particular transaction are considered transaction costs and must be deducted from both pooled fund gross returns and pooled fund net returns. These items (also referred to as "brokerage expenses") are direct costs incurred upon implementation of a particular investment transaction and are considered transaction costs. It is recommended that these transaction costs be accounted for through the capital returns. Please note that the acquisition and disposition transaction costs described earlier are different from investment management fees specifically associated with acquisition and disposition services performed by the firm. It is common practice in the real estate industry to have investment management agreements separate the investment management fee into one or more of the following components: base investment management, acquisition, disposition, and financing. In this scenario, the fees specifically relating to acquisition and disposition are typically considered to be part of the investment management fee because these relate to the investment management responsibilities performed by the firm in formulating its investment decisions as part of the normal investment decision-making process. Financing fees, if applicable, are typically identified separately in the investment management agreement and are classified as transaction costs because they are usually related to post-acquisition refinancing.

The term "net investment income" is intended to reflect the effect of ownership and financing structures and includes all underlying property-level activity. Investment-level returns are distinct from property-level returns. Investment-level returns reflect the effect of ownership and financing structures and include all underlying property-level activity. Property-level returns exclude all of the non-property (investment-level) balance sheet items, as well as income and expenses, and include only those income and expenses that directly relate to the operation of the property. Property-level returns are not used for reporting performance in compliance with the GIPS standards, although they may be shown as supplemental information.

Income Return

The income return measures the investment income earned on all investments (including cash and cash equivalents) during the measurement period, net of all non-recoverable expenditures, interest expense on debt, and property taxes. The income return is computed as a percentage of the capital employed. Capital employed is defined as the "weighted average equity" (weighted average capital) during the measurement period. Capital employed does not include any income return or capital return earned during the measurement period. Beginning capital is adjusted by weighting the external cash flows that occurred during the period.

The numerator in the gross income return represents the investment income for the pooled fund during the period, including any income earned during the period at the investment level, and also reflects all income, fees, and expenses at the property level.

The formula for gross income return is as follows:

$$r_t^{GI} = \frac{NII_t + AF_t + PF_t^I}{V_t^B + \sum_{j=1}^{J}\left(CF_{j,t} \times W_{j,t}\right)}.$$

The numerator in the net income return represents the net investment income for the pooled fund during the period. This figure would include any income earned and expenses and fees deducted at the investment level and all income, fees, and expenses at the property level.

The formula for net income return is as follows:

$$r_t^{NI} = \frac{NII_t}{V_t^B + \sum_{j=1}^{J}\left(CF_{j,t} \times W_{j,t}\right)}.$$

 |

Capital Return

The capital return is the change in value of the real estate investments and cash and/or cash equivalent assets held throughout the measurement period, adjusted for all capital expenditures (subtracted) and net proceeds from sales (added). The capital return is computed as a percentage of the capital employed. Capital return is also known as "capital appreciation return" or "appreciation return."

The capital return numerator reflects the change (increase or decrease) in investment value adjusted for capital improvements, sales, refinancing, and net investment income activity. The numerator includes both realized gains/losses and the change in unrealized gains/losses from the prior period.

The net capital return reflects the deduction of any performance-based (incentive) fees attributable to the capital component for performance calculation purposes. This figure would exclude any performance-based fees attributable to the income component for performance calculation purposes.

The formula for gross capital return is as follows:

$$r_t^{GC} = \frac{V_t^E - V_t^B - \sum_{j=1}^{J} CF_{j,t} - NII_t + PF_t^C + FC_t}{V_t^B + \sum_{j=1}^{J}\left(CF_{j,t} \times W_{j,t}\right)}.$$

The formula for net capital return is as follows:

$$r_t^{NC} = \frac{V_t^E - V_t^B - \sum_{j=1}^{J} CF_{j,t} - NII_t}{V_t^B + \sum_{j=1}^{J}\left(CF_{j,t} \times W_{j,t}\right)}.$$

Total Return

The total return is the percentage change in value of real estate investments, including all capital return and income return components, expressed as a percentage of the capital employed over the measurement period. The total return numerator measures the change (increase or decrease) in investment value from both income (loss) and realized and unrealized gains and losses.

The formula for gross total return is as follows:

$$r_t^{GT} = \frac{V_t^E - V_t^B - \sum_{j=1}^{J} CF_{j,t} + AF_t + PF_t^I + PF_t^C + FC_t}{V_t^B + \sum_{j=1}^{J}\left(CF_{j,t} \times W_{j,t}\right)}.$$

The formula for net total return is as follows:

$$r_t^{NT} = \frac{V_t^E - V_t^B - \sum_{j=1}^{J} CF_{j,t}}{V_t^B + \sum_{j=1}^{J}\left(CF_{j,t} \times W_{j,t}\right)}.$$

The formulas for calculating gross component returns and gross total returns assume that no administrative fees were charged. If administrative fees are charged to the fund, the firm should adjust the numerator in the gross return formulas to add back any administrative fees.

All performance results, both total returns and component returns, must be clearly identified so that prospective investors can properly interpret and compare performance. In order to interpret performance data, prospective investors need to know what the performance results represent.

Provision 6.B.10

For POOLED FUNDS OF FUNDS, the FIRM SHOULD present the percentage, if any, of POOLED FUND assets that is invested in DIRECT INVESTMENTS (rather than in fund investment vehicles) as of each annual period end.

Discussion

Direct investments by a fund of funds are investments made directly in companies rather than investments made through pooled funds. Direct investments may augment the strategy used in the investment in underlying pooled funds. Direct investments may have different terms and conditions that might change the return characteristics of the fund of funds, such as a different fee structure. By presenting the percentage of investments dedicated to direct investments as of each annual period end, the firm is providing additional transparency and allowing the prospective investor to factor in additional criteria when analyzing the returns included in the GIPS Pooled Fund Report for the fund of funds. If no assets are invested in direct investments, this recommendation is not applicable.

Provision 6.B.11

If the FIRM has COMMITTED CAPITAL, the FIRM SHOULD present FIRM-wide uncalled COMMITTED CAPITAL as of each annual period end.

Discussion

Committed capital is defined as pledges of capital to an investment vehicle by investors (limited partners and the general partner) or the firm and is typically drawn down over a period of time.

Uncalled committed capital, also known as dry powder, is the amount of capital that has not yet been drawn. If a firm has committed capital, it is recommended that the firm present total firm-wide uncalled committed capital as of each annual period end. This information provides prospective investors a more complete picture of the capital that is currently committed to a future investment. If the firm chooses to present firm-wide uncalled committed capital, it may present this amount separately from total firm assets. The firm may also choose to present the combination of total firm assets and firm-wide uncalled committed capital. Provision 6.A.7 discusses the requirements relating to the presentation of firm-wide uncalled committed capital in a GIPS Pooled Fund Report.

Provision 6.B.12

The FIRM SHOULD present the total FAIR VALUE of the FIRM'S co-investments related to the POOLED FUND as of each annual period end.

Discussion

Direct investments are investments made directly in companies rather than investments through pooled fund investments. Co-investments are a type of direct investment in which pooled fund investors invest additional capital alongside the pooled fund's investments. It is recommended that the firm present the total fair value of the firm's co-investments related to the pooled fund as of the most recent annual period end. This information will give prospective investors a more complete picture of the nature of the investments related to the pooled fund.

6.C. Disclosure—Requirements

Provision 6.C.1

Once the FIRM has met all the applicable REQUIREMENTS of the GIPS standards, the FIRM MUST disclose its compliance with the GIPS standards using one of the following compliance statements. The compliance statement for a POOLED FUND MUST only be used in a GIPS POOLED FUND REPORT.

a. For a FIRM that is verified:

   "[Insert name of FIRM] claims compliance with the Global Investment Performance Standards (GIPS®) and has prepared and presented this report in compliance with the GIPS standards. [Insert name of FIRM] has been independently verified for the periods [insert dates]. The verification report(s) is/are available upon request.

"A firm that claims compliance with the GIPS standards must establish policies and procedures for complying with all the applicable requirements of the GIPS standards. Verification provides assurance on whether the firm's policies and procedures related to composite and pooled fund maintenance, as well as the calculation, presentation, and distribution of performance, have been designed in compliance with the GIPS standards and have been implemented on a firm-wide basis. Verification does not provide assurance on the accuracy of any specific performance report."

b. For POOLED FUNDS of a verified FIRM that have also had a PERFORMANCE EXAMINATION:

"[Insert name of FIRM] claims compliance with the Global Investment Performance Standards (GIPS®) and has prepared and presented this report in compliance with the GIPS standards. [Insert name of FIRM] has been independently verified for the periods [insert dates].

"A firm that claims compliance with the GIPS standards must establish policies and procedures for complying with all the applicable requirements of the GIPS standards. Verification provides assurance on whether the firm's policies and procedures related to composite and pooled fund maintenance, as well as the calculation, presentation, and distribution of performance, have been designed in compliance with the GIPS standards and have been implemented on a firm-wide basis. The [insert name of POOLED FUND] has had a performance examination for the periods [insert dates]. The verification and performance examination reports are available upon request."

The compliance statement for a FIRM that is verified or for POOLED FUNDS of a verified FIRM that have also had a PERFORMANCE EXAMINATION is complete only when both paragraphs are shown together, one after the other.

c. For a FIRM that has not been verified:

"[Insert name of FIRM] claims compliance with the Global Investment Performance Standards (GIPS®) and has prepared and presented this report in compliance with the GIPS standards. [Insert name of FIRM] has not been independently verified."

The FIRM MUST NOT exclude any portion of the respective compliance statement. Any modifications to the compliance statement MUST be additive.

Discussion

A firm meeting all the requirements of the GIPS standards must use one of the three compliance statements in each of its GIPS Pooled Fund Reports. The English version of the compliance statements is the controlling version. If a firm chooses to translate the claim of compliance into a language for which there is no official translation of the GIPS standards, the firm must take care to ensure that the translation used reflects the required wording of the claim of compliance used in Provisions 6.C.1.a, 6.C.1.b, or 6.C.1.c.

It is acceptable to combine both paragraphs of the claim of compliance for a verified firm (Provision 6.C.1.a) into a single paragraph. If the paragraphs are not combined, the claim of compliance for a verified firm is complete only when both paragraphs are shown together, one after the other. A firm may not separate the two required paragraphs from each other.

The same is true for the claim of compliance for a pooled fund that has also had a performance examination (Provision 6.C.1.b). Both paragraphs of the claim of compliance may be combined into a single paragraph. If the paragraphs are not combined, the claim of compliance is complete only when both paragraphs are shown together, one after the other. A firm may not separate the two required paragraphs from each other.

When preparing the GIPS Pooled Fund Report for a pooled fund that has had a performance examination, the firm may choose to use either the verification or performance examination compliance statement. For example, a firm might choose to use the verification compliance statement for all GIPS Reports, including GIPS Reports for composites or pooled funds that have had a performance examination, if it wishes to standardize the compliance statement for all GIPS Reports throughout the firm. In this situation, the firm may also disclose that a specific composite or pooled fund has had a performance examination.

The language in each compliance statement must not exclude any portion of the respective compliance statement, with one exception. In the second paragraph of both 6.C.1.a and 6.C.1.b, there is a reference to "composite and pooled fund maintenance." The firm may delete the words "composite and" if no composites are included within the definition of the firm.

There may also be instances where it may be appropriate for a firm to modify the language slightly. For example, a firm may modify the language to include the name of the firm's verifier, if the firm wishes to disclose this information. A firm may also need to modify the language to add more details about the name of the firm that has been verified or the dates of the verification if the verification period was not continuous. Any modifications must be additive and must not result in a compliance statement that is false or misleading.

Provision 6.C.2

The FIRM MUST disclose the following: "GIPS® is a registered trademark of CFA Institute. CFA Institute does not endorse or promote this organization, nor does it warrant the accuracy or quality of the content contained herein."

Discussion

"GIPS®" is a registered trademark of CFA Institute, and firms are required to acknowledge this in all GIPS Pooled Fund Reports. The required disclosure may appear in the body of the GIPS Pooled Fund Report or in a footnote to the report. The term "this organization", which is included in the required disclosure, refers to any entity associated with the GIPS Pooled Fund Report, either the firm or the verifier.

CFA Institute (owner of the GIPS® trademark) may take appropriate action against any firm that misuses the mark "GIPS®" or any compliance statement, including false claims of compliance with the GIPS standards. CFA Institute members, CFA Program charterholders, CFA candidates, CIPM Program certificants, and CIPM candidates who misuse the term "GIPS" or any compliance statement, misrepresent their performance history or the performance history of their firm, or falsely claim compliance with the GIPS standards are also subject to disciplinary sanctions under the CFA Institute Code of Ethics and Standards of Professional Conduct. Possible disciplinary sanctions include public censure, suspension of membership, and revocation of the CFA charter or CIPM certificate.

Regulators with jurisdiction over firms claiming compliance with the GIPS standards may also take enforcement actions against firms that falsely claim compliance with the GIPS standards.

Firms may also use the following language to replace the first sentence in this required disclosure: "GIPS® is a registered trademark owned by CFA Institute." See the GIPS Standards Trademark Usage Guidelines on the CFA Institute website (www.cfainstitute.org) for additional guidance on the proper use of "GIPS".

Provision 6.C.3

The FIRM MUST disclose the definition of the FIRM used to determine TOTAL FIRM ASSETS and FIRM-wide compliance.

Discussion

To claim compliance with the GIPS standards, a firm must comply with all applicable requirements of the GIPS standards on a firm-wide basis. Accordingly, the firm must determine exactly how it will be defined for the purpose of compliance. The GIPS standards require that a firm must be defined as an investment firm, subsidiary, or division held out to the public as a distinct business entity.

A distinct business entity is a unit, division, department, or office that is organizationally and functionally segregated from other units, divisions, departments, or offices, that retains discretion over the assets it manages, and that should have autonomy over the investment decision-making process.

Possible criteria that can be used to determine this status include:

- being a legal entity,
- having a distinct market or client type (e.g., institutional, retail, private client), and
- using a separate and distinct investment process.

See Provision 1.A.2 for a more detailed discussion of defining the firm.

Because there are often a number of closely related units or divisions within larger investment management entities, it is critical to disclose the precise definition of the firm that is presenting the performance results and would be responsible for the management of the pooled fund. This provision requires the firm to disclose sufficient details of the entity that is presenting investment performance such that the firm is clearly identified.

Sample Disclosures:

Example 1:

Firm A is a multinational investment firm with offices around the world, including in Japan, Australia, the United Kingdom, and the United States. Although all of its offices are part of the global parent company, each office is registered with the appropriate national regulatory authority, and each is held out to investors and prospective investors as a distinct business entity. The firm has defined its offices in Japan, Australia, the United Kingdom, and the United States as separate firms for the purpose of complying with the GIPS standards. The offices in Japan, the United Kingdom, and the United States claim compliance with the GIPS standards. Firm A's Australia office, however, does not claim compliance with the GIPS standards.

Sample Disclosure for Firm A—US:

"For the purpose of complying with the GIPS standards, the firm is defined as Firm A—US, which serves US clients and investors and is a subsidiary of Firm A, a multinational investment firm with offices globally. Firm A also has subsidiaries in the United Kingdom, Australia, and Japan, which are not included in the definition of the firm for purposes of compliance with the GIPS standards."

Example 2:

Firm B has two divisions, each of which serves a distinct client type. Firm B Institutional Investment Management manages institutional assets. Firm B Retail Investors manages retail assets. The firm has determined that it will create two separate firms for the purpose of complying with the GIPS standards.

Sample Disclosure for Firm B Institutional Investment Management:

"For the purpose of complying with the GIPS standards, the firm is defined as Firm B Institutional Investment Management, the institutional asset management division of Firm B."

Example 3:

Firm C is an investment management firm that offers both active and passive (indexed) investment strategies. For the purpose of complying with the GIPS standards, the firm has decided to create two separate firms: one that offers active investment strategies and one that offers indexed investment strategies.

Sample Disclosure for Firm C–Indexed Investing:

"For the purpose of complying with the GIPS standards, the firm is defined as Firm C—Indexed Investing. Firm C—Indexed Investing is the division of Firm C that offers indexed investment strategies to investors."

Provision 6.C.4

The FIRM MUST disclose the POOLED FUND DESCRIPTION.

Discussion

The pooled fund description is defined as general information regarding the investment mandate, objective, or strategy of the pooled fund. The pooled fund description must include enough information to allow a prospective investor to understand the key characteristics of the pooled fund's investment mandate, objective, or strategy, including:

- the material risks of the pooled fund's strategy,
- how leverage, derivatives, and short positions may be used, if they are a material part of the strategy, and
- if illiquid investments are a material part of the strategy.

The required disclosure of the pooled fund description provides information about the pooled fund's investment strategy that is intended to help a prospective investor who is considering an investment in a pooled fund and is reviewing a GIPS Pooled Fund Report for that pooled fund. The pooled fund description should provide sufficient information to prospective investors to allow them to differentiate the significant features of the pooled fund from other strategies or pooled funds within the firm and to compare products across firms. The disclosed strategy features will likely affect both the historical and expected risk and returns. Along with the required benchmark description (see Provision 6.C.5), the GIPS Pooled Fund Report will allow prospective investors to understand both the investment strategy employed and the benchmark against which the pooled fund's performance is evaluated. This will help prospective investors to compare investments across firms.

If leverage, derivatives, and short positions may be used, and they are a material part of the strategy, this must be disclosed in the pooled fund description. Provision 6.C.15 requires that the firm disclose how leverage, derivatives, and short positions have been used historically, if material. Taken together, these two required disclosures provide a more complete picture about the presence, use, and extent of leverage, derivatives, and short positions. When determining what would be material, the firm must consider whether the disclosure of how leverage, derivatives, and/or short positions may be used and/or have been used historically is likely to affect a prospective investor's view of the risk involved in the pooled fund's strategy. If so, it would be misleading for the firm to fail to disclose their use to these prospective investors when describing the strategy.

Generally, all investment products or strategies have some degree of inherent risk (e.g., market risk), but it is not intended that the pooled fund description identifies every risk of the pooled fund's strategy. Instead, firms must identify those material risks of the strategy, if any, and must disclose those risks. For example, investment concentration, correlation (or lack thereof), liquidity, and exposure to counterparties are features that may need to be included in the pooled fund description.

The key characteristics of some pooled fund strategies may change given market events. Firms should periodically review pooled fund descriptions to ensure they are current.

Sample Disclosures:

"The Large Cap Equity Growth Fund invests in large-capitalization US stocks that are considered to have growth in earnings prospects that is superior to that of the average company within the benchmark, the XYZ Large Cap Growth Index. The targeted tracking error between the pooled fund and the benchmark is less than 3%."

"The Leveraged Bond Pooled Fund invests in a diversified range of high-yield corporate and government bonds with the aim of providing investors with a high level of income while seeking to maximize the total return. The fund is invested in domestic and international fixed-income securities of varying maturities. The strategy allows investment in exchange-traded and OTC derivative contracts (including, but not limited to, options, futures, swaps, and forward currency contracts) for the purposes of risk, volatility, and currency exposure management. The strategy allows leverage up to but not exceeding twice the value of the fund's investments through the use of repurchase financing arrangements with counterparties. Inherent in derivative instrument investments is the risk of counterparty default. Leverage may also magnify losses as well as gains to the extent that leverage is employed. The benchmark is the XYZ Capital Global Aggregate Bond Index."

"The Juneau Private Placement Bond Fund invests in investment-grade, long-term, fixed-rate private placement bonds denominated in Canadian dollars, in a variety of industries. Private placement bonds are illiquid investments and have restrictions on transferability. The fund primarily invests in private placement bonds with maturities greater than 10 years that are, therefore, sensitive to changes in interest rates. Investments in the fund are subject to credit risk."

A Sample List of Pooled Fund Descriptions can be found in Appendix D of the GIPS standards.

Provision 6.C.5

The FIRM MUST disclose:

a. The BENCHMARK DESCRIPTION, which MUST include the key features of the BENCHMARK or the name of the BENCHMARK for a readily recognized index or other point of reference.
b. The PERIODICITY of the BENCHMARK if BENCHMARK returns are calculated less frequently than monthly.

Discussion

Firms are required to disclose a description of each benchmark included in a GIPS Pooled Fund Report. The benchmark description is defined as general information regarding the investments, structure, and/or characteristics of the benchmark, and it must include the key features of the benchmark. In the case of a widely recognized benchmark, such as the S&P 500® Index, the name of the benchmark will satisfy this requirement. (S&P 500® is a registered trademark of Standard & Poor's Financial Services LLC.) Each firm must decide for itself whether a benchmark is widely recognized. If the firm is not certain as to whether the benchmark is widely known, the firm must include the benchmark description.

If the benchmark returns are calculated less frequently than monthly, the periodicity of the benchmark must be disclosed.

Sample Disclosure for a Widely Recognized Benchmark:

"The benchmark is the S&P 500® Index."

Sample Disclosure for a Benchmark That Is Not Widely Recognized:

"The benchmark is the XYZ World Index, which is designed to measure the equity market performance of developed market countries. The benchmark is market-cap weighted and is composed of all XYZ country-specific developed market indices."

Sample Disclosure for an Index with Returns Calculated Less Frequently than Monthly:

"The ABC Property Index (API) is a quarterly, unleveraged composite total return for private commercial real estate properties held for investment purposes only. All properties in the API have been acquired, at least in part, on behalf of tax-exempt institutional investors."

> **Provision 6.C.6**
>
> When presenting POOLED FUND GROSS RETURNS, the FIRM MUST disclose if any other fees are deducted in addition to TRANSACTION COSTS.

Discussion

A pooled fund gross return is the return on investments reduced by any transaction costs. If a firm presents pooled fund gross returns in a GIPS Pooled Fund Report, the firm must disclose if any other fees are deducted in addition to transaction costs. For example, a pooled fund's gross returns might reflect the deduction of administrative expenses, such as custodian and fund accounting fees. The same is true for a fund of funds. Firms are not required to disclose that returns reflect the deduction of expenses incurred in underlying investments, including investments in other pooled funds.

In cases where fees other than transactions costs have been deducted from the pooled fund gross returns, this disclosure helps prospective investors understand the gross returns being presented and therefore compare performance across firms.

Firms may calculate pooled fund gross returns that do not reflect the deduction of the underlying pooled fund investment management fees only when the firm controls the investment management fees of the underlying pooled funds. In such situations, the firm can present the pooled fund gross returns that are gross of the underlying funds' investment management fees but net of the underlying funds' transaction costs and other expenses. The following represent some situations in which this criterion is met:

- Both underlying funds and the fund of funds are managed by the same firm, and there is effectively a fee rebate or waiver at the fund-of-funds level for those fees charged at the underlying fund level.
- A fund of funds resembles a master-feeder structure that invests in one or multiple underlying funds managed by the same firm, and its investment management fee model is structured so that the investment management fee is either partially or fully charged at the underlying fund level.

Sample Disclosure:

"Gross returns reflect the deduction of administrative expenses but do not reflect the deduction of investment management fees."

Provision 6.C.7

When presenting POOLED FUND NET RETURNS, the FIRM MUST disclose:

a. If POOLED FUND NET RETURNS are calculated using model or actual TOTAL POOLED FUND FEES.

b. If POOLED FUND NET RETURNS are net of any PERFORMANCE-BASED FEES or CARRIED INTEREST.

c. If model INVESTMENT MANAGEMENT FEES or model TOTAL POOLED FUND FEES are used and POOLED FUND GROSS RETURNS are not presented, the model INVESTMENT MANAGEMENT FEE or model TOTAL POOLED FUND FEE used to calculate POOLED FUND NET RETURNS.[48]

d. If model INVESTMENT MANAGEMENT FEES or model TOTAL POOLED FUND FEES are used, the methodology used to calculate POOLED FUND NET RETURNS.

e. If the POOLED FUND has a partnership structure, on which assets the POOLED FUND NET RETURNS are calculated.

f. If the POOLED FUND has multiple share classes, and one share class is used to calculate POOLED FUND NET RETURNS, the share class used to calculate POOLED FUND NET RETURNS.

Discussion

When presenting returns, it is important that there are sufficient disclosures so that prospective investors can understand what the returns actually represent.

Pooled fund net returns are required to reflect the deduction of all fees and expenses, including transaction costs, investment management fees, administrative fees, and other costs. When calculating pooled fund net returns, the fees used in the calculation must include both asset-based and performance-based fees. If the pooled fund net returns are net of any performance-based fees or carried interest, that fact must be disclosed.

A firm must disclose if model or actual total pooled fund fees are used to calculate pooled fund net returns. (See Provision 2.A.33 for an explanation of when model total pooled fund fees

[48] REQUIRED for periods ending on or after 31 December 2020.

may be used.) If model fees are used and gross returns are presented along with the net returns, prospective investors can easily determine the model fee used by deducting the net returns from the gross returns. For periods ending on or after 31 December 2020, however, if model investment management fees or model total pooled fund fees have been used and pooled fund gross returns are not presented, the firm must disclose the model investment management fees or model total pooled fund fees used to calculate the pooled fund net returns. The methodology used in the calculation of pooled fund net returns must be disclosed if model investment management fees or model total pooled fund fees are used.

Because general partner assets are not charged an investment management fee, the inclusion of general partner assets in the calculation of pooled fund net returns will boost net returns relative to the returns actually received by pooled fund investors. Therefore, in order for prospective investors to understand the pooled fund net returns presented in a GIPS Pooled Fund Report, if a pooled fund has a partnership structure, firms must disclose whether returns are calculated based on the general partner assets, the limited partner assets, or total pooled fund assets. To present the most relevant returns for prospective investors, it is common practice for pooled fund net returns to be calculated using only the limited partner assets and cash flows.

Pooled funds often have multiple share classes, with each class typically having different fees and expenses. In addition, there are often restrictions on what type of investor can purchase a particular share class. When a pooled fund has multiple share classes, firms must disclose which share class was used to calculate pooled fund net returns. This information will help prospective investors determine if the returns are based on fees and expenses that are high or low relative to the fund's other share classes. It will also help investors determine if the returns are based on a share class for which they are eligible. If the returns are based on a share class for which they are not eligible, a prospective investor can then request information for a share class for which they are eligible.

Sample Disclosure for Actual Total Pooled Fund Fees:

"Pooled fund net returns are net of actual total pooled fund fees, including incentive fees, which are recorded on an accrual basis. Net returns are calculated using the assets of the limited partners."

Sample Disclosure for Model Total Pooled Fund Fees:

"Net returns are calculated by applying a model total pooled fund fee of 0.4125% on a quarterly basis. This equates to a model annual total pooled fund fee of 1.65%. The model fee is based on the actual administrative expenses as stated in the 2019 audited financial statements and applying the highest tier of the standard fee schedule that a limited partner would pay."

Provision 6.C.8

The FIRM MUST disclose which fees and expenses other than INVESTMENT MANAGEMENT FEES (e.g., research costs) are separately charged by the FIRM to investors, if material.

Discussion

Administrative fees and costs are typically paid from a pooled fund's assets. Investment management fees may be paid from a pooled fund's assets or may be separately charged to investors. In some cases, other fees and expenses, such as investment research costs, may be billed by the firm directly to the investor. When any fees or expenses other than investment management fees are separately charged by the firm to investors, and these fees or expenses are material, the firm must disclose which fees and expenses are separately charged. When determining if additional fees or expenses would be considered material, a firm must consider whether the additional fees or expenses are significant enough to reduce a prospective investor's assessment of the attractiveness of the expected returns of the pooled fund relative to total fees charged. If so, the firm's failure to disclose these additional fees or expenses would violate the principle of full disclosure.

Sample Disclosure:

"In addition to the fees charged directly to the pooled fund and reflected in the pooled fund's net returns, investment research costs are charged directly to investors, as stipulated in the pooled fund offering memo."

Provision 6.C.9

The FIRM MUST disclose or otherwise indicate the reporting currency.

Discussion

The GIPS standards require that firms disclose the currency used to report the numerical information presented in a GIPS Pooled Fund Report. If the firm presents performance in multiple currencies in the same GIPS Pooled Fund Report, the firm must ensure it is clear which currencies are used to calculate and report performance and assets.

Labeling the columns within a GIPS Pooled Fund Report with the appropriate currency symbol would satisfy this requirement, as would a written disclosure. If firms market the pooled fund outside their home market, they should consider whether the currency symbol alone is sufficient. For example, a Canadian firm marketing only in Canada may decide to present only the $ symbol.

 |

If the firm markets the pooled fund in both the United States and Canada, the firm must disclose whether the currency is USD or CAD, because both currencies use the same currency symbol.

All required and recommended information presented in a GIPS Pooled Fund Report must be presented in the same currency. (See Provision 6.A.10.)

Sample Disclosures:

"Valuations are computed and all information is reported in Canadian dollars."

"All numerical information is reported in Japanese yen."

Provision 6.C.10

The FIRM MUST disclose the current FEE SCHEDULE appropriate to PROSPECTIVE INVESTORS.

Discussion

Firms must disclose the current schedule of investment management fees that is applicable to prospective investors for the specific pooled fund. The fee schedule can be asset based, performance based, or a combination of both. Firms are also required to disclose the pooled fund's expense ratio, which includes investment management fees as well as all other pooled fund expenses. See Provision 6.A.5 for a discussion of pooled fund expense ratios.

The fee schedule should be appropriate to the particular prospective investor and must be current. Although a current fee schedule may not assist a prospective investor when interpreting historical performance because the actual fees paid may differ from the fee schedule disclosed, it is the most relevant fee schedule for the prospective investor. The actual fee that the prospective investor may pay (if the investor hires the firm) could also differ from the fee schedule disclosed in the GIPS Pooled Fund Report. For example, the prospective investor may be able to negotiate a lower fee.

If the pooled fund has multiple fee schedules, the firm may use the highest fee schedule as the appropriate fee that can be used for all prospective investors. The firm may also include multiple fee schedules in the GIPS Pooled Fund Report. Including a range of fee schedules (e.g., management fees range from 0.50% to 0.95%) would not satisfy this requirement.

This disclosure requirement is not satisfied if the firm does not include the fee schedule in the GIPS Pooled Fund Report and instead makes reference to another document that includes the fee schedule, such as Form ADV, which is a US regulatory document, or a fund prospectus. The fee schedule may be an exhibit attached to the GIPS Pooled Fund Report. The exhibit may be the pooled fund's offering documents, if the offering documents include the appropriate current fee schedule.

Sample Disclosure:

"The annual fee schedule for Fund XYZ is as follows:

First €10 million	0.80%
Next €40 million	0.60%
Above €50 million	0.30%"

Provision 6.C.11

If the FEE SCHEDULE includes PERFORMANCE-BASED FEES or CARRIED INTEREST, the FIRM MUST disclose the PERFORMANCE-BASED FEE DESCRIPTION or CARRIED INTEREST DESCRIPTION.

Discussion

Sufficient information must be included with any fee schedule included in a GIPS Pooled Fund Report to allow prospective investors to understand the nature of the firm's compensation. If performance-based fees or carried interest are included in the fee schedule, the firm must disclose a description of the performance-based fees and/or carried interest. Relevant information for a performance-based fee includes the performance-based fee rate, hurdle rate, clawback, high watermark, reset frequency, accrual frequency, crystallization schedule, and on what basis fees are charged. Relevant information for carried interest includes the hurdle rate, crystallization schedule, and high watermark.

Sample Disclosure:

"The standard fee schedule is as follows:

Management fee is 0.75% per annum, charged on a quarterly basis on the period-end value of fund net assets.

Performance fee:

The performance fee is earned when the fund's total return, reduced by the pro rata accrued fixed management fee, exceeds the benchmark return (the excess return) and the fund's net asset value is above the high watermark, which is the fund's net asset value as of the last year end when the performance fee crystallized. The performance fee is 10% of the excess return, which is calculated arithmetically, accrued quarterly, and crystallizes annually. Further details of the performance fee calculation are available upon request."

Provision 6.C.12

The FIRM MUST disclose the POOLED FUND INCEPTION DATE and what the POOLED FUND INCEPTION DATE represents.

Discussion

When reviewing the performance data in a GIPS Pooled Fund Report, it is important that prospective investors have sufficient information regarding the length of the pooled fund track record to put the performance presented in the GIPS Pooled Fund Report in perspective. Therefore, the inception date of the pooled fund being presented in the GIPS Pooled Fund Report must be disclosed. Prospective investors can then compare the periods of performance presented in the GIPS Pooled Fund Report with the length of the pooled fund's track record, and they can request additional information for historical periods not included in the GIPS Pooled Fund Report.

Because an inception date may represent a different point in the life of a fund for different funds, a firm must also disclose what the pooled fund inception date represents. For example, for a broad distribution pooled fund, the inception date is the date on which the fund commences operations and begins trading. For a limited distribution fund, the inception date may be based on one of the following dates: (1) when investment management fees are first charged, (2) when the first investment-related cash flow takes place, (3) when the first capital call is made, or (4) when the first committed capital is closed and legally binding. It is only with appropriate disclosure that prospective investors can understand what the inception date represents.

Sample Disclosure for a Broad Distribution Pooled Fund:

"The Small Cap Growth Fund has an inception date of 1 May 2017, the date on which the Fund began operations."

Sample Disclosure for a Limited Distribution Pooled Fund:

"The Global Growth Fund has an inception date of 15 September 2019, the date of the first capital call from the Fund's limited partners."

Provision 6.C.13

The FIRM MUST disclose that the following lists are available upon request, if applicable:

a. List of COMPOSITE DESCRIPTIONS.

b. List of POOLED FUND DESCRIPTIONS for LIMITED DISTRIBUTION POOLED FUNDS.

c. List of BROAD DISTRIBUTION POOLED FUNDS.

Discussion

In each GIPS Pooled Fund Report, firms must disclose that a list of composite descriptions and a list of pooled fund descriptions for limited distribution pooled funds (LDPFs) are available upon request, if applicable to the firm. The firm must also disclose that a list of broad distribution pooled funds (BDPFs) is available upon request, if BDPFs are included within the definition of the firm. The required list of LDPF descriptions and of BDPFs is at the fund level and not the share class level.

If the firm does not sell participation in a fund (e.g., the firm manages the assets but another legal entity distributes the fund and the firm does not sell shares in the fund), the firm must consider the portfolio a segregated account and would include the portfolio in a composite. This would include sub-advised pooled funds. The segregated account would not be included on the list of LDPF descriptions or the list of BDPFs. In addition, a portfolio with a pooled fund wrapper, (i.e., a single-investor pooled fund), which is unitized but is not available to other investors, is also considered a segregated account, would be included in a composite, and would not appear on a list of LDPF descriptions or a list of BDPFs.

As noted in the discussion of Provision 1.A.22, if a pooled fund is included in a composite but the firm offers participation in the fund, either directly or through an agent, the pooled fund must still appear on the required list of LDPF descriptions or the list of BDPFs, as appropriate.

The firm may combine its list of composite descriptions, its list of LDPF descriptions, and its list of BDPFs into one document if it wishes to do so. The firm may also prepare a list of all of the strategies that it offers and may indicate, as part of the strategy description, the types of portfolios (segregated account, LDPF, or BDPF) in which the strategy is available. This list of strategies can be in narrative or table format.

This requirement exists to provide prospective investors with a complete picture of the firm's composites and pooled funds. Prospective investors may then request information that will allow them to evaluate whether the GIPS Pooled Fund Report they have received is the most appropriate and to determine if there are any other GIPS Composite Reports or GIPS Pooled Fund Reports that they should also request to see.

a. List of COMPOSITE DESCRIPTIONS.

If composites are included within the definition of the firm, the firm must disclose, in each GIPS Pooled Fund Report, that the firm's list of composite descriptions is available upon request. The list of composite descriptions itself does not need to be included in each GIPS Pooled Fund Report but must be available upon request. The list of composite descriptions must include the composite description for each current composite, as well as a description for all composites that have terminated in the past five years. The composite descriptions disclosed in GIPS Composite Reports must be consistent with the descriptions included in the list of composite descriptions.

An explanation of composite descriptions can be found in the discussion of Provision 1.A.22. A Sample List of Composite Descriptions can be found in Appendix D of the GIPS standards.

b. List of POOLED FUND DESCRIPTIONS for LIMITED DISTRIBUTION POOLED FUNDS.

If LDPFs are included within the definition of a firm, the firm must disclose, in each GIPS Pooled Fund Report, that the firm's list of descriptions of LDPFs is available upon request. An LDPF is any pooled fund that is not a BDPF. A BDPF is any pooled fund that is regulated under a framework that would permit the general public to purchase or hold the pooled fund's shares and is not exclusively offered in one-on-one presentations. LDPFs are often referred to as "private funds." These funds are typically sold in one-on-one presentations and may not be highly regulated. The list of LDPF descriptions does not need to be included in each GIPS Pooled Fund Report but must be available upon request. The list of LDPF descriptions must include the pooled fund description for each current pooled fund but does not have to include terminated funds. Terminated LDPFs are treated differently from terminated composites because, although a firm can restart a composite strategy when a prospective client hires the firm for a strategy that was previously closed, the firm does not have the same ability to restart a pooled fund. The pooled fund descriptions disclosed in GIPS Pooled Fund Reports must be consistent with the descriptions included in the list of pooled fund descriptions.

The list of LDPF descriptions may be tailored to include only those LDPFs for which a prospective investor is eligible, but the firm is not required to do this.

An explanation of LDPF descriptions can be found in the discussion of Provision 1.A.22. A Sample List of Pooled Fund Descriptions can be found in Appendix D of the GIPS standards.

c. List of BROAD DISTRIBUTION POOLED FUNDS.

In addition to the lists of composite descriptions and LDPF descriptions, firms must also disclose, in each GIPS Pooled Fund Report, that a list of BDPFs is available upon request, if applicable to the firm. A BDPF is any pooled fund that is regulated under a framework that would permit the general public to purchase or hold the pooled fund's shares and is not exclusively offered in one-on-one presentations. These funds are typically sold to the general public and are highly regulated.

Note that the required list of BDPFs is a list of the names of the firm's BDPFs only. No descriptions of the BDPFs are required. The list of BDPF names does not need to be included in each GIPS Pooled Fund Report but must be available upon request. The list of BDPFs must include the names of all current BDPFs but does not need to include terminated BDPFs. Terminated BDPFs are treated differently from terminated composites because, although a firm can restart a composite strategy when a prospective client hires the firm for a strategy that was previously closed, the firm does not have the same ability to restart a pooled fund. If a firm includes information about all of its BDPFs on its website, the firm may provide a link to the website to fulfill the requirement to provide the list of BDPFs upon request.

This list may be tailored to include only those BDPFs for which a prospective investor is eligible, but the firm is not required to do this.

Sample Disclosures:

For Firms with Composites and Limited Distribution Pooled Funds

"A list of composite descriptions and a list of limited distribution pooled fund descriptions are available upon request."

For Firms with Composites, Limited Distribution Pooled Funds, and Broad Distribution Pooled Funds

"A list of composite descriptions, a list of limited distribution pooled fund descriptions, and a list of broad distribution pooled funds are available upon request."

For Firms That Offer Strategies in Multiple Vehicles

"A list of all composite and pooled fund investment strategies offered by the firm, with a description of each strategy, is available upon request. The type of portfolios in which each strategy is available (segregated account, limited distribution pooled fund, or broad distribution pooled fund) is indicated in the description of each strategy."

Provision 6.C.14

The FIRM MUST disclose that policies for valuing investments, calculating performance, and preparing GIPS REPORTS are available upon request.

Discussion

In each GIPS Pooled Fund Report, firms must disclose the availability of policies for valuing investments, calculating performance, and preparing GIPS Reports. The policies are not required to be included in each GIPS Pooled Fund Report but must be available upon request. Firms are not required to provide the related procedures, in addition to the policies, but may do so.

Sample Disclosure:

"Firm XYZ's policies for valuing investments, calculating performance, and preparing GIPS Reports are available upon request."

Provision 6.C.15

The FIRM MUST disclose how leverage, derivatives, and short positions have been used historically, if material.

Discussion

Firms must provide enough information in a GIPS Pooled Fund Report to allow a prospective investor to understand how leverage, derivatives, and short positions have been employed historically and may be used going forward. Although the pooled fund description includes disclosure of the firm's ability to use leverage, derivatives, and short positions (see Provision 6.C.4), Provision 6.C.15 requires that the firm disclose the leverage, derivatives, and short positions that have been used historically, if material. Taken together, these two required disclosures provide a more complete picture of the presence, use, and extent of leverage, derivatives, and short positions.

For example, assume a firm discloses in the pooled fund description that the strategy may employ up to 200% leverage. To satisfy the disclosure requirement in Provision 6.C.15, the firm might state, "Since the inception of the strategy, the leverage has averaged 110% of the pooled fund's value; however, during 2019 the leverage averaged 160%, which greatly increased the sensitivity to market volatility and the potential for realized gains and/or losses."

No disclosure is required if leverage, derivatives, and short positions have not been used or if their use has not been material. When determining what would be material, the firm must consider whether the disclosure of how leverage, derivatives, and/or short positions have been used historically is likely to affect a prospective investor's view of the risk involved in the pooled fund's strategy. If so, it would be misleading for the firm to fail to disclose their use to prospective investors when describing the strategy.

Provision 6.C.16

The FIRM MUST disclose all significant events that would help a PROSPECTIVE INVESTOR interpret the GIPS POOLED FUND REPORT. This disclosure MUST be included for a minimum of one year and for as long as it is relevant to interpreting the track record.

Discussion

The GIPS standards are based on the principles of fair representation and full disclosure. Meeting these objectives requires a good faith commitment on the part of the firm to adhere to the spirit of the GIPS standards. The GIPS standards cannot foresee and cover every situation that might occur. Therefore, this provision requires that firms disclose all significant events that would help explain the firm's GIPS Pooled Fund Report to a prospective investor. The primary goal of this requirement is to provide relevant information to prospective investors so that they can understand the potential effect of the significant event on the pooled fund's investment strategy and the firm.

Significant events are determined by the firm and would include, as examples, a material change in personnel responsible for investment management, significant changes to the investment management process, the loss of historical records resulting from a catastrophic event, or a change in firm ownership. The acquisition of a new entity or selling off part of a firm would also qualify as a significant event, as would the departure of someone who was the single investment decision maker for a strategy.

Depending on the situation, a general statement describing the significant event that has occurred may be sufficient. Other situations may require firms to disclose specific information pertaining to the significant event. The disclosure regarding the significant event must be included in the GIPS Pooled Fund Report for a minimum of one year and for as long as it is relevant to interpreting the performance track record. As an example, a firm that acquires another firm, resulting in a large increase in total firm assets, may disclose this significant event for as long as the large change in total firm assets is included in the GIPS Pooled Fund Report. In contrast, a change in a firm's chief investment officer (CIO) is a change that a firm may believe should be disclosed for one year only.

The firm must consider the underlying principles of the GIPS standards, which are fair representation and full disclosure, when determining how long the disclosure will be included in the GIPS Pooled Fund Report.

Sample Disclosures:

"In June 2017, Firm G determined that the custodian bank used by all of the firm's proprietary mutual funds had failed to file reclaimable withholding tax refund requests with the appropriate

 |

authorities. At that time, all accrued reclaimable withholding taxes were written off, decreasing the Fund's monthly return by 1.06%."

"On 15 April 2018, the quantitative asset management division of Firm Z was sold, resulting in the 2018 decrease in Firm Z's assets."

"In February 2020, the parent company of Firm M announced plans to exit the investment management business and sell Firm M. As of April 2020, a tentative sale of Firm M has been agreed upon but not yet finalized."

Provision 6.C.17

For any performance presented for periods prior to the MINIMUM EFFECTIVE COMPLIANCE DATE that does not comply with the GIPS standards, the FIRM MUST disclose the periods of non-compliance.

Discussion

Firms may link non-GIPS compliant performance to their GIPS-compliant performance provided that only GIPS-compliant performance is presented for periods beginning on or after the minimum effective compliance date, which is 1 January 2006 for private equity and real estate pooled funds and 1 January 2000 for all other pooled funds. (See Provision 1.A.29.) If the firm chooses to present non-compliant performance for periods prior to the minimum effective compliance date, the firm must disclose which periods are not in compliance. Prospective investors and existing investors can then inquire about the reasons why the periods prior to the minimum effective compliance date are not compliant and consider the effects of non-compliance on the historical performance.

If non-compliant performance is included in a GIPS Pooled Fund Report after the minimum effective compliance date, it must be labeled as supplemental information and must not be linked to the GIPS-compliant performance.

Sample Disclosure:

"The performance record for the XYZ Private Equity Fund for 1995 through 1999 is not in compliance with the GIPS standards."

Provision 6.C.18

If the FIRM is redefined, the FIRM MUST disclose the date and description of the redefinition.

Discussion

A firm redefinition occurs when something changes with how the firm is held out to the public or when any of its distinct business entity criteria significantly change. Changes in investment style or personnel are not events that typically cause a firm redefinition. A simple firm name change is also not a sufficient reason to redefine the firm. Corporate restructuring may cause a change with how the firm is held out to the public. As an example, a firm that was defined to include only the institutional division would be redefined when it consolidated the institutional division with the mutual fund/retail division. A merger or acquisition may cause a change in the definition of the firm, but that is not always the case.

Suppose that a firm defines itself as an investment management firm offering active equity strategies to investors. An acquisition that expanded the firm's offerings to include fixed-income strategies would result in a redefinition of the firm, because there would be a change in how the firm holds itself out to the public. An acquisition that simply added additional equity strategies to the firm's offerings would not result in a redefinition of the firm. However, the acquisition is likely to be a significant event that must be disclosed in a GIPS Pooled Fund Report. (See Provision 6.C.16.)

In some cases, as a result of a significant alteration in a firm's structure or organization, a change can be so great that it creates a new firm. See Provision 1.A.2 for guidance on firm definitions.

The GIPS standards require that changes in a firm's organization must not lead to alteration of historical performance (see Provision 1.A.28).

Sample Disclosures:

"As of 1 August 2019, XYZ Firm was redefined to include both the London and Tokyo office of XYZ Company. Previously, the firm was defined to include only the London office."

"As of 1 January 2020, XYZ Investment Management was redefined to include the wrap division."

"Effective 1 January 2019, ABC Capital Management was redefined as an investment management firm offering both equity and fixed-income strategies. Prior to the 31 December 2018 acquisition of Curtone Capital Management, an investment firm offering fixed-income strategies, ABC Capital Management offered only equity strategies."

Provision 6.C.19

If the POOLED FUND'S investment mandate, objective, or strategy is changed, the FIRM MUST disclose the date and description of the change.

Discussion

Investment strategies can change over time. If there is a change in a pooled fund's investment mandate, objective, or strategy, the firm must disclose the date and description of the change.

Sample Disclosure:

"As of 1 July 2017, the strategy for the Fixed Income Pooled Fund includes the use of interest rate futures to modify duration and manage interest rate risk. Prior to this date, the Fund's strategy did not involve the active management of interest rate risk."

Provision 6.C.20

The FIRM MUST disclose changes to the name of the POOLED FUND. This disclosure MUST be included for a minimum of one year and for as long as it is relevant to interpreting the track record.

Discussion

When prospective investors are evaluating pooled funds over time and across firms, it is important that they understand exactly which pooled funds they are assessing. If a firm changes the name of a pooled fund, the change must be disclosed in the GIPS Pooled Fund Report. The name change must be disclosed for a minimum of one year and potentially for more than one year if the firm determines the disclosure is still relevant and meaningful. The firm must consider the underlying principles of the GIPS standards, which are fair representation and full disclosure, when determining how long the disclosure will be included in the GIPS Pooled Fund Report.

Sample Disclosure:

"As of 1 January 2016, the XYZ Index Pooled Fund was renamed the US Equity Large Cap Pooled Fund."

Provision 6.C.21

The FIRM MUST disclose if POOLED FUND returns are gross or net of withholding taxes, if material.

Discussion

Global investing requires recognition of the tax consequences of investing in different countries. The GIPS standards do not require firms to reflect withholding taxes, either reclaimable or non-reclaimable taxes, in a certain manner. Firms may choose whether or not to reflect the effect of withholding taxes when calculating performance. The GIPS standards do recommend that performance be reported net of non-reclaimable withholding taxes on dividends, interest, and capital gains and also recommend that reclaimable foreign withholding taxes be accrued (see Provision 2.B.5). If withholding taxes are material, firms must disclose how withholding taxes are treated when calculating performance. A firm must determine the level at which withholding taxes become material, document this level in its policies and procedures, and apply it consistently.

Sample Disclosure:

"Pooled fund returns are net of all foreign non-reclaimable withholding taxes. Reclaimable withholding taxes are reflected as income if and when received."

Provision 6.C.22

The FIRM MUST disclose if BENCHMARK returns are net of withholding taxes if this information is available.

Discussion

Global investing requires recognition of the tax consequences of investing in different countries. The GIPS standards do not require firms to reflect withholding taxes, either reclaimable or non-reclaimable taxes, in a certain manner. Firms may choose whether or not to reflect the effect of withholding taxes when calculating pooled fund performance and, similarly, whether or not to use a benchmark that reflects the effect of withholding taxes.

As Provision 6.C.21 indicates, if withholding taxes are material, firms must disclose how withholding taxes are treated when calculating performance. To facilitate the comparison of pooled fund returns and benchmark returns, firms must also disclose if the benchmark returns are net of withholding taxes if this information is available. If the benchmark name indicates that the benchmark is net of withholding taxes, no additional disclosure is necessary.

Sample Disclosure:

"Benchmark returns are net of withholding taxes."

Provision 6.C.23

If the GIPS POOLED FUND REPORT conforms with laws and/or regulations that conflict with the REQUIREMENTS of the GIPS standards, the FIRM MUST disclose this fact and disclose the manner in which the laws and/or regulations conflict with the GIPS standards.

Discussion

Firms must comply with all applicable laws and regulations regarding the calculation and presentation of performance. Compliance with applicable laws and regulations, however, does not necessarily result in compliance with the GIPS standards. Firms must also comply with all of the applicable requirements of the GIPS standards. In the rare cases where laws and regulations conflict with the GIPS standards, firms are required to comply with the laws and regulations and disclose the manner in which the laws and/or regulations conflict with the GIPS standards.

This disclosure will assist prospective investors in comparing GIPS Pooled Fund Reports among firms where reporting requirements may differ because of local laws or regulations.

Sample Disclosure:

"Local laws do not allow the presentation of returns of less than one year to prospective investors, which is in conflict with the GIPS standards. Therefore, no performance is presented for this pooled fund for the period from 1 July 2018 (the inception date of the pooled fund) through 31 December 2018."

Provision 6.C.24

The FIRM MUST disclose the use of a SUB-ADVISOR and the periods a SUB-ADVISOR was used.[49]

[49] REQUIRED for periods beginning on or after 1 January 2006.

Discussion

Some firms use a sub-advisor to manage part or all of a particular strategy. For example, if a firm specializes in managing equities, it might hire a sub-advisor (a third-party investment manager) to manage the fixed-income portion of its balanced portfolios. The GIPS standards require that firms include the performance of pooled fund assets assigned to a sub-advisor in the respective pooled fund's performance. In the spirit of full disclosure, a firm must disclose the fact that a sub-advisor was used in the management of the pooled fund and the periods for which a sub-advisor was used. It is not necessary to disclose the name of the sub-advisor. This is required for periods beginning on or after 1 January 2006.

Sample Disclosures:

"A sub-advisor is used to manage the international equity allocation of the Asia Growth Balanced Fund."

"A sub-advisor was used for the management of the Targeted Duration Fixed Income Pooled Fund from its inception in 2001 through 31 December 2018."

Provision 6.C.25

The FIRM MUST disclose if the POOLED FUND'S valuation hierarchy materially differs from the RECOMMENDED valuation hierarchy. (See provision 2.B.6 for the RECOMMENDED valuation hierarchy.)[50]

Discussion

Firms must establish policies and procedures for determining pooled fund investment valuations. For periods beginning on or after 1 January 2011, those valuations must be determined in accordance with the definition of fair value. Provision 2.B.6 includes a recommended valuation hierarchy that firms should incorporate into their policies and procedures for determining fair value for pooled fund investments. Firms must establish a valuation hierarchy on a pooled fund–specific basis. It is acceptable for firms to apply a different valuation hierarchy to specific pooled funds provided the valuation methodology conforms to the definition of fair value. If the valuation hierarchy materially differs from the recommended valuation hierarchy, the firm must disclose this fact. Prospective investors will be informed and then may request additional information about the firm's valuation policies.

---

[50] REQUIRED for periods beginning on or after 1 January 2011.

Sample Disclosure:

"All pooled fund investments are valued using the firm's proprietary valuation models to determine fair value. Our valuation procedures materially differ from the recommended valuation hierarchy in the GIPS standards."

Provision 6.C.26

If the FIRM determines no appropriate BENCHMARK for the POOLED FUND exists, the FIRM MUST disclose why no BENCHMARK is presented.

Discussion

Benchmarks are important tools that aid in the planning, implementation, and evaluation of an investment strategy. They also help facilitate discussions with prospective investors regarding the relationship between pooled fund risk and return. As a result, the GIPS standards require firms to provide benchmark total returns in all GIPS Pooled Fund Reports. The benchmark must reflect the investment mandate, objective, or strategy of the pooled fund. Although there is typically an appropriate benchmark for traditional strategies, it is more common for managers of alternative strategies to determine that no appropriate benchmark for the pooled fund exists. If this is the case, the firm must disclose why no benchmark is presented.

Sample Disclosure:

"Because the pooled fund's strategy is absolute return where investments are permitted in all asset classes, no benchmark is presented because we believe that no benchmark that reflects this strategy exists."

Provision 6.C.27

If the FIRM changes the BENCHMARK, the FIRM MUST disclose:

a. For a prospective BENCHMARK change, the date and description of the change. Changes MUST be disclosed for as long as returns for the prior BENCHMARK are included in the GIPS POOLED FUND REPORT.

b. For a retroactive BENCHMARK change, the date and description of the change. Changes MUST be disclosed for a minimum of one year and for as long as they are relevant to interpreting the track record.

Discussion

Firms must disclose the date and description of any changes to the benchmark over time. A benchmark change can take two forms:

- The benchmark is changed from one benchmark to another on a prospective basis only.
- The benchmark is changed for all periods (i.e., retroactively).

In most cases, the firm should only change the benchmark going forward and not change the benchmark retroactively.

If the firm changes the benchmark prospectively and presents benchmark returns that combine two different benchmarks, the date and description of the change must be disclosed for as long as returns for the prior benchmark are included in the GIPS Pooled Fund Report. For example, assume a firm changes the benchmark for a pooled fund in June 2015, and the change is made prospectively. As long as benchmark returns from 2015 or prior periods are included in the GIPS Pooled Fund Report, the firm must include this disclosure. Firms must also carefully identify the benchmark as a custom benchmark in the GIPS Pooled Fund Report and must make clear that the benchmark returns are not those of the current benchmark for all periods. It would not be appropriate to label the benchmark returns with the name of the current benchmark. The firm must provide information, including labeling of the benchmark, that is sufficient to allow a prospective investor to distinguish the prior benchmark returns from the current benchmark returns.

There may be times when a firm determines that it is appropriate to change the benchmark for a given pooled fund retroactively. For example, because benchmarks are continually evolving, if the firm finds that a new benchmark is a better comparison for an investment strategy, the firm may consider changing the benchmark retroactively. In the case of a retroactive benchmark change, there must be a disclosure of the date and description of the benchmark change, including the fact that the benchmark was changed retroactively. Disclosures related to a retroactive change in a benchmark must be included in the respective GIPS Pooled Fund Report for a minimum of one year and for as long as the disclosures are relevant to interpreting the performance track record. The firm must consider the underlying principles of the GIPS standards, which are fair representation and full disclosure, when determining how long this disclosure will be included in the GIPS Pooled Fund Report.

When a firm changes a benchmark retroactively, the firm is encouraged to continue to also present the old benchmark.

This provision applies to a fundamental change in the benchmark—for example, a change in an index used in calculating the benchmark—rather than to periodic minor changes in benchmark weights and components. If a firm uses a custom benchmark that is a blend of one or more benchmarks, a change in the weights of the constituent benchmarks is not considered a benchmark change within the scope of this provision. For example, the benchmark may change every quarter as part of the normal procedure. In this instance, it is appropriate to disclose that the benchmark is rebalanced quarterly using the weights of the asset classes in the strategy's model portfolio A firm is not required to disclose how the asset class weights have changed each quarter but may do so.

Changes to the benchmark primarily intended to make performance look better by lowering the benchmark return violate the spirit of the GIPS standards.

Sample Disclosure for a Prospective Change:

"Benchmark results presented are a combination of two indices. ABC Index was used prior to 30 September 2015; ABC Value Index is used subsequently."

Sample Disclosure for a Retroactive Change:

"In January 2017, the benchmark was changed from ABC Index to XYZ Index for all periods."

Provision 6.C.28

If a custom BENCHMARK or combination of multiple BENCHMARKS is used, the FIRM MUST:

a. Disclose the BENCHMARK components, weights, and rebalancing process, if applicable.
b. Disclose the calculation methodology.
c. Clearly label the BENCHMARK to indicate that it is a custom BENCHMARK.

Discussion

When custom benchmarks are used, the firm must disclose the benchmark components, weights, and rebalancing process, if applicable, as well as the calculation methodology. For example, if the firm combines two indices, WW Index and XX Index, to create the WWXX benchmark for the pooled fund, the following would be an appropriate disclosure:

"The WWXX benchmark is a combination of 50% WW Index and 50% XX Index, calculated by weighting the respective index returns on a monthly basis."

It is also required that the benchmark be clearly labeled to indicate that it is a custom benchmark. For example, the label for the benchmark returns in a GIPS Pooled Fund Report would read "Custom Benchmark." The benchmark description and required disclosures might read as follows:

"*Custom Benchmark*: The benchmark is 100% hedged. The benchmark is based on a zero-cost one-month rolling hedge, whereby mid spot rates and one-month bid–offer forward points are applied."

In some markets, it has become more common to use benchmarks that reflect the deduction of model fees or other expenses. These net benchmarks are considered custom benchmarks. A firm must not present net benchmark returns compared with only pooled fund gross returns. For example, assume the firm wishes to include a custom benchmark that reflects the deduction of model or actual total pooled fund fees, but the firm presents only pooled fund gross returns in the GIPS Pooled Fund Report. The firm must not present net benchmark returns when only pooled fund gross returns are presented. The firm may use net benchmark returns only when pooled fund net returns are presented. The use of net benchmark returns when only pooled fund gross returns are presented is one instance where disclosure is not sufficient to prevent the information presented from being false and misleading. When a firm includes net benchmark returns in a GIPS Pooled Fund Report, the firm must clearly label the benchmark as a custom net benchmark and disclose the calculation methodology.

It is becoming more common for exchange-traded funds (ETFs) to be used as benchmarks. An ETF is a pooled fund that tracks a specific investment universe that is expressed by an index or a basket of securities and that is listed on an exchange. Unlike a market index, an ETF incurs trading costs and other charges, including taxes. Because of the incurred costs, an ETF may underperform the market index that it tracks. If an ETF is chosen as the benchmark for a strategy, the firm should present pooled fund net returns. As part of the benchmark description for an ETF, the firm must disclose the following items:

- if ETF returns are gross or net of fees and other costs, including transaction costs;
- the ETF expense ratio, if ETF net returns are presented;
- if ETF returns are based on market prices or net asset values (NAVs);
- the timing of the market close used to determine the ETF's valuations; and
- if ETF returns are gross or net of withholding taxes, if this information is available.

If the firm also presents pooled fund gross returns, it should present ETF returns that are grossed up, but it is not required to do so.

Sample Disclosures:

"Benchmark returns are a customized version of the XYZ Index, which is calculated monthly by XYZ Company. The benchmark reflects the deduction of a model fee of 1.00% per annum, which is calculated monthly by deducting 1/12 of 1% from the benchmark return."

"The benchmark is the Special ETF, which tracks the securities included in the Special Index. The ETF returns reflect the deduction of all expenses and transaction costs incurred by the Special ETF and are net of withholding taxes. As of 31 December 2019, the expense ratio was 0.14%. The Special ETF returns reflect market prices, which are determined by the midpoint between the bid and ask prices as of the closing time of the New York Stock Exchange."

Provision 6.C.29

For POOLED FUNDS with at least three annual periods of performance, the FIRM MUST disclose if the three-year annualized EX POST STANDARD DEVIATION of the POOLED FUND and/or BENCHMARK is not presented because 36 monthly returns are not available.

Discussion

For periods ending on or after 1 January 2011, firms must present the three-year annualized ex post standard deviation of the pooled fund and benchmark, which must be calculated using 36 monthly returns, as of each annual period end.

The 2010 edition of the GIPS standards required that a firm disclose, in all cases, if the three-year annualized ex post standard deviation of the pooled fund and/or benchmark is not presented because 36 monthly returns are not available. The 2020 edition of the GIPS standards modifies this requirement. This disclosure is required only if the three-year annualized ex post standard deviation is not presented for pooled funds that have at least three annual periods of performance. This change applies to all periods presented in a GIPS Pooled Fund Report.

If a pooled fund has at least three annual periods of performance but 36 monthly returns are not available for the pooled fund, firms are not required to present the three-year annualized ex post standard deviation for either the benchmark or the pooled fund. This scenario often applies to private market investment pooled funds because they are not required to have monthly returns. Firms must disclose that 36 monthly returns are not available for the pooled fund. (If private market investment pooled funds do have monthly valuations and 36 monthly returns are available, the three-year annualized ex post standard deviation must be presented.) If 36 monthly returns are not available for the pooled fund but are available for the benchmark, a firm is not required to present the three-year annualized ex post standard deviation for the benchmark but may do so.

If 36 monthly returns are not available for the benchmark but are available for the pooled fund, firms are required to present only the three-year annualized ex post standard deviation for the pooled fund. In this instance, because 36 monthly returns are not available for the benchmark, firms must not present a three-year annualized ex post standard deviation for the benchmark using data points other than monthly. Firms must disclose that 36 monthly returns are not available for the benchmark.

Sample Disclosure If 36 Monthly Returns Are Available for the Pooled Fund but Not for the Benchmark:

"The three-year annualized ex post standard deviation of the benchmark is not presented because the benchmark returns are calculated quarterly."

Sample Disclosure If 36 Monthly Returns Are Not Available for the Pooled Fund:

"The three-year annualized ex post standard deviation of the fund and benchmark are not presented because the fund returns are calculated quarterly."

Provision 6.C.30

The FIRM MUST disclose if performance from a past firm or affiliation is presented and for which periods.

Discussion

Provision 1.A.32 includes the portability tests that must be met to determine if performance from a past firm or affiliation may be used to represent the historical performance of a new or acquiring firm and if that performance can be linked to the ongoing performance of the new or acquiring firm. Provision 1.A.33 includes the portability tests that must be met for the new or acquiring firm to use performance from a past firm or affiliation to represent its historical performance when there is a break in the track record between the past firm or affiliation and the new or acquiring firm. In this instance, the track record from the past firm or affiliation may be used if the tests are met, but it must not be linked to the performance of the new or acquiring firm.

If the firm meets the required portability tests and presents performance from a past firm or affiliation in the GIPS Pooled Fund Report, the firm must disclose this fact, as well as the periods for which performance from the past firm or affiliation is presented.

Sample Disclosure:

"The Opportunity Fund was funded in March 2016 and was managed by the Distressed Debt Team at a prior firm. On 15 December 2017, the prior firm sold the line of business that included the Distressed Debt Team to ABC Investments. Fund activity prior to 15 December 2017 is from the prior firm."

Provision 6.C.31

The FIRM MUST disclose any change to the GIPS POOLED FUND REPORT resulting from the correction of a MATERIAL ERROR. Following the correction of the GIPS POOLED FUND REPORT, this disclosure MUST be included for a minimum of one year and for as long as it is relevant to interpreting the track record. This disclosure is not REQUIRED to be included in a GIPS POOLED FUND REPORT that is provided to a PROSPECTIVE INVESTOR that did not receive the GIPS POOLED FUND REPORT containing the MATERIAL ERROR.

Discussion

Firms claiming compliance with the GIPS standards are likely to be faced with situations in which errors are discovered that must be specifically addressed. An error, which can be qualitative or quantitative, can be related to any component of a GIPS Pooled Fund Report that is missing or inaccurate. Errors in GIPS Pooled Fund Reports can result from, but are not limited to, incorrect, incomplete, or missing:

- pooled fund returns or assets,
- firm assets,
- benchmark returns,
- pooled fund inception date,
- three-year annualized ex post standard deviation, or
- disclosures.

Any material error in a GIPS Pooled Fund Report must be corrected and disclosed in a revised GIPS Pooled Fund Report. A firm must define materiality within its error correction policies and procedures.

To adhere to this requirement, a firm must determine the criteria it will use to determine materiality. The following is a definition of materiality that firms might find useful as a starting point for their determination of materiality: "An error is material if the magnitude of the omission or misstatement of performance information, in light of surrounding circumstances, makes it probable that the judgment of a reasonable person relying on the information would have been changed by the omission or misstatement." A firm should have a defined process for determining the objective criteria it will use in determining materiality.

Disclosure of the change in the corrected GIPS Pooled Fund Report resulting from a material error must be included in the GIPS Pooled Fund Report for a minimum of 12 months following the correction of the report and for as long as it is relevant to interpreting the track record. The firm must consider the underlying principles of the GIPS standards, which are fair representation and full disclosure, when determining how long the disclosure will be included in the GIPS Pooled Fund Report that contained the material error.

Disclosure of the change resulting from a material error is not required to be included in a GIPS Pooled Fund Report that is provided to new prospective investors.

The discussion for Provision 1.A.20 provides additional information on error correction, including the determination of materiality, the actions that must be taken when an error in a GIPS Pooled Fund Report is discovered, and an explanation of who must receive the revised GIPS Pooled Fund Report.

Sample Disclosure:

"This GIPS Pooled Fund Report includes a correction of the information provided for the XYZ Index. The annual return for the XYZ Index for 2017 was originally presented as 3.4%. The correct return is 4.3%, as shown in this revised GIPS Pooled Fund Report."

Provision 6.C.32

The FIRM MUST disclose if preliminary, estimated values are used to determine FAIR VALUE.

Discussion

The use of preliminary, estimated values as fair value is common for some alternative strategies, including those that invest in underlying funds for which the firm relies on valuations provided by the underlying fund managers. When using preliminary, estimated values as fair value, it is important to remember the underlying principles of the GIPS standards: fair representation and full disclosure. If using preliminary, estimated values, firms must disclose this fact in the relevant GIPS Pooled Fund Report.

Firms that use preliminary, estimated values to determine fair value and subsequently change valuations when final values are received must determine how the firm's error correction policies will be applied. (Please see Provision 1.A.20 for guidance on error correction policies.) Differences between the final and estimated values are not necessarily errors but are treated in a similar manner because the correction of previously presented information may be involved.

In addition to this required disclosure, it is recommended (see Provision 6.B.8) that firms present the percentage of assets in the pooled fund that were valued using preliminary, estimated values as of each annual period end. This information will help prospective investors to interpret the performance record.

Sample Disclosure:

"Preliminary, estimated values were used in the determination of the fair value of the pooled fund's assets."

Provision 6.C.33

If the FIRM changes the type of return(s) presented for the POOLED FUND (e.g., changes from MONEY-WEIGHTED RETURNS to TIME-WEIGHTED RETURNS), the FIRM MUST disclose the change and the date of the change. This disclosure MUST be included for a minimum of one year and for as long as it is relevant to interpreting the track record.

Discussion

A firm must present time-weighted returns (TWRs) in a GIPS Pooled Fund Report unless certain criteria are met that allow money-weighted returns (MWRs) to be presented instead of TWRs. Firms may choose to present MWRs instead of TWRs for a specific pooled fund only if the firm controls the external cash flows into the pooled fund and the pooled fund has at least one of the following characteristics: It is closed-end; fixed life; fixed commitment; or illiquid investments are a significant part of the strategy. (See Provision 1.A.35.)

When a firm changes the type of return presented for a pooled fund, the firm must disclose, in the respective GIPS Pooled Fund Report, the change in the type of return (e.g., from MWR to TWR) and the date of the change. This disclosure must be included in the GIPS Pooled Fund Report for a minimum of one year and for as long as it is relevant and helpful to the firm's prospective investors in interpreting the pooled fund's track record. The firm must consider the underlying principles of the GIPS standards, which are fair representation and full disclosure, when determining how long the disclosure will be included in the GIPS Pooled Fund Report.

When a firm changes the type of return presented for a pooled fund, for example from MWRs to TWRs, the firm must change the returns for all periods. As an example, suppose that a firm is presenting performance for the period from the inception of a pooled fund on 1 January 2013 through 31 December 2020. It decides that it will switch to present TWRs as of 1 January 2020. The firm cannot present MWRs through 31 December 2019 and TWRs from 1 January 2020 through 31 December 2020. The firm must present TWRs from 1 January 2013 (the inception date of the pooled fund) through 31 December 2020 in the GIPS Pooled Fund Report for the period ended 31 December 2020.

Sample Disclosure:

"Beginning with the GIPS Pooled Fund Report for the period ended 31 December 2020, the returns presented for the XYZ Pooled Fund were changed from money-weighted returns to time-weighted returns."

Provision 6.C.34

If the FIRM presents ADDITIONAL RISK MEASURES, the FIRM MUST:

a. Describe any ADDITIONAL RISK MEASURE.
b. Disclose the name of the risk-free rate if a risk-free rate is used in the calculation of the ADDITIONAL RISK MEASURE.

Discussion

Understanding and interpreting investment performance requires the consideration of both risk and return. It is therefore recommended that firms present additional risk measures (i.e., beyond those required to be presented) for the pooled fund and the benchmark. (See Provision 6.B.5.) It is important to keep in mind that additional risk measures should be consistent with the pooled fund's strategy. For example, if the strategy is to track the benchmark, then tracking error would be consistent with that objective.

The GIPS Pooled Fund Report must include a description of any additional risk measure presented. If a risk-free rate is used in the calculation of an additional risk measure, the name of the risk-free rate must be disclosed. The disclosure of the name of the risk-free rate used in the calculation of an additional risk measure is required because of the importance of the selection of an appropriate risk-free rate. With a disclosure regarding the risk-free rate, the firm's prospective investors can better understand and interpret the additional risk measure(s) presented.

Provision 6.C.35

The FIRM MUST disclose if POOLED FUND GROSS RETURNS or POOLED FUND NET RETURNS are used to calculate presented risk measures.

Discussion

To help prospective investors interpret the risk measures presented in a GIPS Pooled Fund Report, the firm must disclose which returns are used in the calculation of the presented risk measures. This applies to both required risk measures (e.g., the three-year annualized ex post standard deviation) and any additional risk measures. As discussed in Provision 2.B.7, it is recommended that firms use gross returns for pooled funds when calculating risk measures.

Sample Disclosures:

"Pooled fund gross returns were used to calculate the three-year annualized ex post standard deviation of the pooled fund."

"Gross returns were used to calculate all risk measures presented in this GIPS Pooled Fund Report."

"Pooled fund net returns were used to calculate the three-year annualized ex post standard deviation of the pooled fund."

Provision 6.C.36

For REAL ESTATE investments that are not in a REAL ESTATE OPEN-END FUND, the FIRM MUST disclose that:[51]

a. EXTERNAL VALUATIONS are obtained, and the frequency for which they are obtained, or
b. The FIRM relies on valuations from financial statement audits.

Discussion

According to Provision 2.A.44, for periods beginning on or after 1 January 2012, real estate investments included in any portfolio except a real estate open-end fund must either:

- have an external valuation at least once every 12 months unless client agreements stipulate otherwise, in which case real estate investments must have an external valuation at least once every 36 months or per the client agreement if the client agreement requires external valuations more frequently than every 36 months; or
- be subject to an annual financial statement audit performed by an independent public accounting firm. The real estate investments must be accounted for at fair value, and the most recent audited financial statements available must contain an unmodified opinion issued by an independent public accounting firm.

Because valuation is such an important issue for real estate investments, firms must inform prospective investors whether they externally value real estate investments and, if so, how frequently, or instead place reliance on valuations from audited financial statements. This disclosure is required for pooled funds that are not a real estate open end fund, for periods ending on or after 31 December 2020.

Sample Disclosures:

"ABC Company obtains external valuations for all real estate investments annually."

"XYZ Company relies on valuations from audited financial statements. The audits are performed by an independent public accounting firm."

[51] REQUIRED for periods ending on or after 31 December 2020.

Provision 6.C.37

When the GIPS POOLED FUND REPORT includes THEORETICAL PERFORMANCE as SUPPLEMENTAL INFORMATION, the FIRM MUST:

a. Disclose that the results are theoretical, are not based on the performance of actual assets, and if the THEORETICAL PERFORMANCE was derived from the retroactive or prospective application of a model.

b. Disclose a basic description of the methodology and assumptions used to calculate the THEORETICAL PERFORMANCE sufficient for the PROSPECTIVE INVESTOR to interpret the THEORETICAL PERFORMANCE, including if it is based on model performance, backtested performance, or hypothetical performance.

c. Disclose whether the THEORETICAL PERFORMANCE reflects the deduction of actual or estimated INVESTMENT MANAGEMENT FEES, TRANSACTION COSTS, or other fees and charges that an actual POOLED FUND investor would have paid or will pay.

d. Clearly label the THEORETICAL PERFORMANCE as SUPPLEMENTAL INFORMATION.

Discussion

To be presented as supplemental information in a GIPS Pooled Fund Report, theoretical performance must relate to the respective pooled fund. The following are examples of theoretical performance that may be included in a GIPS Pooled Fund Report as supplemental information:

- Results created by applying a pooled fund investment strategy or methodology to historical data to indicate how a strategy constructed with the benefit of hindsight would have performed during a certain period in the past had the strategy been in existence during that period.
- Ex ante performance that is linked to actual pooled fund performance, or that is calculated using actual pooled fund performance.
- Results that include the effect of currency hedging that has been applied after-the-fact to the pooled fund. The pooled fund was not originally managed including the currency hedging strategy, and the hedging is not part of the actual pooled fund returns.

When theoretical performance is included as supplemental information in a GIPS Pooled Fund Report, a firm is required to include a number of disclosures to ensure that the recipients of the report, including prospective investors, understand the nature of the information being presented. Among the required disclosures are the source of the theoretical performance, the methodology and assumptions used to calculate the theoretical performance, and the treatment of fees and costs.

Firms must also clearly label the theoretical performance as supplemental information.

 |

Sample Disclosure:

"A return history has been constructed for the period from 1 January 2015 through 31 December 2018 that reflects the application of an investment model used by XYZ Investment Management. The results are theoretical and are not based on the performance of actual assets. The return history is derived from the retroactive application of a model. Taking the constituents of the large-cap index at each month end, those securities that have an above-average dividend yield and an above-average dividend payout ratio were identified and reweighted by market capitalization. The next-month's performance was then applied to those stock weights to derive a model return for the month. These monthly model returns are then linked to provide annual returns. The theoretical performance presented does not reflect the deduction of investment management fees, transaction costs, or other fees and charges."

6.D. Disclosure—Recommendations

Provision 6.D.1

The FIRM SHOULD disclose material changes to valuation policies and/or methodologies.

Discussion

Valuation is a critical component of the performance calculation. Therefore, if a change to a firm's valuation policies and/or methodologies is material, firms should disclose the change in order to enable prospective investors to understand the potential effect of such a change. Some examples of a material change include, but are not limited to, the following:

- new valuation principles adopted by a local accounting standards board,
- adoption of new international standards in lieu of local standards,
- change of economic criteria used to value investments, and
- change from a discounted cash flow basis to a comparables basis.

Sample Disclosure for a Policy Change:

"Prior to 1 March 2016, illiquid securities were valued internally. Subsequently, illiquid securities are valued using a third-party pricing service."

Sample Disclosure for a Methodology Change:

"For periods prior to 1 August 2019, real estate investments were valued on a discounted cash flow basis. As of 1 August 2019, real estate investments are valued on a comparables basis."

Provision 6.D.2

The FIRM SHOULD disclose material changes to calculation policies and/or methodologies.

Discussion

Firms have discretion to determine which policies and methodologies are used for calculating performance. Although these policies and methodologies must adhere to all applicable calculation requirements, firms may choose from a wide variety of policies and methodologies. Firms may change calculation policies and/or methodologies; however, firms must not change a calculation policy or methodology for the sole purpose of increasing performance. If a change to the calculation policies and/or methodologies is material, firms should disclose the change in order to enable prospective investors to understand the potential effect of such a change.

Sample Disclosure:

"Effective 1 January 2010, fund returns are calculated daily, using a true time-weighted return methodology. Previously, fund returns were calculated monthly using the Modified Dietz method."

Provision 6.D.3

The FIRM SHOULD disclose material differences between the BENCHMARK and the POOLED FUND'S investment mandate, objective, or strategy.

Discussion

Firms are required to disclose the pooled fund description (see Provision 6.C.4) and the benchmark description (see Provision 6.C.5) in a GIPS Pooled Fund Report. It is recommended that firms also disclose any material differences between the benchmark and the pooled fund's investment mandate, objective, or strategy. Prospective investors will be better able to evaluate the performance of the strategy relative to the benchmark presented if they understand any material differences between the pooled fund and the benchmark.

Sample Disclosures:

"The Concentrated Equity Pooled Fund focuses its investments on the health care and technology sectors. As of 31 December 2019, 62% of the Fund was invested in the health care and technology sectors, while 18% of the fund's benchmark, the XYZ Index, was invested in these two sectors."

"The Absolute Return Pooled Fund invests in stocks both long and short regardless of country of domicile or market capitalization. The Fund's benchmark is the T-bill rate, which is the hurdle rate, and is composed of materially different investments."

> **Provision 6.D.4**
>
> The FIRM SHOULD disclose the key assumptions used to value investments.

Discussion

Firms are required to disclose that valuation policies are available upon request. (See Provision 6.C.14.) Because valuation is a critical component of the performance calculation, it is recommended that firms also disclose the key assumptions used when valuing pooled fund investments. This will help prospective investors better understand how the firm values investments and compare valuation assumptions for similar strategies used by different firms.

Sample Disclosure:

"Investments are valued using recent market quotations. If there is no publicly traded reference, equity investments are valued using a market multiples approach for similar investments in active markets, and fixed-income investments are valued using inputs such as interest rates, yield curve shape, volatility, prepayments, and credit risk."

> **Provision 6.D.5**
>
> If a parent company contains multiple firms, each FIRM within the parent company SHOULD disclose a list of the other firms contained within the parent company.

Discussion

The term "firm" is used in two different ways in Provision 6.D.5. "FIRM" is used to indicate an entity that claims compliance with the GIPS standards, whereas "firm" is used to indicate an entity that may or may not claim compliance with the GIPS standards. The definition of a firm will be based on the specific circumstances of the firm but must reflect how the firm is held out to the public as a distinct business entity. In some cases, a parent company may have two or more units, divisions, departments, or offices that are defined as separate firms within the context of the GIPS standards. To avoid confusion, a firm claiming compliance with the GIPS standards must be sure that it is clearly defined relative to the other firms within the parent company and that it is apparent which firm is claiming compliance. In the interest of fair representation and full disclosure, firms should disclose a list of the other organizations within the parent company. Firms should also consider indicating which organizations within the parent company claim compliance with the GIPS standards.

Sample Disclosure:

"ABC Institutional Investment Management is the institutional division of ABC parent company. The private banking division of ABC parent company also claims compliance with the GIPS standards, whereas the retail division of ABC parent company does not claim compliance with the GIPS standards."

Provision 6.D.6

If the FIRM adheres to any industry valuation guidelines in addition to the GIPS valuation REQUIREMENTS, the FIRM SHOULD disclose which guidelines have been applied.

Discussion

Some market segments, such as private equity, have developed their own valuation guidelines. For these markets, it is not uncommon for the GIPS standards valuation requirements to be supplemented by other local or international standards because other standards may be more stringent in their requirements.

The disclosure of which industry's valuation guidelines have been used in addition to the GIPS standards valuation requirements will help prospective investors to determine the comparability of GIPS Pooled Fund Reports from different firms and/or jurisdictions.

Sample Disclosure:

"The Global Diversified Distressed Fund adheres to the XYZ Venture Capital Association's valuation guidelines as well as the GIPS standards valuation requirements. The XYZ valuation standards are based on fair value but provide more prescriptive advice in terms of how to value specific investments, such as secondary investments and distressed debt investments."

Provision 6.D.7

When using BENCHMARKS that have limitations, such as peer group BENCHMARKS, the FIRM SHOULD disclose these limitations.

Discussion

Firms must determine which benchmark(s) are most appropriate for pooled fund(s). When determining which benchmarks to present in a GIPS Pooled Fund Report, firms should be guided by the ethical spirit of the GIPS standards.

Some benchmarks with known limitations are often used for certain types of investments. For example, peer group benchmarks, such as hedge fund peer group universe indices, are often used for hedge funds and other alternative investment strategies. Although peer group benchmarks are frequently used to evaluate hedge funds, there are some common problems with hedge fund peer group benchmarks, including the following:

- self-reporting bias (only some hedge funds choose to report performance data),
- survivorship bias (historical returns of closed hedge funds are removed from the peer group benchmark),
- inability to obtain returns for the same periods as the pooled fund, and
- lack of investability (some hedge funds within a peer group benchmark are closed to new investors).

When using benchmarks that exhibit limitations, firms should describe these limitations in the relevant GIPS Pooled Fund Report. This helps prospective investors understand the nature of the benchmark and be aware of any known drawbacks in comparing the risk and return of the benchmark and pooled fund.

Sample Disclosure:

"The benchmark is the Hedge Fund Aggregate Multi-Style Index, which includes more than 100 hedge funds of various styles and strategies. Because this index is based on the data self-reported by the constituent funds, it may have a self-reporting bias. In addition, some funds are closed to new investors and are no longer investable. We believe that no better index exists as a comparison for this pooled fund."

Provision 6.D.8

The FIRM SHOULD disclose how research costs are reflected in returns.

Discussion

The focus on research costs has grown in certain markets. Although research costs are often absorbed by the firm, some firms instead charge research costs directly to investors. To allow prospective investors to understand the firm's policy for the treatment of research costs, firms should disclose if returns do or do not reflect the deduction of research costs.

Sample Disclosures:

"ABC Company bears the costs of investment research. Research costs are not separately charged to investors or to the fund."

"Certain investment research costs are charged directly to investors and are not paid by pooled fund assets. Therefore, fund returns do not reflect the research costs that are charged directly to investors."

7. POOLED FUND MONEY-WEIGHTED RETURN REPORT

The following provisions apply to POOLED FUNDS that include MONEY-WEIGHTED RETURNS in a GIPS POOLED FUND REPORT when the FIRM meets the REQUIREMENTS specified in Provision 1.A.35 and chooses to present MONEY-WEIGHTED RETURNS.

7.A. Presentation and Reporting—Requirements

Provision 7.A.1

The FIRM MUST present in each GIPS POOLED FUND REPORT:

a. The annualized POOLED FUND SINCE-INCEPTION MONEY-WEIGHTED RETURN through the most recent annual period end.

Discussion

To claim compliance, a firm is required to meet all applicable requirements of the GIPS standards on a firm-wide basis for at least a five-year period, or since inception of the firm if the firm has been in existence for less than five years. See Provision 1.A.3 for a discussion of the required periods for initially claiming compliance.

If a firm meets the requirements for presenting money-weighted returns in a GIPS Pooled Fund Report (see Provision 1.A.35) and chooses to do so, the firm must present the annualized pooled fund since-inception money-weighted return (SI-MWR) through the most recent annual period end.

For example, assume a firm presents returns on a calendar year-end basis. If a pooled fund has an inception date of 1 March 2015 and the most recent annual period end is 31 December 2019, the firm must present an annualized pooled fund SI-MWR from 1 March 2015 through 31 December 2019. Although only the annualized pooled fund SI-MWR through the most recent annual period end is required, it is recommended that firms present annualized pooled fund SI-MWRs through each annual period end. (See Provision 7.B.1.) In this example, doing so would mean presenting SI-MWRs from 1 March 2015 through 31 December 2015, 1 March 2015 through 31 December 2016, 1 March 2015 through 31 December 2017, and 1 March 2015 through 31 December 2018.

The SI-MWR from 1 March 2015 through 31 December 2015 must not be annualized because the return is for a period of less than one year.

Firms must clearly label the periods for which SI-MWRs are presented. Firms must select the annual period end for which SI-MWRs will be presented on a pooled fund–specific basis and apply it consistently. For purposes of comparability, best practice would be for a firm to report pooled fund SI-MWRs for periods ending on 31 December.

Firms may present pooled fund gross returns or pooled fund net returns. Firms may also choose to present both pooled fund gross returns and pooled fund net returns in a GIPS Pooled Fund Report.

Provision 7.A.1

The FIRM MUST present in each GIPS POOLED FUND REPORT:

b. When the POOLED FUND has a track record that is less than a full year, the non-annualized POOLED FUND SINCE-INCEPTION MONEY-WEIGHTED RETURN through the initial annual period end.

Discussion

When a pooled fund has a track record of less than a full year, the firm must present the non-annualized since-inception money-weighted return (SI-MWR) through the initial annual period end. Subsequently, the firm must extend the measurement period for the SI-MWR to include the next annual period and calculate an annualized SI-MWR through the most recent annual period end.

SI-MWRs for periods of less than a full year must not be annualized. As an example, a pooled fund that began on 1 December 2020 and has a one-month initial return through 31 December 2020 of 3% (which equates to an annualized return of 42.6%) would be required to present that 3% as the partial year's performance. The annualized return of 42.6% must not be presented. Some spreadsheet and software applications automatically annualize all returns, and firms are reminded that for periods of less than a year, the firm must "de-annualize" any annualized returns that are calculated.

The method chosen to de-annualize a return is at the discretion of the firm, but it must be a geometric calculation. In the situation just presented, the 42.6% annualized return could be de-annualized by one of the following formulas:

$$\left\{\left[(1+0.426)^{\left(\frac{1}{12}\right)}\right]-1\right\}\times 100=3\% \text{ or } \left\{\left[(1+0.426)^{\left(\frac{31}{365}\right)}\right]-1\right\}\times 100=3\%,$$

both resulting in a non-annualized one-month return of 3%.

Provision 7.A.1

The FIRM MUST present in each GIPS POOLED FUND REPORT:

c. When the POOLED FUND terminates, the annualized POOLED FUND SINCE-INCEPTION MONEY-WEIGHTED RETURN through the POOLED FUND TERMINATION DATE.

Discussion

When a pooled fund terminates, the firm must present the annualized pooled fund since-inception money-weighted return (SI-MWR) through the pooled fund termination date. For example, if a pooled fund has an inception date of 1 July 2012 and terminates on 31 August 2019, the GIPS Pooled Fund Report for this pooled fund must include a pooled fund SI-MWR for the period from 1 July 2012 through 31 August 2019.

Provision 7.A.1

The FIRM MUST present in each GIPS POOLED FUND REPORT:

d. The SINCE-INCEPTION MONEY-WEIGHTED RETURN for the BENCHMARK for the same periods as presented for the POOLED FUND, unless the FIRM determines there is no appropriate BENCHMARK.

Discussion

Benchmarks are important tools that aid in the planning, implementation, and evaluation of a pooled fund's investment policy. They also help facilitate discussions with prospective investors regarding the relationship between risk and return. As a result, firms are required to present the since-inception money-weighted return (SI-MWR) for the benchmark for the same periods as presented for the pooled fund, unless the firm determines that there is no appropriate benchmark.

The benchmark presented must be one that reflects the pooled fund's investment mandate, objective, or strategy. A firm may choose to present more than one benchmark in a GIPS Pooled Fund Report but must include all required information for all benchmarks presented in the GIPS Pooled Fund Report.

Because the benchmark selected for a pooled fund must be appropriate for comparison with the performance of the pooled fund, a firm must not compare a time-weighted return (TWR) benchmark with a pooled fund's SI-MWR. Public market indexes by themselves are not directly comparable to an MWR because the market indexes typically use TWRs. The public market equivalent (PME) is a method in which a public market index is used to create a comparable MWR from a series of cash flows that replicate those of the pooled fund and that can be compared with the pooled fund's MWR. When the firm uses a PME, the market index used must be a total return benchmark.

For pooled funds that have a subscription line of credit (LOC), and the firm is required to present pooled fund returns both with and without the subscription LOC (see Provision 7.A.2), the firm must present benchmark returns for the same periods as both pooled fund returns. If the benchmark is a PME, the firm must calculate a PME using the pooled fund cash flows with the subscription LOC as well as the pooled fund cash flows without the subscription LOC.

See Provision 1.A.19 for a discussion of total return benchmarks. See the discussion of Provision 7.C.29 for additional information regarding a PME.

Provision 7.A.1

The FIRM MUST present in each GIPS POOLED FUND REPORT:

e. POOLED FUND assets as of the most recent annual period end.

Discussion

Each GIPS Pooled Fund Report must include the pooled fund assets as of the most recent annual period end. This requirement provides information to prospective investors on the size of the pooled fund, measured by the amount of assets it contains. When the pooled fund strategy uses discretionary leverage, pooled fund assets must be presented net of the discretionary leverage and not grossed up as if the discretionary leverage did not exist. Discretionary leverage refers to loans taken at the discretion of the firm. In contrast, non-discretionary leverage refers to borrowings undertaken by the investor. For example, if the firm is managing a fund that has $200 million in assets, and the firm chooses to borrow $50 million, the fund's net assets are $200 million and its gross assets are $250 million. When calculating pooled fund assets, the firm must use $200 million.

Provision 7.A.1

The FIRM MUST present in each GIPS POOLED FUND REPORT:

f. TOTAL FIRM ASSETS as of the most recent annual period end.[52]

[52] REQUIRED for periods ending on or after 31 December 2020. For periods ending prior to 31 December 2020, FIRMS may present either TOTAL FIRM ASSETS or POOLED FUND assets as a percentage of TOTAL FIRM ASSETS.

 |

Discussion

For periods ending on or after 31 December 2020, the firm must present total firm assets as of the most recent annual period end. For periods ending prior to this date, the firm must present either total firm assets or pooled fund assets as a percentage of total firm assets. Discretionary leverage must be deducted when calculating total firm assets. Discretionary leverage refers to loans taken at the discretion of the firm. In contrast, non-discretionary leverage refers to borrowings undertaken by the investor. For example, if the firm is managing a fund that has $200 million in assets, and the firm chooses to borrow $50 million, the firm must use $200 million when calculating total firm assets, not $250 million. The inclusion of both pooled fund assets and total firm assets in a GIPS Pooled Fund Report will help a prospective investor understand the pooled fund size in relation to total firm assets.

Firms must be sure that assets are not double-counted because counting assets more than once would not fairly represent total firm assets.

See the discussion of Provision 2.A.1 for additional guidance on the calculation of total firm assets.

Provision 7.A.2

If a SUBSCRIPTION LINE OF CREDIT is used, the FIRM MUST present the POOLED FUND SINCE-INCEPTION MONEY-WEIGHTED RETURN both with and without the SUBSCRIPTION LINE OF CREDIT through the most recent annual period end. The FIRM is not REQUIRED to present returns without the SUBSCRIPTION LINE OF CREDIT when the SUBSCRIPTION LINE OF CREDIT has all of the following characteristics.[53]

a. The principal was repaid within 120 days using COMMITTED CAPITAL drawn down through a capital call.
b. No principal was used to fund DISTRIBUTIONS.

Discussion

A subscription line of credit (LOC) is a loan facility that is usually put in place to facilitate administration when firms are calling for funds from investors. A subscription LOC can have a significant effect on returns. However, there has been a lack of consistency in return calculations when a subscription LOC is used. For comparability and transparency, firms that use a subscription LOC must calculate and present the since-inception money-weighted return (SI-MWR) that includes the subscription LOC. For periods ending on or after 31 December 2020, firms are required to

[53] REQUIRED for periods ending on or after 31 December 2020.

also calculate and present a SI-MWR that does not include the subscription LOC unless the subscription LOC has the following two characteristics:

- The principal was repaid within 120 days using committed capital drawn down through a capital call; and
- No principal was used to fund distributions.

If the subscription LOC has both of these characteristics, the firm is not required to calculate and present a SI-MWR that does not include the subscription LOC.

Presenting pooled fund returns with and without the subscription LOC provides prospective investors with a more complete understanding of the pooled fund's performance and the effect of the subscription LOC on the pooled fund's returns.

If returns both with and without the subscription LOC are required to be presented in a GIPS Pooled Fund Report, these returns must be comparable. If the firm presents gross returns only, gross returns with and without the subscription LOC must be presented. If the firm presents net returns only, net returns with and without the subscription LOC must be presented. If the firm presents both gross and net returns, the firm must present gross returns with and without the subscription LOC as well as net returns with and without the subscription LOC.

The SI-MWRs with and without the subscription LOC are required for the SI-MWR that is presented through the most recent annual period end. If a firm chooses to also include SI-MWRs through each annual period end, the SI-MWRs with and without the subscription LOC must be presented in the GIPS Pooled Fund Report.

See Provision 2.A.50 for guidance for calculating returns with and without the subscription LOC.

Provision 7.A.3

The FIRM MUST present the percentage of the total FAIR VALUE of POOLED FUND assets that were valued using subjective unobservable inputs (as described in provision 2.B.6.e) as of the most recent annual period end, if such investments represent a material amount of POOLED FUND assets.

Discussion

Markets are not always liquid, and investment prices are not always objective and/or observable. As the last level of the recommended valuation hierarchy indicates (see Provision 2.B.6), it may be necessary for a firm to use subjective unobservable inputs to value an investment for which markets are not active on the measurement date. Examples of subjective unobservable inputs include an assumed discount rate, an assumed occupancy rate for a commercial building, and the default rate used for the valuation of a security in default. Examples related to insurance-linked securities include assumptions regarding hurricane damage and mortality rates. Unobservable inputs should be used to measure fair value only when observable inputs and prices are not available or appropriate. Unobservable inputs reflect the firm's own assumptions about the assumptions that market participants would use in pricing the investment and should be developed based on the best information available under the circumstances.

Firms must present the percentage of the total fair value of pooled fund assets that were valued using subjective unobservable inputs as of the most recent annual period end, if such investments represent a material amount of pooled fund assets. The amount of pooled fund assets valued using subjective unobservable inputs would be considered material if it would likely influence a reader's judgment regarding the reliability of the valuation. The firm must decide on the criteria it will use to determine when subjective unobservable inputs represent a material amount of pooled fund assets, include these criteria in its policy and procedures, and apply these criteria consistently.

Sample Disclosure:

"As of 31 December 2020, 29% of pooled fund assets were valued using subjective unobservable inputs. These inputs are not supported by market activity and instead are based on internal proprietary pricing models."

Provision 7.A.4

If the POOLED FUND has COMMITTED CAPITAL, the FIRM MUST present the following items as of the most recent annual period end:

a. POOLED FUND SINCE-INCEPTION PAID-IN CAPITAL.
b. POOLED FUND SINCE-INCEPTION DISTRIBUTIONS.
c. POOLED FUND cumulative COMMITTED CAPITAL.
d. TOTAL VALUE to SINCE-INCEPTION PAID-IN CAPITAL (INVESTMENT MULTIPLE or TVPI).
e. SINCE-INCEPTION DISTRIBUTIONS to SINCE-INCEPTION PAID-IN CAPITAL (REALIZATION MULTIPLE or DPI).
f. SINCE-INCEPTION PAID-IN CAPITAL to cumulative COMMITTED CAPITAL (PIC MULTIPLE).
g. RESIDUAL VALUE to SINCE-INCEPTION PAID-IN CAPITAL (UNREALIZED MULTIPLE or RVPI).

Discussion

Although the money-weighted return (MWR) is the basic metric used to report performance for pooled funds where the firm has control over the cash flows, has met the other requirements for presenting an MWR, and has chosen to present MWRs, it is not the only useful metric used to gauge performance. Other measures are also useful to provide additional insight. The MWR by its nature is sensitive to early cash flow events, and the MWR calculation assumes that the residual value, or fair value, of a pooled fund is totally liquid whereas in reality, the residual value may be illiquid. Other metrics have been developed that allow a prospective investor to examine aspects of performance other than simply a rate of return.

a. POOLED FUND SINCE-INCEPTION PAID-IN CAPITAL.

The pooled fund since-inception paid-in capital consists of all capital inflows to a pooled fund by the investors (e.g., limited partners). These inflows are also referred to as contributions to a pooled fund by the investors. Paid-in capital also includes distributions that are subsequently recalled and reinvested into the pooled fund.

b. POOLED FUND SINCE-INCEPTION DISTRIBUTIONS.

Pooled fund since-inception distributions includes all cash and stock distributed from a pooled fund to the investors (e.g., limited partners).

c. POOLED FUND cumulative COMMITTED CAPITAL.

The pooled fund cumulative committed capital represents the total pledges of capital to a pooled fund by the investors (e.g., limited partners). Committed capital can be either drawn (paid-in) or undrawn (dry powder).

d. TOTAL VALUE to SINCE-INCEPTION PAID-IN CAPITAL (INVESTMENT MULTIPLE or TVPI).

The investment multiple, or TVPI, provides investors with a multiple that indicates how many times more the investment is worth compared with the original investment without taking into account the time value of money. Also known as the Multiple of Investment Capital (MOIC), it is equal to the sum of the pooled fund since-inception distributions and its residual value (i.e., fair value) divided by the pooled fund since-inception paid-in capital. The investment multiple is calculated as follows:

$$\text{TVPI} = \frac{\text{Since} - \text{Inception Distributions} + \text{Residual Value}}{\text{Since} - \text{Inception Paid} - \text{In Capital}}$$

TVPI can also be calculated as DPI + RVPI, where

DPI = realization multiple (see Provision 7.A.4.e)

RVPI = unrealized multiple (see Provision 7.A.4.g)

 |

e. SINCE-INCEPTION DISTRIBUTIONS to SINCE-INCEPTION PAID-IN CAPITAL (REALIZATION MULTIPLE or DPI).

The DPI, or realization multiple, measures how much invested capital has actually been returned to investors. It is the amount of invested capital that investors have "realized" and is often viewed as the amount of the TVPI that is "realized." TVPI, also known as the investment multiple, is calculated as total value divided by since-inception paid-in capital. (See Provision 7.A.4.d.) DPI is calculated as follows:

$$\text{DPI} = \frac{\text{Since} - \text{Inception Distributions}}{\text{Since} - \text{Inception Paid} - \text{In Capital}}$$

f. SINCE-INCEPTION PAID-IN CAPITAL to cumulative COMMITTED CAPITAL (PIC MULTIPLE).

The paid-in capital multiple, also known as the PIC multiple or PIC ratio, gives prospective investors information regarding how much committed capital has actually been drawn down or called. It is also known as the "dry-powder ratio" because it measures how much capital has already been invested and therefore indicates how much is left to invest. The PIC multiple is calculated as follows:

$$\text{PIC} = \frac{\text{Since} - \text{Inception Paid} - \text{In Capital}}{\text{Cumulative Committed Capital}}$$

Distributions can be either recallable or non-recallable. If a distribution is recallable, after the pooled fund distributes proceeds to its investors, it can draw down the same capital again, which makes it possible for the pooled fund to draw capital in excess of its total committed capital. A recallable distribution must be treated as an actual distribution and, if and when that distribution is recalled (drawn again), it must be treated as additional paid-in capital.

Recallable distributions affect the performance metric calculations. Firms may wish to consider additional disclosure when there is a material effect on the PIC or realization multiples. If a recallable distribution is re-contributed and reflected as paid-in capital a second time, the result will be that cumulative paid-in capital since inception is higher than total committed capital. It also means that the realization multiple (DPI), unrealized multiple (RVPI), and investment multiple (TVPI) will be lower. (For more information on DPI, RVPI, and TVPI, please see Provisions 7.A.4.e, 7.A.4.g, and 7.A.4.d, respectively). All else being equal, for pooled funds that have had recallable distributions, the denominator will be increased and the PIC multiple will be higher.

g. RESIDUAL VALUE to SINCE-INCEPTION PAID-IN CAPITAL (UNREALIZED MULTIPLE or RVPI).

The unrealized multiple, or RVPI, is the converse of the realization multiple. It is equal to the pooled fund's residual value (or fair value) at the end of the period divided by since-inception paid-in capital. It is calculated as follows:

$$\text{RVPI} = \frac{\text{Residual Value}}{\text{Since} - \text{Inception Paid} - \text{In Capital}}$$

Provision 7.A.5

The FIRM MUST clearly label or identify:

a. The periods that are presented.
b. If POOLED FUND returns are POOLED FUND GROSS RETURNS or POOLED FUND NET RETURNS.
c. If POOLED FUND returns do or do not reflect the SUBSCRIPTION LINE OF CREDIT. This information is REQUIRED only if the FIRM presents returns both with and without the SUBSCRIPTION LINE OF CREDIT.

Discussion

All periods presented in a GIPS Pooled Fund Report must be clearly labeled or identified.

Firms may present pooled fund gross returns or pooled fund net returns in a GIPS Pooled Fund Report and may also choose to present both pooled fund gross returns and pooled fund net returns. For prospective investors to understand the nature of the returns being presented, the returns included in a GIPS Pooled Fund Report must be clearly labeled or identified as either gross returns or net returns.

If a firm uses a subscription line of credit (LOC), and it is required to present returns both with and without this subscription LOC, the firm must clearly indicate whether the pooled fund returns do or do not reflect the subscription LOC. If no subscription LOC is used or the firm is not required to present returns both with and without the subscription LOC, this disclosure is not required.

Provision 7.A.6

If the FIRM includes more than one BENCHMARK in the GIPS POOLED FUND REPORT, the FIRM MUST present and disclose all REQUIRED information for all BENCHMARKS presented.

Discussion

It is permissible to include more than one benchmark in a GIPS Pooled Fund Report. All benchmarks included in a GIPS Pooled Fund Report must adhere to the requirements of the GIPS standards that are applicable to benchmarks. Firms may label benchmarks as primary and secondary benchmarks, but the same requirements and recommendations apply to all benchmarks included in a GIPS Pooled Fund Report. For example, a GIPS Pooled Fund Report must include:

- a description for all benchmarks, and
- a disclosure of changes to (or deletion of) any benchmark.

If the firm designates benchmarks as primary and secondary benchmarks, it must disclose when these designations change (e.g., if a primary benchmark becomes a secondary benchmark), because such a change in designation is considered a benchmark change. In all instances, if multiple benchmarks are presented in a GIPS Pooled Fund Report and one or more of the benchmarks is removed from the GIPS Pooled Fund Report, the firm must disclose this fact. (See Provision 7.C.27.)

An appropriate benchmark for a pooled fund reflects the investment mandate, objective, or strategy of the pooled fund. Additional benchmarks beyond appropriate benchmarks may be presented in a GIPS Pooled Fund Report as supplemental information. There must be sufficient disclosure so that a prospective investor understands the nature of the benchmark and why it is being presented. Disclosure, however, does not necessarily prevent information from being false or misleading. An additional benchmark must never be presented for the sole purpose of providing a favorable comparison to the performance of the pooled fund. To do so would be misleading, regardless of the disclosures accompanying the benchmark.

Provision 7.A.7

The FIRM MUST present the POOLED FUND EXPENSE RATIO appropriate to PROSPECTIVE INVESTORS.

Discussion

Firms must present the expense ratio that is applicable to prospective investors for the specific pooled fund. The pooled fund expense ratio is the ratio of total pooled fund expenses to average net assets. The expense ratio should not reflect transaction costs.

The expense ratio gives prospective investors important insight into the total fees and expenses paid by investors in the fund. For example, a pooled fund expense ratio of 2% indicates that an investor will pay $20 in expenses each year for every $1,000 invested, in addition to transaction costs. An expense ratio also helps investors compare expenses across funds, because even a small difference in fees can have a significant effect over time.

If the pooled fund has multiple share classes, the firm may present multiple expense ratios or may present only the expense ratio appropriate to the prospective investor. The firm may also use the highest expense ratio as the expense ratio that can be used for all prospective investors of the fund. Expense ratios must reflect any performance-based fees or carried interest, if accrued or charged to the pooled fund. Presenting a range of expense ratios (e.g., the expense ratio for all share classes ranges between 0.40% and 0.85%) would not satisfy this requirement.

Because expense ratios can change over time, firms must determine which expense ratio to present. A firm might choose to present the expense ratio as of the most recent annual period end, or the last known expense ratio. When the expense ratio has had a material change resulting from a change in assets or costs, the firm should present a more current expense ratio that reflects what a prospective investor is likely to pay at the current time.

Pooled fund expense ratios that are calculated for periods of less than one year must be annualized. Assume that a pooled fund starts on 1 April, and the firm calculates an expense ratio of 0.75% for the period from 1 April 2019 through 31 December 2019. The firm must present an annualized rate of 1.00%, representing a pooled fund expense ratio for the entire year rather than the 0.75% that represents an expense ratio for only nine months. Presenting an annualized expense ratio facilitates the comparison of expense ratios across funds and firms. Firms may also present the non-annualized expense ratio but must clearly disclose or indicate that the expense ratio is not annualized.

This presentation requirement is not satisfied if the firm does not include the expense ratio in the GIPS Pooled Fund Report and instead makes reference to another document that includes the expense ratio, such as a fund prospectus. The expense ratio may be an exhibit attached to the GIPS Pooled Fund Report. The exhibit may be the pooled fund's offering documents, if the offering documents include the appropriate expense ratio.

Provision 7.A.8

If the FIRM chooses to present POOLED FUND uncalled COMMITTED CAPITAL or a combination of POOLED FUND assets and POOLED FUND uncalled COMMITTED CAPITAL, the FIRM MUST:

a. Present POOLED FUND uncalled COMMITTED CAPITAL for the same periods for which the combination of POOLED FUND assets and POOLED FUND uncalled COMMITTED CAPITAL is presented.
b. Clearly label POOLED FUND uncalled COMMITTED CAPITAL as such.
c. Clearly label the combination of POOLED FUND assets and POOLED FUND uncalled COMMITTED CAPITAL as such.

Discussion

Committed capital is defined as pledges of capital to an investment vehicle by investors (limited partners and the general partner) or the firm and is typically drawn down over a period of time. Uncalled committed capital, also known as dry powder, is the amount of capital that has not yet been drawn. Because uncalled committed capital is not considered actual pooled fund assets, pooled fund uncalled committed capital must not be included in the calculation of pooled fund assets as of 1 January 2020. This is consistent with the requirement to not include uncalled committed capital in total firm assets for periods beginning on or after 1 January 2020. (See Provision 2.A.1.) A firm may report pooled fund uncalled committed capital in addition to the required presentation of pooled fund assets, if it wishes to do so. The inclusion of information on pooled fund uncalled committed capital provides prospective investors with a more complete picture of the firm's investments and the amount of capital that is currently committed to a future investment. If a firm chooses to present information on pooled fund uncalled committed capital it may present pooled fund uncalled committed capital as either:

- a separate value, or
- the combination of pooled fund assets and pooled fund uncalled committed capital.

If a firm chooses to present pooled fund uncalled committed capital as a separate value, the information must be clearly labeled.

If a firm chooses to present the combination of pooled fund assets and pooled fund uncalled committed capital, it must present pooled fund uncalled committed capital for the same periods for which the combination of pooled fund assets and pooled fund uncalled committed capital is presented. Both pooled fund uncalled committed capital and the combination of pooled fund assets and pooled fund uncalled committed capital must be clearly labeled as such.

Provision 7.A.9

If the FIRM chooses to present FIRM-wide uncalled COMMITTED CAPITAL or a combination of TOTAL FIRM ASSETS and FIRM-wide uncalled COMMITTED CAPITAL, the FIRM MUST:

a. Present FIRM-wide uncalled COMMITTED CAPITAL for the same periods for which the combination of TOTAL FIRM ASSETS and FIRM-wide uncalled COMMITTED CAPITAL is presented.
b. Clearly label FIRM-wide uncalled COMMITTED CAPITAL as such.
c. Clearly label the combination of TOTAL FIRM ASSETS and FIRM-wide uncalled COMMITTED CAPITAL as such.

Discussion

Committed capital is defined as pledges of capital to an investment vehicle by investors (limited partners and the general partner) or the firm and is typically drawn down over a period of time. Uncalled committed capital, also known as dry powder, is the amount of capital that has not yet been drawn. For periods beginning on or after 1 January 2020, uncalled committed capital must not be included in total firm assets. (See Provision 2.A.1.) Although firm-wide uncalled committed capital must not be included in the calculation of total firm assets as of 1 January 2020, a firm may report firm-wide uncalled committed capital in addition to the required presentation of total firm assets, if it wishes to do so. The inclusion of information on firm-wide uncalled committed capital provides prospective investors with a more complete picture of the firm's investments and the amount of its capital that is currently committed to a future investment. If a firm chooses to present information on firm-wide uncalled committed capital, it may present firm-wide uncalled committed capital as either:

- a separate value, or
- the combination of total firm assets and firm-wide uncalled committed capital.

If a firm chooses to present firm-wide uncalled committed capital as a separate value, the information must be clearly labeled.

If a firm chooses to present the combination of total firm assets and firm-wide uncalled committed capital, the firm must present firm-wide uncalled committed capital for the same periods for which the combination of total firm assets and firm-wide uncalled committed capital is presented. Both firm-wide uncalled committed capital and the combination of total firm assets and firm-wide uncalled committed capital must be clearly labeled as such.

Provision 7.A.10

If the FIRM chooses to present ADVISORY-ONLY ASSETS that reflect the POOLED FUND'S investment mandate, objective, or strategy or a combination of POOLED FUND assets and ADVISORY-ONLY ASSETS that reflect the POOLED FUND'S investment mandate, objective, or strategy, the FIRM MUST:

a. Present ADVISORY-ONLY ASSETS that reflect the POOLED FUND'S investment mandate, objective, or strategy for the same periods for which the combination of POOLED FUND assets and ADVISORY-ONLY ASSETS that reflect the POOLED FUND'S investment mandate, objective, or strategy is presented.

b. Clearly label ADVISORY-ONLY ASSETS that reflect the POOLED FUND'S investment mandate, objective, or strategy as such.

c. Clearly label the combination of POOLED FUND assets and ADVISORY-ONLY ASSETS that reflect the POOLED FUND'S investment mandate, objective, or strategy as such.

Discussion

Pooled fund advisory-only assets are assets for which the firm provides investment recommendations in line with the pooled fund's strategy but for which the firm has no control over implementation of investment decisions and no trading authority for the assets. Although pooled fund advisory-only assets must not be included in the calculation of pooled fund assets because the firm does not manage these assets, a firm may wish to provide information on pooled fund advisory-only assets that reflect the pooled fund's investment mandate, objective, or strategy, in addition to the required presentation of pooled fund assets. The inclusion of information on pooled fund advisory-only assets provides prospective investors additional information about a firm's business model and the types of investment-related services that it provides. If a firm chooses to present information on pooled fund advisory-only assets, it may present pooled fund advisory-only assets as either:

- a separate value, or
- the combination of pooled fund assets and pooled fund advisory-only assets.

If a firm chooses to present pooled fund advisory-only assets as a separate value, the information must be clearly labeled.

If a firm chooses to present the combination of pooled fund assets and pooled fund advisory-only assets, the firm must present pooled fund advisory-only assets for the same periods for which the combination of pooled fund assets and pooled fund advisory-only assets is presented. Both pooled fund advisory-only assets and the combination of pooled fund assets and pooled fund advisory-only assets must be clearly labeled as such.

Provision 7.A.11

If the FIRM chooses to present FIRM-wide ADVISORY-ONLY ASSETS or a combination of TOTAL FIRM ASSETS and FIRM-wide ADVISORY-ONLY ASSETS, the FIRM MUST:

a. Present FIRM-wide ADVISORY-ONLY ASSETS for the same periods for which the combination of TOTAL FIRM ASSETS and FIRM-wide ADVISORY-ONLY ASSETS is presented.

b. Clearly label FIRM-wide ADVISORY-ONLY ASSETS as such.

c. Clearly label the combination of TOTAL FIRM ASSETS and FIRM-wide ADVISORY-ONLY ASSETS as such.

Discussion

Advisory-only assets are assets for which the firm provides investment recommendations but for which the firm has no control over implementation of investment decisions and no trading authority for the assets. Although firm-wide advisory-only assets must not be included in the calculation of total firm assets because the firm does not manage these assets, a firm may wish to provide information on firm-wide advisory-only assets in addition to the required presentation of total firm assets. The inclusion of information on firm-wide advisory-only assets provides prospective investors additional information about a firm's business model and the types of investment-related services that it provides. If a firm chooses to present information on firm-wide advisory-only assets, it may present firm-wide advisory-only assets as either:

- a separate value, or
- the combination of total firm assets and firm-wide advisory-only assets.

If a firm chooses to present firm-wide advisory-only assets as a separate value, the information must be clearly labeled.

If a firm chooses to present the combination of total firm assets and firm-wide advisory-only assets, the firm must present firm-wide advisory-only assets for the same periods for which the combination of total firm assets and firm-wide advisory-only assets is presented. Both the firm-wide advisory-only assets and the combination of total firm assets and firm-wide advisory-only assets must be clearly labeled as such.

Provision 7.A.12

All REQUIRED and RECOMMENDED information in the GIPS POOLED FUND REPORT MUST be presented in the same currency.

Discussion

Firms must present all required and recommended information in a GIPS Pooled Fund Report in the same currency (e.g., pooled fund and benchmark returns, pooled fund assets, and total firm assets). This requirement is not applicable to the fee schedule. Supplemental information should also be presented in the same currency. If it is not, that fact must be disclosed. Not disclosing this fact could be misleading.

If a firm chooses to present a pooled fund in a different currency, the firm must convert all of the required information into the new currency. If the firm chooses to present performance in multiple currencies in the same GIPS Pooled Fund Report, the firm must convert all of the required information into each of the currencies and ensure it is clear in which currencies performance is reported. The firm must also convert any recommended information it chooses to present in the GIPS Pooled Fund Report containing the converted information.

The GIPS standards do not require or recommend a particular method for converting performance from one currency to another. One option for converting returns into a different currency is to convert the underlying data (values and external cash flows) into the selected currency using the exchange rate on the date of each cash flow or valuation date, and then calculate the pooled fund returns based on the converted data.

It is not acceptable to convert returns by applying the exchange rate as of the current period end to the historical data, including cash flows and valuations, used to calculate returns.

It is up to the firm to determine the pooled fund–specific conversion method. Policies and procedures for converting returns must be established, documented, and applied consistently.

Provision 7.A.13

Any SUPPLEMENTAL INFORMATION included in the GIPS POOLED FUND REPORT:

a. MUST relate directly to the POOLED FUND.
b. MUST NOT contradict or conflict with the REQUIRED or RECOMMENDED information in the GIPS POOLED FUND REPORT.
c. MUST be clearly labeled as SUPPLEMENTAL INFORMATION.

Discussion

Supplemental information is any performance-related information included as part of a GIPS Pooled Fund Report that supplements or enhances the requirements and/or recommendations of the GIPS standards. Performance-related information includes:

- information expressed in terms of investment return and risk, and
- other information and input data that directly relate to the calculation of investment return and risk (e.g., pooled fund holdings), as well as information derived from investment return and risk input data (e.g. performance contribution or attribution).

Supplemental information should provide users of the GIPS Pooled Fund Report with the proper context in which to understand the performance results. Common examples of supplemental information for a GIPS Pooled Fund Report that presents money-weighted returns (MWRs) include the following:

- projected investment-level MWRs,
- projected multiples, and
- benchmark time-weighted returns.

Supplemental information must relate directly to the pooled fund and must not contradict or conflict with the required or recommended information in the GIPS Pooled Fund Report. Examples of information that relates directly to the pooled fund and would be considered supplemental information include segment returns (e.g., country or sector), performance attribution, and pooled fund holdings. An example of information that would conflict with the GIPS standards is an MWR that includes data from a past firm when the firm does not meet the portability tests specified in Provision 1.A.32.

The following is a more complete list of the principles that apply when supplemental information is presented. Supplemental information must:

- satisfy the spirit and principles of the GIPS standards—fair representation and full disclosure,
- comply with all applicable laws and regulations regarding the calculation and presentation of performance,
- not include performance or performance-related information that is false or misleading,
- relate directly to the pooled fund and supplement or enhance the required or recommended information included in the GIPS Pooled Fund Report,
- not contradict or conflict with the required or recommended information in the GIPS Pooled Fund Report,
- be clearly labeled as supplemental information, and
- not be shown with greater prominence than the required pooled fund information.

7.B. Presentation and Reporting—Recommendations

Provision 7.B.1

The FIRM SHOULD present annualized SINCE-INCEPTION MONEY-WEIGHTED POOLED FUND GROSS RETURNS and SINCE-INCEPTION MONEY-WEIGHTED POOLED FUND NET RETURNS as of each annual period end.

Discussion

A firm is required to present either a since-inception money-weighted pooled fund gross return or since-inception money-weighted pooled fund net return in a GIPS Pooled Fund Report that presents money-weighted returns. Each type of return provides important information to prospective investors.

Because a since-inception money-weighted pooled fund gross return is the return on investments reduced by any transaction costs, it is the best measure of the firm's investment management ability and can be thought of as the "investment return." In addition, because fees are sometimes negotiable, pooled fund gross returns show the firm's expertise in managing assets without the effect of the firm's or investor's negotiating skills. Gross returns also allow prospective investors to better compare performance between firms.

Since-inception money-weighted pooled fund net returns reflect the deduction of all pooled fund fees and costs, including investment management fees, administrative fees, and other costs. Pooled fund net returns therefore provide the best indication to prospective investors of the returns that the firm's investors in a particular fund received or would have received over time, after taking into account the effect of all fees and costs associated with the pooled fund.

Because both pooled fund gross returns and pooled fund net returns provide important information to prospective investors, it is recommended that firms present both since-inception money-weighted pooled fund gross returns and since-inception money-weighted pooled fund net returns in a GIPS Pooled Fund Report.

Also, while a firm is required to present only the annualized pooled fund since-inception money-weighed return (SI-MWR) through the most recent annual period end, it is recommended that the firm also present SI-MWRs as of each annual period end. Doing so will provide prospective investors with a more complete picture of the performance of the pooled fund over time.

Provision 7.B.2

If the POOLED FUND has COMMITTED CAPITAL, the FIRM SHOULD present the following items as of each annual period end:

a. POOLED FUND SINCE-INCEPTION PAID-IN CAPITAL.

b. POOLED FUND SINCE-INCEPTION DISTRIBUTIONS.

c. POOLED FUND cumulative COMMITTED CAPITAL.

d. TOTAL VALUE to SINCE-INCEPTION PAID-IN CAPITAL (INVESTMENT MULTIPLE or TVPI).

e. SINCE-INCEPTION DISTRIBUTIONS to SINCE-INCEPTION PAID-IN CAPITAL (REALIZATION MULTIPLE or DPI).

f. SINCE-INCEPTION PAID-IN CAPITAL to cumulative COMMITTED CAPITAL (PIC MULTIPLE).

g. RESIDUAL VALUE to SINCE-INCEPTION PAID-IN CAPITAL (UNREALIZED MULTIPLE or RVPI).

Discussion

Firms are required to present the pooled fund since-inception money-weighted return (SI-MWR), through the most recent annual period end, as well as the since-inception paid-in capital, since-inception distributions, cumulative committed capital, investment multiple (TVPI), realization multiple (DPI), PIC multiple, and unrealized multiple (RVPI), as of the most recent annual period end. If firms choose to present additional SI-MWRs through prior annual period ends, firms are recommended to also present the same metrics as of each additional period end for which returns are presented. See Provision 7.A.4 for further discussion of these metrics.

Provision 7.B.3

The FIRM SHOULD present PROPRIETARY ASSETS as a percentage of POOLED FUND assets as of the most recent annual period end.

Discussion

Proprietary assets are assets owned by the firm, the firm's management, and/or the firm's parent company that are managed by the firm. General partner assets in a pooled fund are considered proprietary assets. Knowing how much of a pooled fund's assets are proprietary and how much are managed for external investors provides prospective investors with additional insight regarding the pooled fund, especially when a significant percentage of the pooled fund's assets are proprietary. If a pooled fund includes proprietary assets, it is recommended that firms present proprietary assets as a percentage of pooled fund assets as of the most recent annual period end.

Provision 7.B.4

The FIRM SHOULD present an appropriate EX POST risk measure for the POOLED FUND and the BENCHMARK. The same EX POST risk measure SHOULD be presented for the POOLED FUND and the BENCHMARK.

Discussion

Evaluating past performance requires an understanding of the risks taken to achieve the results. Although firms are required to include a qualitative narrative of material risks as part of the pooled fund description, firms should also include an ex post risk measure for the pooled fund and benchmark. Any risk measure presented must be calculated on an ex post basis and be based on actual historical data. Some examples of ex post risk measures that may be presented include drawdown measures, interest rate risk measures (e.g., duration), credit risk measures (e.g., credit spread), and liquidity risk measures. Because no quantitative risk measure is required for pooled funds that present money-weighted returns, all risk measures presented are considered additional risk measures.

If the firm chooses to present an ex post risk measure for the pooled fund and benchmark, the same ex post risk measure should be presented for the pooled fund and benchmark. The risk measure must be one that the firm determines is appropriate for the pooled fund. When choosing an appropriate ex post risk measure to present, the firm should satisfy itself that there are sufficient data points for the selected risk measure to be statistically significant so as not to be misleading. Firms are required to describe any additional risk measure that is included in the GIPS Pooled Fund Report (see Provision 7.C.36).

Provision 7.B.5

If the FIRM uses preliminary, estimated values as FAIR VALUE, the FIRM SHOULD present the percentage of assets in the POOLED FUND that were valued using preliminary, estimated values as of the most recent annual period end.

Discussion

The use of preliminary, estimated values as fair value is common for some alternative strategies, including those that invest in underlying funds for which the firm relies on valuations provided by the underlying fund managers. When using preliminary, estimated values as fair value, it is important to remember the underlying principles of the GIPS standards: fair representation and full disclosure. If using preliminary, estimated values, firms must disclose this fact in the relevant GIPS Pooled Fund Report (see Provision 7.C.34). It is recommended that the firm also present the percentage of assets in the pooled fund that were valued using preliminary, estimated values as of the most recent annual period end. This provides important information that allows prospective investors to better assess the valuations and performance record presented.

Provision 7.B.6

For POOLED FUNDS OF FUNDS, the FIRM SHOULD present the percentage, if any, of POOLED FUND assets that is invested in DIRECT INVESTMENTS (rather than in fund investment vehicles) as of the most recent annual period end.

Discussion

Direct investments by a fund of funds are investments made directly in companies rather than investments made through pooled funds. Direct investments may augment the strategy used in the investment in underlying pooled funds. Direct investments may have different terms and conditions that might change the fund of funds' return characteristics, such as a different fee structure. By presenting the percentage of investments dedicated to direct investments as of the most recent annual period end, the firm is providing additional transparency and allowing the prospective investor to factor in additional criteria when analyzing the returns included in the GIPS Pooled Fund Report for the fund of funds. If no assets are invested in direct investments, this recommendation is not applicable.

Provision 7.B.7

If the FIRM has COMMITTED CAPITAL, the FIRM SHOULD present FIRM-wide uncalled COMMITTED CAPITAL as of the most recent annual period end.

Discussion

Committed capital is defined as pledges of capital to an investment vehicle by investors (limited partners and the general partner) or the firm and is typically drawn down over a period of time. Uncalled committed capital, also known as dry powder, is the amount of capital that has not yet been drawn. If a firm has committed capital, it is recommended that the firm present total firm-wide uncalled committed capital as of the most recent annual period end. This information provides prospective investors a more complete picture of the capital that is currently committed to a future investment. If the firm chooses to present firm-wide uncalled committed capital, it may present this amount separately from total firm assets. The firm may also choose to present the combination of total firm assets and firm-wide uncalled committed capital. Provision 7.A.9 discusses the requirements relating to the presentation of firm-wide uncalled committed capital in a GIPS Pooled Fund Report.

Provision 7.B.8

The FIRM SHOULD present the total FAIR VALUE of the FIRM'S co-investments related to the POOLED FUND as of the most recent annual period end.

Discussion

Direct investments are investments made directly in companies rather than investments made through pooled fund investments. Co-investments are a type of direct investment in which pooled fund investors invest additional capital alongside the pooled fund's investments. It is recommended that the firm present the total fair value of the firm's co-investments related to the pooled fund as of the most recent annual period end. This information will give prospective investors a more complete picture of the nature of the investments related to the pooled fund.

7.C. Disclosure—Requirements

Provision 7.C.1

Once the FIRM has met all the applicable REQUIREMENTS of the GIPS standards, the FIRM MUST disclose its compliance with the GIPS standards using one of the following compliance statements. The compliance statement for a POOLED FUND MUST only be used in a GIPS POOLED FUND REPORT.

a. For a FIRM that is verified:

"[Insert name of FIRM] claims compliance with the Global Investment Performance Standards (GIPS®) and has prepared and presented this report in compliance with the GIPS standards. [Insert name of FIRM] has been independently verified for the periods [insert dates]. The verification report(s) is/are available upon request.

"A firm that claims compliance with the GIPS standards must establish policies and procedures for complying with all the applicable requirements of the GIPS standards. Verification provides assurance on whether the firm's policies and procedures related to composite and pooled fund maintenance, as well as the calculation, presentation, and distribution of performance, have been designed in compliance with the GIPS standards and have been implemented on a firm-wide basis. Verification does not provide assurance on the accuracy of any specific performance report."

b. For POOLED FUNDS of a verified FIRM that have also had a PERFORMANCE EXAMINATION:

"[Insert name of FIRM] claims compliance with the Global Investment Performance Standards (GIPS®) and has prepared and presented this report in compliance with the GIPS standards. [Insert name of FIRM] has been independently verified for the periods [insert dates].

"A firm that claims compliance with the GIPS standards must establish policies and procedures for complying with all the applicable requirements of the GIPS standards. Verification provides assurance on whether the firm's policies and procedures related to composite and pooled fund maintenance, as well as the calculation, presentation, and distribution of performance, have been designed in compliance with the GIPS standards and have been implemented on a firm-wide basis. The [insert name of POOLED FUND] has had a performance examination for the periods [insert dates]. The verification and performance examination reports are available upon request."

The compliance statement for a FIRM that is verified or for POOLED FUNDS of a verified FIRM that have also had a PERFORMANCE EXAMINATION is complete only when both paragraphs are shown together, one after the other.

c. For a FIRM that has not been verified:

"[Insert name of FIRM] claims compliance with the Global Investment Performance Standards (GIPS®) and has prepared and presented this report in compliance with the GIPS standards. [Insert name of FIRM] has not been independently verified."

The FIRM MUST NOT exclude any portion of the respective compliance statement. Any modifications to the compliance statement MUST be additive.

Discussion

A firm meeting all the requirements of the GIPS standards must use one of the three compliance statements in each of its GIPS Pooled Fund Reports. The English version of the compliance statements is the controlling version. If a firm chooses to translate the claim of compliance into a language for which there is no official translation of the GIPS standards, the firm must take care to ensure that the translation used reflects the required wording of the claim of compliance used in Provisions 7.C.1.a, 7.C.1.b, or 7.C.1.c.

It is acceptable to combine both paragraphs of the claim of compliance for a verified firm (Provision 7.C.1.a) into a single paragraph. If the paragraphs are not combined, the claim of compliance for a verified firm is complete only when both paragraphs are shown together, one after the other. A firm may not separate the two required paragraphs from each other.

The same is true for the claim of compliance for a pooled fund that has also had a performance examination (Provision 7.C.1.b). Both paragraphs of the claim of compliance may be combined into a single paragraph. If the paragraphs are not combined, the claim of compliance is complete only when both paragraphs are shown together, one after the other. A firm may not separate the two required paragraphs from each other.

When preparing the GIPS Pooled Fund Report for a pooled fund that has had a performance examination, the firm may choose to use either the verification or performance examination compliance statement. For example, a firm might choose to use the verification compliance statement for all GIPS Reports, including GIPS Reports for pooled funds and composites that have had a performance examination, if it wishes to standardize the compliance statement for all GIPS Reports throughout the firm. In this situation, the firm may also disclose that a specific pooled fund has had a performance examination.

The language in each compliance statement must not exclude any portion of the respective compliance statement, with one exception. In the second paragraph of both 7.C.1.a and 7.C.1.b, there is a reference to "composite and pooled fund maintenance." The firm may delete the words "composite and" if no composites are included within the definition of the firm.

There may also be instances where it may be appropriate for a firm to modify the language slightly. For example, a firm may modify the language to include the name of the firm's verifier, if the firm wishes to disclose this information. A firm may also need to modify the language to add more details about the name of the firm that has been verified or the dates of the verification if the verification period was not continuous. Any modifications must be additive and must not result in a compliance statement that is false or misleading.

Provision 7.C.2

The FIRM MUST disclose the following: "GIPS® is a registered trademark of CFA Institute. CFA Institute does not endorse or promote this organization, nor does it warrant the accuracy or quality of the content contained herein."

Discussion

"GIPS®" is a registered trademark of CFA Institute, and firms are required to acknowledge this fact in all GIPS Pooled Fund Reports. The required disclosure may appear in the body of the GIPS Pooled Fund Report or in a footnote to the report. The term "this organization", which is included in the required disclosure, refers to any entity associated with the GIPS Pooled Fund Report, either the firm or the verifier.

CFA Institute (owner of the GIPS® trademark) may take appropriate action against any firm that misuses the mark "GIPS®" or any compliance statement, including false claims of compliance with the GIPS standards. CFA Institute members, CFA Program charterholders, CFA candidates, CIPM Program certificants, and CIPM candidates who misuse the term "GIPS" or any compliance statement, misrepresent their performance history or the performance history of their firm, or falsely claim compliance with the GIPS standards are also subject to disciplinary sanctions under the CFA Institute Code of Ethics and Standards of Professional Conduct. Possible disciplinary sanctions include public censure, suspension of membership, and revocation of the CFA charter or CIPM certificate.

Regulators with jurisdiction over firms claiming compliance with the GIPS standards may also take enforcement actions against firms that falsely claim compliance with the GIPS standards.

Firms may also use the following language to replace the first sentence in this required disclosure: "GIPS® is a registered trademark owned by CFA Institute." See the GIPS Standards Trademark Usage Guidelines on the CFA Institute website (www.cfainstitute.org) for additional guidance on the proper use of "GIPS".

Provision 7.C.3

The FIRM MUST disclose the definition of the FIRM used to determine TOTAL FIRM ASSETS and FIRM-wide compliance.

Discussion

To claim compliance with the GIPS standards, a firm must comply with all applicable requirements of the GIPS standards on a firm-wide basis. Accordingly, the firm must determine exactly how it will be defined for the purpose of compliance. The GIPS standards require that a firm must be defined as an investment firm, subsidiary, or division held out to the public as a distinct business entity.

A distinct business entity is a unit, division, department, or office that is organizationally and functionally segregated from other units, divisions, departments, or offices; that retains discretion over the assets it manages; and that should have autonomy over the investment decision-making process.

Possible criteria that can be used to determine this status include:

- being a legal entity,
- having a distinct market or client type (e.g., institutional, retail, private client), and
- using a separate and distinct investment process.

See Provision 1.A.2 for a more detailed discussion of defining the firm.

Because there are often a number of closely related units or divisions within larger investment management entities, it is critical to disclose the precise definition of the firm that is presenting the performance results and would be responsible for the management of the pooled fund's assets. This provision requires the firm to disclose sufficient details of the entity that is presenting investment performance such that the firm is clearly identified.

Sample Disclosures:

Example 1:

Firm A is a multinational investment firm with offices around the world, including in Japan, Australia, the United Kingdom, and the United States. Although all of its offices are part of the global parent company, each office is registered with the appropriate national regulatory authority, and each is held out to the public as a distinct business entity. The firm has defined its offices in Japan, Australia, the United Kingdom, and the United States as separate firms for the purpose of complying with the GIPS standards. The offices in Japan, the United Kingdom, and the

United States claim compliance with the GIPS standards. Firm A's Australia office, however, does not claim compliance with the GIPS standards.

Sample Disclosure for Firm A—US:

"For the purpose of complying with the GIPS standards, the firm is defined as Firm A—US, which serves US clients and investors and is a subsidiary of Firm A, a multinational investment firm with offices globally. Firm A also has subsidiaries in the United Kingdom, Australia, and Japan, which are not included in the definition of the firm for purposes of compliance with the GIPS standards."

Example 2:

Firm B has two divisions, each of which serves a distinct client type. Firm B Institutional Investment Management manages institutional assets. Firm B Retail Investors manages retail assets. The firm has determined that it will create two separate firms for the purpose of complying with the GIPS standards.

Sample Disclosure for Firm B Institutional Investment Management:

"For the purpose of complying with the GIPS standards, the firm is defined as Firm B Institutional Investment Management, the institutional asset management division of Firm B."

Example 3:

Firm C is an investment management firm that offers both active and passive (indexed) investment strategies. For the purpose of complying with the GIPS standards, the firm has decided to create two separate firms: one that offers active investment strategies and one that offers indexed investment strategies.

Sample Disclosure for Firm C—Indexed Investing

"For the purpose of complying with the GIPS standards, the firm is defined as Firm C—Indexed Investing. Firm C—Indexed Investing is the division of Firm C that offers indexed investment strategies to investors."

Provision 7.C.4

The FIRM MUST disclose the POOLED FUND DESCRIPTION.

Discussion

The pooled fund description is defined as general information regarding the investment mandate, objective, or strategy of the pooled fund. The pooled fund description must include enough information to allow a prospective investor to understand the key characteristics of the pooled fund's investment mandate, objective, or strategy, including:

- the material risks of the pooled fund's strategy,
- how leverage, derivatives, and short positions may be used, if they are a material part of the strategy, and
- if illiquid investments are a material part of the strategy.

The required disclosure of the pooled fund description provides information about the pooled fund's investment strategy that is intended to help a prospective investor who is considering an investment in a pooled fund and is reviewing a GIPS Pooled Fund Report for that pooled fund. The pooled fund description should provide sufficient information to prospective investors to allow them to differentiate the significant features of the pooled fund from other strategies or pooled funds within the firm and to compare products across firms. The disclosed strategy features will likely affect both the historical and expected risk and returns. Along with the required benchmark description (see Provision 7.C.5), the GIPS Pooled Fund Report will allow prospective investors to understand both the investment strategy employed and the benchmark against which the pooled fund's performance is evaluated. This will help prospective investors to compare investments across firms.

If leverage, derivatives, and short positions may be used, and they are a material part of the strategy, this must be disclosed in the pooled fund description. Provision 7.C.15 requires that the firm disclose how leverage, derivatives, and short positions have been used historically, if material. Taken together, these two required disclosures provide a more complete picture about the presence, use, and extent of leverage, derivatives, and short positions. When determining what would be material, the firm must consider whether the disclosure of how leverage, derivatives, and/or short positions may be used and/or have been used historically is likely to affect a prospective investor's view of the risk involved in the pooled fund strategy. If so, it would be misleading for the firm to fail to disclose their use to prospective investors when describing the strategy.

Generally, all investment products or strategies have some degree of inherent risk (e.g., market risk), but it is not intended that the pooled fund description identifies every risk of the pooled fund's strategy. Instead, firms must identify those material risks of the strategy, if any, and must disclose those risks. For example, investment concentration, correlation (or lack thereof), liquidity, and exposure to counterparties are features that may need to be included in the pooled fund description.

The key characteristics of some pooled fund strategies may change given market events. Firms should periodically review pooled fund descriptions to ensure they are current.

 |

Sample Disclosure:

"The Armor Distressed Debt Fund's returns reflect the EUR share class. The fund invests at least 85% of its assets in distressed euro-denominated bonds that have credit ratings of CCC or lower by at least one major credit rating agency. Key risks include widening corporate spreads and defaults, high levels of government debt, and elevated political tensions, which could lead to abrupt changes in monetary policy by the European Central Bank (ECB). A material amount of the fund's investments may be illiquid."

A Sample List of Pooled Fund Descriptions can be found in Appendix D of the GIPS standards.

Provision 7.C.5

The FIRM MUST disclose the BENCHMARK DESCRIPTION, which MUST include the key features of the BENCHMARK or the name of the BENCHMARK for a readily recognized index or other point of reference.

Discussion

Firms are required to disclose a description of each benchmark included in a GIPS Pooled Fund Report. The benchmark description is defined as general information regarding the investments, structure, and/or characteristics of the benchmark, and it must include the key features of the benchmark. In the case of a widely-recognized benchmark, the name of the benchmark will satisfy this requirement. There are few money-weighted return benchmarks that would be considered widely recognized. If the firm presents a public market equivalent (PME) as a benchmark, the benchmark description must include the name of the market index that is used to calculate the PME. Given the unique nature of a PME, if the market index used to calculate the PME is not readily recognized, the firm must also disclose the description of this benchmark. See the discussion of Provision 7.C.29 for an explanation of a PME. Each firm must decide for itself whether a benchmark is widely recognized. If the firm is not certain as to whether the benchmark is widely known, the firm must include the benchmark description.

Sample Disclosure:

"The custom benchmark return is calculated by applying the investment cash flows of the Armor Distressed Debt Fund to the XYZ Eurozone Distressed Debt Bond Index. The index reflects a portfolio of euro-denominated distressed debt bonds issued in Eurozone countries that generally have credit ratings of CCC or lower from the main rating agencies and are listed on the XYZ platforms."

Provision 7.C.6

When presenting POOLED FUND GROSS RETURNS, the FIRM MUST disclose if any other fees are deducted in addition to TRANSACTION COSTS.

Discussion

A pooled fund gross return is the return on investments reduced by any transaction costs. If a firm presents a pooled fund gross return in a GIPS Pooled Fund Report, the firm must disclose if any other fees are deducted in addition to actual transaction costs. For example, a pooled fund's gross return might reflect the deduction of administrative expenses, such as custodian and fund accounting fees. The same is true for a fund of funds. Firms are not required to disclose that returns reflect the deduction of expenses incurred in underlying investments, including investments in other pooled funds.

In cases where fees other than transactions costs have been deducted from the gross returns, this disclosure helps prospective investors understand the gross returns being presented and therefore compare performance across firms.

Firms may calculate pooled fund gross returns that do not reflect the deduction of the underlying pooled fund investment management fees only when the firm controls the investment management fees of the underlying pooled funds. In such situations, the firm can present the pooled fund gross returns that are gross of the underlying funds' investment management fees but net of the underlying funds' transaction costs and other expenses. The following represent some situations in which this criterion is met:

- Both underlying funds and the fund of funds are managed by the same firm and there is effectively a fee rebate or waiver at the fund-of-funds level for those fees charged at the underlying fund level.
- A fund of funds resembles a master-feeder structure that invests in one or multiple underlying funds managed by the same firm, and its investment management fee model is structured so that the investment management fee is either partially or fully charged at the underlying fund level.

Sample Disclosure:

"Gross returns reflect the deduction of administrative expenses but do not reflect the deduction of investment management fees."

 |

Provision 7.C.7

When presenting POOLED FUND NET RETURNS, the FIRM MUST disclose:

a. If POOLED FUND NET RETURNS are calculated using model or actual TOTAL POOLED FUND FEES.

b. If POOLED FUND NET RETURNS are net of any PERFORMANCE-BASED FEES or CARRIED INTEREST.

c. If model INVESTMENT MANAGEMENT FEES or model TOTAL POOLED FUND FEES are used and POOLED FUND GROSS RETURNS are not presented, the model INVESTMENT MANAGEMENT FEE or model TOTAL POOLED FUND FEE used to calculate POOLED FUND NET RETURNS.[54]

d. If model INVESTMENT MANAGEMENT FEES or model TOTAL POOLED FUND FEES are used, the methodology used to calculate POOLED FUND NET RETURNS.

e. If the POOLED FUND has a partnership structure, on which assets the POOLED FUND NET RETURNS are calculated.

f. If the POOLED FUND has multiple share classes, and one share class is used to calculate POOLED FUND NET RETURNS, the share class used to calculate POOLED FUND NET RETURNS.

Discussion

When presenting returns, it is important that there are sufficient disclosures so that prospective investors can understand what the returns actually represent.

Pooled fund net returns are required to reflect the deduction of all fees and expenses, including transaction costs, investment management fees, administrative fees, and other costs. When calculating pooled fund net returns, the fees used in the calculation must include both asset-based and performance-based fees. If the pooled fund net returns are net of any performance-based fees or carried interest, that fact must be disclosed.

A firm must disclose if model or actual total pooled fund fees are used to calculate pooled fund net returns. (See Provision 2.A.33 for an explanation of when model total pooled fund fees may be used.) Given the nature of a money-weighted return calculation, in most instances firms will use actual investment management fees and actual total pooled fund fees. However, there may be cases where it is appropriate to use model fees, such as when a pooled fund is seeded with firm capital and no investment management fees are charged. If model fees are used, and gross returns are presented along with the net returns, prospective investors can easily determine the model fee used by deducting the net returns from the gross returns. For periods ending on or after 31 December 2020, however, if model investment management fees or model total pooled fund fees are used and pooled fund gross returns are not presented, the firm must disclose the model

[54] REQUIRED for periods ending on or after 31 December 2020.

investment management fees or model total pooled fund fees used to calculate pooled fund net returns. The methodology used in the calculation of pooled fund net returns must also be disclosed if model investment management fees or model total pooled fund fees are used. Given the nature of a money-weighted return calculation, in most instances firms will use actual total pooled fund fees. In some cases, however, it may be appropriate to use model fees, such as when a pooled fund is seeded with firm capital and no fees or expenses are charged.

Because general partner assets are not charged an investment management fee, the inclusion of general partner assets in the calculation of pooled fund net returns will boost net returns relative to the returns actually received by pooled fund investors. Therefore, in order for prospective investors to understand the pooled fund net returns presented in a GIPS Pooled Fund Report, if a pooled fund has a partnership structure, firms must disclose whether returns are calculated based on the general partner assets, the limited partner assets, or total pooled fund assets. To present the most relevant returns for prospective investors, it is common practice for pooled fund net returns to be calculated using only the limited partner assets and cash flows.

Pooled funds often have multiple share classes, with each class typically having different fees and expenses. In addition, there are often restrictions on what type of investor can purchase a particular share class. When a pooled fund has multiple share classes, firms must disclose which share class was used to calculate pooled fund net returns. This information will help prospective investors determine if the returns are based on fees and expenses that are high or low relative to the fund's other share classes. It will also help investors determine if the returns are based on a share class for which they are eligible. If the returns are based on a share class for which they are not eligible, a prospective investor can then request information for a share class for which they are eligible.

Sample Disclosure for Actual Total Pooled Fund Fees:

"Pooled fund net returns are net of actual total pooled fund fees, including incentive fees, which are recorded on an accrual basis. Net returns are calculated using the assets of the limited partners."

Sample Disclosure for Model Total Pooled Fund Fees:

"Net returns are calculated by applying a model total pooled fund fee of 0.4125% on a quarterly basis. This equates to a model annual total pooled fund fee of 1.65%. The model fee is based on the actual administrative expenses as stated in the 2019 audited financial statements and applying the highest tier of the standard fee schedule that a limited partner would pay."

Provision 7.C.8

The FIRM MUST disclose which fees and expenses other than INVESTMENT MANAGEMENT FEES (e.g., research costs) are separately charged by the FIRM to investors, if material.

Discussion

Administrative fees and costs are typically paid from a pooled fund's assets. Investment management fees may be paid from a pooled fund's assets or may be separately charged to investors. In some cases, other fees and expenses, such as investment research costs, may be billed by the firm directly to the investor. When any fees and expenses other than investment management fees are separately charged by the firm to investors, and these fees and expenses are material, the firm must disclose which fees and expenses are separately charged. When determining if additional fees or expenses would be considered material, a firm must consider whether the additional fees or expenses are significant enough to reduce a prospective investor's assessment of the attractiveness of the expected returns of the pooled fund relative to total fees charged. If so, the firm's failure to disclose these additional fees or expenses would violate the principle of full disclosure.

Sample Disclosure:

"In addition to the fees charged directly to the pooled fund and reflected in the pooled fund's net return, investment research costs are charged directly to investors, as stipulated in the pooled fund offering memo."

Provision 7.C.9

The FIRM MUST disclose or otherwise indicate the reporting currency.

Discussion

The GIPS standards require that firms disclose the currency used to report the numerical information presented in a GIPS Pooled Fund Report. If the firm presents performance in multiple currencies in the same GIPS Pooled Fund Report, the firm must ensure it is clear which currencies are used to calculate performance and assets.

Labeling the columns within a GIPS Pooled Fund Report with the appropriate currency symbol would satisfy this requirement, as would a written disclosure. If firms market the strategy outside their home market, they should consider whether the currency symbol alone is sufficient. For example, a Canadian firm marketing only in Canada may decide to present only the $ symbol. If the firm markets the strategy in both the United States and Canada, the firm must disclose whether the currency is USD or CAD, because both currencies use the same currency symbol.

All required and recommended information presented in a GIPS Pooled Fund Report must be presented in the same currency. (See Provision 7.A.12.)

Sample Disclosures:

"Valuations are computed and all information is reported in Canadian dollars."

"All numerical information is reported in Japanese yen."

Provision 7.C.10

The FIRM MUST disclose the current FEE SCHEDULE appropriate to PROSPECTIVE INVESTORS.

Discussion

Firms must disclose the current schedule of investment management fees that is applicable to prospective investors for the specific pooled fund. The fee schedule can be asset-based, performance based, or a combination of both. Firms are also required to disclose the pooled fund's expense ratio, which includes investment management fees as well as all other pooled fund expenses. See Provision 7.A.7 for a discussion of pooled fund expense ratios.

The fee schedule should be appropriate to the particular prospective investors and must be current. Although a current fee schedule may not assist a prospective investor when interpreting historical performance because the actual fees paid may differ from the fee schedule disclosed, it is the most relevant fee schedule for the prospective investor. The actual fee that the prospective investor may pay (if the investor hires the firm) could also differ from the fee schedule disclosed in the GIPS Pooled Fund Report. For example, the prospective investor may be able to negotiate a lower fee.

If the pooled fund has multiple fee schedules, the firm may use the highest fee schedule as the appropriate fee that can be used for all prospective investors. The firm may also include multiple fee schedules in the GIPS Pooled Fund Report. Including a range of fee schedules (e.g., management fees range from 0.50% to 0.95%) would not satisfy this requirement.

This disclosure requirement is not satisfied if the firm does not include the fee schedule in the GIPS Pooled Fund Report and instead makes reference to another document that includes the fee schedule, such as Form ADV, which is a US regulatory document, or a fund prospectus. The fee schedule may be an exhibit attached to the GIPS Pooled Fund Report. The exhibit may be the pooled fund's offering documents, if the offering documents include the appropriate current fee schedule.

Sample Disclosure:

"The annual fee schedule for Fund XYZ is as follows:

First €10 million	0.80%
Next €40 million	0.60%
Above €50 million	0.30%"

Provision 7.C.11

If the FEE SCHEDULE includes PERFORMANCE-BASED FEES or CARRIED INTEREST, the FIRM MUST disclose the PERFORMANCE-BASED FEE DESCRIPTION or CARRIED INTEREST DESCRIPTION.

Discussion

Sufficient information must be included with any fee schedule included in a GIPS Pooled Fund Report to allow prospective investors to understand the nature of the firm's compensation. If performance-based fees or carried interest are included in the fee schedule, the firm must disclose a description of the performance-based fees and/or carried interest. Relevant information for a performance-based fee includes the performance-based fee rate, hurdle rate, clawback, high watermark, reset frequency, accrual frequency, crystallization schedule, and on what basis fees are charged. Relevant information for carried interest includes the hurdle rate, crystallization schedule, and high watermark.

Sample Disclosure:

"The standard fee schedule is as follows:

> Management fee is 0.75% per annum, charged on a quarterly basis on the period-end value of fund net assets.
>
> Performance fee:
>
> The performance fee is earned when the fund's total return, reduced by the pro rata accrued fixed management fee, exceeds the benchmark return (the excess return) and the fund's net asset value is above the high watermark, which is the fund's net asset value as of the last year end when the performance fee crystallized. The performance fee is 10% of the excess return, which is calculated arithmetically, accrued quarterly, and crystallizes annually. Further details of the performance fee calculation are available upon request."

Provision 7.C.12

The FIRM MUST disclose the POOLED FUND INCEPTION DATE and what the POOLED FUND INCEPTION DATE represents.

Discussion

Because an inception date may represent a different point in the life of a fund for different funds, a firm must disclose the pooled fund inception date and what the pooled fund inception date represents. For example, for a broad distribution pooled fund, the inception date is the date on which the fund commences operations and begins trading. For a limited distribution fund, the inception date may be based on one of the following dates: (1) when investment management fees are first charged, (2) when the first investment-related cash flow takes place, (3) when the first capital call is made, or (4) when the first committed capital is closed and legally binding. It is only with appropriate disclosure that prospective investors can understand what the inception date represents.

Sample Disclosure for a Broad Distribution Pooled Fund:

"The Small-Cap Growth Fund has an inception date of 1 May 2017, the date on which the Fund began operations."

Sample Disclosure for a Limited Distribution Pooled Fund:

"The Global Growth Fund has an inception date of 15 September 2019, the date of the first capital call from the Fund's limited partners."

Provision 7.C.13

The FIRM MUST disclose that the following lists are available upon request, if applicable:

a. List of COMPOSITE DESCRIPTIONS.
b. List of POOLED FUND DESCRIPTIONS for LIMITED DISTRIBUTION POOLED FUNDS.
c. List of BROAD DISTRIBUTION POOLED FUNDS.

Discussion

In each GIPS Pooled Fund Report, firms must disclose that a list of composite descriptions and a list of pooled fund descriptions for limited distribution pooled funds (LDPFs) are available upon request, if applicable to the firm. The firm must also disclose that a list of broad distribution pooled funds (BDPFs) is available upon request, if BDPFs are included within the definition of the firm. The required list of LDPF descriptions and of BDPFs is at the fund level and not the share class level.

If the firm does not sell participation in a fund (e.g., the firm manages the assets but another legal entity distributes the fund and the firm does not sell shares in the fund), the firm must consider the portfolio a segregated account and would include the portfolio in a composite. This would include sub-advised pooled funds. The segregated account would not be included on the list of LDPF descriptions or the list of BDPFs. In addition, a portfolio with a pooled fund wrapper (i.e., a single-investor pooled fund), which is unitized but is not available to other investors, is also considered a segregated account, would be included in a composite, and would not appear on a list of LDPF descriptions or a list of BDPFs.

As noted in the discussion of Provision 1.A.22, if a pooled fund is included in a composite but the firm offers participation in the fund, either directly or through an agent, the pooled fund must still appear on the required list of LDPF descriptions or the list of BDPFs, as appropriate.

The firm may combine its list of composite descriptions, its list of LDPF descriptions, and its list of BDPFs into one document, if it wishes to do so. The firm may also prepare a list of all the strategies that it offers and may indicate, as part of the strategy description, the types of portfolios (segregated account, LDPF, or BDPF) in which the strategy is available. This list of strategies can be in narrative or table format.

This requirement exists to provide prospective investors with a complete picture of the firm's composites and pooled funds. Prospective investors may then request information that will allow them to evaluate whether the GIPS Pooled Fund Report they have received is the most appropriate and to determine if there are any other GIPS Composite Reports or GIPS Pooled Fund Reports that they should also request to see.

a. List of COMPOSITE DESCRIPTIONS.

If composites are included within the definition of the firm, the firm must disclose, in each GIPS Pooled Fund Report, that the firm's list of composite descriptions is available upon request. The list of composite descriptions itself does not need to be included in each GIPS Pooled Fund Report but must be available upon request. The list of composite descriptions must include the composite description for each current composite, as well as a description for all composites that have terminated in the past five years. The composite descriptions disclosed in GIPS Composite Reports must be consistent with the descriptions included in the list of composite descriptions.

An explanation of composite descriptions can be found in the discussion of Provision 1.A.22. A Sample List of Composite Descriptions can be found in Appendix D of the GIPS standards.

b. List of POOLED FUND DESCRIPTIONS for LIMITED DISTRIBUTION POOLED FUNDS.

If LDPFs are included within the definition of a firm, the firm must disclose, in each GIPS Pooled Fund Report, that the firm's list of descriptions of LDPFs is available upon request. An LDPF is any pooled fund that is not a BDPF. A BDPF is any pooled fund that is regulated under a framework that would permit the general public to purchase or hold the pooled fund's shares and is not exclusively offered in one-on-one presentations. LDPFs are often referred to as "private funds." These funds are typically sold in one-on-one presentations and may not be highly regulated. The list of

LDPF descriptions does not need to be included in each GIPS Pooled Fund Report but must be available upon request. The list of LDPF descriptions must include the pooled fund description for each current pooled fund but does not have to include terminated funds. Terminated LDPFs are treated differently from terminated composites because, although a firm can restart a composite strategy when a prospective client hires the firm for a strategy that was previously closed, the firm does not have the same ability to restart a pooled fund. The pooled fund descriptions disclosed in GIPS Pooled Fund Reports must be consistent with the descriptions included in the list of pooled fund descriptions.

The list of LDPF descriptions may be tailored to include only those LDPFs for which a prospective investor is eligible, but the firm is not required to do this.

An explanation of LDPF descriptions can be found in the discussion of Provision 1.A.22. A Sample List of Pooled Fund Descriptions can be found in Appendix D of the GIPS standards.

c. List of BROAD DISTRIBUTION POOLED FUNDS.

In addition to the lists of composite descriptions and LDPF descriptions, firms must also disclose, in each GIPS Pooled Fund Report, that a list of BDPFs is available upon request, if applicable to the firm. A BDPF is any pooled fund that is regulated under a framework that would permit the general public to purchase or hold the pooled fund's shares and is not exclusively offered in one-on-one presentations. These funds are typically sold to the general public and are highly regulated.

Note that the required list of BDPFs is a list of the names of the firm's BDPFs only. No descriptions of the BDPFs are required. The list of BDPF names does not need to be included in each GIPS Pooled Fund Report but must be available upon request. The list of BDPFs must include the names of all current BDPFs but does not need to include terminated BDPFs. Terminated BDPFs are treated differently from terminated composites because, although a firm can restart a composite strategy when a prospective client hires the firm for a strategy that was previously closed, the firm does not have the same ability to restart a pooled fund. If a firm includes information about all of its BDPFs on its website, the firm may provide a link to the website to fulfill the requirement to provide the list of BDPFs upon request.

This list may be tailored to include only those BDPFs for which a prospective investor is eligible, but the firm is not required to do this.

Sample Disclosures:

For Firms with Composites and Limited Distribution Pooled Funds

"A list of composite descriptions and a list of limited distribution pooled fund descriptions are available upon request."

For Firms with Composites, Limited Distribution Pooled Funds, and Broad Distribution Pooled Funds

"A list of composite descriptions, a list of limited distribution pooled fund descriptions, and a list of broad distribution pooled funds are available upon request."

For Firms That Offer Strategies in Multiple Vehicles

"A list of all composite and pooled fund investment strategies offered by the firm, with a description of each strategy, is available upon request. The type of portfolios in which each strategy is available (segregated account, limited distribution pooled fund, or broad distribution pooled fund) is indicated in the description of each strategy."

Provision 7.C.14

The FIRM MUST disclose that policies for valuing investments, calculating performance, and preparing GIPS REPORTS are available upon request.

Discussion

In each GIPS Pooled Fund Report, firms must disclose the availability of policies for valuing investments, calculating performance, and preparing GIPS Reports. The policies are not required to be included in each GIPS Pooled Fund Report but must be available upon request. Firms are not required to provide the related procedures, in addition to the policies, but may do so.

Sample Disclosure:

"Firm XYZ's policies for valuing investments, calculating performance, and preparing GIPS Reports are available upon request."

Provision 7.C.15

The FIRM MUST disclose how leverage, derivatives, and short positions have been used historically, if material.

Discussion

Firms must provide enough information in a GIPS Pooled Fund Report to allow a prospective investor to understand how leverage, derivatives, and short positions have been employed historically and may be used going forward. Although the pooled fund description includes disclosure of the firm's ability to use leverage, derivatives, and short positions (see Provision 7.C.4), Provision 7.C.15 requires that the firm disclose the leverage, derivatives, and short positions that have been used historically, if material. Taken together, these two required disclosures provide a more complete picture of the presence, use, and extent of leverage, derivatives, and short positions.

For example, assume a firm discloses in the pooled fund description that the strategy may employ up to 200% leverage. To satisfy the disclosure requirement in Provision 7.C.15, the firm might state, "Since the inception of the pooled fund, the leverage has averaged 110% of the pooled fund's value; however, during 2019 the leverage averaged 160%, which greatly increased the sensitivity to market volatility and the potential for realized gains and/or losses."

No disclosure is required if leverage, derivatives, and short positions have not been used or if their use has not been material. When determining what would be material, the firm must consider whether the disclosure of how leverage, derivatives, and/or short positions have been used historically is likely to affect a prospective investor's view of the risk involved in the pooled fund's strategy. If so, it would be misleading for the firm to fail to disclose their use to prospective investors when describing the strategy.

Provision 7.C.16

The FIRM MUST disclose all significant events that would help a PROSPECTIVE INVESTOR interpret the GIPS POOLED FUND REPORT. This disclosure MUST be included for a minimum of one year and for as long as it is relevant to interpreting the track record.

Discussion

The GIPS standards are based on the principles of fair representation and full disclosure. Meeting these objectives requires a good faith commitment on the part of the firm to adhere to the spirit of the GIPS standards. The GIPS standards cannot foresee and cover every situation that might occur. Therefore, this provision requires that firms disclose all significant events that would help explain the firm's GIPS Pooled Fund Report to a prospective investor. The primary goal of this requirement is to provide relevant information to prospective investors so that they can understand the potential effect of the significant event on the pooled fund's investment strategy and the firm.

Significant events are determined by the firm and would include, as examples, a material change in personnel responsible for investment management, significant changes to the investment management process, the loss of historical records resulting from a catastrophic event, or a change in firm ownership. The acquisition of a new entity or selling off part of a firm would also qualify as a significant event, as would the departure of someone who was the single investment decision maker for a strategy.

Depending on the situation, a general statement describing the significant event that has occurred may be sufficient. Other situations may require firms to disclose specific information pertaining to the significant event. The disclosure regarding the significant event must be included in the GIPS Pooled Fund Report for a minimum of one year and for as long as it is relevant to interpreting the performance track record. As an example, a firm that acquires another firm, resulting in a large increase in total firm assets, may disclose this significant event for as long as the large change in total firm assets is included in the GIPS Pooled Fund Report. In contrast, a change in a firm's chief investment officer is a change that a firm may believe should be disclosed for one year only.

The firm must consider the underlying principles of the GIPS standards, which are fair representation and full disclosure, when determining how long the disclosure will be included in the GIPS Pooled Fund Report.

Sample Disclosures:

"In June 2017, Firm G determined that the custodian bank used by all of the firm's proprietary mutual funds had failed to file reclaimable withholding tax refund requests with the appropriate authorities. At that time, all accrued reclaimable withholding taxes were written off, decreasing the Fund's monthly return by 1.06%."

"On 15 April 2018, the quantitative asset management division of Firm Z was sold, resulting in the 2018 decrease in Firm Z's assets."

"In February 2020, the parent company of Firm M announced plans to exit the investment management business and sell Firm M. As of April 2020, a tentative sale of Firm M has been agreed upon but not yet finalized."

Provision 7.C.17

For any performance presented for periods prior to the MINIMUM EFFECTIVE COMPLIANCE DATE that does not comply with the GIPS standards, the FIRM MUST disclose the periods of non-compliance.

Discussion

In a GIPS Pooled Fund Report that includes money-weighted returns (MWRs), firms may present non-GIPS compliant performance only for periods ending before the minimum effective compliance date, which is 1 January 2006 for private equity and real estate pooled funds and 1 January 2000 for all other pooled funds. (See Provision 1.A.30.) If the firm chooses to present non-compliant performance for periods prior to the minimum effective compliance date, the firm must disclose which periods are not in compliance. Prospective investors and existing investors can then inquire about the reasons why the performance prior to the minimum effective compliance date is not compliant and consider the effects of non-compliance on the historical performance.

The measurement period for a pooled fund's since-inception money-weighted return (SI-MWR) is the period from the pooled fund's inception date through the end of the period being reported. The beginning date remains constant and the ending date is extended as the measurement period becomes longer. It is necessary to use the period-end date of a SI-MWR to determine the non-compliant period.

Determining the period of compliance for an MWR calculation requires consideration of cash flows and valuations. When calculating MWRs, quarterly or more frequent cash flows must be used prior to 1 January 2020, and daily cash flows must be used as of 1 January 2020. For periods ending on or after 1 January 2011, the pooled fund must be valued in accordance with the definition of fair value. See the discussion of Provision 2.A.19 for information on valuation requirements for periods ending prior to that date.

Given that the minimum effective compliance dates are so distant, and that firms are required to present only one SI-MWR (the SI-MWR through the most recent annual period end), it is not expected that the minimum effective compliance date will have an effect on many firms that present pooled fund MWRs.

If non-compliant performance for periods ending on or after the minimum effective compliance date is included in a GIPS Pooled Fund Report, it must be labeled as supplemental information.

Sample Disclosure:

"The returns for the XYZ Private Equity Fund for periods ending prior to 31 December 2005 are not in compliance with the GIPS standards."

Provision 7.C.18

If the FIRM is redefined, the FIRM MUST disclose the date and description of the redefinition.

Discussion

A firm redefinition occurs when something changes with how the firm is held out to the public, or when any of its distinct business entity criteria significantly change. Changes in investment style or personnel are not events that typically cause a firm redefinition. A simple firm name change is also not a sufficient reason to redefine the firm. Corporate restructuring may cause a change with how the firm is held out to the public. As an example, a firm that was defined to include only the institutional division would be redefined when it consolidated the institutional division with the mutual fund/retail division. A merger or acquisition may cause a change in the definition of the firm, but that is not always the case.

Suppose that a firm defines itself as an investment management firm offering active equity strategies to investors. An acquisition that expanded the firm's offerings to include fixed-income strategies would result in a redefinition of the firm, because there would be a change in how the firm holds itself out to the public. An acquisition that simply added additional equity strategies to the firm's offerings would not result in a redefinition of the firm. However, the acquisition is likely to be a significant event that must be disclosed in a GIPS Pooled Fund Report. (See Provision 7.C.16.)

In some cases, as a result of a significant alteration in a firm's structure or organization, a change can be so great that it creates a new firm. See Provision 1.A.2 for guidance on firm definitions.

The GIPS standards require that changes in a firm's organization must not lead to alteration of historical performance (see Provision 1.A.28).

Sample Disclosures:

"As of 1 August 2019, XYZ Firm was redefined to include both the London and Tokyo office of XYZ Company. Previously, the firm was defined to include only the London office."

"As of 1 January 2020, XYZ Investment Management was redefined to include the wrap division."

"Effective 1 January 2019, ABC Capital Management was redefined as an investment management firm offering both equity and fixed-income strategies. Prior to the 31 December 2018 acquisition of Curtone Capital Management, an investment firm offering fixed-income strategies, ABC Capital Management offered only equity strategies."

Provision 7.C.19

If the POOLED FUND's investment mandate, objective, or strategy is changed, the FIRM MUST disclose the date and description of the change.

Discussion

Investment strategies can change over time. If there is a change in a pooled fund's investment mandate, objective, or strategy, the firm must disclose the date and description of the change.

Sample Disclosure:

"As of 1 July 2017, the strategy for the Fixed Income Pooled Fund includes the use of interest rate futures to modify duration and manage interest rate risk. Prior to this date, the Fund's strategy did not involve the active management of interest rate risk."

Provision 7.C.20

The FIRM MUST disclose changes to the name of the POOLED FUND. This disclosure MUST be included for a minimum of one year and for as long as it is relevant to interpreting the track record.

Discussion

When prospective investors are evaluating pooled funds over time and across firms, it is important that they understand exactly which pooled funds they are assessing. If a firm changes the name of a pooled fund, the change must be disclosed in the GIPS Pooled Fund Report. The name change must be disclosed for a minimum of one year and potentially for more than one year if the firm determines the disclosure is still relevant and meaningful. The firm must consider the underlying principles of the GIPS standards, which are fair representation and full disclosure, when determining how long the disclosure will be included in the GIPS Pooled Fund Report.

Sample Disclosure:

"As of 1 January 2016, the Small-Cap Fund was renamed the US Equity Opportunity Fund."

Provision 7.C.21

The FIRM MUST disclose if POOLED FUND returns are gross or net of withholding taxes, if material.

Discussion

Global investing requires recognition of the tax consequences of investing in different countries. The GIPS standards do not require firms to reflect withholding taxes, either reclaimable or non-reclaimable taxes, in a certain manner. Firms may choose whether or not to reflect the effect of withholding taxes when calculating performance. The GIPS standards do recommend that performance be reported net of non-reclaimable withholding taxes on dividends, interest, and capital gains and also recommend that reclaimable foreign withholding taxes be accrued (see Provision 2.B.5). If withholding taxes are material, firms must disclose how withholding taxes are treated when calculating performance. A firm must determine the level at which withholding taxes become material, document this level in its policies and procedures, and apply it consistently.

Sample Disclosure:

"Pooled fund returns are net of all foreign non-reclaimable withholding taxes. Reclaimable withholding taxes are reflected as income if and when received."

Provision 7.C.22

The FIRM MUST disclose if BENCHMARK returns are net of withholding taxes if this information is available.

Discussion

Global investing requires recognition of the tax consequences of investing in different countries. The GIPS standards do not require firms to reflect withholding taxes, either reclaimable or non-reclaimable taxes, in a certain manner. Firms may choose whether or not to reflect the effect of withholding taxes when calculating pooled fund performance and, similarly, whether or not to use a benchmark that reflects the effect of withholding taxes.

As Provision 7.C.21 indicates, if withholding taxes are material, firms must disclose how withholding taxes are treated when calculating performance. To facilitate the comparison of pooled fund returns and benchmark returns, firms must also disclose if the benchmark returns are net of withholding taxes if this information is available. If the benchmark name indicates that the benchmark is net of withholding taxes, no additional disclosure is necessary.

Sample Disclosure:

"Benchmark returns are net of withholding taxes."

Provision 7.C.23

If the GIPS POOLED FUND REPORT conforms with laws and/or regulations that conflict with the REQUIREMENTS of the GIPS standards, the FIRM MUST disclose this fact and disclose the manner in which the laws and/or regulations conflict with the GIPS standards.

Discussion

Firms must comply with all applicable laws and regulations regarding the calculation and presentation of performance. Compliance with applicable laws and regulations, however, does not necessarily result in compliance with the GIPS standards. Firms must also comply with all of the applicable requirements of the GIPS standards. In the rare cases where laws and regulations conflict with the GIPS standards, firms are required to comply with the laws and regulations and disclose the manner in which the laws and/or regulations conflict with the GIPS standards.

This disclosure will assist prospective investors in comparing GIPS Pooled Fund Reports among firms where reporting requirements may differ because of local laws or regulations.

Sample Disclosure:

"We present since-inception money-weighted returns through each annual period end. Local laws do not allow the presentation of returns of less than one year to prospective investors, which is in conflict with the GIPS standards. Therefore, no performance is presented for this pooled fund for the period from 1 July 2018 (the inception date of the pooled fund) to 31 December 2018."

Provision 7.C.24

The FIRM MUST disclose the use of a SUB-ADVISOR and the periods a SUB-ADVISOR was used.[55]

Discussion

Some firms use a sub-advisor to manage part or all of a particular strategy. For example, if a firm specializes in managing equities, it might hire a sub-advisor (a third-party investment manager) to manage the fixed-income portion of its balanced portfolios. The GIPS standards require that firms include the performance of pooled fund assets assigned to a sub-advisor in the respective pooled fund's performance. In the spirit of full disclosure, a firm must disclose the fact that a sub-advisor was used in the management of the pooled fund and the periods for which a sub-advisor was used. It is not necessary to disclose the name of the sub-advisor. This is required for periods beginning on or after 1 January 2006.

Sample Disclosures:

"A sub-advisor is used to manage the international equity allocation of the Asia Growth Balanced Fund."

[55] REQUIRED for periods beginning on or after 1 January 2006.

"A sub-advisor was used for the management of the Global Private Equity Fund from its inception in 2001 through 31 December 2018."

Provision 7.C.25

The FIRM MUST disclose if the POOLED FUND's valuation hierarchy materially differs from the RECOMMENDED valuation hierarchy.[56] (See provision 2.B.6 for the RECOMMENDED valuation hierarchy.)

Discussion

Firms must establish policies and procedures for determining pooled fund investment valuations. For periods beginning on or after 1 January 2011, those valuations must be determined in accordance with the definition of fair value. Provision 2.B.6 includes a recommended valuation hierarchy that firms should incorporate into their policies and procedures for determining fair value for pooled fund investments. Firms must establish a valuation hierarchy on a pooled fund–specific basis. It is acceptable for firms to apply a different valuation hierarchy to specific pooled funds provided the valuation methodology conforms to the definition of fair value. If the valuation hierarchy materially differs from the recommended valuation hierarchy, the firm must disclose this fact. Prospective investors will be informed and then may request additional information about the firm's valuation policies.

Sample Disclosure:

"All pooled fund investments are valued using the firm's proprietary valuation models to determine fair value. Our valuation procedures materially differ from the recommended valuation hierarchy in the GIPS standards."

Provision 7.C.26

If the FIRM determines no appropriate BENCHMARK for the POOLED FUND exists, the FIRM MUST disclose why no BENCHMARK is presented.

[56] REQUIRED for periods beginning on or after 1 January 2011.

Discussion

Benchmarks are important tools that aid in the planning, implementation, and evaluation of an investment strategy. They also help facilitate discussions with prospective investors regarding the relationship between pooled fund risk and return. As a result, the GIPS standards require firms to provide benchmark total returns in all GIPS Pooled Fund Reports. The benchmark must reflect the investment mandate, objective, or strategy of the pooled fund. Although there is typically an appropriate benchmark for traditional strategies, it is more common for managers of alternative strategies to determine that no appropriate benchmark for the pooled fund exists. If this is the case, the firm must disclose why no benchmark is presented.

Sample Disclosure:

"Because the pooled fund's strategy is absolute return where investments are permitted in all asset classes, no benchmark is presented because we believe that no benchmark that reflects this strategy exists."

Provision 7.C.27

If the FIRM changes the BENCHMARK, the FIRM MUST disclose:

a. For a prospective BENCHMARK change, the date and description of the change. Changes MUST be disclosed for as long as returns for the prior BENCHMARK are included in the GIPS POOLED FUND REPORT.

b. For a retroactive BENCHMARK change, the date and description of the change. Changes MUST be disclosed for a minimum of one year and for as long as it is relevant to interpreting the track record.

Discussion

Firms must disclose the date and description of any changes to the benchmark over time. A benchmark change can take two forms:

- The benchmark is changed from one benchmark to another on a prospective basis only.
- The benchmark is changed for all periods (i.e., retroactively).

In most cases, the firm should only change the benchmark going forward and not change the benchmark retroactively.

If the firm changes the benchmark prospectively and presents benchmark returns that combine two different benchmarks, the date and description of the change must be disclosed for as long as returns for the prior benchmark are included in the GIPS Pooled Fund Report. Given the nature of a money-weighted return (MWR), however, it is not expected that this situation would apply to a GIPS Pooled Fund Report that includes MWRs.

There may be times when a firm determines that it is appropriate to change the benchmark for a given pooled fund retroactively. For example, because benchmarks are continually evolving, if the firm finds that a new benchmark is a better comparison for an investment strategy, the firm may consider changing the benchmark retroactively. In the case of a retroactive benchmark change, there must be a disclosure of the date and description of the benchmark change, including the fact that the benchmark was changed retroactively. Disclosures related to a retroactive change in a benchmark must be included in the respective GIPS Pooled Fund Report for a minimum of one year and for as long as the disclosures are relevant to interpreting the performance track record. The firm must consider the underlying principles of the GIPS standards, which are fair representation and full disclosure, when determining how long this disclosure will be included in the GIPS Pooled Fund Report.

When a firm changes a benchmark retroactively, the firm is encouraged to continue to also present the old benchmark.

Changes to the benchmark primarily intended to make performance look better by lowering the benchmark return violate the spirit of the GIPS standards.

Sample Disclosure:

"In January 2017, the benchmark was changed from ABC Index to XYZ Index for all periods."

Provision 7.C.28

If a custom BENCHMARK or combination of multiple BENCHMARKS is used, the FIRM MUST:

a. Disclose the BENCHMARK components, weights, and rebalancing process, if applicable.
b. Disclose the calculation methodology.
c. Clearly label the BENCHMARK to indicate that it is a custom BENCHMARK.

Discussion

When custom benchmarks are used, the firm must disclose the benchmark components, weights, and rebalancing process, if applicable. Given the nature of money-weighted return (MWR) calculations, this disclosure will rarely apply to a GIPS Pooled Fund Report that presents MWRs.

Instead, it is expected that a firm would use a public market equivalent (PME) as a custom benchmark. See the discussion of Provision 7.C.29 for an explanation of a PME. A PME must be clearly labeled as such, and the methodology used to calculate the PME must be disclosed.

A firm may calculate a PME that is gross or net of pooled fund fees. A PME that is net of pooled fund fees is calculated using the same cash flows that are used to calculate the pooled fund net return. A firm may use a net PME benchmark only when pooled fund net returns are presented. The use of a net benchmark when only pooled fund gross returns are presented is one instance where disclosure is not sufficient to prevent the information presented from being false and misleading. When a firm includes a net benchmark in a GIPS Pooled Fund Report, the firm must clearly label the benchmark as a custom benchmark and disclose the calculation methodology.

Sample Disclosure for a PME Benchmark:

"The benchmark is the public market equivalent (PME) of the ABC Mid-Cap Equity Index, which tracks the performance of US mid-cap companies. The PME is a method by which a public market index is used to create a since-inception money-weighted return that is comparable to a fund's since-inception money-weighted return from a series of cash flows that are the same as those of the fund and uses a theoretical investment value. The theoretical investment value is derived by buying and selling the public market index using the dates and amounts of actual pooled fund cash flows."

Provision 7.C.29

The FIRM MUST disclose the calculation methodology used for the BENCHMARK. If the FIRM presents the PUBLIC MARKET EQUIVALENT of a POOLED FUND as a BENCHMARK, the FIRM MUST also disclose the index used to calculate the PUBLIC MARKET EQUIVALENT.

Discussion

The benchmark selected for a pooled fund must be appropriate for comparison with the performance of the pooled fund. Unlike benchmarks for publicly traded securities, however, industry benchmarks for private market investments are less widely available or are available only through certain commercial vendors. Firms may use public market indices as a benchmark for private market investments, but the public market indices by themselves are not directly comparable to a money-weighted return (MWR) because the market indices typically use a time-weighted return. The public market equivalent (PME) is a method where a public market index is used to create a comparable MWR from a series of cash flows that replicate those of the pooled fund and that can be compared with the MWR of the pooled fund.

The GIPS standards require that the calculation methodology for the benchmark be disclosed. This information provides transparency as to the comparability of performance between the pooled fund and the benchmark. If a PME is used as a benchmark, the firm must disclose which public market index is used to create the PME.

Sample Disclosure for a Non-PME Benchmark:

"The benchmark is the since-inception money-weighted return for the ACME Advisory US Venture Capital Funds Universe – 2018 Vintage Year. The vintage year is determined by the date of the first capital call for each fund in the universe."

Sample Disclosure for a PME Benchmark:

"The benchmark is the public market equivalent (PME) of the ABC Mid-Cap Equity Index, which tracks the performance of US mid-cap companies. The PME is a method by which a public market index is used to create a since-inception money-weighted return that is comparable to a fund's since-inception money-weighted return from a series of cash flows that are the same as those of the fund and uses a theoretical investment value. The theoretical investment value is derived by buying and selling the public market index using the dates and amounts of actual pooled fund cash flows."

Provision 7.C.30

The FIRM MUST disclose if performance from a past firm or affiliation is presented, and for which periods.

Discussion

Although firms often think about time-weighted returns when considering portability issues, it is also possible for a money-weighted return to span two firms. Provision 1.A.32 includes the tests that must be met to determine if performance from a past firm or affiliation may be used to represent the historical performance of a new or acquiring firm and if that performance can be linked to the ongoing performance of the new or acquiring firm. Provision 1.A.33 includes the portability tests that must be met for the new or acquiring firm to use performance from a past firm or affiliation to represent its historical performance when there is a break in the track record between the past firm or affiliation and the new or acquiring firm. In this instance, the track record from the past firm or affiliation may be used if the tests are met, but the track record must not be linked to performance of the new or acquiring firm. A current since-inception money-weighted return (SI-MWR) must be calculated using only the performance after the break. A SI-MWR from the beginning of the track record up until the break may also be presented if the tests in Provision 1.A.33 are met. The current SI-MWR for the period after the break in performance and the SI-MWR representing performance prior to the break must not be linked, however, and each must be clearly labeled.

If the firm meets the required portability tests and presents performance from a past firm or affiliation in the GIPS Pooled Fund Report, the firm must disclose this fact, as well as the periods for which performance from the past firm or affiliation is presented.

Sample Disclosure:

"The Opportunity Fund was funded in March 2016 and was managed by the Distressed Debt Team at a prior firm. On 15 December 2017, the prior firm sold the line of business that included the Distressed Debt Team to ABC Investments. Fund activity prior to 15 December 2017 is from the prior firm."

Provision 7.C.31

The FIRM MUST disclose the frequency of EXTERNAL CASH FLOWS used in the MONEY-WEIGHTED RETURN calculation if daily frequency was not used.

Discussion

When calculating money-weighted returns (MWRs), quarterly or more frequent cash flows must be used prior to 1 January 2020, and daily cash flows must be used as of 1 January 2020. A historical cash flow stream may therefore include daily, monthly and/or quarterly cash flows. When constructing such a cash flow stream historically, and daily cash flows are not used, the firm must assume that all quarterly and monthly cash flows occurred on a particular date in the month or quarter regardless of the actual date of the cash flow. For example, all monthly or quarterly cash flows might be dated as if they occurred on the last day of the month, regardless of the actual date of the cash flow. See Provision 2.A.29 for an example of how quarterly and monthly cash flows can be reflected in an MWR calculation.

The MWR calculation is sensitive to the relative timing of cash flows and, especially early in the life of a fund, returns calculated using a quarterly cash flow dating convention can differ from returns calculated using a monthly or daily convention. Accordingly, firms are required to disclose the frequency of cash flows used in the MWR calculation if daily cash flows are not used for periods prior to 1 January 2020. It is recommended that firms use daily cash flows for all periods.

Sample Disclosure:

"The money-weighted return calculation incorporates monthly cash flows for periods prior to 1 January 2020 and daily cash flows thereafter."

Provision 7.C.32

If a SUBSCRIPTION LINE OF CREDIT is used, and the FIRM is REQUIRED to present returns both with and without the SUBSCRIPTION LINE OF CREDIT, the FIRM MUST disclose:

a. The purpose for using the SUBSCRIPTION LINE OF CREDIT.
b. The size of the SUBSCRIPTION LINE OF CREDIT as of the most recent annual period end.
c. The SUBSCRIPTION LINE OF CREDIT amount outstanding as of the most recent annual period end.

Discussion

Subscription lines of credit are being used by more firms and for longer periods, and they may have a significant effect on returns. It is therefore important that prospective investors have sufficient information about any subscription line of credit (LOC) that could influence pooled fund performance.

In those situations in which a subscription LOC is used and the firm is required to present returns both with and without the subscription LOC (see Provision 7.A.2), the firm must disclose the purpose of the subscription LOC so that prospective investors can better understand why the subscription LOC exists. In some cases, the subscription LOC is short term in nature and is put in place simply to facilitate administration when capital is being called from investors. In other cases, the subscription LOC is longer term and is used to delay the capital calls from investors. To help prospective investors put the subscription LOC in perspective, the firm must also disclose both the size of the subscription LOC and the subscription LOC amount outstanding as of the most recent annual period end.

Sample Disclosures:

"A $100M subscription line of credit is in place as bridge financing to reduce the number of capital calls made to fund investors. As of 31 December 2020, $40M is outstanding."

"A $250M subscription line of credit is in place and is used to finance investments. During the past two years, the subscription LOC was fully drawn but was repaid as of 31 December 2019."

Provision 7.C.33

The FIRM MUST disclose any change to the GIPS POOLED FUND REPORT resulting from the correction of a MATERIAL ERROR. Following the correction of the GIPS POOLED FUND REPORT, this disclosure MUST be included for a minimum of one year and for as long as it is relevant to interpreting the track record. This disclosure is not REQUIRED to be included in a GIPS POOLED FUND REPORT that is provided to a PROSPECTIVE INVESTOR that did not receive the GIPS POOLED FUND REPORT containing the MATERIAL ERROR.

Discussion

Firms claiming compliance with the GIPS standards are likely to be faced with situations in which errors are discovered that must be specifically addressed. An error, which can be qualitative or quantitative, can be related to any component of a GIPS Pooled Fund Report that is missing or inaccurate. Errors in GIPS Pooled Fund Reports can result from, but are not limited to, incorrect, incomplete, or missing:

- pooled fund returns or assets,
- firm assets,
- benchmark returns, or
- disclosures.

Any material error in a GIPS Pooled Fund Report must be corrected and disclosed in a corrected GIPS Pooled Fund Report. A firm must define materiality within its error correction policies and procedures.

To adhere to this requirement, a firm must determine the criteria it will use to determine materiality. The following is a definition of materiality that firms might find useful as a starting point for their determination of materiality. "An error is material if the magnitude of the omission or misstatement of performance information, in light of surrounding circumstances, makes it probable that the judgment of a reasonable person relying on the information would have been changed by the omission or misstatement." A firm should have a defined process for determining the objective criteria it will use in determining materiality.

Disclosure of the change in the corrected GIPS Pooled Fund Report resulting from a material error must be included in the GIPS Pooled Fund Report for a minimum of 12 months following the correction of the report and for as long as it is relevant to interpreting the track record. The firm must consider the underlying principles of the GIPS standards, which are fair representation and full disclosure, when determining how long the disclosure will be included in the GIPS Pooled Fund Report that contained the material error.

Disclosure of the change resulting from a material error is not required to be included in a GIPS Pooled Fund Report that is provided to new prospective investors.

The discussion for Provision 1.A.20 provides additional information on error correction, including determination of materiality, the actions that must be taken when an error in a GIPS Pooled Fund Report is discovered, and an explanation of who must receive the revised GIPS Pooled Fund Report.

Sample Disclosure:

"This GIPS Pooled Fund Report includes a correction of the information provided for the XYZ Peer Universe. The since-inception internal rate of return for the XYZ Peer Universe through 31 December 2020 was originally presented as 3.4%. The correct return is 4.3%, as shown in this revised GIPS Pooled Fund Report."

> **Provision 7.C.34**
>
> The FIRM MUST disclose if preliminary, estimated values are used to determine FAIR VALUE.

Discussion

The use of preliminary, estimated values as fair value is common for some alternative strategies, including those that invest in underlying funds, for which the firm relies on valuations provided by the underlying fund managers. When using preliminary, estimated values as fair value, it is important to remember the underlying principles of the GIPS standards: fair representation and full disclosure. If using preliminary, estimated values, firms must disclose this fact in the relevant GIPS Pooled Fund Report.

Firms that use preliminary, estimated values to determine fair value and subsequently change valuations when final values are received must determine how the firm's error correction policies will be applied. (Please see Provision 1.A.20 for guidance on error correction policies.) Differences between the final and estimated values are not necessarily errors but are treated in a similar manner because the correction of previously presented information may be involved.

In addition to this required disclosure, it is recommended (see Provision 7.B.5) that firms present the percentage of assets in the pooled fund that were valued using preliminary, estimated values as of the most recent annual period end. This information will help prospective investors to interpret the performance record.

Sample Disclosure:

"Preliminary, estimated values were used in the determination of the fair value of the pooled fund's assets."

Provision 7.C.35

If the FIRM changes the type of return(s) presented for the POOLED FUND (e.g., changes from TIME-WEIGHTED RETURNS to MONEY-WEIGHTED RETURNS), the FIRM MUST disclose the change and the date of the change. This disclosure MUST be included for a minimum of one year and for as long as it is relevant to interpreting the track record.

Discussion

A firm must present time-weighted returns (TWRs) in a GIPS Pooled Fund Report unless certain criteria are met that allow money-weighted returns (MWRs) to be presented instead of TWRs. Firms may choose to present MWRs instead of TWRs for a specific pooled fund only if the firm controls the external cash flows into the pooled fund and the pooled fund has at least one of the following characteristics: it is closed-end; fixed life; fixed commitment; or illiquid investments are a significant part of the strategy. (See Provision 1.A.35.)

When a firm changes the type of return presented for a pooled fund, the firm must disclose, in the respective GIPS Pooled Fund Report, the change in the type of return (e.g., from TWR to MWR) and the date of the change. This disclosure must be included in the GIPS Pooled Fund Report for a minimum of one year and for as long as it is relevant and helpful to the firm's prospective investors in interpreting the pooled fund's track record. The firm must consider the underlying principles of the GIPS standards, which are fair representation and full disclosure, when determining how long the disclosure will be included in the GIPS Pooled Fund Report.

When a firm changes the type of return presented for a pooled fund, for example from TWRs to MWRs, the firm must change the returns for all periods. As an example, suppose that a firm is presenting TWRs for a pooled fund from the inception of a pooled fund on 1 January 2013 through 31 December 2019. It decides that it will switch to present MWRs as of 1 January 2020. The firm cannot present TWRs through 31 December 2019 and an MWR from 1 January 2020 through 31 December 2020. The firm must present the since-inception MWR for the period from 1 January 2013 (the inception date of the pooled fund) through 31 December 2020 in the GIPS Pooled Fund Report for the period ended 31 December 2020.

Sample Disclosure:

"Beginning with the GIPS Pooled Fund Report for the period ended 31 December 2020, the returns presented for Fund XYZ were changed from time-weighted returns to money-weighted returns."

Provision 7.C.36

If the FIRM presents ADDITIONAL RISK MEASURES, the FIRM MUST:

a. Describe any ADDITIONAL RISK MEASURE.

b. Disclose the name of the risk-free rate if a risk-free rate is used in the calculation of the ADDITIONAL RISK MEASURE.

Discussion

There is no required risk measure for a GIPS Pooled Fund Report that presents money-weighted returns. However, understanding and interpreting investment performance requires the consideration of both risk and return. It is therefore recommended that firms present additional risk measures for the pooled fund and the benchmark. (Because no quantitative risk measure is required for pooled funds that present money-weighted returns, all risk measures presented are considered additional risk measures. See Provision 7.B.4.) It is important to keep in mind that additional risk measures should be consistent with the pooled fund's strategy. For example, if the strategy includes managing foreign currency risk, the presentation of a hedge ratio would be consistent with that objective.

The GIPS Pooled Fund Report must include a description of any additional risk measure presented. If a risk-free rate is used in the calculation of an additional risk measure, the name of the risk-free rate must be disclosed. The disclosure of the name of the risk-free rate used in the calculation of an additional risk measure is required because of the importance of the selection of an appropriate risk-free rate. With a disclosure regarding the risk-free rate, the firm's prospective investors can better understand and interpret the additional risk measure(s) presented.

Provision 7.C.37

The FIRM MUST disclose if POOLED FUND GROSS RETURNS or POOLED FUND NET RETURNS are used to calculate presented risk measures.

Discussion

To help prospective investors interpret the risk measures presented in a GIPS Pooled Fund Report, the firm must disclose which returns—pooled fund gross returns or pooled fund net returns—are used in the calculation of the presented risk measures.

Sample Disclosure:

"Pooled fund net returns were used to calculate drawdown."

Provision 7.C.38

For REAL ESTATE investments that are not in a REAL ESTATE OPEN-END FUND, the FIRM MUST disclose that:[57]

a. EXTERNAL VALUATIONS are obtained, and the frequency with which they are obtained, or

b. The FIRM relies on valuations from financial statement audits.

Discussion

According to Provision 2.A.44, for periods beginning on or after 1 January 2012, real estate investments included in any portfolio except a real estate open-end fund must either:

- have an external valuation at least once every 12 months unless client agreements stipulate otherwise, in which case real estate investments must have an external valuation at least once every 36 months or per the client agreement if the investor agreement requires external valuations more frequently than every 36 months; or
- be subject to an annual financial statement audit performed by an independent public accounting firm. The real estate investments must be accounted for at fair value, and the most recent audited financial statements available must contain an unmodified opinion issued by an independent public accounting firm.

Because valuation is such an important issue for real estate investments, firms must inform prospective investors whether they externally value real estate investments and, if so, how frequently, or instead place reliance on valuations from audited financial statements. This disclosure is required for pooled funds that are not a real estate open-end fund, for periods ending on or after 31 December 2020.

Sample Disclosures:

"ABC Company obtains external valuations for all real estate investments annually."

"XYZ Company relies on valuations from audited financial statements. The audits are performed by an independent public accounting firm."

[57] REQUIRED for periods ending on or after 31 December 2020.

Provision 7.C.39

When the GIPS POOLED FUND REPORT includes THEORETICAL PERFORMANCE as SUPPLEMENTAL INFORMATION, the FIRM MUST:

a. Disclose that the results are theoretical, are not based on the performance of actual assets, and if the THEORETICAL PERFORMANCE was derived from the retroactive or prospective application of a model.
b. Disclose a basic description of the methodology and assumptions used to calculate the THEORETICAL PERFORMANCE sufficient for the PROSPECTIVE INVESTOR to interpret the THEORETICAL PERFORMANCE, including if it is based on model performance, backtested performance, or hypothetical performance.
c. Disclose whether the THEORETICAL PERFORMANCE reflects the deduction of actual or estimated INVESTMENT MANAGEMENT FEES, TRANSACTION COSTS, or other fees and charges that an actual POOLED FUND investor would have paid or will pay.
d. Clearly label the THEORETICAL PERFORMANCE as SUPPLEMENTAL INFORMATION.

Discussion

To be presented as supplemental information in a GIPS Pooled Fund Report, theoretical performance must relate to the respective pooled fund. The following are examples of theoretical performance that may be included in a GIPS Pooled Fund Report as supplemental information:

- Results created by applying a pooled fund investment strategy or methodology to historical data to indicate how a strategy constructed with the benefit of hindsight would have performed during a certain period in the past had the strategy been in existence during that period.
- Ex ante performance that is calculated by combining actual pooled fund cash flows with projected future cash flows.
- Results that include the effect of currency hedging that has been applied after the fact to the pooled fund when the pooled fund was not originally managed including the currency hedging strategy, and the hedging is not part of the actual pooled fund returns.

When theoretical performance is included as supplemental information in a GIPS Pooled Fund Report, a firm is required to include a number of disclosures to ensure that the recipients of the report, including prospective investors, understand the nature of the information being presented. Among the required disclosures are the source of the theoretical performance, the methodology and assumptions used to calculate the theoretical performance, and the treatment of fees and costs.

Firms must also clearly label the theoretical performance as supplemental information.

Sample Disclosure:

"A return history has been constructed for the period from 1 January 2015 through 31 December 2018 that reflects the application of an investment model used by XYZ Investment Management. The results are theoretical and are not based on the performance of actual assets. The return history is derived from the retroactive application of a model. The model assumes that an investment was made in the top 20 individual funds that have been identified as funds that meet the model's ESG screening criteria currently, and assumes an equal amount was invested in each fund on an assumed quarterly capital call. The first capital call was assumed to occur on 31 December 2014. The since-inception internal rate of return for the model does not reflect the deduction of investment management fees, transaction costs or other fees and charges."

7.D. Disclosure—Recommendations

Provision 7.D.1

The FIRM SHOULD disclose material changes to valuation policies and/or methodologies.

Discussion

Valuation is a critical component of the performance calculation. Therefore, if a change to a firm's valuation policies and/or methodologies is material, firms should disclose the change in order to enable prospective investors to understand the potential effect of such a change.

Some examples of a material change include, but are not limited to, the following:

- new valuation principles adopted by a local accounting standards board,
- adoption of new international standards in lieu of local standards,
- change of economic criteria used to value investments, and
- change from a discounted cash flow basis to a comparables basis.

Sample Disclosure for a Policy Change:

"Prior to 1 March 2016, illiquid securities were valued internally. Subsequently, illiquid securities are valued using a third-party pricing service."

Sample Disclosure for a Methodology Change:

"For periods prior to 1 August 2019, real estate investments were valued on a discounted cash flow basis. As of 1 August 2019, real estate investments are valued on a comparables basis."

Provision 7.D.2

The FIRM SHOULD disclose material changes to calculation policies and/or methodologies.

Discussion

Firms have discretion to determine which policies and methodologies are used for calculating performance. Although these policies and methodologies must adhere to all applicable calculation requirements, firms may choose from a wide variety of policies and methodologies. Firms may change calculation policies and/or methodologies; however, firms must not change a calculation policy or methodology for the sole purpose of increasing performance. If a change to the calculation policies and/or methodologies is material, firms should disclose the change in order to enable prospective investors to understand the potential effect of such a change.

Sample Disclosure:

"Prior to 2019, the internal rate of return method was used to calculate since-inception money-weighted returns. Subsequently, the Modified Dietz method is used for all periods."

Provision 7.D.3

The FIRM SHOULD disclose material differences between the BENCHMARK and the POOLED FUND's investment mandate, objective, or strategy.

Discussion

Firms are required to disclose the pooled fund description (see Provision 7.C.4) and the benchmark description (see Provision 7.C.5) in a GIPS Pooled Fund Report. It is recommended that firms also disclose any material differences between the benchmark and the pooled fund's investment mandate, objective, or strategy. Prospective investors will be better able to evaluate the performance of the strategy relative to the benchmark presented if they understand any material differences between the pooled fund and the benchmark.

Sample Disclosure:

"The Small-Cap Opportunities Fund is a venture capital fund that invests in small-cap startups in all sectors, with a focus on the health care and financial services sectors. The benchmark for the Fund is the public market equivalent (PME) of the ABC Small-Cap Index, which tracks the performance of US small-cap companies. The investment strategy of the Fund differs from the small-cap investment strategies represented by the PME because the Fund concentrates its investments. As of 31 December 2019, 62% of the Fund was invested in the health care and financial services sectors, and 18% of the index was invested in these two sectors."

Provision 7.D.4

The FIRM SHOULD disclose the key assumptions used to value investments.

Discussion

Firms are required to disclose that valuation policies are available upon request. (See Provision 7.C.14.) Because valuation is a critical component of the performance calculation, it is recommended that firms also disclose the key assumptions used when valuing pooled fund investments. This will help prospective investors better understand how the firm values investments and compare valuation assumptions for similar strategies used by different firms.

Sample Disclosure:

"The firm uses valuations reported by the general partners of the underlying pooled funds."

Provision 7.D.5

If a parent company contains multiple firms, each FIRM within the parent company SHOULD disclose a list of the other firms contained within the parent company.

Discussion

The term "firm" is used in two different ways in Provision 7.D.5. "FIRM" is used to indicate an entity that claims compliance with the GIPS standards, whereas "firm" is used to indicate an entity that may or may not claim compliance with the GIPS standards. The definition of a firm will be based on the specific circumstances of the firm but must reflect how the firm is held out to the public as a distinct business entity. In some cases, a parent company may have two or more units, divisions, departments, or offices that are defined as separate firms within the context of the GIPS standards. To avoid confusion, a firm claiming compliance with the GIPS standards must be sure that it is clearly defined relative to the other firms within the parent company and that it is apparent which firm is claiming compliance. In the interest of fair representation and full disclosure, firms should disclose a list of the other organizations within the parent company. Firms should also consider indicating which organizations within the parent company claim compliance with the GIPS standards.

Sample Disclosure:

"ABC Institutional Investment Management is the institutional division of ABC parent company. The private banking division of ABC parent company also claims compliance with the GIPS standards, whereas the retail division of ABC parent company does not claim compliance with the GIPS standards."

Provision 7.D.6

If the FIRM adheres to any industry valuation guidelines in addition to the GIPS valuation REQUIREMENTS, the FIRM SHOULD disclose which guidelines have been applied.

Discussion

Some market segments, such as private equity, have developed their own valuation guidelines. For these markets, it is not uncommon for the GIPS standards valuation requirements to be supplemented by other local or international standards because other standards may be more stringent in their requirements.

The disclosure of which industry's valuation guidelines have been used in addition to the GIPS standards valuation requirements will help prospective investors to determine the comparability of GIPS Pooled Fund Reports from different firms and/or jurisdictions.

Sample Disclosure:

"The Global Diversified Distressed Fund adheres to the XYZ Venture Capital Association's valuation guidelines as well as the GIPS standards valuation requirements. The XYZ valuation standards are based on fair value but provide more prescriptive advice in terms of how to value specific investments, such as secondary investments and distressed debt investments."

Provision 7.D.7

When using BENCHMARKS that have limitations, such as peer group BENCHMARKS, the FIRM SHOULD disclose these limitations.

Discussion

Firms must determine which benchmark(s) are most appropriate for pooled fund(s). When determining which benchmarks to present in a GIPS Pooled Fund Report, firms should be guided by the ethical spirit of the GIPS standards.

Some benchmarks with known limitations are often used for certain types of investments. For example, peer group benchmarks, such as hedge fund peer group universe indices, are often used for hedge funds and other alternative investment strategies. Although peer group benchmarks are frequently used to evaluate hedge funds, there are some common problems with hedge fund peer group benchmarks, including the following:

- self-reporting bias (only some hedge funds choose to report performance data),
- survivorship bias (historical returns of closed hedge funds are removed from the peer group benchmark),
- inability to obtain returns for the same periods as the pooled fund, and
- lack of investability (some hedge funds within a peer group benchmark are closed to new investors).

When using benchmarks that exhibit limitations, firms should describe these limitations in the relevant GIPS Pooled Fund Report. This helps prospective investors understand the nature of the benchmark and be aware of any known drawbacks in comparing the risk and return of the benchmark and pooled fund.

Sample Disclosure:

"The benchmark is the Hedge Fund Aggregate Multi-Style Index, which includes more than 100 hedge funds of various styles and strategies. Because this index is based on the data self-reported by the constituent funds, it may have a self-reporting bias. In addition, some funds are closed to new investors and are no longer investable. We believe that no better index exists as a comparison for the pooled fund."

Provision 7.D.8

The FIRM SHOULD disclose how research costs are reflected in returns.

Discussion

The focus on research costs has grown in certain markets. Although research costs are often absorbed by the firm, some firms instead charge research costs directly to investors. To allow

 |

prospective investors to understand the firm's policy for the treatment of research costs, firms should disclose if returns do or do not reflect the deduction of research costs.

Sample Disclosures:

"ABC Company bears the costs of investment research. Research costs are not separately charged to investors nor to the fund."

"Certain investment research costs are charged directly to investors and are not paid from pooled fund assets. Therefore, fund returns do not reflect the research costs that are charged directly to investors."

8. GIPS ADVERTISING GUIDELINES

Purpose of the GIPS Advertising Guidelines

The GIPS Advertising Guidelines provide firms with options for advertising when mentioning the firm's claim of compliance. The GIPS Advertising Guidelines do not replace the GIPS standards, nor do they absolve firms from presenting GIPS Composite Reports and GIPS Pooled Fund Reports as required by the GIPS standards. These guidelines apply only to firms that already satisfy all the applicable requirements of the GIPS standards on a firm-wide basis and prepare an advertisement that adheres to the requirements of the GIPS Advertising Guidelines (a "GIPS Advertisement"). Firms may also choose to include a GIPS Composite Report or GIPS Pooled Fund Report in the advertisement.

Definitions

Advertisement

For the GIPS Advertising Guidelines, an advertisement includes any materials that are distributed to or designed for use in newspapers, magazines, firm brochures, pooled fund fact sheets, pooled fund offering documents, letters, media, websites, or any other written or electronic material distributed to more than one party, and there is no contact between the firm and the reader of the advertisement. One-on-one presentations and individual client reporting are not considered advertisements.

GIPS Advertisement

A GIPS Advertisement is an advertisement by a GIPS-compliant firm that adheres to the requirements of the GIPS Advertising Guidelines.

Relationship of the GIPS Advertising Guidelines to Regulatory Requirements

When preparing GIPS Advertisements, firms must also adhere to all applicable laws and regulations governing advertisements. Firms are encouraged to seek legal or regulatory counsel because additional disclosures may be required. In cases where applicable laws or regulations conflict with the requirements of the GIPS standards or the GIPS Advertising Guidelines, firms are required to comply with the laws or regulations.

Other Information

The GIPS Advertisement may include other information beyond what is required or recommended under the GIPS Advertising Guidelines provided the information is shown with equal or lesser prominence relative to the information required or recommended by the GIPS Advertising Guidelines and the information does not conflict with the requirements or recommendations of the GIPS standards or the GIPS Advertising Guidelines. Firms must adhere to the principles of fair representation and full disclosure when advertising and must not present performance or performance-related information that is false or misleading.

8.A. Fundamental Requirements of the GIPS Advertising Guidelines

Provision 8.A.1

The GIPS Advertising Guidelines apply only to FIRMS that already claim compliance with the GIPS standards.

Discussion

A firm that claims compliance with the GIPS standards has three options with respect to preparing an advertisement:

- Prepare the advertisement in accordance with the GIPS Advertising Guidelines.
- Include a GIPS Report in the advertisement.
- Do not mention the GIPS standards in the advertisement.

A firm that chooses to claim compliance in an advertisement must either meet the requirements of the GIPS Advertising Guidelines or include a GIPS Report in the advertisement. Firms are not required to claim compliance with the GIPS standards in advertisements.

Firms claiming compliance with the GIPS standards must ensure that all performance or performance-related information in marketing materials is not false or misleading and adheres to the guiding principles of fair representation and full disclosure, whether or not the materials contain a claim of compliance with the GIPS standards.

Provision 8.A.2

A FIRM that chooses to claim compliance in a GIPS ADVERTISEMENT MUST comply with all applicable REQUIREMENTS of the GIPS Advertising Guidelines.

Discussion

If a firm chooses to advertise its claim of compliance with the GIPS standards by creating a GIPS Advertisement, it must comply with all applicable requirements of the GIPS Advertising Guidelines. The firm must also adhere to all applicable laws and regulations governing advertisements.

Provision 8.A.3

The FIRM MUST maintain all data and information necessary to support all items included in a GIPS ADVERTISEMENT.

Discussion

A fundamental principle of the GIPS standards is the need for firms to be able to ensure the validity of their claim of compliance. It is, therefore, important for current and prospective clients and investors, verifiers, and regulators to have confidence that all items included in a GIPS Advertisement are supported by the appropriate records.

Firms must maintain records to be able to recalculate their performance history, as well as substantiate all other information included in a GIPS Advertisement, for all periods shown. This requirement applies to all periods for which performance is presented in the GIPS Advertisement. This requirement is consistent with the regulatory requirements of many countries. In some jurisdictions, however, regulators require records to be kept for longer periods than those required by the GIPS standards. Care should be taken to ensure that the firm follows the strictest of the recordkeeping requirements applicable to the firm.

It is understood that the required data may not be immediately available. For example, data may need to be retrieved from an offsite location or from a third-party service provider. However, the data and information required to be maintained by this provision must be available in a usable format within a reasonable time frame. In all instances, either paper (hard-copy) records or electronically stored records will suffice. If records are stored electronically, the records must be accessible and able to be printed or downloaded, if needed. Records stored in a system that is not operable and from which data cannot be retrieved will not satisfy the recordkeeping requirements.

Please refer to Provision 1.A.25 for more information about the records required to be retained to support a GIPS Advertisement.

Provision 8.A.4

Returns for periods of less than one year included in a GIPS ADVERTISEMENT MUST NOT be annualized.

Discussion

Composite or pooled fund performance reflects only the performance of actual assets managed by the firm. When returns for periods of less than one year are annualized, the partial-year return is "extended" in order to create an annual return. The extrapolation of the partial-year return produces a simulated return and does not reflect the performance of actual assets. Therefore, performance for periods of less than one year must not be annualized in a GIPS Advertisement.

Care must be taken when money-weighted returns (MWRs) are calculated and the composite or pooled fund has less than a year of performance. Many firms use Excel to calculate MWRs using the XIRR function. The XIRR function calculates an annualized internal rate of return (IRR) (an IRR is a method that can be used to calculate an MWR). When calculating an XIRR for a period of less than one year, the annualized return generated must be "de-annualized."

The non-annualized since inception IRR (SI-IRR) can be calculated as follows:

$$R_{SI-IRR} = \left[(1 + r_{SI-IRR})^{\frac{TD}{365}} \right] - 1,$$

where

R_{SI-IRR} = non-annualized since-inception internal rate of return

r_{SI-IRR} = annualized since-inception internal rate of return

TD = total number of calendar days in the measurement period (less than one year)

For example, a portfolio is funded with $1,000,000 cash on 1 September 2020. Another $75,000 is contributed on 10 September 2020. At the end of the month, 30 September 2020, the portfolio is valued at $1,100,000. Also assume that end-of-day cash flows are used. Using Excel's XIRR formula, the annualized SI-IRR is 34.41%.

Dates	External Cash Flows & Ending Valuation		Explanation
1-Sep-2020	$	1,000,000	Contribution
10-Sep-2020	$	75,000	Contribution
30-Sep-2020	$	1,100,000	Portfolio value as of 30 September 2020
		34.41%	Calculated annualized return using XIRR

To calculate the non-annualized return in Excel using the non-annualized SI-IRR formula, the calculation is as follows:

= (1+0.3441)^(29/365)–1

= 2.38%

Provision 8.A.5

When TIME-WEIGHTED RETURNS are presented in a GIPS ADVERTISEMENT, the FIRM MUST NOT LINK non-GIPS-compliant performance for periods beginning on or after the MINIMUM EFFECTIVE COMPLIANCE DATE to GIPS-compliant performance. The FIRM may LINK non-GIPS-compliant performance to GIPS-compliant performance in a GIPS ADVERTISEMENT provided that only GIPS-compliant performance is presented for periods beginning on or after the MINIMUM EFFECTIVE COMPLIANCE DATE.

Discussion

The minimum effective compliance date is the date after which only GIPS-compliant performance may be presented in GIPS Advertisements. When presenting time-weighted returns in a GIPS Advertisement, the firm must not link non-GIPS-compliant performance for periods beginning on or after the minimum effective compliance date to GIPS-compliant performance. Most composites and pooled funds have a minimum effective compliance date of 1 January 2000. Therefore, for these composites and pooled funds, performance for periods beginning on or after 1 January 2000 that does not comply with the GIPS standards must not be presented as part of a GIPS Advertisement.

Real estate and private equity composites and pooled funds and wrap fee composites have a different minimum effective compliance date of 1 January 2006. For these composites and pooled funds, performance for periods beginning on or after 1 January 2006 that does not comply with the GIPS standards must not be presented in a GIPS Advertisement.

The GIPS standards allow firms to link non-GIPS-compliant performance to the composite's or pooled fund's GIPS-compliant history in a GIPS Advertisement provided that only GIPS-compliant performance is presented for periods beginning on or after the minimum effective compliance date. Firms are reminded, however, that they must comply with all applicable laws and regulations regarding the calculation and presentation of performance. Firms that manage broad distribution pooled funds (BDPFs) are typically required by laws or regulations to present the BDPF's performance for specified periods in the advertisement. These required performance periods may include periods for which the firm does not claim compliance with the GIPS standards. A firm that claims compliance with the GIPS standards may, therefore, link non-GIPS-compliant performance for any period to GIPS-compliant performance in a GIPS Advertisement when calculating returns that are required by laws or regulations to be presented for a BDPF's advertisement, as well as in any other materials outside of a GIPS Advertisement or GIPS Report in which the firm is required to present such information. However, if a firm chooses to prepare a GIPS Pooled Fund Report for a BDPF, the firm must consider the minimum effective compliance date. See Provision 1.A.29. The firm must also disclose any conflict with the GIPS standards or GIPS Advertising Guidelines. See Provision 8.G.15.

Provision 8.A.6

When MONEY-WEIGHTED RETURNS are presented in a GIPS ADVERTISEMENT, the FIRM MUST NOT present non-GIPS-compliant performance for periods ending on or after the MINIMUM EFFECTIVE COMPLIANCE DATE. The FIRM may present non-GIPS-compliant performance in a GIPS ADVERTISEMENT provided that only GIPS-compliant performance is presented for periods ending on or after the MINIMUM EFFECTIVE COMPLIANCE DATE.[c]

Discussion

The minimum effective compliance date is the date after which only GIPS-compliant performance may be presented by a firm in GIPS Advertisements. For money-weighted returns, the firm must not present non-GIPS-compliant performance for periods ending on or after the minimum effective compliance date. Most composites and pooled funds have a minimum effective compliance date of 1 January 2000. For these composites and pooled funds, performance for periods ending on or after 1 January 2000 that does not comply with the GIPS standards must not be presented as part of a GIPS Advertisement. Real estate and private equity composites and pooled funds have a minimum effective compliance date of 1 January 2006. For these composites and pooled funds, performance for periods ending on or after 1 January 2006 that does not comply with the GIPS standards must not be presented in a GIPS Advertisement. For any performance presented

[c] The 2020 edition of the GIPS standards incorrectly uses the word "link" versus "present."

 |

for periods ended prior to the minimum effective compliance date that does not comply with the GIPS standards in a GIPS Advertisement, firms must disclose the periods of non-compliance.

The measurement period for a since-inception money-weighted return (MWR) is the period from the inception date of the composite or pooled fund through the end of the period that is being reported. The beginning date remains constant and the ending date is extended as the measurement period becomes longer. The period-end date will determine what is a compliant time period for GIPS Advertisement purposes.

The inception date is always incorporated into a since-inception MWR in contrast to a time-weighted return (TWR), which does not necessarily incorporate since-inception results. It could be argued that the since-inception basis of MWR reporting would mean that any period of historical non-compliance could make the current period also non-compliant because the current calculation includes inputs from periods for which the firm did not claim compliance with the GIPS standards. This is not the case, however—a firm may present returns that use inputs (i.e., cash flows) from periods for which the firm did not claim compliance as long as the inputs meet any applicable requirements of the GIPS standards. Daily external cash flows must be used within any GIPS-compliant since-inception MWR calculation as of 1 January 2020. Prior to 1 January 2020, quarterly or more-frequent external cash flows must be used.

Firms are reminded that they must comply with all applicable laws and regulations regarding the calculation and presentation of performance and they must not present performance or performance-related information that is false or misleading.

Provision 8.A.7

COMPOSITE returns included in a GIPS ADVERTISEMENT MUST be derived from the returns included in or that will be included in the corresponding GIPS COMPOSITE REPORT.

Discussion

In the spirit of fair representation and full disclosure, all composite returns included in a GIPS Advertisement must be derived from the returns that have been included in or that will be included in the corresponding GIPS Composite Report. This requirement is to ensure consistency in the performance reported by a firm. If a GIPS Advertisement is more current than the corresponding GIPS Composite Report, it is permissible to include more-recent performance in the GIPS Advertisement, as long as this performance will be included in the GIPS Composite Report when it is updated or would be included in the GIPS Composite Report if it were issued as of the date of the GIPS Advertisement.

Provision 8.A.8

Disclosures included in a GIPS ADVERTISEMENT for a COMPOSITE MUST be consistent with the related disclosure included in the corresponding GIPS COMPOSITE REPORT, unless the disclosure included in the GIPS ADVERTISEMENT is more current and has not yet been reflected in the corresponding GIPS COMPOSITE REPORT.

Discussion

In the spirit of fair representation and full disclosure, all disclosures included in a GIPS Advertisement must be consistent with the disclosures that have been included in or that will be included in the corresponding GIPS Composite Report. This requirement is to ensure consistency in information reported by a firm. If a GIPS Advertisement is more current than the corresponding GIPS Composite Report, it is permissible to include a more current disclosure in the GIPS Advertisement, as long as the more current disclosure will be included in the GIPS Composite Report when it is updated or would be included in the GIPS Composite Report if it were issued as of the date of the GIPS Advertisement.

Provision 8.A.9

LIMITED DISTRIBUTION POOLED FUND returns included in a GIPS ADVERTISEMENT MUST be derived from the returns included in or that will be included in the corresponding GIPS POOLED FUND REPORT.

Discussion

In the spirit of fair representation and full disclosure, all limited distribution pooled fund (LDPF) returns included in a GIPS Advertisement must be derived from the returns that have been included in or that will be included in the corresponding GIPS Pooled Fund Report. This requirement is to ensure consistency in the performance reported by a firm. If a GIPS Advertisement is more current than the corresponding GIPS Pooled Fund Report, it is permissible to include more-recent performance in the GIPS Advertisement, as long as this performance will be included in the GIPS Pooled Fund Report when it is updated or would be included in the GIPS Pooled Fund Report if it were issued as of the date of the GIPS Advertisement.

If the firm does not prepare a GIPS Pooled Fund Report for the LDPF but instead includes the LDPF in a composite for which a GIPS Composite Report is prepared, the LDPF returns presented in a GIPS Advertisement must be derived from the returns that would be included in a GIPS Pooled Fund Report for that LDPF if a GIPS Pooled Fund Report for that LDPF were created.

(See Provision 2.A.26 for information regarding the calculation of time-weighted returns for pooled funds that are not included in composites and Provision 2.A.29 for information regarding the calculation of money-weighted returns for pooled funds that are not included in composites.)

Provision 8.A.10

Disclosures included in a GIPS ADVERTISEMENT for a LIMITED DISTRIBUTION POOLED FUND MUST be consistent with the related disclosure included in the corresponding GIPS POOLED FUND REPORT, unless the disclosure included in the GIPS ADVERTISEMENT is more current and has not yet been reflected in the corresponding GIPS POOLED FUND REPORT.

Discussion

In the spirit of fair representation and full disclosure, all disclosures included in a GIPS Advertisement for a limited distribution pooled fund (LDPF) must be consistent with the disclosures included in or that will be included in the corresponding GIPS Pooled Fund Report. This requirement is to ensure consistency in information reported by a firm. If a GIPS Advertisement is more current than the corresponding GIPS Pooled Fund Report, it is permissible to include a more current disclosure in the GIPS Advertisement, as long as the more current disclosure will be included in the GIPS Pooled Fund Report when it is updated or would be included in the GIPS Pooled Fund Report if it were issued as of the date of the GIPS Advertisement.

If the firm does not prepare a GIPS Pooled Fund Report for the LDPF but instead includes the LDPF in a composite for which a GIPS Composite Report is prepared, the disclosures presented in a GIPS Advertisement for the LDPF must be consistent with the related disclosures that would be included in a GIPS Pooled Fund Report if a GIPS Pooled Fund Report for that LDPF were created.

Provision 8.A.11

BENCHMARK returns included in a GIPS ADVERTISEMENT MUST be TOTAL RETURNS.

Discussion

Because the GIPS standards require that benchmark returns presented in a GIPS Advertisement be total returns, a price-only index would not satisfy the requirements of the GIPS Advertising Guidelines. This also applies to benchmarks that are components of a blended benchmark. A price-only benchmark may be presented in a GIPS Advertisement only if it is presented in addition to a total return benchmark. It must be labeled as a price-only benchmark, and there must be sufficient disclosures so that a prospective client or prospective investor understands the difference between the return of a price-only benchmark and the return of a total return benchmark. Firms must not present only a price-only benchmark in a GIPS Advertisement, even if no appropriate total return benchmark is available for a specific composite or pooled fund. If a firm determines that no appropriate benchmark for the composite or pooled fund exists, it must not present a benchmark.

Some benchmarks may appear to be price-only benchmarks because they do not include income, but they should be considered total return benchmarks. These include the following:

- public market equivalent (PME) benchmarks,
- commodity benchmarks, and similar benchmarks, that do not have income because of the nature of the benchmark constituents, and
- target returns, such as an 8% hurdle rate.

The public market equivalent (PME) is a method in which a public market index is used to create a comparable money-weighted return (MWR) from a series of cash flows that replicate those of the pooled fund or composite and that can be compared with the MWR of the pooled fund or composite. When the firm uses a PME, the market index used must be a total return benchmark.

The benchmark presented in the GIPS Advertisement must be consistent with the benchmark presented in the corresponding GIPS Composite Report or GIPS Pooled Fund Report. If more than one benchmark is included in the corresponding GIPS Composite Report or GIPS Pooled Fund Report, the firm should consider whether multiple benchmarks should be presented in the GIPS Advertisement.

Provision 8.A.12

The FIRM MUST clearly label or identify:

a. The name of the COMPOSITE OR POOLED FUND for which the GIPS ADVERTISEMENT is prepared.
b. The name of any BENCHMARK included in the GIPS ADVERTISEMENT.
c. The periods that are presented in the GIPS ADVERTISEMENT.

Discussion

The items presented in a GIPS Advertisement must be clearly labeled or identified so there is clarity regarding the information being presented. Among the items included in a GIPS Advertisement that must be clearly identified or labeled are:

- the name of the composite or pooled fund for which the GIPS Advertisement is prepared,
- the name of any benchmark included in the GIPS Advertisement, and
- the time periods presented.

The name of the benchmark is particularly important when a customized benchmark is used. Firms may need to include more than the name of a customized benchmark when more information is needed for a reader to understand the information presented. For example, if a firm includes a custom benchmark that is net of model fees and costs, simply stating that the benchmark is a custom benchmark would not allow a reader to understand the benchmark returns. It would be appropriate to disclose that the benchmark is net of fees and costs as well as the fees and costs that were used.

Provision 8.A.13

Other information beyond what is REQUIRED OR RECOMMENDED under the GIPS Advertising Guidelines (e.g., COMPOSITE OR POOLED FUND returns for additional periods) MUST be presented with equal or lesser prominence relative to the information REQUIRED OR RECOMMENDED by the GIPS Advertising Guidelines. This information MUST NOT conflict with the REQUIREMENTS OR RECOMMENDATIONS of the GIPS standards or the GIPS Advertising Guidelines.

Discussion

A GIPS Advertisement may include information beyond what is required or recommended under the GIPS Advertising Guidelines. For example, returns for periods in addition to the required periods may be shown. However, information beyond what is required or recommended must:

- be shown with equal or lesser prominence relative to the information that is required or recommended,
- not conflict with the requirements or recommendations of the GIPS standards or the GIPS Advertising Guidelines,
- not be false or misleading, and
- adhere to the principles of fair representation and full disclosure.

As an example, assume that a GIPS Advertisement for a composite includes all information required by the GIPS Advertising Guidelines in a size 10 font. Including backtested hypothetical performance in size 18 font would not be allowed because this information would not be shown with equal or lesser prominence.

Provision 8.A.14

All REQUIRED and RECOMMENDED information in a GIPS ADVERTISEMENT MUST be presented in the same currency.

Discussion

Firms must present all required and recommended information in a GIPS Advertisement in the same currency (e.g., composite or pooled fund and benchmark returns). Any information beyond what is required or recommended by the GIPS Advertising Guidelines should also be presented in the same currency. If it is not, that fact must be disclosed. It would be misleading for the firm to not disclose this fact.

If a firm chooses to present a composite or pooled fund in a different currency, the firm must convert all of the required information into the new currency. If the firm chooses to present performance in multiple currencies in the same GIPS Advertisement, the firm must convert all of the required information into each of the currencies and ensure it is clear in which currencies performance is reported. The firm must also convert any recommended information it chooses to present in the GIPS Advertisement containing the converted information. See Provision 4.A.12 for guidance on converting composite time-weighted returns and Provision 7.A.12 for converting pooled fund money-weighted returns.

8.B. GIPS Advertisements That Do Not Include Performance

Provision 8.B.1

The FIRM MUST disclose the GIPS Advertising Guidelines compliance statement:

> "[Insert name of FIRM] claims compliance with the Global Investment Performance Standards (GIPS®)."

Discussion

A firm has two ways of advertising its claim of compliance with the GIPS standards: 1) by following the GIPS Advertising Guidelines or 2) by including a GIPS Composite Report or a GIPS Pooled Fund Report in its advertisement. If a firm chooses to advertise its claim of compliance by following the GIPS Advertising Guidelines, it must include the following compliance statement in the GIPS Advertisement.

> "[Insert name of FIRM] claims compliance with the Global Investment Performance Standards (GIPS®)."

The compliance statement required by the GIPS Advertising Guidelines is different from the compliance statement required to be disclosed in a GIPS Composite Report or GIPS Pooled Fund Report. The GIPS Advertising Guidelines compliance statement must appear exactly as presented in this provision and may not be reworded in any way. The English version of the compliance statement is the controlling version. If a firm chooses to translate the compliance statement into a language for which there is no official translation of the GIPS standards, the firm must take care to ensure that the translation used reflects the required wording of the compliance statement.

Provision 8.B.2

The FIRM MUST disclose the following: "GIPS® is a registered trademark of CFA Institute. CFA Institute does not endorse or promote this organization, nor does it warrant the accuracy or quality of the content contained herein."

Discussion

"GIPS®" is a registered trademark of CFA Institute, and firms are required to acknowledge this in all GIPS Advertisements. The required disclosure may appear in the body of the GIPS Advertisement or in a footnote to the GIPS Advertisement. The term "this organization," which is included in the required disclosure, refers to any entity associated with the GIPS Advertisement, either the firm or the verifier.

CFA Institute (owner of the GIPS® trademark) may take appropriate action against any firm that misuses the mark "GIPS®" or any compliance statement, including false claims of compliance with the GIPS standards. CFA Institute members, CFA Program charterholders, CFA candidates, CIPM Program certificants, and CIPM candidates who misuse the term "GIPS" or any compliance statement, misrepresent their performance history or the performance history of their firm, or falsely claim compliance with the GIPS standards are also subject to disciplinary sanctions under the CFA Institute Code of Ethics and Standards of Professional Conduct. Possible disciplinary sanctions include public censure, suspension of membership, and revocation of the CFA charter or CIPM certificate.

Regulators with jurisdiction over firms claiming compliance with the GIPS standards may also take enforcement actions against firms that falsely claim compliance with the GIPS standards.

Firms may also use the following language to replace the first sentence in this required disclosure: "GIPS® is a registered trademark owned by CFA Institute." See the GIPS Standards Trademark Usage Guidelines on the CFA Institute website (www.cfainstitute.org) for additional guidance on the proper use of "GIPS".

Provision 8.B.3

The FIRM MUST disclose how to obtain GIPS-compliant performance information for the FIRM'S strategies and products.

Discussion

An advertisement is typically brief and provides limited information regarding the firm and its strategies and products. A reader of a GIPS Advertisement may want to receive additional information in order to have a more complete understanding of a firm's investment offerings, including performance. It is, therefore, required that firms disclose in a GIPS Advertisement that does not include performance how to obtain GIPS-compliant performance information. GIPS-compliant performance information includes GIPS Reports and the firm's required list of composite descriptions, list of limited distribution pooled fund descriptions, and list of broad distribution pooled funds.

Sample Disclosure:

"To receive additional information regarding Ava Advisors, including GIPS-compliant performance information for Ava Advisors' strategies and products, contact Lucia Bear at +41 34 5678910 or write Ava Advisors, One Squirrel Street, Uetikon, Switzerland or lbear@avaadvisors.com."

COMPOSITES

8.C. GIPS Advertisements for a Composite That Include Performance—Requirements

Provision 8.C.1

If TIME-WEIGHTED RETURNS are presented in the corresponding GIPS COMPOSITE REPORT, the FIRM MUST present COMPOSITE TOTAL RETURNS according to one of the following:

a. One-, three-, and five-year annualized COMPOSITE returns through the most recent period. If the COMPOSITE has been in existence for less than five years, the FIRM MUST also present the annualized return since the COMPOSITE INCEPTION DATE.

b. The period-to-date COMPOSITE return in addition to one-, three-, and five-year annualized COMPOSITE returns through the same period as presented in the corresponding GIPS COMPOSITE REPORT. If the COMPOSITE has been in existence for less than five years, the FIRM MUST also present the annualized return since the COMPOSITE INCEPTION DATE.

c. The period-to-date COMPOSITE return in addition to five years of annual COMPOSITE returns (or for each annual period since the COMPOSITE INCEPTION DATE if the COMPOSITE has been in existence for less than five years). The annual returns MUST be calculated through the same period as presented in the corresponding GIPS COMPOSITE REPORT.

d. The annualized COMPOSITE return for the total period that includes all periods presented in the corresponding GIPS COMPOSITE REPORT, through either:

   i. The most recent period end, or

   ii. The most recent annual period end.

Discussion

Provision 8.C.1 does not require a firm presenting time-weighted returns in a GIPS Advertisement to include all four options (a through d) mentioned in the provision. Rather, a firm must present performance in accordance with one of the options described in the provision. A GIPS Advertisement must also adhere to all applicable laws and regulations governing advertisements.

Three of the four options in Provision 8.C.1 include the presentation of annualized composite returns, which represent the geometric average annual compound return achieved over the defined period of more than one year. Annualized performance is permitted only for periods of one year or more.

The formula for calculating annualized performance is as follows:

$$\text{Annualized Return (\%)} = [(1 + R)^{1/n}] - 1,$$

where R is the cumulative return for the period, which is calculated by geometrically linking the sub-period returns during the period, and n is the number of years in the period.

For example, assume a composite's cumulative return for a five-year period is 150.0%. It has a five-year average annual compound return, or annualized return, of 20.11%, which is calculated as:

$$[(1+1.50)^{\frac{1}{5}}]-1=0.2011=20.11\%.$$

If instead the 150% is earned over 12.5 years, the 12.5-year average annual compound return, or annualized return, is 7.61%, which is calculated as:

$$[(1+1.50)^{\frac{1}{12.5}}]-1=0.0761=7.61\%.$$

If the firm chooses to comply with Provision 8.C.1.a, it must present the one-, three-, and five-year annualized composite returns through the most recent period end. If the composite has been in existence for less than five years, the firm must also present the annualized composite return from the composite inception date through the most recent period end, in addition to the most recent one-year return (and the three-year annualized return, if the composite has been in existence for three years or longer).

The most recent period-end date is as of the most recent month- or quarter-end date.
For example, if preparing a GIPS Advertisement in May, the most recent quarter end would be 31 March and the most recent month end would be 30 April. The firm may choose whether to use month-end or quarter-end periods.

If the firm chooses to comply with Provision 8.C.1.b, it must present the period-to-date composite return in addition to the one-, three-, and five-year annualized composite returns through the same period as presented in the corresponding GIPS Composite Report. For example, if the GIPS Composite Report includes calendar-year annual returns, then the annualized returns in the GIPS Advertisements must be through the most recent 31 December. If the composite has been in existence for less than five years, the firm must also present the annualized composite return from the composite inception date through the most recent period end (either month or quarter end), in addition to the one-year return (and the three-year annualized return, if the composite has been in existence for three years or longer).

If the firm chooses to comply with Provision 8.C.1.c, it must present the period-to-date composite return in addition to five years of annual composite returns. If the composite has been in existence for less than five years, the firm must present the annual composite returns for each annual period since the composite's inception date. The annual returns must be calculated through the same period as presented in the corresponding GIPS Composite Report.

If the firm chooses to comply with Provision 8.C.1.d, it must present the annualized composite return for the total period that includes all periods presented in the corresponding GIPS Composite Report through either: a) the most recent month or quarter period end or b) the most recent annual period end. If the composite has been in existence for less than one year, the return must not be annualized.

In the spirit of fair representation and full disclosure, Provision 8.A.7 requires that all composite returns included in a GIPS Advertisement must be derived from the returns that have been included in or that will be included in the corresponding GIPS Composite Report. This is to ensure consistency in the performance reported by a firm. If a GIPS Advertisement is more current than the corresponding GIPS Composite Report, it is permissible to include more recent performance in the GIPS Advertisement, as long as this performance will be included in the GIPS Composite Report when it is updated or would be included in the GIPS Composite Report if it were issued as of the date of the GIPS Advertisement.

Provision 8.C.2

If MONEY-WEIGHTED RETURNS are presented in the corresponding GIPS COMPOSITE REPORT, the FIRM MUST present the annualized (for periods longer than one year) or non-annualized (for periods less than one year) COMPOSITE SINCE-INCEPTION MONEY-WEIGHTED RETURN through either:

a. The most recent period end, or
b. The most recent annual period end.

Discussion

If the firm meets the criteria to present a money-weighted return (MWR) instead of a time-weighted return in a GIPS Composite Report (see Provision 1.A.35) and has chosen to do so, it must present an MWR in the corresponding GIPS Advertisement. The return presented must be the annualized (for periods longer than one year) or non-annualized (for periods less than one year) since-inception MWR through either: a) the most recent period end (i.e., through the most recent month or quarter end) or b) the most recent annual period end.

In the spirit of fair representation and full disclosure, Provision 8.A.7 requires that all composite returns included in a GIPS Advertisement must be derived from the returns that have been included in or that will be included in the corresponding GIPS Composite Report. This requirement is to ensure consistency in the performance reported by a firm. If a GIPS Advertisement is more current than the corresponding GIPS Composite Report, it is permissible to include more-recent performance in the GIPS Advertisement, as long as this performance will be included in the GIPS Composite Report when it is updated or would be included in the GIPS Composite Report if it were issued as of the date of the GIPS Advertisement.

Provision 8.C.3

The FIRM MUST clearly label COMPOSITE returns as GROSS-OF-FEES or NET-OF-FEES.

Discussion

Firms may present either gross-of-fees composite returns or net-of-fees composite returns in a GIPS Advertisement and may also choose to present both gross-of-fees and net-of-fees returns. For prospective clients to understand the nature of the returns being presented, all returns presented must be clearly labeled as gross-of-fees or net-of-fees.

A firm may present net-of-fees returns in a GIPS Advertisement even if the corresponding GIPS Composite Report includes only gross-of-fees returns, or the firm may present gross-of-fees returns even if the corresponding GIPS Composite Report presents only net-of-fees returns, as long as the returns presented in the GIPS Advertisement are derived from the returns that would be included in the corresponding GIPS Composite Report.

Firms advertising performance results must adhere to all applicable laws and regulations, including those governing advertisements. In some jurisdictions, laws or regulations require performance in an advertisement to be presented net-of-fees. Whether or not laws or regulations specify which returns must be presented in an advertisement, firms must clearly indicate whether returns are presented gross-of-fees or net-of-fees so that the reader of the advertisement has a clear understanding of the returns that are presented.

Provision 8.C.4

The FIRM MUST present BENCHMARK returns for the same BENCHMARK as presented in the corresponding GIPS COMPOSITE REPORT, if the corresponding GIPS COMPOSITE REPORT includes BENCHMARK returns. BENCHMARK returns MUST be of the same return type (TIME-WEIGHTED RETURNS or MONEY-WEIGHTED RETURNS), in the same currency, and for the same periods for which the COMPOSITE returns are presented.

 |

Discussion

As described in Provisions 8.C.1 and 8.C.2, firms that present performance in a GIPS Advertisement for a composite have various options for the time periods used in presenting time-weighted returns (TWRs) and money-weighted returns (MWRs). Once an option is selected, the firm must present the total returns for the benchmark(s) for the same periods as the composite returns. The benchmark must be the same benchmark as presented in the corresponding GIPS Composite Report and must also be the same return type (TWR or MWR) and in the same currency as the composite returns. If more than one benchmark is included in the GIPS Composite Report, the firm should consider whether multiple benchmarks should be presented in the GIPS Advertisement.

This requirement is an acknowledgement that a comparison of benchmark and composite returns will help the reader of the GIPS Advertisement determine how well the composite has performed relative to the benchmark.

Provision 8.C.5

The FIRM MUST disclose or otherwise indicate the reporting currency.

Discussion

The GIPS standards require that firms disclose the currency used to report the numerical information presented in a GIPS Advertisement. If the firm presents performance in multiple currencies in the same GIPS Advertisement, the firm must ensure it is clear which currencies are used to calculate and report performance.

Labeling the columns within a GIPS Advertisement with the appropriate currency symbol would satisfy this requirement, as would a written disclosure. If firms advertise the strategy outside their home market, they should consider whether the currency symbol alone is sufficient. For example, a Canadian firm advertising only in Canada may decide to present only the $ symbol. If the firm advertises the strategy in both the United States and Canada, the firm must disclose whether the currency is USD or CAD, because both currencies use the same currency symbol.

All required and recommended information presented in a GIPS Advertisement must be presented in the same currency. (See Provision 8.A.14.)

Sample Disclosures

"Valuations are computed and all information is reported in Canadian dollars."

"Performance is reported in Japanese yen."

Provision 8.C.6

The FIRM MUST disclose the GIPS Advertising Guidelines compliance statement:

> "[Insert name of FIRM] claims compliance with the Global Investment Performance Standards (GIPS®)."

Discussion

A firm has two ways of advertising its claim of compliance with the GIPS standards: 1) by following the GIPS Advertising Guidelines or 2) by including a GIPS Composite Report or a GIPS Pooled Fund Report in its advertisement. If a firm chooses to advertise its claim of compliance by following the GIPS Advertising Guidelines, it must include the following compliance statement in the GIPS Advertisement:

> "[Insert name of FIRM] claims compliance with the Global Investment Performance Standards (GIPS®)."

The compliance statement required by the GIPS Advertising Guidelines is different from the compliance statement required to be disclosed in a GIPS Composite Report or GIPS Pooled Fund Report. The GIPS Advertising Guidelines compliance statement must appear exactly as presented in this provision and may not be reworded in any way. The English version of the compliance statement is the controlling version. If a firm chooses to translate the compliance statement into a language for which there is no official translation of the GIPS standards, the firm must take care to ensure that the translation used reflects the required wording of the compliance statement.

Provision 8.C.7

The FIRM MUST disclose the following: "GIPS® is a registered trademark of CFA Institute. CFA Institute does not endorse or promote this organization, nor does it warrant the accuracy or quality of the content contained herein."

Discussion

"GIPS®" is a registered trademark of CFA Institute, and firms are required to acknowledge this in all GIPS Advertisements. The required disclosure may appear in the body of the GIPS Advertisement or in a footnote to the GIPS Advertisement. The term "this organization," which is included in the required disclosure, refers to any entity associated with the GIPS Advertisement, either the firm or the verifier.

CFA Institute (owner of the GIPS® trademark) may take appropriate action against any firm that misuses the mark "GIPS®" or any compliance statement, including false claims of compliance with the GIPS standards. CFA Institute members, CFA Program charterholders, CFA candidates, CIPM Program certificants, and CIPM candidates who misuse the term "GIPS" or any compliance statement, misrepresent their performance history or the performance history of their firm, or falsely claim compliance with the GIPS standards are also subject to disciplinary sanctions under the CFA Institute Code of Ethics and Standards of Professional Conduct. Possible disciplinary sanctions include public censure, suspension of membership, and revocation of the CFA charter or CIPM certificate.

Regulators with jurisdiction over firms claiming compliance with the GIPS standards may also take enforcement actions against firms that falsely claim compliance with the GIPS standards.

Firms may also use the following language to replace the first sentence in this required disclosure: "GIPS® is a registered trademark owned by CFA Institute." See the GIPS Standards Trademark Usage Guidelines on the CFA Institute website (www.cfainstitute.org) for additional guidance on the proper use of "GIPS".

Provision 8.C.8

The FIRM MUST disclose how to obtain a GIPS COMPOSITE REPORT.

Discussion

An advertisement is typically brief and provides limited information regarding the firm and its strategies and products. A reader of a GIPS Advertisement may want to receive additional information on the firm's investment strategies, including a GIPS Composite Report for the strategy presented in the advertisement. Firms are, therefore, required to disclose in a GIPS Advertisement how to obtain a GIPS Composite Report.

Sample Disclosure for a Composite:

"To receive additional information regarding Ava Advisors, including a GIPS Composite Report for the strategy presented in this advertisement, contact Lucia Bear at +41 34 5678910 or write Ava Advisors, One Squirrel Street, Uetikon, Switzerland or lbear@avaadvisors.com."

Provision 8.C.9

The FIRM MUST disclose if the GIPS ADVERTISEMENT conforms with laws or regulations that conflict with the REQUIREMENTS OR RECOMMENDATIONS of the GIPS standards or the GIPS Advertising Guidelines, as well as the manner in which the laws or regulations conflict with the GIPS standards or the GIPS Advertising Guidelines.

Discussion

Firms must comply with all applicable laws and regulations regarding the calculation and presentation of performance, including the advertising of performance. Compliance with applicable laws and regulations, however, does not necessarily result in compliance with the GIPS Advertising Guidelines. Firms must also comply with all of the applicable requirements of the GIPS Advertising Guidelines when preparing an advertisement in accordance with the GIPS Advertising Guidelines. When laws and regulations conflict with the GIPS Advertising Guidelines, firms are required to comply with the laws and regulations and disclose the manner in which the laws or regulations conflict with the GIPS Advertising Guidelines.

This disclosure will assist readers of the GIPS Advertisement in comparing GIPS Advertisements among firms where reporting requirements may differ because of local laws or regulations.

Sample Disclosure:

"Local laws do not allow the presentation of returns of less than one year in an advertisement, which is in conflict with the GIPS Advertising Guidelines. Therefore, no performance is presented for this composite for the period from 1 July 2018 (the inception date of the composite) through 31 December 2018."

8.D. GIPS Advertisements for a Composite That Include Performance—Recommendations

Provision 8.D.1

The FIRM SHOULD disclose the COMPOSITE DESCRIPTION.

 |

Discussion

To help a reader of a GIPS Advertisement more fully understand the composite being presented, it is recommended that a firm disclose the composite description in the GIPS Advertisement. The composite description is general information regarding the investment mandate, objective, or strategy of the composite. The composite description must include all key features of the composite and must include enough information to allow a reader of the advertisement to understand the key characteristics of the composite's investment mandate, objective, or strategy, including:

- the material risks of the composite's strategy,
- how leverage, derivatives, and short positions may be used, if they are a material part of the strategy, and
- if illiquid investments are a material part of the strategy.

The recommended disclosure of the composite description provides information about the composite's investment strategy that is intended to help a reader of the GIPS Advertisement who is reviewing a GIPS Advertisement for that composite. The composite description should provide sufficient information to readers of the advertisement to allow them to differentiate the significant features of the composite's strategy from other strategies within the firm and to compare products across firms. The disclosed strategy features will likely affect both the historical and expected risk and returns. Along with the recommended disclosure of the benchmark description (see Provision 8.D.3), the GIPS Advertisement will allow the reader to understand both the investment strategy employed and the benchmark against which the composite's performance is evaluated. This will help the reader to compare investments across firms.

If leverage, derivatives, and short positions may be used, and they are a material part of the strategy, this must be disclosed in the composite description. Provision 8.D.2 recommends that the firm disclose how leverage, derivatives, and short positions have been used historically, if material. Taken together, these two recommended disclosures provide a more complete picture about the presence, use, and extent of leverage, derivatives, and short positions. When determining what would be material, the firm must consider whether the disclosure of how leverage, derivatives, and/or short positions are used and/or have been used historically is likely to affect a reader's view of the risk involved in the strategy. If so, the firm must consider if it would be misleading for the firm to fail to disclose their use to the reader when describing the strategy.

Generally, all investment products or strategies have some degree of inherent risk (e.g., market risk), but it is not intended that the composite description identifies every risk of the strategy. Instead, firms must identify those material risks of the strategy, if any, and must disclose those risks. For example, investment concentration, correlation (or lack thereof), liquidity, and exposure to counterparties are features that may need to be included in the composite description. (See Provision 3.A.5 for additional guidance on composite descriptions.)

The key characteristics of some strategies may change in response to market events. Firms should periodically review composite descriptions to ensure they are current.

Given the abbreviated nature of an advertisement, there may be times when firms may wish to use a shorter composite description in a GIPS Advertisement rather than the composite description used in the corresponding GIPS Composite Report. The following examples illustrate how a composite description can be shortened for an advertisement while still conveying the essential features of the composite's strategy.

Sample Disclosures:

Composite Description Included in a GIPS Composite Report

"The Leveraged Bond Composite includes all institutional segregated portfolios invested in a diversified range of high-yield corporate and government bonds with the aim of providing investors with a high level of income while seeking to maximize the total return. The portfolios are invested in domestic and international fixed-income securities of varying maturities. The strategy allows investment in exchange-traded and OTC derivative contracts (including, but not limited to, options, futures, swaps, and forward currency contracts) for the purposes of risk, volatility, and currency exposure management. The strategy allows leverage up to but not exceeding twice the value of a portfolio's investments through the use of repurchase financing arrangements with counterparties. Inherent in derivative instrument investments is the risk of counterparty default. Leverage may also magnify losses as well as gains to the extent that leverage is used. The benchmark is the XYZ Capital Global Aggregate Bond Index."

Composite Description Included in a GIPS Advertisement

"The Leveraged Bond Composite's strategy invests in a diversified range of high-yield corporate and government bonds. The portfolios are invested in domestic and international fixed-income securities of varying maturities. The strategy allows investment in exchange-traded and OTC derivatives for the purposes of risk, volatility, and currency exposure management. The strategy allows leverage up to but not exceeding twice the value of a portfolio's investments. The benchmark is the XYZ Capital Global Aggregate Bond Index."

Provision 8.D.2

The FIRM SHOULD disclose how leverage, derivatives, and short positions have been used historically, if material.

 |

Discussion

It is recommended that firms provide enough information in a GIPS Advertisement to allow a reader to understand how leverage, derivatives, and short positions have been employed historically and may be used going forward. Although the recommended disclosure of the composite description (Provision 8.D.1) would include disclosure of the firm's ability to use leverage, derivatives, and short positions, Provision 8.D.2 recommends that the firm disclose how leverage, derivatives, and short positions have been used historically, if material. Taken together, these two recommended disclosures provide a more complete picture of the presence, use, and extent of leverage, derivatives, and short positions.

For example, assume a firm discloses in the composite description that the strategy may employ up to 200% leverage. To satisfy the disclosure recommendation in Provision 8.D.2, the firm might state, "Since the inception of the strategy, the leverage has averaged 110% of the composite's value; during 2019, however, the leverage averaged 160%, which greatly increased the sensitivity to market volatility and the potential for realized gains and/or losses."

When determining what would be material, the firm must consider whether the disclosure of how leverage, derivatives, and/or short positions have been used historically is likely to affect a reader's view of the risk involved in the strategy. If so, the firm must consider if it would be misleading to fail to disclose their use when describing the strategy.

Provision 8.D.3

The FIRM SHOULD disclose the BENCHMARK DESCRIPTION, which must include the key features of the BENCHMARK or the name of the BENCHMARK for a readily recognized index or other point of reference.

Discussion

Firms are recommended to disclose a description of each benchmark included in a GIPS Advertisement. The benchmark description is defined as general information regarding the investments, structure, and/or characteristics of the benchmark, and it must include the key features of the benchmark. In the case of a widely recognized benchmark, such as the S&P 500® Index, the name of the benchmark will satisfy this recommendation. (S&P 500® is a registered trademark of Standard & Poor's Financial Services LLC.) Each firm must decide for itself whether a benchmark is widely recognized. If the firm is not certain as to whether the benchmark is widely known, it is recommended that the firm include the benchmark description.

Sample Disclosure for a Widely Recognized Benchmark:

"The benchmark is the S&P 500® Index."

Sample Disclosure for a Benchmark That Is Not Widely Recognized:

"The benchmark is the XYZ World Total Return Index, which is designed to measure the equity market performance of developed market countries. The benchmark is market-cap weighted and is composed of all XYZ country-specific developed market indices."

> **Provision 8.D.4**
>
> If the FIRM determines no appropriate BENCHMARK for the COMPOSITE exists, the FIRM SHOULD disclose why no BENCHMARK is presented.

Discussion

Benchmarks are important tools that aid in the planning, implementation, and evaluation of an investment strategy. They also provide information to the reader of a GIPS Advertisement regarding the relationship between a composite's risk and return. As a result, the GIPS standards require firms to provide benchmark total returns in all GIPS Advertisements, unless the firm determines that no appropriate benchmark for the composite exists. The benchmark must reflect the investment mandate, objective, or strategy of the composite. Although there is typically an appropriate benchmark for traditional strategies, it is more common for managers of alternative strategies to determine that no appropriate benchmark for the composite exists. If this is the case, it is recommended that the firm disclose why no benchmark is presented.

Sample Disclosure:

"Because the composite's strategy is absolute return where investments are permitted in all asset classes, as a result no benchmark is presented because we believe that no benchmark that reflects this strategy exists."

> **Provision 8.D.5**
>
> The FIRM SHOULD disclose the definition of the FIRM.

Discussion

To claim compliance with the GIPS standards, a firm must comply with all applicable requirements of the GIPS standards on a firm-wide basis. Accordingly, the firm must determine exactly how it will be defined for the purpose of compliance. The GIPS standards require that a firm must be defined as an investment firm, subsidiary, or division held out to the public as a distinct business entity.

A distinct business entity is a unit, division, department, or office that is organizationally and functionally segregated from other units, divisions, departments, or offices, that retains discretion over the assets it manages, and that should have autonomy over the investment decision-making process.

Possible criteria that can be used to determine this status include:

- being a legal entity,
- having a distinct market or client type (e.g., institutional, retail, private client), and
- using a separate and distinct investment process.

See Provision 1.A.2 for a more detailed discussion of defining the firm.

Because there are often a number of closely related units or divisions within larger investment management entities, the precise definition of the firm that is presenting the performance results and would be responsible for the management of the assets is important information for those who are reading the GIPS Advertisement. This provision, therefore, recommends that the firm disclose sufficient details of the entity that is presenting investment performance such that the firm is clearly identified.

Sample Disclosure:

"For the purpose of complying with the GIPS standards, the firm is defined as Firm B Institutional Investment Management, the institutional asset management division of Firm B."

LIMITED DISTRIBUTION POOLED FUNDS

8.E. GIPS Advertisements for a Limited Distribution Pooled Fund That Include Performance—Requirements

Provision 8.E.1

If TIME-WEIGHTED RETURNS are presented in the corresponding GIPS REPORT, the FIRM MUST present TIME-WEIGHTED RETURNS for the POOLED FUND according to one of the following:

a. One-, three-, and five-year annualized returns through the most recent period. If the POOLED FUND has been in existence for less than five years, the FIRM MUST also present the annualized return since the POOLED FUND INCEPTION DATE.

b. The period-to-date return in addition to one-, three-, and five-year annualized returns through the same period as presented in the corresponding GIPS REPORT. If the POOLED FUND has been in existence for less than five years, the FIRM MUST also present the annualized return since the POOLED FUND INCEPTION DATE.

c. The period-to-date return in addition to five years of annual returns (or for each annual period since the POOLED FUND INCEPTION DATE if the POOLED FUND has been in existence for less than five years). The annual returns MUST be calculated through the same period as presented in the corresponding GIPS REPORT.

d. The annualized POOLED FUND return for the total period that includes all periods presented in the corresponding GIPS REPORT, through either:

   i. The most recent period end, or

   ii. The most recent annual period end.

Discussion

Provision 8.E.1 does not require a firm presenting time-weighted returns in a GIPS Advertisement to include all four options (a through d) mentioned in the provision. Rather, a firm must present performance in accordance with one of the options described in the provision. A GIPS Advertisement must also adhere to all applicable laws and regulations governing advertisements.

Three of the four options in Provision 8.E.1 include the presentation of annualized pooled fund returns, which represent the geometric average annual compound return achieved over the

 |

defined period of more than one year. Annualized performance is permitted only for periods of one year or more.

The formula for calculating annualized performance is as follows:

$$\text{Annualized Return (\%)} = [(1 + R)^{1/n}] - 1,$$

where R is the cumulative return for the period, which is calculated by geometrically linking the sub-period returns during the period, and n is the number of years in the period.

For example, assume a pooled fund's cumulative return for a five-year period is 150.0%. It has a five-year average annual compound return, or annualized return, of 20.11%, which is calculated as:

$$[(1+1.50)^{\frac{1}{5}}]-1=0.2011=20.11\%.$$

If instead the 150% is earned over 12.5 years, the 12.5-year average annual compound return, or annualized return, is 7.61%, which is calculated as:

$$[(1+1.50)^{\frac{1}{12.5}}]-1=0.0761=7.61\%.$$

If the firm chooses to comply with Provision 8.E.1.a, it must present the one-, three-, and five-year annualized pooled fund returns through the most recent period end. If the pooled fund has been in existence for less than five years, the firm must also present the annualized pooled fund return from the pooled fund inception date through the most recent period end, in addition to the most recent one-year return (and the three-year annualized return, if the pooled fund has been in existence for three years or longer).

The most recent period-end date is as of the most recent month- or quarter-end date. For example, if preparing a GIPS Advertisement in May, the most recent quarter end would be 31 March and the most recent month end would be 30 April. The firm may choose whether to use month-end or quarter-end periods.

If the firm chooses to comply with Provision 8.E.1.b, it must present the period-to-date pooled fund return in addition to the one-, three-, and five-year annualized pooled fund returns through the same period as presented in the corresponding GIPS Pooled Fund Report. For example, if the GIPS Pooled Fund Report includes calendar-year annual returns, then the annualized returns in the GIPS Advertisements must be through the most recent 31 December. If the pooled fund has been in existence for less than five years, the firm must also present the annualized pooled fund return from the pooled fund inception date through the most recent period end (either month or quarter end) in addition to the one-year return (and the three-year annualized return, if the pooled fund has been in existence for three years or longer).

If the firm chooses to comply with Provision 8.E.1.c, it must present the period-to-date pooled fund return in addition to five years of annual pooled fund returns. If the pooled fund has been in existence for less than five years, the firm must present the annual pooled fund returns for each annual period since the pooled fund's inception date. The annual returns must be calculated through the same period as presented in the corresponding GIPS Pooled Fund Report.

If the firm chooses to comply with Provision 8.E.1.d, it must present the annualized pooled fund return for the total period that includes all periods presented in the corresponding GIPS Pooled Fund Report through either: a) the most recent month or quarter period end or b) the most recent annual period end. If the pooled fund has been in existence for less than one year, the return must not be annualized.

In the spirit of fair representation and full disclosure, Provision 8.A.9 requires that limited distribution pooled fund (LDPF) returns included in a GIPS Advertisement must be derived from the returns that have been included in or that will be included in the corresponding GIPS Pooled Fund Report. This requirement is to ensure consistency in the performance reported by a firm. If a GIPS Advertisement is more current than the corresponding GIPS Pooled Fund Report, it is permissible to include more-recent performance in the GIPS Advertisement, as long as this performance will be included in the GIPS Pooled Fund Report when it is updated or would be included in the GIPS Report if it were issued as of the date of the GIPS Advertisement.

If the firm does not prepare a GIPS Pooled Fund Report for the LDPF but instead includes the LDPF in a composite for which a GIPS Composite Report is prepared, the LDPF returns presented in a GIPS Advertisement must be derived from the returns that would be included in a GIPS Pooled Fund Report for that LDPF if a GIPS Pooled Fund Report for that LDPF were created. (See Provision 2.A.26 for information regarding the calculation of time-weighted returns for pooled funds that are not included in composites.)

Provision 8.E.2

If MONEY-WEIGHTED RETURNS are presented in the corresponding GIPS REPORT, the FIRM MUST present the annualized (for periods longer than one year) or non-annualized (for periods less than one year) SINCE-INCEPTION MONEY-WEIGHTED RETURN for the POOLED FUND through either:

a. The most recent period end, or
b. The most recent annual period end.

Discussion

If the firm meets the criteria to present a money-weighted return (MWR) instead of a time-weighted return in a GIPS Pooled Fund Report (see Provision 1.A.35) and has chosen to do so, it must present an MWR in the corresponding GIPS Advertisement. The return presented must be the annualized (for periods longer than one year) or non-annualized (for periods less than one year) since-inception MWR through either: a) the most recent period end (i.e., through the most recent month or quarter end) or b) the most recent annual period end.

In the spirit of fair representation and full disclosure, Provision 8.A.9 requires that all limited distribution pooled fund (LDPF) returns included in a GIPS Advertisement must be derived from the returns that have been included in or that will be included in the corresponding GIPS Pooled Fund Report. This is to ensure consistency in the performance reported by a firm. If a GIPS Advertisement is more current than the corresponding GIPS Pooled Fund Report, it is permissible to include more-recent performance in the GIPS Advertisement, as long as this performance will be included in the GIPS Pooled Fund Report when it is updated or would be included in the GIPS Pooled Fund Report if it were issued as of the date of the GIPS Advertisement.

If the firm does not prepare a GIPS Pooled Fund Report for the LDPF but instead includes the LDPF in a composite for which a GIPS Composite Report is prepared, the LDPF returns presented in a GIPS Advertisement must be derived from the returns that would be included in a GIPS Pooled Fund Report for that LDPF if a GIPS Pooled Fund Report for that LDPF were created. (See Provision 2.A.29 for information regarding the calculation of money-weighted returns for pooled funds that are not included in composites.)

Provision 8.E.3

The FIRM MUST clearly label POOLED FUND returns as gross or net of TOTAL POOLED FUND FEES.

Discussion

Firms may present pooled fund returns as either gross or net of total pooled fund fees in a GIPS Advertisement and may also choose to present returns both gross and net of total pooled fund fees. For readers of the GIPS Advertisement to understand the nature of the returns being presented, all returns presented must be clearly labeled as gross of total pooled fund fees or net of total pooled fund fees.

A firm may present returns net of total pooled fund fees in a GIPS Advertisement even if the corresponding GIPS Pooled Fund Report includes only returns that are gross of total pooled fund fees. The firm may also present returns that are gross of total pooled fund fees even if the corresponding GIPS Pooled Fund Report presents only returns that are net of total pooled fund fees. The returns presented in the GIPS Advertisement must be consistent with the returns that would be included in the corresponding GIPS Pooled Fund Report.

If the firm does not prepare a GIPS Pooled Fund Report for the limited distribution pooled fund (LDPF) but instead includes the LDPF in a composite for which a GIPS Composite Report is prepared, the LDPF returns presented in a GIPS Advertisement, whether they are gross or net returns, must be consistent with the returns that would be included in the corresponding GIPS Pooled Fund Report for that LDPF if a GIPS Pooled Fund Report for that LDPF were created. (See Provision 2.A.26 for information regarding the calculation of time-weighted returns for pooled funds that are not included in composites and Provision 2.A.29 for information regarding the calculation of money-weighted returns for pooled funds that are not included in composites.)

Firms advertising performance results must adhere to all applicable laws and regulations, including those governing advertisements. In some jurisdictions, laws or regulations require performance in a pooled fund advertisement to be presented net of total pooled fund fees. Whether or not laws or regulations specify which returns must be presented in an advertisement, firms must clearly indicate whether returns are presented gross or net of total pooled fund fees so that the reader of the advertisement has a clear understanding of the returns that are presented.

Provision 8.E.4

The FIRM MUST present BENCHMARK returns for the same BENCHMARK as presented in the corresponding GIPS REPORT, if the corresponding GIPS REPORT includes BENCHMARK returns. BENCHMARK returns MUST be of the same return type (TIME-WEIGHTED RETURNS or MONEY-WEIGHTED RETURNS), in the same currency, and for the same periods for which the POOLED FUND returns are presented.

Discussion

As described in Provisions 8.E.1 and 8.E.2, firms that present performance in a GIPS Advertisement for a limited distribution pooled fund have various options for the time periods used in presenting time-weighted returns (TWRs) and money-weighted returns (MWRs). Once an option is selected, the firm must present the total returns for the benchmark(s) for the same periods as the pooled fund returns. The benchmark must be the same benchmark as presented in the corresponding GIPS Pooled Fund Report and must also be the same return type (TWR or MWR) and in the same currency as the pooled fund returns. If more than one benchmark is included in the GIPS Pooled Fund Report, the firm should consider whether multiple benchmarks should be presented in the GIPS Advertisement.

If the firm does not prepare a GIPS Pooled Fund Report for the limited distribution pooled fund (LDPF) but instead includes the LDPF in a composite for which a GIPS Composite Report is prepared, the benchmark presented in the GIPS Advertisement must be consistent with the benchmark that would be included in the corresponding GIPS Pooled Fund Report if a GIPS Pooled Fund Report for that LDPF were created.

This requirement is an acknowledgement that a comparison of benchmark and pooled fund returns will help the reader of the GIPS Advertisement determine how well the pooled fund has performed relative to the benchmark.

Provision 8.E.5

The FIRM MUST disclose or otherwise indicate the reporting currency.

Discussion

The GIPS standards require that firms disclose the currency used to report the numerical information presented in a GIPS Advertisement. If the firm presents performance in multiple currencies in the same GIPS Advertisement, the firm must ensure it is clear which currencies are used to calculate and report performance.

Labeling the columns within a GIPS Advertisement with the appropriate currency symbol would satisfy this requirement, as would a written disclosure. If firms advertise the strategy outside their home market, they should consider whether the currency symbol alone is sufficient. For example, a Canadian firm advertising only in Canada may decide to present only the $ symbol. If the firm advertises the strategy in both the United States and Canada, the firm must disclose whether the currency is USD or CAD, because both currencies use the same currency symbol.

All required and recommended information presented in a GIPS Advertisement must be presented in the same currency. (See Provision 8.A.14.)

Sample Disclosures:

"Valuations are computed and all information is reported in Canadian dollars."

"Performance is reported in Japanese yen."

Provision 8.E.6

The FIRM MUST disclose the GIPS Advertising Guidelines compliance statement:

> "[Insert name of FIRM] claims compliance with the Global Investment Performance Standards (GIPS®)."

Discussion

A firm has two ways of advertising its claim of compliance with the GIPS standards: 1) by following the GIPS Advertising Guidelines or 2) by including a GIPS Composite Report or a GIPS Pooled Fund Report in its advertisement. If a firm chooses to advertise its claim of compliance by following the GIPS Advertising Guidelines, it must include the following compliance statement in the GIPS Advertisement:

> "[Insert name of FIRM] claims compliance with the Global Investment Performance Standards (GIPS®)."

The compliance statement required by the GIPS Advertising Guidelines is different from the compliance statement required to be disclosed in a GIPS Composite Report or GIPS Pooled Fund Report. The GIPS Advertising Guidelines compliance statement must appear exactly as presented in this provision and may not be reworded in any way. The English version of the compliance statement is the controlling version. If a firm chooses to translate the compliance statement into a language for which there is no official translation of the GIPS standards, the firm must take care to ensure that the translation used reflects the required wording of the compliance statement.

Provision 8.E.7

The FIRM MUST disclose the following: "GIPS® is a registered trademark of CFA Institute. CFA Institute does not endorse or promote this organization, nor does it warrant the accuracy or quality of the content contained herein."

Discussion

"GIPS®" is a registered trademark of CFA Institute, and firms are required to acknowledge this in all GIPS Advertisements. The required disclosure may appear in the body of the GIPS Advertisement or in a footnote to the GIPS Advertisement. The term "this organization," which is included in the required disclosure, refers to any entity associated with the GIPS Advertisement, either the firm or the verifier.

CFA Institute (owner of the GIPS® trademark) may take appropriate action against any firm that misuses the mark "GIPS®" or any compliance statement, including false claims of compliance with the GIPS standards. CFA Institute members, CFA Program charterholders, CFA candidates, CIPM Program certificants, and CIPM candidates who misuse the term "GIPS" or any compliance statement, misrepresent their performance history or the performance history of their firm, or falsely claim compliance with the GIPS standards are also subject to disciplinary sanctions under the CFA Institute Code of Ethics and Standards of Professional Conduct. Possible disciplinary sanctions include public censure, suspension of membership, and revocation of the CFA charter or CIPM certificate.

Regulators with jurisdiction over firms claiming compliance with the GIPS standards may also take enforcement actions against firms that falsely claim compliance with the GIPS standards.

Firms may also use the following language to replace the first sentence in this required disclosure: "GIPS® is a registered trademark owned by CFA Institute." See the GIPS Standards Trademark Usage Guidelines on the CFA Institute website (www.cfainstitute.org) for additional guidance on the proper use of "GIPS".

Provision 8.E.8

The FIRM MUST disclose how to obtain a GIPS REPORT.

Discussion

An advertisement is typically brief and provides limited information regarding the firm and its strategies and products. A reader of a GIPS Advertisement may want to receive additional information on the firm's investment strategies and pooled funds, including a GIPS Report for the pooled fund presented in the advertisement. It is, therefore, required that firms disclose in a GIPS Advertisement how to obtain a GIPS Report.

Sample Disclosure for a Limited Distribution Pooled Fund:

"To receive additional information regarding Ava Advisors, including a GIPS Report for the pooled fund presented in this advertisement, contact Lucia Bear at +41 34 5678910 or write Ava Advisors, One Squirrel Street, Uetikon, Switzerland or lbear@avaadvisors.com."

Provision 8.E.9

The FIRM MUST disclose if the GIPS ADVERTISEMENT conforms with laws or regulations that conflict with the REQUIREMENTS or RECOMMENDATIONS of the GIPS standards or the GIPS Advertising Guidelines, as well as the manner in which the laws or regulations conflict with the GIPS standards or the GIPS Advertising Guidelines.

Discussion

Firms must comply with all applicable laws and regulations regarding the calculation and presentation of performance, including the advertising of performance. Compliance with applicable laws and regulations, however, does not necessarily result in compliance with the GIPS

Advertising Guidelines. Firms must also comply with all of the applicable requirements of the GIPS Advertising Guidelines when preparing an advertisement in accordance with the GIPS Advertising Guidelines. When laws and regulations conflict with the GIPS Advertising Guidelines, firms are required to comply with the laws and regulations and disclose the manner in which the laws or regulations conflict with the GIPS standards or the GIPS Advertising Guidelines.

This disclosure will assist readers of the GIPS Advertisement in comparing GIPS Advertisements among firms where reporting requirements may differ because of local laws or regulations.

Sample Disclosure:

"Local laws do not allow the presentation of returns of less than one year in an advertisement, which is in conflict with the GIPS Advertising Guidelines. Therefore, no performance is presented for this pooled fund for the period from 1 July 2018 (the inception date of the pooled fund) through 31 December 2018."

8.F. GIPS Advertisements for a Limited Distribution Pooled Fund That Include Performance—Recommendations

Provision 8.F.1

The FIRM SHOULD disclose the POOLED FUND DESCRIPTION.

Discussion

To help a reader of a GIPS Advertisement more fully understand the pooled fund being presented, it is recommended that a firm disclose the pooled fund description in the advertisement. The pooled fund description is general information regarding the investment mandate, objective, or strategy of the pooled fund. The pooled fund description must include all key features of the pooled fund and must include enough information to allow a reader of the advertisement to understand the key characteristics of the pooled fund's investment mandate, objective, or strategy, including:

- the material risks of the pooled fund's strategy,
- how leverage, derivatives, and short positions may be used, if they are a material part of the strategy, and
- if illiquid investments are a material part of the strategy.

The recommended disclosure of the pooled fund description provides information about the pooled fund's investment strategy that is intended to help a reader of the GIPS Advertisement who is reviewing a GIPS Advertisement for that pooled fund. The pooled fund description should provide sufficient information to the reader to allow them to differentiate the significant features of the pooled fund's strategy from other strategies or pooled funds within the firm and to compare products across firms. The disclosed strategy features will likely affect both the historical and expected risk and returns. Along with the recommended disclosure of the benchmark description (see Provision 8.F.3), the GIPS Advertisement will allow the reader to understand both the investment strategy employed and the benchmark against which the pooled fund's performance is evaluated. This will help the reader to compare investments across firms.

If leverage, derivatives, and short positions may be used, and they are a material part of the strategy, this must be disclosed in the pooled fund description. Provision 8.F.2 recommends that the firm disclose how leverage, derivatives, and short positions have been used historically, if material. Taken together, these two recommended disclosures provide a more complete picture about the presence, use, and extent of leverage, derivatives, and short positions. When determining what would be material, the firm must consider whether the disclosure of how leverage, derivatives, and/or short positions are used and/or have been used historically is likely to affect a reader's view of the risk involved in the pooled fund strategy. If so, the firm must consider if it would be misleading for the firm to fail to disclose their use to the reader when describing the strategy.

Generally, all investment products or strategies have some degree of inherent risk (e.g., market risk), but it is not intended that the pooled fund description identifies every risk of the strategy. Instead, firms must identify those material risks of the strategy, if any, and must disclose those risks. For example, investment concentration, correlation (or lack thereof), liquidity, and exposure to counterparties are features that may need to be included in the pooled fund description.

The key characteristics of some pooled fund strategies may change in response to market events. Firms should periodically review pooled fund descriptions to ensure they are current.

A sample list of pooled fund descriptions can be found in Appendix D: Sample Lists.

Given the abbreviated nature of an advertisement, there may be times when firms may wish to use a shorter pooled fund description in a GIPS Advertisement than the pooled fund description used in the corresponding GIPS Report. The following examples illustrate how a pooled fund description can be shortened for use in an advertisement while still conveying the essential features of the pooled fund's strategy.

Sample Disclosures for a Limited Distribution Pooled Fund:

Pooled Fund Description Included in a GIPS Pooled Fund Report

"The 2018 Venture Capital Fund seeks long-term capital appreciation by acquiring minority interests in early-stage technology companies. The Fund invests in technology companies in Europe, Asia Pacific, and emerging markets. European venture investments are more concentrated than in the other regions and are focused on a few high-quality companies. Exit opportunities include IPOs, trade sales, and secondary sales. Opportunities in China and India will be targeted for investment, and an allocation to Chinese high-tech will be at least 10% of the invested capital over the Fund's life. International venture capital investments are generally illiquid and are subject to currency risk. If investment opportunities and/or exit strategies become limited, the life of the fund may be extended, and capital calls and distributions may be delayed. The Fund is benchmarked to the XYZ Venture Capital Index."

Pooled Fund Description Included in a GIPS Advertisement

"The 2018 Venture Capital Fund invests in early-stage technology companies in Europe, Asia Pacific (with at least 10% allocation to China), and emerging markets. Exit opportunities include IPOs, trade sales, and secondary sales. International venture capital investments are generally illiquid and are subject to currency risk. If investment opportunities and/or exit strategies become limited, the life of the fund may be extended, and capital calls and distributions may be delayed. The Fund is benchmarked to the XYZ Venture Capital Index."

Provision 8.F.2

The FIRM SHOULD disclose how leverage, derivatives, and short positions have been used historically, if material.

Discussion

It is recommended that firms provide enough information in a GIPS Advertisement to allow a reader to understand how leverage, derivatives, and short positions have been employed historically and may be used going forward. Although the recommended disclosure of the pooled fund description (Provision 8.F.1) would include disclosure of the firm's ability to use leverage, derivatives, and short positions, Provision 8.F.2 recommends that the firm disclose how leverage, derivatives, and short positions have been used historically, if material. Taken together, these two recommended disclosures provide a more complete picture of the presence, use, and extent of leverage, derivatives, and short positions.

For example, assume a firm discloses in the pooled fund description that the strategy may employ up to 200% leverage. To satisfy the disclosure recommendation in Provision 8.F.2, the firm might state, "Since the inception of the pooled fund, the leverage has averaged 110% of the pooled fund's value; however, during 2019, the leverage averaged 160%, which greatly increased the sensitivity to market volatility and the potential for realized gains and/or losses."

When determining what would be material, the firm must consider whether the disclosure of how leverage, derivatives, and/or short positions have been used historically is likely to affect a reader's view of the risk involved in the strategy. If so, the firm must consider if it would be misleading to fail to disclose their use when describing the strategy.

Provision 8.F.3

The FIRM SHOULD disclose the BENCHMARK DESCRIPTION, which MUST include the key features of the BENCHMARK or the name of the BENCHMARK for a readily recognized index or other point of reference.

Discussion

Firms are recommended to disclose a description of each benchmark included in a GIPS Advertisement. The benchmark description is defined as general information regarding the investments, structure, and/or characteristics of the benchmark, and it must include the key features of the benchmark. In the case of a widely recognized benchmark, such as the S&P 500® Index, the name of the benchmark will satisfy this recommendation. (S&P 500® is a registered trademark of Standard & Poor's Financial Services LLC.) Each firm must decide for itself whether a benchmark is widely recognized. If the firm is not certain as to whether the benchmark is widely known, it is recommended that the firm include the benchmark description.

Sample Disclosure for a Widely Recognized Benchmark:

"The benchmark is the S&P 500® Index."

Sample Disclosure for a Benchmark That Is Not Widely Recognized:

"The custom benchmark return is calculated by applying the investment cash flows of the Armor Distressed Debt Fund to the XYZ Eurozone Distressed Debt Bond Total Return Index. The index reflects a portfolio of euro-denominated distressed debt bonds issued in Eurozone countries that generally have credit ratings of CCC or lower from the main rating agencies and are listed on the XYZ platforms."

Provision 8.F.4

If the FIRM determines no appropriate BENCHMARK for the POOLED FUND exists, the FIRM SHOULD disclose why no BENCHMARK is presented.

Discussion

Benchmarks are important tools that aid in the planning, implementation, and evaluation of an investment strategy. They also provide information to the reader of a GIPS Advertisement regarding the relationship between a pooled fund's risk and return. As a result, the GIPS standards require firms to provide benchmark total returns in all GIPS Advertisements, unless the firm determines that no appropriate benchmark for the pooled fund's strategy exists. The benchmark must reflect the investment mandate, objective, or strategy of the pooled fund. Although there is typically an appropriate benchmark for traditional pooled fund strategies, it is more common for managers of alternative pooled fund strategies to determine that no appropriate benchmark for the pooled fund exists. If this is the case, it is recommended that the firm disclose why no benchmark is presented.

Sample Disclosure:

"Because the pooled fund's strategy is absolute return where investments are permitted in all asset classes, as a result no benchmark is presented because we believe that no benchmark that reflects this strategy exists."

Provision 8.F.5

The FIRM SHOULD disclose the definition of the FIRM.

Discussion

To claim compliance with the GIPS standards, a firm must comply with all applicable requirements of the GIPS standards on a firm-wide basis. Accordingly, the firm must determine exactly how it will be defined for the purpose of compliance. The GIPS standards require that a firm must be defined as an investment firm, subsidiary, or division held out to the public as a distinct business entity.

A distinct business entity is a unit, division, department, or office that is organizationally and functionally segregated from other units, divisions, departments, or offices, that retains discretion over the assets it manages, and that should have autonomy over the investment decision-making process.

Possible criteria that can be used to determine this status include:

- being a legal entity,
- having a distinct market or client type (e.g., institutional, retail, private client), and
- using a separate and distinct investment process.

See Provision 1.A.2 for a more detailed discussion of defining the firm.

Because there are often a number of closely related units or divisions within larger investment management entities, the precise definition of the firm that is presenting the performance results and would be responsible for the management of the pooled fund's assets is important information for those who are reading the GIPS Advertisement. This provision, therefore, recommends that the firm disclose sufficient details of the entity that is presenting investment performance such that the firm is clearly identified.

Sample Disclosure

"For the purpose of complying with the GIPS standards, the firm is defined as Firm B Institutional Investment Management, the institutional asset management division of Firm B."

BROAD DISTRIBUTION POOLED FUNDS

8.G. GIPS Advertisements for a Broad Distribution Pooled Fund That Include Performance—Requirements

Provision 8.G.1

If laws or regulations mandate specific POOLED FUND returns, the FIRM MUST present POOLED FUND returns according to the methodology and for the periods REQUIRED by laws or regulations.

Discussion

Laws or regulations typically specify how broad distribution pooled fund (BDPF) returns must be presented in an advertisement. If laws or regulations mandate a specific methodology for calculating BDPF returns, and specific time periods for which BDPF returns must be presented in an advertisement, a firm must follow the laws or regulations. If laws or regulations do not mandate a specific methodology and/or periodicity, the firm must instead follow the requirements in Provision 8.G.2.

Provisions 8.G.1 and 8.G.2 address only the methodology and time periods required for the presentation of returns in a GIPS Advertisement for a BDPF. Firms must comply with all of the other applicable requirements of laws or regulations and the GIPS Advertising Guidelines as well.

Provision 8.G.2

If specific periods are not mandated by laws or regulations, POOLED FUND returns MUST be presented consistent with one of the following options:

a. One-, three-, and five-year annualized returns through the most recent period. If the POOLED FUND has been in existence for less than five years, the FIRM MUST also present the annualized return since the POOLED FUND INCEPTION DATE.

b. The period-to-date return in addition to one-, three-, and five-year annualized returns through the most recent period. If the POOLED FUND has been in existence for less than five years, the FIRM MUST also present the annualized return since the POOLED FUND INCEPTION DATE.

c. The period-to-date return in addition to five years of annual returns (or for each annual period since the POOLED FUND INCEPTION DATE if the POOLED FUND has been in existence for less than five years).

d. The annualized POOLED FUND return since the POOLED FUND INCEPTION DATE through the most recent period.

Discussion

Provision 8.G.2 does not require a firm presenting time-weighted returns in a GIPS Advertisement to include all four options (a through d) mentioned in the provision. Rather, a firm must present performance in accordance with laws or regulations (Provision 8.G.1) or one of the options described in Provision 8.G.2. A GIPS Advertisement must also adhere to all applicable laws and regulations governing advertisements.

Three of the four options in Provision 8.G.2 include the presentation of annualized pooled fund returns, which represent the geometric average annual compound return achieved over the defined period of more than one year. Annualized performance is permitted only for periods of one year or more.

The formula for calculating annualized performance is as follows:

$$\text{Annualized Return (\%)} = [(1 + R)^{1/n}] - 1,$$

where R is the cumulative return for the period, which is calculated by geometrically linking the sub-period returns during the period, and n is the number of years in the period.

For example, assume a pooled fund's cumulative return for a five-year period is 150.0%. It has a five-year average annual compound return, or annualized return, of 20.11%, which is calculated as:

$$[(1+1.50)^{\frac{1}{5}}]-1=0.2011=20.11\%.$$

If instead the 150% is earned over 12.5 years, the 12.5-year average annual compound return, or annualized return, is 7.61%, which is calculated as:

$$[(1+1.50)^{\frac{1}{12.5}}]-1=0.0761=7.61\%.$$

If the firm chooses to comply with Provision 8.G.2.a, it must present the one-, three-, and five-year annualized pooled fund returns through the most recent period end. If the pooled fund has been in existence for less than five years, the firm must also present the annualized pooled fund return from the pooled fund inception date through the most recent period end, in addition to the most recent one-year return (and the three-year annualized return, if the pooled fund has been in existence for three years or longer).

The most recent period-end date is as of the most recent month- or quarter-end date. For example, if preparing a GIPS Advertisement in May, the most recent quarter end would be 31 March and the most recent month end would be 30 April. The firm may choose whether to use month-end or quarter-end periods.

If the firm chooses to comply with Provision 8.G.2.b, it must present the period-to-date pooled fund return in addition to the one-, three-, and five-year annualized pooled fund returns through the most recent period end (either month or quarter end). If the pooled fund has been in existence for less than five years, the firm must also present the annualized pooled fund return from the pooled fund inception date through the most recent period end (either month or quarter end) in addition to the one-year return (and the three-year annualized return, if the pooled fund has been in existence for three years or longer).

If the firm chooses to comply with Provision 8.G.2.c, it must present the period-to-date pooled fund return in addition to five years of annual pooled fund returns (or for each annual period since the pooled fund inception date if the pooled fund has been in existence for less than five years).

If the firm chooses to comply with Provision 8.G.2.d, it must present the annualized pooled fund return from the pooled fund inception date through the most recent period end (either month or quarter end). If the pooled fund has been in existence for less than one year, the return must not be annualized.

The GIPS standards require firms to present time-weighted returns (TWRs) unless very specific circumstances are met. As discussed in Provision 1.A.35, a firm may present money-weighted returns (MWRs) instead of TWRs only if the firm has control over the external cash flows into and out of the pooled fund and the pooled fund has at least one of the following characteristics:

- closed-end
- fixed life
- fixed commitment
- illiquid investments as a significant part of the investment strategy.

A firm typically does not know the investors in a broad distribution pooled fund (BDPF) and therefore would be unable to call capital. Most BDPFs also would not meet at least one of the four specified characteristics. For these reasons, the discussion of BDPF returns presented in a GIPS Advertisement focuses on TWRs. However, MWRs may be presented in a GIPS Advertisement for a BDPF if required by laws or regulations. (See Provision 8.G.1.) If the presentation of an MWR for a BDPF is mandated by laws or regulations, the MWR presented must be the annualized (for periods longer than one year) or non-annualized (for periods less than one year) since-inception MWR through the most recent period end, unless a different period is specified by laws or regulations. Firms must follow the calculation methodology specified by laws or regulations. If local laws and regulations do not specify a calculation methodology, firms should follow the requirements for calculating MWRs included in Provision 2.A.29.

When laws or regulations do not require MWRs for BDPFs, firms may include MWRs in a GIPS Advertisement along with TWRs.

Provision 8.G.3

If the GIPS ADVERTISEMENT is created for a specific POOLED FUND share class, and POOLED FUND NET RETURNS are presented, POOLED FUND NET RETURNS MUST reflect the fees and expenses of that specific share class.

Discussion

Broad distribution pooled funds often have many share classes, each with different fees and expenses. If the GIPS Advertisement is created for a specific pooled fund share class, the pooled fund returns presented in the GIPS Advertisement must reflect the fees and expenses of that specific share class.

 |

Provision 8.G.4

If the GIPS ADVERTISEMENT is not created for a specific share class and POOLED FUND NET RETURNS are presented, POOLED FUND NET RETURNS MUST reflect the fees and expenses of:

a. The share class with the maximum fee that is available for general distribution, or

b. All share classes.

Discussion

Broad distribution pooled funds (BDPFs) often have many share classes, each with different fees and expenses. It is important that the pooled fund net returns presented in a GIPS Advertisement reflect the appropriate fees and expenses so the returns are not false or misleading. If a BDPF has multiple share classes, and the GIPS Advertisement is not created for a specific share class, the firm has two options in terms of the fees and expenses that must be reflected in the pooled fund net returns presented in the GIPS Advertisement.

The first option is for the firm to present pooled fund net returns that reflect the fees and expenses of the share class that has the maximum fee and that is available for general distribution. A share class of a BDPF is considered available for general distribution if the share class is available to anyone who is qualified to invest in that pooled fund. For example, suppose that a mutual fund has only two share classes:

- a retail share class that requires a minimum initial investment of $500, which is the lowest minimum investment for any share class in the fund, and
- an institutional share class that has a minimum initial investment of $1,000,000.

The retail share class is considered to be available for general distribution because it is available to any investor willing to make the minimum initial investment of $500 that is necessary to invest in the fund. The institutional share class is not considered to be available for general distribution because investment in that share class is limited to those investors who are willing to make a significantly larger investment in the fund. In this case, the retail share class is the only class of shares of the fund that is available for general distribution. It is, therefore, the fees and expense of the retail share class that must be reflected in the pooled fund net returns. If there are multiple retail share classes, the firm must use the fees and expenses of the retail share class with the highest fees and expenses that is available for general distribution.

The second option is to include information on all share classes by presenting either:

- all share classes, with the returns for each share class presented individually reflecting the fees and expenses of that share class, or
- a combined weighted average net return that reflects the fees and expenses of all share classes.

Regardless of the method chosen by a firm to present returns that appropriately reflect fees and expenses for a BDPF with multiple share classes, it is important to have sufficient disclosures so that prospective investors understand what fees and expenses are reflected in the BDPF's net returns. For example, if the firm chooses to present a combined weighted average net return that reflects the fees and expenses of all share classes, it may be appropriate to disclose that the return does not necessarily reflect the return of any individual investor. It may also be appropriate to provide details for how a reader of the advertisement would be able to obtain additional information on fees and expenses or any other information included in the GIPS Advertisement.

Provision 8.G.5

The FIRM MUST clearly label POOLED FUND returns as gross or net of TOTAL POOLED FUND FEES.

Discussion

Firms may present pooled fund returns as either gross or net of total pooled fund fees in a GIPS Advertisement and may also choose to present returns both gross and net of total pooled fund fees. For readers of the GIPS Advertisement to understand the nature of the returns being presented, all returns presented must be clearly labeled as gross of total pooled fund fees or net of total pooled fund fees.

Firms advertising performance results must adhere to all applicable laws and regulations, including those governing advertisements. In some jurisdictions, laws or regulations require performance in a pooled fund advertisement to be presented net of total pooled fund fees. Whether or not laws or regulations specify which returns must be presented in an advertisement, firms must clearly indicate whether returns are presented gross or net of total pooled fund fees so that the reader of the advertisement has a clear understanding of the returns that are presented.

Provision 8.G.6

The FIRM MUST present BENCHMARK TOTAL RETURNS for the same periods for which the POOLED FUND is presented, unless the FIRM determines there is no appropriate BENCHMARK.

Discussion

As described in Provisions 8.G.1 and 8.G.2, firms that present performance in a GIPS Advertisement for a broad distribution pooled fund have various options for the periods used in presenting returns. Once an option is selected, the firm must present benchmark total returns for the same periods for which pooled fund returns are presented. The benchmark must be in the same currency as the pooled fund returns presented in the GIPS Advertisement. This requirement is an acknowledgement that a comparison of benchmark and pooled fund returns will help the reader of the GIPS Advertisement determine how well the pooled fund has performed relative to the benchmark.

Provision 8.G.7

The FIRM MUST disclose the current EXPENSE RATIO and which fees and expenses are included in the EXPENSE RATIO. The FIRM MUST disclose if PERFORMANCE-BASED FEES are not reflected in the EXPENSE RATIO, if applicable.

Discussion

Firms must disclose the current expense ratio as well as which fees and expenses are included in the expense ratio. The pooled fund expense ratio is the ratio of total pooled fund expenses to average net assets. The expense ratio should not reflect transaction costs. The expense ratio gives readers of the GIPS Advertisement insight into the total fees and expenses involved in an investment in the fund. For example, a pooled fund expense ratio of 1.00% indicates that an investor will pay $10 in expenses each year for every $1,000 invested, in addition to transaction costs. An expense ratio also helps investors compare expenses across funds, because even a small difference in fees can have a significant effect over time.

Because expense ratios can change over time, firms must determine which expense ratio to present. A firm might choose to present the expense ratio as of the most recent annual period end, or the last known expense ratio. When the expense ratio has had a material change resulting from a change in assets or costs, the firm should present a more current expense ratio that reflects what a prospective investor is likely to pay at the current time.

If the pooled fund has multiple share classes, the firm may present multiple expense ratios or may present the expense ratio for the share class that has the highest expense ratio and is available for general distribution. Presenting a range of expense ratios (e.g., the expense ratio for all share classes ranges between 0.40% and 0.85%) would not satisfy this requirement. Performance-based fees are expected to be included in the expense ratio. If laws or regulations do not allow the inclusion of performance-based fees in the calculation of the expense ratio, the firm must disclose that performance-based fees are not reflected in the expense ratio.

Pooled fund expense ratios that are calculated for periods of less than one year must be annualized. For example, assume that a pooled fund starts on 1 April, and the firm calculates an expense ratio of 0.75% for the period from 1 April 2019 through 31 December 2019. The firm must present an annualized rate of 1.00%, representing a pooled fund expense ratio for the entire year, rather than the 0.75% that represents an expense ratio for only nine months. Presenting an annualized expense ratio facilitates the comparison of expense ratios across funds and firms. Firms may also present the non-annualized expense ratio but must clearly disclose or indicate that the expense ratio is not annualized.

Sample Disclosure:

"The Fund's expense ratio (annual, Class A) is 1.00%. The expense ratio is calculated based on the Fund's average net assets during the Fund's most recently completed fiscal year and has not been adjusted for current asset levels. The expense ratio includes operating costs, including administrative, compliance, distribution, management, marketing, shareholder services, and record-keeping fees. Please see the Fund's prospectus for additional details."

Provision 8.G.8

The FIRM MUST disclose or otherwise indicate the reporting currency.

Discussion

The GIPS standards require that firms disclose the currency used to report the numerical information presented in a GIPS Advertisement. If the firm presents performance in multiple currencies in the same GIPS Advertisement, the firm must ensure it is clear which currencies are used to calculate and report performance.

Labeling the columns within a GIPS Advertisement with the appropriate currency symbol would satisfy this requirement, as would a written disclosure. If firms advertise the strategy outside their home market, they should consider whether the currency symbol alone is sufficient. For example, a Canadian firm advertising only in Canada may decide to present only the $ symbol. If the firm advertises the strategy in both the United States and Canada, the firm must disclose whether the currency is USD or CAD, because both currencies use the same currency symbol.

All required and recommended information presented in a GIPS Advertising Report must be presented in the same currency. (See Provision 8.A.14.)

Sample Disclosures:

"Valuations are computed and all information is reported in Canadian dollars."

"Performance is reported in Japanese yen."

Provision 8.G.9

The FIRM MUST disclose the POOLED FUND DESCRIPTION.

Discussion

To help a reader of a GIPS Advertisement more fully understand the pooled fund being presented, a firm must disclose the pooled fund description in the advertisement. The pooled fund description is general information regarding the investment mandate, objective, or strategy of the pooled fund. The pooled fund description must include all key features of the pooled fund and must include enough information to allow a reader of the advertisement to understand the key characteristics of the pooled fund's investment mandate, objective, or strategy, including:

- the material risks of the pooled fund's strategy,
- how leverage, derivatives, and short positions may be used, if they are a material part of the strategy, and
- if illiquid investments are a material part of the strategy.

The required disclosure of the pooled fund description provides information about the pooled fund's investment strategy that is intended to help the reader of the GIPS Advertisement who is reviewing a GIPS Advertisement for that pooled fund. The pooled fund description should provide sufficient information to the reader to allow them to differentiate the significant features of the pooled fund's strategy from other strategies or pooled funds within the firm and to compare products across firms. The disclosed strategy features will likely affect both the historical and expected risk and returns. Along with the required disclosure of the benchmark description (see Provision 8.G.12), the GIPS Advertisement will allow the reader to understand both the investment strategy employed and the benchmark against which the pooled fund's performance is evaluated. This will help the reader to compare investments across firms.

If leverage, derivatives, and short positions may be used, and they are a material part of the strategy, this must be disclosed in the pooled fund description. When determining what would be material, the firm must consider whether the disclosure of how leverage, derivatives, and/or short positions are used and/or have been used historically is likely to affect a prospective investor's view of the risk involved in the strategy. If so, it would be misleading for the firm to fail to disclose their use to these prospective investors when describing the strategy. Firms should also disclose how leverage, derivative, and short positions have been used historically, if material. Doing so would provide a more complete picture about the presence, use, and extent of leverage, derivatives, and short positions.

Generally, all investment products or strategies have some degree of inherent risk (e.g., market risk), but it is not intended that the pooled fund description identifies every risk of the pooled fund's strategy. Instead, firms must identify those material risks of the strategy, if any, and must disclose those risks. For example, investment concentration, correlation (or lack thereof), liquidity, and exposure to counterparties are features that may need to be included in the pooled fund description.

The key characteristics of some pooled fund strategies may change in response to market events. Firms should periodically review pooled fund descriptions to ensure they are current.

A sample list of pooled fund descriptions can be found in Appendix D: Sample Lists.

Sample Disclosures for a Firm's US Fixed-Income Fund:

Given the abbreviated nature of an advertisement, there may be times when firms may wish to use a shorter pooled fund description in a GIPS Advertisement than is used in other materials. The following example illustrates how a pooled fund description can be shortened for an advertisement while still conveying the essential features of the pooled fund's strategy.

Longer Version of the US Fixed-Income Fund Description

"The Fund is designed to maximize total return by investing in a portfolio of investment-grade intermediate- and long-term debt securities. The Fund will primarily invest in corporate bonds, US Treasuries, other US government and agency securities, and asset-backed, mortgage-related, and mortgage-backed securities. The Fund will invest at least 80% of its assets in bonds and up to 20% in cash and cash equivalents. The Fund is subject to general market risk, interest rate risk, credit (issuer and counterparty) risk, and liquidity risk. General market risk is the risk that the value of the securities owned by the Fund may underperform because of factors affecting particular industries or securities markets generally. Interest rate risk is the risk the values of bonds will change as a result of changes in interest rates. If rates increase, the value of bonds declines in general. Credit risk is the risk the value of investments may change because of changes in creditworthiness of issuers of debt securities and default of counterparties in investment transactions. Liquidity risk is the risk the Fund may have a loss when it sells securities to raise cash for redemption requests by shareholders."

Shorter Version of the US Fixed-Income Fund Description

"The Fund invests in a portfolio of US investment-grade intermediate- and long-term debt securities, such as corporate bonds, US Treasuries, other US government and agency securities, and asset-backed and mortgage-backed securities. Up to 20% may be held in cash and cash equivalents. The fixed-income investments must be rated investment grade or above. The Fund is subject to general market risk, interest rate risk, credit (issuer and counterparty) risk, and liquidity risk. The Fund's benchmark is the XYZ Bond Index."

Provision 8.G.10

If laws or regulations mandate specific information about the POOLED FUND'S risk, as either a qualitative narrative or a quantitative metric, the FIRM MUST disclose this information.

Discussion

If laws or regulations mandate firms to include in an advertisement specific information about the pooled fund's risk, as either a qualitative narrative or a quantitative metric, the firm must disclose this information. This requirement applies only to the information mandated by the applicable laws or regulations to be included in an advertisement, not to other documents of the pooled fund. For example, local laws and regulations may require that funds present specific risk indicators in prospectuses, regulatory factsheets, or investor documents but not in advertisements. In this case, such risk indicators are not required to be presented in GIPS Advertisements.

When laws and regulations conflict with the GIPS standards or the GIPS Advertising Guidelines, firms are required to comply with the laws and regulations and disclose the manner in which the laws or regulations conflict with the GIPS standards or the GIPS Advertising Guidelines.

Provision 8.G.11

If laws or regulations do not mandate specific information about the POOLED FUND'S risk, the FIRM MUST choose and present an appropriate risk measure or qualitative disclosure that a PROSPECTIVE INVESTOR is likely to understand.

Discussion

Understanding and interpreting investment performance requires the consideration of both risk and return. An indication of risk is, therefore, required in all GIPS Advertisements for broad distribution pooled funds (BDPFs). If local laws or regulations do not mandate that specific information about a pooled fund's risk be included in an advertisement for a BDPF (see Provision 8.G.10), firms must choose and present an appropriate risk measure or a qualitative narrative disclosure of risk. Firms should choose a risk measure that is well known or that can be clearly presented and explained in the GIPS Advertisement so that a broad audience is likely to understand the degree of risk that the risk indicator is intended to convey.

It is important to keep in mind that risk measures should be consistent with the pooled fund's strategy. For example, if the strategy is to track the benchmark, then tracking error would be consistent with that objective.

Provision 8.G.12

The FIRM MUST disclose the BENCHMARK DESCRIPTION, which MUST include the key features of the BENCHMARK or the name of the BENCHMARK for a readily recognized index or other point of reference.

Discussion

Firms are required to disclose a description of each benchmark included in a GIPS Advertisement for a broad distribution pooled fund. The benchmark description is defined as general information regarding the investments, structure, and/or characteristics of the benchmark, and it must include the key features of the benchmark. In the case of a widely recognized benchmark, such as the S&P 500® Total Return Index, the name of the benchmark will satisfy this requirement. (S&P 500® is a registered trademark of Standard & Poor's Financial Services LLC.) Each firm must decide for itself whether a benchmark is widely recognized. If the firm is not certain as to whether the benchmark is widely known, the firm must include the benchmark description.

Sample Disclosure for a Widely Recognized Benchmark:

"The benchmark is the S&P 500® Index."

Sample Disclosure for a Benchmark That Is Not Widely Recognized:

"The benchmark is the XYZ World Total Return Index, which is designed to measure the equity market performance of developed market countries. The benchmark is market-cap weighted and is composed of all XYZ country-specific developed market indices."

Provision 8.G.13

The FIRM MUST disclose the GIPS Advertising Guidelines compliance statement:

> "[Insert name of FIRM] claims compliance with the Global Investment Performance Standards (GIPS®)."

Discussion

A firm has two ways of advertising its claim of compliance with the GIPS standards: 1) by following the GIPS Advertising Guidelines or 2) by including a GIPS Composite Report or a GIPS

 |

Pooled Fund Report in its advertisement. If a firm chooses to advertise its compliance by following the GIPS Advertising Guidelines, it must include the following claim of compliance in the GIPS Advertisement:

> "[Insert name of FIRM] claims compliance with the Global Investment Performance Standards (GIPS®)."

The compliance statement required by the GIPS Advertising Guidelines is different from the compliance statement required to be disclosed in a GIPS Composite Report or GIPS Pooled Fund Report. The GIPS Advertising Guidelines compliance statement must appear exactly as presented in this provision and may not be reworded in any way. The English version of the compliance statement is the controlling version. If a firm chooses to translate the compliance statement into a language for which there is no official translation of the GIPS standards, the firm must take care to ensure that the translation used reflects the required wording of the compliance statement.

Provision 8.G.14

The FIRM MUST disclose the following: "GIPS® is a registered trademark of CFA Institute. CFA Institute does not endorse or promote this organization, nor does it warrant the accuracy or quality of the content contained herein."

Discussion

"GIPS®" is a registered trademark of CFA Institute, and firms are required to acknowledge this in all GIPS Advertisements. The required disclosure may appear in the body of the GIPS Advertisement or in a footnote to the GIPS Advertisement. The term "this organization," which is included in the required disclosure, refers to any entity associated with the GIPS Advertisement, either the firm or the verifier.

CFA Institute (owner of the GIPS® trademark) may take appropriate action against any firm that misuses the mark "GIPS®" or any compliance statement, including false claims of compliance with the GIPS standards. CFA Institute members, CFA Program charterholders, CFA candidates, CIPM Program certificants, and CIPM candidates who misuse the term "GIPS" or any compliance statement, misrepresent their performance history or the performance history of their firm, or falsely claim compliance with the GIPS standards are also subject to disciplinary sanctions under the CFA Institute Code of Ethics and Standards of Professional Conduct. Possible disciplinary sanctions include public censure, suspension of membership, and revocation of the CFA charter or CIPM certificate.

Regulators with jurisdiction over firms claiming compliance with the GIPS standards may also take enforcement actions against firms that falsely claim compliance with the GIPS standards.

Firms may also use the following language to replace the first sentence in this required disclosure: "GIPS® is a registered trademark owned by CFA Institute." See the GIPS Standards Trademark Usage Guidelines on the CFA Institute website (www.cfainstitute.org) for additional guidance on the proper use of "GIPS".

Provision 8.G.15

The FIRM MUST disclose if the GIPS ADVERTISEMENT conforms with laws or regulations that conflict with the REQUIREMENTS OR RECOMMENDATIONS of the GIPS standards or the GIPS Advertising Guidelines, as well as the manner in which the laws or regulations conflict with the GIPS standards or the GIPS Advertising Guidelines.

Discussion

Firms must comply with all applicable laws and regulations regarding the calculation and presentation of performance, including the advertising of performance. Compliance with applicable laws and regulations, however, does not necessarily result in compliance with the GIPS Advertising Guidelines. Firms must also comply with all of the applicable requirements of the GIPS standards, including the GIPS Advertising Guidelines, when preparing an advertisement in accordance with the GIPS Advertising Guidelines. When laws and regulations conflict with the GIPS standards or the GIPS Advertising Guidelines, firms are required to comply with the laws and regulations and disclose the manner in which the laws or regulations conflict with the GIPS standards or the GIPS Advertising Guidelines.

This disclosure will assist readers of the GIPS Advertisement in comparing GIPS Advertisements among firms where reporting requirements may differ because of local laws or regulations.

Sample Disclosure:

"Local laws do not allow the presentation of returns of less than one year in an advertisement, which is in conflict with the GIPS Advertising Guidelines. Therefore, no performance is presented for this composite for the period from 1 July 2018 (the inception date of the composite) through 31 December 2018."

8.H. GIPS Advertisements for a Broad Distribution Pooled Fund That Include Performance—Recommendations

Provision 8.H.1

If the FIRM determines no appropriate BENCHMARK for the POOLED FUND exists, the FIRM SHOULD disclose why no BENCHMARK is presented.

Discussion

Benchmarks are important tools that aid in the planning, implementation, and evaluation of an investment strategy. They also provide information to the reader of a GIPS Advertisement regarding the relationship between a pooled fund's risk and return. As a result, the GIPS standards require firms to provide benchmark total returns in all GIPS Advertisements for a broad distribution pooled fund unless the firm determines that no appropriate benchmark for the pooled fund's strategy exists. The benchmark must reflect the investment mandate, objective, or strategy of the pooled fund. Although there is typically an appropriate benchmark for traditional pooled fund strategies, it is more common for managers of alternative pooled fund strategies to determine that no appropriate benchmark for the pooled fund exists. If this is the case, it is recommended that the firm disclose why no benchmark is presented.

Sample Disclosure:

"Because the pooled fund's strategy is absolute return where investments are permitted in all asset classes, no benchmark is presented because we believe that no benchmark that reflects this strategy exists."

Provision 8.H.2

The FIRM SHOULD disclose the POOLED FUND'S SALES CHARGES AND LOADS.

Discussion

In order for the reader of the GIPS Advertisement to have a clear understanding of the costs of buying or selling shares in a broad distribution pooled fund, it is recommended that firms disclose the pooled fund's sales charges and loads. This information may be an important factor in a reader's decision as to whether or not to buy shares of a particular fund.

Sales charges and loads may also be referred to as "term commission," "entry and exit fees," "front-end," "back-end," "deferred fees," "subscription and redemption fees," "cost of sales/purchase of funds," "up-front fees," and "trail commission."

Sample Disclosures:

"The Fund has a maximum entry fee of 5.00% and an exit charge of 1.00%. In some cases, an investor might pay less. Please refer to your financial advisor or distributor for the actual entry and exit changes."

"The sales charge (load) imposed on purchases, as well as the sales charge (load) on reinvested distributions is 3.00%. There are no distribution and/or service (12b-1) fees."

Provision 8.H.3

The FIRM SHOULD disclose how SALES CHARGES AND LOADS are reflected in the POOLED FUND'S returns, if applicable.

Discussion

In order to help readers of a GIPS Advertisement understand what costs are reflected in a pooled fund's returns, it is recommended that firms disclose whether or not sales charges and loads are reflected in (i.e., deducted from) the pooled fund's returns. Sales charges and loads, which are typically charged on the front end or back end, should not be included in the calculation of the pooled fund's returns, because regulators in some countries do not allow the inclusion of such charges when calculating pooled fund returns. If sales charges and loads have been deducted when calculating the pooled fund's returns, the deduction of such charges should be disclosed. If sales charges and loads are not reflected in the pooled fund's returns, it is important that readers understand that purchasing and selling shares of the pooled fund will result in costs that are not reflected in the pooled fund returns presented in the GIPS Advertisement. This recommended disclosure will also help readers in comparing pooled fund returns across funds and firms.

Sales charges and loads may also be referred to as "term commission," "entry and exit fees," "front-end," "back-end," "differed fees," "subscription and redemption fees," "cost of sales/purchase of funds," "up-front fees," and "trail commission."

 |

Sample Disclosure When the Pooled Fund's Returns Reflect the Deduction of Sales Charges and Loads:

"The Fund has a maximum entry fee of 5.00% and an exit charge of 1.00%. The pooled fund's net returns reflect the deduction of both entry and exit fees."

Sample Disclosure When the Pooled Fund's Returns Do Not Reflect the Deduction of Sales Charges and Loads:

"The Fund has sales charges and loads that total 1.50%. Sales charges and loads, which reduce the potential growth of a shareholder's investment, have not been reflected in the Fund's net returns presented in this advertisement."

Provision 8.H.4

The FIRM SHOULD disclose the definition of the FIRM.

Discussion

To claim compliance with the GIPS standards, a firm must comply with all applicable requirements of the GIPS standards on a firm-wide basis. Accordingly, the firm must determine exactly how it will be defined for the purpose of compliance. The GIPS standards require that a firm must be defined as an investment firm, subsidiary, or division held out to the public as a distinct business entity.

A distinct business entity is a unit, division, department, or office that is organizationally and functionally segregated from other units, divisions, departments, or offices, that retains discretion over the assets it manages, and that should have autonomy over the investment decision-making process.

Possible criteria that can be used to determine this status include:

- being a legal entity,
- having a distinct market or client type (e.g., institutional, retail, private client), and
- using a separate and distinct investment process.

See Provision 1.A.2 for a more detailed discussion of defining the firm.

Because there are often a number of closely related units or divisions within larger investment management entities, the precise definition of the firm that is presenting the performance results and would be responsible for the management of the pooled fund's assets is important information for those who are reading the GIPS Advertisement. This provision, therefore, recommends that the firm disclose sufficient details of the entity that is presenting investment performance such that the firm is clearly identified.

Sample Disclosure:

"For the purpose of complying with the GIPS standards, the firm is defined as Firm B Institutional Investment Management, the institutional asset management division of Firm B."

Made in the USA
Monee, IL
16 September 2026

63227620R00308